Davis, Lee (Lee Allyn)

Man-made catastrophes.

$40.00

DATE			

Man-made Catastrophes

MAN-MADE CATASTROPHES

FROM THE BURNING OF ROME TO THE LOCKERBIE CRASH

Lee Davis

New York

MAN-MADE CATASTROPHES: FROM THE BURNING OF ROME TO THE LOCKERBIE CRASH

Facts On File, Inc.
460 Park Avenue South
New York NY 10016
USA

Library of Congress Cataloging-in-Publication Data

Davis, Lee Allyn.
Man-made catastrophes : from the burning of Rome to the Lockerbie crash / Lee Allyn Davis.
p. cm.
Includes bibliographical references and index.
ISBN 0-8160-2035-3 (acid-free paper)
1. Disasters. I. Title.
D24.D38 1991
904—dc20 91-41859

A British CIP catalogue record for this book is available from the British Library.

Facts On File books are available at special discounts when purchased in bulk quantities for businesses, associations, institutions or sales promotions. Please call our Special Sales Department in New York at 212/683-2244 (dial 800/322-8755 except in NY, AK or HI) or in Oxford at 865/728399.

Text design by Ron Monteleone
Jacket design by Soloway/Mitchell
Composition and manufacturing by the Maple-Vail Book Manufacturing Group
Printed in the United States of America

10 9 8 7 6 5 4 3 2 1

This book is printed on acid-free paper.

To Lisa.
That's all.

CONTENTS

ACKNOWLEDGMENTS

It is the custom, as if it were an awards ceremony, to thank everybody but your dog and your least favorite relative for help in the birthing of a book. That is not going to be the practice on this page. If I were to name all of the people over the passage of three years who, while I was writing about and therefore living through some of the world's worst times, kept me from getting depressed to the point of paralysis, I would compile a cast of—well—hundreds.

So, I won't, but will, instead, express my gratitude to the major players in this drama of disasters:

Particularly to Mary Lou Barber, who forfeited half a summer to help me endlessly and immeasurably in the accumulation of a small mountain range of reference material;

To Diane Johnston, who cut through a continent of red tape at the New York Public Library and made the portion of my life spent there infinitely more productive than it otherwise would have been;

To Jean Kaleda, Edana McCaffery Cichanowicz, Joanne Brooks, Patricia S. Tormey and the rest of the research staff at the Riverhead Free Library; to Shirley Van Derof, Phyllis Acard, Karen Hewlett, Susan LaVista, Jane Vail, Elva Stanley, Robert Allard, Jan Camarda and Nancy Foley of the Westhampton Free Library; to Selma Kelson and the research staff of the Patchogue-Medford Library; to the research staff of the library at the Southampton Campus of Long Island University; to the research staff of the print division of the Library of Congress;

To Elizabeth Hooks, of the American Red Cross photo library; to Reynaldo Reyes, of the United Nations photo library; to Pedro Soto, of the CARE photo library; to Michael Benson, Larry Crabil and particularly Bill McGruder of the National Transportation Safety Board; to Tim Cronen of the library of the Smithsonian Institution Air and Space Museum;

To Tom Deja for his picture research; to Fred Robertson for his patient photography of disintegrating copies of old newspapers;

To my agents, Elizabeth and Ed Knappman, for causing this to happen in the first place;

To my editors at Facts On File, during the long course of the birth of this book: Kate Kelly and Neal Maillet.

And to all of those unnamed friends and spiritual advisors who kept me sane for three years—my deepest and heartfelt thanks.

Lee Davis
Westhampton, N.Y.

• • • • •

INTRODUCTION

• • • • •

Stupidity.

Neglect.

Avariciousness.

The three weird sisters, the archetypal three of man-made disasters, wend their way through practically every one of the several hundred entries in this volume, often in triplicate and duplicate.

Although "human error" is the euphemism that is used in journalism to describe the reasons for most man-made disasters, it is not altogether accurate. True, the mistakes that a conductor or engineer makes in judging distances when rounding a blind curve are human errors, as are the misreadings of instruments in an industrial plant about to blow apart. Human error is present when an airline pilot, using his best judgment, miscalculates the fuel left in rapidly emptying tanks or the distance to a runway. And human error is present when a navigator of a ship, in a panic situation, steers out of the safety of deep water into the disaster of a reef.

But more often than not, other forces have made that human error easy to commit, and certain to cause a cataclysm. Human sloth and corporate greed often figure in the faulty instrument provided the engineer in the doomed plant, in the failure to provide a proper evacuation plan for a nuclear facility, in the decision of a captain who goes to bed and leaves the bridge to a midshipman in treacherous waters, in the failure of the management of a building or a discotheque to provide the proper fire exits for its patrons, in the neglect of the owners of a shipping line to provide the proper number of lifeboats or the correct filling in life jackets for its passengers.

And in man-made disasters, government often plays an ill-starring role. The cover-ups that are universally present after nuclear disasters have occurred, the misinformation before they happen and the failure to conduct proper inspections of such vital parts as the O-rings in space vehicles have all indicated government culpability.

If, then, there is any constant thread that weaves through the fabric of man-made disasters, it is the presence of those three weird sisters, Stupidity, Neglect and Avariciousness, their pervasiveness before, during and after the disasters and the uncomfortable truth that without them, some of the worst of these disasters never would have occurred.

To carry the Shakespearian analogy still further:

Another basic characteristic of man-made disaster is its inevitability, the inexorable passage of fate once a particular person or group of persons sets that fate in motion. The Shakespearian tragic hero (as distinguished from the Greek tragic hero) has a series of choices. If he makes the correct choice, he wins and faces only complications that result in comedy. If he makes the wrong choice, or a series of wrong choices, he faces his ineluctable doom. For once the first domino has been knocked over, that's it. The rest are bound to follow, with all the inevitability of a law in physics.

And that, too, is another characteristic of many man-made disasters. One error in design is committed; one fatal shortcut is tried by management; one chance too many is taken by a pilot or an engineer; one unwise challenge to fate or inevitability is made by anyone, and the rest is sadness.

At least in the realm of natural disasters, which seem to conform to the Greek theory of tragedy, one can blame it on fate itself, represented by the overwhelming presence of the overpowering forces of nature. People may admittedly be in the wrong place at the wrong time when a tidal wave or a hurricane or an earthquake strikes. But they did not *initiate* the coming of the tidal wave or hurricane or earthquake.

And in the broad spectrum of man-made disasters, it is true that natural forces *have* taken a hand. Ships have gone down in sudden storms and faceless fogs; airliners have been struck by lightning or have been the victims of sudden wind shears; small fires have been fanned into conflagrations by sudden wind gusts. Freezing temperatures certainly played a role in bringing about the *Challenger* space disaster. And it might even be argued that natural, explosive gases in coal mines were placed there, not by man, but by nature.

But except for very few instances, these presences are *secondary*, and it is what occurs *before* or *during* these emergencies that matters in man-made disasters. The judgment of the captain of a ship or an airplane, the decisions made by fire chiefs or rescue squads, the advice given by experts to engineers fighting to bring an industrial plant under control spell the difference between disasters and accidents. And once those Shakespearian dominoes have been set in motion by that act of bad judgment, ignorance, badly placed cowardice or misplaced bravado, the dividing line between trouble and cataclysm is crossed. And there is no going back.

Now, a word about degree:

In his introduction to his play *Death of a Salesman,* Arthur Miller separates the merely pathetic from the truly tragic by using the image of a man being hit by a falling piano.

The situation is this:

A piano is being moved into a fifth-floor apartment via a block and tackle. It hovers outside a window, five stories above a city sidewalk.

An unsuspecting man turns the corner, whistling. He strolls down the sidewalk, and then, just as he gets underneath the piano, a rope breaks. The piano falls, crushing the man.

The next day, an article, headed "Man Hit by Falling Piano," appears in the newspapers. It reports the facts and nothing else.

Is that, asks Miller, pathetic or tragic?

It's pathetic, according to Miller, because you don't know where the man came from or where he was going. If, on the other hand, you knew, for instance, that he had just paid the last installment on his mortgage and was on the way to the jewelry store to pick up the engagement ring to give to the love of his life, it would be tragic. Summing it up, Miller concludes, "You are in the presence of tragedy when you are in the presence of a man who has missed his joy. But the awareness of the joy, and the awareness that it has been missed must be there."

Well, there is both tragedy and patheticness in *Manmade Catastrophes.* Because of its encyclopedic nature, there is neither the space nor the information to include on these pages all of the joys that have been missed by the millions who have died. But it is there, by implication, and wherever it has been possible, it has been included.

There is no greater disaster than the one that occurred to you last year, yesterday or in the last instant. And the reason for this is that you knew the joy and you know the vacuum that is left when it has been missed. So, in the catastrophes that consume this volume, there are millions of people to whom that particular disaster was far more than pathetic. It was the supreme tragedy of their existence.

And all of this would be terribly depressing, if that were all. But there is a reason that we revere our tragedies more than our comedies, why we feel, when they are over, the uplift that the Greeks termed catharsis and that Aristotle, in his *Poetics,* decreed must be present in every true tragedy. It's composed of two qualities: bravery and knowledge. Tragic heroes go to their deaths bravely and learn from their errors before they die.

So, while there is terrible, horrible, disgusting cowardice on these pages—particularly, for some odd reason, in the recital of maritime disasters (they seem to have brought out the very worst in us)—there is also noble bravery, too. Time after time, there are vignettes of remarkable, indelible acts of courage that shine like stars in an otherwise dark sky of disaster: The families who went back to their cabins and donned their evening clothes before stoically going down with the *Titanic;* for instance; the heroic conductors and engineers of out-of-control trains who hurtled to their deaths with their hands on brakes that burned out beneath them; the rescuers that risked their lives to go into burning buildings or soon-to-explode mine shafts; the pilots of planes that brought their crippled birds in with minimum loss of life; the flight attendants and crews who faced down terrorists. The list is long and bright, and proof that there is a goodness and a courage in human beings that no disaster can entirely destroy.

There is also a unique quality in the comparison of categories in this volume. Some categories have almost disappeared in the lexicon of extreme disasters. Lighter-than-air catastrophes, mine explosions, railroad wrecks and the sinking of transatlantic liners, for instance, are clustered in the past. Others, such as political unrest, fires, airplane crashes and industrial disasters, remain constant. And still others, such as terrorism, nuclear accidents and space disasters, grow in number, frequency and size as time unfolds. And there is the undeniable conclusion that the worst of these has yet to happen.

There are old favorites in this volume: the *Titanic,* the *Hindenburg,* the Chicago Fire. And there are new favorites: Bhopal, Chernobyl, the *Challenger* and Three Mile Island. And there are disasters that, for one reason or another, either have not found their way into record books or, because of lack of information or withheld information, remain incomplete stories.

Take, for instance, the worst disaster at sea ever reported. Supposedly, 6,000 Chinese Nationalist soldiers lost their lives in the sinking of a troopship near Manchuria in 1949. But there are no official records, no eyewitness reports, no historians' loggings of this incident that this writer could find after exhaustive research.

Or take the strange case of the *Wilhelm Gustloff.* Its sinking brought about the worst loss of civilian life at sea in all of history. And yet it has scarcely been mentioned in history books of its period, and finding even the few details available took considerable digging. That the *Wilhelm Gustloff* was a German hospital and troopship and that she was sunk by an unidentified Soviet submarine at the very end of World War II undoubtedly accounts for the lack of information. And yet here was a disaster with casualties that were nearly five times that of the *Titanic,* and the incident has remained buried for 45 years in some back room of history.

Finally, take the silence of the Soviet Union after the enormous explosion that shook the Ural Mountains, at a nuclear dump site near the city of Kasli, in 1957. Although the CIA and, presumably, the governments of other Western countries were aware of the explosion, no news of it leaked out until a Soviet scientist, Dr. Zhores Medvedev, emigrated to the West and published a reference to it in a scientific journal. And even then, heads of atomic energy commissions worldwide scoffed at the news. If it had not been for the determination of Medvedev to assert his newfound freedom of expression, this catastrophe might well have remained buried under an international mountain range of official denials.

That these little-known or unknown disasters exist is a final characteristic of man-made disasters. There is no necessity to cover up a natural disaster. But because of the origin of man-made disasters, there has often, unfortunately, been ample—if persuasive—reason to alter or suppress the facts, figures, origins and particularly, in the case of nuclear disasters, the implications of these catastrophes.

Still, the search for these tales with unhappy endings is worth the effort and the collection—to sometimes show human beings at their worst, true, but also to often show them at their most noble and heroic, meeting disaster with courage or simple acceptance and learning from it.

And it is for this last reason, incidentally, that, except for four cases in which helpless civilians were the victims, disasters that took place during a war were omitted. War is, in itself, humankind's very worst self-created disaster. And the fact that humankind has not yet learned that war's endless horror and universal devastation are the most eloquent argument against its recommitment is yet another reason to exclude it from a survey of disasters created by human beings. It is, using Arthur Miller's definition, the most pathetic and least tragic of human enterprises culminating in disasters, one that brings to mind John Wilkes Booth's last words, "Useless, useless, useless . . ."

It is hoped, then, that, utilizing this criteria, this volume of man-made cataclysms does contain some nobility, some surviving dignity and an ultimate sense that, even given catastrophic circumstances, some of us, as King Arthur says at the end of *Camelot,* "do shine."

AIR CRASHES

. . . .

• • • • •

THE WORST RECORDED AIR CRASHES

• • • • •

N.B.: For air crashes caused by terrorist bombs or hijacking, see CIVIL UNREST AND TERRORISM.

* Detailed in text

Africa
* Mediterranean coast (Dec. 21, 1923) French dirigible *Dixmude*

Antarctica
* (Nov. 28, 1979) New Zealand DC-10

Atlantic Ocean
(Aug. 1, 1948) French Latecoere 631 Flying Boat
* (Aug. 14, 1958) KLM Super Constellation
* (Feb. 8, 1965) Eastern DC7-B
(June 23, 1985) Air India Boeing 747SR

Austria
* Innsbruck (Feb. 29, 1964) British Eagle International Britannia

Belgium
Berg (Feb. 15, 1961) Sabena Boeing 707
Bali (April 27, 1974) Pan Am Boeing 707

Brazil
Azul (July 16, 1961) Argentine Airlines Boeing 707
Rio de Janeiro (Feb. 25, 1960) U.S. Navy transport; REAL DC-3

Cameroon
* Douala (Mar. 4, 1962) Trans-African British Caledonian DC-7C

Canada
Newfoundland
* Gander (Dec. 12, 1985) Arrow Air DC-8
Ontario
* Toronto (July 5, 1970) Air Canada DC-8
Quebec
* Issoudun (Aug. 11, 1957) Maritime Central Airways DC-4
* Montreal (Nov. 29, 1963) Trans-Canada DC-8 F
* Toronto (July 5, 1970) Air Canada DC-8

Chile
* Andes Mountains (Feb. 6, 1965) Chilean Linea Aera Nacionale DC-6B

China
Shanghai (Dec. 25, 1946) 3 China Air transport planes

Colombia
* Bogota (July 24, 1938) Colombian military stunt plane
Bogota (Feb. 15, 1947) Avianca DC-4

Cyprus
Nicosia (April 20, 1967) Swiss Gobe Britannia

Czechoslovakia
* Bratislava (Nov. 24, 1966) TABSO Bulgarian Ilyushin-18

Dominican Republic
Santo Domingo (Feb. 15, 1970) Dominican DC-9

Egypt
Aswan (Mar. 20, 1969) United Arab IL-18
Cairo (Aug. 31, 1950) TWA Constellation
* Cairo (May 20, 1965) Pakistan International Boeing 707

France
* Beauvais (Oct. 5, 1930) British dirigible R-101
* Grenoble (Nov. 13, 1950) Canadian Curtis-Reid Air-Tours
Nice (Sept. 11, 1968) Air France Caravelle
Paris
* (June 3, 1962) Air France Boeing 707
(July 11, 1973) Brazilian Boeing 707
* (Mar. 3, 1974) Turkish Airlines Douglas DC-10
Pyrenees (June 3, 1967) British Air Ferry Ltd. DC-6

Germany
* East Berlin (Aug. 14, 1972) Interflug Ilyushin-62
Edelweiler (Aug. 11, 1955) 2 U.S. Air Force Flying Boxcars
* Johannisthal (Oct. 17, 1913) German naval dirigible LZ-18
* Munich (Dec. 17, 1960) U.S. Air Force C-131 Convair

Great Britain
England
* London (June 18, 1972) BEA Trident 1
Wales
* Cardiff (Mar. 12, 1950) British Avro Tudor V

Greece
Athens (Dec. 8, 1969) Olympia Airways DC-6B

Guam
(Sept. 19, 1960) World Airways DC6-B

India
Bombay
(July 7, 1962) Alitalia DC-8
* (Jan. 1, 1978) Air India Boeing 747
* New Delhi (June 14, 1972) Japan Airlines DC-8

Indonesia
Bali (April 27, 1974) Pan Am Boeing 707

Ireland
Shannon (Sept. 19, 1961) President Airlines DC-6

Italy
Milan (June 26, 1959) TWA Super Constellation
* Palermo (May 5, 1972) Alitalia DC-8

Japan
Hokkaido (Feb. 1, 1954) U.S. Air Force C-46

* Morioka (July 30, 1971) All-Nippon Boeing 727; Japanese Air Force F-86
* Mount Fuji (Mar. 5, 1966) BOAC Boeing 707
* Mount Ogura (Aug. 12, 1985) Japan Airlines Boeing 747SR
Tokyo
* (June 18, 1953) U.S. Air Force C-124
* (Feb. 4, 1966) All-Nippon Airways Boeing 727

Libya
Ghadames (May 10, 1961) Air France Starliner

Mexico
Guadalahara (June 2, 1958) Lockheed Constellation

Morocco
Casablanca
(May 18, 1958) Sabena DC-6B
* (July 12, 1961) Czechoslovak Ilyushin-18
Imzizen (Aug. 3, 1975) Alia Boeing 707
Mt. Mallaytine (Dec. 23, 1973) Sabena Caravelle
Rabat (Sept. 12, 1961) Air France Caravelle

New Guinea
(July 16, 1957) KLM Super Constellation

Nigeria
(Nov. 20, 1969) Nigerian Airlines DC-10
(Jan. 22, 1973) Nigerian Airlines Boeing 707

Pacific Ocean
(Mar. 16, 1962) Flying Tiger Super Constellation

Pakistan
* Karachi (Mar. 3, 1953) Canadian Pacific Comet Jet

Peru
Cuzco (Aug. 9, 1970) Peruvian Electra
Jungle (Dec. 24, 1971) Peruvian Electra
* Lima (Nov. 27, 1962) Varig Airlines Boeing 707

Puerto Rico
* San Juan (April 11, 1952) Pan Am DC-4

Saudi Arabia
* Riyadh (Aug. 19, 1980) Saudi Airlines Lockheed Tristar

South Vietnam
(Dec. 24, 1966) U.S. military C-44
Saigon (April 4, 1975) U.S. Air Force Galaxy C-58

Spain
* Barcelona (July 3, 1970) Dan-Air British Comet
Canary Islands
* Santa Cruz de Tenerife (Dec. 3, 1972) Spantax Airlines Convair 990-A
* Santa Cruz de Tenerife (Mar. 27, 1977) KLM Boeing 747; Pan Am Boeing 747
* Granada (Oct. 2, 1964) Union Transports Africain Douglas DC-6
* Ibiza (Jan. 7, 1972) Iberia Caravelle

Sri Lanka
Colombo (Dec. 4, 1974) Dutch DC-8

Switzerland
* Basel (April 10, 1973) BEA Vanguard
Zurich (Sept. 2, 1963) Swissair Caravelle

Turkey
Ankara (Feb. 4, 1963) Turkish Air Force C-47

United States (see also Guam; Puerto Rico)
Alaska
* Anchorage (June 3, 1963) Northwest DC-7 charter
* Juneau (Sept. 4, 1971) Alaska Airlines Boeing 727
Arizona
* Grand Canyon (June 30, 1956) TWA Super Constellation; United DC-7
California
El Toro (June 25, 1965) U.S. Air Force C-135
Lake Tahoe (Mar. 1, 1964) Paradise Airlines Constellation
Simi Mountains (July 12, 1949) Standard Airlines
Hawaii
Honolulu (Mar. 22, 1955) U.S. Navy DC-6
Illinois
* Chicago (May 25, 1979) American DC-10
Hinsdale (Sept. 1, 1961) TWA Constellation
Indiana
* Shelbyville (Aug. 9, 1969) Allegheny DC-9; Piper Cherokee
Maryland
* Elkton (Dec. 8, 1963) Pan Am Boeing 707
Fort Deposit (May 30, 1947) Eastern DC-4
Massachusetts
Boston
* (Oct. 4, 1960) Eastern Electra
* (July 31, 1973) Delta DC-9
Michigan
* South Haven (June 24, 1950) Northwest DC-4
New Jersey
Asbury Park (June 20, 1956) Venezuelan Airlines Constellation
* Coast (April 14, 1933) U.S. dirigible *Akron*
Elizabeth (Dec. 16, 1951) Miami Airlines C-46
* Lakehurst (May 6, 1937) German zeppelin *Hindenburg*
New York
* Brooklyn (Dec. 16, 1960) United DC-8; TWA Super Constellation
* Cove Neck, L.I. (Jan. 25, 1990) Avianca Boeing 707
New York City
* (July 28, 1945) Army Air Corps B-25
(May 29, 1947) United DC-4
* (Feb. 3, 1959) American Lockheed Electra
(Mar. 1, 1962) American Boeing 707
(June 24, 1975) Eastern Boeing 727
North Carolina
* Hendersonville (July 19, 1967) Piedmont Boeing 727; Cessna 310
Ohio
* Ava (Sept. 3, 1925) U.S. Army dirigible *Shenandoah*
Pennsylvania
Mt. Carmel (June 17, 1948) United DC-6
Texas
* Dawson (May 3, 1968) Braniff Lockheed Electra

Utah
* Bryce Canyon (Oct. 24, 1947) United DC-6

Virginia
* Richmond (Nov. 8, 1961) Imperial Airlines Lockheed Constellation

Washington
* Moses Lake (Dec. 20, 1952) U.S. Air Force C-124

Washington, D.C.
(Nov. 1, 1949) Eastern DC-4; Bolivian P-38

Wyoming
Laramie (Oct. 6, 1955) United DC-4

USSR
Irkutsk (Aug. 11, 1971) Soviet Aeroflot Tupolev-104
Kanash (Oct. 17, 1958) Soviet Aeroflot Tupolev-104
Kharkov (May 18, 1972) Soviet Aeroflot Tupolev-104
* Kranaya Polyana (Oct. 14, 1972) Aeroflot Ilyushin-62
Leningrad (Dec. 31, 1970) Soviet Aeroflot Ilyushin-18

Venezuela
* La Coruba (Mar. 16, 1969) Venezuelan DC-8

West Indies
* Guadaloupe (June 22, 1962) Air France Boeing 707

Yugoslavia
* Ljubljana (Sept. 1, 1966) Britannia Airways 102

CHRONOLOGY

1913
Oct. 17
* Johannisthal, Germany; German naval dirigible LZ-18

1923
Dec. 21
* Mediterranean coast of Africa; French dirigible *Dixmude*

1925
Sept. 3
* Ava, Ohio; U.S. Army dirigible *Shenandoah*

1930
Oct. 5
* Beauvais, France; British dirigible R-101

1933
April 14
* Coast of New Jersey; U.S. dirigible *Akron*

1937
May 6
* Lakehurst, New Jersey; German zeppelin *Hindenburg*

1938
July 24
* Bogota, Colombia; Colombian military stunt plane

1945
July 28
* New York, New York; Army Air Corps B-25

N.B.: For air crashes caused by terrorist bombs or hijacking, see CIVIL UNREST AND TERRORISM.

* Detailed in text

1946
Dec. 25
Shanghai, China; 3 China Air transport planes

1947
Feb. 15
Bogota, Colombia; Avianca DC-4
May 29
New York, New York; United DC-4
May 30
Fort Deposit, Maryland; Eastern DC-4
Oct. 24
* Bryce Canyon, Utah; United DC-6

1948
June 17
Mt. Carmel, Pennsylvania; United DC-6
Aug. 1
Atlantic Ocean; French Latecoere 631 Flying Boat

1949
July 12
Simi Mountains, California; Standard Airlines
Nov. 1
Washington, D.C.; Eastern DC-4; Bolivian P-38

1950
Mar. 12
* Cardiff, Wales; British Avro Tudor V
Aug. 31
Cairo, Egypt; TWA Constellation
Nov. 13
* Grenoble, France; Canadian Curtis Reid Air-Tours

1951
Dec. 16
Elizabeth, New Jersey; Miami Airlines C-46

1952
April 11
* San Juan, Puerto Rico; Pan Am DC-4
Dec. 20
* Moses Lake, Washington; U.S. Air Force C-124

1953
Mar. 3
* Karachi, Pakistan; Canadian Pacific Comet Jet
June 18
* Tokyo, Japan; U.S. Air Force C-124

1954
Feb. 1
Hokkaido, Japan; U.S. Air Force C-46

1955
Aug. 11
Edelweiler, Germany; 2 U.S. Air Force Flying Boxcars
Oct. 6
Laramie, Wyoming; United DC-4

1956
June 30
* Grand Canyon, Arizona; TWA Super Constellation; United DC-7

1957
July 16
* New Guinea; KLM Super Constellation
Aug. 11
* Quebec, Canada; Maritime Central Airways DC-4

1958
May 18
Casablanca, Morocco; Sabena DC-6B
June 2
Guadalajara, Mexico; Lockheed Constellation
Aug. 14
* Atlantic Ocean; KLM Super Constellation
Oct. 17
Kanash, USSR; Soviet Aeroflot Tupolev-104

1959
Feb. 3
* New York, New York; American Lockheed Electra
June 26
Milan, Italy; TWA Super Constellation

1960
Feb. 25
Rio de Janeiro, Brazil; U.S. Navy transport; REAL DC-3
Sept. 19
Guam; World Airways DC6-B
Oct. 4
* Boston, Massachusetts; Eastern Electra
Dec. 16
* Brooklyn, New York; United DC-8; TWA Super Constellation
Dec. 17
* Munich, Germany; U.S. Air Force C-131 Convair

1961
Feb. 15
Berg, Belgium; Sabena Boeing 707
May 10
Ghadames, Libya; Air France Starliner
July 12
* Casablanca, Morocco; Czechoslovak Ilyushin-18
July 16
Azul, Brazil; Argentine Airlines Boeing 707
Sept. 1
Hinsdale, Illinois; TWA Constellation
Sept. 10
Shannon, Ireland; President Airlines DC-6
Sept. 12
Rabat, Morocco; Air France Caravelle
Nov. 8
* Richmond, Virginia; Imperial Airlines Lockheed Constellation

1962
Mar. 1
New York, New York; American Boeing 707
Mar. 4
* Douala, Cameroon; Trans-African British Caledonian DC-7C
Mar. 16
Pacific Ocean; Flying Tiger Super Constellation
June 3
* Paris, France; Air France Boeing 707
June 22
* Guadaloupe, West Indies; Air France Boeing 707
July 7
Bombay, India; Alitalia DC-8
Nov. 27
* Lima, Peru; Varig Airlines Boeing 707

1963
Feb. 4
Ankara, Turkey; Turkish Air Force C-47
June 3
* Anchorage, Alaska; Northwest DC-7 charter
Sept. 2
Zurich, Switzerland; Swissaire Caravelle
Nov. 29
* Montreal, Canada; Trans-Canada DC-8F
Dec. 8
* Elkton, Maryland; Pan Am Boeing 707

1964
Feb. 29
* Innsbruck, Austria; British Eagle International Britannia
Mar. 1
Lake Tahoe, California; Paradise Airlines Constellation
Oct. 2
* Granada, Spain; Union transports Africain DC-6

1965
Feb. 6
* Andes Mountains, Chile; Chilean Linea Aera Nacionale DC-6B
Feb. 8
* Atlantic Ocean; Eastern DC7-B
May 20
* Cairo, Egypt; Pakistan International Boeing 707
June 25
El Toro, California; U.S. Air Force C-135

1966
Feb. 4
* Tokyo, Japan; All Nippon Airways Boeing 727
Mar. 5
* Mount Fuji, Japan; BOAC Boeing 707
Sept. 1
* Ljubljana, Yugoslavia; Britannia Airways 102
Nov. 24
* Bratislava, Czechoslovakia; TABSO Bulgarian Ilyushin-18
Dec. 24
South Vietnam; U.S. military C-44

1967
April 20
Nicosia, Cyprus; Swiss Gobe Britannia
June 3
Pyrenees, France; British Air Ferry Ltd. DC-6
July 19
* Hendersonville, North Carolina; Piedmont Boeing 727; Cessna 310

1968
May 3
* Dawson, Texas; Braniff Lockheed Electra
Sept. 11
Nice, France; Air France Caravelle

1969
Mar. 16
* La Coruba, Venezuela; Venezuelan DC-8
Mar. 20
Aswan, Egypt; United Arab IL-18

Aug. 9
* Shelbyville, Indiana; Allegheny DC-9; Piper Cherokee
Nov. 20
Nigeria; Nigerian Airlines DC-10
Dec. 8
Athens, Greece; Olympia Airways DC-6B

1970
Feb. 15
Santo Domingo, Dominican Republic; Dominican DC-9
July 3
* Barcelona, Spain; Dan-Air British Comet
July 5
Toronto, Canada; Air Canada DC-8
Aug. 9
Cuzco, Peru; Peruvian Electra
Dec. 31
Leningrad, USSR; Soviet Aeroflot Ilyushin-18

1971
July 30
* Morioka, Japan; All-Nippon Boeing 727; Japanese Air Force F-86
Sept. 4
* Juneau, Alaska; Alaska Airlines Boeing 727
Dec. 24
Jungle, Peru; Peruvian Electra

1972
Jan. 7
* Ibiza, Spain; Iberia Caravelle
Mar. 18
Kharkov, USSR; Soviet Aeroflot Tupolev-104
May 5
* Palermo, Italy; Alitalia DC-8
June 14
* New Delhi, India; Japan Airlines DC-8
June 18
* London, Great Britain; BEA Trident 1
Aug. 14
East Berlin, Germany; Interflug Ilyushin-62
Oct. 14
* Kranaya Polyana, USSR; Aeroflot Ilyushin-62
Dec. 3
* Santa Cruz de Tenerife, Canary Islands; Spantax Airlines Convair 990-A

1973
Jan. 22
Nigeria; Nigerian Airlines Boeing 70
April 10
* Basel, Switzerland; BEA Vanguard
July 11
Paris, France; Brazilian Boeing 707
July 31
* Boston, Massachusetts; Delta DC-9
Dec. 23
Mt. Mallaytine, Morocco; Sabena Caravelle

1974
Mar. 3
* Paris, France; Turkish Airlines Douglas DC-10
April 27
Bali, Indonesia; Pan Am Boeing 707
Dec. 4
Colombo, Sri Lanka; Dutch DC-8

1975
April 4
Saigon, South Vietnam; U.S. Air Force Galaxy C-58
June 24
New York, New York; Eastern Boeing 727
Aug. 3
* Imzizen, Morocco; Alia Boeing 707

1977
Mar. 27
* Santa Cruz de Tenerife, Canary Islands; KLM Boeing 747; Pan Am Boeing 747

1979
May 25
* Chicago, Illinois; American DC-10
Nov. 8
* Antarctica; New Zealand DC-10

1980
Aug. 19
* Riyadh, Saudi Arabia; Saudi Airlines Lockheed Tristar

1985
June 23
Atlantic Ocean; Air India Boeing 747SR
Aug. 12
* Mount Ogura, Japan; Japan Airlines Boeing 747SR
Dec. 12
* Gander, Newfoundland, Canada; Arrow Air DC-8

1990
Jan. 25
* Cove Neck, Long Island, New York; Avianca Boeing 707

• • • • •

AIR CRASHES

• • • • •

Commercial air travel has come a long way from the days of the old Ford Tri-Star. In 1928, a trip on TWA (Transcontinental and Western Airlines then) was a true adventure. According to engineer Arthur Raymond, quoted in Paul Eddy, Elaine Potter and Bruce Page's book *Destination Disaster,* "They gave us cotton wool to stuff in our ears, the 'Tin Goose' was so noisy. The thing vibrated so much it shook the eyeglasses right off your nose. In order to talk to the guy across the aisle you had to shout at the top of your lungs. The higher we went, to get over the mountains, the colder it got in the cabin. My feet nearly froze . . . When the plane landed on a puddle-splotched runway, a spray of mud, sucked in by the cabin air vents, splattered everybody."

Improvements were clearly necessary; Raymond and his cohorts at the Douglas Company set about "building comfort and putting wings on it," as Raymond phrased it. By 1933, the commercial airliner as we know it today had been built, at least in an elementary outline. Its configuration—a pilot's cabin up front, engines encased in cowlings on the wings, a row of portholes through which passengers peered (apprehensively or otherwise) at the clouds, the sky and the arrival or departure of the ground—was established early in the DC-1 (D for Douglas, C for Commercial, 1 for first).

The craft was a model of noisy luxury. Each of its upholstered seats had a reading lamp and a footrest. The galley at the rear was equipped with electric hot plates and a lavatory. The cabin was heated and contained a ventilation system designed to let in more air than noise, and the "stewardess" was, before her transformation into "flight attendant," more than a waitress and psychiatrist. She was also a registered nurse.

And so began a multibillion dollar industry that now makes practically every corner of the globe accessible to those who use it—and millions do, every year.

Its safety record is exemplary. Considering the burgeoning number of flights, the diverse distances and destinations and the number of passengers carried each day in absolute comfort and safety, it is impossible not to say that flying is a safe method of transportation.

And yet, large segments of the public are still deathly afraid of flying. Some refuse to fly. Some fly with their hearts in their throats and their fingers digging into armrests or their companion's arms. Others board flights with grim resignation. And their resignation has a basis: Once aboard an airplane, the passenger is, admittedly, helpless. There's no stopping the plane in midflight to debark, no way of seeing ahead or behind, no escape hatch in the sky. Strapped into his or her seat, the airline passenger is at the total mercy of the crew in the cockpit and the fates surrounding the plane.

And, unfortunately, those crews have not always been skillful, nor has fate been kind. As in any man-made disaster, human failure has played a feature role. And there are a huge number of people who can fail in the chain of command behind the orderly flying of a commercial airliner. There are the engineers who design the craft, the mechanics who service it, the flight personnel who fly it and the controllers who guide it from airport to airport. There are the groups who make the rules regulating commercial flying, and the politicians behind the regulatory bodies.

Who, for instance, can argue that for a while, at least, the skies became dramatically more dangerous when, in 1981, President Reagan fired most of the country's experienced air controllers? And as the skies become more and more crowded, as they inevitably will, air control, pilot training and the technology to prevent turning the more than 2,000 near misses that occur in the sky into fatal collisions will become more and more of an issue and a burning necessity, overseen by government agencies and government policy-makers.

Having said all of this, the one human failure that no amount of technology or skill can cure is that of bad judgment under pressure. As highly trained, as experienced and as cool under grueling circumstances as airline pilots are today, they are nevertheless human and can make mistakes. And, in the case of commercial aviation, as the following section will show, these mistakes can—and often do—result in terrible tragedy.

There are other factors besides human failures: Faulty design and the metal fatigue that comes from long use have caused crashes. Weather has been a constant hazard. And terrorism, whether individual or state sponsored, has picked the airlines as its prime target.

So, the fear of flying, which is really a fear of crashing, has its realistic roots. The statistics are grim, and although air crashes occur infrequently now, they receive enormous media coverage because of the sheer magnitude of the loss of life.

New technology—transponders, three-dimensional radar, wind-shear protection, etc.—is being developed in the interest of safer flying. Efforts to build better, safer airports will certainly diminish the number of crashes, for the statistics reveal that most troubles with aircraft and consequent crashes occur during landing or takeoff. And that has held true, whether the aircraft is a lighter-than-air blimp or a jetliner.

Therefore, improvements in safety have concentrated on takeoff and landing procedures, and in the agonizingly slow rebuilding of the air control system to the level of safety it possessed before it was decimated in 1981.

There is no doubt that air travel is safe. And there is also no doubt that it could be safer.

The criteria for inclusion of crashes in this section centered upon the number of fatalities and the severity of the crash. But statistics alone were not the constant arbiters, and for a logical reason: A 1990 casualty figure could not realistically be applied to the 1930s, when planes were smaller and fewer people were flying. Thus the casualty figures were matched with the time in which they occurred.

Other, lesser crashes were included if they were of a particularly unusual nature or the only crash of a particular type.

Airplane disasters involving terrorism can be found in the section CIVIL UNREST AND TERRORISM.

GLOSSARY

• • • • •

Airline lingo, technical terms and the alphabet soup of regulatory agencies have become part of the national vocabulary. Thus, the following glossary explains terms used in this section.

ADF Automatic Direction Finder
ALPA Airline Pilots Association
Alpha-Numeric System A method of radar identification of individual aircraft by letter and numbers
Altimeter A device displaying the height of a plane from the ground or sea level
AOPA Aircraft Owners and Pilots Association
ARTC Air Route Traffic Control
ARTS Automatic Radar Traffic Control System
ASDE Air Surface Detection Radar
ATC Air Traffic Control
Attitude The horizontal direction of an aircraft
AWLS All Weather Landing System
CAB Civil Aeronautics Board
CAS Collision Avoidance System
FAA Federal Aviation Administration
Flaps A series of hinged wing extensions whose angle can be changed to provide greater lift for landings and takeoffs
Handoff The transfer of control of an in-flight aircraft from one radar center to another
HICAT High altitude clear air turbulence
IFR Instrument Flight Rules
LOCAT Low Altitude Clear Air Turbulence
Mayday The international SOS, from the French *m'aidez*
Overrun The failure of an aircraft to halt its forward progress before reaching the end of the runway
Propjet An aircraft whose motion is caused by a propeller turned by a jet engine; also known as turboprop
Rotate The change of an aircraft's attitude by bringing the nose up, as in takeoff or landing
SST Supersonic transport

Transponder A device that can be actuated to make a specific plane more readily identified on a controller's radarscope

Turbojet An aircraft driven by a jet engine using a turbine-driven air compressor

Undershoot A landing attempt in which the aircraft hits the ground before reaching the runway

VASI Visual Approach Slope Instruments

VFR Visual Flight Rules

VTOL Vertical Takeoff and Landing

• • • • • • • • • • • • • • • •

AFRICA
MEDITERRANEAN COAST

December 21, 1923

• • • • • • • • • • • • • • • •

The state-of-the-art airship Dixmude, *one of France's proudest lighter-than-air ships, exploded when it was struck by lightning over the Mediterranean coast of Africa, on December 21, 1923. All 52 crew members aboard died.*

The golden age of dirigibles, from World War I until the *Hindenburg* disaster (see p. 39), was characterized by opulence, experimentation and isolated horrors. When an early dirigible caught fire, there was no hope for survivors, since the hydrogen that kept these liners of the sky aloft before 1923 was enormously combustible, turning metal white hot in moments.

There was a certain sad irony about the loss of the French dirigible *Dixmude* on December 21, 1923 over the Mediterranean coast of Africa: It was the French who had built the first successful power-driven airship, *La France,* in 1884. And in 1923, the very year the *Dixmude* apparently exploded when its hydrogen-filled skin was struck by lightning, noncombustible helium was successfully introduced in the United States-built *Shenandoah.*

The *Dixmude* had actually been constructed by the Germans as a fighting ship during World War I. It was a state-of-the-art airship, fast, sleek and marvelously outfitted. Turned over to the victorious French in 1920 and christened the *Dixmude,* it went about establishing records. On August 10 of that year, it made the trip from Maubeuge to Cuers in a record 24 hours and 25 minutes. It established a world endurance record when it flew from France to Tunisia in 118 hours and 41 minutes on September 25, 1923.

Three months later, on December 21, the *Dixmude,* now a survey craft for the French Navy, set out for Algeria from Cuers-Pierrefeu, on a course that was designed to locate freshwater sources in the Sahara. Fifty miles south of Biskra, the ship's commander, Lieutenant de Vaisseau du Plessis de Grenadan, was informed that he was headed for heavy weather. His reply to the radioed report was a change of course.

But apparently the storm system was all-encompassing, and the *Dixmude* soon found itself in the midst of a raging, towering thunderstorm. An hour and a half later, the airship succumbed to the gale and began to fall toward the Mediterranean. A distraught Commander de Grenadan radioed that he was making an emergency landing in the water.

This was the last message received from the *Dixmude.* Planes and ships sent to retrieve the ship and its survivors in the area from which the commander had radioed found no traces of it, nor did those who scoured the Sahara nearby.

Villagers along the coast reported seeing a huge fireball in the sky at about the time of the last radio message. Experts concluded that the ship had been struck by lightning and had exploded, flinging fragments of itself and its crew to the elements.

Of the 52 crew members aboard, only the body of Commander de Grenadan was recovered—by two Sicilian fisherman, hauling in their nets two days later.

ANTARCTICA

November 28, 1979

• • • • • • • • • • • • • • • •

An Air New Zealand DC-10 on a sightseeing flight, hampered by low visibility, unpredictable wind currents and a possibly malfunctioning navigation system, slammed into the side of the 12,400-foot-high volcano Mount Erebus on November 28, 1979. Two hundred fifty-seven died in the crash.

Air New Zealand began a series of sightseeing flights over Antarctica in 1978. Popular with tourists, they were looked on askance by representatives of the National Science Foundation, the coordinators of an extensive scientific program in Antarctica. The planes disrupted both wildlife and the atmosphere, as they dipped and circled over the scientific encampments at the end of the earth.

On November 28, 1979 the fourth flight of the season took off from Auckland, New Zealand at 8:21 A.M. It was a nonstop flight that was scheduled to circle over the South

Pole and then land at Christchurch at about 5 P.M. There was a low cloud cover near Mount Erebus, a 12,400-foot active volcano located on Ross Island, off the Antarctica coast about 30 miles north of the U.S. military and scientific station at McCurdo Sound. This was a disappointment; a circle of the volcano was always a high point of the tour.

The temperature in the area was approximately 15 degrees Fahrenheit, and, at that time of year, there was daylight almost around the clock.

At 1 P.M., the pilot of the DC-10, Captain Tim Collins, radioed Auckland that he was descending from his 10,000-foot altitude to 2,000 feet, apparently in an attempt to pierce the cloud cover and give the sightseers a closer, unimpeded view of the volcano.

It was the last anyone would hear from the Air New Zealand flight. It slammed into the side of the mountain about 1,500 feet from its base, exploded and caught fire. No one would survive.

It would be seven hours before rescuers in a U.S. Navy Hercules C-130 would sight the wreckage, pinpointing it for ground rescue crew to arrive by sled. That night, blinding snowstorms roared into the area, keeping the rescue teams from getting to the site and helicopters from landing at it. It would be two days before the search could be resumed and a helicopter pad built.

Only 90 of the 257 bodies would ever be found. The rest, rescuers reasoned, had slipped into crevices or were buried too deeply under the snow to be found.

The "black box" flight recorder was retrieved, and its story was one of instantaneous disaster with almost no warning. Seconds before impact, an alarm sound reverberated in the cockpit from the ground proximity warning system, telling the crew that the plane had descended too low.

Captain Collins was an experienced pilot. A later inquiry determined that there must have been a malfunction in the navigation system of the airplane. This malfunction, coupled with the low visibility and compounded by the hazardous mountain wind currents, was thought to be the cause of the crash.

ATLANTIC OCEAN

August 14, 1958

• • • • • • • • • • • • • • • • • •

KLM Flight 607-E, a Super Constellation, bound from Brussels to New York exploded over the North Atlantic 130 miles off the Irish coast at 11:35 P.M. on August 14, 1958. There were no survivors.

At 11:05 P.M., on August 14, 1958, at the height of the tourist season, KLM Flight 607-E left Shannon, Ireland bound for New York, with 99 passengers and crew aboard. The weather was calm in Ireland; there were no obstacles to a safe and smooth flight to the United States.

A half hour later, the pilot radioed his position to Shannon; he was 130 miles west of the Irish coast, and all was proceeding normally.

It would be the last word to be uttered from Flight 607-E. Somewhere west of the last report, the flight disappeared from radar screens and radio frequencies. Rescue ships were dispatched, and by daylight the next day, bodies and pieces of wreckage were fished from the Atlantic. There had apparently been a midair explosion that had blown apart the airliner without warning. This was before the era of terrorist bombings, so only two theories—weather or a mechanical malfunction—were given credence for the origin of the explosion. Neither would ever be proven conclusively. Whether it was from lightning in a sudden electrical storm (not an uncommon occurrence over the North Atlantic) or mechanical failure no one was able to ascertain from the wreckage.

And there were no survivors.

ATLANTIC OCEAN

February 8, 1965

• • • • • • • • • • • • • • • • • •

Sabotage was suspected in the crash, shortly after takeoff from Kennedy Airport, of Eastern Airlines Flight 663, a DC7-B, off the coast of Long Island. All 84 aboard died.

Eastern Airlines Flight 663 to Richmond, Virginia took off in normal fashion from New York's Kennedy Airport at 6:20 P.M. on February 8, 1965, looped out over the ocean and banked over Jones Beach, Long Island preparatory to gaining cruising altitude.

Captain Stephen Marshall, the pilot of a flight coming in from Puerto Rico, later testified that he saw the aircraft take "an exceptionally deep turn," hang in the air for a moment and then plunge into the Atlantic Ocean, where it exploded upon impact.

At that same moment, Kennedy radar lost the flight from its screens and radioed an emergency alert. A seaman stationed at the top of a watchtower at Short Beach Station, Long Island reported seeing a "red ball of fire about ten feet high above the water" and hearing something that sounded like a small firecracker exploding. Other witnesses in nearby Lido Beach reported seeing and hearing the same thing, which led investigators later to suspect sabotage as the cause of the crash.

Coast Guard ships discovered the oil slick that identified the crash site eight miles south of Jones Beach, Long Island. There were no survivors. All 84 people aboard perished.

AUSTRIA
INNSBRUCK

February 29, 1964

• • • • • • • • • • • • • • • • • •

A British Eagle International Airlines Bristol Britannia failed to make an instrument landing at Innsbruck Airport on the night of February 29, 1964 and smashed into Mount Glungezer. All 88 aboard were killed.

There are scary descents into certain airports in the world. Several Caribbean islands are noted for "white knuckle" landing sites, including the St. Thomas airport in the U.S. Virgin Islands. But at least these airports are situated in areas in which the weather is usually clear and placid.

Not so the airport at Innsbruck, Austria, in the heart of the Austrian Alps and the midst of some of the best ski country on earth. Ringed by 8,000-foot-high mountains, it lies in a bowl that requires a steep and rapid descent from 10,000 feet. Few unseasoned travelers who have ever landed there forget the experience or wish to repeat it.

The night of February 29, 1964 was foggy and still. British Eagle International Airlines, Britain's largest independent airline in 1964, flew regularly from London to Innsbruck, and one of its Bristol Britannias, piloted by Captain E. Williams, attempted an instrument landing in the midst of the fog. The plane never made it to the runway.

Some 12 miles from the airport, flying 100 feet below the necessary altitude to clear the surrounding peaks, the plane smashed into Mount Glungezer, cracked apart and slid into a gorge. All 88 people aboard were killed.

CAMEROON
DOUALA

March 4, 1962

• • • • • • • • • • • • • • • • • •

There has never been an explanation for the crash on takeoff of a Trans-African British Caledonian DC-7C at Douala Airport, in Cameroon, on March 4, 1962. All 111 aboard died in the crash.

The mystery of the sudden crash, on takeoff, of a Caledonian DC-7C from Douala Airport in Cameroon on March 4, 1962 has never been solved. A charter owned by the Trans-African Coach Company and loaded with 111 persons, it had originated in Mozambique and had made an eventless stop at Lisbon. Its destination was Luxembourg.

All seemed to be in order as the DC-7C left the runway on the last leg of its journey. But a mere two minutes after it became airborne, the plane plunged to the ground, bursting into flames and killing all 111 aboard. No incendiary device was discovered in the wreckage, no distress call was radioed to the airport and no mechanical failure was found in the smoldering wreckage of the plane.

CANADA
NEWFOUNDLAND
GANDER

December 12, 1985

• • • • • • • • • • • • • • • • • •

A combination of human error and malfeasance on the part of Arrow Air Charter combined to send an Arrow Air DC-8 plunging to earth after takeoff from Newfoundland's Gander Airport on December 12, 1985. All 258 American servicemen aboard died.

In 1982, a multinational peacekeeping force was deployed in the Sinai Peninsula after Egypt made peace with Israel. With troops from 11 countries, this 2,500-member force was given the job of patrolling borders and generally supervising the security arrangements of the peace treaty, which had been signed in 1979.

In 1985, the American contingent consisted of men in the Third Battalion, 502d Infantry of the 101st Airborne Division. By December of that year, they had put in their requisite six months of duty, and by December 11, one-third of the battalion had been rotated to its home base at Fort Campbell, Kentucky. At Cairo Airport that day, the second shipment of men boarded a DC-8, chartered by the military from Arrow Airlines of Miami. They were on their way home for Christmas.

By the time they left Cologne, Germany, their next stop, there were 250 soldiers and eight crew members aboard the jet. They flew overnight to Newfoundland, their last refueling stop before proceeding on to Kentucky, where Welcome Home banners, a brass band and eager relatives would be waiting to greet them.

The DC-8 touched down at Gander at 4:08 A.M. on December 12, 1985. Six minutes later, it was "on the blocks," refueling. The weather was miserable but not unusual: There was a light drizzle formed from fog, snow and freezing rain. The temperature was 25 degrees Fahrenheit. Visibility was 12 miles, with broken clouds at 1,200 feet.

It was a quick refueling, and there was no attempt to apply de-icing material to the plane's wings.

At 5:10 A.M. the plane left the maintenance area, and at 5:15 it took off, with 258 people and 101,000 pounds of fuel. It had scarcely cleared the runway when it veered suddenly to the right, shuddered for a moment and then plunged into a spruce and birch forest, skidding through it, leveling trees and then exploding in a huge burst of sound and fire.

"I saw this explosion," Bob Cole, a Gander truck driver, later told reporters. "I never saw nothing to match it in my life."

"It was just like a sunset," added Lucy Parsons, an airport worker.

Within eight minutes, volunteer fire fighters, Royal Canadian Mounties and military personnel from the Gander base had reached the scene. The explosion had ignited brushfires over a wide area. "There were bits of fuselage everywhere, no big pieces," Keith Head, a Gander fireman, said. Charred bodies were strewn over the landscape. There were no survivors. All 258 were killed in the gigantic explosion caused by a combination of the impact of the crash and the full load of fuel.

There were many unanswered questions, and boards of inquiry were convened in both Canada and the United States. Two pieces of information emerged soon after the crash: The right outboard engine was in a reverse mode, and this could have accounted for the veering to the right of the plane just before it went down. But investigators were quick to point out that the impact of the crash might have thrown the controls into this mode; that had happened in other crashes.

Second, it was disclosed that the crew had underestimated the weight of passengers and fuel by at least six tons.

The last disclosure led Congress to investigate Arrow Air, and the disclosures that were aired in this investigation were frightening. Former pilots for the line came forth and told Congress that the airline often pushed pilots until they would fall asleep in the cockpit. And it performed absolutely minimal maintenance on its airplanes.

Further examination of the craft that crashed revealed other disquieting information, stories of a pocketknife having to be used to open the forward cargo door, and windows that were taped shut. The DC-8 had had mechanical difficulties earlier that year and was forced to abort two takeoffs in the past six months.

In the wake of all of this, Arrow Air declared bankruptcy and went into Chapter 11 on January 21, 1986.

The final conclusion regarding the cause of the crash settled on the right outboard engine. It was delivering less power than the other three engines at the moment of impact. Whether its reversal on takeoff came from an inattentive crew or yet another mechanical malfunction of that particular DC-8 no one will ever know. That information died with the crew and passengers of the Arrow Air DC-8.

CANADA
ONTARIO
TORONTO

July 5, 1970

• • • • • • • • • • • • • • • •

Incorrectly deployed wing spoilers caused the crash of an Air Canada DC-8 on landing at Toronto Airport on July 5, 1970. All 108 aboard were killed.

The last moments of pilot Peter Hamilton and co-pilot Donald Rowland, commanding an Air Canada DC-8 over Toronto Airport on the morning of July 5, 1970, were heard and recorded by ground controllers. The succession of events was terrifying, and yet these two went about their work with a calmness that was astonishing. Rowland even apologized at one point to Hamilton for prematurely engaging a braking device.

The flight was a routine one for the veteran team who had flown together many times, though not always peacefully. Captain Hamilton was a strong believer in challenging his airline's approved procedures for arming jet spoilers (wing slats to brake jets after they land) early, as high as 2,000 feet. Rowland believed in following company orders, and they had reportedly gotten into a heated argument in Vienna earlier that year over Hamilton's ignoring of the rule. As a result, a lopsided compromise was reached between the two: Hamilton agreed to arm the spoilers at 60 feet.

The danger in even arming these spoilers is one of mistakes under stress. If the spoiler is merely armed, it is set to automatically engage when the landing gear touches the runway. To do this, the pilot or co-pilot lifts a lever.

If the spoiler is deployed, it "spoils" the airflow over the top of the wing and reduces lift, thus braking the plane. To deploy the spoiler, the pilot or co-pilot pulls the same lever that arms the spoiler.

The cockpit recorder, recovered after the crash, told the tale: Rowland, the co-pilot, inadvertently *deployed* the spoilers just before touchdown. "No-no-no," the captain shouted.

"Sorry—Oh! Sorry, Pete," answered Rowland, and simultaneously the right wing hit the ground.

The outboard engine fell off. The plane, suddenly lighter by 4,000 pounds, was catapulted back into the air.

Captain Hamilton regained control and announced to the control tower that he would circle once again and attempt to land. But before he could complete the circle, the inboard engine ripped away from the plane, taking part of the right wing with it.

The plane began to break up. Hamilton and Rowland fought to regain control, adjusting, trying to stabilize the wildly pitching, disintegrating plane. Finally, the forces of balance and gravity won out, and the plane heeled over and dove to earth, breaking apart as it fell and crashing into a populated area alongside the airport. All 108 aboard were killed.

CANADA
QUEBEC
ISSOUDUN

August 11, 1957

• • • • • • • • • • • • • • • • •

An overloaded maritime Central Charter DC-4, piloted by a man with a record of intentionally causing accidents, was flung to the ground in a fierce thunderstorm over Issoudun, near Quebec, on the morning of August 11, 1957. There was one survivor—a baby. Seventy-seven passengers and crew died.

Bizarre as it may seem, Norman Ramsay, the pilot of the ill-fated Maritime Central Charter DC-4 that plunged to earth near Quebec on the morning of August 11, 1957, had been discharged three years previously by Trans-Canada Airlines for intentionally plunging his aircraft into the ground. Since that time he had been under psychiatric care.

That incident had involved a Super Constellation flight from Tampa, Florida to Toronto on December 17, 1954. Coming in for a landing 400 feet below the minimum required altitude, he had simply flown the plane into the turf near the runway. Miraculously, none of the 44 passengers or crew was seriously injured.

Three years later, after his psychiatrist had pronounced him unfit to fly (all of this was revealed in the later board of inquiry findings), Captain Ramsay was piloting an overloaded charter, packed with veterans of the Canadian contingent of the British Expeditionary Force in France, who had gone back to view the battlefields where they had fought in World War I. The DC-4 had been designed to carry 49 passengers. On this trip, from London to Toronto, it would be carrying 73.

The plane took off from Heathrow Airport in London at 5:55 P.M. on the night of August 10. The overloaded plane had difficulty clearing the runway but finally managed it, and the weather report signaled clear weather all the way to Montreal. Refueling stops were planned in Reykjavik, Iceland and Montreal, unless headwinds forced an earlier stop in Quebec.

By the time the plane left Iceland, at 1:12 A.M., the crew had been on duty for 20 hours and had flown almost constantly for 15 or 16 hours. It would be daylight before they would reach Seven Island and Mont Joli, near Quebec city. When they did, they had a mere 122 gallons of fuel left. Most pilots would have elected to land and refuel. Ramsay elected to continue on. He radioed his position.

It would be the last communication received from the plane.

West of Quebec, an enormous thunderstorm loomed up directly in the flight's path. Had they had extra fuel, the flight crew could have climbed above it or skirted around it. Ramsay had only one choice: He entered the storm, and that proved to be a fatal decision. Somewhere over Issoudun, near Quebec, the forces of the thunderstorm flung the DC-4 into the ground with such force that some of its fuselage and all of its motors dug in to depths of up to 84 feet. There was only one survivor—an infant child, whom rescuers, arriving a disgraceful five and a half hours later, discovered sitting in the unoccupied pilot's seat, a considerable distance from the main body of the wreck.

Only 20 bodies could be identified. The others were damaged beyond recognition. Local authorities were given the responsibility of protecting the site until Department of Transport crash investigators could arrive the next day. But these local authorities apparently ignored their mandate. Hundreds of curious souvenir hunters from Quebec and elsewhere roamed the wreckage, carrying away personal possessions of the dead passengers and removing thousands of small parts of the aircraft that might have pieced together the last moments of the doomed flight.

CANADA
QUEBEC
MONTREAL

November 29, 1963

• • • • • • • • • • • • • • • • •

Trans-Canada Flight 831, a DC-8F, encountered severe turbulence after taking off from Montreal Airport on November 29, 1963 and plunged to the ground. All 118 aboard were killed.

Instrument failure was blamed for the crash, on takeoff, of a Trans-Canada DC-8F at Montreal Airport on November 29, 1963.

Flight 831 was an enormously popular one, for its route and for its timing. "A Friday night businessman's milk-run" is the way it was described, as it made its slow way from Montreal to Toronto and points west every night after work.

At 6:10 P.M. on November 29, 1963, the departure time of Flight 831, a torrential rainstorm whipped across the runways of Montreal Airport. Roadways from downtown Montreal to the airport were jammed with stalled traffic, and by 6:22, when the gates closed, eight of the scheduled 118 passengers had still not reached the terminal. The plane nevertheless filled to capacity. Flight 831 always had a full complement of standbys waiting to board.

The flight deck was manned by two veterans, Captain John Snider and co-pilot Harry Dyck. Their weather report read overcast with light rain and fog, visibility four miles, surface wind 12 mph from the northeast. The takeoff, at 6:20, was without event.

The ship climbed to 3,000 feet, and the captain requested permission to make a left-hand turn northwestward, over Riviere-des-Milles-Iles and the small village of Ste.-Therese, in the foothills of the Laurentian Mountains.

Four miles northwest of this village, something went terribly wrong. The jet dove to earth, striking the ground with such force that the shock was recorded on the seismograph at the College Brebeuf in Montreal. The plane dug a crater several times its size in depth and circumference, and its 51,000 pounds of JP4 fuel ignited, sending a pyre of flame and smoke 500 feet in the air. The heat was so intense that rescuers found little left to identify. All 118 passengers and crew apparently died instantly.

Two reasons were later given for the crash: First, there is a particular type of near-ground turbulence called geostrophic convection, which usually happens at night and in rain showers, often to the rear of cold fronts. Simply explained, it is a wind that travels over the ground and is wafted upward because of trees, buildings, hills and other irregularities of the landscape. According to Fred McClement, in his book *It Doesn't Matter Where You Sit,* "[These winds] become dangerous to jets during the takeoff and approach procedures when speeds are lower, turns are being made, and when no trouble is expected."

There was no doubt in the minds of investigators of the crash that the plane encountered some turbulence as it was banking into its northwest turn, and that would mean that the pilot and co-pilot would be relying on their instruments more than usual. The one instrument on which they would be relying most would be the plane's artificial horizon—a circular instrument with a floating ball dial that indicates whether the aircraft is in level flight.

Activated by a vertical gyroscope, this artificial horizon has a built-in danger signal to warn of malfunctioning. The worst-case scenario is one in which the gyro fails, the artificial horizon follows the failed gyro, and the pilot, following the misinformation of the instrument, goes into a dive. At 6,000 feet, the height at which Flight 831 was flying when its fatal trouble occurred, it would be impossible to bring any jet out of a dive.

This was the informed speculation that led the board of inquiry to its conclusions about the possible reason for the crash: a failed gyroscope. As a result of the tragedy, the installation of flight recorders in all turbine-powered aircraft in Canada was required, as well as an improved vertical gyroscope system.

CHILE
ANDES MOUNTAINS

February 6, 1965

• • • • • • • • • • • • • • • •

An ill-maintained Aera Nacionale DC-6B with 87 tourists aboard lost radio contact with Santiago, Chile on February 6, 1965, entered a cloud bank and crashed into the side of San Jose Mountain. All aboard were killed.

It may be fortunate that the jets of the major airlines fly at altitudes too high to view the majestic but dangerous peaks of the Andes. Most adventurous tourists view them close at hand, at ground level. But others, particularly those who want to get an intimate glimpse of the famous statue of Christ of the Andes, erected in Uspallata Pass on the Argentine-Chilean border, must take smaller, propeller-driven planes, which are subjected to the unpredictable air currents and weather of the high Andes.

Such was the case when a soccer team, sightseers and tourists climbed aboard an Aera Nacionale DC-6B at the Santiago airport on February 6, 1965. It was the height of the summer tourist season, and the plane was packed with 87 passengers eager to catch a glimpse of the fabled statue and the peaks that surround it.

The plane was old and, some said afterward, ill maintained. No reason is known for its loss of radio contact 20 minutes after takeoff. A heavy cloud cover shrouded the Andes near Santiago and completely obscured San Jose Mountain and its ancient gorge, El Volcan Pass. The DC-6B disappeared into the cloud cover.

A waterworks engineer spotted it flying overhead, in the direction of the pass. A loud explosion followed, and the engineer immediately reported his sighting to the Santiago airport. Some time later, rescuers discovered the wreckage of the aircraft strewn along the slope of the mountain. There were no survivors.

COLOMBIA
BOGOTA

July 24, 1938

• • • • • • • • • • • • • • • • • •

A military stunt plane flying too close to the packed stands at a military air show at the opening of the Campo de Marte in Bogota, Colombia on July 24, 1938 broke up and slashed through the crowd of 50,000. Fifty-three spectators were killed by falling debris.

The 155th anniversary of the birth of Simon Bolivar, the patriot-dictator who liberated South America from Spain, and the opening of the Campo de Marte, a military exercise field, were celebrated in Bogota, Colombia with a military air show. Fifty thousand spectators packed several metal-roofed stands that sunny afternoon to applaud the daredevil acrobatics of a hand-picked group of military fliers.

The low-flying antics of these pilots did not please Dr. Eduardo Santos, president of Colombia, and he complained more than once to War Minister Alberto Pumarejo about the reckless disregard of safety unfolding before them.

The president's evaluation of the situation turned out to be correct. Within minutes after his last complaint to the war minister, a plane piloted by a Lieutenant Abadia clipped the end of one stand with its wing tip, rolled sideways, sheered away a set of steps leading to the stand and burst into flame. The propeller, separated from its engine, preceded the flaming wreck as it plowed into the stands, incinerating and slashing hundreds of screaming, terrified and trapped spectators.

Some, their clothes on fire, bolted for the open fields; others were pinned to their seats by pieces of wreckage. Fifty-three persons perished in this needless disaster.

CZECHOSLOVAKIA
BRATISLAVA

November 24, 1966

• • • • • • • • • • • • • • • • • •

An Ilyushin-18 owned by TABSO Airlines disappeared into a snowstorm on the night of November 24, 1966 and plunged into a peak of the Carpathian Mountains near Bratislava, Czechoslovakia. All 82 aboard died.

The TABSO Airlines Soviet-built Ilyushin-18 was not scheduled to stop at Bratislava on the night of November 24, 1966. Its normal run took it from Sofia to Budapest and Prague, but for some reason, it made an unscheduled stop at Bratislava.

The stop could have been caused by the weather, which was bad. There were high winds, and just as the liner began to taxi onto the runway, preparatory to takeoff, the skies seemed to open, and it began to snow heavily. Apparently disregarding the weather, the airport gave the aircraft clearance for takeoff.

The four-engine turboprop roared forward and within minutes was obscured from view by the snowstorm. Minutes later, it slammed into the side of a peak in the Carpathian Mountains, which surround Bratislava like a dangerous fence. All 82 people aboard were killed, including Bulgarian opera star Katya Popova.

EGYPT
CAIRO

May 20, 1965

• • • • • • • • • • • • • • • • • •

Hampered by dangerous landing conditions at Egypt's Cairo Airport, a Pakistan International Airways Boeing 707 crashed on landing on the night of May 20, 1965. All 124 aboard were killed.

Cairo Airport in the early 1960s was a nightmare. For years it had been the talk of the industry, and finally, by 1965, members of the International Pilots' Association refused to make night landings at Cairo.

There were numerous hazards. First, there was inadequate lighting, making it difficult to define the parameters of each runway. In addition, some of the runways were eccentrically configured. One in particular was heavily sloped and approachable only by an abrupt dropping of a plane for a distance of almost 1,000 feet. Finally there was a shortage of rescue equipment.

Heeding the boycott by the IPA, authorities had begun to make improvements. But their priorities and the way they deployed them were mysterious. Their first purchase was up-to-date rescue equipment, but this was kept locked away.

The price for this laxity was paid by 124 people who died in the wreckage of a Pakistan International Airways Boeing 707, which, approaching the airport at far too steep a decline, crash-landed on the night of May 20, 1965. The tragedy finally brought about the improvements that could have prevented it.

FRANCE
BEAUVAIS

October 5, 1930

• • • • • • • • • • • • • • • • •

A combination of bad weather, bad judgment and faulty design sent the R-101, Britain's mammoth dirigible, to the ground on October 5, 1930. Forty-nine died.

The R-101, Britain's entry in the speed and passenger sweepstakes of giant dirigibles in the 1920s and 1930s, was buffeted by an enormous storm on the night of October 5, 1930. Its passengers and crew were flung from one side of the gondola to the other. Yet Lieutenant H. C. Irwin, the commander of the dirigible, radioed to his home base in Cardington, England: "After an excellent supper our distinguished passengers smoked a final cigar and, having sighted the French coast, have now gone to rest after the excitement of the leave-taking."

A sister ship to the R-100, the R-101 was an imposing construction. Seven hundred seventy-seven feet in length, it had a hydrogen capacity of five million cubic feet. Powered by six Rolls-Royce Condor engines, it was capable of lifting 150 tons and had accommodations for 100 passengers.

But the R-101 had been in trouble from the first moment out of the factory. On its maiden voyage, on October 14, 1929, its engines had malfunctioned. The fabric of its skin had seemed faulty.

The British government had been aware of these problems, and yet, in an international dirigible competition with Germany and France, it had still pushed for a long trip.

Thus, on October 5, 1930, 52 crew members and four distinguished observers, including Lord Thomson, who had argued most strongly in Parliament for the trip, boarded the R-101 for a trip to the Orient.

There were two portents of disaster. Four tons of water used as ballast were accidentally thrown overboard while the dirigible was still tied to its mooring. Second, a storm was brewing on the Channel, and that was exactly where the R-101 was heading.

Nevertheless, at 6:40 P.M., the R-101 left its mooring mast and headed directly into the storm. Cruising altitude was supposed to be 1,000 feet, but it could not maintain that altitude, dropping abruptly to 700, then shooting up to 1,100. One of the engines stopped partway across the Channel. Still, Lieutenant Irwin pressed cheerily on.

The storm did not abate when they passed over the French coastline. Thirty-five-knot winds buffeted the R-101, driving it lower and lower. By 1:00 A.M., at a village called Poix, the ship's altitude was a mere 250 feet and descending.

An hour later, the R-101 had reached Beauvais. It was now skimming trees and rooftops, headed for what seemed like a gentle and safe landing in a large field outside town. The field, however, was not altogether without obstacles. At one end was a ridge of hills, and the R-101 headed straight for it, crashing into the ridge and igniting its load of hydrogen. The entire ship was consumed in roaring flames in an instant, and 48 crew members and Lord Thomson were burned to death.

FRANCE
GRENOBLE

November 13, 1950

• • • • • • • • • • • • • • • • • •

Bad weather forced a Canadian Curtis-Reid Air-Tours charter flight to ram into Mont Obiou, near Grenoble, France, on November 13, 1950. There were no survivors.

A charter flight loaded with pilgrims returning from a Holy Year pilgrimage to the Vatican encountered severe weather conditions over the French Alps on November 13, 1950. A mere 10 days before, an Air India plane, flying the same route, had flown into the face of Mount Blanc, killing 48 passengers.

The Canadian Curtis-Reid Air-Tours charter flight, carrying 58 passengers who had, that very morning, had an audience with Pope Pius XII, was lost in heavy fog and rain. Some time in the early evening of November 13, it rammed into the side of Mont Obiou, an 8,500-foot peak near Grenoble.

Rescuers would find no survivors among the pilgrims, many of whom, in death, clutched pictures of the pope.

FRANCE
PARIS

June 3, 1962

• • • • • • • • • • • • • • • • • •

Pilot error in failing to abort the takeoff of an overloaded Air France Boeing 707 from Paris's Orly Airport on June 3, 1962 was blamed for its fiery crash. One hundred thirty passengers and crew members were killed; two flight attendants survived.

An Air France Boeing 707 carrying 132 passengers—most of them the leading figures in the cultural life of Atlanta, Georgia—gained eight feet of altitude, fell to the runway at Paris's Orly Airport, skidded forward, hit a row of approach lights at the end of the runway and exploded.

The group, all members of the Atlanta Art Association, had been touring some of Europe's leading museums and repositories of art—the Louvre, the Tate, the Uffizi Gallery and St. Mark's. It was a full flight but not overcrowded. However, for some reason never explained, the pilot seemed to have difficulty raising the jet from the runway. A board of inquiry later speculated that he was experiencing heavy loads on his elevators and tried to abort the takeoff before he reached the end of the runway. Apparently, he made his decision too late to arrest the forward ground speed of the aircraft. The brakes were applied, and all of the engines were thrown into reverse, but the plane, loaded to capacity with jet fuel, was blown to bits when it struck the approach lights and some cherry trees beyond.

One hundred thirty people were killed. The only two survivors were two flight attendants, Jacqueline Gillet and Francoise Authie, who were strapped into seats in the tail section, which broke loose just before the explosion and threw them clear.

Horribly enough, Mr. and Mrs. Milton Bevington of Atlanta carried through with a plan they always practiced when they traveled but never believed would achieve its intended result: They always flew in different airplanes, reasoning that if one crashed, the other would survive to take care of their children. Mrs. Bevington boarded the plane, and her husband watched the entire catastrophe from the terminal.

FRANCE
PARIS

March 3, 1974

• • • • • • • • • • • • • • • • •

In the worst crash in the history of aviation to that date, Turkish Airlines Flight 981, a Douglas DC-10, suddenly lost compression and control when a faulty cargo door blew off, forcing the craft to crash in a turnip field near Paris. All 346 people aboard perished.

The worst crash in the history of aviation to that date was caused by negligence, ignorance, tampering and a poorly designed hatch door. And what is worse, a similar accident that occurred two years earlier should have alerted the experts and those in charge to the problems that were repeated in this tragedy.

On June 6, 1972 an American Airlines DC-10 developed trouble 11,000 feet over Windsor, Ontario. Its rear hatch door blew off, tearing a hole in the fuselage, decompressing the interior of the plane, collapsing part of the passenger cabin floor, sending huge clouds of fog and iron filings through the plane and severing some of the control cables.

For a few feverish minutes, the stunned pilot, Captain Bryce McCormick, and his first officer, Peter Paige Whitney, were certain that they were about to dive to their deaths. The throttles had been slammed backward into idling speed, rendering the plane's engines almost useless. But Captain McCormick gave the plane full throttle, thus preventing its nose from dropping.

Fortunately, his hydraulic lines had not been severed, and he was able to control the plane well enough to return to Detroit—the flight's origination point—and land safely, with no casualties.

The board of inquiry investigating this accident determined that the latching mechanism of the cargo door was faulty and weak enough to give way under pressure. Thus, recommendations were made immediately to McDonnell Douglas to make the following three modifications in all DC-10 cargo doors:

1. The locking pins of the cargo door were to be reconfigured, so that in the "closed" position they would overlap the latches by one-quarter of an inch, instead of $1/32$ of an inch.
2. A support plate was required to prevent the upper torque tube from bending under pressure as it did in the Windsor incident.
3. The tube carrying the locking pins was to be modified to prevent a false signal through the microswitch system.

Apparently, the modifications were not strictly enforced. Not only were they not made on some DC-10s already flying, but two were actually manufactured in the following two years with the same defects in the cargo door. One of these, plane number 29, was sold to Hava Yollari of Turkish Airlines.

On Sunday, March 3, 1974, this DC-10, as Flight 981, took off from Orly Airport in Paris, headed for London. It was loaded with 346 persons, an unusually high passenger-load caused by an engineer's strike at London's Heathrow Airport. Because of the strike, all British European Airways flights were grounded and their passengers transferred to other flights. THY Flight 981 usually flew half full, but this time it turned away passengers, including the British Bury St. Edmunds Rugby team.

Flight 981 had originated in Istanbul at 9 A.M. that morning. Along with all other airlines flying DC-10s, THY had been warned, because of the Windsor incident, to be vigilant when closing the cargo door and to check its locking mechanism carefully.

However, even with careful maintenance, the door's locking mechanism was missing the support plate that was to have been installed after the Windsor incident. Thus, for the 63 weeks it had been operating, ship 29 was in essentially the same condition that the American Airlines flight was in when it had lost its cargo door at 11,000 feet. In addition, a later investigation revealed that the locking pins on this rear cargo door were also misrigged, so that even a slight vibration could dislodge them. Someone had turned the rod on ship 29's rear door the wrong way.

At Orly, THY's maintenance was managed by an outside contractor, SAMOR. The last person to close the rear cargo door was an Algerian expatriate, Mohammed Mahmoudi. He followed his instructions exactly, but not being a trained mechanic, he did not notice that the door closed more easily than it should. Furthermore, he was not assigned to make the final visual inspection of the door through a small peephole. If that inspection had been made, it would have revealed that the locking pins were in the "unsafe" position.

This visual inspection was to be done by either the THY station mechanic or the flight engineer. But on March 3, 1974 Osman Zeytin, the THY station mechanic at Orly, was on vacation in Istanbul. And none of the airport workers saw a flight engineer check the peephole.

The third safety backup was a light in the cockpit that would have revealed to the crew that the door was not securely locked, but it did not light.

Thus, Flight 981 was doomed from the moment it took off, at 12:30 P.M. The captain, Mejak Berkoz, and his copilot, Oral Ulusman, both seasoned fliers, climbed to 11,500 feet and headed east over the village of Coulommiers, where they were to change course north, to London.

At 11,500 feet, there were approximately five tons of air pressure pushing against the mislatched cargo door. The door blew open. The bolts gave way, the latch talons were pulled from the spools and the door flew backward, ripped from its hinges by the aircraft's slip stream.

As in the Windsor incident, the DC-10 rapidly decompressed. The loss of pressure buckled part of the passenger cabin, and the last two rows of seats in the left-hand aisle, with the six passengers strapped into them, were sucked into the cavity and ejected through the hole in the plane's fuselage. They would fall two and a half miles and land in a turnip field near the village of St. Pathus.

The other 340 people aboard Flight 981 only had a minute and a half to live. This time, the buckling of the floor apparently severed all of the control cables, as the dialogue in the cockpit, recorded by the cockpit voice recorder, later revealed:

Voices: "Oops Aw, aw."
A klaxon sounds.
Berkoz: What happened?
Ulusman: The cabin blew out.
Berkoz: Are you sure? Bring it up, pull her nose up.
Ulusman: I can't bring it up—she doesn't respond.
Ozer: Nothing is left.
Ulusman: Seven thousand feet.
A klaxon sounds, warning that the plane has gone over the maximum speed.
Berkoz: Hydraulics?
Ulusman: We have lost it . . . oops, oops.
Berkoz: It looks like we are going to hit the ground. Speed. Oops.
The sound of the initial impact.

Flight 981 hit the ground at 497 miles per hour. None of the passengers and crew survived. The violence of the impact shredded the plane and its inhabitants. Only 40 bodies, including the six who were sucked out of the plane when the door blew off, were found more or less intact and thus were easily identifiable. The rest were disintegrated into approximately 18,000 fragments, which medical personnel and police methodically and scrupulously gathered over the next days.

The FAA board of inquiry discovered the next day that the hatch door was missing its support plate, and there was evidence it had never been fitted. "Human failure" was the final conclusion of the investigation, and according to Paul Eddy, Elaine Potter and Bruce Page, in their examination of negligence in flight, *Destination Disaster,* the blame was placed, at a later annual meeting of McDonnell Douglas, "specifically [on] the failure of an 'illiterate' baggage handler (Mohammed Mahmoudi) to close the cargo door properly."

Hearing of this, the union to which Mahmoudi belonged threatened to boycott DC-10s at all French airports, and an emissary was dispatched from the American Embassy in Paris to union headquarters, where he apologized on behalf of the U.S. government.

Senate hearings were also held, and inspection and improvements on the latching mechanisms of the rear cargo doors on all DC-10s were made mandatory. If they had been made so after the Windsor incident, 346 people would not have perished in this, aviation's worst disaster to date.

GERMANY
EAST BERLIN

August 14, 1972

• • • • • • • • • • • • • • • • • •

One hundred fifty-six persons died in the midair explosion of an Interflug Ilyushin-62 flying from East Berlin to Burgas, Bulgaria. No official explanation for the tragedy has been released by East German authorities.

Confusion and mystery have muddled the facts about the midair explosion of Interflug's Ilyushin-62 on a flight from East Berlin to Burgas, Bulgaria. The aircraft apparently took off without incident from Schonefeld Airport in East Berlin on August 14, 1972, climbed to 100 feet, exploded and hurtled to earth, killing 148 passengers and eight crew members.

Western journalists heard conflicting eyewitness reports—one eyewitness saw flames; the other did not—and the East German authorities refused to release the findings of a board of inquiry.

GERMANY
JOHANNISTHAL

October 17, 1913

• • • • • • • • • • • • • • • • • •

A ripped hull, overheated gas and faulty design were responsible for the crash of the German naval dirigible LZ-18 on October 17, 1913 over Johannisthal, Germany. Twenty-eight died in the fiery crash.

Felix Prietzker was a prize student of Count Ferdinand von Zeppelin, the designer and constructor of Germany's first dirigible, *Luftschiff Zeppelin Number 1.* That ship was the prototype for all of the airships that would ferry military personnel and passengers across the continent and across the Atlantic for the next 40 years.

But Prietzker was no slave to a master designer. His design for the L.2, which became known as the LZ-18, was a marked modification of Count von Zeppelin's original. First, the gondolas, which carried the crew, passengers and control instruments for the ship, were fitted considerably closer to the ship than in the original design. Then a series of windscreens, designed for greater maneuverability, were attached to its bow. According to other engineers, these windscreens created a dangerous situation because they were of metal and were positioned very close to the skin of the ship's hydrogen-filled hull. As air pressure fluctuated, the hull changed in shape and size, and the abrasion of these windscreens against it was a matter of extreme concern to some aircraft engineers.

Prietzker, however, was unconcerned about what he considered to be a fancied danger, and so he pressed ahead with the construction of this airborne leviathan, which was 518 feet, 2 inches in length and was powered by four 165-horsepower Maybach engines mounted on the ship's two gondolas.

The ship, commissioned by and delivered to the German Navy in the autumn of 1913, made its maiden voyage under ironic circumstances. The flight, on September 9, 1913, was an uneventful one. But it occurred at almost the same time that its prototype and sister ship, the L.1, encountered a fierce storm over Helgoland and plummeted into the sea, killing 14 of its crew.

The German naval dirigible LZ-18 plunged to earth in a fiery crash on October 17, 1913, killing 28—the highest death toll in an air crash to that date. Library of Congress

The LZ-18 had, however, passed its first test, and a more elaborate trip was planned for October 17, 1913. This one would take the designer Prietzker and 27 others, including some zeppelin consultants and admiralty officers, on a tour of the German countryside from its berth in Johannisthal.

The airship launched smoothly, floated serenely upward from its post and reached its cruising level of 1,500 feet. The warmth of the morning expanded the hydrogen in the hull, lightening the ship, and it rose easily. At 1,500 feet, the engines were engaged, preparatory to directing the ship westward.

But no sooner had the engines started than a tongue of flame shot outward from the forward engine gondola. Within seconds, the flame had doubled back on itself—blocked, fatally, by the windscreen—and both gondolas and hull were consumed by a roaring, cataclysmic fire. The ship crumpled, its white-hot ribbing bright against the blueness of the morning sky, and as crew members and passengers frantically broke gondola windows to escape, the great ship nosed earthward.

The gondolas hit the ground first, but before the men inside could escape, the white-hot hull collapsed around them. Only three men survived the crash, but they were too severely burned to survive the day. All in all, 28 died—the highest death toll in an air crash to that date.

A board of inquiry named the cause of the crash: a rent in the hull, which allowed the overheated gas to escape and ignite the ship's skin. Prietzker's windscreens, which had directed the burning hydrogen back to the engines and the gondolas, both focused and accelerated the fatal process.

GERMANY
MUNICH

December 17,1960

• • • • • • • • • • • • • • • • • •

A U.S. Air Force C-131 Convair went out of control over Munich, Germany on December 17, 1960 and plunged into the crowded city. Fifty-three people died; 20 were on the plane, 33 on the ground.

Airlines are particularly careful to give thickly populated urban areas wide berths. The chances of an airplane falling into a crowded city street are thus remote; yet, bizarre accidents have been known to happen. Just such an incident took place at the height of the Christmas shopping season in Munich, on December 17, 1960.

That city's Bayerstrasse was thronged with holiday shoppers in the late afternoon of December 17. The thoroughfare is flanked by rows of shops. The public transportation system of the city serves this wide boulevard well; a major trolley line runs down the middle of it.

Outside the city, the Munich-Riem Airport was also crowded. At the section that serviced U.S. military aircraft, a Convair C-131 loaded 18 military service dependents for the brief ride to London. A thick fog had settled over the city and the airport, but the Convair took off on schedule.

Minutes after it became airborne, the C-131 developed engine trouble. The pilot radioed his plight to the Munich-Riem Airport, which in turn contacted the fire brigades in Munich. The plane was out of control and over the city. There was a distinct danger that it could lose power and plunge into Munich itself.

Tragically, that is exactly what happened. The pilot fought to control his aircraft, banking sharply to avoid several tall buildings, then slicing the steeple from Saint Paul's Church and finally, with a roar, diving into the middle of the holiday crowds on the Bayerstrasse.

The plane collided squarely with a crowded trolley, exploding upon impact, setting fire to the car, the street and some buildings bordering the crash site. Passengers in the trolley who might have escaped the fire were trapped inside behind closed and now useless electric doors. Fifty-three people—20 on the plane and 33 on the ground—died.

GREAT BRITAIN
ENGLAND
LONDON

June 18, 1972

• • • • • • • • • • • • • • • • • •

Overloading was the apparent cause of the crash of a BEA Trident 1 shortly after takeoff from Heathrow Airport in London on June 18, 1972. All 118 aboard died, and no official reason for the crash was ever given.

A worldwide pilots' strike had been threatened for the summer of 1972, in protest over the lackadaisical attitude individual Western governments had taken toward the steadily increasing incidents of air terrorism and skyjacking. As a result, flights in Europe in June 1972 were full and occasionally overfull.

This was apparently the case with a British European Airways Trident 1, bound for Brussels, at London's Heathrow Airport on June 18, 1972. The weather was clear; flying conditions were ideal. The plane had been inspected and appeared to be taking off normally, if sluggishly. It was overloaded with 118 passengers and crew.

The plane cleared the runway and retracted its landing gear, preparatory to climbing to cruising altitude. And then, like a wounded bird, it fell out of the sky into a field beyond the runway it had just cleared. The aircraft split upon impact, scattering bits and pieces of its fuselage, wings and engines all over the field.

Rescue crews rushed to the scene immediately, dousing the huge fires fed by the large amount of jet fuel aboard. Two passengers survived the impact but died later: A young girl was pulled from the wreckage by police, but she expired before an ambulance could arrive for her. An older man, found in the field, was taken to a London hospital, but he too died before the end of the day. The precise cause of the crash was never determined.

GREAT BRITAIN
WALES
CARDIFF

March 12, 1950

• • • • • • • • • • • • • • • • •

No reason has been given for the crash on landing of a charter Avro Tudor V at Cardiff, Wales on March 12, 1950. Eighty soccer fans and crew members died; three men survived.

The legion of unexplained crashes under ideal conditions seems to be endless. One such incident is the odd crash of a chartered Avro Tudor V prop plane that carried 78 Welsh soccer fans returning from a triumphant match in Dublin to their deaths.

It was a one-hour, commuter-length flight from Dublin. The weather was nonthreatening; Llandow Airport at Cardiff was clear and ready to accept the landing of the aircraft.

The Avro circled and approached—far too low. Just short of the runway, the plane's forward section hit the ground, and the plane flipped over.

There was no fire, just an eerie, other-worldly silence surrounding this bizarre but fatal accident. Evan Thomas, a farmer who was one of the first rescuers on the scene, reported to the newspapers, "The smoke from the engines was curling from the wreckage. Through it walked two men. They were the only things that moved."

Three men survived the crash. Eighty other soccer fans and crew members were crushed to death.

INDIA
BOMBAY

January 1, 1978

• • • • • • • • • • • • • • • • •

No official explanation was given for the midair explosion of an Air India Boeing 747 over Bombay on January 1, 1978. All 213 aboard were killed.

A mysterious and unexplained explosion aboard an Air India jumbo jet bound from Bombay to the Persian Gulf emirate of Dubai blew the plane apart and killed 213 persons on January 1, 1978.

Residents of the western Bombay suburb of Bandra said they saw the Boeing 747 break in two after the explosion and plummet into the Arabian Sea two miles offshore. It had only been airborne for four and half minutes and had begun to bank to the left to set itself on its course when it suddenly blew apart and plunged into the sea.

Search parties and rescue crews failed to turn up any survivors. All 213 aboard perished in this bizarre tragedy.

INDIA
NEW DELHI

June 14, 1972

• • • • • • • • • • • • • • • • •

Terrorism was suspected but never proved in the midair explosion of a Japan Airlines DC-8 over New Delhi on June 14, 1972. Eighty-seven died; six survived.

A suspicion of terrorist sabotage surrounded the mysterious crash of a Japan Airlines DC-8 jet at New Delhi's Palam International Airport on June 14, 1972. Only two weeks before, Japanese terrorists had massacred 25 innocent people in the International Airport in Tel Aviv, and threats of retaliation had been made. But investigators would never adequately prove this theory.

The plane had departed from Tokyo and was proceeding with a normal, clear-weather landing when it suddenly burst into flames, heeled over and crashed into the farmland that rimmed the airport, near the Jamuna River. Authorities reasoned that there was an explosion, either before or on impact, since pieces of the plane and its passengers were strewn over a two-mile radius. Eighty-seven died in the wreck and six survived, but their testimony cast no light upon the events that led to the crash.

ITALY
PALERMO

May 5, 1972

• • • • • • • • • • • • • • • • •

Pilot error caused the crash of an Alitalia DC-8 into Montagna Lunga, near Palermo, on May 5, 1972. All 115 aboard were killed.

Palermo's Punta Raisi Airport is a treacherous trap. Ringed by high mountains, it has claimed even the most careful of pilots. Night landings are exercises in care, skill and prayer, and most airlines try not to land or take off after dark at this, one of Europe's most dangerous landing fields.

On the night of May 5, 1972 an Alitalia DC-8 jet from Rome attempted to land at Punta Raisi. The pilot, a veteran of the run, apparently misjudged his approach and came in too low to clear the mountain range. Minutes before he should have safely touched down on the runway, he slammed into the side of Montagna Lunga, a 12,250-foot peak near the airport. The plane exploded on impact, setting forest fires that would burn for days. Every one of the 115 crew members and passengers aboard perished in the crash.

JAPAN
MORIOKA
July 30, 1971

• • • • • • • • • • • • • • • • •

A Japanese Air Force F-86 Sabre jet without radar collided in midair with an All-Nippon Boeing 727 on July 30, 1971. Pilot error was blamed in this crash that killed all 162 passengers aboard the jet. The military jet pilot parachuted to safety.

The year 1971 was particularly bad for near collisions in the sky. There were 600 of these near misses reported in the United States that year, and 200 in Japan. There were just too many civilian and military aircraft flying in close proximity to one another in the two countries, and experts felt that a tragedy was bound to occur. It did, on July 30, over Morioka, in the so-called Japanese Alps.

Flight 58, an All-Nippon Boeing 727 was loaded largely with members of a Japanese society dedicated to the memory of war dead. They had just been to Hokkaido on a pilgrimage and were heading back to Tokyo. The takeoff from Chitose Airport was uneventful; it was a clear day, and visibility was good. They reached their cruising level of 28,000 feet easily and without incident.

In the same area, Sergeant Yoshimi Ichikawa, a student pilot with 21 hours in the air, was at the controls of a Japanese Air Force F-86 Sabre jet. Neither he nor his instructor, Captain Tamotsu Kuma, who was flying in another Sabre jet, had the benefit of radar.

The airliner did, and thus it is somewhat puzzling that its commander did not see the military aircraft until it was too late. The planes collided in midair. The airliner exploded upon impact, and pieces of it and its passengers were scattered over mountaintops. All 162 jet passengers would die in this tragedy, but Ichikawa, the student pilot of the jet, would parachute to safety.

He was immediately arrested and charged with involuntary homicide, but he would be acquitted.

JAPAN
MOUNT FUJI
March 5, 1966

• • • • • • • • • • • • • • • • •

Pilot error and wind conditions claimed a BOAC Boeing 707 on March 5, 1966. The aircraft collided with Mount Fuji, killing 124 people.

A terrible crash had taken place a month before at Tokyo International Airport (see p. 26), and as BOAC Flight 911 taxied out for takeoff, its passengers could plainly see the charred remnants of that catastrophe. None of them could have known that within a few minutes, a second tragedy, almost as grim as the first, would snuff out their lives.

The Boeing 707 was carrying a full passenger load the afternoon of March 5, 1966, but its takeoff was without effort. It reached 6,000 feet and circled close to Mount Fuji, which was clearly visible in the sharp afternoon sunlight.

What was not visible, to either passengers or flight crew, were the killer air currents that circle Mount Fuji. Of the force and nature of tornadoes, they are a pilot's anathema, and captains of aircraft give them wide berth. But for some reason that will never be explained, the pilot of BOAC Flight 911 did not avoid the mountain and its lethal winds by a wide enough margin.

Caught in the winds, the airliner blew apart in midair, flinging wreckage and bodies against the slopes of Mount Fuji. One hundred twenty-four people—all those aboard—died, raising the total number of crash victims at or near Tokyo International Airport in one month to 257.

JAPAN
MOUNT OGURA
August 12, 1985

• • • • • • • • • • • • • • • • •

Improper repairs of a Japan Airlines Boeing 747SR led to the loss of part of the airplane's tail section and loss of control of the aircraft, which crashed into the side of Mount Ogura, Japan. The worst air disaster in the world involving a single passenger plane, it claimed 475 lives. Forty-nine passengers survived.

The worse air disaster in the world involving a single passenger plane occurred on a mountainside in central Japan on the evening of Monday, August 12, 1985. A Japan Airlines jumbo jet veered eratically in an uncontrolled path and slammed into the side of Moung Ogura, one of Japan's highest peaks. There were 524 people aboard; only 49 of them survived.

Japan Airlines Flight 123 left Tokyo's Haneda Airport at 6:15 P.M. for its 250-mile flight to Osaka. Travel had been especially heavy in the last few days. Thousands of Japanese were returning to their hometowns for a traditional midsummer festival known as Obon, in which the souls of ancestors are honored.

Rescuers comb the wreckage of Japan Airlines Flight 123 after it crashed into Mount Ogura, north of Tokyo, on August 12, 1985. Five hundred twenty died in the crash of the Boeing 747 en route from Tokyo to Osaka. National Transportation Safety Board

The plane was a Boeing 747SR, especially configured for Japan, where flights with 500 passengers were not uncommon. This one was completely filled.

The aircraft had seen a lot of service and, seven years before, had made a hard landing at Osaka. The impact had damaged the lower rear fuselage, and Boeing maintenance people had supposedly repaired it.

Thirteen minutes after takeoff, Flight 123 was clearly in trouble. The pilot, Masami Takahama, radioed that the right rear passenger door had "broken." One of the survivors, Yumi Ochia, an off-duty assistant purser for Japan Airlines, said later that there was a loud noise that originated in the rear of the plane and over her head. Following it, there was an instant "whiteout" as a thick fog filled the cabin—a sure indication that the cabin pressure had dropped and water vapor had condensed.

The plane had reached its cruising altitude of 24,000 feet by now, and the crew immediately radioed Tokyo for permission to drop to 20,000 feet.

But a far greater problem than reduced cabin pressure had been created by whatever caused the loud noise heard by the off-duty purser. The impact of it had been great enough to force the plane's nose up. And worse, it had apparently done something major to the craft's control system. Among the 43 sensors placed throughout the airliner, the one in the rear, near the horizontal stabilizer, had registered the greatest shock. It had broken off. Captain Takahama was unable to control the plane.

"Immediate trouble, request turn back to Haneda," a crew member radioed to Tokyo at 6:25 P.M., seconds after the first transmission. Four times over the next 30 minutes, the captain radioed that he had no control of the plane. He was attempting to steer it by alternately increasing and throttling down engine power.

By 6:45, the plane had lost an appreciable amount of altitude. It was flying at only 9,300 feet, and the captain had all but lost complete control. "We may be finished," he said to his co-pilot. At the same time, the black box recorder picked up a voice in the background announcing emergency-landing instructions in the cabin.

Ten minutes later, Tokyo radioed Flight 123 that it could land either at Haneda or at a U.S. air base in Yokota, northwest of Tokyo.

But by then, Flight 123 had stopped answering. One minute after the clearance had been given for an emergency landing, it had slammed into the side of Mount Ogura, in Gumma prefecture, 70 miles northwest of Tokyo. It exploded on impact, setting fire to acres of forest on the side of the mountain.

An eyewitness later told the Japan Broadcasting Corporation that she had watched the plane crash in "a big flame" after it flew over her house. The explosion was "followed by a white smoke which turned into a black mushroom-like-cloud," she said.

It would be 14 hours before the first rescue teams, composed of three dozen airborne troops, could be lowered onto the mountain by helicopters, joined by local police who hiked through a steady rain to the crash site.

At first, sabotage was thought to be the culprit. But a Japanese Navy destroyer on routine patrol reported finding a section of the plane's tail in Sagami Bay, just off the Miura Peninsula, southwest of Tokyo and 80 miles southeast of the crash site. The tail had apparently fallen off.

Now the history of the aircraft began to help solve the mystery of the crash and the 32 terrible minutes that preceded it. One of the first questions to be solved was what had caused the rudder and other hydraulic systems to stop functioning.

The answer was in the repairs made seven years previously to a ruptured bulkhead. They had been improperly made, even though they had been done by a team flown by Boeing to Japan. Shaped somewhat like an umbrella canopy, the bulkhead was at the very back of the passenger cabin and separated the highly pressurized cabin, from the unpressurized tail section, which was immediately behind it.

A single line of rivets was used for part of the repair, instead of the double line of rivets called for in the manual. With the expected metal fatigue brought on by seven years of constant use, the improper repair eventually gave way. And the results were monumentally tragic.

The blame apparently was not entirely Boeing's, at least in the minds of some officials and employees of Japan Airlines. Shortly after the findings of the investigative panel were released, there was a major shake-up in the executive structure of Japan Airlines. The president and two executives were replaced.

But this was not the end of the aftermath of this record catastrope. On September 21, police in Yokohama were called to the home of Hiro Tominaga, a Japan Airlines maintenance official who had been negotiating compensation payments with families of the crash victims.

Tominaga was found on the floor of his home, dead of knife wounds inflicted to his neck and chest. A four-inch-long knife was found near his body. A note nearby read, "I am atoning with my death."

JAPAN
TOKYO

June 18, 1953

• • • • • • • • • • • • • • • • •

Unspecified engine trouble caused the crash of a U.S. Air Force C-124 Globemaster shortly after takeoff from Tachikawa Air Base, near Tokyo, on June 18, 1953. All 129 aboard perished.

A United States Air Force C-124 Globemaster, a double-deck transport, was loaded with 129 military passengers and crew when it took off from Tachikawa Air Base, near Tokyo, on June 18, 1953.

The flight was routine during the Korean War. Relief personnel were being ferried to Korea; the wounded and those in need of R and R would board the return trip to Japan. The weather was clear; the takeoff was clean.

But four minutes after takeoff, the flight developed engine trouble. One engine quit completely, and the pilot radioed that he would be returning to the field. He never did. Less than five minutes later, the plane dove into a rice paddy, exploding and bursting into flames. None of the 129 aboard survived, and no cause for the crash was ever established.

JAPAN
TOKYO

February 4, 1966

• • • • • • • • • • • • • • • • •

No official reason was ever given for the crash of an All-Nippon Airways Boeing 727 landing at Tokyo International Airport on February 4, 1966. All 133 persons aboard died.

The year 1966 was a terrible one for air crashes at Tokyo International Airport. Two took place within one month of each other, on February 4 and March 5 (see p. 24). The precise reasons for both crashes would remain forever unexplained.

At a little before 7 P.M. on February 4, 1966, an All-Nippon Airways Boeing 727, arriving from Sapporo and piloted by veteran captain Masaki Takahashi, radioed for clearance to land. The weather was cloudless and calm.

The controllers in the tower cleared the flight for landing, and the 727 began its long circle of approach over Tokyo Bay.

At exactly 6:59 P.M., it disappeared from the controllers' radar screens. A few minutes later, when it should have been coming in for its final approach, it did not appear. And then, the tragic news arrived, by telephone: Fishermen had seen a "pillar of fire" soar overhead and dive into Tokyo Bay.

Rescue efforts went on through the night, but it would be dawn before bodies and the remains of the plane could be brought to the surface. No one survived. One hundred thirty-three people died.

MOROCCO
CASABLANCA

July 12, 1961

• • • • • • • • • • • • • • • • • • •

A fear of exposing Soviet military secrets to the West caused the pilot of a Czechoslovakian Airlines Ilyushin-18 to ignore instructions to divert from fogbound Casablanca Airport to a nearby U.S. air base. The plane crashed, killing all 72 aboard.

International politics seem to have figured prominently in the terrible tragedy that befell the passengers in a Ceskoslovenske Aerolinie (Czechoslovakian Airlines) Ilyushin-18 flight from Zurich to Prague, via Morocco.

The flight was scheduled to stop at Casablanca on the evening of July 12, 1961. But Casablanca was completely blanketed with a heavy fog, and the airport had closed down. Josef Mikus, the veteran pilot captaining the flight, was denied permission to land and told to divert to the U.S. air base at Nouasseur, a mere 15 minutes away. It was still open and relatively fog free.

The plane had plenty of fuel. It could easily have made the distance to the U.S. air base. However, Captain Mikus knew that there were several Soviet flying instructors aboard, on their way to train revolutionaries in Ghana and Guinea. Furthermore, there was a huge cargo load of films and pamphlets also destined for these two insurrection-torn African republics. To Mikus, landing at an American military base was tantamount to landing in the arms of the enemy.

At least that was the explanation given by authorities afterward, after Mikus ignored the instructions of the control tower at Casablanca and nosed his turboprop in for an instrument landing. But without help from the controllers, Mikus and his plane had no chance of success. Midway to its landing, the aircraft hit a power line. The heavy cable ripped two engines from the plane's wings, hurling them into midair, where they exploded. Two towers collapsed inward, toward the plane, which was flung heavily to earth.

It would take 25 minutes for rescuers to reach the scene of the crash, and even then, according to the I.C.A.O. (International Civil Aviation Organization) *Accident Digest,* Number 13, "When the police arrived at the scene . . . calls for help were heard coming from the wreckage, and an attempt was made to rescue the passengers, but a fire started, and it was impossible to continue operations."

All 72 persons aboard died.

NEW GUINEA
BIAK ISLAND

July 16, 1957

• • • • • • • • • • • • • • • • • • •

An unexplained engine explosion hurtled a KLM Super Constellation into the sea shortly after takeoff from Biak Island, New Guinea on July 16, 1957. Fifty-seven died.

A KLM Super Constellation took off in pleasant weather on the afternoon of July 16, 1957 bound from Biak Island in Dutch Guinea to Amsterdam. Within moments an engine exploded. The pilot, Captain Bob de Roos, fought for control of the plane while his co-pilot went about the methodical closing down of the engine.

But no amount of closing down could reverse the forces the explosion had started. Within minutes, the remaining engines were afire and useless. Without power, and with most of the wing controls also useless, the aircraft nosed over and plunged into the sea, a mere five miles from its takeoff point.

The forward part of the plane disappeared instantly beneath the surface of the water. The extreme tail section broke off and floated. Papuan natives, seeing the plane hurtling over their heads and into the sea, set off immediately in canoes. Their speed and skill and calmness saved 11 terrified passengers huddled in the detached but still floating tail section. Fifty-seven other passengers, trapped in the rest of the fuselage, drowned or were burned to death.

PAKISTAN
KARACHI

March 3, 1953

• • • • • • • • • • • • • • • • • • •

Pilot error was blamed for the first fatal jetliner crash in history, on takeoff from Karachi Airport on March 3, 1953.

On a test run, the Canadian Pacific Comet 1A turbojet burst into flames on impact, killing all 11 men aboard.

The first fatal jetliner crash in airline history took place while deHaviland was in the process of refining the design of its Comet 1A turbojet. The Comet was not a trouble-free airplane; only six months before this catastrophe, one had crashed near Rome. But none of the technical and flying crew aboard were injured.

On March 3, 1953 the Comet that had been sold to Canadian Pacific Airlines was being tested by 11 technicians and crew members. It had been loaded with 5,000 extra gallons of fuel before takeoff—an enormous addition of weight and enough to tip its nose dangerously up as it struggled to become airborne.

Had he seen that this would put the plane in danger of crashing, the pilot could have aborted the takeoff. The pilot apparently did not, and thus the board of inquiry later attributed what happened next to "pilot error."

Unable to lift off, the plane overshot the runway, climbed a few feet in the air, wavered and struck a brick culvert with one wing. This spun it off course, and it immediately slammed into and then through a wall. The fuel ignited; the plane burst into consuming flames, and all 11 men aboard were incinerated.

PERU
LIMA

November 27, 1962

• • • • • • • • • • • • • • • •

No explanation was given for the crash, in clear weather in the Andes near Lima, of a Varig Airlines Boeing 707 on November 27, 1962. All 97 aboard perished.

The Andes have claimed numerous victims in a number of air crashes (see p. 16). Some passengers have survived to write books and magazine articles about their collisions with these needle-like peaks. However, there would be no survivors of the crash of a Varig Airlines Boeing 707 in the late afternoon of November 27, 1962 and no record of the reasons for the mysterious crash in clear weather.

The flight from Rio de Janeiro to Los Angeles encountered trouble just before it was to land in Lima, Peru. At 5:30 P.M., the pilot radioed the airport in Lima, stating that there was trouble with the aircraft. Before he could explain further, transmission abruptly ended.

It would be 3:00 A.M. before a search party would reach the demolished plane, strewn over the face of a peak in the Andes. All 97 aboard were dead.

PUERTO RICO
SAN JUAN

April 11, 1952

• • • • • • • • • • • • • • • •

The failure of airline personnel to follow basic safety procedures during a ditch at sea near San Juan killed 52 people aboard a Pan American DC-4 on April 11, 1952. Seven survived.

A failure to follow basic procedure by the cabin and cockpit crew aboard a Pan American DC-4 on April 11, 1952 accounted for 52 needless fatalities.

The flight took off uneventfully from San Juan, Puerto Rico bound for New York. But nine minutes into the flight, the plane developed engine trouble. With one of its motors inoperable, it began to descend. The pilot had time to decide between ditching the plane in the sea, four miles from Puerto Rico, or taking his chances over land. He opted to go down at sea and informed the San Juan tower of his intent.

Once this course had been determined, it was up to the crew to prepare the passengers for the ditching effort by informing them of the location of life jackets and rubber rafts—both of which were aboard in sufficient quantity to save everyone. But this crucial and elementary drill was never carried out.

As a result, when the aircraft struck the water and floated, passengers panicked. To compound the terror, the crew opened the wrong doors to debark the passengers and let enormous amounts of water into the cabin, thus hastening the sinking of the craft. Terrified, confused and without life jackets, the passengers huddled on the plane's wing. Only one life raft was inflated, and this floated off with only seven survivors aboard.

Three minutes later, the aircraft sank beneath 15-foot waves, carrying 52 passengers to a watery death. A handful managed to stay afloat until ships could rescue them.

SAUDI ARABIA
RIYADH

August 19, 1980

• • • • • • • • • • • • • • • •

A combination of the failure of airline personnel to follow evacuation procedures and the Saudi Airlines practice of cooking over open butane stoves aboard its aircraft resulted in death by fire aboard a Saudi Airlines Lockheed L-1011

The death of all 310 passengers aboard this Saudi Airlines Lockheed-1011 at Riyadh was a result of the Saudi custom of allowing passengers to cook on board and a failure of airline personnel to follow proper evacuation procedures. National Transportation Safety Board

TriStar on the ground at Riyadh, Saudi Arabia on August 19, 1980. All 310 aboard died.

Three hundred ten passengers and crew were aboard a Saudi Airlines Lockheed L-1011 TriStar on the afternoon of August 19, 1980. The flight had originated in Karachi, Pakistan and was on its way to Jidda, after a short stopover in Riyadh. Among the passengers were some devout Muslims, who were allowed to bring two butane cooking stoves aboard so that they could observe their dietary laws in flight. U.S. carriers would blanch at this practice, but it was routine in the Middle East.

The flight departed from Riyadh without incident. But shortly after takeoff, when the plane was approximately 80 miles from the airport, the pilot radioed that there was a fire aboard and he was returning. He was given clearance and landed safely. The plane taxied to the end of the runway and onto a side area.

Rescue teams rushed to it, expecting the passengers to pour from the escape hatches. But before fire fighters could reach the plane, it burst thunderously into flames. Heavy smoke billowed from every opening, and the heat was intense. No one could approach the aircraft, not even in a protective asbestos suit. Fire trucks sprayed the consumed airliner with foam. It was all that could be done for the moment.

When teams were finally able to cut their way into the wreckage, they found an appalling sight. Passengers were piled up in mounds of fused and charred flesh near the escape hatches. There had obviously been a stampede when the plane landed. But none of the hatches were open or even unlocked. The crew's escape hatch in the cockpit was also, strangely, firmly latched. Every single person on the aircraft had died in the fire.

There was a fire extinguisher alongside one of the butane cooking stoves, and this must have been where the fire began. But why hadn't the crew opened the escape hatches?

Investigators posited three possibilities:

1. From the position of the bodies, it was obvious that there had been mass panic aboard the craft. Those in the back had rushed to the front, and this mayhem might have blocked the efforts of the crew to open the exits.
2. It was entirely possible that by the time the plane had taxied to a stop at Riyadh airport, all aboard had been asphyxiated.
3. The escape system on the plane was designed so that the hatches could not be opened from the inside unless the cabin had been depressurized. For some reason, the cabin pressure had not been released by the crew, and thus the escape hatches could not be opened by anyone.

A series of lawsuits by relatives of some of the 310 who perished aboard the plane attempted to prove negligence in the use of flammable materials within the aircraft, and that certainly contributed to the intensity of the blaze. But the reason that the plane remained sealed will never be known.

SPAIN
BARCELONA

July 3, 1970

• • • • • • • • • • • • • • • • • •

No official reason was given for the disappearance of a Dan-Air Airlines Comet over the Mediterranean near Barcelona on July 3, 1970. All 112 persons aboard died.

The Comet turbojet probably should have been retired from service soon after it was first built. In its 25 years of existence, it had many fatal accidents (see p. 28), and one of the worst of these occurred over the Mediterranean, near Barcelona, on the night of July 3, 1970.

A group of tourists, weary of the dampness of England, boarded a chartered, British-built Dan-Air Airlines Comet in Manchester, England at midday on July 3. All were headed to Barcelona, the Costa Brava and vacations in the sun.

The flight was uneventful until the aircraft was within 12 miles of its destination. The pilot radioed to the Barcelona tower at 7:00 P.M. that he was 12 miles away, flying at an altitude of 6,000 feet. This was the last anyone heard from the ill-fated flight. Observers along the coast reported seeing a large plane disappear into the sea approximately 20 miles from Mataro, up the coast from Barcelona.

Search boats were sent out, but no wreckage or bodies nor a trace of the plane or the 112 persons aboard was ever found.

SPAIN
CANARY ISLANDS
SANTA CRUZ DE TENERIFE

December 3, 1972

• • • • • • • • • • • • • • • • • •

In the fourth worst air crash up to that time, a Spantax Airlines Charter Convair 990-A Coronados lost an engine over Santa Cruz de Tenerife, in the Canary Islands, and plunged to earth. All 155 aboard perished.

The Spanish-owned Canary Islands, off the coast of Africa, are a paradise and a winter refuge for thousands of Scandinavians and Germans. The local joke is that there is more German, Danish and Swedish spoken on the islands from September through May than there is Spanish.

A majority of these northern European tourists reach Grand Canary, as the main island is called, by charter airline. A priest in Denmark has operated a huge charter operation for years, which annually ferries thousands of Danes on holiday to and from Grand Canary.

Other, smaller charter lines fly into Los Rodeos Airport on Santa Cruz de Tenerife, one of the six smaller islands. Spantax Airlines, a Spanish charter carrier, is one example, and on December 3, 1972 it chartered one of its Convair 990-A Coronados to a group of Bavarian bus operators on holiday. The group, sunburned and happy, boarded the plane on a cloudless afternoon, and the takeoff was smooth and uneventful.

But 1,000 feet into the air, an engine of the Convair suddenly burst into flames. The plane wavered, stalled and then plunged to earth, exploding mightily upon impact.

Military personnel and civilians from a military base near the crash site reached the conflagration of twisted steel in moments. There was one survivor, a woman, who succumbed to her burns four hours later. One hundred fifty-five persons perished in the crash.

SPAIN
CANARY ISLANDS
SANTA CRUZ DE TENERIFE

March 27, 1977

• • • • • • • • • • • • • • • • • •

In the worst accident in the history of civil aviation, two charter Boeing 747s, one belonging to KLM, the other to Pan Am, collided on the ground in a fog at Los Rodeos Airport on Santa Cruz de Tenerife, on March 27, 1977. A combination of delays caused by a terrorist incident and the misunderstanding of the Spanish-speaking airport controllers by the Dutch crew of the KLM jet culminated in the death of all 249 aboard the KLM plane and 321 aboard the Pan Am 747.

Ironically, the deadliest accident in civil aviation history took place on the ground. And it involved two Boeing 747s that never would have been there in the first place had it not been for a small, fanatical group of militant separatists who had set off a small bomb near the florist's shop in the Las Palmas Airport earlier that day.

A Pan American Airways charter jet from Los Angeles via New York was taking passengers to Las Palmas to hook up with a Mediterranean cruise, and a KLM charter jet loaded with Dutch tourists had been diverted to Santa Cruz de Tenerife because the Las Palmas Airport had been shut down. Santa Cruz de Tenerife is ill equipped and unsuited for jumbo jets, or for most aircraft, for that matter. It is noted for the sudden fogs that close in on it at various times of the day and the year and for the dearth of equipment it possesses.

Still, it was probably the difficulty the Dutch crew of the KLM 747 had in understanding the Spanish-accented English of the control tower that was ultimately responsible for this terrible tragedy, which ultimately claimed the lives of 570 people.

The planes had been delayed on the ground nearly two hours when both were finally cleared for takeoff. There was one main runway at the airport and a small holding area at the end of the runway.

Finally, at 4:40 P.M., the KLM jet was given clearance to taxi to the end of the runway first, with the Pan Am jet behind it. When the Dutch craft reached the end of the runway, it would turn around and take off, while the Pan Am jet would taxi off and wait in the small side space. There would be plenty of time for both maneuvers.

It was extremely foggy, and the Pan Am jet had difficulty keeping the KLM jet in sight. Eventually, its taillights disappeared entirely into the mist. The Pan Am pilot reached the turnoff when suddenly he saw the lights of the KLM bearing down on him, at full throttle, in a takeoff. "What's he doing? He'll kill us all!" shouted the Pan Am pilot, as he frantically tried to pull his plane off the runway and into a field of high grass.

It was too late. The KLM jet smashed full force into the Pan Am 747 and then went on to tear through it. Both planes exploded in a giant roar of igniting jet fuel. Black clouds rose in the air, and the cries of the dying pierced the blackness like knives. Blood was everywhere.

Every single person on the KLM died. Because the Pan Am craft had partially left the runway, those in the front of the plane survived. "It exploded from the back," said Lynda Daniel, a 20-year-old Los Angeles college student. "We were sitting next to the emergency exit and it blew off. Most of the people sitting in the first six seats made it. People started climbing over me, and I saw flames, so I decided to get out."

Fire consumed most of both of the jets, and some of the bodies were burned beyond recognition. All 249 aboard the KLM jet were dead. Three hundred twenty-one died on the Pan Am 747, in a tragedy that never should have occurred.

SPAIN
GRANADA

October 2, 1964

• • • • • • • • • • • • • • • • • •

No explanation has been found for the mysterious plunge into the Mediterranean near Granada of a Union Transports Africain Douglas DC-6 on October 2, 1964. All 80 aboard perished.

The Douglas DC-6 was a reliable plane, a piston-powered workhorse that carried thousands of passengers during the last days before jets took over the industry. Its efficiency and its fuel capacity allowed it to make intercontinental flights. Still, the DC-6 had its problems. Its engines were enormously complicated, using up most of their own power in the supercharger needed to force air into their hungry induction systems, and depending for their successful operation on intricate cooling systems and electrical equipment. The technology of the modem jet resolved these problems.

Still, in 1964, DC-6s flew well and often. One such plane was maintained by the French-owned Union Transports Africain, and on October 2, 1964 it was filled with 73 passengers and seven crew members on their way from Palma, on the island of Majorca, to Mauritania, in West Africa. The aircraft took off from Palma, headed west and south near Granada, and then abruptly lost altitude and dove into the Mediterranean.

Ships from several countries searched throughout the area where other ships had seen the DC-6 descend, but neither people nor wreckage was ever found. Nor was the reason for the crash ever determined.

SPAIN
IBIZA

January 7, 1972

• • • • • • • • • • • • • • • • • •

Pilot error was blamed for the smashing of an Iberia Airlines Caravelle into a mountainside on the island of Ibiza on January 7, 1972. One hundred seven died.

Ibiza is one of the gems of the Balearic Islands, located in the western Mediterranean off the coast of Spain. Although Majorca is the best known of this string of three islands (Minorca is the third), easily accessible in less than an hour by air from Valencia and Barcelona, Ibiza is the preference of artists and tourists who prefer splendid isolation and Roman and Phoenician ruins. A mere 221 square miles of terraced towns, it attracts discriminating tourists particularly during the winter holiday season.

On January 7, 1972, 98 Spanish tourists, fresh from spending the Christmas and New Year's holidays on Ibiza, boarded Iberia Airlines Flight 602, a Caravelle, for their short return to the mainland. The flight took off from Ibiza Airport at approximately 2:00 P.M. Ten minutes later, it smashed into a mountain in the Atalayasa range, a semicircle of mountains rimming the city.

Although the precise cause of the accident was never discovered, the plane's pilot, Jose Luis Ballester, apparently misjudged his climb after takeoff and failed to clear the top of the mountain ridge. Wreckage and bodies were strewn over a one-mile radius. There were no survivors. All 107 aboard died in the crash and its consequent fire.

SWITZERLAND
BASEL

April 10, 1973

• • • • • • • • • • • • • • • • •

Pilot error caused the crash of a BEA Vanguard charter jet into a mountainside south of Basel, Switzerland on April 10, 1973. One hundred seven died; 39 survived.

Mrs. Brenda Hopkins was very active in the Axbridge, England Ladies' Guild, and she thought it would be a wonderful and original idea to organize a one-day air excursion to Switzerland. Some of the women could go to Lucerne to shop; others could visit the Swiss Industries Fair in Basel.

Seventy guild members liked the idea and joined the 60 or so other passengers on a chartered four-engine Vanguard turboprop that left Bristol for Basel bright and early on the morning of April 10, 1973.

It was snowing in Basel but not very hard. It was possible to make an instrument landing at the Basel airport, and officials there gave the pilot clearance to do so. He circled the airport once, then passed directly over it and made a wide circle southward. The control tower tried to reach him, but there was neither radar nor radio contact.

The reason was a calamitous one: The plane had slammed into a wooded hillside 1,800 feet high near the village of Hochwald, eight miles south of Basel. First, the wing had snagged on the branches of trees clinging to the side of the hill, and that had flipped it over on its back. Then, skidding through the three-foot-deep snow, it had dissembled, coming apart in several sections.

The tail portion remained relatively intact, and it was here that the 39 survivors of the crash were located. They huddled together in the shelter of their piece of an airplane, singing hymns and staying close, until rescuers arrived.

A farmer first saw the wreck and phoned police, who asked him and his fellow farmers to clear a path to the plane with their tractors. The farmers complied, allowing rescuers to finally reach the site of the wreck. Swiss army helicopters were unable to locate the wreck through the snow.

A local doctor and some farmers did what they could for the survivors and the injured. For the dead, some of whom were still hanging from their seat belts in the upside-down pieces of the plane, nothing could be done. One hundred seven people, most of them British mothers and housewives out on a once-in-a-lifetime one-day outing, were dead.

UNITED STATES
ALASKA
ANCHORAGE

June 3, 1963

• • • • • • • • • • • • • • • • •

No official reason was given for the mysterious crash of a Northwest Airlines DC-7 charter carrying U.S. military personnel over the Pacific Ocean near Anchorage, Alaska on June 3, 1963. All 101 aboard died.

A military charter flight of Northwest Airlines took off from McChord Air Force Base in Washington State at 7:30 A.M. on June 3, 1963. Its destination was Anchorage, Alaska, and it carried 101 passengers and crew members.

At 10:06 A.M., Captain Albert F. Olsen, the pilot of the flight, requested permission from the air station at Sandspit, British Columbia to change altitude from 14,000 to 18,000 feet. This sort of request is usually weather related, and it seems logical that Captain Olsen and his flight were encountering some turbulence.

The tower at Sandspit radioed back, advising him to maintain his present altitude until they could get clearance from Anchorage. Their communication with Anchorage revealed that there was a Pacific Northern Airlines plane already in the vicinity at that altitude, but the Northwest flight was given permission to ascend to 16,000 feet. Sandspit attempted to reach the Northwest flight to advise them of this but was met with nothing but silence.

The radio operators repeated their attempts to rouse the flight, but to no avail. They contacted the Pacific Northern Airlines flight to try to reach the military charter. They had no better luck.

On the ocean below, a fishing boat trolling off the Alaska coast picked up a faint distress signal. It radioed back to Anchorage, and rescuers immediately set out to comb the area for wreckage. Six Coast Guard cutters, three Royal Canadian Air Force planes and 12 U.S. planes converged on the area near the fishermen.

Finally, one of the RCAF pilots reported seeing debris floating in the sea off Graham Island, where the Sandspit air base was located. By the time the Coast Guard cutters reached the site a 55-knot wind had whipped the sea to a wild froth, and fog and darkness had begun to close in. No survivors were found. All 101 perished in this mysterious crash at sea.

UNITED STATES
ALASKA
JUNEAU

September 4, 1971

• • • • • • • • • • • • • • • • • •

Alaska Airlines Flight 1866, a Boeing 727, crashed into Mount Fairweather, near Juneau Airport, during a heavy storm at midnight, September 4, 1971. All 109 passengers and crew aboard died.

A raging storm roared around the Juneau Airport at midnight on September 4, 1971. Alaska Airlines Flight 1866, a Boeing 727, requested permission for an instrument landing. Unfortunately, the Juneau Airport's instrument landing capabilities were elementary and inadequate for the weather conditions that night. There was no localizer, a device that lines up an incoming airplane with the center of the runway, and there was no glide slope device to warn the pilot that his craft had veered off the assigned approach and was heading in another, dangerous direction.

That is exactly what happened with Flight 1866. Coming in for an approach, it was apparently blown off its course and slammed into Mount Fairweather, near the airport. The plane exploded into flames on impact. None of the 109 passengers and crew members survived.

UNITED STATES
ARIZONA
GRAND CANYON

June 30, 1956

• • • • • • • • • • • • • • • • • •

Human error on the part of an air controller caused the first midair collision in U.S. commercial airliner history and the worst air disaster to date when a United Airlines DC-7 collided with a TWA Super Constellation over the Grand Canyon on June 30, 1956. All 128 aboard both planes died.

The first midair collision of commercial airliners in the United States took place in a thunderstorm over Arizona's Grand Canyon on the afternoon of June 30, 1956. The enormity of the tragedy and the senseless set of circumstances that led up to it did have a positive result: the creation of the Airways Modernization Board and, a year later, the passage of the Federal Aviation Act, which set up the Federal Aviation Administration (FAA) as a separate entity.

If the two planes, a TWA Super Constellation and a United Airlines DC-7, had been covered by radar, the collision might not have occurred. But at the time both were operating beyond the boundaries of the existing radar control units and thus were relying purely on radio contact with nearby airports to maintain safe altitudes.

TWA Flight 2 and United Airlines Flight 718 took off from Los Angeles International Airport three minutes apart. The TWA flight, piloted by Captain Jack Gandy, was a half hour late for its scheduled trip to Kansas City. It was assigned a flight altitude of 19,000 feet. The United flight was on time, headed for Chicago, and given a flight level assignment of 21,000 feet. Essentially, then, the two would be flying over the same route for most of their trip but separated by 2,000 feet—a safe distance.

Near Salt Lake City, Gandy radioed Los Angeles and requested permission to climb to 21,000 feet. The 19,000-foot level kept him in clouds and turbulence, and he wanted to rise above it. Ground control in Los Angeles radioed Salt Lake City, which warned that the United flight was at 21,000 feet and very near the Constellation.

Los Angeles radioed the TWA flight, ordering it to maintain its level of 19,000 feet.

And then, an incredible sequence of events took place. Captain Gandy radioed Los Angeles again, requesting a "1,000-foot top." This meant that the Constellation would be able to fly 1,000 feet above the cloud cover, which would determine the altitude. Gandy must have realized the danger in this request; the ground controller in Los Angeles also must have realized it. But, incredibly, permission was given to TWA Flight 2 to climb to a 1,000-foot top.

And that was the fatal decision that would put both planes on a collision course. Had the sky remained clear above the cloud cover, they might have seen and missed each other. But at 10:30 A.M., a thunderhead poked its head above the carpet of clouds below. Both planes entered the gray cloud, and somewhere over the Painted Desert the United Airlines DC-7 plowed into the side of the TWA Constellation, blowing it apart.

Damaged beyond control, the DC-7 pitched over into a steep dive, its crew shouting into the radio, "Salt Lake! United 718! We're going in!" The plane plowed into two enormous buttes—Chuar and Temple—in the Painted Desert, exploding on impact.

The planes and all of their combined 128 passengers and crews were fragmented and scattered for miles. Rescue helicopters, arriving hours later, found no survivors and no intact corpses. Those in the TWA Constellation had been incinerated; those in the United DC-7 had died on impact.

The new regulations drawn up by the newly formed FAA after the crash were better than nothing but hardly effective, considering what had happened to bring them about.

A continental control was instituted on December 1, 1957 effective above 24,000 feet (Remember, this collision occurred at 21,000 feet). This meant that all aircraft would be under positive control whether they were flying on or off the airways. The regulation was mandatory under conditions of restricted visibility but could be ignored during good weather.

UNITED STATES
ILLINOIS
CHICAGO

May 25, 1979

• • • • • • • • • • • • • • • • •

Faulty maintenance by American Airlines mechanics caused the worst disaster in U.S. aviation history. Mishandling of engine repair caused the left engine of an American Airlines DC-10 to fall off in flight near Chicago on May 25, 1979, and the plane lunged to earth, killing all 277 aboard and two on the ground.

The worst disaster in U.S. aviation history occurred on the afternoon of the beginning of the Memorial Day holiday, May 25, 1979. American Airlines Flight 191, a DC-10 bound for Los Angeles and loaded with 277 passengers and a full complement of jet fuel, took off from Runway 14 of Chicago's O'Hare Airport at 3 P.M., nearly on time. The weather was clear and the winds mild.

And then, those who had come to see their friends and family off to the West Coast looked on in horror as the plane reached an altitude of 400 feet, wavered, rolled to the left, stalled and then plunged into the small abandoned Ravenswood Airport, near O'Hare. There was an enormous explosion of jet fuel, and a pyre of flame and black smoke rose high enough to be seen in downtown Chicago's Loop, 10 miles away. The heat from the blaze was hellish. It would be hours before rescue workers could penetrate the intense heat given off by the flames, much less touch the white-hot metal of what was left of the airplane.

The passengers and crew did not have a chance of survival. Every one of them, plus two men working nearby on the ground, were either incinerated or blown to pieces by the impact of the plane hitting the ground. A mobile-home park located near the crash site suffered fire damage when flaming pieces of the plane were flung through the

The worst disaster in United States aviation history in the making. American Airlines Flight 191 rolls sharply to the left moments after losing its left engine over Chicago's O'Hare Airport. National Transportation Safety Board

air and landed on the roofs of its homes. A block away, a Standard Oil Company gasoline storage facility stood unharmed. If the plane had hit it, there would have been no stopping the fire.

It would be later that night before the remains of those killed in the crash would be removed and daybreak the next day before the last of them would be carried off by ambulances serving duty as hearses.

At first, the reason for the crash eluded the experts. Why should an airliner just nose over and dive to earth in the midst of a perfectly normal takeoff? An eyewitness, Winann Johnson, described what happened: "I saw this silver cylinder thing fall from the plane onto the runway," she told reporters. "It burst into flames and then smothered real quickly."

A federal judge immediately impounded all DC-10s in the United States, including those of foreign airlines. The industry erupted in indignation, but the court acted in the interest of public safety, until it could be determined if this was a problem endemic to the DC-10.

Further investigation concluded that the left pylon, which supports the left turbofan engine under the wing, ripped away as the aircraft was lifting into the air.

Investigators maintained that the pylon also had ripped out hydraulic lines. As soon as this happened, the left wing's leading edge flaps, or slats, retracted prematurely. Since slats provide lift at low takeoff speeds, the loss of the left slats caused the left wing to stall and drop while the right wing still had normal lift.

The reason for the malfunction of the pylon was traced to American Airlines' maintenance procedures. McDonnell Douglas recommended that the engines be removed in a two-step procedure: first the engine, then the pylon. But American Airlines mechanics, untrained in this procedure, repeatedly removed the whole assembly with a forklift.

So, every single American Airlines DC-10 then in operation was in danger of repeating the tragic experience of Flight 191. Immediate inspections and corrections were made worldwide, and eventually the DC-10 was pronounced safe to fly. The lesson learned was at a monstrous cost.

UNITED STATES
INDIANA
SHELBYVILLE

August 9, 1969

• • • • • • • • • • • • • • • • • •

Student pilot error and the lack of a transponder were responsible for the midair collision of an Allegheny Airlines DC-9 and a Piper Cherokee over Shelbyville, Indiana on August 9, 1969. Eighty-three were killed.

All of the regulations in the world probably could not have prevented the midair collision between an Allegheny Airlines DC-9 and a Piper Cherokee over Shelbyville, Indiana on August 9, 1969. The fear that haunts both commercial airline pilots and passengers was realized when a plumber, on his first solo flight, came propeller to fuselage with a commercial aircraft coming in for a landing.

The DC-9 was covered by radar at Weir Cook Airport in Indianapolis as it headed in on a calm, sunlit summer afternoon. It could not have been a more routine landing. The single-engine Cherokee carrying the student pilot did not, however, carry a transponder, which would have immediately alerted the tower of its whereabouts.

As the DC-9 circled for its final approach, the Cherokee approached it from the side. The airliner almost cleared the path of the private plane, but not quite. The Cherokee smashed into the DC-9's tail, knocking out its controls and sending it into a dive. Both planes were flying too low to regain altitude and safety. Each smashed into the ground, killing everyone aboard both craft. Eight-three people lost their lives in one of the most unexpected and unpredictable air crashes in U.S. aviation history.

UNITED STATES
MARYLAND
ELKTON

December 8, 1963

• • • • • • • • • • • • • • • • • •

A combination of lightning and jet fuel with a high flash point caused the explosion of a Pan Am Boeing 707 in the skies over Elkton, Maryland on December 8, 1963. Seventy-three people died.

A series of circumstances that converged on the night of December 8, 1964 resulted in a fatal tragedy for everyone aboard Pan Am Flight 214, en route from San Juan International Airport to Philadelphia via Baltimore. Most of those aboard were heading home after vacations in the West Indies. Seventy-one of the flight's original 144 passengers deplaned in Baltimore. They were the lucky ones.

The Boeing 707 assigned to Flight 214 was the oldest jet in service at that time but it showed no signs of metal fatigue. It was, however, burdened with a far more lethal problem. Like other commercial airplanes during the 1960s, it used cost-efficiency JP4 fuel, a mixture of gasoline and kerosene with a high flash point.

There are three kinds of fuel commonly used in civil aviation. Gasoline is used only for piston-engine planes and is highly volatile. Turbine aircraft can use kerosene, similar to domestic paraffin. It has low volatility and is the most widely used jet fuel. The third kind is JP4, the kerosene-gasoline combination called "wide-cut gasoline." It has a flash point of minus four degrees Fahrenheit, a phenomenally low ignition level, which means that it will ignite even though the outside temperature is well below freezing.

The Pan Am Boeing 707 was equipped with fuel vents to equalize the pressure on the inside of the tanks with the pressure on the outside. In 1959, a TWA Constellation blew apart over Italy while it was flying through an electrical storm. A later investigation revealed that the explosion occurred near a wing-tank fuel vent.

At the end of May 1963, seven months before Pan Am Flight 214 took off from San Juan, Lockheed engineers sent a report to the FAA noting that "lightning can ignite an inflammable mixture spewing out of the vent. It would not be necessary for the lightning to actually strike the vent. It could strike anywhere on the aircraft and bleed off into the path of the flammable vapors."

There was plenty of lightning in the air over Philadelphia and Baltimore on the night of December 3, 1963. It had been an unusually mild December, and a cold front moving through the area was setting off huge downpours and fierce lightning. Commercial aircraft were stacked in holding patterns all up and down the East Coast of the United States.

Pan Am Flight 214 took off from Baltimore at 8:25 for the short flight to Philadelphia and almost immediately entered a holding pattern. It circled over New Castle, Maryland in a configuration that would take it directly over Elkton. It was told to hold at 5,000 feet, an altitude that was buffeted by high turbulence and icing.

Shortly thereafter, the Pan Am jet radioed for permission to break the pattern and land at Philadelphia. It was advised to wait until the weather, which was improving, cleared somewhat. The Pan Am crew responded with patience.

Nothing happened for a few moments, and then, at 8:58 P.M., a distress call from the Pan Am Clipper erupted over the radios of every liner in the vicinity and every control tower below: "Mayday . . . Mayday . . . Mayday . . . Clipper two one four out of control . . . here we go."

A thousand feet above, a National jet radioed, "Clipper two fourteen is going down in flames."

It had been struck by lightning, and the lightning had ignited the fuel and blown the left wing off the plane. All control had been lost.

Gerald Cornell, a resident of Elkton, later reported to the CAB: "The sky lit up like a tremendous bolt of lightning . . . then there was a loud explosion, like thunder outside of my house . . . then we saw the plane burst into flames and fall apart."

Other eyewitness reports, collected during the postcrash investigation, were similar. Joseph Dopirak saw a falling jet "coming straight down with only one wing." It blew into a thousand pieces when it struck the ground, he added. Jerry Greenwald, a skater, was close enough to see the one-winged craft plummeting through the sky with bodies tumbling out of it.

Pieced together by the investigation (the flight recorder was useless—it had struck the ground with such force that it had blown apart), the sequence of events unfolded thus: A massive lightning strike occurred first in the left reserve tank and spread to the center tank and the right reserve tank, causing multiple explosions, which in turn tore off the entire left outer wing, resulting in an immediate loss of control. The explosions of fuel continued, scattering bodies and pieces of the aircraft all over the countryside.

As a result of this tragedy, a lightning protection committee was formed in the FAA to study lightning protection systems and their feasibility. Quietly, the use of JP4 fuel was banned on the fleet of planes reserved for flights of the president of the United States and his staff and replaced by the safer but costlier JP5.

UNITED STATES
MASSACHUSETTS
BOSTON

October 4, 1960

• • • • • • • • • • • • • • • • •

A flock of birds sucked into the turbines of the engines of an Eastern Airlines Electra caused it to lose control and crash into Boston Harbor on October 4, 1960. Sixty-one died; 10 were rescued.

Flocks of birds are a recurrent and unexpected danger to jets. Groups of birds soaring around airports can be, and frequently are, ingested into the engines of jetliners. In jet travel's early years, this occurrence would bring an engine to a complete stop, thus threatening takeoffs and landings. Modern jet engines, manufactured after the mid-1970s, are designed to handle "bird strike," as the phenomenon is now called, without failing.

But jet travel was in its infancy on October 4, 1960, when Eastern Airlines Flight 375, a propjet Electra flying to Philadelphia, took off from Boston's Logan Airport. It was a clear late afternoon, and the plane lifted off at 5:48 P.M., all four of its engines in prime working order. Its takeoff pattern took it over Boston Harbor, where it began a slow turn.

And at that moment, Flight 375 encountered a flock of starlings. The birds were sucked up by the turbines of the engines, stopping the port inboard engine and causing it to catch fire. The aircraft, out of control, dropped like a punctured parachute into the waters of Boston Harbor at the Pleasant Park Channel.

The waters were choppy that evening, with a strong set, but there were five yachts anchored nearby. Divers from these boats went into the water and managed to rescue 10 passengers, still strapped in their floating seats. None of the other 61 passengers and crew members survived.

At first, FAA investigation focused on the Lockheed Electra, a trouble-plagued plane, but close scrutiny of the wreckage revealed one of the first examples of "bird strike" as a hazard to safe jet travel.

Pieces of a Delta Airlines DC-9 dot the landscape following the unexplained crash of the liner on its approach to Logan Airport in Boston, on July 31, 1973. National Transportation Safety Board

UNITED STATES
MASSACHUSETTS
BOSTON

July 31, 1973

• • • • • • • • • • • • • • • •

Malfunctioning instruments and delayed rescue attempts may have accounted for the deaths in the otherwise unexplained crash of a Delta Airlines DC-9 on landing at Boston's Logan Airport on July 31, 1973. Eighty-eight died.

Not wanting to miss an important business meeting because of weather delays, Charles R. Mealy summoned a flight attendant on Delta Flight 723 to his seat as the aircraft, a DC-9, was taxiing out on the fog-shrouded runway at Manchester, New Hampshire. When the flight attendant arrived, Mealy announced that he had to leave the flight. "I want to get off this plane" were his exact words, as reported later to local reporters.

The flight attendant informed the captain, who turned the plane around and delivered Mealy to the terminal. An hour later, Mealy would be one of two survivors of Delta Airlines 723, bound from Manchester to Boston on the morning of July 31, 1973.

The weather was still but cloudy, the fog banks reaching almost to the ground. The aircraft took off without incident from Manchester and made the short flight to the airspace over Boston. But at 11:08 A.M., while attempting to make an IFR, or instrument landing, at Boston's Logan Airport, the jet crashed in a huge, thunderous ball of fire, killing 88 passengers and crew and leaving only one person—Air Force Sergeant Leopold Chouinard—alive. Chouinard would survive, but without either of his legs.

The cause of the crash would never be determined, but one factor revealed in the subsequent FAA investigation might have contributed toward it, and another might have worsened it. First, the particular Delta DC-9 involved in the crash had a history of malfunctioning instruments. It was entirely possible that the pilot was receiving wrong information or no information at all from some of his instruments as he relied entirely on them to come into Logan Airport at zero visibility.

Second, the Logan tower was apparently unaware that the flight had crashed until six minutes after it had happened. Those precious six minutes of rescue time might have saved more than one life, though Harris A. Cusick and Geoffrey F. Keating, two airport construction workers who happened to be in the vicinity of the crash site, rushed immediately to it but found only a horribly burned Chouinard alive. The FAA did conclude, however, that had fire fighters been on the scene earlier and extinguished the roaring, lethal blaze, more might have been saved.

UNITED STATES
MICHIGAN
SOUTH HAVEN

June 24, 1950

• • • • • • • • • • • • • • • • • •

The cause of the crash of a Northwest Airlines DC-4 into Lake Michigan on June 24, 1950, in heavy weather, has never been determined. All 58 aboard died.

Like so many airline disasters, the cause of the worst commercial air crash to that date has never been explained. A stormy night. A calm radio transmission. And then silence. The scenario has been played over and over, and each replay brings renewed efforts to improve communication and safety. The "black box"—the voice recorder that freezes the concluding moments of an airliner's life—has aided today's crash investigators, but there was no such voice recorder aboard a Northwest Airlines DC-4 traveling through heavy weather from New York to Minneapolis and thence to Seattle on June 24, 1950.

The storm was particularly fierce over Michigan, and the captain of the aircraft, Robert Lind, requested permission to drop from a turbulent 3,500 feet to what he hoped would be a calmer 2,500 feet. His request was denied. Traffic was particularly heavy at 2,500 feet, dangerously so.

Captain Lind accepted the turnaway and radioed his position. He was over Lake Michigan, near the shore village of South Haven. Then there was silence. Some time shortly after that message, the DC-4 and its load of 58 passengers and crew plunged into the waters of Lake Michigan.

A score of planes and rescue boats, including the destroyer escort *Daniel A. Joy* were sent to the location. It would be the *Daniel A. Joy* that would spot the telltale oil slick that indicated the aircraft's fate. A week later, divers would bring up all 58 bodies and the twisted fuselage of the Northwest airliner.

UNITED STATES
NEW JERSEY
COAST

April 14, 1933

• • • • • • • • • • • • • • • • • •

Human error in piloting and design caused the airship Akron *to crash in a thunderstorm off the coast of New Jersey on April 14, 1933. Seventy-three were killed; three were rescued.*

The history of lighter-than-air travel is not a pretty one. A noble experiment that has now been refined, its early years were marked with incompetence, trial and tragedy. France (see p. 11), Germany (see pp. 21 and 39) and Great Britain (see p. 18) all suffered grisly calamities in their race to put faster and more efficient lighter-than-air craft into the skies. And two of the United States' early efforts at utilizing and improving on the designs of Baron von Zeppelin crashed disastrously.

First there was the *Shenandoah* (see p. 46). Then there was the *Akron,* a ship with a load of troubles. From its maiden flight in August 1931, problems had arisen with the *Akron*'s structure and instrumentation. On a transcontinental trip to California from its home base at Lakehurst, New Jersey in 1932, two girders had unexpectedly and unexplainably collapsed, thus reducing the rigidity of the ship's hull. The $5 million 758-foot-long leviathan (the largest ship in the air at that time) then limped to San Diego, where it killed two sailors at its landing post. A sudden gust of wind lifted it upward, carrying away the men who were trying to tie it down. The two lost their grips on the ropes and plunged to their deaths.

Even under ordinary conditions, the *Akron* did not behave properly. Its instruments malfunctioned; struts and braces gave way regularly. It was a tragedy waiting to happen, and, with an assist from human failure, it fulfilled its promise on April 14, 1933.

Assigned by the U.S. Navy to take radio compass dimensions along the New England coastline, the *Akron* was ordered aloft on a day when wind and fog had grounded all commercial passenger planes in the Northeast. There were violent thunderstorms off the coast, and the *Akron* drifted straight toward one of the worst of them. Even though the *Akron* was filled with helium and not the highly inflammable hydrogen that had claimed earlier airships, it was still vulnerable to updrafts and lightning strikes on its skin.

According to the later inquiry, two misjudgments were made at this point—one by the *Akron*'s commanding officer, Captain McCord, and one by his adjutant, Lieutenant Commander Wiley. First, Captain McCord, upon seeing a giant thunderhead looming up before them, ordered a course change by 15 degrees. The order was evidently misunderstood to be 50 degrees, enough of an error to send the *Akron* and its crew directly into the storm rather than around it.

The ship plunged forward, sucked by the winds of the thunderhead into its very center. Within moments, its altitude had dropped from 1,600 to 700 feet, and this precipitated the second, fatal mistake. Commander Wiley ordered the ship's water ballast to be dumped into the sea, reasoning that this would give them the necessary altitude.

It did, but far too suddenly. The ship bounced upward, severing its rubber cables and smashing its controls. It was helpless in the elements, and it dove, nose forward, into the sea, smashing apart upon impact and splaying pieces of itself and its crew into the water.

Rescuers were dispatched immediately, among them the crew of a J-3 nonrigid blimp. But the same weather system that destroyed the *Akron* also forced the J-3 to crash into the sea, drowning two of its crew of seven.

Boats rescued the remainder of the J-3's personnel and three men from the *Akron* including Commander Wiley. Seventy-three others, including Rear Admiral Henry V. Butler, perished in the crash.

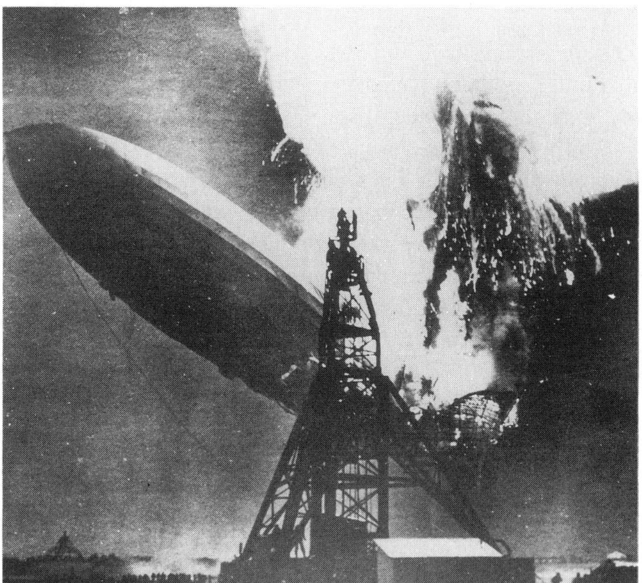

The German dirigible* Hindenburg *burns at its mooring post in Lakehurst, New Jersey on May 6, 1937. This spectacular finale to the age of lighter-than-air transportation was blamed on exhaust sparks igniting escaping gas, static electricity caused by a sudden rainstorm or sabotage. Smithsonian Institution

UNITED STATES
NEW JERSEY
LAKEHURST

May 6, 1937

• • • • • • • • • • • • • • • • • • •

Exhaust sparks igniting escaping gas, static electricity caused by a sudden rainstorm or sabotage caused the fiery crash of the giant dirigible Hindenburg *as it floated near its mooring mast in Lakehurst, New Jersey after a triumphant transatlantic voyage. Thirty-one died; 61 survived.*

For millions, the lost era of lighter-than-air passenger flight will forever by symbolized by the catastrophic conclusion to the stunning career of the world's largest and fastest airship, the *Hindenburg.* The subject of countless books, studies and a feature film, the fiery crash of this 804-foot giant of the skies forms a part of the fabric of every television retrospective of the 1930s—indeed, of every electronic or print recapturing of that age. The tortured voice of Chicago radio station WLS's announcer Herbert Morrison recording those last cataclysmic moments has been rebroadcast countless times: "Oh! oh! oh! It's burst into flames! . . . Get this, Scotty! . . . Get out of the way, please . . . this is terrible, oh my . . ."

It was the true end of an era, and a dream.

In the beginning, when the first ships were designed and built, it was believed that super airship transatlantic air travel would become faster than that of transatlantic ship travel, but no less luxurious. The *Hindenburg* was the apotheosis of the dream, the true super airship, with its nonstop range of 8,000 miles, a 97-passenger capacity in spacious staterooms, lounges and dining rooms, 61 crew members, four 1,100-horsepower Mercedes-Benz engines and 16 gas compartments holding seven million cubic feet of—hydrogen.

And this was the puzzling and eventually fatal question that gnawed at the dream: Why, when helium, which was so much safer and saner, was available and widely used, did the *Hindenburg*'s manufacturers and its directors choose to employ the far more dangerous and explosive hydrogen?

The surface answer has to do with maneuverability. Hydrogen-filled airships are easier to maneuver than helium-filled ones. But there were deeper reasons, too, that had to do with the sort of pride that presupposes immortality, and the *Hindenburg* was a proud ship. Its 36 passengers on the fateful trip from Europe to America of May 6, 1937 paid premium prices of $400 each for the privilege of crossing on this state-of-the-art, luxurious leviathan. And this trip must have been particularly luxurious. The ratio of crew members to passengers was almost two to one.

Although its speed of 85 miles per hour allowed it to cross the Atlantic in one-fifth the time of the surface liners, the *Hindenburg,* like any lighter-than-air craft, was vulnerable and subject to weather conditions and air currents. A series of squalls and crosswinds had hampered the particular crossing of May 6, 1937, and Captain Max Pruss radioed ahead to Lakehurst, New Jersey. Instead of arriving at their estimated hour of 5:00 A.M., the ship would dock at sunset.

The army of reporters, cameramen, spectators and passengers arriving to board the *Hindenburg* for its return trip to Europe probably breathed sighs of relief and caught a few extra hours of sleep.

And so, the ship sailed serenely westward, a craft that had proven itself to be speedy, reliable and safe. It had made 10 transatlantic crossings in 1936 alone, and it was the pride of Germany's emerging Third Reich.

At 3:12 P.M., the *Hindenburg* hove into view near Lakehurst. But as preparations were being made for its docking at the huge mooring mast, surrounded by a landing crew composed of sailors and marines, a sudden rain squall came up. Captain Pruss and his second officer, Captain Ernst Lehmann, thought it wiser to wait out the squall.

By 6:00 P.M. the skies had cleared, and the *Hindenburg* began its majestic descent to the mooring mast. The trapdoors in its bows flipped open, flinging its landing cables groundward. Some of the passengers crowded at the windows of the passenger gondolas; others relaxed in the lounges.

But Captain Pruss was bringing the *Hindenburg* in too fast. He ordered the two rear engines to full reverse and at the same time released 1,000 gallons of water ballast. At exactly 7:23 P.M., Chief Boatswain's Mate R. H. Ward, who was part of the landing crew on the ground, looked up and saw a slight fluttering of the fabric near the number-two gas cell, toward the stern of the ship. Gas was obviously escaping, and there were exhaust sparks erupting from the suddenly reversed engines nearby.

Whether it was this that caused the hydrogen in that gas cell to ignite and explode, or static electricity caused by the sudden rainstorm or, as some darkly hinted, sabotage, the catastrophe spread like a Sierra Nevada forest fire in fast motion.

The tail section of the *Hindenburg* detonated with a ground-shaking impact. Superheated flames shot fiery fingers up into the sky and toward the ground. Like a runaway river of fire, the flames ran forward, engulfing the giant ship in seconds as, one by one, the liner's 16 gas cells exploded. The metal frame, heated to the melting point, drooped by the tail and began to tear apart. The nose poked skyward for a moment, then reversed itself and headed toward the ground.

The approximately 1,000 spectators and press people waiting for the majestic ship to dock could not believe their eyes. WLS's Herbert Morrison provided the most dramatic and vivid coverage of the catastrophe and was later dismissed by his station for failing to maintain his equilibrium: "Here it comes," he exulted, as the ship neared the mooring mast. "And what a sight it is, a thrilling one, a marvelous sight. The sun is striking the windows of the observation deck on the westward side and sparkling like glittering jewels on the background of black velvet . . ."

And then the far less poetic reality: "Oh, oh, oh! It's burst into flames . . . Get this Scotty . . . get out of the way, please, oh, this is terrible, oh my, get out of the way please! It's burning, bursting into flames and is falling just short of the mast. Oh! This is one of the worst . . . Oh! It's a terrific sight . . . Oh, all the humanity . . ." and Morrison burst into tears.

The searing, white-hot heat from the burning hydrogen reached out and tightened the faces of the horrified spectators. On the ship, everything from pandemonium to stoic acceptance was occurring. Some crew members and passengers leaped from the now-descending ship to the landing cables. Very few made it; more fell to their deaths.

The longer passengers and crew stayed aboard the collapsing giant, the more severely burned they became. Those who leaped at the last minute were seen to be human torches, their clothes burned away, their hair on fire. One German businessman turned his back on the smashed windows of the gondola, through which his flaming companions were leaping, and walked into the interior wall of flame that was now turning the liner into a twisted mountain of molten steel.

As the *Hindenburg* settled to earth, collapsing like a spent balloon, sailors rushed into the still-molten hull, finding and dragging out possible survivors. Some passengers and crew leaped for the ground at the last minute and suffered only broken bones. Others did not survive even the short fall. Some perished in the flames, burned to an unrecognized mass. Others survived to die of their burns later in ambulances or hospitals.

It would be 10:45 P.M. that night before the wreckage would cool enough for some sort of accounting. Of the 92 people aboard, 61 survived. Thirty-one died, as did the dream of luxury transcontinental travel in lighter-than-air craft.

UNITED STATES
NEW YORK
BROOKLYN

December 16, 1960

• • • • • • • • • • • • • • • •

Human error on the part of both flight crews and controllers was deemed responsible for the midair collision of a United Airlines DC-8 and a TWA Super Constellation over New York City on December 16, 1960. One hundred twenty-eight aboard the two liners and eight on the ground in Brooklyn died.

Almost five years after the terrible midair collision of a TWA Super Constellation and a United Airlines DC-7 over the Grand Canyon (see p. 33), two planes representing the same airlines were involved in another appalling midair wreck, this time over New York City.

A light snow was falling on the morning of December 16, 1960. A 17-inch snowfall had blanketed New York City a few days before. The temperature was 33 degrees.

United Airlines Flight 826, a DC-8 was coming in from Columbus and Dayton, Ohio, headed for Idlewild (now called Kennedy) Airport. TWA Flight 266, a Super Constellation, was arriving from Chicago, headed for LaGuardia Airport.

Because of the intermittent snow, both flights were on IFR (Instrument Flight Rules) and were being monitored by New York center radar—a system installed as a result of the Grand Canyon collision.

At about 10 A.M., the TWA flight was cleared to descend to 9,000 feet. Once TWA Captain David Wollman reached that altitude, he was told to contact LaGuardia approach control. This meant that each flight was now being monitored by different facilities.

Wreckage is strewn over Sterling Place, Brooklyn after the midair collision of a United Airlines DC-8 and a TWA Super Constellation on December 16, 1960. One hundred twenty-eight aboard the two liners and eight on the ground died. National Transportation Safety Board

At roughly the same time, the United flight, captained by R. H. Sawyer, was being given a revised route by New York center to Preston, a radio check point, with instructions to descend from 11,000 feet to 5,000 feet. "Looks like you'll be able to make Preston at 5,000," said the New York center.

"Will try," United answered.

"If holding is necessary at Preston S.W. one minute pattern right turns . . ." radioed the center.

"Roger, we're out of 6 for 5."

"826, Roger, and you received the holding instructions at Preston. Radar service is terminated. Contact Idlewild approach control."

"Good day," was the cutoff from United.

It was the LaGuardia approach control that first noticed something threatening on its radar screen. At 10:30, it radioed the TWA flight, "Unidentified target approaching . . . six miles."

FAA tests in 1958 determined that pilots could not distinguish traffic until it was three to five miles distant. The same tests, quoted in "Captain X" 's study of airline safety, *Safety Last,* concluded that a pilot flying at 600 miles per hour will travel 920 feet before he can definitely determine if an object he spots out of the corner of his eye is a cloud, a speck of dirt on the windshield or another aircraft. According to the study, "2,680 feet will be used up while he decides whether to climb, dive, or turn left or right; . . . 4,792 feet will slip by before he can make the plane respond to his actions. A jet pilot would need a bare minimum of 9,584 feet before he could spot a target and maneuver to miss it, under excellent conditions: clear day, eyes focused for distant vision, no distractions, and a well-rested crew."

"Unidentified object three miles . . . two o'clock," continued the approach control at LaGuardia.

"Roger," acknowledged the TWA flight.

At 10:33, the United flight radioed approach control at Idlewild: "Approaching Preston at 5,000."

Approach control advised him to maintain altitude and that little or no delay was expected. This was followed by a weather report and landing instructions.

There was no mandatory acknowledgment from the United flight, possibly because at this moment, Captain Sawyer realized that they were not over Preston at all but over Staten Island, New York and headed on a direct collision course for the TWA Constellation.

A moment later, the United DC-8 slammed into the Constellation, its wing ripping a jagged hole in the other plane's fuselage, which in turn ripped off one of the DC-8's jet engines. The Constellation spiraled to earth, crashing into Miller Field, a small military airport on Staten Island. Fortunately, there was no one on the ground below, although everyone aboard the Constellation was killed instantly.

Meanwhile, the DC-8 limped toward LaGuardia, hoping to be able to make an emergency landing there. But it never made it. Over Brooklyn, it lost altitude and plunged into a thickly populated part of that borough. The plane first hit the snow-covered roof of a four-story apartment house and then bounced down to Sterling Place, where parts of the fuselage split apart and skidded down city streets. The major part of the plane smashed into the ironically named Pillar of Fire Church, setting it and 10 nearby buildings ablaze.

Pieces of the flaming wreckage, with charred corpses still strapped in their seats, were deposited in streets adjoining the main conflagration. One 11-year-old boy was rushed to Methodist Hospital, where 10 surgeons fought to save his life but failed. There were no survivors. One hundred twenty-eight people aboard the two airliners and eight on the ground in Brooklyn died.

Charges and countercharges punctuated the follow-up investigation, which fixed the blame on the deceased crew of the United DC-8. The CAB determined that the pilots had failed to report that one of their two key radio navigation instruments was not functioning. Therefore, they were unable to report the plane's exact position. Furthermore, they had raced through the five-mile buffer zone designed to separate LaGuardia and Idlewild traffic.

But there were other factors at work: A trainee had been working the LaGuardia radar at the time. The United flight had not been carefully monitored. And there was no direct phone communication between the two approach-control facilities at Idlewild and LaGuardia.

Lawsuits totaling $77 million were filed against the two airlines and the FAA by the relatives of the victims. The suits were settled for about $29 million, with United taking 60% of the responsibility, the FAA 25% and TWA 15%.

As in the aftermath of the earlier TWA-United midair collision, new safety measures were instituted. Speed for aircraft entering the terminal areas was decreased. Extra controllers were added at busy airports.

A new phone system was installed between the two approach centers, and a system of positive radar handoffs became mandatory. This meant that a controller could not relinquish his or her guidance of a flight until the receiving controller had the blip on his or her radar scope and that blip was positively identified.

Today, transponders and three-dimensional radar have decreased the incidence of midair collisions. But it took this horrendous one to prod airports to put them into use.

UNITED STATES
NEW YORK
COVE NECK, LONG ISLAND

January 25, 1990

• • • • • • • • • • • • • • • •

A Federal Transportation Board inquiry determined that faulty judgments by the crew were responsible when an Avianca Boeing 707 ran out of gas and crashed into the residential area of Cove Neck, Long Island on January 25, 1990. But a series of factors were involved in the tragedy, which resulted in the death of 73 aboard the jet. Eighty-five survived.

The ancient adage about a nail in a horseshoe eventually becoming responsible for the loss of a war was illustrated in the fatal crash of Avianca Flight 52 on the stormy night of January 25, 1990. The word "emergency" was not uttered by the co-pilot when the Boeing 707, critically short of fuel, was being held in a circling pattern before landing at New York's John F. Kennedy Airport. Words the co-pilot did use—"priority" and "low on fuel"—should have indicated an emergency. But the controller, testifying at postcrash hearings, stated that the official word "emergency," which would have triggered an immediate response and brought the flight in safely, was never heard. So, instead of being brought in, the flight was given directions that would exhaust its fuel and cause its crash.

Still, airplane crashes almost always involve many factors. Those in effect that night included foul weather, a shortage of experienced controllers, an unrealistic estimate of the number of aircraft that could be handled at Kennedy given the weather conditions, a failure by a local controller to hear all of the co-pilot's transmissions, the tentativeness of the co-pilot's messages to controllers, the difficulty of communication between flight crews and controllers speaking different languages and the decision of the pilot to abort a landing pass. All of these factored into the incident, and any combination of two or more of them might have caused that tragic loss of life.

At 7:33 A.M. on January 25, 1990, the Central Flow Control Facility in Washington, D.C. warned airlines that it was going to be a bad day for flying on the East Coast. Gusty winds and marginal flying weather would force ground delay procedures at both New York's Kennedy and Boston's Logan airports, the advisory warned.

At 9:30 A.M., Central Flow Advisory 21 was issued, stating that at Kennedy a ground delay program would be implemented at 2 P.M., the time at which peak traffic would begin. Because of low ceiling and visibility, Kennedy would be "reducing the acceptance rate [of aircraft] from 38 to 30 an hour." On a good day, Kennedy is capable of ac-

The wreckage of the Avianca Boeing 707 that crashed in Cove Neck, Long Island on January 25, 1990 is flung over a large part of this thickly populated suburban community. Fortunately no one on the ground was killed. National Transportation Safety Board

cepting 60 flights an hour, but since it is an international airport, and international flights are supposedly exempt from acceptance-rate reductions, this seemed to be a generous figure for the conditions.

And it proved to be so. By the time the Avianca flight approached Kennedy, planes were being held up to 80 minutes on the ground and in the air. Despite the fact that the Avianca flight was an international one, it too was put into a holding pattern.

The flight, with 158 aboard, had originated in Bogota, Colombia and had refueled at Medellin. It had battled strong winds as it made its way up the east coast of the United States.

A few hours earlier, an air controller supervisor at Kennedy had recommended that because of the driving winds and rain, the number of planes allowed to land per hour be further reduced, from the optimum 60 to 22. He was overruled, and the number was set at 33.

Thus, at 8:07, when the Avianca flight entered Kennedy airspace, it was stacked in a holding pattern off the coast of New Jersey about 40 miles south of Kennedy. At that time it was being monitored by a regional control center responsible for traffic in and around the New York area.

By 8:45, the plane had made three wide circles, and its fuel was getting low. Regional controller Philip Brogan contacted the flight and told it that it would be held at least until 9:05. The pilot and co-pilot of the Avianca flight conferred, and the co-pilot radioed back, "I think we need priority."

Brogan inquired about their alternate airport and how long they could hold.

The co-pilot replied that their alternate was Boston but that it was full of traffic. And then, the co-pilot added the phrase that should have tipped off the controllers that an emergency was in the making: "It was Boston but we can't do it now, we . . . run out of fuel now."

Brogan immediately handed off the plane to local controllers to guide it in its approach to Kennedy. But the handoff controller, Jeffrey Potash, was on the phone coordinating the transfer, and he did not hear the comment about running out of fuel. Nothing was said about it to Scott Machose, the local controller.

Had he known this, Machose would undoubtedly have brought the flight in immediately. But instead, he placed the plane in yet another hold, called a "spin," over Long Island. He would keep the flight in this pattern for six and a half minutes, while more precious fuel was burned.

Meanwhile, a thick fog had settled in over Kennedy, making its runway lights invisible from 1,300 feet away.

At 9:07, 77 minutes after it had first entered its holding pattern, the Avianca flight was cleared for landing. It was 27 miles from the airport. The crew was confident that they would make it.

At 9:09, the co-pilot told the pilot, "They are giving us priority."

"Tell me things louder because I'm not hearing it," complained the pilot.

At 9:20, the co-pilot informed the captain: "Yes sir, we are cleared to land."

The plane was flying at 150 miles per hour, and it was just four minutes from a safe landing. "All set for landing," the engineer assured the pilot.

The pilot nosed the plane toward the invisible runway. At 9:23, the Avianca's warning system tripped, setting off a horn that warned that it was descending too steeply. "The runway. Where is it?" the pilot asked the co-pilot.

"I don't see it. I don't see it," he answered. The pilot pulled the nose of the plane up, aborting the landing. "Tell them we are in emergency," he said to the co-pilot.

"Once again, we're running out of fuel," the co-pilot radioed to ground control. He failed to use the critical word "emergency," which triggers immediate clearance.

"Declare emergency," said the pilot again. "Did you tell him?"

"Yes, I already advised him," responded the co-pilot.

"Did you already advise him we don't have fuel?"

"Yes sir. I already advise him . . . and he's going to get us back."

The pilot asked for a bearing. The co-pilot gave him the wrong bearing, taking the plane another precious minute out of its way.

Now, at 9:26, the controller told the crew to fly out another 15 miles northeast before coming back for a second approach. "Is that fine with your fuel?" he asked the co-pilot.

The co-pilot paused a moment and then answered, "I guess so. Thank you very much."

And that was the last, fatal decision. Five minutes later, as the plane began to line up its approach over Long Island's north shore, the engineer announced, "Flame out. Flame out on engine number four."

Four seconds later, the second of the plane's four engines stopped.

"Show me the runway," the pilot called.

"We just, ah, lost two engines and, ah, we need priority please," radioed the co-pilot to the ground.

"You're 20.6 nautical miles from runway 22 left, and cleared for instrument landing," answered ground control.

But it was too late. The remaining two engines had stopped, and the 707 glided silently for almost two minutes before it slammed into a hillside behind a huge estate in Cove Neck, Long Island.

With a roar, it split apart, spewing baggage, bodies and pieces of the plane over the landscape. Local fire departments rushed to the scene, and all through that long and rainy night, rescuers toiled, bringing 85 survivors—some of them horribly injured—out of the mangled wreckage. Seventy-three, including the entire cockpit crew, died in the crash.

UNITED STATES
NEW YORK
NEW YORK

July 28, 1945

• • • • • • • • • • • • • • • •

Pilot misjudgment was responsible for a B-25 Mitchell bomber crashing into New York's Empire State Building on July 28, 1945 in a heavy fog. The crew of three and 11 workers in the building were killed.

One of the more bizarre airplane crashes in the history of aviation occurred on a foggy Saturday morning in July 1945. It involved the collision of a U.S. Army Air Corps B-25 Mitchell bomber with New York City's Empire State Building. The experts at the time said the odds of this sort of accident happening at all were 10,000 to 1. But it happened.

The morning of July 28, 1945 was a murky one in New York City. A heavy fog had rolled in from the Atlantic Ocean overnight, and the sun had not yet burned it away.

Twenty-seven-year-old Lieutenant Colonel William F. Smith Jr., a highly decorated West Point graduate, was flying a B-25 on a short trip from New Bedford, Massachusetts to New York's LaGuardia Airport. The plane was carrying a crew of three and one passenger. At approximately 9:30 A.M., LaGuardia ground control redirected him to Newark, New Jersey. LaGuardia was socked in with fog, ceiling zero and forward visibility about three miles. "The Empire State Building is not visible," added the ground controller, in an unconsciously prophetic afterthought.

Smith and his crew headed for Newark in a path that would take them squarely over the island of Manhattan. Fifteen minutes after receiving his wave-off from LaGuardia, Smith found himself a mere 500 feet above Rockefeller Center's towers, more than 40 stories high. According to observers on the ground, he climbed abruptly out of that danger and disappeared into the mist.

But apparently Smith did not climb high enough. Two minutes later, the bomber, flying at 225 miles per hour, smashed squarely into the north side of the 78th and 79th floors of the Empire State Building—the highest building in the world at the time. The fuel in the engines exploded on impact, and the plane's two propeller-driven engines scissored their way through the concrete walls of the building. One engine emerged on the south side of the skyscraper, became airborne for a brief moment over 33rd Street and descended in a long loop through the skylight of the penthouse sculpture studio of Henry Hering. The other flaming engine demolished the elevator door on the 79th floor, snapping the cable of the elevator car. One woman was riding in it, and she began the long plunge to the bottom. Fortunately the elevator's automatic braking device engaged, and she was saved from a plummet to the basement. But just as she stopped, part of the engine hit the top of the car, caving it in.

The plane broke into several pieces. Part of a wing careened a block east onto Madison Avenue. Pieces of the fuselage dug into the walls of nearby skyscrapers as if they had been shot through a high-powered machine gun.

If this had happened on a weekday, the Empire State Building would have been thickly populated with close to 50,000 office workers and tourists. But it was Saturday, and only a handful of workers were at their desks in the 79th-floor offices of the War Relief Services of the National Catholic Welfare Conference. Eleven of them were killed; some of them burned to death; others were crushed. One man was flung through a window. His charred body would be discovered on a 72nd-story ledge of the Empire State Building. Twenty-five were badly injured. All three servicemen on the plane died violently.

Firemen appeared on the scene quickly and doused the blaze. For weeks, until war-appropriated material could be secured for repairs, a gaping hole 18 by 20 feet would exist in the side of the Empire State Building. A tarpaulin was used to cover it, but it was continually blown loose.

The woman who fell 79 stories in the elevator shaft survived, thanks to the quick thinking of Coast Guard hospital apprentice Donald Maloney, who just happened to be strolling by the Empire State Building. He ran to a drugstore and commandeered syringes, hypodermics and other medical necessities. He then dashed into the building, climbed down through the crumpled roof of the elevator cab, and administered a shot of morphine to the injured woman and saved her life.

UNITED STATES
NEW YORK
QUEENS

February 3, 1959

• • • • • • • • • • • • • • • •

Failure to read new instrumentation correctly resulted in the crash, during an instrument landing, of an American Airlines Lockheed Electra at New York's LaGuardia Airport on February 3, 1959. Sixty-six died; seven survived.

"Undershoot," the technical term for a landing attempt in which the aircraft touches down on the ground before reaching the runway, does not necessarily result in a catastrophic accident. However, Runway 22 at New York's LaGuardia Airport begins on the bank of the East River. Even a minimal undershoot there can be at least wet and at most calamitous; and it was the latter that occurred there on the fog-shrouded evening of February 3, 1959.

The American Airlines flight, which originated in Chicago, was required to make an instrument landing because of a heavy blanket of fog and rain that had all but closed down LaGuardia. Veteran pilot Albert DeWitt was at the controls of the flight's aircraft, a brand-new Lockheed Electra propjet. The 12-day-old plane contained the latest in instrumentation, including a new altimeter designed for precision but configured differently than the altimeters DeWitt and other veteran pilots were used to relying on in instrument landings.

It was the misreading of this new altimeter that was later considered to be a possible cause of the crash. Considering the fact that the last radio transmission from DeWitt contained no inkling of trouble, it was concluded in the follow-up investigation that the captain misread his altimeter and approached too low. Since LaGuardia lacked a backup radio beam to warn off undershooting pilots, this misreading would not have been challenged.

For whatever reason, five minutes after clearance, the American Airlines Electra disappeared from the radar and dove into the waters of the East River at 135 miles per hour. The slow speed allowed part of the fuselage and the tail section to survive the plunge, and those who were in the rear lounge or the rear seats found themselves with enough time to escape.

A businessman and two flight attendants were among a small group of seven that pulled themselves up onto the still-floating tail section. Some others, including flight engineer Warren Cook, managed to escape from the shattered plane underwater. Despite extreme injuries, Cook helped other passengers swim to safety.

Immediate rescue came from a tugboat, the *H. Thomas Teti Jr.*, which was towing several barges. Captain Samuel Nickerson, in command of the tug, summarily cut his barges loose and made for the wreck, taking the seven survivors aboard.

They were the only ones to live. Sixty-six others died.

UNITED STATES
NORTH CAROLINA
HENDERSONVILLE

July 19, 1967

• • • • • • • • • • • • • • • •

Failure to heed instructions by the pilot of a small plane was blamed for the midair collision of a Cessna 310 and a Piedmont Boeing 727 over Hendersonville, North Carolina on July 19, 1967. Eighty-two died.

Fear of falling from an airplane is part of the fear of flying. Like the dream from which the sleeper awakes just before he or she hits the earth, it haunts those who think of flying as an unnatural way to pass between two points. But rarely is this fear realized.

A tragic exception took place on July 19, 1967 over Hendersonville, North Carolina. On that day, a Piedmont Boeing 727 took off from the Ashville-Henderson Airport with no difficulty and with no warning of danger from ground control. On time and on course, the liner continued to climb toward its cruising altitude.

At the same time, a twin-engine Cessna 310, carrying two businessmen bound for Ashville and piloted by veteran charter flyer David Addison, was headed toward the airport. Addison was 12 miles off his flight path, and ground control at Ashville-Henderson radioed to him to turn north. This he apparently failed to do, for barely three minutes later the Cessna plowed directly into the Piedmont 727.

The Cessna blew up immediately, atomizing itself and its occupants. The airliner, a gaping hole in its forward fuselage, lurched forward for a few feet, and then the jet fuel in its wing tanks ignited, and it, too, exploded. Cargo and passengers were flung free of the plane and rained like grisly confetti onto the countryside. Corpses landed in trees and on roads; two crashed through the roofs of houses; one fell onto the pavement near the gas pumps of a service station. The plane itself dove into a patch of woods, setting the trees on fire. Eighty-two people on both planes died. There were no survivors.

UNITED STATES
OHIO
AVA

September 3, 1925

• • • • • • • • • • • • • • • •

Political considerations apparently outweighed weather and safety factors when the Shenandoah, *America's proudest lighter-than-air ship, was forced by local votegetters to fly in bad weather over Ohio. On September 3, 1925 the ship went down in a pasture and broke apart, killing 14 crew members. Twenty-eight survived.*

The early days of dirigible travel are dotted with terrible tragedies. Every major ship—the *Akron* (see p. 38), the *Dixmude* (see p. 11), the *Hindenburg* (see p. 39) and the *Shenandoah*—crashed, with a consequent loss of life.

All were tragic, but the crash of the *Shenandoah*, America's prize entry in the international long-range and high-speed dirigible derby, was the one most tainted by controversy. "The Secretary of the Navy wanted to play politics by sending the ship over the Middle-Western cities," complained the embittered widow of the *Shenandoah*'s commander, F. R. McCrary. "My husband was very much opposed to making the flight at this time because of the weather conditions he knew so well. He asked officials at Washington to delay the flight until a better season."

The famous Colonel Billy Mitchell charged that the *Shenandoah*'s fatal journey was nothing but a propaganda trip, and zeppelin captain Anton Heinen dubbed it "murder."

There was some basis to the charges. September, despite its unpredictable weather in the Midwest, was the month of country fairs, and there were a number of politicians from these states who were facing reelection. They apparently felt that a majestic flyover by the *Shenandoah* would help them with their local constituencies.

Patterned after the German L-49, the 680-foot-long ship was built in 1919 and, like the *Akron*, was plagued with problems almost from its first launching. The problems were not exclusive to the *Shenandoah*; all lighter-than-air ships were, ultimately, expensive, impractical and dangerous. According to pioneer aviator Laurence La Tourette Driggs, quoted by Jay Robert Nash in his book *Darkest Hours:* "When the heavy winds blew, she could neither leave nor enter her hangar. When ordinary storms broke about her, she was in peril. When no mooring mast was handy, she required 500 men to catch her and hold her to earth. When rain drops clung to her envelope, she feared to attempt landing under their weight until they evaporated. When every condition was favorable, she sailed through the skies majestically—*but to what purpose?*"

Political considerations forced the* Shenandoah *to fly in bad weather and thus crash on September 3, 1925 near Ava, Ohio. The wrecked carcass of the once-proud airship was picked clean by souvenir hunters the following day. Smithsonian Institution

Not a high recommendation for the pride of the U.S. Navy, which for safety reasons was filled with helium instead of the hydrogen that would explode and incinerate the *Hindenburg* and its crew and passengers in 1937. Ironically, the *Shenandoah* encountered its first problems at the very mooring mast, at Lakehurst, New Jersey, that would be the scene of the *Hindenburg* disaster.

On January 16, 1924, a sudden storm, with winds up to 65 miles per hour, raged through Lakehurst while the *Shenandoah* was moored. The constant pounding of the winds eventually loosened the ships' mooring cables, and it broke loose, with a skeleton crew aboard. The crew acted swiftly, redistributing ballast and fuel just in time to avoid a plunge into some spiky pine trees beyond the airfield. Buying time, they then took the *Shenandoah* up to balmier altitudes and waited until dawn when they would be able to land the craft safely.

Later that same year, the *Shenandoah* made a safe and highly publicized long-distance flight of 9,317 miles back and forth across the United States. Benign weather, good luck and the skill of Commander Zachary Lansdowne turned the trip into a triumph, establishing a speed record of 19 days, nine hours for the round-trip from Lakehurst to Los Angeles and back.

The September 1925 voyage was another experience altogether. The commander and everyone concerned were aware of two negative factors: The weather was bad and perhaps dangerous and the flight was only really necessary to midwest politicians. Nevertheless, the navy men obeyed orders and left Lakehurst on September 2, bound for the fairgrounds of the Midwest.

By 4:00 A.M. on the third, they had reached Ohio and were immediately beset first by huge headwinds and then by a twister line squall. The turbulence tore at the *Shen-*

andoah, rocking it, plunging it earthward and knocking it skyward. Lansdowne fought the weather with all of the skill he could muster. He dipped the *Shenandoah*'s nose earthward to provide a better, less-battering aerodynamic flow; he maneuvered the rudder and elevators and gave its engines full power, but the ship was at the complete mercy of the up-and-down drafts and lateral winds that shot it upward from 2,000 feet to nearly 7,000 feet.

Now the *Shenandoah* began to come apart. Pieces of its envelope shredded and the engines stopped. It was carrying far too much ballast to stay for more than a moment at 7,000 feet, and it began to dive precipitously. In an attempt to lighten the ship and stop the fall, the commander ordered that everything that could be torn loose from the interior of the *Shenandoah* be tossed overboard.

Lieutenant Charles E. Rosendahl took six men with him, and they clambered to the keel of the ship to release helium with hand valves. But no sooner had they arrived at their destination than the ship began to break apart. It ultimately split in two. First, its control compartment and its Commander plummeted earthward, where all would be crushed inside the gondola.

Then, liberated from the weight of the gondola, the nose shot up to 10,000 feet, with Rosendahl and his men clinging to struts and grillwork. They continued to work frantically, releasing helium until the nose drifted, like a parachute, toward Sharon, Ohio, 12 miles from the point at which the gondola had carried Lansdowne and 10 of his men to their deaths.

While they were on their way down, Rosendahl effected one of the most spectacular rescues in the annals of aviation. Lieutenant J. B. Anderson, ordered by Commander Lansdowne to release a ballast of 800 gallons of gas, was crossing a catwalk when the ship broke apart and plummeted earthward. Anderson lost his balance and dove for a strut. He was hanging from this when the nose portion sailed close. Rosendahl lassoed Anderson with a rope just as the lieutenant lost his hold of the strut and was about to fall. Several men held onto the rope; it played out and held fast as Anderson fell the length of it. He hung suspended for a heart-stopping moment and then was hauled safely to the nose section by Rosendahl and his men.

Once the nose portion landed in an orchard owned by farmer Ernest Nichols, the sailors and Nichols tied it to several trees and a fence. Borrowing the farmer's shotgun, Chief Machinist's Mate Shine S. Halliburton shot holes in the remaining helium bags to prevent the nose portion from becoming airborne again. Meanwhile, the tail section, with 25 men in it, floated down into a nearby field.

The *Shenandoah* lay in pieces, its former glory gone forever. Fourteen crew members were dead; 28 survived. By the next day, souvenir hunters would loot the wreck of the belongings of the dead and even haul off portions of the ship that might have aided in an investigation of the crash.

UNITED STATES
TEXAS
DAWSON

May 3, 1968

• • • • • • • • • • • • • • • • • •

No explanation has been given for the explosion and crash of a Braniff Lockheed Electra near Dawson, Texas on May 3, 1968. All 88 aboard died.

The explosion and crash of a Braniff Lockheed Electra in a rainstorm near Dawson, Texas has never been explained. En route from Houston to Dallas on the night of May 3, 1968, the plane radioed no distress signal, nor was there any indication that the crew was aware of any mechanical difficulty.

And yet, somewhere outside Dawson, the plane simply exploded and plunged to earth, killing all 88 persons aboard.

There was some speculation that the endemic problem of engine mount defects that had caused several earlier crashes of the four-engine, turboprop Electras (see pp. 36 and 45) might have been responsible. But no huge midair explosions occurred in those accidents; wings had been torn off by the loosening of the engine mounts. And no evidence of a bomb was discovered in the wreckage.

Thus, the Braniff crash of May 3, 1968 would remain forever a mystery.

UNITED STATES
UTAH
BRYCE CANYON

October 24, 1947

• • • • • • • • • • • • • • • • • •

Faulty design was determined to be the culprit in the crash of a United Airlines DC-6 on October 24, 1947 as it was descending for a landing at Bryce Canyon Airport, Utah. Fifty-two died.

A design fault caused the calamitous crash of a United Airlines DC-6 on October 24, 1947 just short of the runway to Bryce Canyon Airport, Utah. One of the DC-6's fuel vents had been located near a heater air scoop. Fuel being automatically transferred from one tank to the other during flight often tended to spill, and fuel vapor could then make contact with the electric coils of the cabin heating system. The result: an inevitable fire. One occurred aboard the United DC-6 and another, less than a month later, aboard an American Airlines DC-6 over Gallup, New Mexico.

The latter fire would not result in a crash. The fire aboard the United Airlines plane would, and the drama of its unfolding was spelled out by Captain E. L. MacMillan as he called in at various dangerous moments to air control at Salt Lake City.

The flight took off on time from Los Angeles and was two hours into its journey to New York when the fire was discovered in the cargo department. Heavy clouds of thick smoke were pouring from the hold into the passenger cabin, and crew members with fire extinguishers were trying to control it when MacMillan radioed his first message of distress. "We have baggage fire aboard," MacMillan said. "We are coming to Bryce Canyon. We have smoked-filled plane. Unable to put fire out yet."

Five minutes later, the crew had controlled the fire, but there was no way of telling how much structural damage it had caused. "The tail fire is going out," radioed MacMillan. "We may get down and we may not."

With these chilling words as a directive, Bryce Canyon Airport was prepared for a crash landing. The sky was clear, the runway was made ready and rescue apparatus stood by.

"We may make it. Think we have a chance now," said the captain. "Approaching the strip."

It all seemed easy. But then there was a shout from MacMillan: "The tail is gone!" he yelled. And that was the last word the airport would receive.

Now out of control, the DC-6 was on a glide path that, had it remained intact, would have taken it safely to the Bryce Canyon Airport runway. But fifty feet before the beginning of the runway, there was a small hill. If MacMillan had been able to keep his craft aloft for only a few seconds more, he would have cleared it.

He did not. The DC-6 plowed into the top of the hill and exploded. Its four engines shot 50 feet ahead, skidding to a stop along the runway. Some passengers were flung from the wreckage; others burned within it. Rescuers rushing to the scene could save no one. All 52 aboard died.

As a result of the crash of the United DC-6 and the subsequent fire aboard the American airliner, all DC-6s were grounded by the order of the CAB in November 1947, and the design flaw was corrected.

UNITED STATES
VIRGINIA
RICHMOND

November 8, 1961

• • • • • • • • • • • • • • • • •

Ancient equipment and a failure to profit from the past were the almost certain causes of a catastrophic crash of an Imperial Airlines Lockheed Constellation near Richmond, Virginia on November 8, 1961. Seventy-seven died. Two survived.

In the 1950s and 1960s, the U.S. Army made it a practice to employ the lowest-bidding commercial carriers to ferry its personnel around the United States. However, low bidding in the charter airline business can be dangerous, and Imperial Airlines, one of the army's winners, was a dangerous carrier. Its record was appalling, its equipment outdated.

A quick glance at the airline's record with the army alone should have convinced both the FAA and the U.S. government that its contract with Imperial should have been long since abrogated.

In 1953, one of its DC-3s crashed near Centralia, California, killing 21. Eighteen of the victims were soldiers.

In 1959, Imperial was fined $1,000 by the FAA for loading 30 marines into an unairworthy C-46.

Earlier in 1961, three of Imperial's four pilots had had their licenses lifted by the FAA for "flying their aircraft under conditions dangerous to servicemen aboard."

Imperial's entire fleet consisted of four moth-eaten, patched-together planes, one of which, a 1946 model Lockheed Constellation, was pressed into service to ferry 74 army recruits from various locations to Fort Jackson, South Carolina.

Early on November 8, 1961, the Constellation began its journey at Newark Airport, where 30 recruits climbed aboard. Its first stop was Wilkes-Barre, Pennsylvania, where 31 more boarded. A final 13 were picked up at Baltimore, Maryland for the last leg of the flight to South Carolina.

Shortly after leaving Baltimore, the ship's captain, Ronald Conway, began to have trouble with the Constellation. By the time he radioed Byrd Airport at Richmond, Virginia to request permission for an emergency landing, two of his four engines had stopped.

The airport gave him clearance, and he circled for an approach. Partway through the circle, a third engine quit, but he was a seasoned pilot and could probably have made a landing with only one engine running if another malfunction had not suddenly occurred. The nose landing gear refused to lock.

Still, Conway might have brought it in. But on his second pass at the runway, the plane made a sudden lurch and heeled over into an abrupt dive toward the earth. It hit a forest, traversed a swamp and exploded, killing all 74 soldiers and three of the crew members. Conway and flight engineer William Poythree managed to escape through the cockpit hatch and were thus the only survivors of a crash that never should have happened.

UNITED STATES
WASHINGTON
MOSES LAKE

December 20, 1952

• • • • • • • • • • • • • • • • • •

Pilot error was blamed for the crash, on takeoff, of a U.S. Air Force C-124 over Moses Lake, Washington on December 20, 1952. Eighty-seven were killed; 44 survived.

Pilot error was judged responsible for the crash of a U.S. Air Force C-124 double-decker transport on the morning of December 20, 1952 at Larson Air Force Base, near Moses Lake, Washington.

The plane, carrying 131 servicemen, took off with apparent ease and climbed into the cloudless sky. But at a crucial moment in the takeoff, the pilot apparently failed to unlock the rudder and elevators from the plane's automatic locking gear. A knob on the throttle pedestal is ordinarily moved by the pilot on takeoff from the locked position to the unlocked position—a matter of two notches. If the knob is not moved, the plane can fly but cannot maneuver.

For some reason, the knob was not moved to its proper notch, and two minutes after it took off, the plane plummeted to earth, crashing into a snow-covered field and igniting immediately.

Emergency crews were dispatched forthwith to the fiercely burning wreck, and rescuers in asbestos suits carried survivors from the conflagration. No one in the nose section lived; 87 died, either in the crash or at a nearby hospital. Forty-four were rescued, but some of them were crippled for life.

U.S.S.R.
KRANAYA POLYANA

October 14, 1972

• • • • • • • • • • • • • • • • • •

Pilot error was responsible for the crash of a Soviet Aeroflot Ilyushin-62 on approach, in bad weather, to the Kranaya Polyana airport on October 14, 1972. One hundred seventy-six were killed.

The weather was abominable over Moscow on October 14, 1972. A heavy mist broken by intermittent periods of rain reduced visibility to practically nothing. Not only that, the instrument-landing apparatus at Sheremetevo International Airport was temporarily inoperative. The following afternoon, a British European Airways flight would be diverted to Stockholm when the pilot decided that the combination of bad visibility and an out-of-order landing system was a situation he was unwilling to battle.

The same decision should have been made the night before by the pilot of an Ilyushin-62 reportedly chartered from the Soviet airline Aeroflot by the state travel agency Intourist. At 9:00 P.M. that night, he approached the airport and requested clearance for landing. He was granted it but reminded that there were no instrument-landing capabilities.

The flight had left Paris at noon that day with a full passenger load that included 102 French citizens. Early that evening, all but one of these French passengers had disembarked at a stop in Leningrad. Thirty-eight Chileans, five Algerians, three Italians, two Lebanese, a Frenchman, a Briton and 111 Russians were still aboard when it departed for the last leg of its flight to Moscow.

The pilot circled the field and came in for a landing. It was impossible to see the runway. He circled twice more and aborted each time. Finally, on the fourth try, he apparently felt that he had the runway in sight. But he was tragically wrong. He was three miles away from the airport, on the outskirts of the small village of Kranaya Polyana. The plane struck the ground with enough force to explode and send fiery sparks 100 feet into the misty night sky.

Everyone aboard—176 passengers and crew members—died, making this the worse commercial airline crash in the world to that date. The Soviet news agency Tass stubbornly refused to release details of the crash at first. Soviet authorities even tried to misdirect Western newspeople to the village of Chernaya Gryaz, seven miles from the site of the crash.

But because there were foreign nationals killed in the crash, the Soviets finally released the statistics and a terse story about the disaster.

VENEZUELA
LA CORUBA

March 16, 1969

• • • • • • • • • • • • • • • • • •

Pilot error was blamed for the crash, on takeoff, of a VIASA DC-9 at La Coruba, Venezuela on March 16, 1969. Eighty-four died in the airplane; 76 were killed on the ground.

Maracaibo, a city of 800,000 in the northeastern part of Venezuela, is that country's oil capital. As such, it attracts a large number of foreign businesspeople. So at 11 P.M. on March 16, 1969, 46 Americans were among those on board a VIASA DC-9, en route from Caracas to Miami, which took off from Maracaibo's Grano de Oro Airport.

The flight lasted only two minutes, and it would never rise higher than 150 feet.

According to witnesses, the plane wavered for a moment and then glided toward the ground. On its descent it struck a high tension wire and exploded, sending flaming wreckage into the suburb of La Coruba, just outside Maracaibo. Five square blocks of the town were obliterated by fire and falling parts of the plane. The entire neighborhood resembled a war zone.

Fire and ambulance crews immediately dashed to the scene of the crash. All 74 passengers and 10 crew members aboard the plane perished. There was no hope whatsoever for their survival.

The carnage was appalling. Rescue workers sifted through the wreckage, looking for survivors, sending the injured off to hospitals and caring for those who were less seriously hurt. Roman Catholic priests roamed through the crash area trying to console relatives of the victims and performing last rites for the dead. Boy Scouts went from house to house asking for sheets in which to wrap the dead.

Seventy-one died on the ground; five more would die later in hospitals from their injuries. A total of 160 people perished in this crash, the worst in commercial aviation up to that time. The reason was given as "pilot error."

WEST INDIES
GUADALOUPE

June 22, 1962

• • • • • • • • • • • • • • • •

An Air France Boeing 707 crashed on landing at Guadaloupe on June 22, 1962. The cause of the crash was never ascertained. All 113 aboard died.

The year 1962 was not a good one for Boeing 707s. No less than five of them went down in 1962, killing 456 persons. The 707, a modification by Boeing of its KC-135 tanker, was first flown on December 20, 1957 and was received with great enthusiasm, despite the fact that the early models gained a reputation among pilots of flying "like civil bombers." They burned fuel heavily, but their pure-jet engines gave them a 25% speed margin over Viscounts and Electras, their chief competition, which made them ideal for transcontinental and transoceanic travel.

In 1962 Air France had a bad record for safety. In the period from 1950 to 1968, 812 Air France passengers had been killed. Like the Boeing 707, Air France resolved its deficiencies and developed into a model of safety. But not, unfortunately, before both were involved in a tragic crash on the French Caribbean island of Guadaloupe.

The island's airport, like most in the West Indies, is anything but spacious, and landing on it involves both skill and luck. Ringed by mountains, it demands a steep descent and constant attention on the part of the crew.

On June 22, 1962, an Air France 707 approached the airport at Guadaloupe for a routine landing. It smashed squarely into Dos D'Ane (the Donkey's Back), a rugged mountain peak overlooking the airport's runways. All 113 aboard were killed in the resultant explosion and fire.

No specific reason was ever discovered for the crash. Attention focused on the 707 in the FAA investigation, but no design flaws that could have led to the tragedy were found.

YUGOSLAVIA
LJUBLJANA

September 1, 1966

• • • • • • • • • • • • • • • •

Pilot error was the reason given for the crash on landing at Ljubljana, Yugoslavia of a charter Britannia Airways 102 on September 1, 1966. Ninety-seven died; 20 survived.

One hundred twelve British tourists chartered a turboprop airliner from Britannia Airways in September 1966 for a vacation in Yugoslavia. But because of pilot error, only 20 of them would survive the trip.

The aircraft made the journey from London's Heathrow Airport without trouble. The weather and the approach to the airport in Ljubljana, a city of 200,000 north and west of Zagreb and Belgrade, were clear. But the flight was obviously off course when it approached the landing field, and controllers advised the pilot of his error. He was 110 yards off course and 600 feet too low.

The crew apparently received this information and failed to act on it. The plane descended on the wrong path and at the wrong altitude. Then, according to one of the survivors, Arthur Rowcliff, "The plane slowed down. Then it started to vibrate. A few seconds later we crashed, bounced back in the air and finally fell down. We were thrown clear with our seats."

The aircraft had plowed into a ridge full of fir trees, leaped into the air and then plummeted to earth, where it burst into flames. Those who, like Rowcliff and his family, were thrown clear survived. The others perished in the inferno that erupted when the plane struck the ground. The ultimate death toll would be 97.

CIVIL UNREST AND TERRORISM

THE WORST RECORDED CIVIL UNREST AND TERRORISM

CIVIL UNREST

* Detailed in text

Armenia/Turkey
- * Armenian massacres by Turks (1895–1922)

Austria
- Vienna
- General strike following Nazi acquittal for political murder (1927)

Burundi
- Marangara
- * Tribal confrontation (1988)

China
- Beijing
- * Massacre in Tiananmen Square (1989)
- Northern Provinces
- * Boxer Uprising (1900)

Czechoslovakia
- Uprising crushed (1977)

Egypt
- Insurrections over exorbitant taxes (189 B.C.)

Europe
- * The Holocaust—attempted genocide of European Jews by Nazis (1939–45)

France
- Paris
- * St. Bartholomew's Day massacre of 2,000 Huguenots (1572)
- Massacre of Champs de Mars (1791)
- * Reign of Terror and White Terror (1793–95)
- Rouen
- Burning of Joan of Arc at stake (1431)
- Vassy
- 1,200 French Huguenots slain (1562)

Germany
- Alsace
- First *Bundschuh*, or peasants' revolt (1493)

Great Britain
- England
- Nationalist uprisings in north and west crushed by William I (1068)
- London
- Evil May Day riots—60 hanged on Cardinal Wolsey's orders (1517)
- * Gunpowder Plot—Guy Fawkes arrested in cellars of Parliament (1605)
- Manchester
- Peterloo massacre (1819)

Hungary
- * Uprising crushed (1956)

India
- Amritsar
- * Massacre (1919)
- Riot between Sikhs and Hindus (1984)
- Mandai, Tripura; Assam
- * Tribal massacre (1980)
- Ethnic violence (1983)

Ireland
- Irish railway strike (1920)

Japan
- Edo
- Yetuna, new shogun, overcomes two rebellions (1651)
- Satsuma
- Revolt crushed (1877)

Northern Ireland
- Violence begins (1971–72); 467 Irish killed in 1972

Poland
- Warsaw
- Massacre when Russian troops fire on demonstrators (1861)

Rome
- Gaius Gracchus killed in riot; his reforms abolished (121 B.C.)
- * Revolt of slaves and gladiators under Spartacus; crushed by Pompey and Crassus (71 B.C.)

Russia
- St. Petersburg
- * Decembrist Revolt crushed (1825)

South Africa
- Matabele
- Revolt against British South Africa Company; crushed by Starr Jameson (1893)

United States
- California
- Los Angeles
- * Race riots in Watts (1965)
- Colorado
- Sand Creek
- * Massacre of Cheyenne and Arapaho Indians (1864)
- Illinois
- Chicago
- * Race riots (1919)
- Strike against Republic Steel (1937)
- * Police riot at Democratic National convention (1968)
- Massachusetts
- Boston
- Boston Massacre between civilians and troops (1770)
- New York
- New York
- * Draft riots (1863)
- Ohio
- Kent
- * Killing of Kent State students by Ohio National Guard (1970)
- Virginia
- Southampton
- Revolt of slaves led by Nat Turner (1831)
- Washington, D.C.
- * Bonus Army march (1932)

TERRORISM

Belgium
Red Brigade tries to kidnap and kill Alexander Haig, NATO commander (1979)
Brazil
Rio de Janeiro
* First of diplomatic kidnappings: Charles Elbrick, U.S. ambassador to Brazil (1969)
France
Paris
Orly Airport bombed by Armenians (ASALA) (1983)
Germany
Lufthansa hijacking (1977)
Munich
* Olympic Games massacre (1972)
Neo-Nazi plants bomb at Bierfest (1980)
West Berlin
La Belle discotheque bombing (1986)
Great Britain
England
Birmingham
Provisional IRA sets series of bombs (1974)
Brighton
IRA bomb almost wipes out Margaret Thatcher and entire British cabinet (1984)
London
* Harrods attacked by car bomb planted by Provisional IRA (1983)
Scotland
* Pan Am jet blown up over Lockerbie (1988)
Greece
Athens
TWA plane from Tel Aviv attacked by National Arab Youth for the Liberation of Palestine (Libyan sponsored) (1974)
India
Bombay
Airliner explodes; Sikh terrorists suspected (1985)
JAL hijacking (1977)
Iran
Tehran
* U.S. Embassy held hostage (1979–81)

Ireland
Irish Sea
* Air India Boeing 747 from Toronto to London blown up and crashes into Irish Sea (1985)
Israel
Entebbe Airport; first defeat for international terrorism (1976)
Sinai Desert
* Israeli Phantoms shoot down Libyan Boeing 707 (1973)
Tel Aviv
* Lod (Lydda) Airport; first transnational terrorist attack, between Palestine Liberation Front and Japanese Red Army (1972)
Italy
Bologna
* Neo-fascist terrorists bomb central train station (1980)
Rome
First Palestinian hijacking (1968)
NALYP bombing and hijacking of Pan Am Airliner (1973)
Rome and Vienna, Austria
Coordinated attacks on El Al check-in desks (1985)
Vatican City
Pope John Paul II severely wounded by Turkish Grey Wolves; Bulgarian Secret Service charged with complicity (1981)
Japan
Tokyo
First of Japanese Red Army's international actions
Hijacking of JAL plane to North Korea (1970)
Jordan
* Dawson's field
Five planes hijacked; leads to Black September formation (1970)
Lebanon
Beirut
U.S. Embassy destroyed by car bomb (1983)
* Marine barracks bombed (1983)
* TWA Flight 847 hijacked (1985)
Malta
Hijacking; 58 killed after Israeli commandos rush plane (1985)
Mediterranean Sea
* *Achille Lauro* hijacking (1985)
Netherlands
Rotterdam
Fatah blows up fuel tanks (1971)
Saudi Arabia
Mecca
Muslim extremists kill 150 in Grand Mosque (1979)
Spain
Majorca
Lufthansa flight hijacked by PFLP/Baader-Meinhof (1977)
Sweden
Stockholm
West Germany Embassy blown up by Rote Armee Fraktion (1975)
Syria
Damascus
* Bombing (1981)
United States
California
Berkeley
Patricia Hearst kidnapped by SLA (1974)
New York
New York
FLN bomb exploded in Fraunces Tavern (1975)
LaGuardia Airport bombing (1975)
Washington, D.C.
* Muslim hostage taking (1977)

CHRONOLOGY

CIVIL UNREST

* Detailed in text

189 B.C.
Insurrections; Egypt
121 B.C.
Gaius Gracchus killed in riot; Rome
71 B.C.
* Revolt of slaves and gladiators; Rome
1068
Nationalist uprisings; England
1431
Burning of Joan of Arc; Rouen, France
1493
First peasants' revolt; Alsace, Germany
1517
May 1
Evil May Day riots; London
1562
Slaying of French Huguenots; Vassy, France
1572
Aug. 24
* St. Bartholomew's Day massacre; Paris
1605
Nov. 5
* Gunpowder Plot; London
1651
Shogun overcomes two rebellions; Edo, Japan
1770
Boston Massacre; Boston
1791
Massacre of Champs de Mars; Paris
1793–95
* Reign of Terror and White Terror; Paris
1819
Peterloo massacre; Manchester, England
1825
Dec. 14
* Decembrist Revolt; St. Petersburg, Russia
1831
Revolt of slaves led by Nat Turner; Southampton, Virginia
1861
Massacre of demonstrators; Warsaw, Poland
1863
July 13–15
* Draft riots; New York City
1864
Nov. 29
* Massacre of Cheyenne and Arapaho Indians; Colorado
1877
Revolt; Satsuma, Japan
1893
Revolt against British South Africa Company; Matabele, South Africa
1895–1922
* Armenian massacres; Armenia/Turkey
1900
June
* Boxer Rebellion; Northern Provinces, China
1919
April 13
* Amritsar massacre; Amritsar, India
July 27–Aug. 3
* Race riots; Chicago, Illinois
1920
Irish railway strike; Ireland
1927
General strike; Vienna, Austria
1932
May 20–July 28
* Bonus Army march; Washington, D.C.
1937
Republic Steel strike; Chicago, Illinois
1939–45
* The Holocaust; Europe
1956
Nov. 4
* Hungarian uprising; Hungary
1965
Aug. 11–29
* Race riots; Los Angeles, California
1968
Aug. 25–30
* Police riot at Democratic National Convention; Chicago, Illinois
1970
May 4
* Killing of Kent State students by Ohio National Guard; Kent, Ohio
1971
Violence begins; Northern Ireland
1977
General uprising; Czechoslovakia
1980
June 7–8
* Ethnic violence; Mandai, Tripura, India
1983
Feb. 18
* Ethnic violence; Mandai, Assam, India
1984
Riot between Sikhs and Hindus; Amritsar, India
1988
Aug. 14–21
* Tribal confrontation; Burundi, Africa
1989
April 18–June 4
* Massacre in Tiananmen Square; Beijing, China

TERRORISM

1968
July 22
First Palestinian hijacking; Rome, Italy
1969
Sept. 9
* First diplomatic kidnapping; Rio de Janeiro, Brazil
1970
Sept. 6–8
* Five planes hijacked; Dawson's Field, Jordan
1971
Mar. 4
Fuel tanks blown up; Rotterdam, the Netherlands
1972
May 3
* First transitional terrorist attack; Tel Aviv, Israel
Sept. 5
* Olympic Games massacre; Munich, Germany
1973
Feb. 21
* Israeli jets down Libyan 707 airliner; Sinai Desert, Israel
Sept. 5
Pan Am airliner bombed; Rome, Italy
Sept. 7
TWA airliner blown up; Athens, Greece
1974
Feb. 5
Patricia Hearst kidnapped by SLA; Berkeley, California
Nov. 21
* IRA bombings; Birmingham, England
1975
Dec. 24
FLN bomb explodes in Fraunces Tavern; New York, N.Y.
1976
June 27
First defeat for terrorists; Entebbe Airport, Uganda
1977
Mar. 9–11
* Muslims take hostages; Washington, D.C.
Sept. 28
JAL hijacking; Bombay, India
Oct. 13
Lufthansa hijacking; Majorca, Spain
1979
June 29
Red Brigade attempt on Alexander Haig; Belgium
Nov. 4
* U.S. Embassy held hostage until 1981; Tehran, Iran
1980
Aug. 1
* Neo-fascist bombing of train station; Bologna, Italy
Aug. 1
Neo-Nazi bomb at *Bierfest;* Munich, Germany
1981
May 13
Attempt on Pope John Paul II's life; Vatican City, Italy
Nov. 29
* Bombing; Damascus, Syria
1983
July 15
Orly Airport bombing; Paris, France
Oct. 23
* Marine barracks bombed; Beirut, Lebanon
Dec. 17
* IRA Christmas bombing of Harrods; London
1984
Oct. 12
IRA attempt on Margaret Thatcher; Brighton, England
1985
June 14–18
* TWA Flight 847 hijacked; Beirut, Lebanon
June 22
* Air India 747 blown up; Irish Sea
Oct. 7–9
* *Achille Lauro* hijacking; Mediterranean Sea
Nov. 23
Egyptair hijacking; Malta
1986
April 5
La Belle discotheque bombing; West Berlin; Germany
April 15
U.S. aircraft attack Libya; Libya
1988
Dec. 21
* Pan Am flight bombed; Lockerbie, Scotland

CIVIL UNREST AND TERRORISM

There is a single, dark thread that runs through and binds together the two categories of this section, and the name of it is motivation. Each of these similar undertakings—civil unrest and terrorism—is motivated by a belief.

That belief may be as simple as a fancied slight or as complex as a philosophy; as closely held as a catechism or as widely held as a form of government, a system of laws or an ordering of ideas. The point of the matter is that in each of the incidents described or listed in this section, the action taken was done so with the purpose of either *overthrowing* a particular ideology or political system or *promulgating* a particular ideology or political system.

What qualifies these events as disasters is that, no matter the purpose, nothing was achieved through them. They were either failures, or they brought about the reverse of their intention. The world, or *their* world, was made worse for their actions. The collective loss of life in the American Revolution is not a disaster; the collective loss of life in the Decembrist Revolt of 1825 is, because it failed to accomplish its objective. The loss of life in any airplane crash is catastrophic, but it acquires a new dimension of tragedy when it is the result of a terrorist's bomb.

Political and civil unrest often results in mass assassination. It either involves large groups of people who have been whipped into a fanatic frenzy by leaders who appeal to their dedication to a cause, or it is the massing of the forces of a particular *government* with a particular point of view against a mass of people with an opposing viewpoint. Extended to an international status, it becomes war. Confined to a specific location, it is defined as riot. Extended within the borders of one specific country, it becomes civil war.

The events in this section are, with two exceptions, confined to riots. The remaining two events, included because they are of such horrific dimensions that they cannot be denied space, are two attempts at genocide: the Armenian Massacres (see below) and the Nazi Holocaust (see p. 68).

CIVIL UNREST

ARMENIA/TURKEY

1895–1922

Religious intolerance was the core cause for the 27-year attempt by Turkey to commit genocide upon Armenia and its populace. Two million Armenians were massacred, and Armenia as a country was eliminated from the map of the world.

Genocide is one of humankind's lower forms of activity, and one of the most dramatic exemplifications of this was the horrendous massacre, from 1895 to 1922, of Armenians by the Turkish government. During those 27 years, two million Armenian men, women and children were murdered, often after prolonged and barbaric torture. Others were driven across deserts or to ports of debarkation. The purpose was to totally annihilate the Armenian minority in Turkey as a holy necessity. Armenians were Christians; Turks were Muslims, and it became a holy war—traditionally the most savage sort of conflict.

Founded by Haik, a descendant of Noah, Armenia originally occupied the land at the source of the Tigris and Euphrates rivers in Asia Minor. Eventually, it became known as an incorporation of northeast Turkey, the Armenian Soviet Socialist Republic, and parts of Iranian Azerbaijan.

A mother grieves over her dead child in a field near Aleppo, in the midst of the Armenian massacres. Two million Armenians were killed over a period of 27 years by Turks, who eventually erased Armenia from the map of the world. Library of Congress

Long a disputed territory that was fought over by Persia, Russia and Turkey, Armenia became the scene of turmoil and oppression for centuries. The Turkish Ottoman Empire invaded Armenia in the 15th century and held all of it by the 16th century.

Although Armenians became successful merchants in Turkey, they were always an oppressed minority because of their religion. Saint Gregory the Illuminator established Christianity in Armenia in the third century, and the autonomous Gregorian church became the centerpiece of Armenian culture and belief. Thus, this country without a portfolio was also an island of Christianity in a vast sea of Muslims, and it was this religious identity that the Ottoman Empire, under Sultan Abd al-Hamid II, used as its reason for launching the first volley in an attempt to exterminate all Armenian infidels from what once was the Armenian Empire.

The Sassoun massacres in January 1895 were merely the first steps in a 27-year-long genocidal campaign. Over three years, 300,000 Armenians perished either by the efforts of government troops, starvation or disease. Troops would swoop down on Armenian settlements with the orders "Exterminate, root and branch. Whoever spares man, woman, or child is disloyal."

Thus, when the troops entered a town, they butchered all Armenians without discrimination. Women were raped and then killed. According to the *New York Times* on January 1, 1895, a priest in one village was taken to the roof of his church, hacked to pieces and then set afire. A large group of women and girls was herded into the church, raped and then locked in as soldiers set fire to the church.

In Moosh, Alyan and 14 other villages in the Sassoun district, 7,500 Armenians were butchered in the grisliest of ways. Some escaped into the hills, but starvation eventually drove them back to the villages, where they were set upon by waiting soldiers. Fires were built, and three- and four-year-old children were tossed, alive, into them.

The priests of the church were particular targets for the soldiers. In Ashpig, Der Bedrase, the priest of Geliguson, was stabbed by 40 soldiers wielding bayonets, and his eyes were dug out before he was tossed into a shallow grave he himself was forced to dig. Der Hohannes, the priest of Senmal, faced an even more gruesome ordeal. According to an eyewitness: "The soldiers took out Der Hohannes's eyes, seized his hands, and compelled him to dance. Not only was he deprived of his beard, the insignia of his priestly office, but the cruel creatures took along with the razor some of the skin and flesh as well. Having pierced his throat, they forced him to drink water . . . It flowed from the ghastly cut, down on either side. His head was kicked this way and that, as if a football. Human flesh taken from some of his mangled people was put into his mouth. He, too, was pitched into the ditch with more than two score of men that had the promise of safety if they would cease resistance and surrender."

This was only the beginning. In April 1909, hundreds of thousands of Armenians were butchered in the Massacre of Adana.

By 1913, mass deportations were organized, and tens of thousands of men, women and children were made to march across deserts without food or water. Along the way, they were whipped, bludgeoned, bayoneted and torn limb from limb. Women were raped in front of their husbands and children and then murdered and tossed by the side of the road.

In Marash and in Zeytoon, there were uprisings of Armenian youths, but they were summarily crushed. If soldiers did not kill the Armenians, mobs did, with shovels, axes and blacksmith tools.

In 1915, the deportations increased. Tens of thousands of Armenians were driven ruthlessly from one city to another and back again. On August 7, the prisons in Zeytoon and Fundajak were thrown open, and Armenian prisoners, chained together, were led through the streets to their slaughter. Some were hanged from scaffolds in the center of various villages; the rest were marched to the foot of Mount Aghur and shot.

Not all Armenians were slaughtered or deported. Some were saved for slave labor. Twelve thousand of them worked on the beds of various railroad lines around northeastern Turkey. Overseen by German officers (World War I was now in progress, and Turkey was Germany's ally), these men, women and children were rationed a loaf of bread a day and some water and counted themselves lucky. They were, at least, alive.

Concentration camps of Armenians living in tents sprang up on the countryside, and on June 14, 1916, another mass deportation imprisoned or killed thousands more. Hungry, thirsty, naked, dirty and near death, these Armenians were relentlessly tortured and then killed. When the survivors were led on a deportation march, they were frequently separated from their families. Those who became exhausted fell by the side of the road, where shooting had come to be a kind fate.

Abraham Hartunian, a pastor who survived despite having an eye gouged out and being shot twice in the hip, wrote of this deportation:

> *Corpses! Corpses! Murdered! Mutilated! . . . Stepping over them like ghosts of the dead, we walked and walked . . . Armenians were being massacred on the way between Baghtche and Marash . . . Here were the bodies of those driven out before us and shot, stabbed, savagely slaughtered [but] the previous convoys had experienced more.*
>
> *The men in our group who struck the eyes of the zaptiye [Turkish police] were separated, taken a little distance away, and shot. Everyone expected his turn to come next. The old man whose young son had died in Baghtche was walking along beside me with his daughter-in-law and two small grandchildren . . . But now, unable to walk, he was getting in the way of those behind. A* zaptiye *saw him. He came and kicked him and, dragging him out of the group, tripped him into a ditch nearby and emptied his gun into his breast.*

At various places along the march, Muslim mobs from nearby villages waited with guns, axes and sacks. Told they would be blessed by Allah if they robbed and killed Armenians, they did.

"Night fell," wrote Hartunian in his memoir, *Neither to Laugh nor to Weep,*

> *and the prettier women were taken aside and raped. Among them was an extremely beautiful girl, about twenty-five years of age . . . one after the other, the* zaptiye *. . . raped [her] and then, killing her, threw her mutilated corpse to one side because they could not agree who should have her.*
>
> *Many women were stripped naked and lined up, and their abdomens slashed one by one, were thrown into ditches and wells to die in infinite agony. The* kaymakum *of Der-el-Zor, holding a fifteen-year-old girl before him, directed his words to a murderous band and then, throwing her to the ground, clubbed her to death with the order, "So you must kill all Armenians, without remorse."*
>
> *Convoy after convoy was driven night and day unceasingly, robbed, raped, then brought to the edge of streams and forbidden to drink at the point of the gun. Under the burning sun, thousands perished from hunger and thirst.*
>
> *Many were gathered in one place and burned alive. One of these, left half dead and later rescued, told me that for days she had remained with the corpses and had lived eating their flesh.*

The chronicle of horror was endless. Finally, in 1919, when British troops entered Armenia, an end to the massacres seemed to be in sight. But in one final genocidal sweep, the Turks massacred thousands of Armenians as the British troops were landing. British forces did little to stop these raids, and the remaining Armenians began to lose hope again.

In 1920, the French occupied Turkey. Even so, in that year alone 15,000 Armenians were annihilated in Marash; 160 Armenian girls were taken from an American girl's seminary in Hadjin, raped in the Turkish harems and then massacred; 3,000 Armenians on the road from Marash to Adana were buried in snow and died and further massacres were planned under the eyes of the French.

The 1920 massacres were as brutal as any that had gone before. According to Hartunian, "Children were ripped open before their parents, their hearts taken out and stuffed down their mothers' throats. Mothers were crucified naked to doors, and before their very eyes their small ones were fixed to the floor with swords and left writhing."

By the middle of 1920, the Turks were in full revolt against the French and massacred Armenians at will. Open warfare erupted. Turks burned Armenian homes and businesses; Armenians burned Turkish mosques. The Armenians were eventually overcome, and the Turkish government confiscated the houses, vineyards and fields of dead or fugitive Armenians.

At the end of the year, the Treaty of Sevres was signed, restoring Armenia as a sovereign state. Most Armenians who could, left. There was no guarantee that the massacres that had raged for nearly 27 years would not begin again.

BURUNDI
MARANGARA

August 14–21, 1988

• • • • • • • • • • • • • • • • •

Long-standing animosity between the central African tribes of the Tutsis and Hutus resulted in mass slaughters between

August 14 and 21, 1988. Five thousand people, mostly women and children, were killed; thousands were wounded, many seriously. Forty-seven thousand refugees crossed into neighboring Rwanda; nearly 150,000 were made homeless.

For three centuries, highly charged, emotional confrontation has existed between the central African tribes of the Tutsis and the Hutus. The Tutsis arrived from Somalia and Ethiopia in the 16th and 17th centuries and established themselves as a kind of feudal aristocracy over the Hutus. Tall, cattle-raising people, they set up a ruling regime that denied the short-statured Hutu farmers equal rights. Belgium, which later ruled Burundi as a colony, exacerbated the problem by allowing the Tutsis to dominate education, government and the army. When Burundi achieved independence in 1972, war broke out between the two tribes.

Between August 14 and 21, 1988, the Hutus, armed with rocks and knives, attacked Tutsi villages. The reprisals by the Tutsi army were swift and devastating. Hutu villages were burned to the ground. Women and children were shot, mutilated and beaten. Five thousand victims on both sides of the conflict were killed.

As a result of the violence, 47,000 refugees poured across the border into neighboring Rwanda, and the government of Burundi estimated that nearly 150,000 were made homeless by the slaughter. Hospitals were filled with the wounded, most of whom were suffering from infections resulting from wounds that went untreated for weeks while they hid from soldiers in the underbrush. The result was a multitude of amputations, some of them on children only two years old.

The government of Burundi applied to the United Nations for $15 million in aid, but with the government's own army responsible for the massacres, the world body took a negative view of the request.

CHINA
BEIJING

April 18–June 4, 1989

• • • • • • • • • • • • • • • • •

Pro-democracy demonstrations begun by several thousand students in Tiananmen Square, Beijing on April 18, 1989 swelled to one million in mid-May, during a visit by Mikhail Gorbachev. On June 3–4, army troops sent by the government massacred over 1,000 students and workers, injured more than 10,000 and crushed the uprising.

Life in present-day Communist China is as controlled as if the government were a puppet master and its populace puppets. Government officials assign people jobs, determine where they may live and decide how many children they may have.

Thus, the eventual magnitude of the protest demonstration that filled Beijing's Tiananmen Square throughout most of the spring of 1989 must have come as a startling surprise to both the Communist government of Deng Xiaoping and the demonstrators themselves. Not that gatherings of protesters have no precedence in China. Ironically, it was dissenting students, on May 4, 1919, that played a key role in the founding of China's Communist movement, and it was student demonstrations that followed the death of Chou En-lai in 1976 that helped Deng Xiaoping ascend to power.

In 1976, tens of thousands of mourners opposed the ascension to leadership of the so-called Gang of Four after the deaths of Mao Tse-tung and Chou En-lai, and Deng, accused of being behind the protests, was purged. Three years later, in 1979, the same protesters pasted posters on what became known as Democracy Wall, and they were encouraged by Deng, who was making a comeback. But after he and his allies secured power, he reversed himself and clamped down on them.

Deng was a conservative force. Student protests and prodemocracy marches in 1986, spreading from the provinces to Beijing, became a factor in the downfall of Hu Yaobang, whom Deng accused of failing to stem the protests.

By 1989, Deng was in his 80s and surrounded by likeminded, conservative Communists. In the age of Gorbachev and glasnost, China was ruled by neo-Stalinist hardliners, who practiced a policy of restraining criticism, stifling independence and maintaining a party monopoly on power.

There had been no more dramatic assertion of this than the 1987 ouster of Hu Yaobang, the leader of the Chinese Communist party and the heir apparent to the aging Deng Xiaoping. His removal came about because of his advocacy of intellectual freedom in China, an advocacy that launched a wave of public support from university students throughout China.

On April 15, 1989, Hu Yaobang died, and his death, as his public stands in life, led to yet another outpouring of mourning, support and protest from China's students.

In the predawn hours of April 18, more than 10,000 of them marched through the capital of Beijing, chanting democratic slogans, singing revolutionary songs and eulogizing Hu Yaobang. At the height of the demonstration, several thousand students peeled off and marched to the Communist party headquarters, where some of them attempted to force their way in to see the nation's leaders. Still others staged a sit-in in front of the Great Hall of the

People, at one end of the square, chanting a series of demands, among them freedom of the press, a reappraisal of Hu, a repudiation of past crackdowns on intellectuals and a disclosure of the income and assets of China's leaders and their children. Late in the day, several officials emerged from the hall and accepted a list of demands, assuring the students that they would study them.

Thus the Beijing spring began in a friendly, if public, fashion.

By Friday night, April 21, the government had grown perceptibly nervous and issued a ban on all public demonstrations. In defiance of the ban, more than 100,000 students gathered in Tiananmen Square. By the next morning, thousands of them had set up an encampment, thus foiling government attempts to close off the area and prevent a mass rally.

Later that morning, as the students chanted democratic slogans, party leaders arrived at the Great Hall for memorial services for Hu Yaobang. In the streets, students were conducting their own memorial by singing the "Internationale," which begins, "Rise up, you who refuse to be slaves . . ." During the day, attracted by cries of "Beijing citizens, follow us!" workers began to join the students in the square.

By Sunday the 23d, protests had ignited in other parts of China. In Xian, according to the official New China News Agency, protesters, after watching the official memorial service on television in the public square, attacked the provincial government headquarters, injuring 130 officers and burning 20 houses, setting fire to 10 vehicles and attacking a tourist bus loaded with terrified vacationers.

In Beijing, the demonstrators were far more peaceful, and most left the square by the morning of the 23d, vowing to boycott classes until May 4, the 70th anniversary of the famous 1919 demonstrations.

But by Thursday the 27th, despite the presence of police barricades and army troops in trucks, they were back again, 150,000 strong, marching for 14 hours. This time, at least 75,000 workers joined in, and thousands more lined the route of the march. Workers applauded the students from the street, waved encouragement from office windows and sent food and drinks to the demonstrators. It was the first time the pro-democracy movement had spilled over from students and intellectuals to the ordinary workers of China, and the demonstrators escalated their demands to include populist themes such as increased funding for education and an attempt to control inflation.

Toward the end of the demonstration, crowds burst through the last police barricade surrounding Tiananmen Square. Nearly 1,000 soldiers in 20 trucks were surrounded by mobs who clambered onto the hoods and sides of the vehicles and appeared, according to Western newspeople, about to lynch the terrified soldiers.

But now a distinctive characteristic of the student demonstrations began to assert itself. Students, waving their identification badges, came to the soldiers' rescue, clearing a way for their retreat and shouting "Brothers, go home and till your fields!"

No such gentleness came from the rulers of the country, who in the next two days adopted a stiff line of resistance to the demands in the street.

But the threats seemed to have no effect. A day after the initial demonstrations, the government offered to hold a dialogue with the students, provided they returned to their universities "at once." In the eyes of the students, the pronouncement amounted to a rejection, and new demonstrations spread to Shanghai, Nanjing and other provincial cities.

The impasse continued through early May, and on Saturday, May 13, 2,000 students began a hunger strike in Tiananmen Square, vowing to remain there until their demands were met. On May 14, an unannounced Politburo meeting reportedly endorsed the moderate line of the Communist party leader, Zhao Ziyang, who hinted at the possibility of greater democracy in China.

It may have been a ploy to clear the square for the May 15 visit of Mikhail Gorbachev, who was coming to seal the reconciliation of the world's two largest Communist nations. The demonstrators now became an embarrassment to Deng and his hardliners. A welcoming ceremony for Gorbachev to be held in Tiananmen Square had to be rescheduled, in an abbreviated form, at the airport, after protesters refused to end their vigil and hunger strike in the capital's center.

During the night of May 14, the crowds in the square swelled to 80,000, and by the night of May 15, during a state dinner for Gorbachev, 150,000 rallied around the hunger strikers, who were now being tended by a team of medical students, distributing salt tablets and glucose. By morning, more than 100 hunger strikers had lost consciousness and were taken to hospitals.

By Wednesday the 17th, an astonishing crowd of more than one million Chinese citizens had gathered in the streets of Beijing, bringing the capital and much of the country to a virtual standstill. As more ambulances carried more unconscious hunger strikers to hospitals, a high school teacher cried to a *New York Times* reporter, "Our hearts bleed when we hear the sound of ambulances. [The students] are no longer children. They are the hope of China."

This sort of escalation could no longer be denied by either the Chinese leadership or Gorbachev, who mildly endorsed the demonstrators' aims as he went on to Shanghai, where scores of thousands of people took to the streets to demand democracy and show their support for the Beijing hunger strikers.

Now, Prime Minister Li Peng came to the fore, appearing on television and warning that chaos in Beijing was spreading all over the country. It was time for it to stop, he added, but the million people in the streets of Beijing braved a driving rain to defy him.

To defuse the situation, Li and the Communist party leader, Zhao Ziyang, went to Tiananmen Square to visit some of the hunger strikers, whose ranks had swollen to 3,000. Furthermore, the government capitulated on a key demand by arranging a nationally televised meeting between Li and student leaders. The meeting was an emotional one in which a tearful Zhao Ziyang stated to the young protesters, "You've come too late. You have good intentions. You want our country to become better. The problems you have raised will eventually be resolved. But things are complicated, and there must be a process to resolve these problems."

To the young men, the process was obviously in the streets, where cries for the ouster of Deng and Li Peng were rising and rings of students and protesters guarded the hunger strikers. A makeshift loudspeaker system had been erected, and a copying machine ground out stacks of pamphlets, which were eagerly scooped up by the surrounding crowds. An elderly police officer spoke to reporters. "The student movement is terrific!" he enthused. "If the government commands a crackdown, will I obey their order? No, I will go against it!"

On Saturday, May 20, that crackdown began. Martial law was proclaimed in Beijing, and 1,000 troops were dispatched to the city. At the same time, Deng asserted his authority and removed Zhao Ziyang from his leadership of the party for being too conciliatory with the students. In his place, Deng named Li Peng as both prime minister and party leader. Authorities shut off drinking water fountains in the square.

But the demonstrators held fast. Troops were met by thousands of citizens who rushed into the streets to block their progress. By midday, one million people defied the martial law edict and choked the thoroughfares, surrounding army convoys and threatening them. Once more, students locked arms and protected the soldiers, while citizens pleaded with the army to leave. "You are my army," said a Chinese businesswoman, "You are our brothers and sisters. You are Chinese. Our interests are the same as yours. We believe you have a conscience. You must not crush the movement." Twenty-one army trucks were blocked by workers on the outskirts of the city.

Meanwhile, the government was gathering its forces. Deng stripped Zhao not only of his party leadership but of his right to order troop movements. Foreign television journalists were forced to stop their transmissions, although print journalists continued to roam through the crowds.

And the crowds grew, exceeding one million in Beijing. In Xian, 300,000 demonstrators brought that city to a standstill. In Hong Kong, 500,000 marched. In Shanghai, protesters carried banners reading "Li Peng does not represent us" and "Li Peng, do not use the people's army against the people."

Rumors of an approaching, brutal repression began to circulate among the students, and on May 26, many of them prepared their wills. On Saturday, May 27, some of the leaders called for an end to the occupation of Beijing's main square. Two weeks of living there had spawned impossible health hazards. Garbage carpeted the premises; the refuse, reheated by the 90-degree spring heat, produced a stupendous stench. "It is very difficult to continue our sit-in," Wuer Kaixi, a student leader, said. "As leaders, we have responsibility for students' health and the difficulties are obvious. Hygiene is extremely bad and the food is insufficient." Student leaders proposed an evacuation of the square and called for large-scale demonstrations for greater democracy and the resignation of Prime Minister Li.

But two days later, on Monday, May 29, a crowd of nearly 100,000 workers and students cheered loudly as a 27-foot sculpture, constructed by art students and modeled after the Statue of Liberty, was dragged to the square in several pieces on tricycle carts, reassembled and put in place. The plans to leave had obviously been rescinded, if not totally reversed.

The military, now under the direction of Prime Minister Li Peng, regrouped. On Friday, June 2, 2,000 unarmed troops again marched on Beijing; and again, tens of thousands of citizens turned them back. But this time, the confrontation was more volatile. Eight hundred riot police officers fired tear gas to clear an area outside Communist party headquarters, and 30 people outside the Beijing Hotel were beaten.

But these were isolated incidents. In the rest of the city, soldiers, who seemed to be peasants from distant areas, looked unenthusiastic about their mission. Halted by the citizenry, they sat down along the side of the road and listened while students and workers talked earnestly to them. "You are the people's army," a young worker told several soldiers. "The students' movement is patriotic, and you mustn't use violence against it. Think about it." Most of the soldiers apparently did; some cried. It seemed as if once again, the students and workers had stopped the government.

But those would be the last peaceful moments in Beijing's Tiananmen Square. Shortly after midnight on Sunday, June 4, tens of thousands of seasoned, hardened army troops from the provinces converged on Beijing, supported by tanks and armored personnel carriers. As citizens rushed out to block their paths, they opened fire, killing the protesters and running over their bodies.

Horrified, the citizenry charged the soldiers with greater force, but they were crushed by onrushing tanks, shot and bayoneted by the imperturbable soldiers, who were apparently deaf to the pleas not to kill their fellow citizens.

In the main square, news had been received as early as Saturday afternoon that an armed force was on its way. In hopes of a nonviolent, peaceful end to the confrontation, students had purposely destroyed guns and bombs they had accumulated. "We dismantled the bombs by pouring out the gasoline," a student leader later told the *San Francisco Examiner.* "We wanted to avoid any chance that they would be used by criminals, or be treated as 'evidence' that the students had committed violent acts against the troops."

Student leaders broadcast warnings to those in the square that bloodshed might come and advised them to leave. Some did, but approximately 150,000 remained.

Shortly after midnight, the first two armored vehicles appeared, speeding down the side of the square. Thick formations of heavily armed, helmeted soldiers followed. Machine gun emplacements were set up on the roof of the History Museum.

The students retreated to the Heroes Monument, near the art students' statue of liberty named the Goddess of Democracy and Freedom.

Negotiations were taking place between the student leaders and army commanders for a peaceful retreat of the students. But at 4 A.M., in the midst of these negotiations, the lights in the square were suddenly turned off. The talks continued for another 40 minutes in the dark, and then, abruptly, red flares flooded the area with light. Thousands of additional soldiers had gathered under cover of darkness, and now they rushed into the square, setting up more machine gun emplacements. Interspersed between them were riot police, carrying electric cattle prods and rubber truncheons. They waded into the mobs of students, beating them mercilessly, kicking them and then shooting them.

Armored vehicles roared into the square now, blocking it off entirely, except for a small opening in the direction of the History Museum. The students were trapped. Soldiers continued to advance, smashing the students' broadcasting and printing equipment and dragging the students down from the steps of the Heroes Monument.

It was their only refuge; apparently, the army did not want to damage this national symbol with gunfire. Students retreated again and again to the monument. Soldiers and riot police followed, rushed them, clubbed them and drove them into the street, where they were machine-gunned or shot by automatic rifle fire. Wave after wave of gunfire and clubbing continued until some students, in desperation, tried to escape through the gap between the armored vehicles near the museum. But the gap was soon closed, and the vehicles ringing the square now charged the students, crushing them beneath their tracks and wheels.

Citizens and workers tried to charge the soldiers but were beaten or killed. By 5 A.M., Tiananmen Square had been swept clean of students and workers. Blood was everywhere, and bodies were strewn for blocks. Reporters saw people gunned down, beaten, crushed. As bullets careened over their heads, one hysterical student begged a *New York Times* reporter, "We appeal to your country. Our government is mad. We need help from abroad, especially America. There must be something that America can do." Another sobbed, "Maybe we'll fail today. Maybe we'll fail tomorrow. But someday we will succeed. It's a historical inevitability."

The wounded, the dying and the dead were brought to hospitals. In Beijing Tongren Hospital, one mile southeast of the square, a doctor told reporters for the *Times,* "As doctors we often see deaths. But we've never seen a tragedy like this. Every room in the hospital is covered with blood."

All day on Sunday, troops crossed the city, and the sound of gunfire constantly reverberated through its streets. Rumors sped through the city as rapidly as the military vehicles. The university was about to be assaulted. It had been set afire. There were 20,000 dead; 200,000 dead.

Some soldiers were killed. Thirty-one military vehicles and 23 police cars were burned. A soldier who had shot a young child was overpowered by a large crowd in the Chongwenmen district early Sunday morning, hanged from a bridge and then burned.

But the casualties were primarily among the citizenry. A 24-year-old government official, fleeing from a barrage of bullets near the square, happened upon some wounded and bleeding victims. He stopped to help them. An army officer slammed his pistol into the side of his head. "Don't stir or you will be dead," he said, and a dozen soldiers ran up and began to beat the young samaritan with bricks and rifle butts. "I never thought they could be so brutal," he told a *Times* reporter later at the Union Medical College Hospital. At the same hospital, a doctor showed a reporter bullet holes in the side of an ambulance. Late Sunday afternoon, shoppers on a major side street in Wangfujing, one of the major shopping districts, were shot and killed when troops unexplainably opened fire on them. Altogether, more than 1,000 students, workers and unwary citizens were killed, and 10,000 were injured, in one of the bloodiest peacetime massacres in modern history.

To this day, the Communist government of China states that it did not happen. The official version ignores the bodies, the blackened, twisted remains of barricades, the residue of blood on the Heroes Monument, the eyewitness reports of international reporters. A 42-year-old factory worker who described the slaughter to ABC News was later shown on state television, his head bowed, confessing that he never saw anything and that he was a counterrevolutionary. "I apologize for bringing great harm to the party and the country," he added.

Further television pictures showed soldiers peacefully cleaning up the debris in the square. Three hundred people were killed, many of them soldiers, according to the official version. "Not a single student was killed in Tiananmen Square," said an army commander. Later, the government amended his remarks to admit 23 student deaths.

Worldwide repugnance produced indignant public statements from the government of China. It attacked the United States for interfering in China's affairs when President George Bush protested the killing of civilians by suspending arms sales and visits by military officials between the two countries.

By Wednesday, June 7, the army was still in control in Beijing and still flexing its muscles. It fired into two diplomatic compounds that housed thousands of foreign diplomats and journalists. Stony-faced troops then surrounded the compounds for two hours, after which the United States Embassy sent its marine guards to help evacuate Americans who wanted to leave. The exodus of foreign nationals rose to flood stage, although diplomats remained in the city. Shortly after the incident at the compounds, the army began to evacuate Beijing.

Tension and unrest remained in the capital city. More than 1,000 students were arrested; state television news characterized them as "thugs" and assailed them for supporting the "counterrevolutionary rebellion." Trials were held; scores of students and workers were sentenced to public executions.

Purges occurred throughout the country. Other executions took place in Shanghai. The world was horrified; China remained defiant, chastising its critics for meddling in its internal affairs. A cloak was drawn around the country. Dissidence was muffled, then eliminated. And the world turned its attention elsewhere.

In December 1989, President Bush, apparently trying to maintain the open lines of communication between China and the United States established by former president Richard Nixon, tried to reestablish economic ties with Beijing by sending national security advisor Brent Scowcroft on a secret mission to the Chinese capital. Congress learned of the visits, and objected to the mission. Some members sensed the behind-the-scenes influence of Nixon and Henry Kissinger, his former secretary of state.

In May 1991, President Bush again tried to reestablish Most Favored Nation Trading Status for China, with no assurances of an improvement in human rights. Congress again refused to support him, but in March, 1992, they gave in to Mr. Bush and awarded China most favored nation status. Meanwhile, Deng and his hardliners held China tightly under their control, maintaining it as the last neo-Stalinst stronghold in the world.

CHINA
NORTHERN PROVINCES

June 1900

• • • • • • • • • • • • • • • •

Long-festering hostility between Chinese conservatives and foreign partitioners climaxed in the disastrous Boxer Rebellion of June 1900. Thousands of Western missionaries and residents were killed; hundreds more were injured, and China was left vulnerable to Western powers.

The Orient was opened in the 16th century to Western interests, but only temporarily. Within a very short time, the door was slammed shut to Western commerce and reform, and it would be the beginning of the 19th century before that door was forced open again by the British.

Canton, China was opened to trade in 1834, and this was Britain's opportunity to establish a large foothold in China. In 1839, when China took action to enforce its prohibition of opium importing and proceeded to destroy supplies of opium belonging to British exporters in Canton Harbor, Great Britain instigated the so-called Opium War. The British used modern firearms, and the Chinese were quickly defeated.

Over the next 20 years Western interests took hold in China. Hong Kong became a British colony. Seventeen ports, including Foochow and Shanghai, were opened to Western trade, and France, Russia, Germany and the United States participated in widening the treaty, opening more "treaty ports" and establishing residences for diplomats, businessmen and missionaries.

This was not done without fierce resistance from the Chinese, who fought back periodically. In 1859, Chinese troops attempted to block the entry of diplomats into Peking. British and French forces not only reversed this, but they also occupied all of Peking and burned the imperial summer palace to the ground.

By the 1890s, China was further weakened by its unsuccessful war with Japan and the partitioning of China into foreign spheres of influence. But anti-Western, anti-foreign sentiment was as pervasive as it had been in the 16th century.

Some of this was focused in a powerful secret society

Dismembered bodies are grisly evidence of executions in Canton during the Boxer Rebellion, a grim conflict between Chinese conservatives and Western partitioners. Illustrated London News

called Ho Ch'uan, which in Chinese means "righteous, harmonious fists." In English, this translated, much more prosaically, into "Boxers."

It was no small neighborhood club. Its adherents were fierce and dedicated, and by 1898, there were 140,000 members who had little love for the foreigners whom they saw as usurpers of their country's economy, land, culture and pride.

Ruling at this time was the dowager empress and regent Tz'u Hsi. She was a strict adherent to the old values of China and no friend of the West. In 1875, she named her infant nephew Kuang Hsu to the throne, even though he was not a direct heir. Then, in 1898, she resumed the regency herself, after Kuang Hsu attempted to institute political reforms of which she did not approve.

The dowager empress tacitly approved of the growth and aims of the Boxers, and, given support by the war party at court, they began in late 1899 to conduct raids against foreign missions and Chinese Christians. These forays were waged in the northern provinces—Chihi, Shansi and Shantung, in Manchuria and in inner Mongolia. Western interests had built railroads in these provinces, and some of the earlier actions were directed against the railroads and Western landlords.

As the Boxer Rebellion—as it was eventually known—began to grow, it became more deadly and widespread. Western missionaries were massacred and their dwellings burned to the ground. The land around Peking became a battleground. Telegraph wires from Peking to Pau-ting-Fu were cut; bridges were destroyed. Finally, French, British, Russian and German troops took up positions, and the Boxers massed for an attack. Meanwhile, in the Imperial Palace, the Ultra Conservative party, headed by the dowager empress, opposed Prince Ching and his Moderate party, who argued that the Boxers should be repressed.

During the first week of June 1900, the Boxers struck, 140,000 strong, and occupied Peking. For eight weeks, they attacked missionary outposts, foreign missions and installations. They were most vicious when encountering Chinese Christians. A Professor Headland of Peking University, speaking to the *New York Times* on June 4, said, "I don't believe the Boxers intend to kill any foreigners unless they get mixed up in fights. They want to carry off

A contemporary Chinese print depicts the Boxer Rebellion of 1900. Library of Congress

some, perhaps, in order to get a ransom for them; but they are intent on killing off the native Christians."

For most of the summer of 1900, the Boxers held the northern provinces of China, and foreign interests were muted, if not murdered. And then, in August, as they had on several previous occasions, a force of British, French, Russian, American, German and Japanese troops retook the provinces, killing great numbers of Boxers and driving the rest into hiding.

There would be sporadic raids on missions for another two years. But the Boxer Rebellion would be, for all intents and purposes, crushed, and the Western powers would exact more economic and trade advantages from China, plus $333 million in reparations and an agreement to allow foreign troops to be stationed in Peking. Japan wanted considerably more from the nation that had allowed and encouraged the Boxers to rebell, but disagreements among the Western powers, plus the intervention of the United States, which advocated an end to the further partitioning of China, prevented these wishes from being fulfilled.

The Boxer Rebellion, then, was worse than a failure. It left China in debt and a subject nation to foreign powers.

EUROPE

1939–45

• • • • • • • • • • • • • • • •

Adolf Hitler's determination to exterminate "inferior" races and establish a master race resulted in the six-year-long "Final Solution," or Holocaust, as it was eventually called. Between 1939 and 1945, Nazis systematically murdered five million European Jews, three million Russians and two million Slavs.

In 1939, there were 10 million Jews in Europe. In 1945, at the end of World War II, there were fewer than five million. To Adolf Hitler, the chancellor of the Third Reich, they, along with the Slavs of eastern Europe, were *Untermenschen*, or subhumans, and therefore destined for either slave labor or extermination.

The Nuremberg trials revealed that, in defiance of the Geneva Convention, the Nazis routinely killed prisoners of war, but none so thoroughly, gruesomely or energetically as Russian and Slavic POWs. Two million Russian prisoners of war died in German captivity from starvation, exposure and disease. The remaining million have never been accounted for; at Nuremberg, a good case was made that most of them either died from the above causes or were exterminated by the S.D. (S.S. Security Service).

But this was a small effort compared with the grand plan of the Third Reich, the elimination of all European Jews, a genocide of a magnitude even larger than that of the Turks during the Armenian massacres (see p. 59). It would be an act of unparalleled barbarism, possibly the most inhuman act in the history of the world.

The so-called Final Solution had its roots in a speech made by Adolf Hitler before the Reichstag on January 30, 1939, in which he stated, "If the international Jewish financiers . . . should succeed in plunging the nations into a world war the result will be—the annihilation of the Jewish race throughout Europe."

As early as 1939, systematic incarceration had already begun, with the *Einsatz* groups, organized by Heinrich Himmler and Reinhard Heydrich. These specially trained squads followed the German armies into Poland and rounded up Jews, locking them in ghettos. Two years later, between June 1941 and June 1942, at the beginning of the Russian campaign, this was escalated to extermination. Jews and Soviet commissars were rounded up in each village that was conquered; they were ordered to dig mass graves and then remove their clothing. They were shot at the edge of the grave and shoveled into it. More than 500,000 Jews in White Russia were killed this way.

Later the method was refined. Otto Ohlendorf, testifying at Nuremberg, described it thus: "The *Einsatz* unit would

enter a village or town and order the prominent Jewish citizens to call together all Jews for the purpose of 'resettlement.' They were required to hand over their valuables, and shortly before execution to surrender their outer clothing. They were transported to the place of executions, usually an antitank ditch, in trucks . . ."

In the spring of 1942, Himmler ordered the method of killing to be changed from shooting to gassing. For this, gas vans were constructed by two Berlin firms. Resembling closed trucks, the vans were loaded with up to 25 persons, ostensibly to be taken away for "resettlement." The motor was turned on, and the gas—carbon monoxide—was directed into the van.

However, these vans proved too small to handle the massacres that Hitler and Himmler envisioned, and so the Final Solution evolved to its final, most efficient and horrible phase. According to the Nuremberg statistics, all of the 30-odd principal Nazi concentration camps were really death camps, where millions were killed by torture, starvation or planned execution.

It was at the extermination camps, called the *Vernichtunglager*, where the killing was most widespread and gruesome. The most renowned of these was Auschwitz, in Poland, where four enormous gas chambers with adjoining crematoria killed up to 6,000 Jews a day.

Following the earlier methods of the *Einsatz* units, the Jews rounded up by the Nazis in occupied countries were ordered to gather their valuables and report for resettlement. They were packed like animals into freight cars and transported to the death camps at Auschwitz, Treblinka, Belzec, Sobibor and Chelmno in Poland, where extermination was carried out by gassing, or to smaller installations such as Riga, Vilnius, Minsk, Kaunas and Lvov, where it was done by firing squads.

In either case, "selection" would take place at the railroad siding at which the prisoners debarked from the train. According to Auschwitz commandant Rudolf Hoess, "We had two S.S. doctors on duty . . . to examine the incoming transports of prisoners. These would be marched by one of the doctors, who would make spot decisions as they walked by. Those who were fit to work were sent into the camp. Others were sent immediately to the extermination plants. Children of tender years were invariably exterminated since by reason of their youth they were unable to work."

Even those who were to be killed immediately were deluded into thinking they were being "resettled." Some were given lovely picture postcards marked "Waldsee," inscribed with a reassuring but viciously ironic message:

> *We are doing very well here. We have work and we are well treated. We await your arrival.*

"At Auschwitz," continued Hoess at his trial at Nuremberg, "we endeavored to fool the victims into thinking that they were to go through a delousing process. Of course, frequently they realized our true intentions and we sometimes had riots and difficulties. Very frequently women would hide their children under their clothes but of course when we found them we would send the children in to be exterminated."

The grim charade continued until almost the last days of Auschwitz. The gas chambers were disguised as plain-looking buildings fronted by green lawns punctuated by lush and colorful flower beds. At the entrance, which bore a sign that read "BATHS," an orchestra of young women prisoners played Offenbach and Lehar.

The prisoners were ordered to remove their clothing and were sometimes even given towels. Once 2,000 of them were within the "showers," the doors were slammed shut and barred. It was at this moment that all those inside knew they had been deceived and would die, and so, the stampedes would begin. Mountains of humanity would pile up at the door, and many of the doomed would be trampled or clawed to death in this first desperate surge toward freedom.

Meanwhile, on the roof of the gas chamber, the S.S. would be at work. Concealed in the lawns and flower beds were the mushroom-shaped lids of the vents that ran into the chambers. Orderlies opened the vents and stood ready with amethyst crystals of hydrogen cyanide or Zyklon B, which had originally been manufactured as a strong disinfectant and were now supplied to the extermination camps by Tesch and Stabenow of Hamburg and Degesch of Dessau, two German firms that had received the patent from I. G. Farben. The former supplied two tons of the crystals a month, and the latter three-quarters of a ton.

A Sergeant Moll would give the order, "*Na, gib ihnen schon zu fressen,*" ("All right, give them something to chew on"). The crystals would be poured into the openings, and the openings would then be sealed.

The executioners watched the death throes of those inside through heavy glass portholes. According to Gerald Reitlinger, "they piled up in one blue, clammy, blood-spattered pyramid, clawing and mauling each other even in death."

It took as long as 30 minutes for the killing process to be consummated, and then pumps drew out the poisonous fumes. The huge door leading into the "baths" was opened, and Jewish male inmates, the *Sonderkommando* who were given adequate food and promised their lives, were let in to do their work. Protected with gas masks and rubber boots, they wielded heavy water hoses. Their first task was to wash away the blood and defecation. Then they went through the bodies, extracting gold teeth and hair. Once this had been accomplished, they loaded the naked and mutilated corpses onto lifts or railroad wagons that took them to the furnaces, where they were burned, and their ashes were either scattered into the Sola River or sold as fertilizer.

The gold fillings were later melted down and shipped, along with other valuables taken from the Jews at the railroad siding, to the Reichsbank, where, under a secret agreement between Himmler and the bank's president, Dr. Walther Funk, they were deposited to the credit of the S.S. in an account given the cover name "Max Heiliger."

The gas chambers and crematoria were the result of a disgusting partnership between German industry and the German military. There was spirited bidding to win the contracts for the crematoria, and the firm of I. A. Topf and Sons of Erfurt, manufacturers of heating equipment, won.

Even the efficient construction of the crematoria was no match for the speed at which the Third Reich carried out its extermination policy. In 46 days during the summer of 1944, at Auschwitz alone, between 250,000 and 300,000 Hungarian Jews were put to death. Midway through this period, the gas chambers fell behind, and mass graves were again dug by the victims before they were shot and thrown into them. The bodies were set on fire, after which bulldozers were used to cover over the mass mausoleums. The Russians who liberated the camp and confiscated its records estimated that close to four million died at Auschwitz alone, but later estimates reduced the figure to approximately one million.

Combined with a systematic and almost unimaginably barbaric series of "medical experiments"—operations without anesthesia to test pain thresholds, high altitude experiments, freezing experiments—and the stripping of skin from the bodies of the dead or merely dying, to be tanned and formed into lamp shades and other decorations for the S.S., plus the systematic killing of all of the inhabitants of various places in Poland and Russia—the Warsaw Ghetto and the village of Lidice, for example—this attempted genocide and massacre of the innocents has no parallel in all of history. That it occurred in the 20th century is a discouraging affirmation that man seems to be eternally ca-

The brutal slaughter of French Huguenots in the streets of Paris, the famous St. Bartholomew's Day Massacre of August 24, 1572, is depicted in a period drawing. New York Public Library

pable of inflicting the worst and most senseless disasters upon his fellow man.

FRANCE
PARIS

August 24, 1572

• • • • • • • • • • • • • • • •

The continuing confrontation between Catholics and Protestants in France in the 16th century culminated in a massacre of 2,000 French Huguenots, gathered in Paris on August 24, 1572 to celebrate both St. Bartholomew's Day and the wedding of Henry of Navarre and Margaret of Valois.

One of the bloodiest and most barbaric incidents in the so-called Wars of Religion which raged through France from 1562 to 1598, took place on St. Bartholomew's Day, August 24, 1572 in Paris and later throughout France. Ostensibly it was an attack upon Huguenots for practicing their Protestantism. But palace intrigue and politics were also involved that day.

The Protestant reform movement began in France at the start of the 16th century, but it was given a tangible symbol in 1559, when the first French national synod was held and the Presbyterian church, modeled after John Calvin's reform in Geneva, was founded. The adherents of Protestantism in France were then known as Huguenots—from the German word *Eidgenossen*, meaning sworn companions or confederates. The confederacy extended across class lines but failed to mute the persecution of the Huguenots in France.

In 1560, the Conspiracy of Amboise brought about a fierce confrontation and heavy toll upon the Huguenots. The object of the plot was to allow the House of Bourbon to usurp the power of the Guse family, represented on the throne by Francis II. The plan was to march on the royal castle, abduct the king, and arrest Francois, duc de Guse, and his brother Charles, who was also cardinal of Lorraine.

The cardinal, however, got wind of the plot before it could be put into motion, and the rebel forces were set upon before they could organize themselves. A brutal slaughter followed, and for weeks the bodies of conspirators were hung from the castle and from every tree in sight. The Huguenots were enraged, and the first of the Wars of Religion, in 1562, was a direct result of this slaughter and its grisly aftermath.

By 1572, two of these civil wars had been fought, each ending in reconciliation. But in August 1572 the peace ended violently. That month, the Huguenot nobility was gathered in Paris to attend the wedding of Henry of Navarre (he would later become King Henry IV) and Catherine de' Medici's daughter, Margaret of Valois.

Catherine de' Medici and the duc d'Anjou (later King Henry III), with the reluctant help of King Charles IX, tried, on August 22, to capture the duc de Coligny, the commander of the Huguenots in the second War of Religion and their most respected representative. The attempt failed, and Catherine and her cohorts then determined to kill Coligny and as many Huguenots as they could.

On August 24, St. Bartholomew's Day, while French Huguenots gathered in Paris to celebrate the day and the wedding, the soldiers of the king swooped down on them, massacring every Huguenot in sight. Leaders and ordinary citizens were cut down ruthlessly, and before the day was over, 2,000 Huguenots lay dead in the streets of Paris.

During the next few days, the massacre spread to the countryside and to other cities in France, and within days, the Huguenots regrouped, and the Third War of Religion began. Two more wars would be fought after this, and though the wars themselves would end in 1598, true freedom from oppression for Protestants in France would not come until 1905, when church and state were finally declared separate.

FRANCE
PARIS

1793–95

• • • • • • • • • • • • • • • •

Between 23,000 and 40,000 were executed during the double reign of terror that followed the French Revolution in 1793–95.

Excess may seem a tame word to define the French Revolution's Reign of Terror and its aftermath, the White Terror. But consider the statistics of the Reign of Terror: In Paris alone between May 1793 and June 1794, 1,251 people were executed, either by the guillotine or in mass drownings, called *noyades.* Between March 1793 and August 1794, when the Reign of Terror ended and the White Terror began, 16,594 death sentences were handed down by the Revolutionary Tribunal.

It was, in each case, retribution that set the sentences, and they arose from many complex causes. The French Revolution marked the end of feudalism in France, but it also meant the potential beginning of anarchy. In order to prevent this, the Committee of Public Safety was created, in April 1793, and none too soon. In September 1793, spurred by hunger, thousands rioted in the streets of Paris, and there was a fear that these riots had been fomented by Royalists and counterrevolutionaries.

Under the dominant guidance of Maximilien Robespierre, the committee announced its goals: to eliminate all internal counterrevolutionary elements (ever since the execution of Louis XVI, in January 1793, Royalists had been organizing to overthrow the revolution), to raise new armies (Austria and Prussia, soon to be joined by Great Britain, had taken advantage of a perceived weakened France and had gone to war against it) and to regulate the national economy (hungry people were rioting people, and civil order was necessary).

But the Reign of Terror, a retributive set of mock trials and multiple public executions carried out by Revolutionary tribunals, was counterproductive in its sweeping excess. Defense and preliminary cross-questioning of the accused were abolished, and juries could convict on nothing more than moral proof. And there were only two choices: acquittal or death.

The bases for conviction were general and chilling: "Those who have aided and abetted the plans of the enemies of France by persecuting and slandering patriotism, those who have sought to spread a spirit of discouragement, to deprave the morality of the people, to undermine the purity and energy of revolutionary principles, all those who, by whatever means and under whatever pretext, have attacked the liberty, the unity and the security of the Republic or have worked to prevent these from being established on a firm, lasting basis . . ."

Small wonder, then, that at one time, the Paris prisons held 8,000 prisoners, which in turn led to fears of a prison revolt. Thus, tribunals were held and executions were swift. According to Fouquier-Tinville, the public prosecutor at the Revolutionary Tribunal, "heads were falling like tiles."

Robespierre, however, was overthrown on July 24, 1794, and now the opposition took over. The Thermodorian Reaction, or White Terror, began, and by the first of March, 1795 the Monteuil section of the National Convention demanded death for the death dealers of the Reign of Terror: "What are you waiting for, in order to cleanse the land of these cannibals? Do not their ghastly hue and sunken eyes proclaim enough their foster parents? Have them arrested . . . The Trenchant blade of the law will deprive them of the air they have too long infested."

On February 2, 1795, in Lyons, the first massacre of imprisoned ex-terrorists was carried out. Thousands more would be murdered, individually and in large numbers, while the convention looked on, mindful that inflation, famine and the numbing cold of the winter of 1795 were eating away at the loyalty of the people of Paris and the rest of France. Mass killings tended to keep them indoors and discouraged rioting.

But the White Terror continued through the spring of 1795. All over France, prisons were broken into and prisoners massacred. At Tarascon, in June, Jacobins were hurled into the Rhone from the walls of the Chateau du roi Rene, and there were other such atrocities committed in Salon, Nimes and Pont-Saint-Esprit. "Wherever you look there is throat-cutting," lamented a deputy of the convention.

Finally these excesses produced a reaction, and a calmer return to the values of freedom and the Rights of Man established by the revolution prevailed. The so-called War of the Black Collars in the summer of 1795 rounded up the executioners of the White Terror; far right members of the Council of Deputies were arrested; and a general amnesty was extended for "deeds exclusively connected with the Revolution."

It had ended, but the terror on both sides had greatly weakened the purpose of the French Revolution.

GREAT BRITAIN
ENGLAND
LONDON

November 5, 1605

• • • • • • • • • • • • • • • • • •

The presence of harsh penal laws against English Catholics in 1605 led to the ill-fated Gunpowder Plot to blow up Parliament on November 5, 1605. It failed; all of the conspirators were executed.

Anti-Catholic sentiment ran deep in England at the beginning of the 17th century, and it had official and royal sanction. There were harsh penal laws designed to all but prohibit the practice of Catholicism, and in protest against them, a plot was originated in 1605 to blow up both Parliament and King James I. It would take place on November 5, the opening day of Parliament, which was normally given over to ceremony. The king would be in attendance.

Three young men, Robert Catesby, John Wright and Thomas Winter, originated the plan. They were soon joined by Christopher Wright, Robert Winter, Robert Keyes, Thomas Percy, John Grant, Sir Evirard Digby, Francis Tresham, Ambrose Rookwood, Thomas Bates and Guy Fawkes—the last a convert to Catholicism who served as a soldier with the Spanish in Flanders.

The plan was straightforward: Blow up the entire government and set in place a Catholic monarchy. Like all grand designs, it was too good to be kept secret. At any rate, by the middle of 1605, when Thomas Percy had rented a subcellar under the House of Lords, and the conspirators had stocked it with 36 barrels of gunpowder, overlaid with steel bars and firewood, the grand design was known throughout much of the Catholic community of London, including Henry Garnett, the superior of the English Jesuits.

Members of Parliament, however, did not know of the Gunpowder Plot until October 26, when Francis Tresham sent a letter to his brother-in-law, Lord Monteague, warning him not to attend Parliament on November 5. The planners might as well have announced it in the middle of Piccadilly. Lord Monteague informed his colleagues, among them the first earl of Salisbury, who, in short order, discovered the cellar and its lethal provinder.

On the night of November 4, Guy Fawkes, who because of his military background had been elected to detonate the dynamite, crept quietly into the cellar, to check the fuses and the powder. Soldiers were waiting for him and arrested him on the spot. He was taken to the Tower of London and under torture revealed the names of his co-conspirators.

Soldiers fanned out throughout London and began to make arrests. Catesby tried to fight his way through the arresting party and was killed. Percy, the renter of the cellar, was shot and mortally wounded while trying to flee from his captors. The rest were captured and either imprisoned, killed outright or sentenced to be hanged. Among those hanged in November 1606 were Henry Garnett (the superior of English Jesuits), Thomas and Robert Winter and Guy Fawkes.

Rather than making the lot of Catholics in England better, the Gunpowder Plot worsened their lives. Instead of erasing repressive laws against the practice of their religion, the aborted plot caused the enactment of harsher, more repressive ones. And to this day in England, Guy Fawkes Day is celebrated on November 5 with fireworks and bonfires and the image of Guy Fawkes hanged in effigy.

HUNGARY
BUDAPEST

November 4, 1956

• • • • • • • • • • • • • • • • • •

Hungarian Freedom Fighters, fired by the success of the Polish uprising and a Russian-appointed regime, declared independence on October 23, 1956 with a student uprising. On November 4, 1956, Russian tanks reclaimed Budapest and Hungary. Twenty-five thousand Hungarians were killed in the fighting; thousands more were killed in the ensuing executions.

Today it seems almost inconceivable that tens of thousands of Hungarians lost their lives and their hope in one week of fierce fighting against the Stalinist regime that had held Hungary captive since World War II. Nor does it seem possible that both the United Nations and the Western powers—themselves involved in the "Suez crisis"—could stand by and watch as a bloodbath of staggering proportions took place, while the victims pleaded, over their radio station, for help from the rest of the world.

Yet, it happened, from Tuesday, October 23, 1956, when the first student uprising occurred, until Sunday, November 4, 1956, when Russian tanks reclaimed Budapest.

The world had a chance to help, but did not. Perhaps it was bad timing. Events choose their moments, and this was not the most propitious moment for Hungary to find its freedom.

The impetus for the Hungarian uprising came with the death of Joseph Stalin in March 1953, which was surrounded by a maelstrom of plots and threats. Stalin's tyrannical hold on Russia and the lands it had acquired at the end of World War II was so complete and so ruthless that it carried with it the seeds of an inevitable revolt.

There were demonstrations in East Germany and Czechoslovakia, and in Yugoslavia there was Tito, who preferred his own brand of communism to that of the Stalinist loyalists. So in May 1955, Nikita Khrushchev formed the Warsaw Pact, a treaty of mutual friendship, cooperation and mutual aid, uniting the satellites as an answer to NATO.

But within the Warsaw Pact, there was discontent. In Poznan, Poland on June 28, 1955, a strike occurred. It was put down ruthlessly. Russian tanks and troops arrived, surrounded the city for two days, killed 113 people and broke the strike.

Almost simultaneously, Anastas Mikoyan arrived in Hungary, where a group of intellectuals were already expressing discontent about life under Stalinism. Matyas Rakosi, the head of Hungary's Central Committee, was notoriously repressive, employing the AVH, or Secret Police, to enforce his edicts and intimidate the Politburo. He was opposed by Imre Nagy, a moderate. If Mikoyan had, on that visit to Budapest, replaced Rakosi with Nagy, the Hungarian Revolution might never have taken place. He did not. He replaced Rakosi with Erno Gero, Moscow's handpicked man and one of Rakosi's henchmen.

Meanwhile, crisis erupted in Poland. Riots over the Poznan killings sprang up in Warsaw. The army and Polish students faced each other. To defuse the situation, Khrushchev met with Polish leaders and announced that the Soviet government would allow a form of communism to exist in Poland that was not precisely Russian. The Hungarians thus learned that it was possible to stand up to the Russians and win. They congratulated Poland and made plans for their own revolution.

From October 19 through 21, 1956, Hungarian students and intellectuals escalated their demands for the withdrawal of Soviet troops from Hungary. Meetings were held. A large student demonstration was scheduled for Tuesday, October 23 in Budapest. It was first forbidden; then the prohibition order was withdrawn.

The demonstration took place, and its makeup would have made Lenin smile. It was a spirited alliance of workers and intellectuals—just the mix that Lenin said was indispensable to a revolution.

By that night, the revolution was well under way. The intellectuals, students and workers wanted Nagy; Gero was determined to remain in place. The demonstrators in the streets had created a 16-point manifesto, and they went to the radio station to request that these 16 points be broadcast. According to a UN report filed later, an army major volunteered to present the paper to the head of broadcasting, but as he approached the main entrance to the building, he was gunned down by police.

And so the bloodshed began. Tear gas was lobbed into the crowd, and AVH men, the Hungarian equivalent of the KGB, opened fire, killing a number of people and wounding more. Tanks arrived, but the commander in charge informed everyone that he was a worker and would not participate in a massacre.

The crowd was now armed with machine guns and rifles, driving vans and trucks taken from factories. On Dozsa Gyorgy Street, an immense bronze statue of Stalin was hauled down, with the help of metalworkers using blowtorches. Red stars and other Communist emblems were shot off buildings, and Russian bookshops were looted.

By the next day, Nagy had been installed as prime minister, but the Russians were still in control. Russian tanks reinforced the AVH, which had taken up positions around the city.

The Hungarian Army soon joined the street demonstrators. Most important, a heavily decorated war hero, Colonel Pal Maleter, ordered to lead a formation of five tanks against the insurgents, made a fateful decision. "Once I arrived there," he later said, "it quickly became clear to me that those who were fighting for their freedom were not bandits, but loyal sons of Hungary. As a result I informed the Minister of Defense that I was going over to the insurgents."

On the 25th, a huge group of demonstrators advanced on Parliament Square, demanding Gero's resignation. They were unarmed. Russian tanks and AVH men opened fire on them, killing an estimated 600 unarmed civilians. It was a ghastly massacre, and the Russians replaced Gero as first secretary of the party with Janos Kadar.

The fighting in the streets increased. After the Parliament Square massacre, AVH men were hunted down and strung up on trees. Sometimes they were found to be carrying their pay—10 times that of a worker—and the money was then pinned to their bodies.

A revolutionary cabinet was now formed, with Nagy at its head. By Sunday, October 28, a cease-fire was negotiated, and the Russians appeared to be allowing Nagy and his followers to assume control. It was, to the jubilant insurgents, Poland all over again.

On Monday, according to the United Press, "Soviet tanks crunched out of this war-battered capital [Budapest] . . . carrying their dead with them. They left a wrecked city where the stench of death already [rose] from the smoking ruins." An announcement was made that the AVH would be abolished. Nagy set about tying the various strands of the revolution together. Hungary was free, despite the fighting in the streets.

Meanwhile, in the outside world, Great Britain and France were making plans to take the Suez Canal by force. On the morning of October 31, the news reached Hungary. Nagy fell into a mild depression. "God damn them!" one of the ministers exploded. "Aren't we going to put out feelers to the Western Powers *even now?*"

"Certainly not *now,*" Nagy replied.

The Russian withdrawal from Hungary seemed to be inexplicably stalled. Reports from the countryside told of tanks stopping and soldiers grouping. Communications circulated that trainloads of soldiers estimated at more than 75,000 men accompanied by 2,500 tanks were moving across the frontiers from Russia, Romania and Czechoslovakia. The new, free government of Hungary sent telegrams to the Kremlin questioning this apparent violation of the October 28 agreement of conditions for a cease-fire. By Saturday, November 3, a Russian military delegation arrived at Parliament to negotiate the withdrawal of Soviet troops.

Joseph Cardinal Mindszenty, who had been arrested and convicted of conspiracy in December 1945, was freed, and he gave a radio address. At 8 o'clock that evening, General Maleter drove to Tokol, outside Budapest, to renew negotiations at the Russian military headquarters.

He would never return. Shortly after midnight, General Serov, chief of the Soviet Security Police, would arrest the entire Hungarian delegation.

At 5 A.M. on November 4, 1956, Imre Nagy went on Hungarian radio. He was broadcasting from the Parliament building, where he had spent the night. His words contained a heartrending urgency:

"Attention! Attention! Attention! Attention!

". . . This is Imre Nagy speaking, the president of the Council of Ministers of the Hungarian People's Republic.

Today at daybreak Soviet forces started an attack against our capital, obviously with the intention to overthrow the legal Hungarian democratic government.

"Our troops are fighting.

"The government is in its place.

"I notify the people of our country and the entire world of this fact."

Free Radio Kossuth would continue to broadcast bulletins to the world throughout the day. The reports would increase in intensity and despair. Gyula Hay, the playwright and friend of Nagy, broadcast the most impassioned one:

"This is the Hungarian Writers' Association speaking to all writers, scientists, writers' associations, academies and scientific organizations of the world. We appeal for help to all intellectuals in all countries. Our time is limited. You know the facts. There is no need to review them. Help Hungary! Help the writers, scientists, workers, peasants and all Hungarian intellectuals. Help! Help! Help!"

Kadar had gone over to the Russians and now announced a breakaway government. Nagy took refuge in the Yugoslavian embassy, with his other cabinet ministers.

Heavy artillery opened up on the city. Soviet tanks rolled into Budapest and rumbled through its streets. When sniper fire came from a building, they blasted the entire building to oblivion. The Hungarian News Agency painted the picture: "People are jumping up at the tanks, throwing hand-grenades inside and then slamming the driver's windows. The Hungarian people are not afraid of death. It is only a pity that we can't stand for long."

The fighting roared on for three days and nights, sputtered and then died. The Soviet tanks had completely retaken Hungary, and all of the cries for help had gone unanswered. At exactly the moment that Soviet tanks entered Budapest, British and French paratroopers were dropped at Port Said, Egypt, and America and the United Nations were busy bringing about a cease-fire there.

In a later interview on television, President Dwight Eisenhower said, "The thing started in such a way, you know, that everybody was a little bit fooled, I think, and when suddenly the Soviets came in strength with their tank divisions, and it was a *fait accompli,* it was a great tragedy and disaster."

It certainly was for the Hungarians. The government of Janos Kadar took over and negotiated amnesty for Nagy and his associates. They were loaded into a bus that was to take them to their homes. But before it could leave the Yugoslavian embassy, the bus was boarded by Soviet military personnel, who commandeered it and took it to the headquarters of the Soviet Military Command. The two Yugoslavian diplomats who were to accompany the former Hungarian officials to safety were ordered to return to the embassy, and Nagy and his associates were arrested and imprisoned outside the country at Sinaia in Romania.

In June 1958, those who had not died in captivity were executed: Nagy, General Pal Maleter, the journalist Miklos Gimes and Nagy's secretary, Jozsef Szilagyi. In total, 2,000 were executed and 20,000 were imprisoned after the uprising. An estimated 25,000 died in the street fighting.

The border with Austria remained open for a few weeks after the revolution, and 200,000 refugees streamed across it. Housed in camps and shelters in Austria, they moved on to whatever countries in the West would accept them. Among the refugees were some of the finest minds in Hungary.

Shortly after this, barbed-wire enclosures went up, and the Iron Curtain was firmly redrawn around Hungary. It would be 35 years before it would be torn down again, this time through diplomacy.

INDIA
AMRITSAR

April 13, 1919

• • • • • • • • • • • • • • • • •

Several thousand Indians, gathering in defiance of a British ban on public meetings, were fired upon in the Sikh Holy Shrine of Jalianwala Bagh on April 13, 1919 by soldiers under the direction of Brigadier General R. E. H. Dyer. Three hundred seventy nine Indians died in the barrage; 1,200 were wounded. None was armed.

Amritsar, a city in the northwestern Indian state of Punjab, was for centuries a center of the Sikh religion, a healing spiritual philosophy designed to reconcile Hindu and Muslim concepts. At the center of the city, in the middle of a placid lake, the Golden Temple still stands, the holiest place in the world for Sikhs.

Thus it is particularly poignant and ironic that one of the two most devisive and bloody events in modern Indian history (the other was the Indian Mutiny of 1857) should take place in Amritsar. Nothing would be quite the same after the Amritsar Massacre of 1919. Great Britain, for all that it had accomplished and all it had promised, would never be counted trustworthy by Indians again, and Mohandas Gandhi's star would rise precipitously as a result of the slaughter.

As early as 1861, the first steps toward Indian independence were taken when Indian councillors were appointed by the British colonial government, and provincial councils with Indian members were formed. In 1885, the Indian National Congress was established, and two factions split it immediately. One, led by Gopal Krishna Gokhale, was in favor of a dominion status for India; the other, led by Bal Gangadhar Tilak, agitated for complete independence.

With the coming of World War I, both factions united behind Britain, but as the war wore on, famine, an influenza epidemic and a feeling that independence was a distant dream began to pervade India, and the two potential ruling parties started to regard Britain as an enemy to be overthrown.

During this period, Britain dangled the carrot of eventual self-government, with the Montagu declaration in 1917 and the Montagu-Chelmsford report of 1918. But it did little to settle the unrest, and in 1919 the Rowlatt Acts were passed, which provided for the arrest and imprisonment of political agitators without trial.

It was like throwing gasoline on a fire. India drifted between self-determination and authoritarian rule, and in the middle there was rioting, particularly in the Punjab. On April 10, 1919, in Amritsar, two nationalist leaders were arrested and deported. The crowds began to grow in the streets of the city. One group tried to enter the European cantonment but was turned away. They began to riot.

General R. E. H. Dyer, under the orders of Sir Michael O'Dwyer, one of the architects of the Rowlatt bills, restored order, and all public meetings and assemblies were declared illegal.

In defiance, a public meeting of several thousand Indians was held on April 13 in the Jalianwala Bagh, an enclosed park. Hearing of this, General Dyer took 90 Gurkhas and Baluchi soldiers and two armored cars to the Jalianwala Bagh. He blocked the only exit from the park with the armored vehicles and, without a word of warning, began to fire into the densely packed crowd.

One thousand six hundred five rounds were pumped into the screaming, panicked mass of men, women and children. Officially, 379 were killed and 1,200 injured, but the Hunter Report (see below) eventually set the casualty figures at 1,200 killed and 3,600 injured. General Dyer finally withdrew, but he kept his armored cars in place, preventing medical personnel from entering the park to tend to the wounded, or survivors from carrying the wounded out.

The brutality continued. More fierce demonstrations erupted. The following day, a mob rioting and burning at another spot was bombed and machine-gunned from the air by British forces. On April 15, martial law was declared in Amritsar, and it would remain in place until June 9. During this time, Indians were forced to crawl on all fours past a spot on the street where a woman missionary had been attacked. Public floggings were ordered for such offenses as, according to the Hunter Report, "the contravention of the curfew order, failure to salaam to a commissioned officer, for disrespect to a European, for taking a commandeered car without leave, refusal to sell milk, and for similar contraventions."

In October 1919, the British government convened the Hunter commission of inquiry to investigate the massacre. The panel was composed of four British and four Indian members. However, three of the British members were civil servants, and all four of the Indians were moderates.

General Dyer appeared before them, and he was absolutely unrepentant. "If more troops had been at hand," he testified, "the casualties would have been greater in proportion. It was no longer a question of merely dispersing the crowd but one of producing a sufficient moral effect from a military point of view not only on those who were present, but more especially throughout the Punjab."

The panel condemned him and his actions, but in mild terms such as "unfortunate" and "injudicious." Mohandas Gandhi set about putting into practice *Satygraha,* or nonviolent civil disobedience. It became the policy of the Indian National Congress and it in effect ended British control of India. Great Britain would no longer be able to rule by force, despite the fact that it would repeatedly jail Gandhi and incite those other Indians who did not follow his philosophy of nonviolence to riot.

Ultimately, Gandhi would prevail in most of his goals—except in the uniting of Hindus and Muslims, which the British creation of Pakistan successfully buried—and the British would leave. By that time, Dyer would be removed from his command but lauded by much of the British press and people.

Still, even the staunch supporters of Dyer and O'Dwyer, who had once cried, "There is another force greater than Gandhi's soul force!" would have to admit that the Amritsar Massacre was a turning point. From that moment on, the struggle for Indian independence would admit no compromise, and the good faith of British concessions would nevermore be believed.

INDIA
MANDAI, TRIPURA; ASSAM

June 7–8, 1980;
Feb. 18, 1983

• • • • • • • • • • • • • • • •

Driven by Hindu-Muslim hatred, tribal youth organizations conducted raids on Indian villages, massacring Muslims. In the two worst incidents on June 7–8, 1980 and February 18, 1983, 5,500 Bengali immigrants were massacred; 1,000 were wounded; 300,000 were made homeless.

The most savage and disastrous confrontations between people have been ethnic and religious ones. Consider the

Holocaust of World War II (see p. 68), the Armenian massacres (see p. 59) or, closer to home, the Chicago race riots (see p. 84) and the Watts riots (see p. 80). When a cause is perceived to be a religious one, cruelty can apparently be justified and swallowed up in the cause. "Men never do evil so fully and so happily as when they do it for conscience's sake," said Pascal, and this has never seemed so true as in the confrontations between those driven by differing beliefs.

When Great Britain partitioned India in 1946, isolating its Muslim population in Pakistan and its Hindu population in India, it sowed the seeds of religious confrontation. Hindus in Pakistan were driven out by Muslims and settled in the northeastern provinces of West Bengal and Bangladesh, which was, until 1971, East Bengal. The Bengalis, concentrated mostly in the adjoining states of Tripura and Assam, were predominantly Hindus. The native tribal people who lived there were mostly Muslims.

Thus, the Bengalis were looked upon as foreigners, immigrants and Hindus, a combination the tribespeople regarded with bigoted distaste. In 1980, the situation erupted when tribal youth organizations, dedicated to the expulsion of "foreigners," began systematic massacres.

The first such massacre to reach the attention of the world occurred in Mandai, in Tripura state. Adjoining the border of Bangladesh, the village had long been a Bengali dwelling place; some of its inhabitants had lived there a generation, ever since the partition. Others were new immigrants.

On June 7 and 8, tribal gangs swooped down on the village and laid waste to it. Armed with guns, spears, swords, scythes and bows and arrows, they emptied houses, chased men, women and children out into the flatlands around the village and slaughtered them, crushing their heads and severing their limbs. Children were run through with spears. Three hundred fifty people were killed in this massacre, which left not one person alive in the village of Mandai.

As news of the massacre began to emerge from India, officials in Tripura admitted that nearly 700 people had died in the past year after similar raids, which had rendered 200,000 homeless and had necessitated the setting up of 100 camps to house them.

The Communist-led government of Tripura, which had displaced Prime Minister Indira Gandhi's Congress Party in the 1977 elections, was charged with incompetence and blamed for not controlling the situation. The Tripura government counterchanged the New Delhi government with indifference.

Two weeks later, on June 22, Tarun Basu, a reporter for the New Delhi weekly current affairs journal *Contour*, uncovered a staggering fact: Four thousand Bengalis had been slaughtered by tribesmen during the month of June, and the government of Tripura had burned many of the bodies to cover up the slayings.

This resulted in an immediate tightening of security for the Bengalis which lasted for three years. Then, an important state election was scheduled to elect a 126-member state legislature and 12 members of the national parliament from the neighboring state of Assam. In this case, the settlements were Muslim, and the tribespeople Hindus. This time, an added political dimension, a motive to prevent Muslims from electing Muslims to the legislature and parliament, was added.

The village of Bhagduba Habi in the center of the state was typical. There, Bengali-speaking Muslims who went to vote found themselves surrounded by hostile Assamese tribespeople who turned them back from the polling places. Those who did manage to vote were found murdered the next day.

And then the worst massacres occurred. On Friday, February 18, the violence was particularly vicious. In Bhagduba Habi, old people, women and children were chased into the outlying fields, tortured and killed. Reporters arriving the next day counted 157 bodies, mostly those of children, lined up in rice fields, being readied for mass burial.

On that same day, 17 Muslim villages were attacked in a 20-square-mile area about 50 miles northeast of Gauhati, the state capital. Out of a population of 12,000, 1,200 were slaughtered. Retaliatory attacks against Hindu villages swelled the figure to 1,500. Police, trying to restore order, killed 127. Eight hundred wounded were treated in hastily set up camps.

Once again, the government of India stepped in. In Gauhati, the capital of Assam, the High Court released four prominent leaders of the anti-immigrant movement, hoping to defuse the situation.

With thousands of voters boycotting the voting and thousands more prevented from voting, the Congress Party of Prime Minister Indira Gandhi swept to a landslide victory in the state legislature. Troops would maintain peace. But Indira Gandhi's term in office would be short. One year later, she would be assassinated.

ROME

71 B.C.

• • • • • • • • • • • • • • • • •

The gathering of freed slaves and gladiators, attempting to sever themselves from Roman rule and escape to the Alps, was crushed by the Roman generals Crassus and

The crushing of the uprising of the slaves and gladiators and the death of their leader, Spartacus, are depicted in a 19th-century drawing. New York Public Library (H. Vogel)

Pompey in 71 B.C. *Six thousand slaves and gladiators were crucified.*

In Ancient Rome, slaves were usually enemy soldiers who had been defeated and captured in battle. One of these was Spartacus, a Thracian captured when Rome defeated and annexed Thrace during the first century B.C.

Taken to Capua, Spartacus was installed in the gladiator school there. But in 73 B.C., leading 78 men armed with kitchen knives, he escaped from Capua and established an army of runaway slaves that would eventually number 100,000.

Their first attacks were ragtag ones, made with makeshift swords. Compensating for a lack of organization and skill, they excelled in fierce resolve. As time went on, they defeated more and more Roman legions, appropriating their weaponry and improving their organization. Slave prisons were invaded, and their inmates joined the swelling ranks.

The Roman Senate first sent small armies headed by praetors into the field. They were roundly defeated. The Senate then dispatched consular armies, and they too were beaten. It was time to unite several armies under one consul. Pompey was abroad, fighting in Spain. The second choice was Marcus Crassus, better known for his real estate astuteness than his fighting skills. But Crassus was ambitious, and he brought a strong organizational hand to his resolve to crush the slave revolt. This was a distinct advantage over Spartacus's command. His army was effective but unruly.

It had been Spartacus's aim to fight his way north from Capua and then leave Italy and strike out for the Alps. He wanted nothing more than to return to Thrace. His army laid waste to southern Italy and Campania and developed a taste for plundering. They were in no hurry to leave.

It would be a fatal error. The Roman army under Crassus was given time to organize and arm itself and to force the slave army into a formal battle, a situation both Crassus and Spartacus knew the slave army could not win.

The battle took place near Rhegium, in the toe of Italy, where Crassus trapped the slave army. It was a rout. A heavy snowstorm provided cover for a third of the slaves, who managed to flee from this battle. The remaining two-thirds broke into two fleeing armies, and Spartacus met Crassus on the field near Lucania. He died in a hand-to-hand battle with the Roman consul.

Meanwhile, Pompey had returned from Spain and caught the rest of the escaping slave army. His troops annihilated them, and those they did not kill in battle they crucified. Six thousand slaves on crosses lined the highway from Capua to Rome.

Ironically, the armies of Pompey and Crassus found 3,000 Roman prisoners in the abandoned camp of the rebels. They were unharmed.

RUSSIA
ST. PETERSBURG

December 14, 1825

• • • • • • • • • • • • • • • • •

The Decembrists, a secret society of army officers who had served in Europe and were influenced by Western liberal ideals, revolted against Czar Nicholas I on December 14, 1825. The coup failed, and several hundred officers were killed.

There is a certain mystical fascination about the reign and life of Czar Alexander I. It was he who defeated Napoleon in 1812. It was he who advocated a benign, liberal treaty with France afterward. It was he who then, after 1812, began to subscribe to a sort of general Christian ideal but, in contradiction to its teachings, began to suppress any liberal movements in Russia, calling them "threats to Christian morality." He supported Metternich in crushing all national movements and, under the influence of Juliana Krudenar, created the Holy Alliance to uphold Christian morality in Europe.

In Russia, he established military colonies and paraded them as Christian enclaves. They were actually little serfdoms, in which the common soldiers were treated like chattel.

Alexander I died in 1825. Or possibly he didn't. Rumors maintain that he actually went to Siberia and became a hermit. In 1926 his grave was opened, and it was found to be empty. The mystery remains unsolved to this day.

When Alexander disappeared in 1825, the throne passed unexpectedly to his brother Nicholas I. Nicholas inherited all of the problems set in place by the repressive measures of Alexander. One of these was the formation of secret societies challenging Alexander and his fervent repressions.

One of the secret societies was called the Decembrists, and they were a unique group. Composed of army officers and aristocrats who had fought Napoleon and had thus spent time in the rest of Europe, they were consumed by new, liberal ideas of existence and government. They advocated the establishment of representative democracy but disagreed about the form it should take in Russia. Some supported a constitutional monarchy; others wanted a democratic republic.

They were not the ideal group to stage a rebellion, but the disappearance of Alexander I and the ensuing confusion offered them an opportunity they chose not to refuse.

It seemed that the assumed death of Alexander, who had remained childless, would necessarily result in the assumption of the throne by the next in line, Constantine. But, unbeknownst to all but a very few, he had renounced the throne in 1822. The confusion led the Decembrists to think that they could challenge the unpopular younger brother, Nicholas I, overwhelm him and demand that Constantine grant a constitution.

Ill organized but determined, they advanced upon Senate Square in St. Petersburg on December 14, 1825, the first day of Nicholas's reign. Fully armed and riding horses, the Decembrists formed themselves into a fighting force.

Nicholas attempted to negotiate. They refused. Artillery opened up on them, and the czar's cavalry charged. Improperly shod, the Decembrists' horses slipped and fell on the icy pavement of Senate Square. The artillery cut down more of them.

Within a short time, the revolt was crushed. Five of the leaders were later executed; hundreds more were killed in Senate Square.

It had been an unsuccessful revolt, but its effects would be felt for years. There was an immediate police repression, ordered by Nicholas I and inherited by his heirs. This inspired considerable revolutionary fever and activity. For a small effort, the Decembrist revolt of December 14, 1825 accomplished much and precipitated more.

UNITED STATES
CALIFORNIA
LOS ANGELES

August 11–29, 1965

• • • • • • • • • • • • • • • • •

Festering racial resentments, poverty and sultry summer weather converged to cause the racial riots of August 11–29, 1965 in Watts. Thirty-four died; 874 were injured; 3,800 were arrested; and there was $20 million in property damage.

There can be no doubt that the 1960s, remembered in retrospect as the age of the flower children, was also a decade of extreme violence—Vietnam; the assassinations of President John F. Kennedy, Robert Kennedy and Dr. Martin Luther King Jr.; and civil unrest (see also the police riot at Democratic National Convention, p. 85, and Kent State killings, p. 91).

The summer of 1965 was a hot and sultry one in Los Angeles, and in the Watts neighborhood, an outwardly neat and well-kept suburban section of Los Angeles, it was seemingly serene. Roughly 20 square miles in area, Watts held about a sixth of Los Angeles County's 523,000 blacks.

Shortly before 8 o'clock on the night of August 11, 1965, at the corner of Imperial and Avalon streets, a white California Highway Patrol officer stopped Marquette Frye, who, with his brother Ronald, was driving erratically. Some 25 people watched while their mother, Mrs. Rena Frye, entered the scene and began to berate her son, who in turn began to berate the police.

The crowd grew and became involved. Stones were thrown. The police radioed for help. By 10 P.M., crowds were stoning city buses, and 80 police officers sealed off the 16-block area in an effort to contain the violence.

It was fruitless. Looters had already moved beyond the sealed-off area, and the Watts riots of 1965 had begun.

By the next night, black youths had acquired firearms and were firing on police from the tops of buildings. Anarchy ruled the streets. Fires were started and fire fighters fired upon. White television crews were mauled and their equipment destroyed.

As the fever mounted over the next two days, roving bands of black teenagers assaulted cars containing whites. By August 13, four people had died, 33 police officers had been injured and 249 rioters had been arrested. And the fierceness and tempo of the riot were increasing.

No whites were safe anywhere near the Watts section of Los Angeles. Whenever a car containing whites entered the area, gangs of teenagers, egged on by shouts of "Kill! Kill!" descended upon it. Black police officers who tried to contain the crowds were jeered, called traitors and then stoned.

Robert Richardson, a black advertising salesman for the *Los Angeles Times* who had entered the area, wrote, "Light skinned Negroes such as myself were targets of rocks and bottles until someone standing nearby would shout, 'He's blood. He's a brother—lay off.'

"As some areas were blockaded during the night, the mobs would move outside, looking for more cars with whites. When there were no whites, they started throwing rocks and bottles at Negro cars. Then, near midnight, they began looting stores owned by whites.

"Everybody got in the looting—children, grownups, old men and women, breaking windows and going into stores.

"Then everybody started drinking—even little kids 8 and 9 years old."

And it was then that teenagers started to fan out, into white neighborhood, up to 20 miles from the riot scene. One group of 25 blacks tossed rocks in San Pedro, in the harbor area; another appeared in Pecoima, a black community in the San Fernando Valley.

Los Angeles Police Chief William Parker did nothing to try to bring peace. His public statements, comparing the rock throwers to "monkeys in a zoo," only fanned the flames.

On the morning of August 13, 2,000 heavily armed National Guard troops converged on Los Angeles. Moving in with machine guns, they fired at rioters, who fled and then regrouped elsewhere. At one point, a group of rioters charged Oak Park Hospital, where those who were injured and wounded in the riots were being treated.

The next day, 20,000 National Guardsman were called up and began to penetrate the riot area. A curfew from 8 P.M. to sunrise was imposed on a 35-square-mile area surrounding the riot scene. Snipers shot from rooftops. Fires began to break out with increasing frequency. There was hardly an unlooted store in Watts or the surrounding area. Twenty-one people had been killed. Nineteen were rioters, one was a sheriff's deputy and one was a fireman. Six hundred had been injured.

Chief Parker appeared on television to assail black leaders in the community, calling them "demogogic . . . pseudo leaders of the Negro community who can't lead at all." There was some evidence that Black Muslims were encouraging the riot and egging teenagers on, but by and large, black civil rights leaders from all over the country issued pleas for the violence to end.

There were not enough fire fighters and equipment to stop the continuing string of fires that blazed through the area. But 2,500 of the 15,000 National Guard troops in

Los Angeles began to secure the riot area, and by late on August 14, the rioting had begun to subside.

The death toll rose that day from 22 to 31. One victim was a 14-year-old girl killed in a traffic accident while fleeing the scene of a looting; one was a five-year-old child shot by a sniper. Bricks, rocks and bullets continued to rain down from rooftops, some striking guardsmen and police, some striking black residents. The guardsmen used rifle fire, tear gas, machine guns and bayonets, and Governor Edmund G. Brown widened the curfew area to 50 square miles.

Meanwhile, violence broke out in Long Beach, south of Los Angeles. One policeman was killed and another wounded when they were ambushed by snipers. Troops were ordered into that city.

Governor Brown came to Watts, surrounded by guardsman, and met with black leaders, trying to calm the atmosphere and effect a reconciliation. Gradually, an embittered calm descended over Los Angeles, and the gasoline bombs, rifles and rocks began to disappear.

A score of relief agencies entered the battle-scarred, smoldering area to begin rehabilitation after five days of riots. Slowly the troops were withdrawn, but the curfew remained in place. Racial tension throughout the city remained for a long time.

Two hundred businesses were totally destroyed; 500 were damaged; $200 million in property damage was estimated. Nearly $2 million in federal funds were allocated to aid in the rebuilding of a 45-square-mile area of Los Angeles. One thousand six hundred people were hired under the antipoverty program of Los Angeles County to aid in the cleanup.

In the last hours of the riots, a black woman was killed by a Guardsman, bringing the death toll to 34.

It would be a long path back for Watts.

UNITED STATES
COLORADO
SAND CREEK

November 29, 1864

• • • • • • • • • • • • • • • • • •

Colonel John M. Chivington's disdain for both Indians and treaties manifested itself in the massacre on November 29, 1864 of peaceful Cheyenne and Arapaho Indians. One hundred forty-eight Indians, mostly women and children, were killed, among them nine Indian chiefs; hundreds of Indians were wounded or mutilated; nine soldiers were killed; 38 soldiers were wounded.

There were many Indian raids along the Platte Road in Colorado in the 1860s. It was the main route of stagecoaches, and there were Cheyennes among the Sioux who were chiefly involved in the raids.

But the encampment of Cheyenne and Arapaho in Sand Creek, Colorado, southeast of Denver and 40 miles northeast of Fort Lyon, was a peaceful one. In fact, a verbal agreement was reached between them and territory governor John Evans. They would be under the protection of Fort Lyon, and a formal treaty signing was to take place in a very short time. Chief Black Kettle flew a huge American flag before his adobe hut at Sand Creek in celebration and expectation.

The camp consisted of 100 lodges of Cheyenne, under Chief Black Kettle, and 10 lodges of Arapaho, under Chief Left Hand. They were certain that any day word would arrive from Kansas that a treaty had been concluded.

However, anything but peace was on the mind of Colonel John M. Chivington. Colonel Chivington commanded a company of Colorado volunteers made up of the Third Colorado Cavalry, each of them "100 days men." They were not trained soldiers, but recruits made up of mining toughs, gamblers, "bull-wackers" and general frontier flotsam. There was no discipline; the men chose their officers by vote and then ignored them. They did not wear uniforms, and the one common thread that united them was a desire to kill Indians.

As early as April 1864, Colonel Chivington and his men had attacked Cheyenne indiscriminately. They had been ordered to go to Kansas and fight the Confederates. Colonel Chivington apparently did not want to do this. An attack on Indians would, he felt, make his company indispensable Indian fighters, too good to send East.

It was no problem for him. He hated Indians with an abiding passion. His standing order was to take no prisoners. Under his command, various companies made repeated raids on Cheyenne villages, killing the inhabitants. In one incident in May, 600 Cheyenne warriors met 100 soldiers led by Lieutenant George S. Eayre. The soldiers would have been killed to a man if it had not been for the intervention of Chief Black Kettle, who ordered his warriors not to fire.

But this had no effect whatsoever on Colonel Chivington's plan to exterminate Cheyenne, and so, at the beginning of November, while Chief Black Kettle and his village waited patiently for the peace treaty to be signed, Colonel Chivington made his own plans to massacre every Indian in Sand Creek.

The Indians there were lulled into a sense of security first by Major E. W. Wynkoop and then by Major Scott J. Anthony, who treated them deferentially from their command posts at Fort Lyon. In fact, Major Anthony as-

Frontier art depicting the slaughter of Cheyenne and Arapaho Indians during the Sand Creek, Colorado massacre on November 29, 1864. Currier and Ives, 1858

sured them that they could continue to live safely, under his protection at Sand Creek, until word came about the treaty.

Meanwhile, Colonel Chivington decided to strike one blow at the "Red Rebels" and endear himself to Colorado voters, whom he would be facing soon, after he was mustered out of the service. He began gathering his troops on November 20. On November 24, they had reached Booneville, a little settlement on the Arkansas River above Fort Lyon. On that day, he ceased all traffic down the Arkansas River, even the mail, so that no one, not even Major Anthony, would know of his approach.

On the morning of November 28, he appeared at Fort Lyon, to the surprise of everyone. He surrounded the fort and stationed sentries with orders to let no one out. He then went into the fort and informed Major Anthony of his plan to attack the camp at Sand Creek. Major Anthony, who by now had become convinced that the camp was a peaceful one, objected. He knew the kind of men Chivington was commanding, and he knew that attacking the camp would precipitate Indian raids from less peaceful tribes. It was foolish, and he told Chivington so. The colonel was adamant and ordered Anthony and his men to accompany him in the attack.

Shortly after midnight on the 28th, the army, 1,000 strong, set out on horseback for Sand Creek, led unwillingly—but at the threat of the loss of his life—by Robert Bent, the brother of George Bent, a white man who was then living with the Cheyenne at Sand Creek.

At dawn of November 29, 1864, the main body of the troops attacked, in a pincer movement, from both sides of the camp. Others made for the pony herds to the south of the camp. The sleeping Indians rushed from their huts in dazed confusion, which immediately melted into screams from the women and children and fierce war cries from the men, who dashed back into their huts for their weapons.

Chief Black Kettle grabbed the pole of the large American flag that flew outside his hut and called to his people not to be afraid. The soldiers would not hurt them.

His words died in the dawn as the soldiers opened fire. The Indians who escaped being hit by the cavalry's bullets scattered. Some dashed for the sand hills; others scurried down the dry creek bed. Two miles upstream, some dug holes in the ground to hide. Wherever they went, soldiers followed. Knots of people were cornered and slaughtered. Others stood and fought; still others were chased and gunned down.

The camp was now empty. The soldiers turned their full attention to killing any Indians running from the site. Black Kettle stood in disbelief before his hut until the camp was almost empty, and then he took his wife and started up the creek after his people. After a few steps his wife was hit. She fell, and he continued on until he found a group of Cheyenne hiding in holes they had dug in the side of the riverbank.

After dark, he returned to where his wife had fallen and found her still alive. She told him, and a later board of inquiry, that the soldiers had fired nine more bullets into her as she lay on the ground. The peace commissioners in 1865 counted her wounds and confirmed her story.

By five P.M. the soldiers withdrew. If they had been better trained, they would have closed in and finished off the rest of the Indians. But being a mob, they feared getting close. Instead, they retraced their way along the creek, killing the wounded and scalping them. Little Bear, a friend of George Bent's, described the scene afterward: "After the fight I came back down the creek and saw these dead bodies all cut up and even the wounded scalped and slashed. I saw one old woman wandering about; her whole scalp had been taken off and the blood was running down into her eyes so that she could not see where to go."

All of that cold night, the surviving Indians from Sand Creek stayed in the hills. George Bent wrote later in his letters to Owl Woman, a Cheyenne, "The men and women who were not wounded worked all through the night, trying to keep the children and the wounded from freezing to death. They gathered grass by the handful, feeding little fires around which the wounded and the children lay; they stripped off their own blankets and clothes to keep us warm . . . Many who had lost wives, husbands, children, or friends went back down the creek and crept over the battleground among the naked and mutilated bodies of the dead."

Before dawn, they made their way east, toward the headwaters of Smoky Hill, 50 miles away, to another Indian encampment. Frightened that the soldiers would pick up their trail and slaughter them before they reached there, they sent some men ahead to get help. By nightfall, a huge contingent of Indians with ponies met them and brought them to Smoky Hill. "As we rode into that camp there was a terrible scene," wrote Bent. "Everyone was crying, even the warriors and the women and children screaming and wailing. Nearly everyone present had lost some relations or friends, and many of them in their grief were gashing themselves with their knives until the blood flowed in streams."

Back at the camp, the soldiers plundered the Cheyenne lodges and captured the pony herds. The disciplined troops returned to Fort Lyon. The 100 days men were too busy plundering and squabbling over the ponies to move. Two days later, they headed for the Arapaho village to massacre its residents. But the Arapaho had long since been warned and had escaped to a place near the Kiowa and Comanche, south of the river.

Colonel Chivington went in triumph to Denver, where he and his men were received as heroes and acclaimed for their victory over Black Kettle and his "hostiles." One evening in a Denver theater, a band of soldiers stepped onstage and exhibited over 100 Cheyenne scalps and tobacco bags made of pieces of skin cut from the bodies of dead Cheyenne, while the orchestra played patriotic airs.

Eventually, the truth of the Sand Creek massacre was heard in Washington, and Chivington was ordered to be court-martialed. But he had long since been mustered out of the service and was beyond the reach of a military court.

Colonel George Shoup, his adjutant and the leader of the 100 days men, was elected to the U.S. Senate.

UNITED STATES
ILLINOIS
CHICAGO

July 27–August 3, 1919

• • • • • • • • • • • • • • • •

The famous Chicago race riots of July 27–August 3, 1919 were caused by ill feeling between blacks and whites after World War I, a small altercation on a Chicago beach and hot summer weather. By their end, 35 were dead and more than 500 were injured.

July 1919 was a hot month in the Midwest. On the 27th, citizens of the South Side of Chicago, Illinois gathered on a South Side beach to escape the heat. The beaches in Chicago in 1919 were divided. Blacks swam on one side of the precaution line; whites swam on the other. That afternoon, several blacks wandered across the barrier after some whites had amused themselves by throwing small stones at black bathers.

The confrontation escalated. Larger rocks were thrown. A black swimmer on a raft was struck by a rock that was flung with enough force to knock him into the lake, where he drowned. A white swimmer was hit by another rock, and he, too, drowned.

A melee broke out on the beach and spilled onto 29th Street. Within hours, the pent-up energy that had been accumulating over a period of months, during which isolated bomb explosions, small fires, shootings and sporadic fistfights had punctuated the days and nights, erupted into full-scale violence.

There had been small, contained racial confrontations in a number of cities that summer: Washington, Detroit and New York had had their battles. Blacks who had fought in the war came home with a new sense of equality but discovered that there was neither equality nor justice in some hiring practices or wage policies. White laborers, perceiving blacks as willing to work for lower wages, were resentful.

In the early evening of July 27, the streets on the South Side, particularly along State Street, were packed with brawling whites and blacks. Rocks, stones and sniper fire flew through the air. Fires were set, and fire apparatus was blocked from extinguishing them. Police poured into the area from other precincts; police were fired on and fired back. By midnight, the situation had turned ugly.

The death toll had risen to 14 by 12 o'clock of the first night; nine victims were white, five were black. Seventy-six had been injured.

The riots continued throughout the next day, and looting began. By nightfall, it had spread into the Stock Yards district to 35th and Halstead streets and all through the "black belt" of Chicago. Every available policeman was rushed to the scene; former soldiers and sailors were deputized; 3,600 men in four regiments of the National Guard and reserve troops were activated.

Rocks flew continuously through the South Side. Elevated trains ceased to run, and telephone wires were cut, isolating the area. Roving bands roamed both black and white neighborhoods, cornering lone blacks or whites and stabbing them on the spot.

By July 29, fighting had spread to the Loop, Chicago's business district, where two blacks were killed and a score of others were captured, kicked and beaten. The toll had climbed to 28 dead and more than 500 injured. By 7 o'clock that night, the rioting had reached the North Side of Chicago, where a crowd of Sicilians attacked a group of black families living in one tenement on West Division Street. They were met with a hail of bullets.

That same night, an unidentified black man riding his bicycle on Lytie Street on the North Side was waylaid by a mob of whites who stabbed him and then shot him 16 times. When he fell dead from his bicycle, his body was splashed with gasoline and set afire.

At the same time, car men on the Chicago Transit System, unhappy over stalled contract negotiations, struck the system, immobilizing it and adding to the general pandemonium. Blacks were hanged in effigy; black policemen in full uniform fired on white policemen. Anarchy ruled.

The following day, blacks, who constituted one third of the work force in the stockyards, failed to report to work. Those whites who did report lay in wait for blacks.

The Stanton Avenue Police Station, in the middle of the "black belt," became an arsenal, as confiscated weapons piled up in it. By evening of the third day of rioting, the "black belt" was threatened with starvation when wholesalers refused to send delivery wagons of meat or groceries into the area.

The Loop was a maelstrom. Abandoned trolley cars were overturned; a black porter was cornered by a mob of whites at Wabash Avenue and Adams Street, where he was beaten, trampled and finally shot to death. Five hundred whites stormed the famed Palmer House, looking for black employees.

Meanwhile, Illinois governor Frank O. Lowden and city officials issued public statements saying that the rioting was under control. It would take another day of rioting for Mayor William Hale Thompson to finally order the 4,000 troops into action. On the evening of July 30, troops began to patrol the streets of the South Side, while blacks fired on them and tossed rocks from side alleys.

Governor Lowden and city officials met that afternoon in the Blackstone Hotel. A mob of whites chasing a lone black man roared past the hotel, interrupting the conference.

That night, whites infiltrated black neighborhoods, set fires and then prevented firemen from putting them out. One hundred twenty-three fires were reported on the night of July 30.

Blacks retaliated, invading white districts. A white woman was gunned down as she innocently walked near 47th Street and Indiana Avenue.

Finally, on July 31, 4,000 troops, backed by 3,000 more in reserve, began to restore order. Still, that day, 32 fires were set between 7:00 A.M. and noon. In several cases, streetcars were stretched sideways across streets, blocking firemen. A huge mob of whites with incendiary devices and a determination to "burn the Black Belt to the ground" were intercepted and turned back by troops.

In other sections of the city, troops thwarted street-corner lynchings. Hearing that the army was in control, a group of black workers attempted to return to their jobs in the stockyards. A mob of white workers met them, pursued them, wrestled them to the ground and began to beat them. The militia appeared on the scene, fixed bayonets and separated the groups, forming a cordon around the terrified workers.

Machine guns were set up at other strategic positions, particularly and ironically at the corner of Garfield Boulevard and Normal Avenue.

Finally, on Friday, August 1, as the Chicago car men voted to accept management's offer of 65 cents an hour and an eight-hour day, the rioting quieted. Six thousand troops still patrolled the South Side, but they were meeting fewer demonstrators. Under their protection, fresh food, milk and ice once again flowed into the "black belt." Fifteen thousand black stockyard workers announced that they would return to work on Monday, August 4.

That Sunday, the third, more violence erupted. Six blocks of black homes near the stockyards were destroyed by fire, and plans for blacks to return to work the next day were abandoned. Snipers hiding in an alley of the eastern section of the riot zone tried to assassinate Captain A. R. Wenhelm of the fourth Illinois Reserve Infantry. As he left his headquarters, snipers on nearby rooftops opened fire on him, and a small group of three blacks leaped out of a side alley and lunged at him and his adjutants with knives. Captain Wenhelm received a knife thrust in his side but escaped alive.

Finally, the next day, order was restored. Thirty-five had been killed; between 500 and 600 had been injured. It would be weeks before blacks would be able to return to work throughout the city, and years before any semblance of peace between blacks and whites would arrive in Chicago.

UNITED STATES
ILLINOIS
CHICAGO

August 25–30, 1968

• • • • • • • • • • • • • • •

Antiwar demonstrators who had gathered outside the Democratic National Convention on August 25–30, 1968 to protest the Vietnam policies of the Johnson administration were beaten and gassed by a police force that had gone momentarily berserk and had been ordered to enforce excessive repression measures by Mayor Richard J. Daley. Hundreds of demonstrators, scores of newspeople and bystanders and some delegates were injured.

In 1968, embittered and discouraged by public reaction to his Vietnam policies, Lyndon Johnson announced that he would not run for reelection. It had been a terrible year for him and for the country. The nation was sharply and irrevocably divided over American involvement in Southeast Asia. In April, Dr. Martin Luther King Jr., an advocate of civil rights, had been assassinated. In June, Robert Kennedy, openly challenging President Johnson's Vietnam stance, and an announced candidate for the Democratic nomination for president, had been assassinated.

Eugene R. McCarthy, a solid opponent of the Vietnam War, was the voice of anti-war youth in the country, but it was generally agreed that the powers in the Democratic Party did not feel that he could challenge Richard Nixon for the presidency in 1968. They favored Hubert Humphrey, vice president under Lyndon Johnson, and therefore an advocate of the Vietnam strategy that had divided the country so bitterly.

Thus, a large contingent of anti-war protesters journeyed to Chicago in August 1968 to make their voices heard and, it was hoped, influence the floor votes at the Democratic Convention.

Fearful of violence, Mayor Richard Daley, who was also the political boss of the Cook County Democratic Committee, ordered a mobilization of police forces to contain the demonstrators and prevent possible riots. In addition, he requested and received from Governor Samuel Shapiro 5,649 Illinois National Guardsmen, to be stationed on round-the-clock duty. On top of this, 6,000 regular army troops received riot control training at Fort Hood, Texas in an exercise called Operation Jackson Park, after the park in Chicago that was expected to be the gathering point for the student demonstrators. On August 25, 5,000 of these troops were flown to Chicago, where they were quartered at the Glenview Naval Air Station and the Great Lakes Naval Training Center outside the city. It was an awesome array of power for a peaceful nation to set up against a portion of its own citizenry.

Meanwhile, approximately 1,000 student protesters gathered, in a carnival mood, in Lincoln Park, on the fringes of one of the posher areas of Chicago. On Sunday night, August 25, at 11 P.M., the curfew hour on all public parks in Chicago, they were ordered out of the park by 400 policemen carrying tear gas launchers and rifles and wearing riot gear. The police drove the crowd into the downtown area of Clark Street and LaSalle Street. Traffic was disrupted, and the police waded into the mob of demonstrators, clubbing them with their nightsticks.

Claude Lewis, a black reporter for the *Philadelphia Bulletin,* was scribbling notes when a policeman approached him and demanded that he hand over his notebook. "He snatched the notebook out of my hand and started swinging away," Mr. Lewis later wrote. The first of many newspeople to be worked over by Chicago police, Mr. Lewis was treated for head lacerations at the Henrotin Hospital that evening.

By the next night, 27 newspaper and television reporters had been roughed up by police despite the fact that they had displayed their press credentials. Delos Hall, a cameraman for the Columbia Broadcasting System, reported to the *New York Times* that he was filming police action when he was clubbed from behind, knocked down and then attacked by several more policemen. He was treated for a blow on the mouth and a cut forehead. James Strickland, a cameraman for the National Broadcasting Company, was struck in the face when he photographed Mr. Hall lying in the street.

At 12:20 on the night of August 26, in Lincoln Park, 300 policemen wearing Plexiglas shields fired tear gas into a crowd of nearly 3,000 youths who had erected a barricade of overturned picnic tables, upon which they had affixed Viet Cong, black anarchist and peace flags. In the crowd was poet Allen Ginsberg, who led 300 protesters in a gentle chanting of "Om," the mystic Sanskrit sound of peace and love.

This apparently deflected most of the police force. They waited to make arrests. Finally, Tom Hayden, one of the protest coordinators, was arrested for the second night in a row. All in all, some 150 protesters had been booked so far, and nearly 60 had been injured.

On August 27, at 12:30, in Lincoln Park, the police again moved into the mob of demonstrators that now numbered 2,000 and began to fire tear gas into it. A group of clergymen and demonstrators, gathered around a 12-foot cross that they had set up in the hope of conducting an all-night prayer vigil, were routed and clubbed.

The 2,000 made their way toward Michigan Avenue to Grant Park, where they merged with some 3,000 Yippies, New Leftists and adherents of the National Mobilization Committee to End the War in Vietnam. Grant Park was directly across the street from the Conrad Hilton Hotel, a center of activity for the Democratic National Convention and the headquarters of all of the major nominees.

August 28 was the climactic—and most brutal—day and night. Police were joined by National Guardsmen in the streets. The Democratic National Convention was nearing its most important business, and Hubert Humphrey was expected to win the nomination. A huge march was planned on the Amphitheatre that housed the convention. Already, news from the streets and some of the violence had invaded the floor of the convention itself.

Alex J. Rosenberg, a delegate from New York, was wrestled from the floor by an orange-arm-banded security guard when he refused to show his credentials. Once in the entryway, he was struck by a policeman and hauled away. Paul O'Dwyer, the Democratic candidate for the U.S. Senate, was roughed up by police when he attempted to intercede, as was Mike Wallace, the CBS television reporter, who was also struck on the chin and hauled from the hall.

Later that night, Robert Maytag, a delegate from Colorado, interrupted the seconding of Hubert Humphrey's nomination for president by shouting into a microphone, "Is there any rule under which Mayor Daley can be compelled to end the police state of terror being perpetrated?" Cheers greeted the interruption while Mayor Daley sat impassively, and no move was made by the Democratic National Convention to deter the attempts to control demonstrators on the streets of Chicago.

Later, in his nomination speech putting George McGovern's name in contention for Democratic nominee for president, Senator Abraham M. Ribicoff of Connecticut said, "If Senator George McGovern were President, we would not have these Gestapo tactics in the streets of Chicago."

Impassive no longer, Mayor Daley and his supporters rose angrily to their feet and tried to shout down Senator Ribicoff, who turned to them and added, "How hard it is to accept the truth."

Outside the convention hall, a steady crescendo of activity had been accumulating all day. That afternoon, a gathering of approximately 15,000 young people had filled Grant Park and gathered around its band shell in a rally designed both to protest the violence in the streets and to prepare the demonstrators to march on the Amphitheatre.

There were skirmishes between police and protesters at the exterior of the gathering. At the band shell, poet Allen Ginsberg again led the group chanting "Om," though his voice by now was cracked from chanting and swallowing tear gas; French author Jean Genet spoke to the crowd through a translator; authors William Burroughs and Norman Mailer exhorted them; comedian Dick Gregory, mounting the platform, said, "You just have to look around you at all the police and soldiers to know you must be doing something right." Entertainers Judy Collins and Peter, Paul and Mary led the crowd in folk songs of the resistance movement, and leaders of the protest led the mob out of the park.

Some groups, such as the Poor People's March, had permits, but more purposely did not. There was manipulation by the more militant leaders of more naive and young and marijuana-smoking youngsters.

At the Congress Street Bridge leading from the park to Michigan Avenue, police and Guardsmen opened up with tear gas and mace, attempting to hold the demonstrators within the park. But the numbers were overwhelming, and between 2,000 and 5,000 youths, led by David Dellinger, the national chairman of the Mobilization Committee to End the War in Vietnam, and poet Allen Ginsberg, headed south on Michigan Avenue toward the Amphitheatre.

The police, moving in in phalanxes and using their clubs as prods, broke up the march, sending protesters fleeing up side streets. Those who escaped the police charges faced a tank and National Guardsmen with machine guns. Newspeople were again clubbed to the ground as demonstrators chanted, "The whole world is watching."

Reverend John Boyles, the Presbyterian chaplain at Yale and a staff worker for candidate Eugene McCarthy, was hauled off to a patrol wagon and charged with breach of the peace. Speaking to a *New York Times* reporter afterward, Mr. Boyles said, "It's an unfounded charge. I was protesting the clubbing of a girl I knew from the McCarthy staff. They were beating her on her head with clubs and I yelled at them 'Don't hit a woman.' At that point I was slugged in the stomach and grabbed by a cop who arrested me."

There were 178 arrests that night alone, and 100 persons, including 25 policemen, were injured.

Shortly after midnight, an uneasy calm settled over the city, as 1,000 National Guardsmen arranged themselves in front of the Conrad Hilton Hotel and 5,000 demonstrators drifted back into Grant Park. A field piece was poised in the lobby; officials had prevented the National Guard from bringing bazookas onto the premises.

Blue police barricades were lined up on the streets, and several dozen people, many of them elderly, watched quietly as protesters and police, illuminated by television lights, chased one another in and out of the park. Suddenly, "for no apparent reason," according to reporters on the scene, the police turned on the spectators and charged the barriers, crushing the spectators against the windows of the Haymarket Inn, a restaurant in the hotel. The plate glass windows gave way, sending screaming women and children backward through the broken shards of glass. The police then ran into the restaurant and beat some of the victims who had fallen through the windows. As they were clubbing them, they arrested some of these bewildered and bleeding citizens.

"Outside," wrote Nora Sayre, who was caught in the crush, "people sobbed with pain as their ribs snapped from being crushed against each other . . . Soon, a line of stick-whipping cops swung in on us. Voiceless from gas, I feebly waved my credentials, and the warrior who was about to hit me said, 'oops, press.' He let me limp into the hotel, where people were being pummelled into the red carpet, while free Pepsi was timidly offered on the sidelines."

In St. Chrysostrom's Church and the sixth-floor offices of the Church Federation of Greater Chicago, volunteer doctors treated the gassed, maced and injured demonstrators. A specially equipped van manned by students of Yale Medical School and the Columbia College of Physicians and Surgeons roamed the riot area to dispense first aid, but police harassed first aid teams and forced the van away by threatening to confiscate it. Dr. Albert S. Braverman, an internist from Manhattan who was helping the wounded, was himself a victim. "I was hit and pushed by a cop while I was coming back from dinner and while wearing my white coat and red cross," he told reporters for the *Times*. "When a friend said I was a doctor, the cop replied, 'I don't give a damn.'"

On the next night, August 29, another march was planned to the Amphitheatre. This time, several delegates joined the 3,000 marchers led by Dick Gregory (Dellinger was in jail, and Rennie Davis, his second, had had his arm broken the night before).

"Such blood . . ." wrote Nora Sayre.

> *Broad bloodstreaks on the pavements showed where bodies had been dragged . . . Each day, scores staggered bleeding through the streets and parks, reeling or dropping, their faces glistening with vaseline—for Mace . . . With two doctors, I walk[ed] five blocks ahead of . . . Dick Gregory . . . to the Amphitheatre; we [saw] the tank with the machine guns that await[ed] them. We turn[ed] back to tell them, discovering that the empty alleys—where we'd planned to disappear if necessary—[were] now crammed with police and Guardsmen.*

Armored personnel carriers and jeeps with barbed-wire barriers mounted on their hoods further blocked the way.

The marchers were ordered to stop at 18th Street and Michigan Avenue, on the advice of the Secret Service. Dick Gregory argued that he had invited the demonstrators to his home on 55th Street and wished to pass. He was denied his request, as were others behind him. He pushed past the barricades and was arrested, as were 422 others, including nine delegates. A steady shuttle of police vans ran between the street corner and a specially convened night court.

Ms. Sayre returned to McCarthy headquarters on the second floor of the Conrad Hilton Hotel. "As I watched the beatings and gassings from a second-floor McCarthy room, " she wrote, "twelve policemen surged in, slamming down the windows, drew the curtains, and told us to turn away and watch the TV set, where Humphrey was starting to speak—'And that's an order.' "

Earlier, in the Convention Hall, Mayor Daley had mounted the podium to defend his police and his tactics. He mentioned that 51 police had been injured but failed to note that 300 demonstrators had also been injured. "The people of Chicago," he said, "will never permit a lawless, violent group of terrorists to menace the lives of millions of people, destroy the purpose of a national political convention and take over the streets."

At dawn, police raided the headquarters of Senator Eugene McCarthy, on the 15th floor of the Conrad Hilton Hotel, herded 30 McCarthy aides from several rooms into elevators and took them to the lobby. In the scuffle, three McCarthy workers were injured seriously enough to require hospital treatment. One required 10 stitches in his head, another, six. The police reported four injuries to their ranks. No arrests were made and no charges filed, but Senator McCarthy postponed his departure to call a news conference to protest the police action, which was, authorities said, in response to complaints that objects were being thrown from the windows of McCarthy headquarters—a charge the aides denied.

That same morning, Frank J. Sullivan, the Chicago Police Department's director of public information, called a news conference. He described the demonstrators as "revolutionaries" and called some of their leaders, including Tom Hayden and Rennie Davis, "Communists who are the allies of the men who are killing American soldiers.

"The intellectuals of America hate Richard J. Daley," he continued, "because he was elected by the people—unlike Walter Cronkite [the CBS anchor man at the convention]."

By August 1, the demonstrators had dispersed, as had the National Guard and police. The army personnel had never been called up, and they quietly boarded planes and returned to their camps. More than 71% of the Chicago citizens polled by local papers approved of the police handling of the demonstrators; many replied that they were certain the protesters were Communists, and J. Edgar Hoover announced an FBI investigation. Nevertheless, the rest of the nation and the world looked upon the riots differently. "The Chicago cops taught us that we were rubble with no protection or defense," wrote Nora Sayre. "In future, we can understand the ghettos' rage."

In September 1969, eight radicals and antiwar activists—David Dellinger, Rennie Davis, Tom Hayden, Abbie Hoffman, Jerry Rubin, Bobby Seale, John Froines and Lee Weiner—were tried in Chicago for conspiracy to riot. Bobby Seale, the head of the Black Panthers, was chained and gagged for outbursts in the courtroom. His case was separated from that of the others. Five of the remaining seven defendants were convicted of intent to riot and sentenced to five years in prison and fines of $5,000 each, the maximum penalties permitted. The riot convictions were eventually overturned on appeal because of improper rulings and conduct by the trial judge, Julius Hoffman. Contempt charges stemming from the trial were also dropped.

UNITED STATES
NEW YORK
NEW YORK

July 13–15, 1863

• • • • • • • • • • • • • • • • • •

The July 11, 1863 Conscription Act, designed to replenish a depleted Union Army during the Civil War, allowed wealthy draftees to buy their way out of the draft for $300. It produced three days of rioting in New York City, from July 13–15, in which 2,000 rioters died, 10,000 rioters were wounded; 60 soldiers died, 300 soldiers were wounded; 76 blacks, turned on by the rioters, were reported "missing"; 18 blacks were hanged; and 5 blacks were drowned.

The Civil War was going poorly for the North in 1863, and in April of that year, President Abraham Lincoln announced that 300,000 men would be drafted according to the Conscription Act of Congress. The process would begin in New York City on July 11.

The act was a discriminatory one, pretending to draft all equally, but was actually skewed so that it drafted only the poor. If a man had $300, he could buy himself out of the army. And it was that provision that ignited riots in the North, the most notable and brutal of them the draft riots of New York City.

During the Civil War, New York City had a population of approximately 815,000, 5% of whom were immigrants with no particular allegiance. More than 203,000 Irish had escaped the potato famine to live in extreme poverty in

The confrontation between police and rioters in front of Horace Greeley's* Tribune *during the draft riots in New York City, July 13–15, 1863. Harper's Weekly

the slums of New York. Illiterate and hardly able to make a living, they were discriminated against in practically every sense. They would form the bulk of those to be drafted on July 11.

When the drums containing random numbers began to spin on the morning of July 11, discontent was not confined to Irish immigrants. There had been inflammatory stories in the papers raging against the unfairness of the draft; there was resentment in the slums toward the affluent and also toward blacks, since they were willing to work for even lower wages than those offered immigrants. There was also objection to the primary reason for the war, which was abolition.

And lower New York was a brutal place. Along Five Points, near its lower tip, the Plug Uglies, the Dead Rabbits and other gangs, composed of men and boys living in subhuman conditions, roamed and pillaged and killed. Any excuse would easily turn them out into the streets, and the draft was a better than ordinary reason for them to move uptown.

Just after dawn on Saturday, July 11, there were rumors that a political organization, the Knights of the Golden Circle, was going to take over the U.S. Arsenal at 7th Avenue and 35th Street. It never materialized.

Meanwhile, a large, hostile crowd gathered at Third Avenue and 46th Street, where the drum was spun, and 1,236 names were drawn. The crowd dispersed, muttering.

Sunday, July 12 was a day of festering for the poor and payments of $300 to the authorities for relief from service by the wealthy whose names had been pulled.

By Monday morning, July 13, the unrest had turned to action. A few fires had been set the night before, but they had been swiftly extinguished with no interference. But early Monday morning, a mob began to move up the West Side, toward the homes of the wealthy bordering Central Park. It gathered in a lot just east of the park at about 8 A.M. and then began to break into segments, snaking their way toward the draft lottery drum at Third Avenue and 46th Street.

The mob gathered around the draft office for six blocks in every direction and toppled carriages, forced pedestrians off sidewalks and knocked the top hats off unwary victims. Crudely written posters appeared, reading NO DRAFT!

The Back Joke Gang, composed of members of Volunteer Engine Company No. 33, heard that their fire chief's number had been picked in the draft, and they were determined to invade the office and smash the drum. They were armed and forced their way into the building, smashed the drum and set fire to the structure (police escaped with the official records). When other fire companies arrived to extinguish the blaze, they were held off by the mob.

Superintendent of Police John A. Kennedy arrived in an open carriage to survey the scene. He was recognized, rushed by the mob, beaten mercilessly and tossed over an embankment. He was only saved from murder by sympathetic bystanders who convinced his attackers that he was already dead.

Now insurrections began all over the city. Police were attacked; precinct houses were raided. The so-called Invalid Corps of wounded soldiers was brought into action. Marching up Third Avenue, they were met with a barrage of bricks, paving stones and a dead cat or two. When one of their men was killed, they were ordered by their officer to shoot into the crowd. They did, killing a woman and six men. The crowd, infuriated, rushed them, shooting some of the soldiers with their own muskets. The battle had been joined. What had begun as a poor man's protest was now an armed fight against any sort of authority.

The city rallied, brought in National Guardsman and deputized more than 1,000 citizens. Before it was over, 10,000 soldiers, cavalry, infantry and dozens of batteries of artillery would roar into New York to beat back the mob.

By noon, the crowd had gathered leaders, and they decided that they needed firearms. They marched on the State Armory at Second Avenue and 21st Street, reserving the Union Steam works, an active munitions plant farther north, for later.

By 4 P.M., they were battering at the armory's main gates, while a contingent of police fired on them from inside the armory. Within minutes, the mob had broken down the gates, and the police had retreated to the 18th Precinct Police Station at 22d Street and Third Avenue. The mob rushed the station and burned it, forcing the police to retreat to the Mulberry Street headquarters.

Inside the armory, the mob armed itself. Fearing the return of the police, they locked and barred the door to the third floor drill room. It would prove to be a fatal error, for when the police returned and began to invade the building, some of the mob set fire to it. All of those on the third floor were incinerated when the ancient building went up like an incendiary torch.

In other parts of the city, the mob sought out the rich and blacks. Blacks were captured and lynched. Bodies—an average of three a day—swung from lampposts, trees and gateways.

Stores were looted and then burned. The provost marshall's office at Broadway and Ninth Street was set afire and its contents hacked up and thrown into the street. A mob moved out to burn Mayor George Opdyke's mansion on First Avenue and police headquarters on Mulberry Street.

A force of 125 policemen managed to beat back the assault on police headquarters. The mob was also turned away from Mayor Opdyke's home. Frustrated, it turned its attention to the Colored Orphan Asylum, which housed 200 orphaned black children, all under 12 years of age. The superintendent gathered his charges, and they escaped out the back way of the building on Fifth Avenue between 43d and 44th streets. When the rioters arrived, they found one girl cowering under a bed. They murdered her on the spot, chopped up the furnishings and set fire not only to the asylum but to several neighboring buildings as well.

By that night, the mob held the town. In Printing House Square, they marched on the *New York Tribune* and its editor and publisher, Horace Greeley. Greeley was chased down Park Row but escaped. When he returned to the *Tribune* building, he found that the police and soldiers had turned it into a fortress. Gatling guns protruded from upstairs windows, and a field howitzer was positioned in the main lobby.

Fires sprang up all over the city. Fire companies trying to extinguish them were shot at or pelted with debris. If a rainstorm had not suddenly come up at 11 P.M., the city might well have met the fate of Chicago, earlier in the century (see p. 181).

During that night, Governor Horatio Seymour conferred with the mayor, and both sent telegrams to the War Department in Washington, requesting that New York regiments that were currently recovering from the Battle of Gettysburg be sent to the city immediately.

That night, 2,000 soldiers, sailors and marines set up positions on the streets and in the buildings of New York City, manning an arsenal of firepower and ready for the worst.

Tuesday, July 14 was Bastille Day in France, and the streets of New York resembled Paris during the revolution. Street barricades were built from wagons, dismantled lampposts, street poles, boxes, barrels, kegs and looted furniture. The barricades blocked off First and Ninth avenues and snaked through the streets from 11th to 14th Street.

The Union Steam Works now became the focal point for the mob, and police and army units gathered around it. Police broke heads, literally, with their truncheons; army units fired into the crowds, killing many.

Colonel H. J. O'Brien, who commanded a regiment of artillery, was particularly aggressive in his use of force. He committed murder en masse, firing his cannon into crowds and tearing them to pieces. Whether it was arrogance or ignorance or a taste for self-destruction that caused him to later go back to the scene of that slaughter, no one will ever know. He *did* go back, alone, on horseback, and was, of course, spotted and pelted with bricks.

Sensing danger, O'Brien dismounted and took refuge in a saloon at the corner of Second Avenue and 19th Street. But after taking on a little bravado fuel, he left the saloon and, brandishing a sword and a pistol, waded out into the midst of a hostile mob. Within minutes, he was clubbed to the ground and kicked mercilessly. A rope was tied around his ankles, and the mob took turns dragging him over the cobblestones.

Finding him still alive, the mob then worked him over with knives and left him in the middle of the street. Later that night, he was discovered by another mob, dragged around again, tossed into his own back garden and assaulted with more knives. His body was discovered by his family that night.

The mob then went on to the Union Steam Works, which it captured, but was eventually routed by 200 policemen. The dead piled up like cordwood around the factory and on the front walks.

Meanwhile, infantry companies ringed the Sub Treasury on Wall Street, and at the Brooklyn Navy Yard, the gunboats *Gertrude, Unadilla, Granite City* and *Tulip* loaded their big guns and stood ready to defend the yard. At the Battery, the ironclad *Passaic* rode at the ready.

Late Tuesday, Secretary of War Edwin M. Stanton informed city officials that five regiments of the Union Army in full war gear were being transported by steam cars and ferries to the city.

On Wednesday, July 15, in an effort to quell the riot, officials informed the press that the insurrection had passed its peak.

This announcement, plus the entry into the city that day of thousands of war-trained veterans, the 74th National Guard, the 26th Michigan, the 152d New York Volunteers and others, finally defused the draft rioters. The combined militia set up their positions and their howitzers, and they were a formidable force that soon demolished the remaining resistance in the city.

For three days, the siege played itself out, in a steadily decreasing spiral. Somewhere in the midst of it, someone at city hall issued a proclamation: "The Conscription Act is now suspended in New York and will not be enforced. The Board of Aldermen at a specially called meeting has voted $2,500,000 for all poor men to buy their way out of army service."

The mobs cheered and thought they had won. But within an hour, the proclamation was declared a hoax, and after a few desperate forays, the mob finally dispersed.

Martial law remained in place for a few days. The police combed poor areas to retrieve stolen items. The toll was never precisely counted, but it was concluded by the newspapers that 2,000 of the rioters had died, and from 8,000 to 10,000 had been wounded. These figures were probably low, because many of the dead and wounded were carried off and hidden.

Only a few police were listed as dead. Some 50 to 60 soldiers were killed, although there was never an official listing by the War Department. Three hundred soldiers were wounded. Seventy-six blacks were listed as "missing," which probably meant dead. Eighteen were lynched. Five were drowned in the Hudson and East rivers.

More than $5 million in property damage was reported, including the loss of the Colored Orphan Asylum, a Protestant mission, three provost marshall offices, three police stations, one armory and a score of factories and stores.

Later, armchair analysts dubbed the draft riots the "Roman Catholic Insurrection," because of the large number of immigrant Irishmen who were involved. But of course, it was not. It was an uprising against a conscription act that was perceived as being clearly discriminatory against the lower middle class and the poor.

UNITED STATES
OHIO
KENT

May 4, 1970

• • • • • • • • • • • • • • • •

Three days of demonstrations by students of Kent State University protesting the U.S. invasion of Cambodia climaxed, on May 4, 1970, in the killing of four students by Ohio National Guardsmen. Nine students were wounded, and the protest movement of college students in the United States lost its momentum.

The 1960s were a turbulent decade, marked by the assassinations of three major American leaders, the most unpopular war in U.S. history and an enormous upsurge in activism among the youth of the country. While the drug culture, spearheaded by Timothy Leary, was urging the flower children to "tune in; turn on; drop out," organizations such as the SDS (Students for a Democratic Society) were urging the youth of America to stand up for their beliefs, and not trust anyone over 30.

It was certainly a divided America. There were those who favored the war in Vietnam—a steadily decreasing number by 1970—and those who were vocally, vociferously against it. In 1968, President Lyndon Johnson had declined to run for president again in part because he did not want to defend further U.S. involvement in Vietnam.

But President Richard Nixon and his vice president, Spiro Agnew, were defenders of the war and foes of the antiwar demonstrators, whom they characterized as "malcontents," "bums," "hippies" and so forth, in spite of the fact that much of the American public had already wearied of a war whose moral justification seemed murky and whose end seemed to be nowhere in sight. Finally, in 1969, bowing to public pressure, the United States began to pull its troops out of Vietnam, while continuing to bomb Communist strongholds in Cambodia.

It was a peculiar way to end a war, and antiwar protests continued on campuses across the United States. On April 8, there were student disturbances in Cleveland, Ohio, and 952 National Guardsmen were called out to quiet them. On April 16 and 17, there were student demonstrations in Oxford, Ohio, and 561 National Guardsmen were called out there. The next day, in Sandusky, more student demonstrations erupted, and 96 National Guardsmen were called up. On April 29, there were rumors that the United States was about to invade Cambodia, and student demonstrations flared up all over the country. At Ohio State University, in Cleveland, it turned into a riot, and 2,861 National Guardsman were called in to quell it. Obviously, Governor James A. Rhodes was not averse to calling up the National Guard to quiet civil demonstrations.

On April 30, 1970, President Nixon appeared on television and announced the U.S. invasion of Cambodia. College campuses all over the country erupted with angry student demonstrations.

Kent State University, in Kent, Ohio, was no exception. Although a small and relatively quiet campus, it had its chapter of SDS, and some of its buildings had been taken over by rebellious students. Yippie leader Jerry Rubin had addressed the students in early April. A year earlier, the students had presented a list of demands to the administration of the university:

1. Abolish ROTC
2. Abolish the Liquid Crystals Institute
3. Abolish the Northeast Ohio Crime Laboratory
4. Abolish the Kent Law Enforcement Training Program.

On May 1, the day after Nixon's announcement, some students at Kent State held a campus ceremony in which they buried the Constitution of the United States. Not all of the campus population was happy about this, but some were fired up, not only by it, but by reports of huge demonstrations on other campuses against the Cambodian invasion.

By 8 o'clock that night, 1,000 of Kent State's 20,000 students had spilled into the streets of downtown Kent and were generally raising hell, climbing up on streetlights, stopping traffic and marching down streets and in and out of stores. Fires were set in the middle of streets. Forty-seven establishments had their windows broken. Mayor LeRoy Satrom, celebrating Law Day at a meeting in the Treadwell Inn in nearby Aurora, received the news badly. He drove swiftly back to Kent and conferred first with the town's police chief, Roy D. Thompson, and then clapped an 8:00 P.M. to 6 A.M. curfew on the town. Damage was first estimated at $100,000; then it was reduced to $50,000, then $16,000, and finally to $10,000. A few arrests were made, but the mayor was prompted to call Columbus and alert the National Guard. By 3:00 A.M., a National Guard officer was in town to assess the situation.

The next morning, May 2, the local *Kent-Courier* carried the following headline: "Nixon Hits Bums Who Blow up College Campuses." All day, the city of Kent was bombarded with false fire alarms, bomb threats and violent rumors. At 5:30 that afternoon, Mayor Satrom, afraid that the students would again invade downtown, called in the Ohio National Guard.

While all of this was going on, Robert White, the president of Kent State University, was in Mason City, Iowa, where he was scheduled to make a major address. It would be Sunday morning, May 3 before he would return.

That Saturday evening, the students set out to burn the rickety old ROTC building on campus. A relic of World War II, it was scheduled for razing anyway. But to the student activists, it symbolized U.S. involvement in Asia. By 8 o'clock, a sizable crowd of around 600 students began to throw rocks at the building. Witnesses later testified that 10 or 15 policemen probably could have stopped matters then and there, but there were none visible.

By 8:30, after several attempts to kindle the building failed, two young men (some said of high school age) entered it and really set it ablaze. A half hour later, the Kent volunteer fire department arrived, but students cut their hoses and roughed up some of the firemen, who then left the campus.

The crowd grew and other incidents erupted. A shed containing archery equipment was set afire. There was talk of setting the president's home ablaze, but it never happened.

Meanwhile, two National Guard generals, Sylvester De Corso and Robert Canterbury, arrived in Kent, and 1,196 Guardsmen, taken off duty in Akron where they were monitoring a teamster's strike, were on their way. By 10 o'clock, the Guard had arrived, and student rioters were again running amuck in downtown Kent. Their actions had become more bizarre and indefensible. Arsonists tried to set fire to various buildings. Rocks were thrown at Guardsmen. The atmosphere turned ugly.

Under the protection of the National Guard, the firemen returned to campus, but by now, the ROTC building was a smoldering wreck. Tear gas forced the students from downtown back to campus and their dormitories, and by midnight everything seemed to be under control. Thirty-one people had been arrested for violation of the curfew.

On Sunday morning, May 3, Governor Rhodes arrived in Kent to personally supervise the situation. He inflamed it, releasing public statements that accused student demonstrators of being "worse than the Brown Shirts and communist element and also the nightriders and the vigilantes. They're the worst type that we harbor in America."

The effect on the campus was depressing at best. There were rumors that the government was going to close the college down, and, indeed, it had been suggested.

But it did not happen, and that Sunday has been described as more like a carnival than anything else. Sightseers wandered onto the campus. Students and Guardsmen fraternized. One coed placed a flower in the muzzle of a Guardsman's gun.

But some members of the faculty were disturbed by the presence of the military on the campus and tried to have them removed. They did not succeed.

That night, the turning point in the confrontation was reached. At 7:00 P.M., students began to gather in groups on the campus. Some Molotov cocktails were found by campus police, and the Guard took up positions. Confrontations occurred, and the Guard threw tear gas again, driving some students back but also driving some 200 of them downtown. There the students were met with an armed tank.

They retreated, and might have gone back to the campus, but they met other students who had decided to sit down in the middle of town, in defiance of the curfew.

Everything escalated. The victory bell on campus began to ring. Helicopters with searchlights flew back and forth over the campus, spraying it with intense light. The Guardsmen fixed bayonets. Student leaders demanded a meeting with President White and Mayor Satrom. Although there had been no guarantees made to keep police and National Guardsmen off campus, a student with a bullhorn assured the crowd that guarantees had been offered, and when the National Guard moved in with fixed bayonets and attacked seven students, the student leaders yelled, "We've been betrayed!"

By 11:40, the Guard had secured the campus. But it was an armed truce.

And then, May 4, 1970 dawned. By 11:00 A.M., after some classes had been dismissed early because of the tensions on the campus, students began to gather. All outdoor demonstrations had been banned, although no martial law had officially been declared by Governor Rhodes (he would declare it, retroactively, after the shootings).

A rally had been called by student leaders for noon. An officer in a jeep tried unsuccessfully to break up the rally peacefully. At 12:00, General Canterbury gave the order to prepare to disperse the students. There were 113 Guardsman on campus at the time. There were approximately 1,100 students.

The Guardsmen began to move out, firing tear gas canisters as they went. The students again broke and ran, hurling the gas canisters, rocks and epithets at the Guardsmen. Waves of soldiers and students swept back and forth across the campus. Tear gas filled the air.

Suddenly, at 12:24 P.M., one group of Guardsmen stopped, wheeled and aimed their rifles at the students, who were some 200 yards away and therefore could not have possibly harmed the soldiers. One shot rang out; there was a period of silence for two seconds, and then a fusillade erupted. Sixty-seven shots were fired in the next 13 seconds, and when it all stopped, 13 bodies were scattered on the grass and the parking area beyond. One was dead; 12 were wounded, some fatally; some would be crippled for life. The closest victim was 71 feet from the National Guard; the farthest, 745 feet.

No one knows who started firing. Several officers frantically stopped it, and the Guard was moved instantly back to the ROTC area.

Horror had replaced confrontation. Jeff Miller, a student, was lying face down, the back of his head blown off, his blood spreading over the parking lot. Allison Krause, Sandra Scheuer and William Schroeder had all been wounded seriously. Ms. Krause, denied oxygen by an ambulance attendant, died on the way to the hospital, as did Sandra Scheuer. William Schroeder would die in the hospital from a chest wound.

On the campus, a terrible standoff developed. Three faculty members, Seymour H. Baron, Mike Lunine and Glenn Frank, became the peacemakers. They prevented an adamant general and a troop of frightened soldiers from causing more bloodshed; they talked reason back into the minds of the students, and a slaughter was averted.

Afterward, the reaction to the May 4 killings was sharply divided. There were those who were sickened by it. The Soviet poet Yevgeny Yevtushenko wrote a poem:

Allison Krause, you were killed because you loved
flowers
. . . Ah, how fragrant are the lilacs,
But you feel nothing.
As the president said of you,
you are a bum.
Each victim is a bum. But it is not his fault.

On the other hand, a Kentucky mother whose three sons attended Kent State and were there during the shooting spoke candidly and chillingly to a researcher for James Michener, who was compiling a book about the incident:

MOTHER:	Anyone who appears on the streets of a city like Kent with long hair, dirty clothes or barefooted deserves to be shot.
RESEARCHER:	Have I your permission to quote that?
MOTHER:	You sure do. It would have been better if the Guard had shot the whole lot of them that morning.
RESEARCHER:	But you had three sons there.
MOTHER:	If they didn't do what the Guards told them, they should have been mowed down.
PROFESSOR OF PSYCHOLOGY	(listening in): Is long hair a justification for shooting someone?
MOTHER:	Yes. We have got to clean up this nation. And we'll start with the long-hairs.
PROFESSOR:	Would you permit one of your sons to be shot simply because he went barefooted?
MOTHER:	Yes.
PROFESSOR:	Where did you get such ideas?
MOTHER:	I teach at the local high school.
PROFESSOR:	You mean you are teaching your students such things?
MOTHER:	Yes. I teach them the truth. That the lazy, the dirty, the ones you see walking the streets and doing nothing ought all to be shot.

The heart went out of student protests that day at Kent State. The war would wind down. Vice President Agnew would resign in disgrace, and President Nixon too would be forced to resign as a result of the Watergate scandal. But a numbed silence, as of the grave, would settle over the campuses of the nation.

UNITED STATES
WASHINGTON, D.C.

May 20–July 28, 1932

• • • • • • • • • • • • • • • • • •

World War I veterans, out of work during the Great Depression, marched on Washington, D.C. in May 1932 to demand that a bonus due them in 1945 be paid immediately. On July 28, an army unit led by General Douglas MacArthur cleared the veterans out and set fire to their encampments. One veteran was killed; scores were injured.

It was, for 20th century America, the worst of times. The stock market crash had spiraled the country downward into depression, and by the summer of 1932, there were more than eight and a half million people out of work.

Many of them were veterans of World War I, men who had fought well and selflessly for their country. They had been promised a bonus, totaling $2 billion, to be paid to them in 1945, when, it was presumed, they would be old enough to need it (this was before Social Security). However, with the country and many of its people in dire straits in 1932, Representative Wright Patman introduced a bill in Congress that would pay these veterans their bonus then rather than in 1945.

But as the congressional session lurched toward its summer recess, the proposal seemed to rest dead in the water. At the end of May, various informal contingents of veterans from all over America began funneling into Washington, hoping to prod Congress into passing the Patman bill.

They had their precedent. In the 1700s, unpaid members of the Continental Army had laid siege to Philadelphia until Congress met their demands. In 1932, the leaders of what would come to be known as the Bonus Expeditionary Force felt that a peaceful, orderly settling into Washington would produce the same effect.

The first contingent of approximately 1,300 men arrived on May 28, in 16 trucks, which were festooned with American flags and provided by the state of Maryland. The city of Washington had hot stew, bread, milk and coffee waiting for the arriving servicemen at a vacant government building on Pennsylvania Avenue. Superintendent of Police Pelham D. Glassford personally supervised the welcome, noting parenthetically that they would all have to vacate the premises within 48 hours.

But every day, for weeks, more and more veterans poured into the capital, as 48-hour deadlines were issued and ignored. It was all very low key and friendly, and General Glassford (he was a retired brigadier general and kept the title) managed to have army rolling kitchens set up to accommodate the new arrivals, who now occupied another vacant building and had begun to erect shanties on the banks of the Potomac. Eventually, their main camp would be located on the Anacostia River and would consist of a small village of slapped together lean-tos, shacks and tents.

Congress reacted with anxiety. Some senators and representatives were sympathetic but concerned about the source of the bonus; others were hostile enough to call the

Members of the "bonus army" of World War I veterans gather outside one of their makeshift dwellings in Washington, D.C. in the summer of 1932. Shortly afterward, a U.S. Army unit led by General Douglas MacArthur routed the protesters and set fire to their encampment. Library of Congress

veterans Communists. (There *was* one contingent of Communists, but the other veterans disowned them, forbidding red flags to be flown and chanting "Eyes front, not left" as they sometimes marched from encampments to the Capitol.)

Senator Carl Lewis of Illinois delivered an address at the National Old Soldiers Home in which he fulminated, "If the veterans persist in terroristic tactics, they will endanger their chances of receiving any favorable treatment whatsoever."

In truth, the burgeoning bonus army could not have been more peaceful. Although some had engaged in violence in commandeering freight trains to get to Washington, once there, they settled docilely in.

By June 4, there were several thousand veterans in Washington, and food supplies were running out. The District commissioners offered trucks to transport the marchers 50 miles from the city. The veterans politely refused.

By June 7, the army had swelled to 7,000, and a parade was planned to demand that the $2.4 billion bonus be paid. "If we have to stay until 1945, we will," said one veteran.

During the next week, families began to arrive, and food was sent from the home states of many of the veterans' companies. Morale was high in the Expeditionary Force, but the patience of the federal government was dwindling. On June 9, Dr. William Fowler, the District health officer, and Dr. James G. Cumming toured the camp on the edge of the Potomac and concluded that the camps constituted the "gravest health menace in the history of the District of Columbia." Dr. Fowler called the situation "frightful," pointing to the presence of insects and the fact that many of the veterans were suffering from exposure and malnutrition.

Still, the army grew, at the rate of 100 men an hour. By June 11, there were 15,000 ex-servicemen camped throughout Washington, and the District authorities confessed that they could no longer handle the problem. It was up to the federal government to take a hand.

June 17 was the day the Senate chose to debate and vote on the Patman bonus bill. The galleries were packed with veterans. The plaza before the Capitol building bulged with 10,000 men. For weeks they had petitioned and met with their representatives. There was no doubt in Congress about the determination of this army.

However, at 8:20 P.M. on June 17, the Senate voted down the Patman Bill, 62 to 18. There was a collective groan from the gallery, and outside, in the plaza, after the results of the vote were announced, there was a momentary ripple of anger and a movement toward the outer fringes of the gathering.

W. W. Walters of Oregon, the elected leader of the army, and his associates calmed the crowd, blowing bugles for formation to march back to the camps. "Go back to your camps," shouted Walters. "We are not telling you to go home. We are going to stay in Washington until we get the bonus, no matter how long it takes. And we are 100 times as good Americans as those men who voted against it. We are just asking you to obey the law and not antagonize the authorities."

On July 2, the army returned to the Capitol steps, protesting the adjournment of Congress without reconsidering the bill, and vowing to remain until it was passed, no matter how long it would take. On July 4, it staged a parade down Pennsylvania Avenue.

As July wore on and the humid summer heat seeped down into the camps and buildings, some veterans returned home. But thousands stayed on. They had no place to go and no jobs. They decided to stick it out.

By the end of July, President Herbert Hoover, who had ordered the gates to the White House chained, now decreed that the bonus army be cleared from Washington.

On the morning of July 28, 1932, General Glassford and his police proceeded to march into the camps and gently remove the veterans, who resisted. It was obvious that the police could not do it alone, and shortly after 2 P.M., Hoover ordered a unit of the U.S. Army, under the command of General Douglas MacArthur, to clear the camps. MacArthur and his forces marched down Pennsylvania Avenue with four troops of cavalry, four companies of infantry, a machine gun squadron and several tanks.

The veterans cheered them, as did a large crowd of spectators gathered at the curb. Suddenly, the army unit charged. Cavalrymen rode pell-mell into the crowd, swinging sabers over their heads. Infantrymen tossed tear gas bombs. Men, women and children, veterans and spectators alike were trampled.

The troops moved on, scattering civilians and veterans, throwing tear gas indiscriminately. The peaceful protest had been transformed into a bloody confrontation. On the steps of one of the vacant, veteran-occupied federal buildings, a policeman was hit by a brick tossed from an upper story. He drew his revolver and fired two shots into the crowd, killing one man, William Hashka, an unemployed veteran from Illinois. Other police officers drew their guns; General Glassford shouted to them to put away their firearms, which they did, but not before pointing them directly at him.

Meanwhile, the army unit, under the orders of General MacArthur, who was acting in direct opposition to his orders from the president, began to burn the shacks of the Anacostia camp. He encountered no resistance. Veterans helped his soldiers torch their own Hooverville. The Washington sky was a bright orange all night as the camps of the bonus army were destroyed, and their inhabitants wandered into the streets, joining the larger army of the unemployed of the Great Depression. By midnight, the forced evacuation was complete.

President Hoover issued a statement, in which he asserted: "An examination of a large number of names discloses the fact that a considerable part of those remaining are not veterans; many are Communists and persons with criminal records."

He tried to soften this by adding, "The veterans amongst these numbers are no doubt unaware of the character of their companions and are being led into violence which no government can tolerate."

But the violence had not occurred until the army ordered by Hoover himself arrived on the scene. It was a case of misjudgment, one among many that would, to a large degree, account for Hoover's defeat at the polls by Franklin D. Roosevelt in November 1932.

• • • • • • • • • • • • • • • •

KEY TO MAJOR TERRORIST ORGANIZATIONS

• • • • • • • • •

AFRICA

South Africa

ANC (African National Congress)

Formed to fight for freedom from white domination in South Africa.

EUROPE

France

Action Directe

Anti-NATO group.

ALNC Armee de liberation nationale corse (Corsican National Liberation Army)
Employed bomb attacks against France in cause of Corsican independence.

Germany

Baader-Meinhof Gang
Urban guerrillas named after Andreas Baader and Ulrike Meinhof, their leaders.

RAF (Red Army Faction)
Present form of Baader-Meinhof Gang, merged with second June Movement, named after date on which a student was shot in West Berlin demonstration.

Greece

November 17
Named in memory of date of student uprising in 1973 against colonels' regime.

Ireland

IRA (Irish Republican Army)
Traditional guerrilla and terrorist group dedicated to unification of Ireland.

PIRA (Provisional Irish Republican Army)
Extremist terrorist group within IRA that has taken over completely and is now solely responsible for terrorism in Northern Ireland and British Isles.

Italy

Red Brigades
Leftist terrorist group.

Spain

ETA Basque Homeland and Liberty
Separatist organizaiton founded in 1959.

FAR EAST

India

All India Sikh Students Federation
Followers of Sant Jarnail Singh Bhindranwale, killed in Amritsar massacre.

Japan

JRA (Japanese Red Army)
Active at home and internationally with Palestinian groups.

LATIN AMERICA

Brazil

ALN (National Liberating Action)
Left-wing terrorist group based in Brazil.

MR-8 (October 8 Revolutionary Movement).
Left-wing terrorist group based in Brazil.

Colombia

M19 (April 19 Movement)
Colombian terrorist organization.

El Salvador

FMLN (Farabunde Marti National Liberation Front)
Antigovernmental groups in El Salvador.

MIDDLE EAST

Abu Nidal Faction
Breakaway from Fatah; based in Libya; responsible for attacks in Europe.

Al-Borkan (The Volcano)
Anti-Qaddafi group; the terrorist wing of the National Front for the Salvation of Libya.

Al Dawa (The Call)
Shiites, mostly Iraqis hostile to Assad regime and supporters of Khomeini.

Fatah
Fatah is Yassir Arafat's power base in the Palestine Liberation Organization (see below) and devotes itself to what he refers to as "the armed struggle."

Force 17
Originally bodyguard of PLO leader Yassir Arafat; conducts raids on Israeli targets.

Grey Wolves
Turkish terrorist group; nationalist and fascist.

Hezbollah (The Party of God)
Lebanese Shiites; part of Islamic Jihad; supported by Iran in order to establish Islamic republic in Lebanon.

Iraqi Islamic Revolution
Tehran-based; opposes President Saddam Hussein of Iraq.

Islamic Amal (Islamic Hope)
Lebanese Shiites.

Islamic Jihad (Islamic Holy War)
Umbrella organization uniting Lebanese, Iranian and Iraqi terrorist groups dedicated to making war on West and installing Shiite Islamic Revolution throughout Middle East.

PLO (Palestine Liberation Organization)
Umbrella for various Palestinian groups, terrorist and otherwise; avowed spokesperson for Palestinians.

PFLP-GC (Popular Front for the Liberation of Palestine—General Command)
Operating under Syrian government orders, headed by Ahmed Jibril; totally terrorist organization.

Palestine Liberation Front
Splinter group of General Command, split itself into three groups: pro-Syrian (commander: Abdul Ghanem); pro-PFLP (commander: Talaat Yaquib); pro-Arafat (commander: Abu Abbas).

UNITED STATES

Alpha 66
Miami-based Cuban exile group, engaged in sabotage, assassination, invasions of Cuba.

CFF (Croation Freedom Fighters)
Separatist group.

FALN (Armed Forces of Puerto Rican National Liberation)
Nationalist guerrilla group.

JDL (Jewish Defense League)
Counterterrorist group attacking Arabs in United States.

Omega 7
Anti-Castro Cuban group based in United States.

SLA (Symbionese Liberation Army)
See Weathermen.

Weathermen (The Weather Underground Organization)
Terrorist organization that preaches solidarity with ethnic minorities.

TERRORISM

• • • • • • • • • •

BRAZIL
RIO DE JANEIRO

September 9, 1969

• • • • • • • • • • • • • • • •

Members of Brazil's ALN and MR-8, demanding the release of 15 political prisoners, kidnapped U.S. ambassador Charles Elbrick on September 9, 1969. The prisoners were freed, and so was Ambassador Elbrick.

The first in a long line of diplomatic kidnappings occurred on September 9, 1969 in Rio de Janeiro, Brazil at 2 P.M., as U.S. ambassador Charles Elbrick's limousine slowly pulled up to his home on Marquis Street.

The kidnappers, members of Brazil's two most extreme, left-wing terrorist groups, the National Liberating Action (ALN) and the October Eight Revolutionary Movement (MR-8), had been waiting all morning in two Volkswagens. Now, the two Volkswagens lurched from the curb and blocked the street, while three unobtrusive loiterers advanced on the limousine with drawn pistols.

They entered the car, held the ambassador at gunpoint and ordered the chauffeur to drive to a nearby, secluded dead-end street. There the ambassador was hustled into a microbus that was parked, its engine running. The microbus sped off at breakneck speed for an unknown destination, leaving, on the seat of the Cadillac, a ransom note. It contained two demands: first, the publication of a 1,000-word document denouncing Brazil's military regime, and second, the release of 15 political prisoners. If the demands were not met within 48 hours, the note trumpeted, "We will be compelled to mete out revolutionary justice."

While the Brazilian government and American representatives mulled this over, they were directed to a second note that was left in a box at a church in downtown Rio. In Elbrick's handwriting it read: "Hurry to meet the conditions for my release."

The Brazilian government agreed to the demands. A few hours later, a note from Elbrick in a Rio supermarket announced that he would be freed as soon as the liberated prisoners arrived safely in Mexico City.

"If they get away with it in Rio," said one American Foreign Service Officer to *U.S. News and World Report,* "no diplomat will be safe anywhere in the world."

They did, and the prophecy would come true. Elbrick was returned safely, and the political prisoners were freed. The pattern had been set, and from 1969 onward, political kidnappings would continue to occur, often with more tragic results.

GERMANY
MUNICH

September 5, 1972

• • • • • • • • • • • • • • •

Israel's Olympic team was captured in Munich's Olympic Village on September 5, 1972 by Black September terrorists seeking to free political prisoners. A bungled rescue attempt by German authorities ended in the deaths of all 11 athletes and three terrorists.

There will hopefully never be another session of the Olympic Games remotely like that which occurred in September 1972 in Munich, Bavaria.

One of the objects of the Games was to contrast the Nazi Germany of 1936—the last time the Games were held there—with the prosperous, democratized West Germany of the 1970s. Instead, they would be interrupted by the horrible massacre of 11 of Israel's top athletes.

Until the fearful events of September 5, the XX Olympiad had been an enormous success. More records had toppled than in any other Olympiad to date.

But while this was occurring, Black September, a fanatical splinter group in Fatah, the PLO fighting unit that drew its recruits from other Palestinian groups working under the PLO umbrella, was planning a dramatic kidnapping plot that would publicize its cause to the world. The week before the Olympics began, several Black September members, bearing a veritable arsenal of Russian-built Kalashnikov submachine guns, pistols and hand grenades, set out for Munich.

Once in Munich, they spread out, and a number of them got jobs among the 30,000 temporary employees of the Olympic Village.

At 4:20 A.M. on the morning of September 5, 1972, two terrorists, wearing sports warm-up suits and carrying athletic equipment, scaled the six-and-one-half-foot fence surrounding the village. Two telephone linemen saw them but thought little of it. They were, as far as they knew, a couple of Olympic athletes who had broken the curfew and were sneaking back to their quarters.

In total, there were eight Black September members within the compound. Pausing momentarily outside the athletic quarters, they either blackened their faces with charcoal or pulled on ski masks and made their way to the Olympic Village apartments that housed 22 Israeli athletes, coaches and officials. Two of them knocked on one door, inquiring, in German, "Is this the Israeli team?" Wrestling coach Moshe Weinberg opened the door a crack, saw the masked gunmen, flung himself against the door and shouted to his roommates to flee. Immediately, Weinberg was riddled by a burst of submachine gunfire through the door. He died on the spot.

Simultaneously, in the other apartments, similar scenarios were being played out. In one, Yosef Gottfreund, an impressively tall wrestling referee, tried to hold off invading terrorists and was knifed to death.

Altogether, 18 Israeli athletes scrambled through windows to safety. Nine who did not make it were bound hand and foot in groups of three and pushed together onto a bed in one of the apartments. As hostages, they would be the bartering chips for the terrorists.

By 6 A.M., Munich police had been alerted, and 600 of them surrounded the area. An ambulance removed Weinberg's body, which had been dragged to a terrace and left by the gunmen.

Police Chief Manfred Schreiber attempted to brazen his way into the apartments. He was met by the group's leader, wearing a white tennis hat and sunglasses. For a moment, it seemed possible for Schreiber to take him hostage, and then, according to Schreiber, the man asked, "Do you want to take me?" He opened his hand and showed a hand grenade to the police chief. The terrorist's thumb was on the grenade's pin.

At 9 A.M., a message in English was tossed from a window. On it was a list of 200 prisoners currently held in Israeli jails. They included Ulrike Meinhof and Andreas Baader, the leaders of a gang of German terrorists who had robbed eight banks, bombed U.S. Army posts and killed three policemen before they were captured the previous June, and Kozo Okamoto, a Japanese Red Army terrorist who took part in the massacre at Tel Aviv's Lod Airport in which 26 people died (see p. 105). All were to be freed, according to the note, before the Israeli athletes would be released.

Furthermore, the Palestinians demanded that they and their prisoners be flown out of West Germany to any Arab nation except Lebanon or Jordan, aboard three airplanes that would leave at agreed upon intervals. Officials had three hours to comply. If they did not, the hostages would be executed at the rate of two every thirty minutes.

International phone lines hummed. West German Interior Minister Hans Dietrich Genscher took personal charge of the negotiations, first offering an unlimited sum of money for the release of the hostages and then offering himself and other West German officials as hostages in place of the athletes. Although he was turned down, he was able to stall for time by stating that he was in touch with Israeli authorities. There were two extensions of the deadline, the first to 3 P.M., the next to 5 P.M.

Meanwhile, 15 volunteer police sharpshooters were brought into the area, and worldwide television coverage showed them crouching in readiness until German authorities realized that the terrorists could also tune them in, at which point they ceased the TV coverage.

The games were suspended at 3:45 P.M. that afternoon, after a request from Israel. By that time, Willie Brandt, West Germany's chancellor, had made the decision to permit the terrorists to fly out of West Germany with the hostages. Speaking of the athletes, Brandt said to newspeople later, "We are responsible for the fate of these people."

By 6 P.M., Genscher had run out of stalling tactics. He was told by Brandt that the Palestinians and their hostages would be taken to Munich's airport and flown out on a Lufthansa 727 jet to any place they named. The terrorists selected Cairo, and a 7 P.M. deadline was set.

In actuality, the Germans were moving their sharpshooters to Furstenfeldbruck Field, and the Arabs were planning a destination other than Cairo.

At 10 P.M., 18 hours after the initial assault, the terrorists herded their prisoners, tied together in single file and blindfolded, out of the building and into a German army bus, which drove them through a tunnel under the village to a lawn 275 yards away.

The green expanse had been converted into a helicopter pad. There were three helicopters there; two took the terrorists and their hostages on the 25-minute ride to Furstenfeldbruck airport; the third went ahead, carrying German officials and Israeli intelligence officers.

The airport was ringed by 500 soldiers. But there were only five sharpshooters to pick off eight terrorists. The rest had unexplainably been left behind at the Olympic Village.

The helicopters landed. The terrorists leaped out and took the German crews hostage. They arranged them in front of their helicopters and proceeded to inspect the 727.

As they walked toward it, the police sharpshooters opened fire. The two Arabs guarding the helicopter crews were killed, and one of the pilots was wounded. One more guerrilla on the tarmac died. The leader dove under a helicopter, fired back and knocked out the floodlights on the field and the radio in the control tower. A Munich police sergeant was gunned down.

The battle would rage for an hour more. Five guerrillas, including their leader, would be killed, and three would surrender. And every one of the hostages would be killed. One group of four was burned to death when a terrorist tossed a grenade into the helicopter in which they were being held. The remaining five would be machine-gunned by their captors.

It would be four hours before the horrendous results of the failed ambush would reach the outside world. Reaction from the Arab world would be divided. Lebanon would offer condolences to Israel. Egypt would charge that German bullets killed them all.

In coming days, Israeli retaliation was swift and fierce. On the eve of Rosh Hashanah, Israeli jets struck Lebanon and Syria with the heaviest strikes since the 1967 war. Arab sources later said that 66 were killed in the raids by 75 jets. Israeli ground troops crossed the Lebanese border to battle commandos who had been mining roads in Israel. Syria put its army on alert. Meanwhile, in Libya, Colonel Qaddafi conducted a martyr's funeral for the dead terrorists.

The three surviving Arabs would be tried and imprisoned, but in November they would be released in exchange for a Lufthansa airliner hijacked in Beirut by other Black September terrorists. In Tripoli, Colonel Qadaffi would give the three a hero's welcome and parade.

GREAT BRITAIN
ENGLAND
LONDON

December 17, 1983

• • • • • • • • • • • • • • • • •

Continuing IRA terrorism attacks on British citizens resulted in the explosion of a car bomb planted by the Provisional IRA during the Christmas shopping season, on December 17, 1983. Six were killed; 94 were wounded.

It was Dalthi O'Connell, one of the founders of the Irish Republican Army, who is credited with inventing the car bomb, the stock-in-trade of terrorists worldwide. By 1983, the Provisional IRA had much experience with setting car bombs, and it was one such device that accounted for the Christmas carnage of Harrods department store in London on December 17, 1983.

There had been warnings issued, via radio, television and newspapers, of possible IRA bombings during the holiday season. Scotland Yard intelligence reports from Northern Ireland had warned of "a Christmas blitz."

At approximately 12:40 P.M. on December 17, the phone rang at the Samaritans, a voluntary charity organization in London. A distinctly Irish-accented voice announced, "Car bomb outside Harrods. Two bombs in Harrods."

The Samaritans called Scotland Yard, and at 1:15 a team of police, including animal handlers and trained dogs, arrived on the scene. They went to work in the store first, trying to trace down the interior bombs, while other police conducted a search of cars on the streets surrounding the giant store. The last Saturday before Christmas, thousands of shoppers jammed the store and the sidewalks surrounding it.

At exactly 1:20, a car not checked by the police suddenly exploded with a thunderous, earsplitting roar. Black smoke and shrapnel erupted as if they had been launched from a volcano. The concussion shattered windows for blocks and instantly killed five shoppers and a policeman. Other unsuspecting pedestrians and shoppers were injured, some horribly, by rainstorms of glass and metal.

Ninety-four would be injured; six would die. Those responsible for the bomb would never be captured.

GREAT BRITAIN
SCOTLAND
LOCKERBIE

December 21, 1988

• • • • • • • • • • • • • • • • •

No clear-cut responsibility was established for the midair terrorist bomb explosion aboard Pan Am Flight 103 from London to New York on December 21, 1988. Two hundred fifty-six people on board the plane and 11 on the ground were killed in the fiery crash.

Pan Am Flight 103, a Boeing 747, took off from London's Heathrow Airport 25 minutes behind schedule, at 6:25 P.M., on December 21, 1988. Aboard were 246 passengers and 10 crew members, among them 35 of 38 Syracuse University students who had been studying abroad and were returning home for Christmas, and Brent Carisson of Sweden, the chief administrative officer of the United Nations' Council for Namibia. Carisson was flying to New York for the signing of an accord on Namibian independence.

Fifty-two minutes later, while Flight 103 was flying at an altitude of 31,000 feet over the small village of Lockerbie, in the extreme southern end of Scotland, a bomb, planted in a tape recorder and radio in the plane's luggage compartment, exploded. The main part of the airplane dropped like a flaming missile, landing near a gas station on the outskirts of Lockerbie, setting fire to the station, a dozen row houses and several cars that were on the A74 highway to Glasgow.

Other pieces of the liner and some bodies were strewn over the countryside in an 80-mile-long arc. It was the worst airline crash in British history, and the worst single plane crash in Pan Am's history. The BBC broadcast horrendous pictures of raging fires, devastated houses and cars and shreds of aircraft wreckage. "The plane came down 400 yards from my house," said Bob Glaster, a retired policeman, to reporters. "There was a ball of fire 300 feet into the air, and debris was falling from the sky. When the smoke cleared a little, I could see bodies lying on the road. At least one dozen houses were destroyed."

The terrible part of the tragedy was that Pan Am and government agencies had been warned of the possibility of the bombing in ample time to prevent it and had been unable to accomplish this. One week before the bombing, the American Embassy in Finland had received a notice saying that an unidentified caller had warned that "there would be a bombing attempt against a Pan American aircraft flying from Frankfurt to the United States." Flight 103 had originated in Frankfurt, on a 727 with the same flight number. In London, at Heathrow Airport, passengers and baggage had been transferred to the larger 747 for the longer leg of the journey to New York.

Later investigation revealed that there was, indeed, increased surveillance of passengers boarding the craft and that embassy personnel scheduled to board the flight were warned of the threat, and many canceled their reservations. The general public was *not* warned, and this would make headlines in the United States, particularly in light of later disclosures (see below).

For many months, because of the plastic nature of the explosive, blame was directed toward two anti-Arafat Palestinian terrorist groups, the PFLP General Command, led by Ahmed Jabril, and the Fatah Revolutionary Council, led by Abu Nidal. Later investigation by Scotland Yard, however, led to the conclusion that the initial investigation linked the bombing to the Iranian callers, or, some speculated, at least a terrorist group sympathetic to Iran.

In November 1990 it was revealed that the U.S. Drug Enforcement Agency regularly used Pan Am Flight 103 to fly informants and suitcases of heroin from the Middle East to Detroit. Nazir Khalid Jafaar, of Detroit, was aboard this flight and involved in this operation.

Pan Am's baggage operation in Frankfurt, it was further revealed, was used to put suitcases of heroin on planes, apparently without the usual security checks, under an arrangement between the drug agency and German authorities. Thus, it was eminently possible that Jafaar, who was either an agent or an informer for the DEA, was the unwitting carrier of the bomb that destroyed Flight 103 and killed 256 people in the air and 11 on the ground on the night of December 21, 1988.

Later information refuted this and intimated that the bomb was planted by Libyan terrorists in retaliation for the 1986 attack on Colonel Muammer el-Qaddafi by American jets. This line of investigation ultimately led to the demand, by Great Britain and the United States, for the extradition for trial of two Libyans, Lamen Khalifa Fhimah and Abdel Basset Ali al-Megrahi. The two, the investigation concluded, had planted the bomb responsible for the crash of Pan Am 103.

The two powers took the charges to the United Nations Security Council in early 1992, asking for sanctions against Libya if Colonel Qaddafi did not turn over the two agents. In March 1992, the Security Council passed Resolution 731, ordering Libya to surrender the two men for prosecution in Britain and the United States and also surrender evidence that could be used against them.

Colonel Qaddafi refused, then agreed to turn them over to representatives of the Arab League, then changed his mind again. In late March, the United Nations Security Council gave the colonel two weeks to conform to Resolution 731 or face sanctions that would cease air travel into and out of that country and severely reduce Libya's diplomatic presence in the rest of the world. As this is written, Colonel Qaddafi's reply was to threaten to cut back on oil exports to various countries sympathetic to the UN resolution.

Even if the two terrorists were handed over, experts and family members of those who perished in the crash announced that this would be settling only a small part of the crime. International politics—specifically, the role of Syria in the Persian Gulf War—were preventing investigators from acting on what they knew about the entire operation, these critics and family members charged. President George Bush's statement that Syria had received a "bum rap" simply did not square with the facts, they noted.

In a statement to *New York Times* columnist A. M. Rosenthal, on March 30, 1992, Steven Emerson, the Washington journalist who, with Brian Duffy, wrote *The Fall of Pan Am 103* in 1990, said:

> *The undisputed intelligence shows that Syria-based and -supported terrorists, led by Ahmed Jabril, head of the Popular Front for the Liberation of Palestine—General Command, planned and organized multiple airplane bombings against U.S., European and Israeli airlines in October 1988.*
>
> *The money and orders for the operation came from Iran, seeking revenge for the shooting down of the Iranian airbus that summer by the U.S. According to intelligence officials, Iranian officials traveled to Germany to oversee the operation and to personally witness the transfer of explosives and bombs.*
>
> *But the plan went awry when Syrian-based terrorists were arrested by German police in late October 1988. Jabril, who had received funding from Libya for at least the previous two years, handed off the operation to Libya, which had its own terrorist infrastructure in place.*

Thus the sequence of events as reconstructed by international investigators: Iran bankrolled it. Syrian-based terrorists planned it. Libyans executed it.

The reason that Pan Am 103 was chosen? According to Vincent Cannistraro, who headed the CIA investigation of the crash until he left the agency in 1990, the Jabril group settled on Pan Am because its surveillance indicated that in Frankfurt the airline was not "reconciling" baggage fully. That is, it was not making sure that every piece of luggage "was identified directly with a passenger before being taken on board."

As this goes to press, nobody has been brought to trial or held accountable in a court of law for the bombing of Pan Am Flight 103.

IRAN
TEHRAN

November 4, 1979—January 20, 1981

• • • • • • • • • • • • • • • • • •

The need for the Ayatollah Khomeini to galvanize anti-Western, pro-Islamic loyalty was the root cause of the taking of the U.S. Embassy in Tehran and the imprisonment of 52 hostages for 444 days.

At a few minutes before 11 A.M. on November 4, 1979, 400 young Iranian "students," later learned to be members of the Revolutionary Guard, cut through chains that joined together the gates of the American Embassy in Tehran, Iran. The Iranian guards stationed at the gates offered no resistance, and the invading crowd soon swarmed over the embassy compound.

It seemed at first to be a mirror image of other temporary embassy takeovers that had occurred in the world in the previous months, and President Jimmy Carter, spending Sunday at Camp David, Maryland, did not even return to Washington when informed of the break-in.

But by the next day, it became apparent to the president and the world that this was a move without precedent. Bound and blindfolded hostages were paraded before angry crowds chanting death to the Great Satan, America.

A year earlier, Shah Mohammad Reza Pahlavi had been deposed by revolutionary forces spurred on by Iran's spiritual leader, the Ayatollah Khomeini. The shah had fled to Mexico, and two weeks before the break-in at the American Embassy in Tehran he had flown to New York, where he was undergoing treatment for cancer. The "students" demanded that the deposed shah be returned to Iran for trial.

The United States refused, and thus began one of the longest standoffs in history. For the next 444 days, a tug of war would pit Iran against the United States, with the hostages as the pawns in the game.

Two weeks after the takeover of the embassy, the militants released 13 hostages—eight black men and five women—who returned to the United States in time for Thanksgiving of that year. The shah's health improved, and Mexico, not wishing to become involved in the U.S.-Iran standoff, refused to let him return. He fled to Panama, where he remained in exile, despite Iran's demands.

That Christmas, the White House tree remained dark out of respect for the hostages, and Americans, using the words of a popular song as their cue, began to tie yellow ribbons around trees, where they would shred and fade until the hostages would finally be set free.

At year's end, 1979, three American clergymen were permitted to hold Christmas services for most of the hostages. The International Court of Justice at The Hague unanimously called for their immediate release, and the secretary general of the United Nations, Kurt Waldheim, went to Tehran to try to mediate the standoff. He was denied meetings with either the hostages or the ayatollah, and his car was mobbed and beaten on by demonstrators.

In mid-January, American television crews and correspondents were expelled from Iran, but by late that month, some hope was held out by the newly elected president of Iran, Abolhassan Bani-Sadr, who criticized the militants and promised to try to calm the situation.

Later that month, six American diplomats who had been hidden in the Canadian Embassy escaped using forged Canadian passports. It was the first good news from Iran in three months.

In February, Bani-Sadr announced that the hostages might be released without the return of the shah, but this hope was dashed quickly by the ayatollah, who refused to allow a United Nations commission to see the hostages.

As winter gave way to spring, President Carter's approval rating began to drop. He was up for reelection the following November, and the hostage crisis was eroding the president's chances for a second term in office. Something had to be done to break the deadlock.

On the day after Easter, President Carter formally broke off diplomatic relations with Iran, ordered all Iranian diplomats out of the United States within 24 hours, asked Congress to allow Americans to settle claims against Iran on the $8 billion in Iranian assets that the government had frozen following the embassy takeover, and announced a trade embargo on Iran. Later that month, he also banned travel to Iran by all Americans except journalists, who had been recently readmitted.

On April 25, the United States government launched a dramatic attempt to rescue the hostages. But in a tangle of confusion and mismanagement, the raid dissolved in ignominious failure. Three of the eight helicopters assigned to the mission dropped out with mechanical failure (they were the wrong kind of machine for the Iranian desert). Without them, the mission was canceled, but not before one of the remaining helicopters collided on the ground with a C-130 transport plane, sending both up in flames. Eight servicemen died in the fire, and the rest fled, leaving the charred bodies of their comrades in the sand of the Iranian desert, 250 miles short of Tehran, their destination.

It was the worst fiasco since the CIA-bungled Bay of Pigs invasion of Cuba in 1961. President Carter would be permanently damaged by the incident. Secretary of State Cyrus Vance, who had opposed the raid from the very first, resigned and was replaced by Edmund Muskie.

In early July 1980, Richard I. Queen, one of the hostages who was suffering from multiple sclerosis, was released. This left 54 still in captivity.

On July 27, the shah died in Egypt of the final effects of his cancer. Now the ayatollah went on Iranian radio and read off a new list of conditions: return of the shah's wealth, cancellation of U.S. claims against Iran, unblocking of Iranian assets frozen in America and a pledge by Washington not to interfere in Iranian affairs. It was a list designed to humble a major power before the resolve and strength of the ayatollah.

But the events of history blunted even the power of the spiritual leader of Iran. A full-scale war broke out between Iran and Iraq as the U.S. elections drew near. The hostages faded from the front pages of the world's newspapers. Behind the scenes, the United States knew that Iran was strapped for spare parts and ammunition. It was also aware that Iran felt that it might be able to gain concessions from a president fighting for reelection.

The United States pledged neutrality in the Iran-Iraq war and hinted that if the hostages were freed, some Iranian assets would be unfrozen and more than $500 million worth of spare parts already purchased by Iran would be delivered.

There was a flurry of rumors, climaxing in the week before the election, that an agreement was imminent. But the ayatollah, as was his pattern, again dashed hopes on the eve of election day, 1980, which was the first anniversary of the hostage seizure.

Jimmy Carter lost the election by a landslide to Ronald Reagan, and the day after, President Carter asserted that the 11th-hour developments in the hostage crisis had been the primary cause of his defeat.

During his final weeks in office, President Carter and his administration, using Algeria as an intermediary, haggled with Iran over the hostages. For the second year, he ordered the Christmas tree at the White House to remain dark, but, responding to a request from the hostages' families, he lit it on Christmas Eve for 417 seconds, one for each day of their captivity.

On Christmas Day, three Iranian Christian clergymen and the papal nuncio held religious services for the hostages, and negotiations resumed. Iran conceded that its claim of $14 billion in frozen assets was high and accepted the U.S. figure of $9.5 billion, of which approximately $2.5 billion was subject to legal claims.

Iran's minister for executive affairs, in a speech to the Iranian parliament, probably put his finger on the real reason for the agreement. "The hostages are like a fruit from which all the juice has been squeezed out," he said. "Let us let them all go."

Thus, at 12:25 P.M. on January 20, 1981, just as the newly elected president, Ronald Reagan, was finishing his inaugural address, an Algerian Airlines 727 lifted off from Mehrabad Airport in Tehran with 54 hostages aboard. "God is Great! Death to America!" chanted the men who had brought the hostages to the airport. As the plane left Iranian airspace, nearly $3 billion of Iranian assets were unfrozen by the United States, and more was made available for Iranian repayment loans. The next day, $8 billion of Iranian assets would be funneled into the Bank of England in a special Algerian account accessible to Iran.

The purpose of the ayatollah had been served. He had humbled a great Western power and had arguably sent an American president down to defeat at the polls.

"With thanks to Almighty God," said Ronald Reagan at an inaugural luncheon, "I have been given a tag line, the get-off line, that everyone wants for the end of a toast or a speech, or anything else."

"I doubt that at any time in our history," said Jimmy Carter from his home in Georgia, "more prayers have reached heaven for any Americans than have those given to God in the last 14 months."

IRELAND
IRISH SEA

June 22, 1985

• • • • • • • • • • • • • • • • • •

On June 22, 1985, a bomb planted by Sikh extremists exploded in an Air India 747 over the Irish Sea. All 329 aboard died in this, the first downing of a jumbo jet by a terrorist bomb.

On June 6, 1984, a violent confrontation took place between Sikhs and Hindus at the Golden Temple in Amritsar, in the Punjab region of India. One thousand two hundred were killed that day when the Indian Army raided the temple, among them Bhai Amrik Singh, a former president of the Sikh Student Federation, a militant terrorist organization that had been outlawed by the Indian government. Leaders vowed revenge, and although a lack of physical evidence precluded positive proof, it is generally accepted that it was the Sikh Student Federation that was responsible for the planting of a bomb that blew an Air India 747 to pieces over the Irish Sea on June 22, 1985.

The flight, bound for London, took off uneventfully from Toronto on the evening of June 21. At 8 A.M. the following morning, air controllers at Shannon Airport made contact with the crew of the flight as it entered Irish airspace. Clearance was given to proceed to London.

And then, at 8:15, the airplane disappeared from Shannon's radar screens. No distress signal was radioed by the jet's captain, Commander Narendra. The flight merely disappeared in an instant.

Rescue boats and helicopters were dispatched immediately. It was a bone-chilling morning, with clouds at 500 feet and heavy rain, and at first it was thought that perhaps a freak of weather had caused the crash. But this was rejected summarily by rescuers, who noted that pieces of the airplane were scattered over a five-square-mile area, indicating that the plane had exploded long before it hit the sea.

None of the bodies recovered from the water were wearing life jackets, indicating that the explosion occurred without warning, and no piece of wreckage was larger than 30 square feet, indicating that the detonation must have been enormous.

That very day, the *New York Times* received a telephone call from a member of the 10th Regiment of the Sikh Student Federation, who claimed responsibility for the bombing. Their purpose was in his words, to "protest Hindu imperialism." Similar calls were placed to other newspapers in Europe and India.

There were no survivors; all 329 aboard the jetliner were killed. It was the first jumbo jet downed by a terrorist bomb. No arrests were made, and no incendiary device was discovered.

ISRAEL
SINAI DESERT

February 21, 1973

• • • • • • • • • • • • • • • • •

Fear that a Libyan jetliner had been hijacked and was flying a bomb aimed at Tel Aviv was the reason given for the downing of the jetliner by Israeli Phantoms on February 21, 1973. All 106 aboard died.

In late January 1973, Israeli intelligence received information that Palestinian guerrillas were planning a suicide mission in which a jetliner would be hijacked, armed with bombs and crashed into the heart of Tel Aviv.

In the early afternoon of February 21 of that year, Libyan Arab Airlines Flight 114, a Boeing 707 piloted by a crew loaned from Air France, took off from Tripoli headed for Cairo. Forty-five minutes before it was to land, it radioed Cairo that it was having radio trouble and had lost its way because of bad weather.

At 1:55, the plane, which had overshot Cairo considerably and had wandered into Israeli airspace over the Sinai Desert, was intercepted on Israeli radar. Proceeding on its course, it penetrated 50 miles into Israeli territory, flying over Israeli military concentrations and a military airfield along the Suez Canal.

Israeli authorities tried to contact the jetliner, but it did not respond, obviously because its radio was malfunctioning. Phantom jets took off from the military airfield and intercepted the jet, advising it to turn back. It again did not answer. Warning shots were fired near it. It still did not respond.

At 2:30, the radio aboard the jetliner finally began to function again. The captain radioed Cairo, stating that he was lost and surrounded by Israeli fighters. And then the radio contact abruptly stopped. The fighters homed in on the jetliner and shot it down. It fell to the earth in the Sinai Desert, killing all but 13 of its passengers. The 13, gravely injured, later died of their wounds, and the death toll rose to 106—every passenger and crew member aboard the aircraft.

Reaction was immediate and outraged. Israeli premier Golda Meir expressed distress and propitiation: "The Government of Israel expresses its deep sorrow at the loss of life resulting from the crash of the Libyan plane in Sinai and regrets that the Libyan pilot did not respond to the repeated warnings that were given in accordance with international procedure."

But even within the Israeli government, Israel Gahli dubbed the incident a "disaster," and ordinary Israeli citizens were horrified that their armed forces had shot down a civilian airliner. Conciliatory statements were released by many major governments and delivered to Libya. President Richard Nixon sent a message of condolence, as did UN secretary-general Kurt Waldheim. Libya denounced it as a "criminal act" and vowed revenge, and in August 1973, five passengers were killed and 55 wounded aboard a TWA plane arriving in Athens from Tel Aviv. Responsibility was claimed by members of the Libyan-sponsored National Arab Youth for the Liberation of Palestine.

ISRAEL
TEL AVIV

May 31, 1972

• • • • • • • • • • • • • • •

An agreement between the PFLP and the Red Army to continue terrorist attacks on Israel resulted in the first transnational terrorist incident at Lod (Lydda) Airport on May 31, 1972. Twenty-six unsuspecting travelers were killed; 76 were wounded.

"How does it happen," asked one dazed and bloodied survivor of the Lydda Airport Massacre of May 31, 1972, "that Japanese kill Puerto Ricans because Arabs hate Israelis?"

It was a microcosmic question that had no reason to be asked until that horrible day. Until that time, each terrorist organization seemed to be autonomous. But some time in late 1971, members of Japan's United Red Army made contact with George Haddash, the leader of the Popular Front for the Liberation of Palestine, PFLP, and met with him in Pyongyang, North Korea. From there, they traveled to Jordan, where, along with members of West Germany's Baader-Meinhof Gang, they underwent guerrilla training.

The Japanese Red Army, an ultra-leftist group, had lost support in Japan earlier that year when, after police had arrested hundreds of its adherents, including five of its leaders, the bodies of 14 young people were discovered. The 14 had been tortured to death for deviating from the Red Army's revolutionary line. Thus, the Japanese terrorist group sought to gain credibility and approval in the terrorist world by aligning itself with the PFLP.

Three of its members, trained in Lebanon, boarded an Air France jet in Paris on May 31, 1973. Passengers aboard Air France jets in 1973 felt safe. France practiced a friendly relationship with Arab countries, and at the beginning of May, although Asher Ben Nathan, Israel's ambassador to France, had called on Herve Alphand, secretary-general of the French Foreign Ministry, to plead for increased security measures on flights to Israel, Alphand had refused him, noting that France and the Arab countries were not enemies.

Air France Flight 132 arrived on time and without incident at Tel Aviv's Lydda, or Lod, Airport on May 31. Passengers debarked and proceeded to luggage conveyor belt number 3.

Three young Japanese tourists claimed their bags from the belt and then began to behave strangely. They removed their jackets and crouched to open their suitcases. When they straightened up, they were all holding Czech-made VZT-58 automatic rifles, which they immediately began firing, rapidly and indiscriminately. They fanned their weapons in wide arcs, mowing down the passengers near them, and then raised the barrels of the rifles to shoot those farther away.

Two of the gunmen then dashed for the tarmac, firing at two parked planes. One killed the other, nearly decapitating him with a brutal burst of automatic gunfire. The third terrorist leaped on the now blood-slick baggage conveyor belt, holding a grenade. He pulled the pin, slipped, fell on the grenade and was blown to bits by its explosion.

The one surviving gunman continued to shoot into the crowd until he ran out of ammunition. As he stopped to reload, an El Al traffic controller, Hanan Zaiton, leaped on him and beat him to the ground. Guards rushed to his aid, and then hauled the terrorist, a 24-year-old college dropout named Kozo Okamoto, into a nearby office.

The airport was strewn with the dead, the dying and the wounded. Twenty-six people, including Dr. Aharon Katchalsky, one of Israel's leading scientists, and 14 Puerto Ricans making a pilgrimage to the Holy Land, were killed. Seventy-six others were injured.

An hour after the killings, a spokesperson for the PFLP announced to local papers that it had recruited the Japanese fanatics "to kill as many people as possible."

It was barbaric and senseless, but it proved that there was no safe haven for the innocent who hoped to escape terrorism in the 1970s.

ITALY
BOLOGNA

August 1, 1980

• • • • • • • • • • • • • • •

To "honor" an accused neo-fascist bomber, neo-fascist terrorists detonated a bomb in the Bologna train station on August 1, 1980 at the beginning of the holiday season. Eighty-four died; 200 were injured.

August is the traditional holiday month in Italy and France, and on August 1, 1980 the Bologna train station was packed to capacity with vacationers and tourists. That morning, a judge in Bologna announced that eight neo-fascists, among them, Mario Tuti, had been indicted and would be tried.

Amid unsuspecting travelers in the Bologna train station, a group of terrorists planted a bomb equivalent in power to 90 pounds of TNT in a corner of the second-class waiting room.

Shortly after 1 P.M., the bomb exploded with a thunderous roar, totally demolishing one wing of the massive train station. A restaurant, two waiting rooms and a train platform were flattened as the roof collapsed on them.

Mayhem followed. The screams of the injured and the shouts of rescuers and survivors ricocheted off the columns and walls of the ruins. It was the worst terrorist disaster in Italy's history, eclipsing the 1968 bombing of a Milan bank, in which 16 people were killed and 16 injured. The toll in Bologna would be 84 dead and 200 injured.

On August 2, while smoke still filtered upward from a wing of the station that now had only two iron girders standing, 10,000 Bolognans turned a left-wing rally into a demonstration against terrorism, and labor unions held a rally in Rome's Colosseum, in which they announced a four-hour strike.

That same day, two calls from terrorist groups were received by police. One claimed responsibility for the blast by the Red Brigades, the far left wing terrorist organization that had kidnapped and killed former Prime Minister Aldo Moro. But the caller incorrectly described the time and location of the bomb.

The other caller claimed to represent the Armed Revolutionary Cells, a neo-fascist organization, eight of whose members were to be tried for the railroad bombing of the Bologna-Florence train six years before. The bombing, it was stated, was to honor Mario Tuti, one of the accused.

Police believed this caller and began an exhaustive investigation that would end a little over a year later, on September 12, 1981, in London, with the arrest of the terrorists who planted the bomb.

JORDAN
DAWSON'S FIELD

September 6–8, 1970

A PFLP guerrilla group's demands for the release of Palestinian prisoners culminated in the 1970s' most spectacular terrorist incident, at Dawson's Field in Jordan. Five civilian jetliners were hijacked; four were flown to Jordan and blown up. One hijacker was killed in the explosion, and 300 passengers were taken hostage.

In what began as the largest, most spectacular hijacking operation of the 1970s, four airliners from four countries were hijacked in one morning and early afternoon. The day was September 6, 1970, and all four hijackings took place shortly after each plane took off from its home airport. All were headed for New York.

The first of these, El Al's Flight 219 from Tel Aviv, a Boeing 707 with 148 passengers and 10 crew members aboard, took off from Amsterdam in the morning. Shortly after takeoff, two hijackers, Patrick Arguello, a Nicaraguan working for the PFLP, and Leila Khaled, a Palestinian, sprang to their feet, shouting. Arguello dashed toward the cockpit door. Schlomo Vider, an El Al steward, pounced on him but was shot in the stomach.

The plane was thrown into a steep dive by its pilot, which flung the hijackers off balance and allowed one of the two Israeli security guards aboard to shoot and kill one hijacker, Arguello. Meanwhile, a passenger overpowered Khaled, and she was tied hand and foot with string and a necktie.

The jet diverted to London's Heathrow Airport, where it made an emergency landing. Vider, with three bullets in his stomach, was taken by ambulance to a hospital, and Khaled was led off to jail. The plane was cleaned up, the passengers reloaded and the flight proceeded to New York.

The other three hijackings were considerably more successful for the hijackers.

Pan Am Flight 93, a Boeing 747 on the last leg of a flight from Brussels to New York, with 152 passengers and a crew of 17 aboard, was hijacked shortly after it left Amsterdam. Apparently confused, the hijackers allowed the plane to land in Beirut, Lebanon and then, after they conferred with PFLP "brothers" at the airport, allowed the plane to take off again and eventually land in Cairo. There the hijackers unloaded passengers and crew and blew up the $23 million craft. The passengers were evacuated the following day to New York and Rome.

Meanwhile, TWA Flight 741, a Boeing 707 on an around-the-world voyage, with 141 passengers and a crew of 10, was commandeered shortly after it took off from Frankfurt and diverted to Dawson's Field, a former World War II RAF base in the Jordanian desert. Dawson's Field had been taken over as a "revolutionary airfield" by the PFLP.

Finally, Swissair Flight 100, a DC-8 with 143 passengers and 12 crew members, was hijacked 10 minutes after it took off from Zurich and was ordered to change its course to the Middle East. It set down at Dawson's Field shortly after the other jet.

A spokesman for the PFLP, speaking from Beirut, announced the reasons for the multiple hijacking: The American planes had been seized, he said, "to give the Americans a lesson after they have supported Israel all these years" and in retaliation for the U.S. involvement in peace negotiations in the Middle East between Israel and the Arabs.

The Swiss plane was captured and held in ransom for the release of three Arab commandos convicted by a Swiss court for an attack on an Israeli airliner at the Zurich airport the previous December.

The spokesman also gave the reason for the hijacking of the El Al jet: "We are fighting Israel; they are our enemy and we will fight them everywhere."

The morning of Sept. 7, the scene was an ominous one. The two planes were poised on the old runways, shimmering with heat. In between was a tent, the hijackers' field headquarters. Nearby was a water truck with a sign in Arabic reading "The Popular Front at your service." Around the periphery of the field were PFLP guerrillas armed with Russian Kalashnikov submachine guns, Katyusha rockets and jeeps with heavy-caliber machine guns.

And 250 yards away was the Jordanian Army, ringing the field in an impenetrable circle of tanks, armored personnel carriers, anti-aircraft guns, communications jeeps, ambulances and fire trucks. Each was pointed directly at the planes. King Hussein of Jordan wanted nothing to do with the hijackers, nor did he want the world to feel that he was in complicity with them.

By noon, the hijackers threatened to blow up the planes and their hostages unless the armor was withdrawn. The Jordanian Army backed off two miles and reformed its circle.

As the days passed and deadlines were made and then extended, the hijackers released women and children, conducted press conferences with appearances by hostages and eventually allowed the International Red Cross to fly in a planeload of relief supplies, and a Jordanian Airlines toilet-cleaning vehicle to service the parked planes.

At midweek, on September 8, the PFLP hijacked another jetliner, a British Overseas Airways Corporation VC-10 carrying 117 passengers and crew. The plane was diverted to Beirut, where it refueled, and then flown to Dawson's Field, where it was forced to land and take up its position with the other two jets. It and its occupants would be held, the PFLP announced, until Leila Khaled was released.

By this time, five governments and the United Nations were involved in negotiations. As the days drifted on, token numbers of hostages were released. Sixty-eight were taken to Amman, Jordan and flown to Nicosia, Cyprus and London; 23 more were transferred to a hotel in Amman; 20 were allowed to fly to Beirut. The hijackers now demanded the release of an unspecified number of Arab guerrillas in Israel.

The parent of the PFLP, the PLO, was growing increasingly restive with the extremist tactics of the guerrillas and began to withdraw its support. Eventually, it would disassociate itself completely from the group, which continued to fire off demands including the release of six Arab guerrillas imprisoned in Germany, the return of two Algerians taken from a BOAC flight by Israelis and the release of 2,000 guerrillas held in Israel.

As the relationship with the PLO continued to deteriorate, the hijackers decided on a dramatic action: They freed 260 passengers and kept 40 and blew up all three jetliners. The hostages, some from each of the negotiating countries—the United States, Britain, West Germany, Switzerland and Israel—were to be held until prisoner exchanges could be arranged with each country.

Eventually, all hostages would be released, but not all Palestinian hostages. Leila Khaled would be returned; the Swiss and West German hostages would be traded, but that would be all.

Foreseeing the consequences of violating Jordanian sovereignty by the actions of George Haddash and his PFLP, PLO leader Yassir Arafat expelled the organization from the PLO for lack of discipline.

King Hussein would eventually drive the PLO from its base in Jordan as a result of the incident, and Black September would be formed.

LEBANON
BEIRUT

October 23, 1983

• • • • • • • • • • • • • • • •

A suicide bomber representing the Islamic Jihad drove an explosive-filled truck into the U.S. Marine compound in Beirut, Lebanon on October 23, 1983. Two hundred forty-one U.S. Marines were killed; 58 French soldiers were also killed in a related attack.

Lebanon was a bloody battlefield in 1983. Beirut, formerly one of the most beautiful cities in the world, was on the way to becoming the demolished, smoking shell it is today. Rival religious factions roared back and forth across it and the rest of Lebanon, and both Syria and Iran financed and supplied some of these groups.

The Islamic Jihad, one of the most fanatical of terrorist groups, was founded at this time, and its chief support came from Syria and Iran, though it was headquartered in Lebanon. Its enemies were the United States, Western Europe, Iraq, Jordan and Egypt. A supercharged religious energy, as much as money and arms, fueled this fledgling terrorist organization. Some Middle East observers, among them correspondents Christopher Dobson and Ronald Payne in their study of terrorism, *The Never Ending War,* assert that it was the Israelis who invaded Lebanon in June 1982. This they say, gave the Islamic terrorists in Lebanon their "launching pad."

After a terrorist attack on its ambassador to Britain in London, the Israeli government ordered its armed forces into Lebanon ostensibly to root out the Palestinians. The attack worked, but it also strengthened the resolve of terrorist groups in that country.

Shortly after the Israeli invasion, and while Israeli troops were surrounding Beirut, President Ronald Reagan sent U.S. Marines into that city to try to restore peace through a forceful presence. Aided by small contingents of French, British and Italian troops, they managed to maintain an uneasy truce.

But Shiite organizations, and particularly the newly formed Jihad, were planning the use of a new and gruesome weapon in the continuing escalation of terrorist attacks against the West and Arab enemies. On Monday, April 18, 1983, a truck loaded with explosives was driven onto the U.S. Embassy grounds and detonated. Forty-five people were killed, including 16 Americans. It was the first such suicide bombing in the Middle East, but it would not be the last; nor would it be the most devastating.

That would come at 6:20 A.M., Sunday, October 23, when a pickup truck approached the south gate of U.S. Marine headquarters in Beirut. It was coming from the direction of Beirut International Airport and was noticed by the sergeant on guard duty. Inside the barracks, some 200 marines were sleeping.

Suddenly, the driver of the truck gunned his motor, sending the truck barreling through a sandbag barrier and into the interior courtyard of the compound. Seconds later, the driver tripped a switch and blew himself and the truck and most of the barracks into small slivers of metal, wood and flesh. The crater left by the bomb was 30 feet deep and 40 feet across, and the explosion had the force of a ton of TNT.

"I haven't seen carnage like this since Vietnam," said Marine Major Robert Jordan, who, with other officers who were quartered elsewhere, rushed to the scene to begin the grisly business of rescue and recovery of bodies.

A few minutes after the initial blast, another car bomb driven by a suicidal terrorist rammed into a building housing a company of French troops and exploded.

Machinery was moved into place to lift girders and concrete from wounded survivors. Lebanese and Italian soldiers aided in the rescue effort. Ships of the U.S. Sixth Fleet went on alert. Helicopters airlifted the wounded to the amphibious assault ship *Iwo Jima* and the battleship *New Jersey,* poised offshore near Beirut harbor. Muslim snipers on rooftops shot at the helicopters.

Two hundred forty-one marines were killed, nearly 100 were wounded, and 58 French soldiers were killed in the related bombing of their quarters.

Retaliation consisted of shells lobbed from the *New Jersey* into known terrorist strongholds. Israeli jets bombed the same targets. Intelligence forces from Israel, the United States, France and Lebanon sifted through the rubble. The 12,000 pounds of TNT and PETN, a plastic explosive that was used in the marine barracks bombing, and hexogen, which was involved in the explosion at the French barracks, plus a $50,000 money order to local mercenaries that was traced to Iranian diplomats clearly implicated both Syria and Iran.

Fourteen terrorists were finally named. They included Palestinians, renegade PLO members, professional terrorists and a fundamentalist mullah. The organization was being financed and supported by Shiite, Syrian and Iranian forces, but its network of supply and its operations were Byzantine in their complexity.

On December 12, the suicide bombers struck again, this time in eight locations in Kuwait. One was the American Embassy, which was destroyed through the same method used in Beirut. The other seven locations included the headquarters of the Raytheon Company, an American outfit that was installing Hawk missiles in Kuwait, and the French Embassy.

The peacekeeping force of American, French and Italian armed forces withdrew from Lebanon, leaving it to be destroyed by warring factions. Special barricades would be erected in front of the White House in Washington to guard against possible suicidal drivers of trucks loaded with explosives. Other government buildings would be provided with concrete pylons.

Apparently because of a dwindling supply of terrorists willing to commit suicide for their cause, this type of terrorist bombing stopped after this incident. But it had made its psychological point and had weakened the West in the Middle East.

LEBANON
BEIRUT

June 14–18, 1985

• • • • • • • • • • • • • • • • • •

The Islamic Jihad was responsible for the hijacking of TWA Flight 847 from June 14 to 18, 1985. Hundreds of passengers were terrorized, 39 men were held hostage and then released, and one U.S. Navy man was killed.

In 1970, the PFLP had staged a spectacular hijacking of five jetliners (see p. 106), and the world had trembled and negotiated. In 1985 the Islamic Jihad and its Shiite special squads decided that another hijacking was necessary to reaffirm the power and purpose of the Islamic revolution and its anti-Western orientation.

But between 1970 and 1985, the world changed. International agreements had, at least on the surface, largely forbidden hostage deals, although Islamic Jihad was well aware that clandestine dealing still existed. The arrangements that would eventually erupt the following November into the Iran-contra scandal were already energetically under way in Tehran.

Still, the incidence of air piracy was distinctly down from 15 years before. In 1970, there were 91 airline hijackings; in 1984, 17. The reduction was partly due to increased airport security. However, security remained lax at two airports, Athens and Beirut, and it was here that the Islamic Jihad concentrated its efforts in 1985.

An Islamic Jihad plan to hijack two American airliners simultaneously was uncovered, but half of the plan was aborted when East German authorities picked up two passengers carrying explosives in their baggage.

TWA Flight 847 was, however, not so lucky. The flight originated in Cairo, stopped in Athens and was then to proceed to Rome, and, as a new flight, to Tel Aviv. Slightly after 10 A.M. on the morning of June 14, after a late arrival from Cairo, the flight became packed to capacity in Athens. There were 145 passengers aboard—120 Americans, a Greek pop singer, some Australians and 21 Catholic pilgrims.

A few minutes after takeoff, two Arab terrorists charged up the aisle, one waving a 9-millimeter pistol, the other brandishing two hand grenades, one in each hand. "Hijack! Hijack!" they screamed. "We have come to die!" A mace-like substance had been thrown prior to their charge, filling the cabin with choking smoke. One of them aimed a karate kick at Uli Derickson, the purser on the flight, slamming her against the cockpit door.

The hijackers, Ali Younis and Ahmed Ghorbieh, kicked in the cockpit door. One held the gun to the head of pilot John Testrake while the other pulled the pins on the twin grenades. Captain Testrake acceded to their demands to divert the liner to Beirut. The hijackers then proceeded to terrorize the passengers, beating some of them mercilessly, forcing the rest to assume agonizing postures in their seats.

At first, Beirut refused permission to land, but Testrake convinced controllers and officials there that they were low on fuel and that the hijackers were hysterically out of control, plucking the pins from hand grenades and reinserting them at the last minute, brutalizing the passengers and committing other violent acts to convince all aboard that they were dedicated in their mission.

The plane landed in Beirut long enough to refuel and release 17 women and two children. In Algiers, the next stop, the terrorists released 22 more women and children. Once more, Flight 847 took off, heading back to Beirut. It was night by now, and the Beirut airport shut off its landing lights, hoping to deter the hijackers from landing.

They had already singled out a young U.S. Navy man, Robert Stetham, and had beaten him badly. Unless they got their way in two minutes, they shouted over the radio to the control tower, they would "let one American loose off the plane." The runway lights were turned on; the plane landed; the hijackers demanded that Shiite leaders be brought to the plane.

Again they were refused; again they threatened to kill one American, and this time they did. They shot Stetham in the head and dumped his body onto the tarmac. They would, they told the tower, begin to kill the other Americans one by one unless a rambling list of demands was met. Among the demands were the cutting off of oil sales to the West, the removal of all Arab money from Western banks and the release of all Shiites imprisoned in Kuwait and Israel.

It was insane, but so, apparently, were the hijackers, who, having found a translator in purser Derickson (one of the hijackers spoke German, and she was German), began to wage psychological warfare on the passengers. Ordered to point out the Jewish passengers, Derickson refused and was beaten. Later, the German-speaking hijacker proposed marriage to her. Shouting and screaming and kicking the passengers one minute, the hijackers would order the flight attendants to make omelettes for everyone the next.

Now, reinforcements arrived. Twenty-five armed Shiites rushed aboard the plane. Twelve remained on the tarmac.

Meanwhile, the U.S. Sixth Fleet was moved in close to the shore of Lebanon, and a 1,800-marine amphibious unit was drawn up in the same area. Squadrons of F-16 fighters were redeployed at bases in Turkey.

Late Friday night, the hijackers ordered the plane to again take off and head for Algiers. There, the Greek government handed them Ali Atweh, a terrorist who had been separated from the original two hijackers at Athens and arrested. The deal was that he was to be traded for Greek pop singer Demis Roussos. But the hijackers reneged on the arrangement, freed a group of 10 Greek passengers and the flight attendants but did not include Roussos.

On Sunday morning, June 16, the plane again took off for Beirut. But by this time, Nabih Berri, the head of the Amal, which was the most respectable part of the Shiite organizations in Lebanon, offered to enter the picture as a mediator. His offer was accepted, and on Monday morning, June 17, Nabih Berri's militia freed the remaining passengers, with the exception of 39 American men, including the pilot and co-pilot. They were taken to three safe houses near Bourj el-Barajneh.

But four days of negotiations with Nabih Berri did not resolve the crisis. Finally, President Ronald Reagan was prevailed upon to contact President Assad of Syria. Appealed to as a head of state, Hassad delivered an ultimatum to Hezbollah: Return the captives, or face a cutoff of supplies and communication from Syria.

The Israelis agreed to release some 500 Shiites, Islamic Jihad surrendered and on Friday, June 30, all 39 men were driven to Damascus, where they boarded a plane that flew them to Frankfurt, West Germany.

MEDITERRANEAN SEA

October 7–9, 1985

A perceived need by the PLO to call world attention to itself led to the bungled, improvised hijacking of the Italian cruise ship Achille Lauro *in the Mediterranean from October 7 to 9, 1985. One American was killed.*

The hijacking of the 23,929-ton Italian luxury liner *Achille Lauro* on October 7, 1985 was planned far in advance by its mastermind, PLF leader Abu Abbas. He and Yassir Arafat had come to the conclusion that, considering their recent failures in landing commandos in Israel, it was time for a major terrorist move that would garner world attention.

Thus, the *Achille Lauro* hijacking was planned in the summer of 1985. Four suicide terrorists were to book passage on this cruise ship that plied the Mediterranean, taking tourists from Genoa to Egypt and the Holy Land. The terrorists would board in Genoa and stay under cover until the ship reached the Israeli port of Ashdod. They would wait behind while the passengers debarked; then, under cover of night, they would leave the ship, infiltrate portside oil-storage tanks and an ammunition depot and blow them and themselves up. At least that is what Abu Abbas told the Middle East News Agency in Belgrade after the incident.

The liner was scheduled to sail from Genoa on October 3, with stops in Naples, Syracuse, Alexandria, Port Said, Limassol, Rhodes and Ashdod. Issa Mohammed Abbas, a relative of Abu Abbas, was placed in charge of the Genoa operation. Masir Kadia, one of Abbas's trustees, had already obtained bookings for the four suicide terrorists, Majed al Molky, Hallah al Hassan, Ali Abdullah and Abdel Ibrahim. They were set to occupy cabin 82.

But from that point onward, the operation proceeded to fall apart. On September 25, three PLO terrorists shot three Israelis aboard a yacht moored in the harbor of Larnaca, Cyprus. On October 1, a squadron of Israeli planes flew 1,500 miles to Tunisia and, in retaliation for the September 25 incident, bombed the headquarters of the PLO, south of Tunis. Sixty-seven Arabs were killed, and all communication between PLO headquarters and Genoa was severed.

On that same day, Italian authorities arrested Issa Mohammed Abbas and confiscated four Kalashnikov automatic weapons, eight grenades and some detonators, which had been hidden in the false bottom of his car's gas tank.

The four young terrorists were left on their own, without their leader and the rest of their supplies. They were armed with their own Kalashnikovs and 9-millimeter pistols, but they lacked the dynamite that would be needed to carry out their mission in Israel.

The *Achille Lauro* left Genoa on October 1. The four remained aboard, silent and unnoticed until October 7. The evening before, the ship had pulled into Alexandria, Egypt, and nearly 600 passengers had debarked to tour the pyramids. The ship left at 10 A.M. for Port Said, where it would retrieve the passengers who had left on the Egyptian tour and proceed with the rest of its itinerary.

When the *Achille Lauro* reached international waters, the four terrorists suddenly smashed into the dining room, firing machine guns and pistols. They held the crew of 80 and the remaining 427 passengers at bay, invaded the bridge and commandeered the vessel, ordering Captain Gerardo de Rosa to sail northward, toward the coast of Syria.

But Syria would not allow the ship to dock, and on Tuesday, October 8, the terrorists broadcast a demand for the immediate release of 50 Palestinians held by the Israelis, or they would begin to kill the passengers one by one, beginning with Americans and Britons.

The only passenger to die was 69-year-old New Yorker Leon Klinghoffer, a crusty gentleman confined to a wheelchair who taunted his captors repeatedly. They shot him and threw his body and the wheelchair overboard.

Meanwhile, an international confrontation was rapidly forming. Italy dispatched paratroops to the British bases on the island of Cyprus, toward which the *Achille Lauro* was now steaming. Specially trained SEAL frogmen commando units of the U.S. Navy and Delta army teams were sent to Sicily.

Realizing that the incident had gone too far, Arafat ordered the operation to be aborted. Abu Abbas, who had planned it all in the first place, emerged as the negotiator, and within hours the hijackers announced that they were willing to free everyone upon landing in Port Said, Egypt.

Once the ship docked in Port Said, the hijackers and Abbas were whisked off to Cairo, much to the indignation of U.S. ambassador Nicholas Veliotes, who telephoned his colleagues in Cairo and gave curt orders: "You tell the foreign ministry that we demand they prosecute the sons of bitches."

This was not done. Instead Egyptian President Hosni Mubarak told U.S. sources that the hijackers had already left and were on their way back to Tunis. Intelligence sources, however, uncovered the real story. Preparations were still being made to put the five Arabs aboard an Egyptair Boeing 737 from Al Maza Airport near Cairo to Tunis. The United States utilized the time to scramble F-14 fighters aboard the USS *Saratoga,* in the Mediterranean.

On the night of October 10, over international waters, four F-14s intercepted the Boeing carrying the hijackers and forced it to land at a joint Italian-NATO base at Sigonella, in Sicily. The high degree of secrecy necessary to carry out the counterhijack displeased Italy mightily, since it was not informed in advance of the U.S. action. A confrontation developed between U.S. and Italian military units at Sigonella, and Italian authorities won out, taking the four terrorists and Abbas to an Italian court.

Abbas was released immediately, again much to the outrage of U.S. authorities, and headed back to Tunis by way of Yugoslavia.

On June 18, 1986, the trial of the *Achille Lauro* hijackers began. Three of the planners of the incident, including Abu Abbas, were tried in absentia and sentenced to life imprisonment—sentences that would never be realized.

The other four were sentenced to prison terms ranging from 15 to 30 years. Magied Youssef al Molqui was later tried for the murder of Leon Klinghoffer, convicted and sentenced to life imprisonment.

SYRIA
DAMASCUS

November 29, 1981

• • • • • • • • • • • • • • • •

Anti-Assad Muslims continuing terrorist attacks on Syrian installations were responsible for the detonation of a car bomb on the crowded streets of Damascus on November 29, 1981. Seventy bystanders and police were killed; scores were wounded.

The terrorist attacks of one faction against another have often been as vicious and devastating as those of terrorist organizations against a common enemy such as Israel or the United States. Syria's Muslim Brotherhood, which operated from Jordan, was relentlessly opposed to the ruling party headed by Syrian president Hafez Assad. Drawn from the more fanatical elements of Syria's population of Sunni Muslims, it repeatedly denounced Assad's ruling clique of Alawites as nonbelievers and, over a five-year period from 1976 to 1981, assassinated hundreds of Alawite members of Assad's ruling Baath party.

In the early afternoon of November 29, 1981, a white Honda minivan pulled up in front of the Azbakiyah Recruiting Center in the middle of a middle-class residential district in downtown Damascus. Sensing trouble, police moved in immediately. The driver of the van, Yasin Ben Muhammad Sarji, a 19-year-old former vegetable vendor and a member of the Muslim Brotherhood, drew a pistol but was killed on the spot.

Within seconds, the van exploded. Its 220 pounds of TNT blew a crater in the street, showered the area with lethal shards of metal and masonry and killed 70 innocent bystanders and police. Three buses burst into flames, and their passengers were counted among the dead.

President Assad blamed the West, describing the terrorists as "agents of Zionism and imperialism," but the Muslim Brotherhood soon drowned him out with its own stated reasons, "to further the Islamic revolution in Syria." It added unmistakably that the bombing was in retaliation for "massacres, arbitrary executions and assassinations against Syrian citizens in their country and abroad."

UNITED STATES
WASHINGTON, D.C.

March 9–11, 1977

• • • • • • • • • • • • • • • •

The assassination by Black Muslims of the family of Hanafi Muslim Hamaas Abdul Khaalis led to a three-day occupation of three Washington, D.C. sites by Khaalis and his followers from March 9 to 11, 1977. One person died; 19 were wounded; 134 were taken hostage.

In the violent 1970s, thousands of blacks took Islamic names, converted to Islam and joined one or another of several Islamic sects. The largest and best known of these was the Chicago-based Black Muslims, who numbered—depending on who was counting—10,000 to 70,000 and claimed among their members boxer Muhammad Ali.

The Black Muslims, however, were considered blasphemous by more devout Muslims, who in the United States numbered some two million. Hamaas Abdul Khaalis, born Ernest Timothy McGhee in Gary, Indiana, was a member of the strict Hanafi sect, a subgroup of the orthodox Sunni Muslims.

In the early 1970s, fierce factional fighting broke out between various Muslim groups, and more than 29 Muslims were murdered in these clashes.

The Washington-based Hanafi group claimed among its 1,000 members basketball star Kareem Abdul-Jabbar, who in 1970 bought the group a mansion. Soon after they took up residence, Khaalis began a verbal war against the Black Muslims. He blamed them and their leader, Elijah Muhammad, for the murder of Malcolm X. At the end of

The three leaders of the Hanafi Muslim siege of Washington, D.C. from March 9 to 11, 1977 are transported to jail in a Red Cross ambulance. American Red Cross

1972, Khaalis wrote letters to 58 Black Muslim ministers, calling their leader "a lying deceiver."

A few days later, when Khaalis was absent from the mansion, a squad of Black Muslims invaded it and killed two adults and six children in gruesome ways. All of the children were related to Khaalis. His 10-day-old son was drowned in a sink before his mother's eyes. Three other children—two his, one a grandchild—were drowned in a bath, and two sons were shot. One of his wives and a daughter were seriously wounded.

Five Black Muslims were arrested and sentenced to life imprisonment, but it was not enough for Khaalis. At 11 A.M. on Wednesday, March 9, 1977, he and 11 followers began a 39-hour siege of three locations in Washington, D.C. Before they were through, 134 hostages would be taken, one man would be dead and 19 hostages would be seriously wounded, one seriously enough to be paralyzed.

The first building to be seized was the eight-story headquarters of B'Nai Brith, the Jewish service organization. Khaalis and six of his commandos, dressed in jeans and work shirts with long knives strapped to heavy steel chains hung on their hips and carrying guitar cases holding an assortment of rifles, shotguns and a crossbow, leaped from a van and invaded the building's lobby. "They killed my babies and shot my women," screamed Khaalis at terrified passengers from an elevator that had just arrived at the lobby. "Now they will listen to us—or heads will roll."

The invaders set up a command quarters and a concentration camp on the eighth floor of the building. Those who protested were slashed with machetes. The men and women were separated and then were bound and taunted.

At 12:30 P.M., another group of commandos took over the Islamic Center on the edge of Rock Creek Park. Khaalis had been chiding the center's director, Dr. Muhammad Abdul Rauf, for months for supporting Elijah Muhammad, the leader of the Black Muslims, and for being an Egyptian. "Your country is seeking peace with the Jews," was Khaalis's charge.

Meanwhile, Israeli prime minister Yitzhak Rabin was accepting an honorary degree from American University. He was hustled directly from the ceremonies to Andrews Air Force Base, where he caught a plane for New York.

At 2:15 P.M., the third attack, carried out by two gunmen dressed in black and carrying a shotgun and a .22-caliber handgun, took over an office on the fifth floor of Washington's city hall. It was here that the murder took place.

Two elevators, one carrying city councilman (later Washington mayor) Marion Barry and councilman Robert Pierce and the other Maurice Williams, a reporter for radio station WHUR, and Steven Colter of the *Washington Afro-American,* arrived simultaneously at the fifth floor. The gunmen opened fire. Williams received the full force of a shotgun blast and was killed on the spot. Pierce was paralyzed, the bullet that hit Barry stopped less than an inch from his heart and the bullet that grazed Colter's skull miraculously missed his brain.

Police snipers and FBI agents had by now surrounded all three locations, and Khaalis phoned his demands to Max Robinson, a reporter for WTOP-TV. The demands were many and hysterical. First, he wanted a current motion picture, *Mohammad, Messenger of God,* starring Anthony Quinn to be withdrawn from all movie houses and shipped out of the country. "It's a joke. It's misrepresenting the Muslim faith," said Khaalis.

"Next thing I want the killers of my babies," continued Khaalis. "I say we want them right there. I want to see how tough they are. I want the one who killed Malcolm [X] too." The leader also wanted the police to reimburse him for the $750 fine he had received for contempt of court during the 1973 trial of the five Black Muslims who had massacred his family. Finally, he wanted Secretary of State Cyrus Vance to be contacted; he gave as his reason: "We are going to kill foreign Muslims at the Islamic Center [and] create an international incident."

"They were a bunch of crazies," said Andrew Hoffman, one of a number of hostages released early in the siege. The city hall commandos seemed to be the most brutal, tying their victims hand and foot, making them lie face down on the floor and poking them continually with shotguns. In the B'Nai Brith building, the terrorists painted over windows to block out visibility for police snipers.

By 6:16 P.M. on Wednesday, the 9th, negotiations had begun with Egyptian ambassador Ashraf Ghorbal and Pakistani ambassador Sahabzada Yaqub-Khan conferring with Khaalis. The White House remained removed. That night, Iran's Ardeshir Zahedi, who had flown in from Paris on the Concorde, joined the negotiations. The offending film was pulled from movie houses in New York and Washington.

The first breakthrough occurred at 5:30 P.M. on Thursday, the 10th, when Khaalis agreed to meet face to face with Yaqub-Khan in the lobby of the B'Nai Brith building. The talks lasted three hours. At the end of that time Yaqub-Khan asked for the release of 30 hostages as a gesture of good faith. Khaalis proposed to let all hostages go, provided he was released without bail.

It would be nearly 2 A.M. on the 11th before the legal tangle of doing this was unraveled, and from then until 5:10 A.M., hostages were released and commandos gave themselves up to police. Later that day, bail was set at $50,000 each for two terrorists and $75,000 for six others. The three gunmen at the Islamic Center, where no hostages were harmed, were let go on their own recognizance along with Khaalis.

Khaalis would recoup his $750 and succeed in having a movie shut down for a few days. But that would be his only accomplishment, aside from the satisfaction of terrorizing most of America for 39 hours.

EXPLOSIONS

• • • • •

THE WORST RECORDED EXPLOSIONS

• • • • •

* Detailed in text

Afghanistan
- * Salang Tunnel (Nov. 2, 1892) Truck collision

Austria
- Skoda (Feb. 6, 1916) Arsenal explosion

Belgium
- Hamont Station (Aug. 3, 1918) Ammunition train

Brazil
- Cubatao (Feb. 25, 1984) Oil pipeline

Canada
- Alberta
- Lethbridge (June 19, 1914) Mine explosion
- British Columbia
- Ferme (May 23, 1902) Mine explosion
- Vancouver Island (May 4, 1887) Mine explosion
- Nova Scotia
- * Halifax (Dec. 6, 1917) Ammunition ship

China
- * Lanchow (Oct. 26, 1935) Arsenal explosion
- * Manchuria (Feb. 12, 1931) Mine explosion
- Peking (May 25, 1925) Arsenal explosion
- Tsingtsing (Mar. 29, 1940) Mine explosion

Colombia
- * Cali (Aug. 7, 1956) Dynamite truck convoy

Cuba
- * Havana (Mar. 4, 1960) Munitions ship *La Coubre*

El Salvador
- Lalibertad (Mar. 14, 1934) Explosives warehouse

France
- * Courrieres (Mar. 10, 1906) Mine explosion
- Mons
- (Dec. 14, 1875) Mine explosion
- (Sept. 7, 1892) Mine explosion
- St. Etienne (July 3, 1889) Mine explosion

Germany
- Alsdorf (Oct. 21, 1930) Mine explosion
- Camphausen (Mar. 17, 1885) Mine explosion
- * Johanngeorgendstadt (Nov. 29, 1949) Mine explosion
- * Oppau (Sept. 21, 1921) (see NUCLEAR AND INDUSTRIAL ACCIDENTS)
- * Volklingen (Feb. 7, 1962) Mine explosions
- Westphalia (Nov. 11, 1908) Mine explosions

Great Britain
- England
- * Barnsley (Dec. 12–13, 1866) Mine explosion
- Durham (Feb. 16, 1909) Mine explosion
- Haydock (June 7, 1878) Mine explosion
- * Hulton (Dec. 21, 1910) Mine explosion
- Lancashire (June 18, 1885) Mine explosion
- Northumberland (Jan. 16, 1862) Mine explosion
- Podmore Hall (Jan. 12, 1918) Mine explosion
- * Sunderland (Aug. 17, 1880) Mine explosion
- Yorkshire (Feb. 19, 1857) Mine explosion
- Scotland
- Lanarkshire (Oct. 22, 1877) Mine explosion
- Wales
  - * Abercane (Sept. 11, 1878) Mine explosion
- Clyfnydd (June 23, 1894) Mine explosion
- Glamorgan (July 15, 1856) Mine explosion
- Monmouthshire (Feb. 6, 1890) Mine explosion
- Pontypridd (Nov. 8, 1867) Mine explosion
- Risca
- (Dec. 1, 1860) Mine explosion
- (July 15, 1880) Mine explosion
- * Sengenhydd (Oct. 14, 1913) Mine explosion
- Wrexham (Sept. 22, 1934) Mine explosion

India
- * Asansol (Feb. 19, 1958) Mine explosion
- * Bombay (April 14, 1944) Steamship explosion
- Chasnala (Dec. 27, 1975) Mine explosion
- * Dharbad (May 28, 1965) Mine explosion

Japan
- * Fukuoka (June 1, 1965) Mine explosion
- Nagasaki (Mar. 29, 1906) Mine explosion
- Otaru (Dec. 27, 1924) Harbor explosion
- Sapporo (July 16, 1920) Mine explosion
- Shimonoseki (April 13, 1915) Mine explosion

Mexico
- Barrotean (Mar. 31, 1969) Mine explosion
- Mexico City (Nov. 19, 1984) Gas storage area

Prussia
- Rhenish (Jan. 28, 1907) Mine explosion
- Upper Silesia (June 10, 1895) Mine explosion

Rhodesia
- * Wankie (June 6, 1972) Mine explosion

Russia
Jusovka (July 1, 1908) Mine explosion
Spain
Cadiz (Aug. 18, 1947) Naval mine and torpedo factory
Switzerland
Berne (June 20, 1921) Mine explosion
Turkey
Kharput (Mar. 1, 1925) Munitions plant
United States
California
* Port Chicago (July 17, 1944) Harbor explosion
Illinois
* Cherry (Nov. 13, 1909) Mine explosion
New Mexico
* Dawson (Oct. 22, 1913) Mine explosion
Pennsylvania
Cheswick (Jan. 24, 1904) Mine explosion
* Jacob's Creek (Dec. 19, 1907) Mine explosion
* Mather (May 19, 1928) Mine explosion
* Plymouth (Sept. 6, 1869) Mine explosion
Tennessee
Coal Creek (May 19, 1902) Mine explosion
* Memphis (April 27, 1865) Steamship *Sultana*
Texas
* New London (Mar. 18, 1937) Gas explosion: school
* Texas City (April 16–18, 1947) Liner *Grandcamp*
Utah
* Castle Gate (Mar. 8, 1924) Mine explosion
* Scofield (May 1, 1900) Mine explosion
Virginia
* Pocahontas (Mar. 13, 1884) Mine explosion
West Virginia
* Eccles (April 28, 1914) Mine explosion
* Monongah (Dec. 6, 1907) Mine explosion
Wyoming
* Hanna (June 30, 1903) Mine explosion
USSR
* Ufa (June 3, 1989) Gas pipeline; passenger trains
Yugoslavia
* Kakanj (June 7, 1965) Mine explosion

CHRONOLOGY

* Detailed in text

1856
July 15
Glamorgan, Wales; mine explosion
1857
Feb. 19
Yorkshire, England; mine explosion
1860
Dec. 1
Risca, Wales; mine explosion
1862
Jan. 16
Northumberland, England; mine explosion
1865
April 27
* Memphis, Tennessee; steamship *Sultana*
1866
Dec. 12–13
* Barnsley, England; mine explosion
1867
Nov. 8
Pontypridd, Wales; mine explosion
1869
Sept. 6
* Plymouth, Pennsylvania; mine explosion
1875
Dec. 14
Mons, France; mine explosion
1877
Oct. 22
Lanarkshire, Scotland; mine explosion
1878
June 7
Haydock, England; mine explosion
Sept. 11
* Abercane, Wales; mine explosion
1880
July 15
Risca, Wales; mine explosion
Aug. 17
* Sunderland, England; mine explosion
1884
Mar. 13
* Pocahontas, Virginia; mine explosion
1885
Mar. 17
Camphausen, Germany; mine explosion
June 18
Lancashire, England; mine explosion
1887
May 4
Vancouver Island, British Columbia; mine explosion
1889
July 3
St.-Etienne, France; mine explosion
1890
Feb. 6
Monmouthshire, Wales; mine explosion
1892
Sept. 7
Mons, France; mine explosion

1894
June 23
Clyfydd, Wales; mine explosion
1895
June 10
Upper Silesia, Prussia; mine explosion
1900
May 1
* Scofield, Utah; mine explosion
1902
May 19
Coal Creek, Tennessee; mine explosion
May 23
Ferme, British Columbia; mine explosion
1903
June 30
* Hanna, Wyoming; mine explosion
1904
Jan. 24
Cheswick, Pennsylvania; mine explosion
1906
Mar. 10
* Courrieres, France; mine explosion
Mar. 29
Nagasaki, Japan; mine explosion
1907
Jan. 28
Rhenish, Prussia; mine explosion
Dec. 6
* Monongah, West Virginia; mine explosion
Dec. 19
* Jacob's Creek, Pennsylvania; mine explosion
1908
July 1
Jusovka, Russia; mine explosion
Nov. 11
Westphalia, Germany; mine explosion
1909
Feb. 16
Durham, England; mine explosion
Nov. 13
* Cherry, Illinois; mine explosion
1910
Dec. 21
* Hulton, England; mine explosion
1913
Oct. 14
* Sengenhydd, Wales; mine explosion
Oct. 22
* Dawson, New Mexico; mine explosion
1914
April 18
* Eccles, West Virginia; mine explosion
June 19
Lethbridge, Alberta; mine explosion
1915
April 13
Shimonoseki, Japan; mine explosion
1916
Feb. 6
Skoda, Austria; arsenal explosion
1917
Dec. 6
* Halifax, Nova Scotia; ammunition ship
1918
Jan. 12
Podmore Hall, England; mine explosion
Aug. 3
Hamont Station, Belgium; ammunition train
1920
July 16
Sapporo, Japan; mine explosion
1921
June 20
Berne, Switzerland; mine explosion
Sept. 21
* Oppau, Germany (See NUCLEAR AND INDUSRIAL ACCIDENTS)
1924
Mar. 8
* Castle Gate, Utah; mine explosion
Dec. 27
Otaru, Japan; harbor explosion
1925
Mar. 1
Kharput, Turkey, munitions plant
May 25
Peking, China; arsenal explosion
1928
May 19
* Mather, Pennsylvania; mine explosion
1930
Oct. 21
Alsdorf, Germany; mine explosion
1931
Feb. 12
* China (Manchuria); mine explosion
1934
Mar. 14
Lalibertad, El Salvador; explosives warehouse
Sept. 22
Wrexham, Wales; mine explosion
1935
Oct. 26
* Lanchow, China; arsenal explosion
1937
Mar. 18
* New London, Texas; gas explosion: school
1940
Mar. 29
Tsingtsing, China; mine explosion
1944
April 14
* Bombay, India; steamship explosion
1947
April 16–18
* Texas City, Texas; liner *Grandcamp*
Aug. 18
Cadiz, Spain; naval mine and torpedo factory
1949
Nov. 29
* Johanngeorgendstadt, East Germany; mine explosion
1956
Aug. 7
* Cali, Colombia; dynamite truck convoy
1958
Feb. 19
* Asansol, India; mine explosion

1960
Mar. 4
* Havana, Cuba; munitions ship *La Coubre*

1962
Feb. 7
* Volklingen, West Germany; mine explosion

1965
May 28
* Dharbad, India; mine explosion

June 1
* Fukuoka, Japan; mine explosion

June 7
* Kakanj, Yugoslavia; mine explosion

1969
Mar. 31
Barrotean, Mexico; mine explosion

1972
June 6
* Wankie, Rhodesia; mine explosion

1975
Dec. 27
Chasnala, India; mine explosion

1982
Nov. 2
* Salang Tunnel, Afghanistan; truck collision

1984
Feb. 25
Cubatao, Brazil; oil pipeline

Nov. 19
Mexico City, Mexico; gas storage area

1989
June 3
* Ufa, USSR; gas pipeline; passenger trains

• • • • •

EXPLOSIONS

• • • • •

Explosions are the most spectacular and dramatic of man-made disasters. Like volcanic eruptions, they occur instantaneously, usually without warning and always with great disturbance to the atmosphere. And their casualty counts are high. Those who die as a result of the initial explosions die cruelly and quickly. Of the secondary catastrophes set off by the blast, fire is the most obvious and pervasive. Thus, those who are not blown to bits are frequently burned to death. And in the case of mine explosions, those who escape either of these fates often expire by asphyxiation.

Historically, the worst and most widespread explosions have occurred in coal mines. Ever since its beginnings in Shropshire, England near the end of the 17th century, coal mining has been one of the most hazardous of all human occupations. Later methods of strip and open-pit mining were relatively safe, but underground coal mining, in which coal is extracted from the earth through long, interconnecting tunnels, has carried its hazards with it from its inception. Black lung disease and blindness are only the beginning. The added hazards of unsafe working conditions, cave-ins and barely accessible mine shafts—as well as low wages—have made the lot of the miner a rough one. And from the very beginning, the threat of explosions in these mines, which sometimes burrowed two miles beneath the earth's surface, has haunted miners and their families.

Coal is generally mined in two ways. The first, a laboriously slow method, is to chip away at the walls of shafts, breaking up the coal into sizable chunks that are then transported by cart to the surface.

The second method, more dangerous and widespread, is to drill holes in the face of the wall of coal, pack the holes with explosives, detonate the explosives and blast the coal into manageable chunks. The trick is to blast only the coal, not the mine, and the failure to maintain that delicate balance has resulted in a multitude of tragedies. As in railroading, human error has played the largest role in explosion disasters, both within mines and in other locations.

The hazard of overexploding is further compounded by the usual presence of toxic and ignitable gases. While the need for constant ventilation in the mines has always been apparent, it has not always successfully or diligently been assured. Early on, furnaces were kept burning beneath the surface of the earth to keep the air circulating, and the dangers of these are obvious. Later, manual and then electric fans circulated the air.

But even the most modern methods of ventilation sometimes fail to remove pockets of noxious and ignitable gases, which are called, in the parlance of mining, "damps." These damps come in different varieties, each of them dangerous. A damp, derived from the German *dampf,* which means fog or vapor, results from the decomposition of coal itself. Released by the process of mining, it is an inevitable by-product.

The various categories are:

Firedamp, which consists of methane and other flammable gases, often mixed with air. Explosive mixtures of firedamp with air usually contain from 1% to 14% methane.

Afterdamp, which is the mixture of gasses remaining after an explosion of firedamp. It consists chiefly of carbon dioxide and nitrogen.

Chokedamp, which is the general name given to any mixture of oxygen-deficient gases that cause suffocation.

And that last description is important, for it is perhaps the most pervasive cause of fatalities in mine explosions. An overload of blasting powder, a careless ignition process or an accident with a miner's lamp can ignite a pocket of firedamp. The explosion kills through the force of the blast and the resultant collapse of the tunnel. Fire spreads through the gases and the ever-present coal dust. This in turn produces afterdamp, which results in chokedamp. These secondary damps remove the oxygen from the air and thus suffocate miners who have survived both the blast and the fire.

The unavoidable presence of damps has always plagued both the operators and workers in mines, and various methods for detecting them have evolved over the ages. Keeping canaries in the depths of the first mines was one way of detecting the presence of damps. The birds have a low tolerance for noxious gases, and their deaths warned miners that damps were present. The Davey safety lamp was one of the first detection devices developed that did not require the deaths of birds. The color and height of the lamp flame indicated the amount of firedamp present. If the flame was extinguished, it was a sign of chokedamp. In modern mines, colorimetric detectors and methanometers are used to detect firedamp.

But no amount or sophistication of detection equipment can overcome human failure, and a quick survey of explosions, both within mines and without, points to human error, miscalculation or carelessness as causes. Too much blasting powder, too little care with a match or a miner's lamp, the storing of old and unstable ammunition in a ship in a crowded harbor (see *Fort Stikine,* Bombay, India, p. 132), a school board's decision to save money by channeling unsafe waste gas into a school (see New London, Texas school, p. 139), governmental cover-up that resulted in the overcrowding of a steamboat (see *Sultana,* Memphis, Tennessee, p. 137) and the misreading of signals by a ship's pilot (see *Mont Blanc,* Halifax, Nova Scotia, p. 123) are all human errors and responsible for the explosions that followed them.

No matter what the cause, the effects of explosions are catastrophic, and the magnitude of the heroism that follows has been correspondingly impressive.

The criterion for inclusion in this section is based on the number of fatalities. A general low figure of 200 deaths was used as a cutoff point, and even that seems generous, considering that the high point of fatalities has reached into the thousands.

• • • • • • • • • • • • • • •

AFGHANISTAN
SALANG TUNNEL

November 2, 1982

• • • • • • • • • • • • • • •

The collision of a Soviet army vehicle with a fuel truck in the Salang Tunnel near Kabul, Afghanistan on November 2, 1982 caused a massive explosion and fire. Three thousand motorists and soldiers trapped in the tunnel died from either the explosion, fire or fumes; hundreds more were injured.

The 1.7-mile-long Salang Tunnel is a gateway between Kabul, Afghanistan and the border of the USSR. Built by the Soviets in the 1970s, it is located 11,100 feet high in the rugged Hindu Kush range, a region in which, in late 1982, there was considerable activity between the Soviet army and Afghan rebels.

On November 2, 1982, a long Soviet army convoy entered the tunnel, which was crowded with civilian buses, cars and trucks. The convoy was traveling from Hairotum, on the Amu Darya, the border stream separating Afghanistan from the Soviet Union. Midway through the tunnel, which is 17 feet wide by 25 feet high, one of the Soviet army vehicles collided with a fuel tanker. With a gigantic roar that echoed from one end of the tunnel to the other, the tanker exploded, sending gouts of flame outward in all directions. Thirty army vehicles containing Soviet soldiers were consumed instantly, their occupants burned to death on the spot.

Flames rocketed along the narrow passage of the tunnel, setting fire to buses and civilian vehicles. Panic spread as quickly as the flames, and those in cars at either end of the tunnel tried to escape. But the Soviet army, thinking the explosion was the beginning of a rebel attack, blocked both ends of the tunnel with tanks, thus killing hundreds more from asphyxiation.

The nightmare was increased by two other factors: It was bitterly cold, and those motorists who were unable to see the cause of the tie-up assumed that it was just another traffic jam and remained in their cars with the engines running. This increased the carbon monoxide level in the tunnel, killing more unwary occupants. And to further complicate the situation, the tunnel's ventilation system had broken down days before and was not operating.

All of these factors combined to kill thousands of trapped and innocent civilians and soldiers alike, either from the blast, fire or asphyxiation. It would take days to retrieve the dead from the tunnel, and reports that inched their way slowly out of Afghanistan (no foreign reporters were allowed into the country in 1982) stated that there was hardly a person in the capital city of Kabul who did not have either a relative or a friend who had died in the disaster. The Soviet dead were taken to Kabul; the Afghan dead and injured had to be transported 70 miles east of Kabul to Jalalabad in Nangathar Province.

The exact number of dead would never be known. Estimates ranged between 2,000 and 3,000, with credence given by eyewitnesses to the higher figure.

CANADA
NOVA SCOTIA
HALIFAX

December 6, 1917

• • • • • • • • • • • • • • •

Eight million tons of TNT ignited to set off the worst accidental explosion in the history of the world when the munitions ship Mont Blanc *collided with the* Imo *in Halifax Harbor on December 6, 1917. Twelve hundred were killed; 8,000 were injured.*

The worst accidental explosion in the history of the world—that of eight million tons of TNT—occurred in Halifax Harbor on the morning of December 6, 1917, at the height of World War I. Commenting to the *Times* of London just after the calamity, Lieutenant Colonel Good of Fredericton opined that he had not seen that much carnage on the battlefields of France. "All that could be seen for a great circumference," he said, "were burning buildings, great mounds of iron and brick in the streets, and dead bodies."

Halifax was, during World War I, a gathering point for transatlantic convoys. Six miles long with a breadth of about one mile, it provided secure deep-water anchorage at times of both high and low tide. There was not a ship afloat that could not be comfortably accommodated at Halifax, and so, on December 7, 1917, a number of ships had gathered there, to be led by the British cruiser HMS *High Flyer* across the U-boat–infested Atlantic to Europe.

A few days earlier, the French freighter *Mont Blanc* had picked up a lethal cargo in New York. The 3,121-ton ship was loaded to the capacity of its hold with TNT, picric acid, gun cotton and barrels of benzene.

The morning of Thursday, December 6 was fog laden in its early hours, making visibility difficult, except for the experienced pilots aboard ships such as the *Mont Blanc,* who were used to the harbor. The *Mont Blanc* arrived at 8:40, and by then the sun had burned off most of the fog. All that was necessary was for the pilot to navigate "The Narrows," a portion of the harbor that slimmed down to a half-mile-wide channel. On the south shore lay the Richmond section of Halifax; on the north, the town of Dartmouth. Slightly beyond it was the berth into which the *Mont Blanc* was to ease, temporarily.

Suddenly, from around a bend in the channel, the Belgian relief ship *Imo* appeared, heading out to sea. Its course was carrying it directly toward the *Mont Blanc.* The captain of the *Mont Blanc* described what happened then to the London *Times:*

> *[Responding to a blast of the* Mont Blanc's *whistle by pilot Frank Mackie,] the* Imo *signaled that she was coming to port which would bring her to the same side with us. We were keeping to starboard and could not understand what the* Imo *meant, but kept our course, hoping that she would come down as she should on the starboard side, which would keep her on the Halifax side of the harbour.*
>
> *. . . Then we put the rudder hard aport to try to pass the* Imo *before she should come to us. At the same time the* Imo *reversed engines. As she was light, without cargo, the reverse brought her around slightly to port, her bow towards our starboard. As a collision was then inevitable, we held so that she would be struck forward of the hold where the picric acid substance, which would not explode, was stored, rather than have her strike where the TNT was stored.*

It was a correct and safe plan, if it had worked. But it did not. The *Imo* slammed into the *Mont Blanc,* gashing a huge hole in her side and setting fire to the benzene. The fire spread alarmingly. Once it reached the TNT, there would be a cataclysmic explosion. The captain knew this and immediately issued an abandon-ship order.

At pier eight, where the *Mont Blanc* was to dock, two simultaneous activities took place: A fire alarm was set, and Halifax's fire brigade rushed to the scene. At the same time, the captain of the British ammunition ship *Pictou,* moored at pier eight, realized the imminent mortal danger and ordered his ship abandoned too.

The two crews reached shore and began to scramble for the woods, which were only a short distance away, nestled against high cliffs that secured the harbor against winds. Workers in the dockside factories, seeing the running, shouting sailors, swarmed out of their factories and offices and, joining them, scrambled up the cliff toward the Citadel, Halifax's ancient fortress.

Only the captain of the cruiser *High Flyer* thought of trying to contain the blaze, and his heroic decision proved to be foolhardy and fatal. He ordered 23 men to man a launch and try to sink the *Mont Blanc* before she exploded.

The men had scarcely boarded the ship when, with a roar like a concentrated bombardment, it exploded, sending pieces of metal, balls of fire and white-hot explosive incendiaries sky high. A huge wall of water was forced outward from the explosion. It doubled back upon itself in a tidal wave that ripped huge ships from their moorings and tossed them up on the shore.

In Halifax, William Barton, eating his breakfast at the Halifax hotel, described it: "In ten seconds it was all over. A low rumbling, an earthquake shock, with everything vibrating, then an indescribable noise, followed by the fall of plaster, and the smashing of glass. A cry went up: 'A German bomb.' "

Richmond, on the other side of the harbor, was hit by pressure waves roaring through the trough of hills with the speed and force of a hurricane. An area two and a half miles in circumference was totally flattened by the blast and its aftermath. The explosion was felt up to 125 miles away; in the immediate vicinity it laid waste to everything. The Intercolonial Railway Station, a brick and stone structure in downtown Halifax, was flattened, crushing crowds of people waiting within. A hundred workers were killed in a sugar refining plant on the docks. Children were just gathering in the area schools to begin their school day. And sadly, every one of the schools would be torn asunder. Of the 550 school children in the Halifax area, only seven would survive.

Now fire began to spread, but every fireman in Halifax lay dead in the midst of the wreckage of all of Halifax's fire equipment. Twenty-five thousand people would ultimately be rendered homeless by either the explosion or its resultant fire.

It could have been considerably worse, but for the tidal wave, an act of heroism and a change in the weather.

The tidal wave caused by the explosion washed over the naval ammunition works at The Narrows, preventing it from catching fire and exploding.

Marine superintendent J. W. Harrison climbed aboard the abandoned British ammunition ship *Pictou,* tied up at pier eight, opened the sea valves and set the vessel adrift. Within minutes, the *Pictou* sank, along with its lethal cargo.

And finally, an hour after the explosion, the weather suddenly turned cold, and it began to snow furiously. The storm extinguished the fires that had been burning out of control and laying waste to large areas of Halifax.

Despite these modifications of a truly cataclysmic disaster, a large part of the city lay in ruins. By afternoon, the city militia would take charge. Trains with supplies from New York and Boston began to arrive, and public buildings were opened for the homeless and injured. Emergency hospitals set up by the Red Cross bulged.

Estimates of the dead ranged from 1,200 to 4,000. The official tally was 1,200 with over 8,000 injured. Ironically, and in contrast, only 12 soldiers from Halifax would lose their lives on the battlefields of Europe during the entire war.

CHINA
LANCHOW

October 26, 1935

• • • • • • • • • • • • • • • • •

Sabotage was suspected but never proved in the explosion of an arsenal in the middle of Lanchow, China on October 26, 1935. Two thousand were killed; thousands were injured.

In late 1935, Lanchow, in western China on the Yellow River, was, as it is today, an important industrial hub. Linked by rail to Peking and Mongolia, and on the highway to Tibet, it was, in 1935, important strategically to both the Kuomintang army of Chiang Kai-shek and the increasingly powerful Communists. In two short months, Lanchow would be the scene of the largest and most effective Communist uprising of the 1930s, and the terrible arsenal explosion in downtown Lanchow on October 26, 1935 may very well have been a grim prelude to that historic happening.

The ancient arsenal, containing thousands of pounds of powder and ammunition belonging to the Kuomintang, exploded with a mighty roar. The force was equal to that of an earthquake or a tornado, and for thousands of square yards around the scene of the explosion, houses were flattened as if they had been visited by a string of tornadoes.

Families sitting down for the midday meal were buried alive and later discovered perfectly in place, but dead. The explosion was so enormous that some residents were literally blown to bits. The portion of the city near the arsenal was totally devastated. Two thousand bodies were recovered, but the total casualty figures were thought to be higher.

CHINA
MANCHURIA

February 12, 1931

• • • • • • • • • • • • • • • • •

A paucity of information available in Manchuria on February 12, 1931 obscured or erased the reason for the gigantic mine explosion of that date. Three thousand died, and an unknown number were injured.

The difficulty of gathering news in Manchuria in 1931, when tensions between the Japanese and Chinese were at their highest, was dramatically represented by the monumental explosion of the Fushun mines, 50 miles east of Mukden, on February 12, 1931. Owned by the Fenchihu Company, the mines produced about seven million tons of coal a year and employed thousands of miners.

On February 12, 1931, 3,000 men were working in the mines when the colliery exploded with a thunderous impact. First reports emerging from the scene stated that all 3,000 had been entombed by the blast, which had collapsed not only the shafts but all entrances to them. On the next day, Japanese sources denied the report, stating that all 3,000 had been rescued.

On the following day, Chinese papers contradicted the Japanese version, reinstating the report that all 3,000 miners had perished in the explosion. No further details were ever released, and in September of that year, the "Manchurian Incident"—the bombing of the Japanese railway near Mukden—began the long slide into the Sino-Japanese War of 1937–45.

COLOMBIA
CALI

August 7, 1956

• • • • • • • • • • • • • • • • • •

No cause has ever been found for the explosion of seven dynamite trucks parked in the middle of Cali, Colombia on the night of August 7, 1956. Twelve hundred died, and thousands were injured in the blast.

It certainly seemed as if it was the work of organized terrorists, and General Gustavo Rojas Pinilla, the president of Colombia, stated that it was something planned and executed by "treacherous and criminal conspirators." But the mystery of who caused seven trucks loaded with dynamite to explode in the middle of the city of Cali, Colombia on the night of August 7, 1956 was never solved.

They were part of a military convoy of 20 trucks loaded with ammunition and dynamite, and they had disembarked at the Pacific port of Buenaventura, on the way to Cali and Bogota.

On August 6, the convoy reached Cali. Thirteen trucks peeled off and headed toward Bogota. Seven remained behind, parked in front of the main railroad terminal, which was also very near the Codazzi army barracks and the heart of the downtown district of this city of 900,000 located in the western part of Colombia.

At a few minutes after midnight on August 7, all seven trucks detonated with an earsplitting roar. Every window within a three-mile radius was shattered; the blast scooped out a huge crater in the street in which the atomized trucks had once been parked. Eight city blocks were obliterated, including the Codazzi barracks, in which 500 sleeping soldiers were killed. Even the bronze doors of Cali's enormous and imposing St. Peter's Cathedral, located a full 13 blocks from the blast site, were blown off.

Twelve hundred people were killed in the explosion, and thousands were injured. And the true cause or the persons who set the blast would never be found.

CUBA
HAVANA

March 4, 1960

• • • • • • • • • • • • • • • • • •

A broken hoist cable allowed a net full of grenades to plummet to the deck of the Belgian ammunition ship La Coubre *in Havana Harbor on March 4, 1960. One hundred were killed in the explosion; scores more were injured.*

A broken cable on a hoist, a pregnant pause, and a net full of grenades plummeted to the deck of the Belgian munitions ship *La Coubre,* tied up in Havana Harbor on the afternoon of March 4, 1960. With a roar that shook buildings on the waterfront and sent shock waves against the hovering helicopter holding Fidel Castro, the ship blew up, scattering pieces of it for blocks and shooting off ammunition in all directions.

Longshoremen, soldiers and crew members aboard the ship were ripped apart by the force of the explosion and the resulting release of live bullets or burned to death by the enormous fire that burst forth after the blast. G. Delgado, a fireman who was called to the dock to fight the fire, was momentarily trapped in the ship's stern when it rolled over, preparatory to sinking. "It looked like a scene from Dante's *Inferno,*" Delgado told reporters. "Bodies and pieces of bodies were all over. God knows how I escaped. Bullets and shrapnel were flying all around me."

One hundred men died in the blast, most of them from the direct explosion of the grenades when they detonated on the deck.

Castro would later blame the explosion on CIA sabotage and even staged a media event in which he ordered two cases of grenades to be dropped 400 feet, from a helicopter onto a ball field. The grenades in these cases did not explode on contact, but six soldiers were killed as grenades detonated when they attempted to clean up the debris.

FRANCE
COURRIERES

March 10, 1906

• • • • • • • • • • • • • • • • • •

The worst mine explosion in French history, in the Courrieres Colliery in northern France on March 10, 1906, was caused by a combination of a smoldering fire in the pit and trapped gases. One thousand sixty miners died; hundreds were injured.

Rescued miners wait to be lifted to the surface after the gigantic mine explosion in the Courrieres Colliery, in which 1,060 miners died. London Illustrated News

The Courrieres Colliery in northern France was part of an enormous complex of coal mines that employed 2,000 men and boys. Located in the mountainous region of Pas-de-Calais, the mines formed a series of subterranean tunnels whose multiple outlets were spaced over several towns. Six of the outlets were near Lens; the rest emerged at Courrieres, Verdun, and other tinier hamlets populated by the families of coal miners. The output of the mines was a particularly combustible coal that was largely used in the manufacture of gas and in smelting.

At 3 o'clock in the afternoon of the day before France's worst mine disaster, a small, smoldering fire began in the Cecil pit of the Courrieres mine, at a depth of 270 meters, in a location in which masonry work was being done. Engineers tried to cope with the small blaze but were unable, through a night and early morning, to extinguish it. They opted to starve it of air and closed the outlet.

Apparently, fissures in the walls allowed combustible gases to creep into the closed-off portion of the tunnel. At 7 A.M., when 1,795 men and boys were working in the mine, the pit exploded with a thunderous roar, spitting cages and debris from the mouth of the shaft and killing several men and horses who were above ground near the shaft

Rescuers inside the Courrieres Colliery. London Illustrated Nes

opening. The roof of the mine office was blown cleanly off.

Rescuers began their work immediately, drawing up the injured, most of whom were terribly burned. Fires poured from every outlet, driving off rescuers and driving down the hopes of the thousands of family members who also rushed to the mine, pushing against the cordons of police that were hastily formed.

Leon Cerf, a survivor, recounted the scene below at the time of the explosion to the *New York Times:*

> *I was working with a gang when the explosion occurred. The foreman immediately shouted for us to follow him, and, dashing into a recess in the gallery, we were followed by a blast of poisonous gases, which, however, rushed by without affecting us. We remained there for eight hours, when, feeling that suffocation was gradually coming upon us, we attempted to escape. We crawled in single file toward the shaft, but several of the men dropped dead on the way, including my son and the foreman. I carried my nephew on my back for forty minutes, and succeeded in saving him. It took us four hours to reach the shaft.*

He was one of the fortunate. Others, trapped farther below, could not be reached by rescuers because of collapsed tunnels and noxious afterdamp and chokedamp. One group of rescuers, descending in a cage, distinctly heard a tapping on water pipes, indicating that there were imprisoned miners nearby. But engineers summoned to the location, listening to the same tapping, dashed hopes by estimating that it would take eight days to dislodge the debris in that part of the shaft. By then, the engineers reasoned, the miners would be dead of either starvation or asphyxiation. During the next few hours of rescue work, the tapping diminished and then ceased.

Rescue workers continued to toil through the night. One party of 40 disappeared into a shaft that collapsed behind them, burying them alive.

A huge mortuary camp was set up, and 400 soldiers were called in to buttress the police presence and control hysterical relatives, crying to see the bodies. Some rescuers descended scores of times into the pits until they themselves collapsed. One rescuer, brought to the surface unconscious, was packed into a closed carriage to be driven home. A group of miners, suspecting that the carriage contained bodies, broke its windows, further injuring the exhausted rescuer.

When hope and rescue work were finally abandoned a week later, the death toll was set at 1,060, making it the greatest single mine calamity in not only France but the European continent to that date.

GERMANY
JOHANNGEORGENDSTADT

November 29, 1949

• • • • • • • • • • • • • • • • •

Soviet security prevented the rest of the world from knowing the cause and details of the explosion in the uranium mine in Johanngeorgendstadt, East Germany on November 29, 1949. Three thousand seven hundred were reportedly killed and an unknown number injured.

Soviet authorities clamped an airtight lid on details of the horrendous explosion in the Soviet uranium mine at Johanngeorgendstadt, in Saxony, East Germany on November 29, 1949. The only report that found its way into Western newspapers came from the chief officer of a fire brigade in Leipzig. The officer escaped from the Soviet zone in December, and brought with him some data on the explosion, which had been large enough to register on seismographs in Europe.

Four thousand workers had been in the mine when the explosion occurred, according to the officer, and only 200 to 300 of them had been rescued, which meant that at least 3,700 had perished in this, one of the worst mine disasters of all time.

Precise details would never be known. Soviet security police cordoned off the mine immediately after the explosion. Eighty members of the Johanngeorgendstadt fire brigade fought the blazes that occurred as a result of the blast. When they finished their work, according to the escaped officer, all 80 were arrested by the Soviet security police and shot to death.

GERMANY
OPPAU

September 21, 1921

• • • • • • • • • • • • • • • • •

See NUCLEAR AND INDUSRIAL ACCIDENTS, p. 250.

GERMANY
VOLKLINGEN

February 7, 1962

• • • • • • • • • • • • • • • • •

Methane gas exploded in the Luisenthal pit in Volklingen, West Germany on February 7, 1962. Two hundred ninety-eight miners were killed; more than 200 were injured.

By 1962, it was thought that the danger from the various damps (firedamp, afterdamp, chokedamp) had been solved.

Colorimetric detectors and the methanometer had replaced earlier, more primitive means of detection, and miners could toil in relative safety.

That security was blasted into oblivion on February 7, 1962 in the Luisenthal pit in Volklingen, West Germany. One of the most modern collieries, it employed 480 men per shift in well-supported shafts on several levels. At precisely 8:00 A.M. that morning, methane gas exploded in the second-level tunnel, igniting a huge fire that licked along this shaft until it found the main one, where it branched upward and downward.

A second explosion followed swiftly on the heels of the first, when flames found more methane at the 1,800-foot level. Chokedamp filled every inch of the tunnel, and multiple explosions followed in quick succession.

The men trapped in the tunnels had almost no chance of survival. They suffocated immediately or were crushed to death when the shaft ceilings collapsed from the multiple explosions. "The injured looked terrible," said one survivor, George Kneip. "Some looked completely black. Many cried in agony. One body was headless."

Two hundred ninety-eight miners were killed and more than 200 injured in this, one of the worst mine disasters in German history.

GREAT BRITAIN
ENGLAND
BARNSLEY

December 12–13, 1866

• • • • • • • • • • • • • • • •

An overabundance of blasting powder caused the explosion in the Oaks Colliery, in Barnsley, England on December 12, 1866. Three hundred forty died; the number of injured was unreported.

The Oaks Colliery, located at Barnsley, a short distance north of London, was one of the largest producers of coal in the South Yorkshire district of England in the 19th century. Over 430 miners toiled in its depths, whose principal shaft was known as the "dip" and along which ran a broad roadway. Adjacent to this was the so-called engine plane, a passage that ran for two miles. Underground, the colliery resembled a small city, with horses that pulled the carts of coal upward housed in underground stalls, and an air circulation system facilitated by a large furnace that burned night and day.

Boys worked alongside men in the 19th century in England. There were no child labor laws to speak of, and the day shift of December 2, 1866 consisted of one-third boys and two-thirds men. Although the mine was worked around the clock, the day shift was the most active, and it was only during this time that coal was removed from the mine.

Three hundred thirty men and boys entered the mine at 6 A.M. on Wednesday morning, December 12. At 1:20 P.M., the ground shook, and a dull, heavy explosion erupted from the mouth of the main shaft of the mine. Dense columns of smoke and dust shot into the air from each of the shafts, and in a few seconds the pit bank was enveloped in a thick black cloud.

The explosion had collapsed all of the air shafts, locking noxious fumes in the tunnels in which the miners worked. Rescuers arrived on the scene almost immediately, and, led by a Mr. T. Diamond, the managing partner in the mine, and Superintendent Greenhalgh, a rescue party immediately lowered itself as far as it could into the main shaft. Eighteen badly injured men were discovered and brought immediately to the surface. That would be the last good news of the day.

The longer they searched, and the more deeply they dug, rescuers found only the bodies of miners, caught by the afterdamp or crushed under falling timbers. The stables were flattened, and 20 horses lay dead there. Many of the miners were frozen in attitudes of prayer; one group of 20 was clustered together in a last gesture of communal protection.

Rescuers worked all day and all night of the 12th, digging out tunnels and transporting an increasing number of bodies to the surface. By 8 A.M. on the morning of the 13th, nearly 800 yards of temporary airways had been constructed, and the searchers had penetrated some of the farthest reaches of the mine's tunnels. Only one level contained fire, and it was minor.

And then, shortly after 8 A.M., some of the 37 rescuers in the mine noticed that the air was being rapidly drawn from them. A miner in the rescue party recognized the signs: Another explosion was in the making. Sixteen of the 37 scrambled to the surface and warned another party that was about to descend that there was danger of another explosion. Incredibly, most of this search party refused to believe the escaped rescuers and descended into the mine anyway.

This second party had just reached the bottom of the shaft, at approximately 9 A.M. on the morning of Thursday, December 13, when a second explosion tore through the tunnels of the Oaks Colliery. Debris and pieces of the rescue party shot out of the newly made openings as if they were part of an artillery barrage.

Forty minutes later, shortly before 10 A.M., a third, lesser explosion rocked the works and made rescuers think twice before resuming their work. By nightfall, the mine had

The giant explosion in the Oaks Colliery in Barnsley, England on December 12, 1866 is graphically portrayed in a contemporary lithograph. Three hundred forty men and boys died in the tragedy. Illustrated London News

apparently quieted, and search parties resumed their digging. Some miraculous rescues occurred; individual miners, nearly dead from chokedamp, managed to climb through the debris and meet the rescue parties, who then raised them to the surface by means of a wooden tub suspended from a makeshift block-and-tackle system.

Not many lived, however. Three hundred forty men, 28 of them rescuers, died in the three explosions.

The reason for the tragedy had been a long time coming, according to a report in the Sheffield, England *Independent:* "It seems that there have been for some time complaints of the heat of the atmosphere from the long distance the air had to travel through the workings," the newspaper report noted. The engine plane had been the only passage used to ventilate the tunnels, and so Mr. Diamond, the managing partner, had determined that December to dig another ventilating tunnel.

Apparently an impatient man, Diamond ordered a maximum amount of blasting powder to be used to expedite the task. On Wednesday morning, December 12, miners Richard Hunt and John Clayton began to use a long drill. They decided that a large charge of dynamite was needed to drive it through to its destination and thus wired up a large charge. William Wilson, the man in charge of operations, learned of this while he was working at another location; realizing the possible consequences of setting off such a charge at that specific place—which was filled with pockets of methane—he dashed to the site where Hunt and Clayton were by now setting a fuse.

He got there too late. The fuse was set and detonated just as he arrived on the scene, and the dynamite went up in a fearful roar, igniting the gas and causing a cataclysmic explosion. Astonishingly, Wilson lived to tell the story. The other two were killed by the blast they set.

GREAT BRITAIN
ENGLAND
HULTON

December 21, 1910

• • • • • • • • • • • • • • •

No cause was determined for the explosion in the Little Hulton Mine in Hulton, England on December 21, 1910. All 360 miners in the mine were killed.

The Little Hulton Mine, owned by the Hulton Colliery Company and located in the small town of that name some four miles from Bolton, England, was entirely demolished by a calamitous explosion and fire on the morning of December 21, 1910.

At a little after 7 A.M., shortly after the morning shift descended into the colliery, an ear-shattering explosion rocked the countryside, wrecked the lift mechanism of the shaft and showered the hills with debris. Almost immediately, an inferno of flames spit out of the head of the shaft, preventng rescuers from entering.

When the fire was finally brought under control, rescuers found their way blocked. The shaft had collapsed entirely below the 400-yard level, burying the entire shift of miners.

For a few hours, the fate of 400 other men working in an adjoining mine was in jeopardy when passageways between the two mines collapsed. But all 400 men of that shift were brought to the surface, including several who were injured by the impact of the explosion.

The fate of the workers in the Little Hulton Mine was just the opposite. Rescuers found small groups of bodies of men who were working above the 400-yard level, and that was all. By 9:30 that night, the fate of the entire shift of 360 boys and men was obvious. None could have survived; they were either crushed, blown apart or asphyxiated. Not one person escaped alive from the mine.

GREAT BRITAIN
ENGLAND
SUNDERLAND

August 17, 1880

• • • • • • • • • • • • • • •

The ignition of afterdamp was responsible for the explosion in the Seaham Colliery in Sunderland, England on August 17, 1880. One hundred sixty-one were killed; scores were injured.

Large collieries proliferated throughout Britain and Wales in the 19th century and the first half of the 20th century, and one of the largest of these was the Seaham Colliery near Sunderland, England. Sixteen hundred miners worked three shifts in this hugely productive mine, churning out coal for the world.

On August 17, 1880, the village of Sunderland had scheduled its annual flower show. Heavily attended, it drew a large percentage of the village and surrounding areas, and it, more than anything else, probably accounted for the saving of hundreds of lives in the early morning tragedy that blasted apart the lowest seams of the mine's main tunnel and killed 161 members of a "light shift" of only 246. The death toll would have been considerably heavier and the mine certainly more thickly populated had it not been for the flower show. Many miners had decided to sleep in and go to the show rather than work this shift.

The explosion, touched off by the ignition of afterdamp—the highly combustible gas given off by coal, which, when it accumulates in the shafts, becomes lethal to humans—was set off by the lighted lamp of an unsuspecting miner, at 2:30 A.M. It collapsed the walls and ceilings of the shaft, burying many of the miners. Others, near the blast, were ripped apart and found in pieces later that day.

The other, latent danger in any mine explosion is the spreading of the afterdamp, which, now released, filled the other tunnels, killing the survivors as quickly and effectively as an army's poison gas.

Ralph Markey, a miner who had survived three previous explosions, was trapped, along with 18 other men, in a pocket of space caused by the collapse of a shaft wall. Speaking later to the *Illustrated London News,* Markey recalled feeling a rush of wind an instant before the blast.

Sizing up the situation, Markey led the men in a digging-out exercise that brought them into one of the main shafts. They followed this for a quarter of a mile, stepping over the corpses of their fellow miners. "A deputy overman named Wardle," recalled Markey "[was] lying insensible, with his face covered with blood, and here [came] the afterdamp."

The group pressed cloths to their faces and tried to crawl under the lethal layer of gas.

Eventually, they reached the elevator shaft, but the cage was useless, jammed halfway between tunnels. At last air filtered down to them, and they posted shouters to continually call up the shaft, while the rest of them prepared tea.

It would be two hours before shouted encouragement reached them, assuring them that rescuers were on their way, and another eight hours before a party led by Stratton, the owner of the mine, would reach them. Eighty-five miners would be rescued; 161 would die in the great colliery explosion of 1880.

GREAT BRITAIN
WALES
ABERCANE

September 11, 1878

• • • • • • • • • • • • • • • •

The cause of the explosion in the Ebbw Vale Steel, Iron and Coal Company's Abercane Colliery in Abercane, Wales on September 11, 1878 was and remains unknown. Two hundred sixty-eight miners died in the explosion; 12 were injured.

The Abercane Colliery, owned by the Ebbw Vale Steel, Iron and Coal Company, was one of the largest collieries in South Wales during the end of the 19th century. Situated a few hundred yards from the Abercane railway station, on the Western Valley section of the Monmouthshire Railway, it nestled in a picturesque valley, in the shadow of the Crumlin Viaduct, one of Wales' most charming and well-visited tourist attractions.

It was not unusual to have a working colliery in the midst of town in the 1800s; the production of bituminous coal was to Wales then what oil wells later became to Oklahoma and Texas. And the Abercane Colliery in its most productive times produced 1,000 tons of "steam" coal daily.

It was also one of the most up-to-date mines in the world. Its winding, pumping and ventilating machinery was the most modern for its day; its use of safety lamps was rigidly enforced.

Thus, the 373 men and boys who entered the mine at 11:00 A.M. on September 12, 1878 felt protected and secure. If there ever was an explosion-proof mine, it was this one. And thus, the reason that the mine exploded with an ear-shattering roar at 12:10 P.M. that day was and would remain an unexplained mystery.

The first explosion was followed by two others of equal force. Within seconds, a huge tongue of flame flew from the main shaft opening, followed by dense clouds of acrid smoke, dust and debris. An enormous fire was obviously burning within the pit, incinerating whoever was there.

The winding gear for the buckets that transported men in and out of the mine was damaged by the explosion and had to be repaired before rescuers could begin their work. When it was back in operation, they brought out 82 men and boys who had been working within a few hundred yards of the shaft opening.

But that would be the extent of the rescue. Descending to the bottom of the 330-yard-deep mine, rescuers found horrible devastation. The underground stables yielded 14 dead horses, 12 terribly burned men and 13 bodies. Most of the ambient tunnels had collapsed, and those that had not were unapproachable. The chokedamp was pervasive and lethal, and rescuers were repeatedly turned back.

Finally, at 2:30 A.M. on September 13, to the despair of hundreds of relatives at the scene, it was decided to flood the mine to prevent further fire and explosions. The bodies of 255 men and boys were buried underground; only the 13 bodies that were discovered near the stables were brought to the surface. It would be one of Wales' worst and most mysterious mine disasters.

GREAT BRITAIN
WALES
SENGENHYDD

October 14, 1913

• • • • • • • • • • • • • • • •

There is no known cause for the greatest mine disaster in the history of Great Britain, the explosion in the Universal Colliery at Sengenhydd, Wales on October 14, 1913. Three hundred forty-three died; 12 were injured.

The greatest mine disaster in the history of Great Britain occurred on the morning of October 14, 1913 at the Universal Colliery at Sengenhydd, South Wales, eight miles from Cardiff.

The colliery consisted of two pits, side by side, the Lancaster and York. At 6:00 A.M. on October 14, 935 men descended into the two mine shafts, beginning the first and most active shift of the day.

At 8:12 A.M., the earth around the mine shafts shook, and an enormous explosion ripped through the Lancaster pit, spewing a fountain of debris and dust skyward and ripping out the pithead gear. Within minutes, plumes of orange flames shot up from the pit opening.

Hundreds of rescuers came on the scene immediately, but they were unable to descend into the Lancaster pit because of the intensity of the fire. Not only was the heat tremendous, but the fire was blocking the only air intake to the shaft. It would be an hour before the fire would be controlled enough to allow the pit gear from the undamaged York pit, 50 yards away, to be set in place so that rescuers could be lowered into the Lancaster shaft.

The teams found a holocaust. The force of the explosion had been enormous. Scores of headless and dismembered bodies were found, but fortunately, so were hundreds of survivors. All in all, 498 men were raised, in groups of 20, to the surface by miners from nearby collieries. Twelve seriously injured men were taken to nearby hospitals.

But that still left nearly 350 men trapped within the collapsed mine shaft. Rescuers attempted to enter these shafts, but the afterdamp threatened to kill them, too, and

An anxious crowd gathers outside the ruined Universal Colliery in Sengenhydd, Wales following the worst mine disaster in the history of Great Britain, on October 14, 1913. Illustrated London News

by nightfall, it was apparent that the only survivors of the explosion were now above ground. By that time, 40,000 people had gathered at the pitheads, hoping for a miracle.

The rescuers dug on into the night, recovering 73 more bodies. Finally, on the morning of October 15, the decision was made to seal the mine. Three hundred forty-three men and boys had lost their lives, and slightly more than 200 of them would be sealed in the mine that morning.

Prince Arthur of Connaught and his bride of only a few weeks sent messages of sympathy to the bereaved families of the dead miners and announced that the royal wedding presents would be exhibited in public for the next month as a means of raising money for relief funds.

INDIA
ASANSOL

February 19, 1958

• • • • • • • • • • • • • • • • • •

A gas explosion collapsed a mine in Asansol, India on February 19, 1958. One hundred eighty-three died; scores were injured.

There is a maze of interlocking tunnels in the mines beneath Asansol, India. Like a mountain with a multitude of subterranean ski trails, separate mines interlock and cross.

On February 19, 1958, gases within one of the tunnels ignited and exploded, setting off a chain reaction of echoing explosions throughout the underground system. Walls caved in; the roofs of shafts collapsed and crushed miners beneath them. To add to the terror, water from underground sources poured into the shafts, filling them and drowning many more men.

It would be six hours before rescuers could even reach the first of a mere 17 men. Of the 200 working that particular shift, 183 died.

INDIA
BOMBAY

April 14, 1944

• • • • • • • • • • • • • • • • • •

No cause was ever discovered for the explosion of the ammunition ship Fort Stikine *in Victoria Dock, Bombay, India on April 14, 1944. One thousand three hundred seventy-six were killed, and more than three thousand were injured.*

Victoria Dock, in Bombay, was nicknamed the Gateway to India. Built up over years of British rule, it was equipped with all of the niceties necessary to supply the residing colonials with their needs and to link India with the rest of the industrialized world.

In 1944, at the height of World War II, it was an abnormally busy place. Armies of the Allies were in omnipresent evidence; troop ships, ships loaded with supplies, aircraft, artillery and ammunition, docked and left regularly. On April 14, 1944, there were no less than 27 ships docked there.

Two months earlier, the Canadian-built cargo ship *Fort Stikine* left Birkinhead, England with 12 dismantled Spitfires, over 1,390 tons of explosives and a million pounds of gold bricks. It was obviously a potential seaborne volcano, and its captain, Alexander J. Naismith, was instructed to remain on the outskirts of the convoy to which it was attached. A well-placed torpedo could cause the *Fort Stikine* to ignite the entire convoy.

However, the voyage from England to Karachi was uneventful. At that port, the Spitfires were unloaded, and a masking cargo of 8,700 bales of raw cotton, several hundred barrels of lubricating oil, a holdful of scrap metal and another holdful of fish manure was added. It was, then, not only a dangerous but also an odoriferous voyage from Karachi to Bombay, and the priority off-load when the ship finally tied up at Victoria Dock was the fish manure.

Five gangs of Indian stevedores began the long task of unloading the masking cargo on April 13, beginning with the fish. The next day, they were still unloading when smoke began to rise out of the number two hold, which held explosives. (Later investigation would turn up no clues regarding its origin. It remains a mystery to this day.)

Firemen were called, and they arrived immediately, but within moments it was obvious that they would need reinforcements. Unfortunately, the man sent out to call for them found a dial-less phone, which he abandoned before the operator could come on the line. He then set off an alarm box that only signaled a minimum fire force—far less than was required to halt the spreading blaze, which was now advancing on the small-arms ammunition.

The cotton bales went up in flames, and despite the fact that 32 hoses were trained on the fire, it was apparent to the sailors aboard that the ship was going to blow. Shortly afterward, the small-arms ammunition exploded, and some of the fire fighters left the ship.

It was time for a quick decision on the part of Captain Naismith: take the ship out into the harbor, away from the docks and other ships, or scuttle it? At 3:30 P.M. on April 14, while he was still making up his mind, the first of a series of major explosions erupted, blowing away the entire bow, from the bridge forward, and killing the captain. Pieces of the ship and shrapnel from the ammunition planed across the water and flew through the air. The 400-foot *Japlanda*, anchored alongside the *Fort Stikine*, was blown 60 feet in the air. It landed on the roof of a shed on the dock, setting the shed on fire.

Everyone in the bow of the ship and everyone on the dock near it was either killed or horribly mangled by the explosion. There was not one single fireman left without at least one arm or leg missing.

Rescuers tried to drag the injured and the dying away from the vessel, but they had no sooner begun their task when a second, bigger explosion destroyed the rest of the ship and the remainder of Bombay Harbor. Every single one of the 27 ships docked there was sunk. Gold bricks soared through the air, landing in the heart of Bombay, killing scores of people as effectively as if the bricks were Japanese or German bombs.

The scrap metal was an even more lethal danger. The enormous cloud caused by the explosion, which rose 3,000 feet in the air, was laced with fragments of metal. Some of the heavier pieces fell on parked cars, flattening them and killing the occupants. Others demolished homes. Over a mile away, Captain Sidney Kielly, walking to his office, was cut in half by a piece of falling metal.

It was a horror beyond description for the unsuspecting residents of Bombay, who were suddenly faced with death raining out of the sky. Every ship, every home, every shed, every building, every square foot of docking in the harbor was blown to bits. It would take days for the Indian fire department, aided by over 7,000 allied troops, to put out the fire, haul off the injured and count the dead. One thousand three hundred seventy-six would die, and more than 3,000 would be injured in this, one of the worst man-made explosions of all time.

INDIA
DHARBAD

May 28, 1965

• • • • • • • • • • • • • • • • • • •

A methane gas ignition was responsible for the explosion in the coal mine in Dharbad, India on May 28, 1965. Three hundred seventy-five were killed; hundreds were injured.

Dharbad, 225 miles northwest of Calcutta, was rocked by an enormous explosion in its coal mine on May 28, 1965. A spark of unknown origin ignited methane in one of its shafts, blasting apart a huge section of the mine and sending coal dust into the air over a four-mile radius.

The force of the explosion was so great that it killed over 100 miners who were working on the surface of the mine; it also demolished the record office, the engine room and several nearby houses. Timbers from the shafts were shot upward and soared like airborne battering rams over the area.

The entire main shaft was consumed by raging flames. It would be several days before rescue workers could even begin to enter it. When they finally did, they would find 375 dead.

JAPAN
FUKUOKA

June 1, 1965

• • • • • • • • • • • • • • • • •

Failure to install safety devices by the management of the Yamano coal mine, near Fukuoka, Japan, led to an explosion in the mine on June 1, 1965. Two hundred thirty-six miners were killed; 37 were injured.

The early to mid-1960s seemed to be a time rife with mine explosions (see pp. 127, 133 and 147). One of these, the explosion in the Yamano coal mine, near Fukuoka, Japan, was the result of negligence on the part of management.

In 1959, an explosion in a pocket of methane gas had killed seven miners and injured 24. The management had been cited for safety lapses and had agreed to correct them to avoid a repetition of the small tragedy.

But by June 1, 1965, when 552 miners were at work in the mine, nothing had been done. No methanometers had been installed; no colorimetric detectors had been purchased. The mine was still a time bomb waiting to ignite.

And ignite it did, with a stupendous roar. Shafts collapsed; great, multi-ton boulders sealed off passages. Miners suffocated on the spot as the chokedamp filled the tunnels. Two hundred seventy-nine miners managed to scramble to the elevators, which were fortunately still working, and ascend to safety. Of the 279, 37 were seriously injured and were carried to the surface by their fellow miners.

It would be two days before rescuers could pierce the sealed off chambers that contained the dead. More than 2,000 relatives had kept vigil, day and night, hoping that there would be some survivors. There were none. Two hundred thirty-six miners were discovered, every one of them dead.

The Trade and Industries minister, Yoshio Sakarauchi, resigned his office the next day, admitting that his office had failed to introduce the obvious safety measures that could have prevented the disaster.

RHODESIA
WANKIE

June 6, 1972

• • • • • • • • • • • • • • • • •

A methane gas ignition caused the explosion that decimated the Wankie Colliery in Rhodesia on June 6, 1972. Four hundred twenty-seven miners were killed; 37 escaped unscathed.

Rhodesia's largest colliery is located in Wankie, in the middle veld of that African republic. The town of Wankie contains 20,000 people, and in one way or another, almost all of them are either employed in the mine or related to those who are working in it.

Thus, when, on the afternoon of June 6, 1972, an enormous explosion rocked the earth around the number two shaft of the Wankie Colliery, it immediately emptied every dwelling and filled every person with an understandable terror. A cable car had been spit out of the mouth of the shaft and lay in mangled ruins some yards beyond. Methane gas poured from the opening, and rescue parties were driven back for hours.

Finally, by nightfall, wearing masks and lights, teams of searchers dug into the earth around the shaft and lowered themselves into it. They discovered 37 men who had miraculously been able to squirrel themselves away from the main tunnel and thus avoid the lethal afterdamp.

Not so 427 other miners of that particular shift. Every one of them died, in one of the worst mine disasters in the history of southern Africa's coal mining.

UNITED STATES
CALIFORNIA
PORT CHICAGO

July 17, 1944

• • • • • • • • • • • • • • • • •

Unstable, outdated ammunition being loaded on the ammunition ships E. A. Bryan *and* Quinault Victory *exploded in Port Chicago, California on July 17, 1944. Three hundred twenty-one were killed; hundreds were injured.*

Port Chicago, a shipping town on San Francisco Bay, received a shot of life from World War II. Moderately active before the conflict, it became one of the main staging areas for naval supply ships headed for action in the Pacific, and it employed enough of the town's residents and brought in enough more to allow Port Chicago to qualify as a boom town.

But on the night of July 17, 1944, that title took on an ironic and tragic significance. Two supply ships, the *E. A. Bryan* and the *Quinault Victory,* were being loaded, and it would take almost until midnight to complete the job. The cargo was TNT and cordite, some of it left over from World War I, some of it newly manufactured, all of it destined for the troops fighting the Japanese.

The last of the shipment had almost been loaded when suddenly an enormous, ground-splitting explosion ripped through the ships and the wharves, sending 50-foot flames into the air that could be seen 50 miles away. San Francisco, Oakland and Alameda felt an earth tremor that most thought was the beginning of a major earthquake.

The shock waves of the detonation spread for 20 miles in all directions; every single building in the town of Port Chicago sustained some damage. Every one of the 1,500 residents was aware that something cataclysmic had happened on what were once the wharves of the town.

When the sun rose, it became clear that the waterfront had disappeared. It had been atomized, as had the ships and the 321 men who had been on them or loading them. There were no recognizable traces of docks, ships or men left.

There was talk of sabotage. There always was after a disaster in wartime. But the official conclusion was that the ancient World War I supplies were unstable and that this was probably the reason for the explosion.

UNITED STATES
ILLINOIS
CHERRY

November 13, 1909

The November 13, 1909 explosion in the St. Paul Company mine in Cherry, Illinois was caused by a miner's torch igniting a pile of hay. Two hundred fifty-nine miners died, and an unknown number were injured.

Until well into the 20th century, mules or horses were used to haul iron carts loaded with coal from the mines of both Europe and America. The animals were fed hay, and this hay was piled, as it was on any farm or factory, in an assigned place.

The choice of this place at the St. Paul Company mine in Cherry, Illinois was an unwise one, to put it charitably. Feed hay was piled next to the entrance to the main shaft of the mine, and at 1:00 P.M. on November 13, 1909 the piled hay caught fire from a discarded miner's torch.

It was a small, smoldering fire at first—hardly noticeable, and that was the problem. By the time the hay had begun to burn vigorously, it was too late. Despite workers' frantic efforts to shove, pull and wheel the bales away from the mine entrance, some of the flames from the fire shot into the shaft, igniting the gases in it. A gigantic explosion rocked the entrance to the mine, and flames quickly spread down the tunnel's timbers, setting off more explosions and forcing lethal smoke and chokedamp into the bowels of the mine.

There was chaos both above and below ground. The first group of six rescuers, led by mine superintendent John Bundy, died from fumes as soon as the elevator cage they rode hit bottom.

Trying to seal off the fire, another mine superintendent, James Steele, ordered the shaft entrance sealed. It merely intensified the heat below, as a second wave of rescuers with oxygen tanks and masks attested. Lowering themselves in one of the elevators, they soon ascended again, fleeing from the unbearable heat that prevented them from entering any of the three tunnels that snaked off from the main shaft.

Five thousand people quickly gathered at the mine, most of them relatives of the 400 men who had been trapped at the time of the explosion. Some men had died at the mouth of the shaft. One Andrew McFadden, ordered by his foreman to stay at the entrance and guard the mules, ignored logic and his fellow fleeing workers and followed orders. He was burned to death, along with the mules he was ordered to protect.

Finally, the shafts cooled enough to permit rescuers to penetrate the various subsidiary shafts and hunt for the living, the dead and the dying. The smoke was blinding, the chokedamp still lethal. Rescuers had to crawl on their bellies, holding on to the rails that had guided the carts to the surface in order to find the tunnels.

Rescuer William Vickers told a reporter for the *New York Times,* "At one point we passed about 65 miners sitting by the roadside, almost in a stupor. I tried to rouse them and encourage them to go on, but they seemed to have given up all hope, and did not stir. I had no time to lose and continued on, expecting to send back relief from the shaft. The sight of my doomed comrades is something that will haunt me until my dying day."

Vickers himself escaped death by minutes. Crawling back to the elevator shaft, he collapsed a few feet from it, and only the alertness of two other rescuers, already in the cage, saved him. The men dragged him to the elevator, just as it began to ascend.

He was one of the last out alive. Thirty-six hours of rescue work turned up 170 men, who were saved. Two hundred fifty-nine others died in the fire, explosion and release of toxic gases.

UNITED STATES
NEW MEXICO
DAWSON

October 22, 1913

• • • • • • • • • • • • • • • • •

The blast that destroyed one of the Stag Canyon Fuel Company's coal mines in Dawson, New Mexico was caused by dynamite charges igniting coal dust in the mine. Two hundred sixty-three miners were killed, and 10 were injured in the explosion.

Dynamite was used frequently in the Stag Canyon Fuel Company's coal mines in Dawson, New Mexico. It was an efficient means of loosening coal from the veins, and it was considered a safe method in this meticulously run mine, which contained all of the most modern safety devices developed by 1913. Sprayers were located at intervals in the shafts to cut down on the presence of ignitable coal dust and chokedamp. Dynamite charges were ignited, not by torch, as they were in some mines, but by electrical impulses activated from safe areas above ground. There were electric fans to assure free circulation of air and prevent the building up of pockets of methane.

Yet with all of these precautions, a series of dynamite detonations set off an uncontrolled explosion at 3:00 P.M. on October 22, 1913. Coal dust that had not been damped down by the sprinkler system was ignited; it exploded, and the force of the explosion collapsed the main shaft, trapping 284 miners.

The explosion also disabled the main air fans, and toxic gases, freed by the explosions, rapidly filled all of the tunnels of the mine. It would be two hours before a rescue team carrying oxygen bottles and equipped with masks could enter. The afterdamp was so thick that, despite their gear, they were overcome and had to be rescued by a backup team.

Only 21 men were saved, and it would be 8 o'clock that night before the lethal gases would abate enough to allow men to enter and pile the dead in carts that had heretofore hauled coal from the mine. Two hundred sixty-three miners, almost the entire shift, perished in the explosion or its aftermath.

UNITED STATES
PENNSYLVANIA
JACOB'S CREEK

December 19, 1907

• • • • • • • • • • • • • • • • •

No cause was ever discovered for the explosion of the Darr Mine of the Pittsburgh Coal Company in Jacob's Creek, Pennsylvania on December 19, 1907. Two hundred thirty-nine miners were killed, and one was injured.

The Darr Mine of the Pittsburgh Coal Company in Jacob's Creek, Pennsylvania was located in the side of a mountain separated by a gorge from Jacob's Creek and the nearby Youghiogheny River. From its entrance, it plunged nearly two miles into the earth. That entrance was almost inaccessible. The only way miners could get to it was via a so-called sky ferry, which was a wooden bucket on a winch that lifted six men at a time from Jacob's Creek to the mine entrance.

The sheer laboriousness of even getting to work made the Darr Mine an unpopular place to work, and so the 240-man shift that was working on the morning of December 19, 1907 was composed mainly of Greek and Italian immigrants.

Life was tempestuous and sad in the nearby mining community of Jacob's Creek. Not only were there bad feelings between the Greeks and Italians, which sometimes erupted into confrontations that bayonet-wielding law enforcers had to break up; there was also the pervasive fear that hung over everyone. The mine was rife with pockets of chokedamp.

Mrs. John Campbell, the wife of the mine foreman, later interviewed by local journalists, admitted, "I have for a long time feared an explosion in the mine, for I knew it was gaseous. My husband and I had talked of it, and he often referred to the gas in the mine."

That explosion finally came, at 11:30 A.M. on December 19, 1907, when a 240-man shift was at work two miles deep in the mine, "About 11:30 o'clock," continued Mrs. Campbell, "there was a loud report and the dishes in my cupboard and on the table were rattled and knocked out of place, while the glass in the windows was shattered . . . I knew what had happened."

Families and supervisors rushed to the site, but the entrance had collapsed. A huge cloud of black smoke drifted out of it and clung to the countryside. "My husband was about due for his dinner when the loud report came," said Mrs. Campbell, "and I looked out the back door toward a manway from the mine, through which he always came to his meals. Instead of my husband I saw a great cloud of dust and smoke pouring out of the mouth of the mine through the manway. It floated upward and disappeared across the river."

Joseph Mapleton, who had been near a side entry, was the only miner to survive the blast. Two hundred thirty-nine of his fellow workers were either blown up, crushed or asphyxiated deep beneath the earth in an unsafe coal mine a long way from their birthplaces.

UNITED STATES
PENNSYLVANIA
MATHER

May 19, 1928

• • • • • • • • • • • • • • • • • •

Gas ignition from an electric locomotive caused the explosion in the Mather shafts of the Pittsburgh Coal Company on May 19, 1928. One hundred ninety-five died; six were injured.

The practice of keeping or releasing canaries in mine shafts to detect noxious or lethal gases was carried to one of its most extreme limits on the evening of May 19, 1928 in Mather, Pennsylvania. One hundred birds were released as part of a rescue effort after the 4:07 P.M. explosion in the Mather coal mine.

One of the Pittsburgh Coal Company's most prolific collieries, the Mather shafts yielded one million tons of anthracite per year and employed 750 men around the clock, 365 days a year. The explosion, caused by the igniting of methane by an electrical arc from a storage-battery locomotive that was later defined by government investigators as "non-permissible," erupted just as shifts were changing. Approximately 400 men were either entering or leaving the main shaft at the time of the detonation; 209 were actually in the mine and directly affected by it.

And affected they were, instantly: one hundred ninety-three died immediately, either from the blast, the collapsing mine shafts or the afterdamp. Two more men died from the effects of the disaster, thus bringing the total to 195. Only eight were saved, in a rescue attempt that went on for three days. Of these eight, six were injured but recovered.

UNITED STATES
PENNSYLVANIA
PLYMOUTH

September 6, 1869

• • • • • • • • • • • • • • • • • •

Sparks from an underground furnace ignited support timbers, which caused an explosion that collapsed adjacent tunnels in the Lackawanna and Western Railroad's Avondale coal mine in Plymouth, Pennsylvania on September 6, 1869. One hundred ten miners were killed; 30 were injured.

Until the end of the 19th century, when electricity made circulating fans possible, it was a standard but hazardous practice to keep a furnace burning, night and day, in the depths of a mine. The theory was that the heat would keep a steady circulation of air that would move the noxious gases and prevent them from accumulating in ignitable pockets.

It was a two-edged sword, as the disaster of September 6, 1869 in Plymouth, Pennsylvania proved. The Avondale coal mine, owned and operated by the Lackawanna and Western Railroad, contained just such a furnace, and on that morning some sparks from it ignited the support timbers of the shaft. This fire was enough to cause a small explosion, which in turn collapsed more of the adjacent tunnels.

According to *Harper's Weekly*, "Whatever fresh air there was in the mine went to feed the fierce flame, while the sulfurous gases, having no longer an outlet, were forced back into the chambers and galleries of the colliery."

Rescuers rushed to the scene, first lowering a dog with a lantern hanging from his neck into the shaft, to test for an abundance of lethal gases. The dog was hauled back up alive, and so the rescue work proceeded. Eighty men were found alive. One hundred ten died of asphyxiation.

UNITED STATES
TENNESSEE
MEMPHIS

April 27, 1865

• • • • • • • • • • • • • • • • • •

One of the worst tragedies in American history, the boiler explosion aboard the steamboat Sultana *in Memphis, Tennessee on April 27, 1865 was caused by human negligence, overloading and an overstoked boiler. Officially, 1,547 deaths were recorded, but this figure is generally thought by historians to be too low; hundreds were injured.*

The month of April 1865 was an eventful one. President Abraham Lincoln was assassinated on April 14. Vice President Andrew Johnson assumed the presidency on April 15. General William Sherman accepted the surrender of General Joseph E. Johnston on April 26, thus bringing the armed resistance of the Confederacy to an end. On the same day, John Wilkes Booth was shot to death in a Virginia barn.

A graphic re-creation of the first discovery of the victims of the explosion in the Lackawanna and Western Railroad's Avondale coal mine in Plymouth, Pennsylvania on September 6, 1869. Frank Leslie's Illustrated Newspaper

Thus, when the steamboat *Sultana* blew up in the Mississippi River just north of Memphis, Tennessee at approximately 2:00 A.M. on April 27, 1865, the horrendous tragedy, one of the worst in U.S. history, went largely unreported and unrecorded. In fact, it would be another 30 years before Congress would enact legislation designed to prevent the sort of disaster that occurred aboard the *Sultana* that night.

Steamboat travel always involved one major hazard, that of an overworked, exploding boiler. From the beginnings of steamboat travel very early in the 19th century until 1850, there had been 185 steamboat explosions resulting in the deaths of 1,400 people.

In just minutes on that one night, at least 1,500 people would meet their deaths in the spectacular explosion of the *Sultana*'s boilers, and the cause would be a compound of personal and political misjudgment.

In 1865, great numbers of Union prisoners were released from the Confederate prisoner of war camps at Cahaba and Andersonville. Vicksburg, Mississippi was the loading point for these emaciated survivors, who wanted nothing more than swift passage northward, to Cairo, Illinois, the debarkation point from which they could then go home.

Thousands of them boarded upriver steamers in the early spring of 1865, bound for safety and familiar sights. By April, however, there were ugly and probably founded rumors that the government was giving all of this lucrative business to one steamboat company, in return for a kickback of one dollar a passenger.

The horrendous explosion of the steamship* Sultana *near Memphis, Tennessee on April 27, 1865. An appalling 1,547 died in one of the worst tragedies in American history. Frank Leslie's Illustrated Newspaper

Anxious to scotch the rumors before they reached the public and official investigatory agencies, government officials at Vicksburg welcomed the arrival of the *Sultana,* which belonged to a rival company. Two years old, the *Sultana* was not a particularly impressive or big boat, weighing in at approximately 1,700 tons. It had a legal load limit of 376 passengers and crew members. Anything exceeding this would demand forced firing of its four tubular boilers, an extremely dangerous practice.

But neither the owners nor the government seemed to care about the regulations or the hazards that spring. By 2 A.M. on April 26, after it had ceased loading its war prisoners and cargo and repaired a faulty steam line leading from one of its boilers, the *Sultana* pulled away from Vicksburg with 2,300 to 2,500 veterans, 75 to 100 civilian passengers and a crew of 80. (The figures concerning both passengers and fatalities have remained approximate, since no accurate records were kept.)

Low in the water and lumbering against the current, the *Sultana* carried the greatest load any steamboat had ever carried on the Mississippi when she left Vicksburg. It would take an unprecedented 17 hours for it to reach Memphis, where she docked shortly after 7:00 P.M. on the 26th.

The coal bins had been almost emptied by the time the *Sultana* reached Memphis, and once she had unloaded 100 hogsheads of sugar, she was taken to the Arkansas side of the river to pick up another 1,000 bushels of coal. Once the ship had been loaded, stokers were ordered to "pour on the coal, and keep this thing moving." A plausible rumor ran along the river then and afterward that the chief engineer wired the safety valves in place so that every available bit of steam was available to drive the side wheels of the *Sultana.*

Midnight came and went, and the boat beat against the current, heading steadily northward. At 2:00 A.M. on the 27th, while most of her passengers slept, the number three boiler exploded with a cataclysmic roar. Hot metal ripped through the ship like white-hot knives. Within minutes, two more boilers exploded, ripping half the steamer apart, collapsing the various decks and crushing those hapless passengers or crewmen who had not been either scalded to death or ripped apart by the metal pieces of boilers.

Some passengers were blown into the water and survived. Others who got through the initial explosion were trapped by the roaring fire that followed it. A small group huddled on the bow of the boat and were quickly pushed into the water by the advancing flames and the collapse of the *Sultana*'s two smokestacks.

Steamboats in the area, hearing the explosion, rushed to the rescue, as did the Union gunboat *Grosbeak.* They found a scene of unbelievable carnage. Having survived the hell of Andersonville, hundreds of homeward bound men were blown apart or burned by a disaster that, in retrospect, was nearly inevitable.

A later investigation failed to either fix the blame for the tragedy or accurately estimate the casualty figures. Trained observers guessed the number of dead to be 1,900, a total generally considered to be too high. A U.S. Army board of review released a figure of 1,238, a total obviously designed to minimize the tragedy. The estimate by customs service officials at Memphis of 1,547 has been the generally agreed on, if inconclusive, one, which makes the death toll of the explosion of the *Sultana* 30 more than that of the much more celebrated sinking of the *Titanic* (see p. 219).

UNITED STATES
TEXAS
NEW LONDON

March 18, 1937

The cataclysmic explosion of natural gas that destroyed the New London, Texas Consolidated School on March 18, 1937 was caused by "wet" gas, used as an economy measure by the school system and ignited by a spark. Two hundred ninety-seven students and teachers were killed, 437 were injured in the worst accident in the history of the American public school system.

On a blackboard that survived the worst disaster in the history of public education in the United States, and the worst explosion in America in terms of deaths since the burning of the *General Slocum* in 1904 (see MARITIME DISASTERS, p. 240), was scrawled, in the writing of an elementary school student in the New London, Texas school: "Oil and natural gas are East Texas' greatest natural gifts. Without them, this school would not be here and none of us would be learning our lessons."

Ironically, the New London school *was* no longer standing on the night of March 18, 1937, and 297 students and faculty were indeed no longer there. They had been killed by an explosion caused by a combination of the natural gas that was East Texas's greatest natural gift and a parsimonious decision by the local school board.

New London, Texas was not an underprivileged community, nor were its educational facilities wanting. On a clear day, you could see 10,000 oil derricks through most of the classroom windows of its Consolidated School, 11 of them on the school grounds themselves. The 1,500-student school facility was the most modern available, built at a cost of $1 million in 1937 depression dollars.

But in January of that year, the school board made a mysterious and tragically unwise decision. Until that time, Union Gas Company had sold the New London school board a natural gas mixed with a pungent odorant. It was safe; it was a so-called dry gas from which impurities had been removed, and it was also cheap. The fuel bills for the school amounted to only $250 to $350 per month.

But the school board decided to economize even more by tapping into a pipeline that carried waste gas from a plant operated by the Parade Oil Company. This was a common practice in East Texas in towns close to oil fields. Most of the time, it caused no problems. But this waste gas was notoriously unstable. "Raw" or "wet" gas had a heating and ignition point that varied widely from hour to hour because of the variety of impurities in it. It was used in many of the homes in New London, and the board members decided it could be used in the school, too.

So it canceled its contract with the Union Gas Company and authorized a school janitor to install a connection that would pipe waste gas through the school's heating system. In testimony given after the tragedy that followed, University of Texas expert E. P. Schoch stated that if just one of the school's main lines was accidentally left flowing for half a day, "the saturation point" would be reached, creating conditions for a potential explosion.

At 3:05 P.M. on Thursday, March 18, 1937, just 10 minutes before dismissal time for 694 high school students and 40 teachers in the Consolidated School, there was a horrific explosion that blew the roof off the school, caved in the walls, shook the ground for 40 miles and buried practically everyone in the building under tons of rubble and steel girders. Several small explosions followed.

Rescue squads, many of them oil workers and many of them parents of children buried in the rubble, rushed to the sickening scene. Men plunged immediately into the debris, and some emerged with terrified but safe children. One rescuer, Don Nelson, came upon a heavy bookcase, tilted against a wall. In the tentlike space formed by it, he found 10 children, frightened beyond belief but safe.

But these were the exceptions. The number of dead was first reported by the Associated Press as 455 children, "crumpled under steel and concrete or squeezed bloodless by the blast." But fortunately this theatrical first report was revised downward to 297 students and teachers. Some were killed so instantaneously that they still had smiles on their faces. Others were mutilated beyond recognition. Their bodies were lined up in the school yard; a consignment of 200 coffins was sent for from Dallas. By the time they arrived, officials were forced to wire for more. Bodies were placed on trucks, and the trucks moved in a steady convoy to improvised morgues.

Meanwhile, the injured—437 of them—were taken to overflowing first-aid stations set up in New London and neighboring Tyler, Overton, Kilgore and Henderson.

Outrage, despair and rage forced immediate hearings into the cause of the accident, which was determined to be an accumulation of wet gas ignited by a spark. The specific spark was never identified, but it was theorized that it could have been from either a light switch or a buildup of static electricity.

A positive result of the New London schoolhouse tragedy was the immediate adoption by oil-producing states of a standard law that prohibited oil companies from allowing tapping of their unprocessed, "wet" gas. By law, it must now be burned at site.

UNITED STATES
TEXAS
TEXAS CITY

April 16–18, 1947

• • • • • • • • • • • • • • • •

Human error caused the worst harbor explosion in American history, the explosion of the French ship Grandcamp *in Texas City Harbor, Texas on April 16, 1947. Seven hundred fifty-two were killed, 3,000 aboard neighboring ships and onshore were injured.*

The worst harbor explosion in American history stretched itself over a three-day period and destroyed fully one-third

Heavy clouds of acrid smoke hang over Texas City, Texas following the cataclysmic explosion of April 16, 1947. American Red Cross

of Texas City, Texas, 10 miles across Galveston Bay from Galveston.

"For God's sake, send the Red Cross—thousands are dying!" yelled an operator into one of the few remaining lines linking Texas City with the world after the explosion. She was not exaggerating, and the worst of it is that the bizarre circumstances leading up to the initial blast indicate that human misjudgment might have been the overriding cause.

The French ship *Grandcamp,* a liberty ship used during World War II to move supplies from manufacturing ports to theaters of war, was loaded with, among other cargo, fertilizer, destined for French farms. The fertilizer was composed of nitrate and ammonia—two components of, among other products, TNT. The fertilizer was in the number four cargo hold of the *Grandcamp.* Next to it, in number five, investigators were told that there was ammunition, but this was either untrue or a military secret. It was neither confirmed nor denied by the government, and in wartime, reporters were not given to pursuing such details.

At 8 A.M. on April 16, 1947, a smoldering fire was discovered in some of the sacks of fertilizer by the ship's carpenter, Julian Gueril. He attempted to extinguish it but could not.

Shortly thereafter, the ship's captain, Charles de Guillebon, ordered the hatch closed and the steam jets turned on. It was an accepted way, under ordinary circumstances, of starving a fire. Under the circumstances of April 16, 1947, it was an unfortunate decision on the part of the ship's captain. Ammonium nitrate decomposes, often violently, at 350 degrees Fahrenheit. The steam easily raised the temperature in the hold to at least that in a very short period of time.

The fertilizer continued to burn, and this prompted the captain to summon the Texas City fire department, which arrived swiftly—within 10 minutes. The water from its hoses seemed to make little impression on the billows of black smoke that poured continuously from the *Grandcamp*'s hold and attracted hundreds of curious onlookers, who now lined the docks.

And then, at exactly 9:12 A.M., the *Grandcamp* exploded, instantly killing everyone aboard and everyone on the nearby dock. It was an awesome, thundering blast, heard as far away as 160 miles and containing the force of a small atom bomb. Its devastation would by no means be confined to the ship and the dock area, where 32 sailors and 227 firemen and observers were instantly killed, chopped up into unidentifiable fragments.

An area of the city 20 blocks by 12 was flattened into smoldering desert in an instant. A one-ton piece of the ship's propeller was flung 13,000 feet and embedded itself in the driveway of a private home. In one of the more incredible side effects of the blast, two private planes, flying 1,000 feet above the explosion site, were blasted out of the air as surely as if they had been hit by anti-aircraft fire.

But that was still only part of it. The Monsanto Company maintained a huge complex in Texas City, and its storage tanks, containing styrene products, were a mere 700 yards away. They went up in flames and black smoke. Farther down the dock, the oil storage tanks of the Humble, Stone and Republic oil companies erupted in flames hundreds of feet high.

The entire Monsanto plant began to buckle and crumble, burying those workers under the debris who had not either escaped or been blown through windows and doors at the moment of the explosion. All in all, 3,300 buildings in Texas City would be completely flattened. The water system would erupt, preventing the fire department from controlling the subsequent fires. A dockside ghetto simply disappeared. The Texas Terminal Railway building went up in flames. An elementary school, with 900 students in attendance, lost all of its windows in the blast, and almost every one of the students was slashed by flying glass. Every electric line and all but one telephone line in the city was knocked down.

The streets were littered with chunks of human flesh, and this was the sight that greeted Red Cross units that sped to the scene from San Antonio, Galveston, Port Arthur, Houston, Dallas and Beaumont. Buildings were crushed. The shock waves of the blast even reached residences several miles away, where a Mrs. Tena Lide was reported to have been lifted up and tossed out of a second-story window by them.

Rescuers did what they could in the unchecked inferno of fire that engulfed Texas City. The city hall was turned into a hospital. "I carried out pieces of bodies all afternoon," a rescue worker told the *New York Times*, "[but] I don't believe they added up to two people."

Meanwhile, back at the dock, a secondary horror was building. The *Highflyer*, docked near the *Grandcamp* and loaded with munitions, had caught fire and was in imminent danger of exploding. Two versions of its last moments survive: One, reported by the Associated Press, had it locked hopelessly with a nearby ship, the *Wilson B. Keene*. In this version, it became impossible for tugs to haul it out to sea. In another version, Deputy Mayor John Hill was quoted as saying, "We asked the tugboats to pull the *Highflyer* out to midstream. They refused. They heard she was carrying ammunition."

For whatever reason, the *Highflyer* remained, blazing, at dockside, and at 1:10 P.M. on April 17 it too blew up, killing most of its crew and hundreds more in the city. Texas City burned for the rest of the night. Most of its surviving residents, like the survivors of the Chicago fire, prepared to evacuate.

Through that night and into the next day, rescue teams continued to comb the city for survivors. McGar's Garage, the city's largest repair shop, became its largest morgue. Five hundred fifty-two bodies, or body parts, were laid out on its floor. Three thousand others were injured. Two hundred were reported missing and thought to have been atomized by the blast. The financial loss would amount to $100 million.

UNITED STATES
UTAH
CASTLE GATE

March 8, 1924

No specific source was discovered for the ignition of accumulated gases that caused the explosion in the Utah Fuel Company's coal mine in Castle Gate, Utah on March 8, 1924. One hundred seventy-three miners were killed; 30 were injured.

National newspapers failed to report the details of the sudden explosion that rocked the Utah Fuel Company's coal mine on the outskirts of Castle Gate, Utah on March 8, 1924.

A mine that was widely touted as safe, with modern ventilation and anti–gas-lock equipment, it was not thought to be a candidate for a disaster.

But that is what occurred. Accumulated gases that the ventilating system apparently failed to disperse ignited—from what source it was never determined—and the mine's main shaft exploded and collapsed. A full shift was at work at the time, and 173 died in the blast.

UNITED STATES
UTAH
SCOFIELD

May 1, 1900

• • • • • • • • • • • • • • • •

Human misjudgment was responsible for the storage of blasting powder underground in the Scofield, Utah coal works. The powder ignited on May 1, 1900, causing an explosion that killed 200 miners.

A particularly grisly explosion in the number four shaft of the Scofield, Utah coal works was caused by neither pockets of gas nor faulty ventilation. This time, it was just plain carelessness.

Thirty kegs of hybrid "blasting powder," as it was colorfully called at the time, were stored in the number four shaft, an act of monumental daring or stupidity, depending on one's point of view. At 10:25 A.M. on May 1, 1900, in the middle of a shift, one of the kegs was ignited. The cause was never determined, for there was not enough of either shaft or men left to be able to piece together a scenario. All 30 kegs detonated with a terrible roar, blowing apart that portion of the number four shaft, atomizing all who were near it and collapsing the walls and ceilings of the tunnel on the remainder of the 140 men at work in that shaft.

Unfortunately, the number one shaft intersected with number four near the keg storage area, and the rolling afterdamp caused by the mass unearthing of bituminous coal floated a lethal cloud into shaft number one, asphyxiating 60 more miners. All in all, 200 men would lose their lives to reckless disregard of safety and sanity on the morning of May 1, 1900 in Scofield, Utah.

UNITED STATES
VIRGINIA
POCAHONTAS

March 13, 1884

• • • • • • • • • • • • • • • •

A combination of overuse of blasting powder and faulty ventilation caused the explosion in the Laurel Mine of the Southwest Virginia Improvement Company in Pocahontas, Virginia on March 13, 1884. One hundred twelve miners were killed; two were injured.

The worst-run mines in America in the 19th century were frequently worked by unsuspecting and hardworking immigrants. In Jacob's Creek, Pennsylvania (see p. 136) they

A young wife discovers the body of her husband, blown from the mouth of the Laurel Mine of the Southwest Virginia Improvement Company in Pocahontas, Virginia on March 13, 1884. One hundred twelve were killed and two were injured in the blast. Frank Leslie's Illustrated Newspaper

were Italians and Greeks. In Pocahontas, Virginia they were Hungarians and Germans. The Virginia mine carried impressive credentials. It was called the Laurel Mine, and it was owned by the Western Railroad Company and operated by the Southwest Virginia Improvement Company, which was apparently dedicated to improving conditions in Virginia other than the lives of its coal miners.

The mine was a monument to carelessness. There were no sprinkler systems in the shafts to cut down on the coal dust and its concomitant destroying gases and the incidence of black lung disease. As in the Scofield, Utah mine (see previous entry), the blasting powder used to dislodge coal from stubborn veins was not stored above ground but deep in the bowels of the mine, where its ignition would cause certain disaster. In addition, the mine had a reputation for being heavy-handed with blasting powder, using more than was necessary and thus endangering safety every time the powder was used. Pockets of lethal gas were everywhere. Ventilation in the mine was accomplished through one fan at the mouth of the shaft—a woefully inadequate proviso that further threatened the well-being of the workers every minute they were underground.

Thus, the accident that had been waiting to happen occurred at 1:00 A.M. on March 13, 1884. The customarily extravagant amount of blasting powder was distributed deep in the main shaft. It was detonated, and suddenly, with an ear-decimating roar, the entire shaft exploded, spewing debris and pieces of miners throughout the Virginia countryside, flattening the shacks built by the miners and their families near the shaft and generally turning the entire site into an inferno.

Like the cork in a champagne bottle, a steam engine and its cars of coal soared out of the shaft's mouth, catapulting its engineer 100 yards to his death and running down two more miners at the shaft's mouth. The shock waves flattened homes and scorched the forest. "The very trees on the mountains, which have withstood the beating storms of ages," wrote the reporter for the *New York Times*, "were shriveled, torn and blasted, their branches scattered in every conceivable direction. Steel, wood and flesh were blown as far as a mile. Even the coal dust was blown over the mountain, and covered the earth on the opposite side to a half of an inch."

As for the miners who were in the mine at the time of the explosion: They were no more. *Frank Leslie's Illustrated Newspaper* later reported that there were "fragments of bodies lodged in tree-tops and on the roofs of houses and sheds."

In every shaft fire emitting from every exit prevented rescuers from entering the decimated mine. Finally, later that day, Colonel George Dodds, a mining engineer, ordered all of the entrances and exits sealed. Fire hoses were hooked up, and the mine was flooded.

Two weeks later, when the mine had cooled enough to allow rescue teams to enter it, squads descended through the acrid and devastated ruins. They found 112 dead miners. Those who had not been killed in the blast were drowned by their rescuers.

UNITED STATES
WEST VIRGINIA
ECCLES

April 28, 1914

• • • • • • • • • • • • • • • • • •

A dynamite blast that ignited gases caused the explosion in the New River Colliers Company mine in Eccles, West Virginia on April 28, 1914. One hundred seventy-nine were killed; 51 were injured.

The New River Colliers Company, owned by the Guggenheim family, maintained a mine in Eccles, West Virginia. At that time, the laws of West Virginia allowed children to work in mines, and five of the miners who would die on the afternoon of April 28, 1914 were 15 years of age.

The disaster occurred at the 500-foot level of the mine's number five shaft at exactly 2:10 P.M., while full shifts were working in each of its six tunnels. A dynamite charge was being set in the shaft at that time, and the blasting fuse ignited a pocket of gas that had accumulated from previous controlled explosions.

This one was far from controlled. It blew apart the shaft, sending enormous tongues of flame all the way to the surface. Every one of the 172 men working in the shaft was killed on the spot. Others were so disfigured that they could only be identified by the brass checks that were distributed to each miner as he entered the shaft opening at the beginning of his shift.

Six miners working in the number six shaft, 250 feet above the blast, were rocked by the explosion but initially unhurt. They attempted to escape by placing handkerchiefs over their faces, but the rising afterdamp overtook them before they could get to a safe place, and all six died of asphyxiation.

Rescue efforts began immediately, and 66 men were retrieved from the number six shaft. One of these died later, bringing the death toll to 179.

UNITED STATES
WEST VIRGINIA
MONONGAH

December 6, 1907

• • • • • • • • • • • • • • • • • •

A runaway rail car severed electrical cable that in turn ignited gases in the Monongah mine in Monongah, West Virginia on December 6, 1907. The resultant explosion killed 362 miners and injured four.

Ironically, in both the Eccles (see previous entry) and Monongah mine disasters, a life insurance salesman was present in the mine, hawking his wares of continuance for the families of miners when these two explosions occurred.

The Monongah catastrophe occurred at 10:28 A.M. on the morning of December 6, 1907, while a full shift of 366 men and one insurance agent were working in the intersecting number six and eight shafts. Shortly before this, a train of coal cars, being guided to the surface by a young miner, became uncoupled. The cars behind the broken coupling rolled backward, down the steep slope into the number six shaft. The miner ran ahead, hoping

Wreckage in the Monongah Mine in Monongah, West Virginia on December 6, 1907. Expectant families and rescuers line the hill that encloses the mine. Three hundred sixty-two miners died in an explosion caused by a runaway rail car. Frank Leslies' Illustrated Newspaper

to cut the electric current before disaster struck. But the switches were too far away. The cars slammed into a wall, severing electric cables that sent up showers of sparks which in turn ignited trapped methane in the tunnel. The enormous blast set off by the ignited gas blew the young train operator out of the mouth of the tunnel.

He survived, but 362 of the 366 men working below the blast would not be as lucky. Every one of them was killed, either by the force of the explosion or the falling timbers and collapsing ceilings and walls of the tunnels in which they were trapped.

The 3,000 residents of the nearby coal miners' shanty village rushed to the mine, to wait out the laborious and heartbreaking rescue efforts. Several hours after the blast, four men, bleeding profusely and nearly dead from breathing the afterdamp, crawled through an outcrop at the top of the number eight shaft. They would be the only survivors.

It would be five full days before rescue parties would be able to reach the grisly sight of the blast and its victims. Three hundred sixty-two miners and the salesman were dead in one of the worst mine explosions in U.S. history.

UNITED STATES
WYOMING
HANNA

June 30, 1903

• • • • • • • • • • • • • • • • •

Blasting powder ignited gas that caused the explosion in the Union Pacific Railroad's Hanna, Wyoming mine on June 30, 1903. One hundred sixty-nine died; 27 were injured.

The Hannah, Wyoming coal mine was nothing of which the Union Pacific Railroad could be proud. It was, in fact, a carefully kept secret, its grim and dangerous presence known only among American miners, most of whom would not work it.

Thus, as in the Eccles and Monongah mines (see p. 144), the company employed recent immigrants at low wages and under inhuman conditions. In Hannah, the vast majority of the immigrant coalminers were Finnish—in fact, the mining village had a distinctly Finnish flavor to it—but there were also groups of Polish and Chinese immigrants and some American blacks.

There were practically no safety precautions taken in the mine. Pockets of methane abounded, and every charge of blasting powder that was ignited was a potential harbinger of calamity.

At 10:30 A.M. on June 30, 1903, blasting powder used to loosen a vein of coal one and a half miles deep in the mine's one shaft ignited a gas pocket and set off an enormous explosion. Two seconds later, in a chain reaction, a second explosion occurred, rippling along the pockets of chokedamp and afterdamp, collapsing huge sections of the shaft and belching forth enormous orange flames that reached above the surface of the mine opening.

All but one of the manways into the mine were clamped shut by the timbers collapsing around them. It was through this manway that 46 men managed to escape. Twenty of these were pulled out by a black miner, William Christian, who repeatedly entered the superheated, choking interior of the mine to haul out the injured, until he himself collapsed.

One hundred sixty-nine men were killed in the dual explosions of June 30, but that would not be the end of the story. The mine would continue to operate on half shifts, even though no precautions were made by management following the 1903 tragedy. Just five years later, on March 28, 1908, another explosion roared through the mine, killing fifty-nine miners. Twenty-seven bodies were found and retrieved, but 32 others were sealed forever in the mine when it was finally closed down for good.

USSR
UFA

June 3, 1989

• • • • • • • • • • • • • • • • • • •

A leak in a liquefied petroleum gas pipeline was ignited by a spark from a passing passenger train near Ufa, USSR on June 3, 1989. The explosion killed 190 and injured 720. Another 270 were presumed dead.

Early in the morning of June 3, 1989, partway between the two Soviet cities of Asha and Ufa in the Ural Mountains of the USSR, a liquefied petroleum gas pipeline erupted. It was a Sunday morning, and the gas, which was being transferred from oil fields in Nizhnevartovsk to refineries in Ufa, was being monitored, presumably by a skeleton crew. Pressure gauges undoubtedly showed a drop in pressure, an indication of a leak. But for some unexplainable reason, instead of investigating the leak, the pipeline operators on duty simply turned up the pumps, thus feeding a mixture of propane, butane and benzene vapors into a ravine leading to a nearby railroad. By the time the vapors had settled into the valley surrounding the train tracks, they were composed mainly of methane, the highly volatile gas responsible for a multitude of mine explosions.

Shortly after this, two trains traveling in opposite directions between the Siberian city of Novosibirsk and the Black Sea town of Adler, passed each other in that ravine. The trains, loaded with vacationers, were not scheduled to pass at that particular point at that particular moment, but one was behind schedule, and as fate would have it, the two were parallel when they entered the valley. The heavy aroma of gas, hanging like a fog to the level of the train windows, became sickeningly apparent to the engineers of both trains as they sped through the pass.

Suddenly, a spark from one of the trains ignited the gas, which exploded with a deafening roar and bright orange flashes of flame. Its force—that of 10,000 tons of TNT—felled every tree within a three-mile radius and blew both locomotives and the 38 cars of the two trains completely off the tracks. Pieces of metal, smashed windows and fragments of bodies were blown in several directions.

A metal-melting fire followed instantly, incinerating the surviving passengers before they could extricate themselves from the mangled coaches.

Speaking later to Tass, the Soviet news agency, a Soviet army officer noted that he had been standing at an open window when he noticed the acrid, petroleum smell coming from the gas leak.

"I sensed that something must be wrong," he said, "but before I could do anything there was a glow and then a thunderous explosion." The officer escaped from the burning car through a broken window.

Rescue squads immediately poured into the region from both Ufa and Asha, and surgeons, burn specialists and medical supplies were airlifted from Moscow throughout the day and night. The final casualty count was appalling: 190 were known dead, at least 270 were missing and presumed dead, and 720 were injured seriously enough to be hospitalized.

YUGOSLAVIA
KAKANJ

June 7, 1965

• • • • • • • • • • • • • • • •

Gas ignited by a blasting fuse set off an explosion in a mine in Kakanj, Yugoslavia on June 7, 1965. One hundred twenty-eight were killed; 41 were injured.

Yugoslavia's worst mine disaster occurred in the small town of Kakanj, just outside Sarajevo, on June 7, 1965. By the middle of the 20th century, modern safety precautions had, in practically all countries, reduced the risk of mine explosions dramatically. But the mine at Kakanj was rife with violations of the government's strictly enforced safety regulations, and on June 7, 1965 the miners working the day shift at the Kakanj mine paid the price. Methane, ignited by a blasting fuse, exploded with a thunderous roar, collapsing the mine's main shaft and setting fire to several adjacent ones.

Fortunately, modern rescue apparatus allowed the rescue parties to haul out small groups of dazed and injured workers. One hundred twenty-eight died.

Six months after the blast, a Belgrade court sentenced six officials of the Kakanj mine to seven and a half years at hard labor for gross negligence and malfeasance.

FIRES

• • • • •

THE WORST RECORDED FIRES

• • • • •

* Detailed in text

Austria
* Vienna (1881) Ring Theatre
Belgium
* Brussels (1967) L'Innovation department store
Brazil
* Niteroi (1961) Gran Circo Norte-Americano
Parana (1962) Coffee plantation fire
* Sao Paulo (1974) Joelmo building
Canada
* Montreal (1927) Laurier Palace Theater
New Brunswick (1825) Forest fire
North Ontario (1916) Forest fire
Carthage
(146 B.C.) Sacking of Carthage
Chile
Santiago
(1863) Jesuit church fire
(1945) Braden copper mine fire
China
Antung (1937) Movie theater fire
Canton (1845) Theater Fire
Chow-t'sun (1924) Fire outside city
* Chungking (1949) Burning of the city
Hankow (1947) Fire on the docks
Tuliuchen (1936) Theater fire
Wuchow (1930) Tea District fire
Colombia
* Bogota (1958) El Almacen Vida department store
Egypt
Cairo (1824) Burning of much of the city
France
Paris
* (1887) Opera Comique
* Paris (1897) Charity bazaar
* St. Laurent du Pont (1970) Cinq-Sept Club discotheque
Germany
* Dresden (1945) Firebombing of city
Great Britain
England
* Exeter (1887) Exeter Theatre
London
(1212) City burned
* (1666) Great Fire of London

Guatemala
* Guatemala City (1960) Guatemala City Insane Asylum
Iran
* Abadan (1978) Movie theater
Jamaica
* Kingston (1980) Eventide nursing home
Japan
Hakodate (1934) Much of the city burned
* Osaka (1972) Playtown Cabaret
Yokohama (1955) Catholic Old Women's Home
Mesopotamia
Babylon (538 B.C.) Burning of Babylon
Mexico
Acapulco (1909) Flores Theater
Puerto Rico
* San Juan (1986) Dupont Plaza Hotel
Rome
* (A.D. 64) Burning of Rome by Nero
Russia
Berditschoft (1883) Circus Ferroni
* Igolkino (1929) Factory fire
Moscow (1570) Burning of city
Saudi Arabia
Mina (1975) Tent city burned
South Korea
* Seoul (1971) Taeyunkak Hotel
Spain
* Madrid (1928) Novedades Theater
Syria
* Amude (1960) Movie theater
Turkey
Constantinople (1729) Burning of 12,000 houses
* Constantinople (1870) Fire originating in Armenian district
Smyrna (1922) Burning of city
United States
Connecticut
* Hartford (1944) Ringling Brothers, Barnum & Bailey Circus
Georgia
* Atlanta (1946) Winecoff Hotel
Illinois
Chicago
* (1871) Great Chicago Fire
* (1903) Iroquois Theater
* (1958) Our Lady of the Angels School
Massachusetts
* Boston (1942) Cocoanut Grove Night Club
Minnesota
* (1918) Forest fire
* Hinckley (1894) Forest fire
Mississippi
* Natchez (1940) Rhythm Night Club
New Jersey
* Coast (1934) See MARITIME DISASTERS, *Morro Castle*
* Hoboken (1900) Docks
New York
* The Bronx (1990) Happy Land Social Club
* Brooklyn (1876) Brooklyn Theatre
* New York (1899) Windsor Hotel
* New York (1904) See MARITIME DISASTERS, *General Slocum*
* New York (1911) Triangle Shirtwaist Factory
Ohio
* Collinwood (1908) Lakeview School

* Columbus (1930) Ohio State Penitentiary

Pennsylvania

* Boyertown (1908) Rhoades Theater

Wisconsin

* Peshtigo (1871) Forest fire

CHRONOLOGY

* Detailed in text

538 B.C.
Babylon, Mesopotamia; Burning of Babylon

146 B.C.
Carthage; Sacking of Carthage

64 A.D.
July 19
* Rome; Burning of Rome by Nero

1212
London, England; Burning of city

1570
Moscow, Russia; Burning of city

1666
Sept. 2–6
* London, England; Great Fire of London

1729
Constantinople, Turkey; Burning of 12,000 houses

1824
Mar. 22
Cairo, Egypt; Burning of much of the city

1825
Nov. 7
New Brunswick, Canada; Forest fire

1845
May
Canton, China; Theater fire

1863
Jan. 17
Santiago, Chile; Jesuit church fire

1870
June 5
* Constantinople, Turkey; Fire originating in Armenian district

1871
Oct. 8
* Chicago, Illinois; Great Chicago Fire
* Peshtigo, Wisconsin; Forest fire

1876
Dec. 5
* Brooklyn, New York; Brooklyn Theatre

1881
Dec. 8
* Vienna, Austria; Ring Theatre

1883
Jan. 13
Berditschoft, Russia; Circus Ferroni

1887
May 25
* Paris, France; Opera Comique
Sept. 4
* Exeter, England; Exeter Theatre

1894
Sept. 1
* Hinckley, Minnesota; Forest fire

1897
May 4
* Paris, France; Charity bazaar

1899
Mar. 17
* New York, New York; Windsor Hotel

1900
June 30
Hoboken, New Jersey; Docks

1903
Dec. 30
* Chicago, Illinois; Iroquois Theatre

1904
June 15
* New York, New York; See MARITIME DISASTERS, *General Slocum*

1908
Jan. 13
Boyertown, Pennsylvania; Rhoades Theater
Mar. 4
* Collinwood, Ohio; Lake View School

1909
Feb. 14
Acapulco, Mexico; Flores Theater

1911
Mar. 25
* New York, New York; Triangle Shirtwaist Factory

1916
July 30
North Ontario, Canada; Forest fire

1918
Oct. 12
* Minnesota; Forest fire

1922
Sept. 13
Smyrna, Turkey; Burning of city

1924
Mar. 24
Chow-t'sun, China; Fire outside city

1927
Jan. 9
* Montreal, Canada; Laurier Palace Theater

1928
Sept. 22
* Madrid, Spain; Novedades Theater

1929
Mar. 12
* Igolkino, Russia; Factory fire

1930
April 21
* Columbus, Ohio; Ohio State Penitentiary
Oct. 19
Wuchow, China; Tea District fire

1934
Mar. 21
Hakodate, Japan; Much of city burned
Sept. 8
* New Jersey Coast; See MARITIME DISASTERS, *Morro Castle*

1936
Mar. 15
Tuliuchen, China; Theater fire

1937
Feb. 13
Antung, China; Movie theater fire

1940
April 23
* Natchez, Mississippi; Rhythm Night Club

1942
Nov. 28
* Boston, Massachusetts; Cocoanut Grove Night Club

1944
July 6
* Hartford, Connecticut; Ringling Brothers, Barnum & Bailey Circus

1945
Feb. 13
* Dresden, Germany; Fire bombing of city
June 19
Santiago, Chile; Braden copper mine fire

1946
Dec. 7
* Atlanta, Georgia; Winecoff Hotel

1947
Dec. 28
Hankow, China; Fire on docks

1949
Sept. 2
* Chungking China; Burning of city

1955
Feb. 17
Yokohama, Japan; Catholic Old Women's Home

1958
Dec. 1
* Chicago, Illinois; Our Lady of the Angels School
Dec. 16
* Bogota, Colombia; El Almacen Vida department store

1960
July 14
* Guatemala City, Guatemala; Guatemala City Insane Asylum
Nov. 13
* Amude, Syria; Movie theater

1961
Dec. 17
* Niteroi, Brazil; Gran Circo Norte-Americano

1962
Sept. 7
Parana, Brazil; Coffee plantation fire

1967
May 22
* Brussels, Belgium; L'Innovation department store

1970
Nov. 1
* St. Laurent du Pont, France; Cinq-Sept Club discotheque

1971
Dec. 25
* Seoul, South Korea; Taeyunkak Hotel

1972
May 13
* Osaka, Japan; Playtown Cabaret

1974
Feb. 1
* Sao Paulo, Brazil; Joelmo building fire

1975
Dec. 12
* Mina, Saudi Arabia; Tent city burned

1978
Aug. 20
* Abadan, Iran; Movie Theater

1980
May 20
* Kingston, Jamaica; Eventide nursing home

1986
Dec. 31
* San Juan, Puerto Rico; Dupont Plaza Hotel

1990
Mar. 25
* Bronx, New York; Happy Land Social Club

• • • • •

FIRES

• • • • •

Even the staunch civil libertarian and guardian of the Bill of Rights, Justice Oliver Wendell Holmes, agreed that the protection of freedom of speech does not extend to a person yelling "Fire!" in a crowded theater. That particular outcry has caused some of the worst catastrophes in history, as a quick glance through this section will amply prove. In fact, pandemonium during a fire is as responsible for its fatalities as the flames themselves or the smoke that causes asphyxiation.

And yet, how can anyone really be blamed for feeling terror at the very thought of a death by burning? Fire has always been a treacherous friend to humankind. It brings comfort, warmth, a romantic glow when the time and the season are right, and it stimulates a fertile imagination (how much of our youth was spent finding forms in the fire that crackled in the family fireplace?).

To the Greeks, fire, along with earth, air and water, was one of the four basic elements from which all things were composed, and the Greeks attached mythological powers to it. One of the greatest of the Greek myths is that of Prometheus, who stole fire from the gods and gave it to man and then suffered eternal torture for his generosity. Other religions have attributed the same fiery origins to either the entire religion or to aspects of it. Vesta, goddess of the hearth, and her virgins guarded the holy fire in ancient Rome. Fire is the earthly representation of the sun in Zoroastrianism. In Kashmir Shaivism, the fire of faith in the efficacy of spiritual practices burns away the karmas of the past and present.

Consider the wonder with which primitive people must have discovered fire—probably witnessing lightning igniting a forest. What a monumental discovery it must have been when these primitives first discovered the uses for fire; they made it the very center of their civilizations, and this continued for thousands and thousands of years. The connection between the Greek colony and the metropolis was the fire kindled in the colony from a brand brought from the mother city's fire. And think of the Olympic flame. And think of the monumental moment in 1827 when an English druggist named John Walker invented the first match.

Fire has warded off the terrors of the dark and the life-robbing chill of the cold. When we love, we say the object of our love warms our heart, and we kindle the flame of love.

But as much as we love fire, we fear it. Rather than die by fire, human beings, over and over, have flung themselves from the tops of high buildings. Were they crazed at the moment? Perhaps. But possibly not. Those who have miraculously survived these falls have affirmed that they would rather have the swift death at the end of a fall than the horrible, prolonged pain of death by fire. Medieval zealots knew this; execution at the stake was one of the most inhuman and barbarous practices ever conceived by humankind.

And it is true; death by fire is an agonizing death, for fire consumes slowly and relentlessly. Some victims have had their lungs burst because the fires around them have superheated the air (3,000 degrees Fahrenheit is the usual temperature in the middle of a firestorm) or robbed it of its oxygen. Toxic gases unleashed by fire cause asphyxiation.

And fire, being as fickle as it is, can turn from benevolent provider to destroyer in an instant. A turned back, a momentary distraction, an error in judgment, and a small fire can become a conflagration. The friendliest campfire, or barbecue, the smallest match struck against the darkness can ignite infernos.

Knossos, in Crete—the greatest metropolis of the world in 1400 B.C.—was destroyed by a fire set by invaders. Carthage, Rome, Ninevah, Babylon, Moscow, London, Constantinople, Smyrna, Copenhagen, Munich, Stockholm, St. Petersburg, Cairo, Chicago, New York—every one of them has either been totally destroyed or severely crippled by fire. It is the most devastating destroyer we know—for no matter what humankind invents, no matter how much radiation its atomic or hydrogen weapons produce, even they assume the secondary, pervasive destruction of fire.

Consider its effect upon the world and its population today. The very atmosphere and the continuum of life are threatened by the wholesale destruction, by fire, of the world's rain forests.

And so, perhaps it is because of humankind's continuing dependence on fire that it is the most devastating of all destructive forces, an energy so pervasive and dangerous that it has produced at least two human professions: fire insurance and fire prevention.

Fire insurance sprang into being as a direct result of the London Fire of 1666. The first organized fire fighters protected the cities of ancient Greece and Rome. Wherever humans gathered, they apparently were aware of the duplicity of fire and the necessity to balance dependence with an equal amount of protection. And even then, if fire wants to destroy, it will, no matter the efforts to control it.

The criteria for inclusion in this section are far more complex than in any other category. First, the decision had to be made regarding the inclusion of fire disasters in the volume on natural disasters or in *Man-made Catastrophes.* Certainly, there are forest fires that are begun by lightning, or the smoldering fires brought on by long droughts. But these are small in number compared with those caused by human error, carelessness or design. Even the worst forest fire in U.S. history, that of the 1871 burn that destroyed the city of Peshtigo, Wisconsin and 23 other villages (see p. 203), did not begin from wholly natural causes. Though it is thought to have started spontaneously, its devastation is directly attributable to the mess left behind by loggers who continued to fell trees during a rainless summer, and to railroad workers who, at the same time, burned debris in the forest.

Even spontaneous combustion in a pile of oil-soaked rags is, ultimately, the responsibility of the human being who piled the rags there in the first place.

Thus, fires rightfully belong in this volume.

In some cases, fire is often the secondary disaster. Explosions cause fires; earthquakes cause fires. And so, whenever it seemed as though the fire damage was specifically caused by another primary source for which there was a category, it was not included in this section—hence, for instance, the omission of the San Francisco Earthquake fire, the 1934 fire aboard the *Morro Castle,* and the 1904 fire aboard the excursion steamboat *General Slocum,* in New York Harbor. The first can be found in the Earthquake section in the volume on natural disasters; the other two can be found in the Maritime Disasters section in this volume.

Although war disasters have been omitted from both volumes, one exception was included in this section: The firebombing of Dresden by Allied bombers in 1945. One hundred thirty-five thousand civilians lost their lives, not from bombs, but from the firestorm set by incendiaries. This was the worst fire catastrophe in the world during any age and, because of this, demanded to be included.

Finally, human suffering and casualty figures again dictated the inclusion or noninclusion of a particular fire. Generally speaking, a cutoff of 75 deaths was utilized, with one exception: the London Fire of 1666.

This fire, in which the bacteria that caused the bubonic plague were incinerated, and out of which modern fire-fighting equipment and materials and the concept of fire insurance evolved, only claimed eight lives. But its impact was enough to warrant—perhaps demand—its inclusion in any compendium of the world's fires.

• • • • • • • • • • • • • • •

AUSTRIA
VIENNA

December 8, 1881

• • • • • • • • • • • • • • •

Human error on the part of a stagehand caused the most tragic theater fire in history, at the Ring Theatre in Vienna, Austria on December 8, 1881. Eight hundred fifty died and hundreds were injured.

The most tragic theater fire in history took place the night after Offenbach's *Les Contes d'Hoffmann* premiered at Vienna's elegant, ornate Ring Theatre. It, like so many human catastrophes, was caused by human carelessness, compounded by human error and inaction.

The Ring Theatre, one of the jewels in the most elegant and artistically productive times in the history of this fabled city, had been built by the imperial government of

Franz Joseph in 1873. Located off the famous Ringstrasse, which was already festooned with the Burgtheatre, the Opera House, the Kunstlerhause and the Musikverein, it immediately became a popular mecca for the city's lovers of popular entertainment.

Vienna under Franz Joseph was alive with the arts at the end of the 19th century. Brahms, the Strauss family and Mahler had all been drawn to it in the same way that Mozart and Beethoven had at the end of the 18th century and the beginning of the 19th. And while the Opera House was the home of grand opera, the masses flocked to the gilded splendor of the Ring Theatre, where the great Sarah Bernhardt and Signor Salvini's dramatic troupe appeared, and the lively and racy operettas of Jacques Offenbach were performed.

Royalty and the rich were also drawn to this theater by its glitter and its comfort, but they rarely arrived on time. Offenbach knew enough to write long overtures to fill in the time between the announced curtain time and their bejeweled entrances after 7:00 P.M.

Thus, on the night of December 8, 1881, the night after *Les Contes d'Hoffmann*'s premier, only the two balconies were full at 6:45 P.M. Eager tradespeople, students, actors and actresses, attracted by critical praise and enthusiastic recommendations of the new Offenbach work, filled these two upper parts of the auditorium, while a few renegade knights and bank directors occupied the few boxes and stalls downstairs.

At that precise moment, a stagehand went about his usual task of lighting the upper row of gas jets above the stage. Possibly he was careless. Possibly the elaborate scenery required for the operetta was too abundantly or negligently hung. For whatever reason, his long-handled igniter set fire to the canvas trappings of several theatrical clouds. Within seconds, the flames swept to the stage curtains. The stage doors were open; the air blowing in through them fanned the flames and billowed the curtains outward, toward the audience. Huge tongues of flame leaped from canvas to canvas onstage and out into the auditorium.

At this point, the iron fire curtain that existed in every completely equipped theater of the time could and should have been lowered. It would have contained the fire onstage, curtailed the draft and snuffed out some of the flames. But, inexplicably, this was not done, nor was the fire brigade summoned, nor was the onstage water hose pressed into service.

Instead, panic spread as quickly as the fire. As the flames shot outward from the stage, crawling up drapes and running in fiery streams across the ceiling, the patrons stood up in their seats, screamed, "Fire!" and began to shove at one another. To compound the hysteria, a stagehand shut off the gas, plunging the entire premises into darkness, save for the light of the rapidly accumulating fire.

The occupants of the stalls and boxes got out safely, walking rapidly to the lobby doors and out to the square, where gilded carriages containing royalty and the wealthy were just beginning to draw up.

In the balconies, the crush of humanity battered its way toward the exits, only to find them blocked by impenetrable walls of fire. Some patrons, pushed or panicked, leaped or fell from the front of the balconies. One woman landed on two other audience members, killing herself and both of them.

Summoned by spectators, the fire brigades arrived, but their ladders were too short to reach even the first balcony. By now, patrons were smashing the Gothic windows behind the balconies and leaping hysterically to their deaths in the square below. Firemen frantically ransacked the theater for drapes from which to fashion life nets, but most had been burned to charred threads. They finally found one huge stage drape, and, shouting to those in the balconies to jump into it, they stretched it taut beneath the balcony rails.

The patrons calmed. A commanding, aristocratic man ordered the children to jump first, then the women and finally the men. One hundred twelve children, women and some men thus survived before the walls began to cave in and the flames and smoke became so intense that the rescue attempt had to be abandoned. Those who remained were either incincerated or crushed under the falling walls and pieces of decor.

Members of the royal family—among them, Franz Joseph's grand nephews Charles, Albrecht, William, Salvatore and Eugene—arrived at the scene, took one look at the inferno before them and, on the spot, began a collection of relief funds for the victims. Crown Prince Rudolf wept openly at the catastrophe, which claimed 850 victims—the highest number of fatalities that would ever be recorded in a European theater fire. Hundreds more were injured.

BELGIUM
BRUSSELS

May 22, 1967

• • • • • • • • • • • • • • • •

Panic and the lack of a sprinkler system combined to cause the tragedy of the L'Innovation department store fire in Brussels, Belgium on May 22, 1967. Three hundred twenty-two died; scores were injured.

Panic kills as many people in mass fires as smoke or flames, and panic accounted for many of the deaths in the store fire with the greatest fatality count in history. Three hundred twenty-two people died in the noontime fire at L'Innovation, the five-story department store located in the heart of the old city in Brussels, Belgium.

Spring is a time of innovative sales, and L'Innovation, true to its name, featured a Salute to American Fashion in May 1967. On May 22, the "million dollar showcase" attracted approximately 2,500 customers to the store. L'Innovation prided itself on its service, and another 1,200 clerks—one for every two customers—were in attendance at the height of the shopping day, when office workers on their lunch hour swelled the ranks of shoppers.

It was nearly noon when a fire broke out in three places on the fourth floor of the crowded store. There was some inconclusive evidence of an accelerant being used to begin the fire, though arson was never proved. Whatever its source, the fire spread rapidly and unchecked. The old building was without a sprinkler system. It did have 15 full-time firemen on duty at all times, to compensate for its lack of mechanical fire-fighting means, but for some reason, only two of the 15 responded to the alarm that day. Their sincere but ineffectual efforts to control the wildly spreading blaze with hand-held fire extinguishers did nothing to stop the gathering holocaust.

All 4,000 people in the store tried to reach the exits and elevators at the same time. Many were trampled to death in this insane rush; others had limbs broken and clothing stripped away. Those who could not reach stairways, elevators or doors fought their way to windows. Some smashed them out with their bare hands and leaped for the street, hoping to land on the forgiving hoods of parked cars. Some did and only suffered broken limbs. Others missed and died.

Firemen, hampered by the narrow, twisting streets of the Old Quarter, took an unconscionable amount of time to arrive on the scene. By the time they finally got there, hundreds of canisters of butane gas, destined for summer campers and stored on the store's roof, exploded, feeding the inferno still further. Desperate people still clinging to upper stories were turned into human torches as the flames consumed the entire building, destroying it totally, and burning to ashes many of the 322 people who perished in the fire.

BRAZIL
NITEROI

December 17, 1961

• • • • • • • • • • • • • • • • • •

Either arson or sparks from a passing train were suspected of causing the worst circus fire ever recorded, in Niteroi, Brazil on December 17, 1961. Three hundred twenty-three died; 500 were injured.

This incredible circus fire killed 323 persons—most of them children—and cruelly burned 500 more. And it all happened in a little more than three minutes.

As part of its annual Christmas week celebration in 1961, Brazil featured the Gran Circo Norte-Americano, a Brazilian version of Ringling Brothers. In the town of Niteroi, which is located across the bay from Rio de Janeiro, the circus played out its thrills and fantasies in a blue and white nylon tent large enough to accommodate high-wire acts, animal acts, clowns and 2,500 spectators.

On the afternoon of December 17, 1961, the tent was packed to capacity. Most of the audience was composed of children, on holiday from school. They were transfixed by the death-defying high-wire acrobatics of the featured trapeze artist, Antonietta Estavanovich. And it was Ms. Estavanovich who first saw the flames. What must have gone through her mind as she soared through the air toward her partner and saw flames beneath her, in the upper wall of the tent, she never said. But by the time she and her partner had spun into the safety net and had headed for the exits, the fire had made its way to the center of the tent and was edging downward along the tent poles.

Within three minutes, the entire tent had become one huge flame, and the screaming children were stampeding. Three hundred of them ran toward the center ring. The tent collapsed around them, suffocating them. Some others fell as the mob surged in several directions, and they were trampled underfoot.

Sergio Pfiel Manhaes, a heroic young Boy Scout, pulled out his knife, cut a hole in the side of the tent, hauled his family through it and then went back into the conflagration and led an adult, blinded by smoke, to safety.

Joao Goulart, the president of Brazil, broke down in tears when he went into the children's ward in Niteroi's Antonio Pedro Hospital to visit the 500 injured. The investigation he ordered turned up no conclusive reason for the fire. Opinion on the cause of the disaster was divided between arson and sparks from a passing train.

BRAZIL
SAO PAULO

February 1, 1974

• • • • • • • • • • • • • • • • • •

An overheated air-conditioning vent ignited plastic construction material piled near it in the Joelmo building, which housed the Crefisul Bank, in Sao Paulo, Brazil on

February 1, 1974. Thrill seekers hampered firemen, and 220 died. Hundreds more were injured.

Sao Paulo is one of the wealthiest cities in Brazil. Boasting a population of six million—roughly the same as Chicago—it also boasts some of the country's most modern office buildings.

But Sao Paulo is lacking in elementary safety protection for its populace. The six million residents of Chicago are serviced by 300 fire stations. The six million in Sao Paulo must rely on a mere 13. Safety codes in most major cities of the world decree that nonflammable materials be used in major office buildings. The interior of the Joelmo building, a skyscraper in downtown Sao Paulo that housed the offices of the Crefisul Bank, was composed almost entirely of highly flammable materials. And these two factors accounted for the deaths of 220 people on February 1, 1974.

It was one of the worst office building disasters in history, and it will be forever memorable for the extremes of human behavior that it revealed. At one end of the spectrum were the acts of touching and staggering heroism on the part of firemen, swinging on ropes high over the streets to rescue panicked victims. At the other, was the crush of spectators straining to watch flaming people fling themselves to their deaths from upper stories. Over 300,000 cars, abandoned by these morbid, sensation-hungry spectators, clogged streets and prevented rescue equipment from getting through.

The fire began in an overheated air-conditioning vent on the 12th floor of the 25-story building. Plastic material piled near the vent quickly ignited and spread to other plastic constructions built into the building. The first six floors of the structure were occupied by a car park; thus, most of the employees trapped by the flames were in upper stories beyond the reach of firemen's ladders, which only extended to the seventh floor.

Some managed to battle their way to exits and ran from the building. Others rushed to save themselves, trampling some of their fellow employees to death. Thirty-four people locked themselves in a washroom and turned on the watertaps, in hope of keeping the flames away. They were discovered the next day, every one of them suffocated to death.

People at some of the windows and on some of the ledges of the building, seeing that the ladders could not reach them, jumped, preferring a quick death to a slow one. One man hit two firemen on a ladder, carrying them with him to their deaths. One woman jumped with a baby in her arms. She died; the baby survived. Twenty-five people tried to leap to the roof of a nearby building. All twenty-five died.

Others heeded the large signs that firemen held up to them reading, "Courage. We are with you. Don't jump."

One heroic fireman, Sergeant Jose Rufino, swung on a rope secured to a nearby building, grabbing 18 survivors and swinging with them on his back to safety. During one attempt, a man leaping from the 16th floor collided with Rufino, peeling the man from the fireman's back and sending him to his death. Rufino managed to hang on to the rope and thus saved himself, but his hands were torn and bleeding when he finally rejoined his fellow firemen.

Helicopters sent to rescue survivors from the roof could not land because of the intensity of the heat and the density of the smoke. At one point, the paint began to scale off the doors of one helicopter. Firemen finally dropped cartons of milk to survivors who had made their way to the building's roof. The detoxifying properties of the milk were credited with keeping these near-victims alive until an army helicopter was brought to the roof of the building. The helicopter landed on the slowly buckling roof and lifted off, in a series of staccato landings and takeoffs, 85 people. As the last 10 people were rescued, the roof collapsed.

It would be four hours before firemen could bring the blaze under any sort of control. Almost all of the interior of the building from the 12th floor upward was reduced to charred and sodden rubble.

There was some talk of sabotage, some reports that a telephone operator at the Crefisul Bank had received an anonymous call the day before saying that a bomb would explode on Friday morning. But the report was never considered in the inquiry that followed the fire. The cause was multiple; 220 people were dead; hundreds had been injured; and the municipality had much to do to prevent a recurrence.

CANADA
MONTREAL

January 9, 1927

• • • • • • • • • • • • • • • •

Employee negligence and political payoffs that allowed fire code violations to exist were the causes of the fire in the Laurier Palace Theater in Montreal, Canada on January 9, 1927. Seventy-eight children died; 30 were severely injured.

Fate is often ironic, as anyone who has reached the age of reasoning can attest. But it was never more so than on the afternoon of January 9, 1927, when 800 patrons, almost all of them children, gathered in Montreal's Laurier Palace Theater to watch a film titled *Get 'Em Young.*

The Laurier Palace was a movie house that had existed well past its prime. It had never entirely conformed to the existing fire code of the city of Montreal and was, in January 1927, operating illegally, without a license. The reason: It had failed to correct hazardous safety conditions, chief among them an absence of unobstructed and well-marked fire exits. That the theater was open at all must have had something to do with local politics, since it was located directly across the street from a police station.

On the afternoon of January 9, the theater was conducting a special children's matinee, and it was packed. Most of the children were well under the age of 16. Approximately 500 filled the orchestra floor; the younger children, aged six and seven, were crammed into the balcony. There were no chaperones present. Only the usual theater staff was there to control the children.

Sometime during the showing of the movie, somebody—an employee, it was charged in the investigation—dropped a lighted cigarette in the middle of the balcony. Within seconds, inflammable material in the seats had ignited, and a conflagration was under way.

The children on the first floor, removed from the immediate fire, escaped unharmed through several exits. But the small children, now choked and blinded by smoke and surrounded by flames, understandably panicked. The only egress from the balcony was by a narrow, unlighted stairway that descended a short way, made a sharp right-angle turn at a landing and then dropped another few steps to a door that was only 37 inches wide. The stairwell itself was a scant 10 inches wider than this cramped doorway.

As the flames shot upward and outward from their beginnings, the young children stampeded for the stairwell. Some managed to get down the stairs safely—their small girths allowed them plenty of room. But then, one child either tripped or was pushed down the stairs. She formed a wedge that blocked off the only escape route for the remaining, screaming youngsters. They plummeted down the stairs, piled up on one another and became wedged into the stairwell.

It would take less than two minutes for the entire balcony to go up in flames, and during that time, the projectionist worked heroically to save nearly 30 children by shoving them, two at a time, through a window in the projection booth onto the top of the theater marquee.

When the firemen arrived, the pile of bodies at the bottom of the stairwell was eight deep and could only be reached by cutting a hole in a side wall. Only a few of the children trapped there were still alive. Seventy-eight young people died, 52 from smoke and asphyxiation, 25 from being crushed to death in the stairwell and one from the flames. Thirty were severely injured.

CHINA
CHUNGKING

September 2, 1949

• • • • • • • • • • • • • • • • •

Arson was suspected in the fire that began in the slum district of Chungking, China on September 2, 1949 and destroyed 10,000 homes and left 100,000 homeless. One thousand seven hundred died in the fire; thousands were injured.

The year was one of extreme turmoil in China, the turning point between Nationalist and Communist control of the country. Until 1947, Chiang Kai Shek's Nationalists, supported by U.S. supplies and money, had tenaciously held on to the control of the country. But by November 1948, when the Chinese Communists, under Mao Tse Tung, captured Mukden and thus the industrial heartland of the country, the standoff between the two factions had all but been won by the Communists. Sweeping inflation, increased police repression and a grinding, endless famine had so eroded public confidence in the Nationalists that a state of civil strife, trembling on the brink of civil war, existed.

In January 1949, Peking fell to the Communists. From April to November, other major cities also fell, most without a fight. Nanking, Han-kou, Shanghai, Canton and eventually Chungking, the Nationalist capital, all surrendered.

In September, the tensions in the city were at their highest point. And on September 2, 1949 at 4:00 P.M., a fire of mysterious origin began in Chungking's slum district. Whether the arsonist was a Communist or whether it was someone directed by the Nationalist government to set the blaze in the hope of turning public opinion against the Communists will probably never be known. In the holocaust's aftermath, the Nationalists rounded up suspected Communists and, a week later, executed for arson a man known to be part of the Communist underground.

The human toll was staggering. The fire, once begun, spread unchecked in several directions. It ate into the residential district, consuming nearly 10,000 homes and leaving more than 100,000 people homeless. It devastated the business district and then, fanned by winds, roared toward the waterfronts of the Yangtze and Chialung rivers. Refugees, running ahead of the advancing wall of fire, had come to this part of the city in the hope of escaping in one of the hundreds of boats docked there. Hundreds of people were burned to death both on the docks and in the moored boats, as the roaring inferno outraced and enveloped them.

Chungking would burn for 18 hours that afternoon and night, and when it was over, more than 1,700 residents of that embattled city would be dead. One day less than a month later, the Nationalists would be in Taiwan, and the civil strife would be at an end. Chungking's terrible fire would be one of its last and most dramatic manifestations.

COLOMBIA
BOGOTA

December 16, 1958

• • • • • • • • • • • • • • •

A light bulb ignited a creche in El Almacen Vida, one of Bogota, Colombia's largest department stores, on December 16, 1958. Eighty-four died in the resultant fire; scores were injured.

One of Bogota, Colombia's biggest department stores is called El Almacen Vida—the Life Department Store. It became anything but that on December 16, 1958. Early in the day, the store was jammed with holiday shoppers, shoving and pushing their way past displays of new merchandise and elaborate Christmas decorations.

One of the most elaborate and effective of these was the creche that was set up in the toy department. Realistic, artistically arranged and highly detailed, it had as its centerpiece Christ lying on a bed of straw. Brightly colored lights outlined the roof of the creche, blending with the general joyous atmosphere of the store.

Sometime during the day, one or more of these brightly burning lights became dislodged and fell into the straw surrounding the figure of Christ. Unnoticed, it set fire to the straw, and this in turn spread to a pile of plastic toys next to the decorations. Within minutes, the entire toy department was engulfed in flames, and the bitter smoke of burning plastic billowed to the ceiling.

Panic spread as hysterical patrons tried to run for the front and largest exits of the store. But the toy department was located near these exits, and a solid wall of flames blocked them.

Some male customers smashed sizable holes in the glass of the store's display windows and scores of survivors gingerly made their way through these openings. But 84 people, trapped by the flames and the smoke in the rear of the store, were burned to death.

A spectacular fire interrupted a performance of Massenet's Mignon at Paris's Opera-Comique on the evening of May 25, 1887. Two hundred died, and the opera house was gutted. Illustrated London News

FRANCE
PARIS

May 25, 1887

• • • • • • • • • • • • • • •

A gaslight igniting scenery followed by human error—the failure to lower a fire curtain—caused the fire in Paris's Opera-Comique on May 25, 1887. Two hundred died.

The venerable Opera-Comique, on Paris's Place Boieldieu, was packed on the evening of May 25, 1887 for a performance of Massenet. The Opera-Comique, like the Ring Theatre in Vienna (see p. 156), was a livelier place than the Opera, and like the Ring Theatre, it would be the scene of a gigantic tragedy that could have been averted, if only the iron fire curtain had been lowered.

As in most 19th-century theater fires, the conflagration at the Opera-Comique started onstage, when a gaslight positioned in the fly space over the stage ignited a piece of canvas scenery. Witnessing this, two singers in the company, Taskin and Soulacroix, stepped to the footlights and tried to calm the immediately restive audience. Had one stagehand had his wits about him and lowered the iron curtain at that moment, the fire would have been contained, and the tragedy that followed would not have occurred.

But this did not happen, and the flames soared out over the audience, sending streamers of black and acrid smoke ahead of them. In other theater fires (see pp. 167, 186 and 196), aristocratic, high-paying customers had no difficulty escaping the conflagration from their stalls and boxes. But in the case of the Opera-Comique, tragedy was more democratic; it spared no one. Obstructions that a uniform fire code would never have allowed blocked everyone's way to exits, and the well-to-do found themselves joining the hysterical, working-class patrons of the galleries, trying to climb to upper windows and the roof, away from the flames.

Outside, the arriving *pompiers* threw up ladders, but few of them could reach the people trapped on ledges, and none of the ladders came close to reaching the roof. In despair, people began to hurl themselves to their deaths from windows and ledges. Firemen rescued whomever they could. Two bejeweled women were taken from a window sill and brought into a nearby druggist's shop, where they were laid upon two nearby counters. They died soon after.

By 11:00 P.M., the upper-story dressing rooms and music library had caught fire, and the roof had collapsed, sending scores of trapped people hurtling through the flames to their deaths. The last two people to be rescued by firemen were huddled on a brick cornice. The woman had passed out and was lowered by rope to the street; the man was guided onto a ladder, which he descended to safety.

The fire was finally brought under control at dawn of the next day. Two hundred bodies were discovered in the wreckage. Most of them had died of asphyxiation; some had been crushed in the stampede or by falling pieces of the opera house.

FRANCE
PARIS

May 4, 1897

• • • • • • • • • • • • • • • • • •

A lamp used to illuminate a kinematograph ignited the structure erected at Paris's annual Grand Bazar de Charite on May 4, 1897. One hundred fifty people died in the fire; hundreds were injured.

A uniform code of fire regulations governing public places was put in place in Paris as a result of a shocking tragedy that, on May 4, 1897, burned to death 150 of the wealthiest women of that city.

The annual Grand Bazar de Charite, designed to raise thousands of francs for the destitute, was held in May 1897 in a 220- by 300-foot structure built especially for the occasion and decorated like a street in a medieval French city.

The decor was not new. It had been used a year before at an exposition at the Palais d'Industrie. Built from linen, coated with turpentine and filled between the surfaces with papier mache, it was clearly a stage set and obviously inflammable.

More than 1,500 socialites packed themselves into the structure on the evening of May 4 to buy semiprecious objects at inflated prices for charity. Midway through the evening, a lamp used to illuminate a kinematograph set fire to the scenery. Within seconds, the flames shot up to the roof, which was made of tarred felt.

There was only one exit, and all 1,500 patrons and society ladies stampeded toward it, while flaming pieces of the roof descended upon them, turning some of the escapees into flaming torches. Within a few moments, the molten roof collapsed and the walls caved in, burying and burning to death 150 people and brutally injuring hundreds more.

FRANCE
ST.-LAURENT-DU-PONT

November 1, 1970

• • • • • • • • • • • • • • • • • •

A dropped, lighted cigarette combined with multiple violations of fire codes caused the fire in the Cinq-Sept Club, a disco in St.-Laurent-du-Pont, France, on November 1, 1970. One hundred forty six patrons died; hundreds were injured.

The Cinq-Sept Club, in the small French village of St.-Laurent-du-Pont, 20 miles south of Grenoble, was a disaster aching to occur. A multiple array of safety violations and a disregard of common sense rendered this huge disco, a gathering place for young people from Grenoble, Aix-les-Bains and Chambery, a dangerous fire trap.

In clear violation of French fire regulations, one of the two required access doors as well as the main entrance was sealed, and the other locked. The two regulation fire exits were unlit; one was hidden by a screen behind the bandstand, and the other was blocked by stacks of chairs. The main entrance itself was an eight-foot-high, spiked turnstile.

The psychedelic decor in this hangar-like club consisted of an arched grotto sculpted from highly flammable polystyrene, another violation of fire regulations. Above the dance floor were tiny alcoves, reachable by one spiral staircase. There were no fire extinguishers on the premises.

And finally, and most astonishing of all, the club possessed no telephone.

A molten roof collapsed on hundreds of society patrons attending the Grand Bazar de Charite at the end of a flash fire on the night of May 4, 1897. Here, the grim job of identifying their remains is conducted. Illustrated London News

On the night of November 1, 1970, the Cinq-Sept was packed with youngsters in their late teens and early twenties gyrating to the sounds of "Storm," a new group from Paris. Around 1:40 A.M., the group had just begun its last set with the Stones' "Satisfaction."

Upstairs, in one of the alcoves, someone dropped a lighted cigarette on a cushion. It immediately caught fire, and several patrons tried to beat it out with their hands and jackets. But the fire was stubborn, and in moments it had spread to the plastic arches that separated the alcoves. A vast tongue of flame shot the length of the dance floor as the plastic arches began to melt, dropping molten lumps of plastic on those near them.

At first, there was an orderliness about the exodus of the crowd. Some in the alcoves descended the staircase and exited through the one obvious and available, if obstructed, exit. Thirty left this way. But moments later, panic took over. The flames and the heat intensified enormously, and heavy, suffocating fumes filled the club, asphyxiating some couples, who were later discovered still locked in each other's arms on the dance floor and near the bar.

One barman hurled himself against one of the emergency exits near him, and he and a handful of patrons escaped through it. Simultaneously, one of the owners, 25-year-old Gilbert Bas, saw an emergency light come on in his office. Walking toward the door, he heard the anguished cries of "Fire!" but did not open the door to the club. With no telephone, he was unable to call the fire department. He exited through his office door and drove almost two kilometers to the fire station to report the fire in person.

Meanwhile, people in the club were dying. The pandemonium induced by panic had pressed the crowd against the turnstile at the main entrance, jamming it. Later rescuers would discover the body of one young man impaled upon one of the spikes of the turnstile.

The club had become an inferno. The corrugated iron roof turned red hot and collapsed on those inside. One hundred forty-four young people would perish horribly in the flames. Two more would die later of their burns, bringing the mortality total to 146.

The next day, morbid curiosity would attract thousands to the tiny village to view the grisly sight. It would take a combined force of 200 policemen and law enforcement officials to move the crowd away from the ruins of the club.

The sheer magnitude of the disaster forced an intense investigation, and the village's mayor, Pierre Perrin, and secretary-general of the prefecture de l'Isere Albert Ulrich were immediately suspended from their jobs. As the investigation progressed, a tangled web of bureaucratic fumbling, backturning and compromise was revealed. There was scarcely a municipal agency that was not involved in some way. The rules were in place. But they had never been enforced.

In June 1971, the mayor and two building contractors were charged with causing injury through negligence. Gilbert Bas, the sole surviving owner (his two partners had died in the blaze), was charged with manslaughter. In November 1971, all were found guilty but received suspended sentences—Bas for two years, Mayor Perrin for 10 months, the three building contractors for 15, 13 and 10 months each.

The fire would go down in record books as the worst in the history of France.

GERMANY
DRESDEN

February 13, 1945

• • • • • • • • • • • • • • • • • •

The Allied firebombing of Dresden on February 13, 1945 caused a fire storm that destroyed the city, killed 135,000 residents and injured hundreds of thousands more.

Picture fire falling from the sky, carried by the wind, consuming land, buildings, people and the very oxygen in the air. This is a fire storm, and this was the ghastly terror that took the lives of 135,000 people during the firebombing of Dresden, Germany, from February 13 through the 15th, 1945.

Before it died, Dresden was a beautiful city, the Florence of Germany, a center of art, architecture, sculpture and music from the 14th century onward. From 1500, it was the seat of Saxon princes, who fostered and collected the art that distinguished the city. By the late 17th and early 18th century, under Frederick Augustus I and Frederick Augustus II, Dresden became a showplace of baroque and rococo architecture. Bach, Handel, Telemann, Wagner and Richard Strauss lived and wrote there, as it developed from a rococo center to a seat of romantic art and German opera. It was one of the loveliest cities in the world and a repository of thousands of pieces of priceless art.

For historians, there were famous collections of watches and chronometers, geometric instruments, arms and armor. In the Zwinger, a former medieval execution field, friezes and statuary from the classic age of Greece were collected.

By the beginning of World War II, Dresden had become the seventh largest city in Germany, with an *Auldstadt,* or old city, that looked as it had in medieval times, with narrow streets, shops, museums, a zoo and a number of ancient churches; and, beyond this, an old/new city with residences and light industry. It was also a rail center, but it was located far enough off the autobahn, which crossed the River Elbe west of the city, not to be choked with the traffic from this main national artery.

The autobahn bridge, the rail yards and the industrial complexes on the city's outskirts were virtually untouched by the fire storm that totally destroyed the city's center in 1945. The bombs and the fire were meant for civilians, and that is who they killed.

It is important to note that the firebombing of Dresden occurred at the end of World War II. In a last-ditch attempt at terrorizing the populace of Great Britain, the Nazis had unleashed V-1 and V-2 rockets. In the five years of the war, England had suffered a total of 60,595 casualties.

There were several tactical reasons for the launching of Operation Thunderclap, a firebomb raid on a leading German city planned for late January or early February 1945, with a combined force of RAF Lancaster bombers and USAAF B-17s: (1) It was needed, it was argued, as a retaliation for the V-2s that had been hitting Britain, in order to lift civilian moral; (2) It was needed to further lower German morale; and (3) It was needed as a bargaining chip for the upcoming Yalta Conference between Churchill, Roosevelt and Stalin. As an internal RAF memo stated it: "The intentions of the attack are to hit the enemy where he will feel it most, behind an already partially collapsed front, to prevent the use of the city in the way of further advance, and incidentally to show the Russians when they arrive what Bomber Command can do." There

Survivors prepare a mass grave for the dead following the firebombing of Dresden, Germany on February 13, 1945. Some 135,000 died, hundreds of thousands were injured and the so-called Florence of Germany was leveled. Library of Congress

were several cities that were considered for the raid, among them Dresden and Berlin.

By now, refugees had swollen the population of Dresden from 600,000 to one million. They lived in huts on the exterior of the city, along with some Allied POWs, some of whom were kept in an abandoned slaughterhouse. Among these was writer Kurt Vonnegut, who would later write, devastatingly, of the Dresden firebombing in his novel *Slaughterhouse 5.*

The Yalta Conference, postponed, opened on February 4, 1945 and concluded on February 11. On February 3, acting on its own, the Eighth U.S. Air Force launched a twin bombing raid on Berlin and Magdeburg. One thousand Flying Fortresses bombed Berlin; 400 Liberators bombed Magdeburg. In the words of author Alexander McKee, in his *Dresden, 1945, The Devil's Tinderbox,* "the basic reasons for making such a raid on Berlin one day before the Yalta Conference opened were political and diplomatic: to make clear to the Russians that, despite some setbacks recently in the Ardennes, the United States of America was a super-power capable of wielding overwhelmingly destructive forces."

Thus, the job had already been done in Berlin. Why Thunderclap still went forward, two days after the end of the Yalta Conference, remains a mystery to this day.

A three-wave attack was planned and became reality on the night of February 13 and the afternoon of the 14th. Two waves of 1,299 Lancasters, carrying a bomb weight of 3906.9 tons, left England on the afternoon of the 13th.

It was Shrove Tuesday, and the streets of Dresden were thronged with people in holiday finery, shopping or merely celebrating. At 10 P.M., the first "Christmas Trees," as the green flares released prior to a bombing were called, appeared over Dresden. There were no anti-aircraft defenses; only the air-raid sirens signaled the beginning of the raid.

The populace headed for bomb shelters and cellars and remained there while the RAF laid down a "carpet" of incendiary bombs. It was over in 15 minutes, and the populace came out to find flames everywhere. The Historical Museum in the old city center was afire, but a great many of its paintings had been removed, along with an immense china collection, to be transported out of the city before the Russians arrived. It was in a lorry parked outside the museum, and although it survived the first foray, it and the lorry would eventually be consumed.

Jets of flames swept up from the charred wreckage of ceilingless buildings and, driven by a west wind, began to travel horizontally across the city.

Meanwhile, the second, much greater force of bombers was on its way. At 1:22 A.M., the sirens sounded again. But by now, the streets were full of refugees from the first attack. The avenues, the parks, every open space was crowded with people trying to settle down for the night away from buildings.

Charlotte Mann, interviewed by Alexander McKee for his book, recalled, "It was as if fire was poured from the sky. Where there was darkness at one moment, we could suddenly see flames lick up . . . as I looked back to the center, I noted that it was just one single sea of flames. Now everyone started to make a run for the outskirts in order to reach some open space."

Margret Fryer, who had been questioned by the Gestapo that day and had escaped the concentration camps, now found herself in an inferno. "Because of flying sparks and the fire-storm I couldn't see anything at first," she recalled.

> *A witches' cauldron was waiting for me out there: no street, only rubble nearly a meter high, glass, girders, stones, craters. I tried to get rid of the sparks by constantly patting them off my coat. It was useless. I stopped doing it, stumbled, and someone behind me called out: "Take your coat off, it's started to burn." In the pervading extreme heat, I hadn't even noticed. I took off the coat and dropped it.*
>
> *Suddenly, I saw people again, right in front of me. They scream and gesticulate with their hands, and then—to my utter horror and amazement—I see how one after the other they simply seem to let themselves drop to the ground. I had a feeling that they were being shot, but my mind could not understand what was really happening. Today I know that these unfortunate people were the victims of lack of oxygen. They fainted and then burnt to cinders . . .*
>
> *It's dreadfully hot . . . I'm standing up, but there's something wrong, everything seems so far away, and I can't hear or see properly any more. I was suffering from lack of oxygen [too]. I must have stumbled forward roughly ten paces when I all at once inhaled fresh air.*

What she had experienced, and what saved her, was the cool winter air rushing in to replace the boiling hot air of the fires and blowing through the inferno of flames that had heated the center of the old town to a temperature of 3,000 degrees Fahrenheit (sandstone begins to alter its form at 1,200 degrees). The cool air was felt by some as a sort of suction that actually collapsed more fragile buildings.

Margret Fryer stumbled on, climbed into a car to rest, was directed out of it and informed that it too had caught fire.

"Dead, dead dead everywhere," she continued.

> *Some completely black like charcoal. Others completely untouched, lying as if they were asleep. Women in aprons, women with children sitting in the trams as if they had just nodded off. Many women, many young girls, many small children, soldiers who were only identifiable as such by the metal buckles on their belts, almost all of them naked. Some clinging to each other in groups as if they were clawing at each other.*
>
> *From some of the debris poked arms, heads, legs, shattered skulls . . . Most people looked as if they had been inflated, with large yellow and brown stains on their bodies. People whose clothes were still glowing . . . my face was a mass of blisters and so were my hands. My eyes were narrow slits and puffed up, my whole body was covered in little black, pitted marks.*

The fire was so fierce it collapsed stone structures. Almost all of the houses lost their roofs, and the walled enclosures then acted like stoves, belching up huge balls of flame and hot smoke. Superheated air rose miles wide and miles high above the infernally flaming city. At 20,000 feet, the crews of the bombers saw the sky as a roseate bowl above them, and the turbulence caused by the rising hot air currents buffeted them about.

Under the collapsed buildings, thousands of people were crushed or suffocated or were simply burned alive. Nearly every household in the city was swelled by refugees, and so the casualties were multiplied over and over.

By now, the flames of the burning city were visible on the ground from 50 miles away. The wind was blowing from the west, which drove those who survived either toward the open flood meadows of the River Elbe to the southeast, where the Grosser Garten, a designated refugee space, lay, or south, through the narrow streets of the old city.

Daylight was darkened in the city by thick clouds from the still-burning buildings. At dawn, the third wave of 1,300 U.S. bombers and 900 Thunderbolts and Mustangs took off from King's Cliffe in Northamptonshire. The people of Dresden were surveying the horrible aftermath.

Annemarie Waehmann, who had survived the bombing of the Friedrichstadt hospital complex, approached what had once been the central station. She smelled "thick smoke everywhere." She continued:

> *As we climbed with great effort over large pieces of walls and roofs which had collapsed and fallen into the street,*

we could hear behind us, beside us, and in front of us, burnt ruins collapsing with dull crashes. The nearer we came to the town center, the worse it became. It looked like a crater landscape, and then we saw the dead. Charred or carbonized corpses, shrunk to half size. Oh dear God! At the Freiburger Platz we saw an ambulance, with the male nurses just about to put a stretcher into it. A number of people were sitting on the ground. But why didn't they move? As we came nearer, we saw it all. They were all dead. Their lungs had been burst by the blast.

When the third noon raid arrived, there was no warning. All of the air-raid sirens had been silenced by fire. No incendiaries were dropped. The idea was to kill the escaping refugees.

Another attack—the fourth—occurred that evening on the outskirts of the city. But the rail yards, the autobahn bridge and the industrial complex were again untouched.

The following day, as it is after every fire storm, rain fell, turning the ghost of a city into a sea of mud, wreckage and half-hidden corpses. The discovered diary of a family named Daniels recorded some of the aftermath:

First they brought [the dead] in wagons to the outskirts of Dresden for burial. Then they burnt them in the Altmarkt. The recoveries and burials took weeks, and there was the danger of epidemics breaking out. It was a miracle we survived. What misery existed. There were children dead whose parents were still alive, and parents dead whose children were left behind. For them, life is hardly worth living any more. We are very grateful that we are still alive and together. When the war is over, all we have to do is build everything up again.

And Dresden was built again, but like Rotterdam, which had been gutted and leveled by the Nazis, it was not, nor would it ever again be, one of the most beautiful cities in the world. That city had died, along with 135,000 people, in the most catastrophic fire ever set or experienced by any humans anywhere on earth in any age.

GREAT BRITAIN
ENGLAND
EXETER

September 4, 1887

• • • • • • • • • • • • • • • • • • • •

A gaslight ignited scenery onstage, causing the fire in the Exeter Theatre in Exeter, England on September 4, 1887. Two hundred were killed; hundreds were injured.

"The bodies were lying so thick [at the bottom of the gallery stairs] that they quite occupied the entire width of

The Exeter Theatre fire in progress on the night of September 4, 1887. The theater, one of the prides of Exeter, England, was totally destroyed; 200 died and hundreds were injured. Illustrated London News

the staircase," said Harry Foot to the *Illustrated London News* on September 5, 1887; "in some cases they were four and five rows deep. At the bottom of the stairs they lay thicker than at the top, almost as if shot down a shoot. In the majority of cases the arms were outstretched beyond the head, as if they had struggled to the last to drag themselves forward; but their legs were rendered immovable by the bodies of those who had followed and partly fallen on them."

Foot and nearly 1,400 other playgoers had attended a performance at the stately Exeter Theatre, one of the prides of the city of Exeter, England, on the night of September 4, 1887. The performance had hardly begun when the nemesis of safety in 19th century theaters (see pp. 156, 161 and 196), an onstage gaslight, ignited some canvas scenery. As in the Ring Theatre disaster in Vienna six years before (see p. 156), the initial ignition occurred in the flies above the stage and slightly behind the top of the proscenium. Overhead gas lamps set fire to the uppermost reaches of a tall piece of scenery, just behind the act drop, and spread rapidly to the act curtain, then to the drapes in front of the proscenium. From there, the flames shot out in lethal sheets into the audience.

The actors onstage and the wealthy in the stalls and boxes were able to file out without injury. Some 900 of them emerged unscathed.

It was, as usual, a different scene entirely in the gallery. There, pandemonium and hysteria took an early toll. Men, women and children fled toward the one stairwell that might allow them to escape the huge, billowing clouds of smoke that were now blotting out whatever light had been left in the theater.

By the time many of them reached the stairwell, it had become a fatal flue, collecting the smoke from other parts of the structure, containing it and shooting it upward. Some gallery patrons were trampled underfoot; others who managed to reach the stairwell suffocated from the smoke, fell in place and blockaded the exit, trapping others behind.

George Cooper, a soldier, William Hunt, a sailor, and the aforementioned patron Harry Foot were among the heroes of the day. Ignoring their own safety, they dashed into the theater, plucking survivors from the steadily accumulating piles of the dead and dying and dragging or carrying them from the flaming theater.

Eventually, the flames reached the lead roof and heated it to the melting point. Flames descended the stairwells, followed by drops of molten lead. It was only at this point that the rescuers abandoned their efforts. "It would have been suicidal to have continued our work," Foot confessed to reporters later.

Two hundred patrons died in this fire, most of them in one stairway.

The Great 1666 Fire of London is depicted in a period painting. Thirteen thousand homes and 87 churches were destroyed; eight people died, and the black plague was thought to be incinerated in the flames. New York Public Library

GREAT BRITAIN
ENGLAND
LONDON

September 2–6, 1666

A fire in the chimney of a bake shop, coupled with a long drought, caused the Great Fire of London on September 2, 1666. Thirteen thousand houses and 87 churches were destroyed; only eight people died.

The Great Fire of London was monumental in many respects. It destroyed 13,000 houses and 87 churches—including Saint Paul's—on 400 streets, laid waste to the Royal Exchange and Guild Hall and reduced a score of other public buildings to charred ashes. It burned for five days and was only stopped by a change in the direction and velocity of the wind. It reduced to rubble a large portion of the largest city in the world at that time and exposed to the public the woeful inadequacy of the fire-fighting apparatus and techniques of the age.

Yet there were positive aspects to this holocaust. If records are at all accurate, it only claimed eight lives. The bubonic plague, which had raged through Europe for decades, disappeared in England, apparently burned out of existence by the Great London Fire of 1666. Scientists theorize that the intense heat incinerated the plague bacillus, thus freeing the British Isles from what would continue to roam the continent of Europe for another 150 years.

The methods of forcing water through hoses by compressed air had been known and feasible since the invention, in 1590 by Cyprian Lucar, of the "portable squirt"—a brass tank powered by three men and used to some effect in fighting the 1666 fire. Decaus's "rare and necessary engine," developed in 1615 and outfitted with a swivel joint, and Hans Hautch's engine at Nuremberg, built in 1655, which was designed to force, by air, a steady stream of water at a fire, were also in limited use. But only the least effective of these, the portable squirt was brought into play during the Great Fire, and even then on a very limited basis. Firemen simply pulled down flaming houses by grappling their walls with iron hooks on poles.

Afterward, however, modern methods of climbing ladders, extinguishing flames and carrying people to safety were begun. After the fire, when a new engine designed to fight fires was invented or introduced, it was not ignored, as it had been before 1666, but tested and, if found effective, was adopted.

Furthermore, as a result of the extent of this calamity, the concept of fire insurance was developed, and less than a year later, the world's first fire insurance policy was written by Dr. Nicholas Barton, who had built houses in the burned-out districts of London following the fire. His policies guaranteed to replace a house if it was destroyed by fire, and he did an immediate, brisk business, which eventually developed into Phoenix Fire Insurance, a firm that is still functioning today.

A long, pervasive drought preceded the London fire, very much like the long dry spell that occurred before the famous Chicago fire of 1871 (see p. 181). That fire began early in the evening. The London conflagration started at 2 in the morning in the chimney of the King's Baker's Shop on Pudding Lane, near London Bridge. From there, borne on a brisk wind, it ignited house after house and worked its way to the Thames wharves, where piles of flammable goods were stored.

The two most important men in the fighting of the Great Fire were Samuel Pepys and William Penn. Pepys, the son of a London tailor, was then secretary of the admiralty, an accomplished musician, a critic of painting, architecture and drama, a charming host and a connoisseur of beautiful women. He also kept a meticulous diary, and it is in the pages of this diary that the most vivid and precise record of the fire was set down:

> *September 2, 1666. Some of the maids sitting up late last night to get things ready against our feast today . . . called us up about three in the morning to tell us of a great fire they saw in the City. So I rose, and slipped on my nightgown, and went to [the] window; and thought it to be on the back side of Mark Lane at the farthest, and so went to bed again and to sleep.*

The next morning, Pepys's wife Jane informed him that 300 houses had been burned down and that all of Fish Street by London Bridge had been consumed. Pepys went to the Thames:

> *I . . . got a boat, and through the bridge, and there saw a lamentable fire, everybody endeavoring to remove their goods, and flinging into the river, or bringing them into lighters that lay off; poor people staying in their houses till the very fire touched them, and then running into boats or clambering from one pair of stairs by the water—one side to another . . . Having stayed and in an hour's time seen the fire rage every way, and nobody, to my sight, endeavoring to quench it, but to remove their goods and leave all to the fire . . . and the wind mighty high and driving into the city; and everything, after so long a drought, proving combustible, even the very stones of churches, I to White Hall.*

At White Hall, Pepys informed the king and the Duke of York of the horrendous state of London and got from them an order to pull down every house that might carry the fire forward.

"At last," he goes on, "met my Lord Mayor in Canning Street, like a man spent, with a handkercher about his neck, to the King's message, he cried, like a fainting woman:

> *'Lord! What can I do? I am spent. People will not obey me. I have been pulling down houses; but the fire overtakes us faster than we can do it . . .' The houses so very thick thereabouts, and full of matter for burning, as pitch and tar in Thames Street, and warehouses of oil and wines and brandy and other things.*

As the days and nights ached forward, the fire seemed to increase. Pepys went back and forth between the lord mayor, the king, and the Duke of York, bearing one repeated order: "Pull down the houses." He laments:

> *and to the fire up and down, it still increasing, and the wind great. So near the fire as we could for smoke; and all over the Thames, with one's faces in the wind you were almost burned with a shower of firedrops . . . and, as it grew darker, appeared more and more; and in corners and upon steeples, and between churches and houses, as far as we could see up the hill of the City, in a most horrid, malicious, bloody flame, not like the fine flame of an ordinary fire . . . We saw the fire as only one entire arch of fire from this to the other side of the bridge, and in a bow up the hill for an arch of above a mile long. It made me weep to see it. The churches, houses, and all on fire and flaming at once; and a horrid noise the flames made, and the cracking of houses at their ruin.*

By the morning of the fifth, William Penn, an important enough personage to command attention both in court and in the city, had taken a hand, and instead of simply pulling down houses, fire brigadiers were now, under his direction, blowing them up.

Pepys looked on:

> *I up to the top of Barking steeple, and there saw the saddest sight of desolation that I ever saw; everywhere great fires, oil cellars and brimstone and other things burning . . .*
>
> *I walked into the town, and find Fenchurch Street, Gracious Street, and Lombard Street all in dust. The exchange a sad sight, nothing standing there of all the statues or pillars but Sir Thomas Gresham's picture in the corner. Into Moorfield's our feet ready to burn walking through the town among hot coals and flint that full of people and poor wretches carrying their goods there . . . Thence homeward, having passed through Cheapside and Newgate market, all burned . . . and took up, which I keep by me, a piece of glass of the Mercers' Chapel in the street, where much more was, so melted and buckled with the heat of the fire like parchment.*

The wind changed; the fire abated. Less than a third of the walled city remained after this cataclysmic fire, which consumed most of London and taught many much about survival and prevention. One of those to learn from it was William Penn's Quaker son, who came to America 16 years later and founded Philadelphia. When he mapped out the city, he made sure it was filled with wide streets that would never become conduits of the sort of fire that he had witnessed as a child in London.

GUATEMALA
GUATEMALA CITY

July 14, 1960

• • • • • • • • • • • • • • • •

Either faulty electrical wiring or a candle collapsing onto flammable material in front of a religious statue ignited the fire in the Guatemala City Insane Asylum on July 14, 1960. Two hundred twenty-five died; 300 were injured.

The Guatemala City Insane Asylum was madness personified. A structure built in 1890, its facilities, its design and its safety had all outlived their capacity by the summer of 1960. Sometime during the early hours of July 14 of that year, a fire began in the asylum, started either by faulty electrical wiring or a candle collapsing onto flammable material in front of a religious statue. Within minutes, the ancient structure was ablaze, and 600 of its 1,500 inmates and attendants were trapped behind nonfunctioning doors.

The children who were housed in the asylum were the first to be evacuated, and every one of them survived. But there were still hundreds of adults who were incapable of saving themselves, and they were driven to wild hysteria by a fire that resisted every effort of the Guatemala City fire department to extinguish it.

Finally, realizing that most of the exits were blocked, and that those that were open were not being used by the patients to free themselves, the fire department, led by Guatemalan president Miguel Ydigoras Fuentes, brought a bulldozer onto the premises and knocked down a wall. Hundreds fled the building to safety through the hole in the wall, but others still had to be led, fighting and screaming, from the flames by rescuers. Thirty-one maximum-security patients, each considered dangerous, were never freed from their cells and burned to death in them.

The fire was brought under control by early morning of the 14th, and by that evening, 27,000 pounds of relief supplies had arrived from the United States. Two hundred twenty-five patients, most of them women, perished in the fire, and 300 were severely injured.

In the grim aftermath, murder and arson in the city increased after the fire. They were attributed to 48 criminally insane inmates who escaped from the burning asylum that night and were never recaptured.

IRAN
ABADAN

August 20, 1978

• • • • • • • • • • • • • • • •

Arson caused a fire in a movie theater in Abadan, Iran on August 20, 1978. Four hundred twenty-two died in the conflagration.

In 1978, Shah Mohammad Reza Pahlavi was trying to Westernize Iran. He ran head on into Muslim extremists, who announced that, in his efforts to emancipate women and redistribute church lands, the shah was violating the teachings of the Koran. Further, the general atmosphere engendered by his "Westernizing" process had resulted in a general laxity on the part of segments of the public in observing the strict dictates of the Muslim holy month of Ramadan. One of the consequences of this that angered the extremists was the showing of movies during Ramadan.

Saturday night, August 20, 1978 was a hot and muggy night in the oil-refining city of Abadan, at the northern tip of the Persian Gulf. A crowd had gathered at the Rex Theatre to see the Persian-language film *The Deer* and escape the heat.

Partway through the evening, a group of Muslim terrorists, aided by two employees of the Rex who were sympathetic to their cause, approached the theater from the outside. They carried several cans of gasoline, which they proceeded to splash on every outside wall. Then, as several of them ignited the gasoline, others, aided by the employees, opened the only exit door and doused the interior section of the theater near it with flaming gasoline. They then slammed the door and locked it.

Inside, the terrified audience went berserk. Flames roared through the building, consuming its interior and the people within. An enormous hill of grappling human beings piled up at the barricaded exit. Those who arrived there first were crushed under the pile; others were overcome by smoke; those at the top were incinerated.

The heat rose to inhuman levels. The entire building was consumed by flames. Some managed to smash windows; still others discovered a roof exit that had been overlooked by the arsonists and escaped. But they were the lucky few. By the time firemen arrived on the scene, smashed windows and broke in the barricaded door, the screaming from within the inferno that was once a theater had stopped.

Four hundred twenty-two people were burned to death, died of suffocation or were trampled to death. Entire families from the working-class neighborhood in which the theater was located were wiped out.

Ten arrests were made the following Monday, and the theater's manager was arrested and charged with negligence for ignoring police orders to hire more employees and guards. It would be one of the last futile gestures of opposition to the Muslim extremists, who would soon command the country.

JAMAICA
KINGSTON

May 20, 1980

• • • • • • • • • • • • • • • • • •

Overcrowding, combined with a short circuit in the wall of Eventide Home, a nursing home in Kingston, Jamaica, caused a fire on May 20, 1980. One hundred fifty-seven perished in the blaze.

On the night of May 20, 1980, there were 204 elderly, indigent women asleep in a 110-year-old, two-story building in a three-building complex called Eventide Home, located in Kingston, Jamaica. The other two buildings housed elderly men and handicapped children, and the entire complex was city owned and city run.

The structure sheltering the women was particularly decrepit and dangerous. Built of highly inflammable pitch pine wood, it had been branded a "tinder box" by Kingston fire chief Allen Ridgeway several times, but the city had ignored his warnings and had packed the building, which had a legal capacity of 180, with 204 elderly women.

"It was a place of indigent people," the fire chief explained to reporters after the fire that destroyed it. "The ratio of indigent rose and the capacity of the complex couldn't be expanded. The normal statutes just couldn't be kept."

And this breaking of its own statutes by the city only intensified the tragedy when the inevitable finally happened. At 1 A.M. on Wednesday, May 20, 1980, a short circuit in the building's electrical system started a fire in one of the walls. By the time anyone had even smelled the smoke, the flames had begun to consume the building. Screaming women, some unable to leave their beds, remained helpless before the onslaught of the flames, which raced with lightning speed through the entire building, collapsing walls and floors and igniting everything burnable within moments.

Some women managed to reach windows, but the fire spread so rapidly that it had become a hopeless situation long before the fire department even arrived. There were neither ladders nor safety nets for them, and the women who jumped from the upper level of the two stories injured themselves seriously.

The fire department arrived on the scene within five minutes. Four minutes later, the entire building collapsed upon itself with a sickening roar that mixed with the piercing screams of the women still trapped within it. A huge funeral pyre, it instantly silenced the last frantic efforts of any remaining survivors. Of the 204 women who had just 20 minutes before been sleeping peacefully within the shelter, only 47 would escape. One hundred fifty-seven died in the flames, most of them burned alive. It would be almost impossible to identify most of them the next day.

The best the fire department could do was to evacuate the children from their nearby shelter. The men, at a far corner of the complex, were not disturbed, and many slept through the entire holocaust.

A political campaign was warming up in Jamaica, and both sides in the contest irresponsibly accused the other of sending arsonists to start the fire. Prime Minister Michael N. Manley informed local radio stations that night that arsonists began the blaze, and a Kingston police spokesman perpetuated the rumor that telephone wires to the complex had been cut shortly before the blaze started. But Fire Chief Ridgeway steadfastly refused to blame arsonists, and his investigation proved that the immediate cause of the fire had been an electrical short circuit. The resultant tragedy was caused by housing helpless people in an overcrowded fire trap.

JAPAN
OSAKA

May 13, 1972

• • • • • • • • • • • • • • • • • •

A short circuit in a room containing oil-soaked rags, plus obscured fire exits, combined to turn the fire in the Playtown Cabaret in Osaka, Japan on May 13, 1972 into a fatal inferno. One hundred eighteen died; 38 were injured.

The sealing or blocking of fire exits is the major cause of fatalities in fires that occur in public places. This was tragically true in the Cinq-Sept fire in France (see p. 162), and it was also true in the Playtown Cabaret fire in Osaka, Japan on May 13, 1972.

The cabaret, a club frequented by businessmen and young couples and overseen by an army of partially clothed hostesses, occupied the top story of the Sennichi department store in Osaka. When the department store closed, the fun began in the cabaret.

On the evening of May 13, 1972, a lone workman in the store, an electrician named Keiji Kewashima, was making some electrical repairs on the third floor. Wires apparently shorted in a room that contained oil-soaked rags, and Kewashima soon found himself surrounded by flames. He ran from the room, shouting a warning that could not possibly be heard three stories above him in the Playtown Cabaret.

Thus the fire spread, unopposed, into the elevator shafts, up the walls and through the ductwork. When it finally reached the cabaret, practically all escape routes had been rendered useless. The cables in the elevator shafts had been burned apart. Flames licked at the outsides of windows. Hallways were filled by blinding, suffocating smoke.

The fire exits that might have provided some safe escape were hidden behind drapes. Later, rescuers would find piles of charred corpses, their hands reaching out as if searching along the superheated walls for the fire exits. An emergency fire chute *was* discovered by some, and 20 people scrambled down it. But halfway to the street, the chute collapsed, sending all 20 to their deaths.

Hysterical patrons, finding themselves trapped, smashed windows with tables and chairs. Some leaped from the windows, killing themselves in the fall. Nineteen tried to jump to the next building. None made it; all died. Others climbed to the roof, but by then the entire building was a roaring, consuming torch, and they were either burned alive or forced to leap to their deaths.

When the firemen finally arrived with their extension ladders, frantic patrons were falling past them to the earth. One hundred eighteen people died from suffocation, burning or falls, and 38 were injured. Only 48 were rescued.

PUERTO RICO
SAN JUAN

December 31, 1986

• • • • • • • • • • • • • • • • •

Labor troubles led to arson that caused the catastrophic fire on New Year's Eve, December 31, 1986 in the Dupont Plaza Hotel in San Juan, Puerto Rico. Ninety-six died; hundreds were injured.

For nearly two weeks preceding New Year's Eve of 1986, there were bad feelings between the management of the 22-story luxury Dupont Plaza Hotel, located in the Candado Beach area of San Juan, Puerto Rico, and Local 901 of the International Brotherhood of Teamsters, which represented the hotel's employees. During those 10 days, three small, smoky fires had broken out and been extinguished in various parts of the hotel. When guests—a great number of them from the United States—called the front desk and mentioned rumors that there had been bomb threats and fires in the hotel, they were told that the rumors were "false and groundless."

The hotel was crowded with holiday celebrants, many of them gambling in its casino, on the afternoon of December 31, 1986. Some of them had received disquieting telephone calls in their rooms that morning, warning that they would be "burned out." Again, when they reported these calls to desk clerks, they were told that they were probably the work of holiday pranksters.

At 1:41 P.M. that afternoon, a phone call was received at a police station near the hotel from a man who identified himself as "Santiago." The message was that a bomb had been planted on the premises of the hotel. Two policemen were dispatched to the Dupont Plaza. There is no record that they made a thorough investigation of the premises, but according to Jose L. Lopez, a senior spokesman for the commonwealth's police department, they did speak with members of the hotel staff, who told them that "there were no problems, everything was normal." The officers, Mr. Lopez said, "went back to the station and made a report."

Meanwhile, members of the hotel staff who belonged to the Teamsters' local and union officials were holding a stormy meeting in the hotel's ballroom. There was a vote on management's latest contract proposal, and it was turned down. A strike was called for midnight.

Among the employees present at the meeting was a 35-year-old maintenance worker named Hector Escudero Aponte. He was particularly frustrated and angered by the attitude and the offer of the hotel's management. He felt, as he later told investigators, that something had to be done to prove that the union meant business. He knew, he thought, how to intimidate management into listening to the union.

The previous day, a shipment of new furniture, wrapped in plastic, had been delivered to the hotel. It was stacked in the ballroom in piles six feet high.

Aponte stopped by the kitchen and picked up a can of Sterno-type cooking fuel. He entered the ballroom a little after 3:00 P.M., placed the canister next to one of the piles of furniture and lit it. It would, he believed produce a nice, contained, but smoky fire. He would later confess that he only meant to start "a small fire that would damage the personal property of the hotel."

But that is not what happened at all.

The six-foot towers of plastic-wrapped furniture became incendiaries. The plastic exploded, sending huge gouts of black smoke and orange flames skyward, through the walls and into the casino.

There were 70 people there, concentrating on winning money to spend at New Year's celebrations and beyond.

According to Kevin W. Condon of Ansonia, Connecticut, "Somebody [at the blackjack table] said there was smoke. But nobody paid any attention, and we continued playing. Then there was a big burst of smoke and we went running toward one of the exits. When someone opened the door, we saw that the whole hallway was covered with [illegible]k smoke. We slammed the door, went running toward [illegible]exit and that was filled with black smoke. Then [illegible]"

[illegible] was fire and for everyone
survivor and
Fire coming
upervisor and

and according
ere closed and
ons, now fully
to the casino,
ows that over-

he poolside pa-
Larry Roberts of
off like crazy,
ver older people

ea bleeding from
said Alexander
uest house across
g across the pool
eir clothing smol-

Meanwhile, terrified hotel gue[illegible] re blinded by the thick smoke that filled the hotel corridors. Puerto Rican law did not specify that sprinkler systems were mandatory in public buildings, and the Dupont Plaza did not have a sprinkler system.

Dominick Pannunzio and his wife, on the 15th floor, opened the door of their room and plunged into a cloud of dark gray smoke. They groped their way to an exit stairwell with a panicking crowd of screaming and shoving people.

"We ran down to the eighth floor," Pannunzio recalled, "and we ran into a solid wall of people, yelling, 'Go up! Go up! You can't get through here!' You couldn't see. Everyone was in panic.

"At the 17th or 18th floor, a bunch of people were coming down yelling, 'Down! Down! You can't go up!' We tried to get into one of the halls but all the doors were locked. People were gagging and falling down."

Finally, a maid let Pannunzio and 20 others into a room that had a balcony. They soaked towels and linens with water from the bathroom sink, held them to their faces and huddled on the room's balcony for four and a half hours before firemen finally rescued them.

The smoke was as dangerous as the flames. The plastic wrapping around the piled furniture in the ballroom was capable of producing noxious fumes, and the furniture itself, as well as other furniture throughout the hotel, was made of a fake leather composed of polyvinyl chloride. When burned, this substance produces hydrochloric acid, which scorches the lungs, the nostrils, the eyes—and can cause death immediately. Most of the dead were discovered near the pool area, the ballroom and the lobby—some of them sitting peacefully in chairs.

A great many guests ascended to the roof of the building, in the hope that helicopters would rescue them. A police helicopter hovered near, but according to radio transmissions received by private pilots, its pilot felt that he could not land because the roof was not flat.

At the same moment another helicopter pilot, Pat Walker, a 41-year-old charter pilot based in St. Thomas, was unloading a flight of four people at San Juan International Airport. The four had flown from the Virgin Islands to a New Year's party in San Juan.

Seeing the thick column of smoke, he radioed authorities who said he was needed and gave him clearance to refuel at Isla Grande and proceed to the Dupont Plaza.

Fortunately, Walker had no timidity about landing on the roof. The closest he could get, however, was to put one landing skid down on its edge. He had no hoist aboard and had to maneuver his helicopter perilously close to the roof. Blinded at times by the column of heat and smoke spiraling upward from the hotel, he coaxed four hysterical women aboard the craft and brought them safely to the ground.

Taking a police officer with him who helped calm the guests and organize the evacuation, Walker returned over and over again during the next 45 minutes, plucking 21 people from the roof of the hotel in his five-passenger Ranger and depositing them safely on the beach below, before larger military helicopters arrived on the scene.

It would be 7:00 that night before the fire was brought under control, and days before the dead, the dying and survivors were removed from the wrecked hotel. Some were found in their rooms, asphyxiated from the smoke that spread through the air-conditioning system. There were bloody towels on the adjoining beach, but a few yards away at the pool, palm trees were pristinely untouched. Paperback books and bottles of suntan lotion were strewn around, dropped by fleeing vacationers.

In the end, 96 died, and hundreds were injured. Hector Escudero Aponte confessed to arson and was sentenced to the maximum 99 years.

ROME

July 19, A.D. 64

• • • • • • • • • • • • • • • •

Imperial arson, ordered by Nero, caused the fire that consumed three of Rome's 14 districts and damaged seven more on July 19, A.D.*64. No fatality or injury figures survive.*

One of the more despicable pictures of ancient times is that of Nero fiddling while Rome burns. But the picture is not entirely accurate. Actually, the mad emperor fingered the lyre while he sang verses from *The Fall of Troy* and watched the conflagration from a safe hilltop.

There is unanimous consent among contemporary historians that Nero ordered this terrible fire set—possibly so that he could expand his already grandiose palace, which occupied two of Rome's seven hills, possibly because he had tired of the drabness of Rome's ancient buildings, possibly because he liked fires.

In any case, Nero departed on a short trip to Actium on July 17, A.D. 64, and on July 19 a mysterious blaze began in the vicinity of the Circus Maximus, at the bottom of the Palatine Hill. From the Circus Maximus, it spread swiftly, helped by a strong wind and the narrow streets of the quarter. It moved on without mercy, consuming buildings that had stood since the time of Romulus, the founder of the city 800 years before. Romulus's temple dedicated to the god Jupiter was one of the many venerable and irreplaceable buildings that burned during the six days and seven nights of the conflagration.

Tacitus, the historian of Rome, described the sorry scene:

> *Terrified, shrieking women, helpless old and young . . . fugitives and lingerers alike—all heightened the confusion. When people looked back, menacing flames sprang up before them or outflanked them. When they escaped to a neighboring quarter, the fire followed—even districts believed remote proved to be involved. Finally, with no idea where or what to flee, they crowded onto the country roads, or lay in the fields. Some who had lost everything—even their food for the day—could have escaped but preferred to die. So did others, who had failed to rescue their loved ones.*

That the fire was officially set was supported by Tacitus, too. "Nobody dared fight the flames," he wrote. "Attempts to do so were prevented by menacing gangs. Torches, too, were openly thrown in, by men crying that they acted under orders."

Finally, before the entire city was destroyed, fire brigades demolished buildings in the fire's path, and it ended, but not before consuming three of the city's 14 districts entirely and severely damaging seven more. Nero forbade homeowners from returning to salvage what they could from the ruins of their homes. The reason? Tacitus answers: "to collect as much loot as possible for himself."

Rumor, based on fact, spread through the city as fast as the fire; Nero had ordered it. To stop the rumor, Nero publicly speculated that the Christians in Rome, among them Saint Peter, were behind the arson that had wreaked such havoc. He ordered mass arrests and public crucifixions. Christians were set afire in Nero's gardens, and others were forced to enter the Circus dressed as animals, where killer dogs tore them to pieces.

According to the historians, even this failed to hide Nero's guilt. He rebuilt the city, after reconstructing his own palace on a hitherto unprecedented scale of opulence. There was a 120-foot-high statue of himself in the entrance hall, a pillared arcade a mile long and gardens containing lakes and complete forests. In the city, rebuilt public buildings were restricted in height, built of nonflammable stone, and porches were dictated as part of their approved design, so that fire fighters could have easy access in case of future fires.

RUSSIA
IGOLKINO

March 12, 1929

• • • • • • • • • • • • • • • •

Drunken negligence on the part of a projectionist, compounded by the overcrowding of a room with inadequate exits above a factory in Igolkino, Russia, caused the March 12, 1929 fire in that city. One hundred twenty died in the blaze.

March 12, 1929 was the 12th anniversary of the abdication of Czar Nicholas II. In the tiny Russian village of Igolkino, 250 miles northeast of Moscow, a group of drunken workers and their families decided to celebrate by viewing Victor Seastrom's classic film *The Wind*. Igolkino possessed no movie theater, but this did not dissuade the celebrants. They commandeered a 24-by-24-foot room above a factory. The factory manager had protested vehemently against the use of the room. First, according to *New York Times* reporter Walter Duranty, "[he] feared the peasants would steal tools stored in the room." But more importantly, and perhaps a bit more believably, he knew that 30 gallons of gasoline had been accidentally spilled on the floor of the room the day before, that there was only one exit from the room and that the windows were too small to accommodate people trying to flee from a fire.

His protestations fell on deaf ears. The village Soviet warned him that he would be arrested if he tried to prevent the workers from using the room. The factory manager acquiesced, and workers, led by Bazarnof, a drunken projectionist who carried the projector and film in one hand and a bottle of vodka in the other, crammed themselves into the fetid room.

Most of the revelers could not have cared less about the motion picture. They in fact shouted for music. Bazarnof complied, turning the running of the film over to an unskilled and equally drunk friend. Lighting up a cigarette and strapping on an accordian, Bazarnof squatted in the doorway of the only exit and began to play Russian folk songs. The substitute projectionist allowed the film to run off the take-up reel and accumulate in a pile on the floor.

Unconcerned, Bazarnof continued to play the accordian. When his cigarette had burned down to a butt, he flipped it. The still-glowing cigarette landed in the middle of the nitrate-treated film and instantly ignited it. The flames rushed to the gasoline-soaked floor, and within seconds the entire room and its occupants were ablaze. Bazarnof leaped up and ran. He did not stop until he reached a nearby village, where, a day later, he was arrested.

Meanwhile, people choked and suffocated on the thick black smoke generated by the ball of fire that had now consumed the room. Some were trampled to death underfoot; others were burned alive.

In the midst of this, someone discovered a trapdoor that opened onto the factory below. One hundred thirty people managed to squeeze through either the trapdoor or the one exit, but 120 died in that 24-by-24-foot cauldron.

One more victim would be claimed in a ghoulish and grisly charade. Furious and distraught over the mayhem and death, the village's peasants vented their rage not on the absent projectionist who had caused the fire, but on the factory manager who had tried to warn their dead comrades away from the firetrap. A mob of workers cornered him, stoned him, beat him unconscious and flung him into the still-raging fire, where he burned to death.

SOUTH KOREA
SEOUL

December 25, 1971

• • • • • • • • • • • • • • • • •

Human negligence in failing to contain a small fire caused by a propane tank explosion in a coffee shop led to the huge fire in the Taeyunkak Hotel in Seoul, South Korea on Christmas Day, December 25, 1971. One hundred sixty-three died in the fire; 50 were injured.

Holiday times seem to be particularly vulnerable to tragedies resulting from human carelessness.

Eight workers and executives of the luxurious 21-story Taeyunkak Hotel in the center of Seoul, Korea were arrested and charged with negligence after the December 25, 1971 fire that raked the hotel with roaring flames and caused the death of 163 persons.

The fire began at 10:00 A.M. when a propane tank used for cooking in a second-floor coffee shop exploded and burst into flames. Under ordinary circumstances, this manageable fire should have been extinguished, or at least contained within the confines of the coffee shop. But it was not, and the flames soared up through conduits and elevator shafts, climbing 20 stories to the hotel's roof within minutes.

Fortunately, because of the Christmas holiday, the offices in the building were unoccupied. Still, 317 people—187 guests and 130 hotel employees—were in the building when the fire began. Again, as in so many fires in public buildings, there were too few fire escapes, and those that existed were blocked by fire, smoke or debris.

Firemen arrived quickly, but an incredible situation developed as soon as they came upon the scene. Amazingly, in a city of skyscrapers, they had ladders that only reached to the fourth floor. Their hoses only drove water as high as the ninth floor, and the flames were shooting out of the building all the way to the 22nd story and beyond.

Panicked, hysterical people began to fling themselves from windows. Even when 13 helicopters arrived, the mayhem and dying scarcely ceased. The roof was consumed in flames; there was no landing space for the helicopters, and so their pilots and crews attempted to rescue survivors by ladder from window ledges. It was a risky exercise for professionals under ideal circumstances. It proved disastrous in this situation. Only a small number of people managed to clamber up the swinging ladders to safety, and two who were rescued from the flames lost their grip and fell to their deaths.

Everything was tried, even the pieced-together poles of circus acrobats, but little could be done for those trapped on the upper floors of this flaming modern hotel, and it was considered fortunate that only 163 people died and approximately 50 were injured.

SPAIN
MADRID

September 22, 1928

• • • • • • • • • • • • • • • • •

A short circuit set fire to scenery in the Novedades Theater in Madrid on September 22, 1928. The resultant fire killed 110 people; 350 were injured, many seriously.

Every major city in Europe seems to have its favorite theater, and in Madrid in the 1920s it was the Novedades Theater. A venerable, ornate wooden structure built in

1860 and converted to electricity soon thereafter, it was in need of further refurbishment in 1928. But the nearly 3,200 spectators who jammed it on the night of September 22, as they did practically every night it was open, were unaware of the old structure's aging innards.

The consequences of time burst into flame during the intermission that evening. A short circuit in the ceiling of a room used to store unused scenery set fire first to the ceiling, then the scenery, then adjacent rooms and finally the auditorium of the theater itself.

The performers, who saw the flames first, were able to escape through their stage exits and entrances. The wealthier patrons on the orchestra floor were, for the most part, either outside or in the outer lobby and thus escaped unharmed.

But as usual in theater fires, the less affluent customers, the working class who could only afford balcony seats, were trapped, hemmed in by the height of the balcony on one side and inadequate, cramped, smoke-filled staircases on the other. Panic struck immediately, and scores were trampled in the rush toward the stairways. Some patrons, shoved by other hysterical audience members, lost their footing and plunged over the balcony rail and into the auditorium.

"Many persons," reported the *New York Times,* "mad with terror tried to fight their way out stabbing with knives right and left or biting, scratching or shoving aside weaker persons in their way."

For each of these despicable acts there were equal numbers of heroic ones. Men carried children on their shoulders through walls of flames and then reentered the inferno to rescue more. A woman usher stood her ground, holding a flashlight on a dark exit so that people could be guided to it. She was discovered dead the next day, still clutching the flashlight.

The two staircases soon became piles of wedged bodies caught between flaming wooden walls. Firemen could do nothing to save the old building. Their ladders could not be raised in the narrow streets bordering the Novedades, and so they watched, helpless, as people threw themselves to the street and their deaths from upper stories of the theater.

One hundred ten died; 350 were injured, some of them for life.

SYRIA
AMUDE

November 13, 1960

• • • • • • • • • • • • • • • • • •

An unexplained explosion in the projection booth of a movie theater in Amude, Syria on November 13, 1960 caused a fire that gutted the building. One hundred fifty-two children attending a special program were killed; 23 were injured.

As in Montreal (see p. 159), a children's movie program in the tiny town of Amude, Syria, near the Turkish border, turned into a fiery nightmare. The Montreal holocaust took place during a special matinee. The Amude disaster occurred at a special evening program, in which 175 children were gathered in the small local movie theater to see a special film.

The children, who accounted for a large part of the village's population under the age of 15, had just begun to settle back and become involved in the film when suddenly, jets of flame shot out of the projection booth, accompanied by pieces of flaming film. In the inquiry that followed, some witnesses said an explosion had occurred in the projection booth; some refuted this. The projectionist was severely burned and thus could neither verify nor dispute it.

In any case, the theater was consumed by raging flames in minutes. There simply was neither enough time nor exits to save most of the children. One hundred fifty-two died from suffocation, trampling or fire. Twenty-three escaped, but every one was badly injured.

TURKEY
CONSTANTINOPLE

June 5, 1870

• • • • • • • • • • • • • • • • • •

Hot charcoals spilled from a brazier onto the wooden steps of a home in the Armenian section of Constantinople, Turkey on June 5, 1870 and fanned by high winds led to a conflagration that destroyed 3,000 homes and set fire to the entire city. Nine hundred residents died.

There seems to be some dispute about some of the details of the great fire that swept through Constantinople, Turkey on Sunday, June 5, 1870. Several versions indicate that it was a balmy spring day, and a large portion of the population was out of the city, enjoying picnics and the country. But these same reports also indicate that a gale-force wind was blowing, and this wind was responsible for the wildfire nature of the disaster. Considering the enormous number of casualties—900 persons burned to death, more than 3,000 buildings destroyed—it would seem that the population was at home, not out battling the winds on open picnic grounds.

A fire brigade rushes down a Constantinople street during the consuming fire of June 5, 1870. Illustrated London News

One detail runs consistently through the chronicles of that terrible day, however: the origins of the fire. An Armenian family in the Valide Tchesme district was definitely at home at dinnertime, and the mother of the household instructed her young daughter to go upstairs, fill an iron pan with burning charcoal and bring it downstairs to the cooking quarters. The daughter obeyed, but on the way back she dropped some of the glowing charcoal on the steps. The gale, blowing through an open window on the staircase, scattered the sparks onto the roof of an adjoining home, and the blaze was under way.

Flames leaped from home to home, leveling both the Armenian and Christian quarters in a matter of hours, and then roared to the docks on the Bosporus and up Feridje, the grand street that contained churches, shops, hospitals, legations and consulates.

The churches, hospitals and diplomatic missions were surrounded by stone walls and sustained little damage. Sir Henry Elliott, the British consul, only suffered a singed silk dressing gown, which he wore while directing fire prevention within his compound. But the damage to the remainder of the city was devastating: 900 dead, 3,000 buildings in ruins, and more than a square mile of Constantinople reduced to rubble.

UNITED STATES
CONNECTICUT
HARTFORD

July 6, 1944

• • • • • • • • • • • • • • • • • •

The most tragic circus fire in history, the Ringling Brothers, Barnum & Bailey fire in Hartford, Connecticut on July 6, 1944, was caused by a combination of arson and a shortage of fireproof materials because of World War II. One hundred sixty-eight died; more than 480 were injured.

The greatest circus tragedy in history and one of America's worst fires resulted from two conspiring causes: World War II and arson.

The 6,000 patrons who half filled the main tent of Ringling Brothers, Barnum & Bailey Circus on Thursday afternoon, July 6, 1944 in Hartford, Connecticut were almost entirely children (two-thirds of the audience was under the age of 12), mothers and grandparents. There were very few young fathers in the audience; most young American men in 1944 were fighting in World War II.

The war had also commandeered something besides young men: Safe fireproofing material of the sort that circuses needed, and had until now used to keep the highly in-

Terrified audience members flee the Barnum and Bailey Circus fire in Hartford, Connecticut on July 6, 1944. American Red Cross

flammable canvas of the big top from burning, had been redirected to the war effort. Thus, Ringling Brothers and Barnum & Bailey had treated their new, $60,000 big top with a stopgap mixture of paraffin and gasoline. It was a fatal mistake. Rather than stopping the fire, it accelerated it. Seeing the extreme effects of its refusal to make fireproofing material available to civilians, the government reversed itself 24 hours after the Hartford circus tragedy.

One more fateful piece fit into the structure of tragedy that afternoon. The management of Ringling Brothers and Barnum & Bailey employed several "firewatchers," who were stationed at strategic points within the tent. The firewatcher stationed at the main entrance became apprehensive about the safety of the crowd near the animal runways. If the roustabouts disassembling the runways should hit some of the huge jacks supporting the stands, they might collapse, reasoned the firewalker, and he left his post to make sure this did not occur.

The fire was deliberately set. It would be six years before the man who set it, Robert Dale Segree, would come forth and confess. But confess he did, in great detail. He had been only 14 years old when he set the fire, but before that he had killed a nine-year-old girl with a rock, had strangled three other people and had set fire to a store, a boat pier, a Salvation Army center, a schoolhouse and various other buildings. He claimed that he was driven to perform such acts by a rider on a fiery red horse who came to him in his dreams. The night before the Hartford holocaust, this rider had appeared, and so, at 2:30 P.M. on July 6, 1944, just as the Flying Wallendas were climbing to their high-wire perch at the top of the tent and as the wild lions, tigers, jaguars and leopards of Alfred Court's wild animal act were being prodded into the wire runways that would direct them out of the main arena and into their outside cages, Robert Dale Segree touched a lighted cigarette to the canvas of the big top, near its main entrance.

And at that moment, the fire started.

It spread swiftly, powered by the paraffin and gasoline coating and helped by a sudden wind that whipped through the main entrance. Three ushers, Paul Runyon, Mike Dare and Kenneth Grinnell, saw the flame when it was still no bigger than a bouquet of roses and, grabbing three buckets of water, dashed toward it. But the heat of the fire was already so great that it scorched their clothes and drove them back before they could empty their buckets.

The crowd did not panic at first, even though there were isolated cries of "Fire!" Most apparently felt that it would be put out, and they filed in orderly fashion toward the multiple exits. Merle Evans instructed his band to keep on playing, and they did, in an attempt to maintain calm.

But none reckoned with the speed of acceleration of the fire. Suddenly, it roared up the wall of the tent and then toward its peak. Large chunks of flaming canvas started to fall onto the exiting audience. And pandemonium began. Evans, sensing that the fire was going out of control, launched into "The Stars and Stripes Forever," the musical equivalent of "hey rube!"; and roustabouts from all over the circus grounds grabbed water buckets and hoses and dashed for the main tent.

Only five minutes had elapsed, and the tent was a collapsing inferno. The three animal runways cut off escape for the reserved-seat section, and these patrons trampled one another in an attempt to get to the main arena. Older people and children, unable to crawl over the runways, fell before them and were buried by others trying to thrash their way past. People, then bodies piled up at the end of each of the runways. Flaming chunks of canvas fell on them, creating ghastly funeral pyres. A hundred people at a time were set afire by these cometlike hunks of flaming canvas.

Thomas E. Murphy, a reporter for the *Hartford Courant,* described the scene:

I saw one woman fail to make it over the runway. She slid back and slumped to the ground. A man tried to fend off the crowd but the pressure was too great. I was slammed against the steel barrier and my knee caught momentarily between the bars. Then, taking my five-year-old son in my hands, I tossed him over the barrier to the ground beyond. The flames at this point were nearly overhead and the heat was becoming unbearable.

At this point, the six gigantic support poles that supported the big top began to tumble, thundering down like falling redwoods, crushing people who were in their path. Merle Evans witnessed this. "[The fire] just kept coming," he said, "and as it raced, the center poles, burned from their grommets, fell one by one." Seeing the hopelessness of the situation, Evans ordered his 29 musicians, their uniforms scorched, to evacuate.

The flying Wallendas had descended from their perches and had crawled out over the tops of the runway cages and escaped. The Wallendas, the roustabouts, policemen and clowns Emmett Kelly and Felix Adler dashed back into the inferno, rescuing whomever they could. They carried out bodies piled up in the entranceways, hoping to clear it for survivors. But by now the tent had collapsed, sealing the fates of those within.

Outside the big top, mayhem took over as mothers tried to run back into the flames in search of their children. One policeman held a distraught woman who screamed, "Let me go! Let me go! For Christ's sake, my kids are in there!"

Bandmaster Evans, sitting on a bench, shook his head. "I have been through storms and blowdowns and circus wrecks," he said, "but never anything like this. I hope to God I never see a thing like this again."

Clown Emmett Kelly, tears running down his cheeks, comforted a sobbing child. "Listen, honey," reporter Murphy heard him say, "listen to the old man. You go way over there . . . and wait for your mommy. She'll be along soon."

In 10 minutes—some said less—168 people died, and more than 480 were injured, many of them seriously. Two-thirds of those killed were children, and almost all of the rest were women.

Help arrived swiftly and in many forms. Fifteen hundred volunteer workers, 1,000 nurse's aides and staff assistants from the Hartford Chapter of the American Red Cross; Connecticut State Police, Hartford Police; civil defense units; soldiers from nearby Camp Bradley; nurses and doctors and fire apparatus from Hartford, East Hartford, West Hartford and Bloomfield. But the fire had spread so rapidly that they could do nothing to save anyone. Thus, more than 100 ambulances took the injured to the municipal hospital; other vehicles took the unidentified dead to the state armory.

An investigation was launched immediately, and five circus officials were indicted on technical charges of manslaughter. It would be 1950 before Segree would come forward to confess his guilt. He would be sentenced on November 4, 1950 on two counts and receive a comparatively mild—when one considers the enormity of his crime—two to 20 years on each count.

Ringling Brothers and Barnum & Bailey would spend the next seven years paying off its debts. There would be 676 suits by relatives of those who died in the fire, and everyone of them would be paid without a court fight. The final total of claims paid was more than $4 million, and since the circus carried only $500,000 worth of liability insurance, the money would come out of the next 10 years' profits. The arbitration agreements have been recorded as one of the most forthright and honest settlements in modern legal history.

UNITED STATES
GEORGIA
ATLANTA

December 7, 1946

• • • • • • • • • • • • • • • •

The worst hotel fire in U.S. history took place in the "fireproof" Winecoff Hotel in Atlanta, Georgia on December 7, 1946. Caused by a smoldering mattress that burst into flames in a momentarily unattended corridor, it killed 119 and injured 100.

For 33 years, W. Frank Winecoff's "fireproof" signature hotel existed safely on Peachtree Street in the heart of downtown Atlanta, Georgia. And then, in the worst hotel fire in the history of the United States, it burned, out of control, with no fire escapes, no sprinkler system, no alarm system and therefore no hope of survival for its 285 guests. That 66 of them escaped unharmed was a miracle. One hundred nineteen died, and more than 100 were injured in one night of terror.

The Winecoff was a substantial, boxy 15-story hotel containing 210 rooms. It was built, true to its claim, of entirely noncombustible materials. The walls and floors were made of steel, reinforced concrete, face brick, marble and terra-cotta. The dividing walls consisted of hollow tile. With this sort of construction, city officials failed to enforce fire codes, and thus the hotel operated in 1946 without outside fire escapes, a sprinkler system or an automatic fire alarm.

At 3:30 A.M. on December 7, 1946, a smoldering mattress, left in the third-floor corridor, burst into flame. It would only go undetected for 10 minutes. The night bellhop, Bill Mobley, delivering ice and ginger ale to room 510 and forced to wait in the hall while that room's inhabitant finished taking a shower, smelled smoke. So did the elevator girl, who informed Comer Rowan, the night clerk. He told her to go to the fifth floor and inform the hotel's engineer, who was making his nightly inspection rounds.

Meanwhile, Rowan himself sprinted to the stairwell in the lobby and looked up. Flames were licking at the walls a few floors over his head.

He dashed back to his desk and called the fire department. The first engine would be on the scene in slightly over a minute; the entire 60-man force would be there in 10. But the fate of everyone in the hotel had already been sealed the moment the flames from the mattress had ignited new paint on the corridor walls, raced down the corridor and entered the center stairwell. Fed by an updraft, the fire became a conflagration, racing for the upper stories. With both elevators now immobilized, the stairway impassable and no fire escapes, there was no safe way out.

Unaware of this, Rowan began to call rooms, warning the guests of the fire. He was only able to complete a few calls before the phone went dead.

The firemen arriving on the scene had two choices: trying to control the fire or trying to rescue the trapped guests, who were by now fashioning makeshift ropes from knotted bedsheets. Some were merely perched on window ledges.

The firemen opted for the second choice and began to run up their ladders, which reached the 10th floor, to try to rescue some of the terrified guests.

Within a few moments, panic erupted, and as the fire and smoke began to reach their rooms, some people began to fling themselves to the street rather than be burned alive. One man trying to lower himself from a bedsheet toward one of the fire ladders was struck by two people who had jumped from a higher floor. All three fell to their deaths. A woman leaped from an upper floor and struck a fireman carrying a woman down a ladder. All three were flung to the sidewalk. The two women were killed; the fireman was seriously injured.

Safety nets were frantically spread, and some of the people survived by jumping into them. Others missed. On the 13th floor, a group of people pooled their bedsheets to make an extra long rope but then defeated themselves fatally when two tried to descend simultaneously. The sheets parted, and they fell. A four-year-old boy, flung from an upper window, would have been killed if a man on the street had not caught him.

Individual acts of bravery abounded. Major Jake Cahill and his wife were rescued by fire ladder. Once they had reached the ground, Major Cahill entered an adjacent building via the alleyway behind the hotel, stripped off his coat, found a wooden plank and, placing it on two adjacent window sills, crawled across it and rescued his mother from her room by guiding her back across the wooden plank. While he was rescuing his mother, someone stole his fountain pen and traveler's checks from his abandoned coat.

Eventually, firemen turned to the fire itself. Entering the lobby, they made their way up the stairwell, a floor at a time. They battered their way into rooms hoping to find survivors and found very few. Most were burned beyond recognition or asphyxiated. In one 11th-floor room, they found a mother kneeling in the bathroom, holding three small children in her arms. The fire had fused their bodies together.

Hospitals in Atlanta, at Fort McPherson and the Atlanta Naval Air Station were crammed with the injured, the dying and the dead. Georgia governor Ellis Arnold and Atlanta mayor William B. Hartsfield launched an immediate investigation and discovered that the Winecoff was not the only hotel in Atlanta without fire escapes, sprinkler systems or automatic alarms. The presence of these, plus proper metal fire doors in the corridors, would have prevented this tragedy.

The hotel's lessees were indicted for involuntary manslaughter, but the charges were dropped six months later. Ironically, 70-year-old W. Frank Winecoff, who had built his fireproof hotel in 1913 and had been given a 10th floor suite in perpetuity, also perished that night, a victim of America's worst hotel fire.

UNITED STATES
ILLINOIS
CHICAGO

October 8, 1871

• • • • • • • • • • • • • • • • • • • •

A combination of a long drought, wooden construction and the overturning of a kerosene lantern in the O'Leary barn on DeKoven Street led to the Great Chicago Fire of October 8, 1871. Some 250 to 300 died, 90,000 were made homeless. There was $196 million in property damage.

Chicago had grown swiftly from a village of 4,000 people in 1840 to a thriving city of 300,000 in 1871. There were 60,000 buildings spread over 36 square miles by that year, and almost all of them were built of wood. Even the stone and brick buildings possessed either tarred or wood-shingle roofs.

The poor of Chicago were legion, and they lived in squalid two- or three-room shacks, flimsy shanties with winter wood piled against their outer walls and ramshackle barns and sheds behind them. Weather-beaten tenements sheltered thousands of people in minuscule cubicles. And all of this was tied together by miles and miles of wooden sidewalks and fences—which would become superhighways for the flames of the Great Chicago Fire, the worst fire disaster to ever occur in the United States.

The condition of rapid growth in Chicago from 1840 to 1871 certainly contributed to the magnitude of the fire. But the weather of the summer preceding it was also a major factor. From July 3 to the beginning of October, Chicago had received only two and a half inches of rain. Every stick of wood in the city was tinder dry; even the leaves on the trees had been scorched and dehydrated by the summer heat and lack of water, and they lay in piles along the sides of the streets.

The beginnings of the Great Chicago Fire, according to accepted belief. This contemporary lithograph captures the moment, on the evening of October 8, 1871, when Mrs. O'Leary and her cow first worked their mischief. Lithography Collection, Smithsonian Institution

The Chicago Fire Department was led by the wise and dedicated and usually frustrated Robert Williams. His manpower and engine power were not exactly immense: 200 men, 17 steam-fired, horsedrawn engines, three hook and ladder trucks and six hose wagons. The 43-year-old Williams, who bore a striking resemblance to Robert E. Lee, had repeatedly asked the city council for more ammunition and troops with which to fight fires, but he had been repeatedly turned down. The council had even refused a fireboat for the Chicago River—a horrendous oversight, considering that the river flowed directly through the city, was flanked by warehouses and wooden docks and intersected by 24 wooden bridges.

Furthermore, during the first week of October, there had been 35 major fires in Chicago, the worst of them at 10:00 P.M. on October 7, one night before the big one. A planing mill on the West Side had caught fire, and before it had been extinguished, some $750,000 in damage had been done.

That very night, author George Francis Train gave a lecture in Farwell Hall in downtown Chicago. "This is the last public address that will be delivered within these walls," he intoned. "A terrible calamity is impending over the city of Chicago. More I cannot say; more I dare not utter."

Whether he had some inside information, or was psychic, or was guessing, nobody ever knew. But he was terribly, absolutely right.

At 8:30 on Sunday night, October 8, 1871, something happened at 137 DeKoven Street on Chicago's West Side. Myth and fancy and the rewriting of history by everyone from local newpaper reporters to screenwriters to Katie O'Leary herself have probably buried forever the true facts. But all narrators agree on one: The Great Fire of Chicago began in the O'Leary barn. All also agree that she kept five cows, had a milk route, had five children and had a neighbor named Patrick McLaughlin.

Then the stories begin to part company. One account, by historian Hal Butler, says that one of the O'Learys' cows was sick, that Katie O'Leary went out to the barn at 8:30 that night to examine the sick animal, examined her, decided to go back into the house to get some salt as a

The wind-whipped flames of the Great Chicago Fire advance on the fleeing refugees in this contemporary painting of the event. Library of Congress

remedy, left a kerosene lamp on the straw-strewn floor and the restless cow kicked it over, igniting the straw.

Katie first told this story and then later denied it.

Another version has her neighbor Patrick McLaughlin knocking on her door, waking her up at 8:30 and asking her for some more milk for a party the McLaughlins were having. In this version, Katie goes to the barn and attempts to milk her cow for the second time that day; the cow resists and kicks over the kerosene lamp.

Another has Patrick McLaughlin sneaking into the barn to milk the cow, which kicks over the lantern.

"Big Jim" O'Leary, Katie's politician-gambler son, played by Tyrone Power in the movie *In Old Chicago,* claimed afterward that some small boys in the neighborhood sneaked into the barn for a smoke and started the blaze.

And still another version has elements formed in the soil throughout the Midwest by a comet many thousands of years ago making the ground—particularly the ground under Katie O'Leary's barn—combustible.

Whatever the ignition, at approximately 8:45 on October 8, 1871, the O'Leary barn went up in flames. Simultaneously, the heat that had gathered under the roof blew a hole through it and puffed out a billow of bright, yellow-red fire surrounded by dense white smoke.

The watchman of Little Giant Company Number 6, whose members had had only four hours sleep after battling the Saturday night blaze at the planing company, was the first to see it, and he routed out the company, which was situated only five blocks away from DeKoven Street and the O'Learys.

As the Little Giant Company started for the fire, a southwest wind kicked up, flinging sparks from the barn toward neighboring structures. Before the engine company arrived on the scene, a second barn, a paint shop and a flimsy wooden home were also on fire. Flames were flinging themselves 50 to 60 feet in the air. The company pulled up at DeKoven and Jefferson, laid a line down through DeKoven and then through the passageway to the O'Leary barn and soon had a solid stream of water directed on the blaze.

Bruno Goll, the owner of a nearby drugstore, ran to a new fire alarm box and turned in the alarm. But the wiring of the box was apparently faulty, and the message never reached the central fire control at the courthouse. This, it turned out, was a key failure, for if reinforcements from other fire companies had arrived within the next half hour, it is generally conceded that the fire could have been contained and extinguished. Instead, it started to spread northward.

Even without the faulty wiring, however, the fire might still have been brought under control if a series of events had not occurred in the courthouse tower. The fire watcher there, Mathias Schafer, spotted the blaze and called down to fire operator William Brown to mark the spot at call box 342, at the corner of Halsted and Canalport, more than a mile from the fire's actual location. Every other engine company in the city, alerted by telegraph, sped toward that spot.

Taking a second look, Schafer realized his error and signaled to Brown to send out another alarm. The fire was not at call box 342, but at call box 319. Astoundingly, Brown refused to send out the second signal, asserting that it would confuse the fire companies. Schafer argued with him, but Brown remained adamant, thus preventing the two most powerful fire engines in the city, housed only a few blocks from the fire, from arriving in time to put it out.

By the time the other companies reached the real scene of the fire, two square blocks of houses and barns were blazing, and the fire was rapidly growing beyond the control of anyone. One company's hose burst; another unit's hose burned up, and a third could not find enough pressure to pump water.

Six blocks north of the O'Leary home was Saint Paul's Catholic Church, bordered by Bateman's Lumber Mill and two furniture factories. The wind-driven blaze now picked up a burning timber and hurled it six blocks through the air. The firebrand hit the steeple of Saint Paul's, setting it and the church ablaze. Within minutes, the fire had spread to the lumberyard. A half million board feet of lumber, 1,000 cords of kindling and almost a million wooden shingles ignited.

An hour passed, and three major fires now blazed in the city. The first fire had split into two columns, rushing north at a terrifying speed. The third was in the nearby Bateman Lumber Mill. Smoke, powered by the terrific heat beneath it, shot up into the wind. Sparks, flaming shingles and pieces of clapboard exploded upward through the smoke like volcanic debris.

The draft caused by the flames, like a suction, and very much like the situation that would exist in Dresden 74 years later (see p. 164), plus the southwest wind, became strong enough to blow people down in the streets. Sparks rained lethally.

Frightened residents began to evacuate their homes. The wind increased, sending flaming ash and debris north toward the downtown district.

Now the three fires merged. Near midnight, the wind hurled pieces of burning wood across the Chicago River, where they set fire to the Parmalee Omnibus and Stage Company, and this fire now spread to the Chicago Gas Works, where two enormous gas storage tanks stood in the direct path of the flames. Tom Burtis, the night superintendent, prevented an unholy explosion from happening

A view of the Great Chicago Fire of 1871 from the West Side, captured in a contemporary lithograph. New York Public Library

by releasing the gas into the North Side Reserve and the Chicago sewers.

But his heroism had mixed results. The gashouse did not explode, but the gas fumes emitting from sewer manholes throughout the South Division erupted in thunderous bursts of fire, which burned uncontrollably and set fire to nearby buildings.

From the gasworks, the fire leaped to a nearby armory where stored ammunition exploded, adding a sense of Armageddon to the already abundant terror of the night.

Hysteria turned the streets into bedlam. Conley's Patch, Chicago's 24-hour red-light district, was soon ablaze and emptying its brothels, saloons and rooming houses of their inhabitants. Drunks were everywhere as the saloons became free houses. Roaming gangs of looters began to strip battered businesses of their stock. Jacob Klein, a resident of the West Side, was killed by several toughs as he was carrying two bolts of cloth from his building. The toughs tried to wrest it from him; he resisted; they crushed his head with a shovel and made off with the cloth.

As the flames advanced on the courthouse, Mayor Roswell Mason telegraphed other cities for help. Fire equipment was immediately loaded onto railroad cars in Aurora, Illinois as well as St. Louis, Cincinnati and Milwaukee. New York City dispatched a special train loaded with men and supplies.

Ex-alderman James Hildreth broke into an armory and had 3,000 pounds of explosives removed. Collaring the mayor, he talked him into authorizing the blowing up of buildings to form firebreaks. Aided by two policemen, Hildreth went out into the city, dynamiting buildings to absolutely no avail. The fire merely leaped across the open spaces where the buildings once stood.

At 1 A.M., a blazing piece of timber struck the tower of the courthouse, setting it on fire. The huge five-and-a-half-ton bell within it was set in motion, to toll continually for an hour until it would fall through the fire-pitted roof to the ground below. Before that happened, the building was evacuated. One hundred sixty prisoners housed in its basement jail were set free to roam and pillage the city. Five murderers were, however, not freed but were handcuffed together and placed in the custody of the police.

The entire business district was engulfed in flames. Two plush new hotels, the Bigelow and the Grand Pacific, had not even opened their doors for business. They never would.

The Palmer House (which would later be rebuilt), the Sherman House and the Tremont House were all consumed by flames. The courthouse, the chamber of commerce, the armory, the opera house, Marshall Field's store, the YMCA, four railroad depots and all of the dockage, every theater, every bank, every newspaper and every hotel in Chicago were among the 3,650 buildings in the south district that would be destroyed during the 30 hours the fire storm blew back and forth across Chicago.

By 3:00 A.M., stone decomposed or exploded, girders melted, streetcar tracks were twisted and the iron wheels of streetcars were transformed into shapeless globs as the firestorm heated to—as one clerk in a paint store attested—3,000 degrees Fahrenheit. The night turned saffron. It was said that a man 20 miles away read a newspaper by the light of the flames.

People living in second-story apartments threw boxes and trunks out of windows in an effort to save their possessions. Many people were struck by these objects, and some were killed. Unscrupulous draymen, capitalizing on hysteria and misery, charged $100 to haul property to safety, drove a few blocks and demanded more. If the property owner could not pay, the goods and the owner were dumped into the street.

Joe Medill, editor of the *Chicago Tribune,* desperately tried to get out an issue of his paper, even as the flames roared around the new, supposedly fireproof *Tribune* building. Although the heat inside was almost unbearable, a few reporters tried to write their stories. But the stories would never be printed. The heat melted the press rollers, and shortly after that, the building burst into flames, sending the reporters out into the streets to join the thousands of hysterical refugees roaming, running, brawling and looting.

And now the ultimate irony occurred. An enormous firebrand, a huge 12-foot-long plank, lifted by the gale-like wind, soared through the air and landed on the roof of the new waterworks building. Smashing through the slates of this fireproof stone building located in the middle of a huge park, it set fire to the wooden support timbers and the walls and completely immobilized the pumping machinery. There was no longer any water for the fire engines, no way to keep the fire from spreading.

At seven in the morning on Monday, October 9, the Galena Elevator and McCormick's Harvester Works caught fire, the flames wrapping around the brick buildings and crushing them. The walls of the great structures folded in and sent out immense gusts of heat and tons of sparks and embers, which hastened the destruction of everything north of the river.

All of the bridges over the south branch of the Chicago River were burned away. Fire engines drew water from the river now and made ineffectual forays into the inferno. By doing this, they managed to keep the fire from doubling back to the south.

One by one, the North Side mansions of the wealthy began to go up in flames. Their owners and their servants managed to save some valuables. Davis Fales, a lawyer, dug a huge hole in his backyard and buried his favorite piano in it. One man was seen burying his family up to their necks in the mud by the river. He then scooped up water and kept them wet, saving them until tugs began to rescue people from the scalding beach.

Samuel Stone, the assistant librarian of the Chicago Historical Society, located at the corner of Dearborn and Ontario streets, did what he could to move valuable documents to the society's basement. One of the most precious of these was the original copy of Abraham Lincoln's Emancipation Proclamation. Stone attempted to smash the glass that protected it but could not. "At this moment," he later told reporters, "again the wind and fire filled the whole heavens, dashing firebrands against the reception room windows." The ceiling began to give way, and Stone escaped, but the Emancipation Proclamation was burned to a cinder.

Finally, on Monday afternoon, the fire began to show signs of burning itself out. Flames only continued to spread in the northern sector. On Monday night, the rain that always follows a fire storm began to fall. It was a soaking rain, and it snuffed out all that remained of the fire.

On Tuesday morning, one could stand in the ashes of Katie O'Leary's barn and look out across 2,200 acres of ash-strewn wasteland. From DeKoven Street to the lake and northward to the prairies, nearly four miles away, there was hardly a board or a brick left standing. Fifteen thousand dwellings, 80 office buildings, 170 factories, 39 churches, 28 hotels, 39 banks, six railroad terminals, nine theaters, 21 public buildings, 1,600 shops and stores, grain elevators, coalyards and lumberyards, breweries and distilleries, warehouses, bridges, wharves and shipping were all gone. Ninety-thousand people were homeless. The property damage was fixed at $196 million, or one-third of the city's wealth.

Fifty-four American fire insurance companies were ruined by the conflagration, some paying as little as three cents on the dollar. The city of Chicago carried no fire insurance, and the $470,000 courthouse, the police and fire stations, schools, bridges and other public property that had been destroyed were a total loss. Interestingly, the biggest item of damage suffered by the city was 122 miles of wooden sidewalks, valued at more than $941,000.

The exact number of dead will never be known. Most authorities, including the Chicago Historical Society, place it at 250. Others say 300. It was amazingly small, considering the extent of the fire.

The famous Civil War general Philip Sheridan, in command of an army post near Chicago, joined forces with Allan Pinkerton's detective agency to enforce the martial law that Mayor Mason imposed on the city.

Relief began to flow into the city overnight. Food, clothing and money poured in from all over the country. Jim Fisk drove around New York in his coach and four, picking up relief bundles. Commodore Vanderbilt ran special trains into Chicago to speed the relief effort. The most generous contribution—$550,000—came from the people of Boston, a city whose main section would be gutted by fire a year later.

The city began to rebuild immediately, although 50,000 of its inhabitants would leave during the first month of its laborious recovery. Still, it recovered, fueled by the sort of spirit represented by real estate agent William D. Kerfoot, who hammered together a wooden shanty from scraps of wood that had not been burned too badly and then opened for business with a sign that read: ALL GONE EXCEPT WIFE, CHILDREN AND ENERGY.

Firemen at work controlling the worst theater fire in U.S. history, Chicago's Iroquois Theatre fire on December 30, 1903. New York Public Library

UNITED STATES
ILLINOIS
CHICAGO

December 30, 1903

• • • • • • • • • • • • • • • • •

The worst theater fire in U.S. history, that of the Iroquois Theatre in Chicago on December 30, 1903, was caused by a combination of negligence in design, blocked fire exits, a snagged fire curtain, an absent stage manager and a calcium light igniting scenery. Five hundred ninety-one died and scores were injured in the resulting inferno.

"Does freedom of speech extend to yelling 'Fire!' in a crowded theater?" Oliver Wendell Holmes asked, and the consequences of this, the instances of ensuing, fatal panic, replay themselves over and over in the worst theater fires in the world. As in Vienna (see p. 156), Brooklyn (see p. 196) and Montreal (see p. 159), this was true in Chicago's Iroquois Theatre, a mere 24 years after the Great Fire (see previous entry). It would be the scene of the worst theater fire in U.S. history.

The Iroquois Theatre was frankly, fabulous. Designed by 29-year-old architect and wunderkind Benjamin H. Marshall in French Renaissance style, it was glamorous, dazzling, plush and fireproof. At least this is what Marshall and co-owners and theatrical entrepreneurs Will J. Davis and Harry J. Powers both believed and advertised. George Williams, building commissioner of the city of Chicago, also deemed it safe after inspecting the theater just 39 days before its cataclysmic final performance.

That it was grand nobody would dispute. It consisted of an ornate foyer with two magnificent staircases, a plushly draped auditorium, an elaborately designed proscenium arch, a mammoth stage, dressing rooms galore and the latest in electrical equipment. It would seat 1,724, but there was standing room for 300 more. It had more exits than any theater in the country—30 in all, 27 of them double-door fire exits—and each floor—orchestra, balcony and gallery—was equipped with emergency exits feeding into the foyer.

But fireproof? William Clendenin, the editor of a magazine called *Fireproof,* toured the premises of the theater before it was finished, and his assessment was far less sanguine that that of its builders and owners. There was no sprinkler system over the stage, he pointed out. There was no ventilating flue above the stage to carry flames up and away from the audience. The skylight above the stage was nailed shut. There was heavy use of wood trim throughout the theater. There was no direct fire alarm connection with the fire department. And on the night of December 30, 1903, all but three of the 30 exits would be locked, some with iron gratings securing them.

Clendenin was dismissed by both the theater owners and the office of the Chicago building inspector. He wrote a scathing editorial about this in *Fireproof,* but it was an exercise in futility; hardly anyone read his magazine.

On November 22, Ed Laughlin, an inspector from the building commissioner's office, inspected the building "from dressing rooms to capstone" and pronounced it "fireproof beyond all doubt."

Two weeks later, Joseph Daugherty, a stagehand, sounded a preliminary alarm, which was also ignored. He informed owner Will J. Davis that there had been a small trash fire backstage, which he had put out. However, when he had tried, as a safety measure, to lower the asbestos curtain, it had snagged on a reflector some 20 feet above the stage floor. Daugherty suggested that, although the actors wanted the reflector there, it should be moved. Davis agreed to take it under advisement but then did nothing about it.

The December 30 matinee performance of a Klaw and Erlanger extravaganza titled *Mr. Bluebeard,* starring comedian Eddie Foy, was more than sold out. There were 2,000 people in the audience that day, 1,724 sitting and the rest standing. The first act passed without incident. Everything was going so well, in fact, that stage manager Bill Carlton left his post backstage and strolled out to the foyer to watch the second act from the front. Several stagehands slipped out for a drink in a nearby saloon.

More importantly, Edward Cummings, a stage carpenter in charge of the electrical mechanism controlling the asbestos curtain, also slipped out to go to the local hardware store.

The second act began with a double octet of eight men and eight women singing a song titled "In the Pale Moonlight." Above them, in one of the wings, spotlight operator William McMullin noticed that his calcium light was dangerously close to a flimsy tormentor. And as he watched, the tormentor caught fire. He tried to snuff out the tiny flame with his hand, but it was just beyond his reach.

The flame twisted upward, and theater fireman Bill Sallers, summoned by McMullin, grabbed an extinguisher and aimed it at the small blaze. The stream fell short.

By now, more and more pieces of scenery were on fire. The stage was filled with 40,000 cubic feet of scenery, wooden sticks, frames, paint and canvas, and 180 drop scenes hung with 75,000 feet of new, oily and highly inflammable manila rope.

The fly space above the stage was a mass of flame, and sparks began to rain down on the double octet. The dance routine wavered and then began to break down. One of the women fainted, and the rest of the dancers panicked and sprinted for the wings. The crowd, not quite sure of the danger, became slightly restive.

Eddie Foy, who smelled the smoke in his dressing room, walked briskly onstage and down to the footlights. "Stay seated," he said to the audience. "It is nothing. It will be out in a minute."

And then, he turned to the conductor in the pit and hissed, "For God's sake, play, play and keep playing!" Like the band on the *Titanic,* the pit orchestra began to play, but by now, several audience members had cried out "Fire!" and the audience had begun to stampede. Foy tried to calm them, pleading with them to walk slowly to the exits. Then, realizing that this was useless, he shouted to the stagehands to lower the asbestos curtain.

The man in charge was gone; fireman Sallers fumbled with the mechanism and finally got it working. But as it had two weeks ago, the right side of the curtain caught on the reflector, 20 feet above the stage floor. The left side descended to 12 feet above the floor and stopped. And the flames licked out from beneath the curtain, into the auditorium.

Foy left the stage just before the entire catwalk and loft rigging thundered to its floor, spouting sparks like a fireworks display. Some of the mechanism landed on the central lightboard, and every light in the theater went out, terrifying the fleeing audience.

Even at this point, the fire was not enormous, and the horror that followed would not have occurred if the dancing girls from the double octet had not run for the stage door. Two stagehands obligingly opened it for them, and the huge draft that swept in through the open door exploded the onstage fire into an enormous fireball. It roared and rolled through the entire theater, spanning the 50-foot space to the balcony in one huge leap and then splitting in two. The lower part swirled under the balcony and out into the foyer; the other half roared upward, to engulf the people in both the balcony and the gallery. Everything in its path burned.

Bedlam ensued. People clawed at one another. Some were stripped naked. Some fell or were pushed over the balcony rail, setting fire to or crushing many of those below. Vicious fights broke out. Men, women and children were trampled.

The 16-year-old ushers on the first floor went berserk, actually holding the doors against the crowd. Abandoning this, they fled for their lives without opening the emergency exits. Some calmer audience members managed to find some of these doors and opened them, only to find that there was a four-foot-high ledge between the door sill and the sidewalk. People dashing out fell, breaking legs and arms and becoming rugs for other terrified escapees.

Almost all of the 800 patrons on the orchestra floor escaped. But in the balcony, more than half of the 1,100 spectators died. There were no exit signs; bewildered and panicked, these hapless humans dashed about trying to find a door. Some did, only to discover that the fire escapes had no ladders to take them to the ground.

The crowd surged like a tidal wave for the 60-foot-high gilt and marble foyer. But all of the exits, from the balcony, the gallery and the orchestra, met here, and the crush became horrendous. People flung themselves over and on one another, falling over balustrades, landing on top of the swirling mass of humanity trapped at the middle of the foyer. And then the flames reached this pile of humanity and fused it into a hill of burning corpses.

Behind this, in the balcony, firemen later found bodies piled six deep in the aisles. Many of the people were nude; others were horribly mangled and mutilated. A few people were still alive, buried under the charred bodies.

It had all taken 15 minutes. That was all, and 591 people were dead. The stage, boxes, main floor, balcony, gallery, all of the wood trim and draperies and even the asbestos curtain—which was discovered to have been made of nothing but paper—were destroyed.

Twelve people were indicted, including the theater owners, building commissioner Williams, and Mayor Harrison. The coroner's inquest was a national sensation for three weeks.

The case went to a grand jury, which exonerated Mayor Harrison and several others but upheld the manslaughter charges against Davis and two minor theater officials and charged Williams with misfeasance.

Not one of them served a jail sentence. All got off on technicalities. None of the relatives of the dead collected on any of the hundreds of damage suits. The only person to serve a jail sentence was the owner of a nearby saloon. His property had been used as a temporary morgue, and he was convicted of robbing the dead.

UNITED STATES
ILLINOIS
CHICAGO

December 1, 1958

• • • • • • • • • • • • • • • •

A lack of fire drill regulations led to tragedy in the fire, begun in a pile of trash in the basement, in Our Lady of the Angel's grade school in Chicago on December 1, 1958. Ninety-three perished in the blaze.

Chicago's Our Lady of the Angels grade school, run by the Sisters of Charity, was an old building, lacking in many amenities and necessities. It did not have a sprinkler system, and it is generally acknowledged that the presence of one might very well have averted the tragedy that occurred on December 1, 1958. However, it was the general breakdown of certain elementary fire drill regulations that probably caused most of the deaths that day.

Ordinarily, school concluded at 3:00 P.M. Just 30 minutes before this, on December 1, 1958, a fire started in a heap of trash in the basement. Two teachers who had classes on the first floor noticed the smell of smoke first. They led their classes out of the building to safety but, inexplicably, did not inform other classes or make any effort to ring the fire alarm.

At 2:42, a janitor found the fire, and he did shout for the parish housekeeper to turn in the alarm. Even then, teachers and students on the second floor were not informed of the steadily increasing blaze. And it was on the second floor that all of the fatalities would occur. By the time the firemen arrived, five minutes later, all of the first-floor classrooms had been safely evacuated.

On the second floor, many students panicked, running through the smoke filled halls, coming up against walls of furiously burning flames in the stairwells, retreating to the classrooms, climbing on windowsills and leaping to their deaths on the sidewalk below.

Horrified firemen and passersby tried to calm the hysterical children and attempted to talk them back into the rooms so that firemen on ladders could safely take them from the windows. But their pleas were drowned out by the screams of the children plummeting to the ground around the fire ladders. Some firemen caught falling youngsters by their legs, their arms, their hair. As quickly as they could, they raced up and down ladders carrying hysterical children, some of them on the brink of asphyxiation.

There were some clear heads in the midst of this madness. One nun instructed her students to crawl under the smoke in the hallway and then roll down the stairs. All did; all survived. Another teacher barricaded the door of her second-floor classroom against the smoke and instructed her charges to pray. They did; firemen appeared at the windows of the classroom and rescued the class.

Priests, passersby and firemen rushed into the rapidly disintegrating building and carried out other children. Of the 1,515 students, 1,425 survived. Ninety students and three nuns died in the fire.

UNITED STATES
MASSACHUSETTS
BOSTON

November 28, 1942

• • • • • • • • • • • • • • • •

A smoldering match carelessly tossed onto an artificial palm caused the tragic fire in Boston's Cocoanut Grove Night Club

The interior of the Cocoanut Grove Night Club after the horrendous fire of November 28, 1942, which claimed 491 lives. American Red Cross

on November 28, 1942. Four hundred ninety-one died, and hundreds were injured

The fad of nightclubs was at its zenith during the years of World War II. Elaborate, multileveled, gaudily decorated and dimly lit, these places of entertainment offered several rooms for several moods. There were small, intimate bars with piano players and an occasional singer, slightly larger cabarets with jazz combos and huge dining rooms with dance floors, big bands, and opulent shows with singers, dancers, acrobats and production numbers.

Boston's Cocoanut Grove Night Club, owned by Barnet Wilansky and located in a one-story building between Piedmont Street and Shawmut Avenue in Boston's mid-town theater district, was typical of this genre. The main entrance through a revolving door opened into a foyer, which connected with the main dining room, complete with a rolling stage. There was a double-door exit from the dining room to Shawmut Avenue and a hallway exit that led to a service door. A new cocktail lounge affixed to the dining room opened in early November 1942 to accommodate the increased crowds of servicemen and war workers.

The Piedmont Street side of the building contained two bars. One, which was part of the main dining area, was called the Caricature Bar; the other several steps down from street level, was dubbed the Melody Lounge. It was the most darkly lit, intimate part of the club, where dates could sit in booths in semidarkness while a pianist played. It was reached by a narrow stairway from the main level.

Throughout, the club was decorated with a forest of artificial palm trees.

On Saturday night, November 28, 1942, the biggest crowd in its history—more than 800 patrons—jammed the Cocoanut Grove. In addition to the soldiers, sailors, marines, coastguardsmen and warplant workers, there was a large contingent of football fans celebrating Holy Cross's unexpected and thorough thrashing of Sugar Bowl–destined Boston College. In the main dining room, movie cowboy Buck Jones entertained a large table of motion picture executives and flunkies.

At 10 P.M., the floor show, headlined by singer Billy Payne, the dance team of Pierce and Roland, acrobatic dancer Miriam Johnson, violinist Helen Fay and a chorus of dancers backed by Mickey Alpert's band, was about to begin.

In the Melody Lounge, which was, like every room in the club, vastly overcrowded, more than 130 people talked, drank or listened to a ragtime piano player. In a corner booth, a soldier unscrewed a light bulb hanging above him.

John Bradley, one of the five bartenders on duty, told Stanley Tomaszewski, a 16-year-old bar boy, to screw the bulb back in. Tomaszewski grabbed a bar stool, informed the unhappy soldier of his mission, climbed up on the stool and attempted to find the light bulb. Failing on his first try, he lit a match, located the bulb and tightened it. The smoldering match, discarded carelessly, landed on an artificial palm. Within seconds, the tree incandesced in a rush of flame. By the time the terrified boy had descended from the bar stool, the fire had leaped from tree to tree, and the ceiling of the Melody Lounge was ablaze. The bartenders rushed over, tearing down drapes and trees, trying to smother the flames, but it was hopeless. The conflagration had begun.

The lounge's occupants panicked and bolted for the narrow flight of stairs leading to the street-level foyer. It was a hopeless horror. Flaming pieces of palm trees rained down on the kicking, clawing mass of people who piled up in the stairwell, turning it into a grim funeral pyre.

In the main dining room, just as the show was about to begin, a young woman, her hair on fire, suddenly dashed across the dance floor, screaming. Panic spread here, too, and customers, overturning tables and battering at one another, ran for the only exit they knew—the revolving door to the street. But before they got there, they ran into the few, fire-seared refugees from the Melody Lounge who had managed to crawl over the mass of bodies on the stairs.

A huge battering ram of humanity slammed against the revolving door, instantly jamming it. Next to the door was an auxiliary exit equipped with a panic lock, designed to open easily if pressure was applied from within. But the door had been bolted, and the first wave of refugees were slammed so tightly against it that they could not locate the bolt.

At the same time, customers in the new cocktail lounge clawed their way to the customer exit on Broadway. But the door opened *inward,* and before the first terrified customers there could pull it toward them, the crush of those behind smashed them up against the now immovable door. More than 100 bodies were later found, piled in a terrible heap against the door.

The lights went out, making the scene more terrifying. Toxic fumes, fed by burning paint and blazing decorative material, killed many before they had a chance to leave their tables in the dining room. Buck Jones was thought to have died this way.

Fifty patrons made their way to the basement. Many of them, unable to find an exit, were asphyxiated. Others did manage to find windows and, breaking them, made their escape. One veteran waiter, Henry W. Bimler, had gone to the basement kitchen immediately. But he found the employee exit locked. He asked the dishwasher for the key, and the dishwasher stentorially refused, saying that only the boss could give him permission to surrender it. Bimler went back upstairs, where he encountered several young women who had become separated from their escorts and now tearfully asked him for help. He guided them back to the kitchen and the nightclub's walk-in refrigerator. He led them into it and walked in himself; firemen later rescued the group—slightly chilled but safe—from the ruins of the club.

Providentially, the Boston Fire Department had been summoned to a minor automobile fire just around the corner from the Cocoanut Grove, and when the alarm went out and someone dashed down the sidewalk yelling that the club was on fire, they only had half a block to travel.

They smashed windows and pried some survivors loose from the piles of humanity at the exits. And several of the entertainers managed to rescue not only their fellow players but a score of patrons as well.

The fire lasted only a few minutes. It spread with awesome speed, consuming the entire premises and then exploding through the roof. The firemen could do little more than hose down the fire and carry out the dead.

Hundreds of morbid onlookers rushed to the scene, hampering rescue efforts. Several naval offices and their men locked arms and formed a human chain to hold back the crowds. Servicemen helped firemen stretch their hoses. When it became apparent that there were not enough ambulances available to carry the injured to hospitals, nearly 100 taxicabs were commandeered. Trucks carried off the dead.

The Boston chapter of the Red Cross sent 500 workers to the scene; the New York Red Cross sent disaster relief workers; civil defense units tended to the injured and dying. Sulfa supplies dipped at hospitals; a special plane reached Boston with an adequate supply an hour later from New York.

By 2 A.M., martial law had been declared, enforced by both civilian and military police. The final toll was sickening: 491 died and hundreds more injured.

In the aftermath of the tragedy, fire safety rules that had fallen into place after the tragic Iroquois Theatre blaze in Chicago in 1903 (see p. 186) were extended to nightclubs, which, until the Cocoanut Grove fire, had been without fire regulations. Capacity limits, sprinkler systems and plainly marked exits became the rule as a result of the terrible and avoidable holocaust of November 28, 1942.

UNITED STATES
MINNESOTA

October 12, 1918

• • • • • • • • • • • • • • • • • •

Ordinary spring and summer smolderings were fanned into Minnesota's worst forest fire by 60-mile-per-hour winds on October 12, 1918. Eight hundred people died.

Minnesota's worst and most extensive forest fire to date began as a six-month-long, expected series of spring and summer brush fires. The peat terrain in northern Minnesota frequently experienced fires in dry seasons, settlers in the area were told, and so the fires glowed silently on with neither incident nor cure.

But at 1:00 P.M. on October 12, 1918, a 60-mile-per-hour wind suddenly sprang up, fanning the glowing ashes into a roaring conflagration, with flames as high as the towering trees they consumed. Fed and nudged by the wind, the fire storm spread wildly, first in a 175-mile stretch of land that ranged from Bemidji to Two Harbors, then from the Mesaba Range in the north to a midway point between Duluth and Minneapolis.

There were scores of settlements, logging towns and summer resorts in the affected area, and the inhabitants scarcely had time to prepare for the onslaught of the fast-advancing forest fire. The tiny village of Brokston, west of Duluth, was the first to be consumed but a special train evacuated every one of its inhabitants. Cloquet, a logging town of 10,000, was similarly evacuated to nearby Carlton, but the fire pursued its inhabitants there, and, adding the population of Carlton to the passengership of the train, they sped 20 miles farther to Superior, where the entire population of the two villages remained in safety.

Resort dwellers fared much less well and much more tragically. Moose Lake was surrounded by a solid wall of fire that closed in on the resort like pincers, and with such force that the fire funneled down a 30-foot well, burning to death a family that had taken refuge there. All 400 people in this town died.

The lake area north of Duluth suffered similar damage. The flames, powered by the relentless gale, licked across large bodies of water, burning to death people who dove into the waters in the hope of escaping the fire. Boatloads of frantic refugees overturned, drowning their occupants. Another 400 perished in the lake region.

The wall of fire advanced on Duluth in two sections, one from the west and one from the north. But just as it was entering the suburbs, the winds shifted, and the city was spared. Nevertheless, 800 people died in this horrendous and wide-reaching forest fire, one of the worst in U.S. history.

UNITED STATES
MINNESOTA
HINCKLEY

September 1, 1894

• • • • • • • • • • • • • • • • • •

Smoldering ashes on a forest floor were fanned into flames by a sudden burst of wind on September 1, 1894 near Hinckley, Minnesota. The resultant forest fire killed 413 people—one-third of the population of the town—and destroyed every building.

A raging forest fire that in many ways equaled the more famous one in nearby Peshtigo, Wisconsin (see p. 203) completely destroyed the town of Hinckley, Minnesota and killed one-third of its population on the afternoon of September 1, 1894. A smoldering beginning (see previous entry) lulled the populace of the small town, located 75 miles from St. Paul, into acceptance of these small fires as the consequence of a summer without rain.

In August of that year, in fact, much of the northwestern United States was beset by forest fires, which gutted 25 other towns in Minnesota, Michigan and Wisconsin. Small settlements in the wilderness, built mainly of wood and existing along railroad lines, these towns fell, one by one, as shifting winds fanned glowing ashes into fulminating fires.

On September 1, 1894, a sudden gust of wind did just this on the outskirts of Hinckley, and a three-story-high wall of flame began to advance on the town. Terrified residents ran for the few bodies of water in the town. But the long drought of the summer had nearly emptied most of the ponds and had lowered the level of the Grindstone River to a knee-high level. The hundreds who threw

Terrified escapees from the devastating forest fire that destroyed one-third of the town of Hinckley, Minnesota on September 1, 1894 run from a burning evacuation train and fling themselves into a swamp. Some were burned to death by the hot mud, but most survived. Frank Leslie's Illustrated Newspaper

themselves into it could not submerge deeply enough to escape the long fingers of flames that rushed across the water and so they burned alive.

Another hazard in this rural community turned out to be stampeding animals, who ran over fleeing townspeople, crushing them to death.

Two trains took hundreds of people from the town, and one of these escapes was miraculously and touchingly dramatic. The Limited, on the St. Paul and Duluth Line, paused at the Hinckley station to receive refugees who had not been able to leave on an earlier Eastern Minnesota Line train. By the time the Limited drew into town, the fire had cut off escape on all sides, and 105 people died trying to reach the train.

Hundreds of others clambered aboard, and the engineer threw the train into forward, heading directly into the wall of fire. Flames poured into his cab, burning him horribly, but he stayed at the controls and physically restrained his fireman from jumping. Meanwhile, passengers lay down on the floor of the wooden coaches, which were now afire.

The engineer got the train to the side of a lake, waved the hundreds of men, women and children who were aboard the train toward the lake and then fell dead of the burns he had just received. The passengers staggered to the lake and flung themselves in. Many had already been cruelly burned, and the mud they spread on their bodies instantly baked on to their skin. Their clothes were in blackened tatters, but most of them survived, thanks to the engineer.

Four hundred thirteen of their fellow townspeople, one-third of the population of Hinckley, did not, however, and there was not a building left standing in the town when the fire that had consumed it roared on.

UNITED STATES
MISSISSIPPI
NATCHEZ

April 23, 1940

• • • • • • • • • • • • • • • •

The ignoring of fire regulations by both owners and officials and a carelessly thrown match were the causes of the fire that devastated the Rhythm Night Club in Natchez, Mississippi on April 23, 1940. One hundred ninety-eight died; 40 were injured.

In the segregated world of Natchez, Mississippi in 1940, there were some small joys for blacks. One of them was the decrepit old St. Catherine Street church, transmogrified into a nightclub that featured nationally famous black jazz musicians. The best, passing through, played here, and every corner of the Rhythm Night Club, as it was called, was packed for these occasions.

The white city government of Natchez neither cared about nor enforced any sort of fire regulations in the club. First, fire surveillance was extremely loose regarding nightclubs in the United States before the Cocoanut Grove fire in 1942 (see p. 188), and second, the club was operating illegally, anyway, and local law enforcement authorities let these kinds of operations function pretty much on their own.

On the night of April 23, 1940, the Rhythm Night Club was full and a little more. More than 250 patrons funneled through its one combination entrance and exit that night and danced, drank and listened to the music under the strung Spanish moss that made the church into a sort of swinging grotto. Its windows had long since been boarded up and decorated on the inside.

Somewhere, sometime during the evening, a carelessly thrown match ignited the Spanish moss. The spread of the fire was immediate and terrible. Stifling smoke and raging flames whipped around the space as if it were the interior of an infernal tornado. Crazed patrons, trying to escape, pounded on the boarded up windows with no success. A battle raged for the front door, and 40 people, most of them men, managed to fight their way through it. All were badly burned, but they at least survived.

The others—198 of them—were forced toward the opposite side of the building by the whirling conflagration. There they died, in enormous piles of fused bodies. The club burned to the ground. Not one person there escaped injury.

UNITED STATES
NEW JERSEY
COAST

September 8, 1934

• • • • • • • • • • • • • • •

See MARITIME DISASTERS, *Morro Castle* (p. 217).

UNITED STATES
NEW JERSEY
HOBOKEN

June 30, 1900

• • • • • • • • • • • • • • •

A smoldering fire of unknown origin in cotton bales piled on the docks in Hoboken, New Jersey on June 30, 1900 suddenly burst into flames, igniting the entire docks and four German Lloyd ships loaded with Sunday sightseers. Three hundred twenty-six died in the blaze; 250 were injured.

The Hoboken piers were busy places in 1900, and their busiest sector housed the ships of the German Lloyd Line. On Saturday, June 30, 1900, four of German Lloyd's most impressive and modern passenger liners were docked at the pier: the magnificent 20,000-ton *Kaiser Wilhelm der Grosse,* the 5,267-ton *Saale,* the 10,000-ton *Bremen* and the 6,398-ton *Main.* The ships were large and famous. The *Main,* commissioned a mere month before, was the modern pride of the German commercial fleet; the leviathan-like *Kaiser Wilhelm,* 648 feet long, held the eastward Atlantic record from New York to Southampton of five days, 17 hours and eight minutes.

A large percentage of the crews of these ships were ashore on leave; a skeleton crew, carpenters and longshoremen were loading and preparing them for departure within the next few days. Roiling the waters around the four vessels were 18 canal boats laden with oil, coal, cotton and gasoline.

It was the practice in 1900 to allow sightseers on board ships in port, and hundreds of them were aboard all four ships that sunny afternoon. Hundreds more lined the Manhattan shoreline, across the North River from Hoboken.

Pier number three was a particularly crowded place. The *Saale* and the *Bremen* were docked there, and stacks of cotton bales sentineled the docks. Next to the cotton were 100 barrels of whiskey, also ready to be loaded aboard.

On Sunday, June 30, 1900, a horrible fire engulfed the Hoboken docks and four German Lloyd ships. Three hundred twenty-six sightseers, passengers, firemen and crew members died in the tragic conflagration. Frank Leslie's Illustrated Newspaper

At approximately 3:55 that afternoon, a smoldering fire of unknown origin in one of the bales of cotton suddenly burst into flames. Within an instant, the fire had spread to the whiskey barrels, which went up with a roar, sending orange and red flames licking skyward toward the storage sheds on the dock. The wood of the pier ignited next, and the flames shot like racing animals toward 200 longshoremen. The longshoremen did not stand on ceremony or curiosity. They ran, with the flames pursuing them. Forty of them were not fast enough and perished in the fire that overtook them.

At the same time, the conflagration was now shooting up the wooden gangplanks to each of the four ships tied up at the German Lloyd docks. Hundred-foot-high flames leaped from pier to pier, igniting warehouses and the wooden decks of the four steamers.

The sightseers were trapped aboard, as flames descended into the living quarters and innards of each ship. The *Kaiser Wilhelm* was farthest from the source of the fire, and a dozen tugs raced to her and pulled her away from the dock and into midstream. With her captain standing at the bridge with two pistols at the ready, the entire crew set to putting out the fire on her. They succeeded, beating back the fires systematically. No one was killed, though many sailors suffered extreme burns.

Chaos consumed the other three liners. They burned out of control, as tugs pulled the *Bremen* and the *Saale* away from the pier and into the waters of the North River. Simultaneously, these tugs took crew members and sightseers off the ships. One hundred four men were rescued from the *Bremen* by the tug *Nettie Tice;* 40 were removed from the *Saale* by the *Westchester.*

But that was a small effort. Most of the personnel and visitors on the ships were below decks when the fire began. With the blaze beginning on the wooden decks, their way to escape was completely cut off. Portholes on all ships were only 11 inches in diameter—far too small to allow an adult to escape.

Sailors on the tugs looked on in horror and helplessness as faces appeared at the portholes with flames reaching up behind them. The *Main,* its steel hull turning red hot and then white hot, was irremovable. Snugged against the flaming pier, it took the full brunt of the fire. A stewardess appeared at one of its portholes, frantically pleading for help. Rescuers tried to pour water through an adjacent porthole to put out the flames around her but could not.

Finally, according to *Munsey's Magazine,* the woman, realizing that it was hopeless, said, "Now listen! Listen! Tell my mother—she lives in Bremen—tell her my last thought was of her—tell her all my money is in the bank—tell her she can have it all—tell her—." And the flames closed around the stewardess.

It would be three hours before all of the frantic people—crew members, visitors and sailors—would die, while rescuers looked on in frustration and fury. Only 15 men, holed up in the bowels of the *Maine* and able to signal via an oil lamp of their whereabouts to the tug crews, were saved on that ship. Rescuers, spotting the lamp at 11:00 P.M, pulled up alongside the ship and began to cut through the red-hot metal. They reached the 15 men, delirious, stripped naked and nearly suffocated. But all survived without aftereffects, except for one elderly sailor who went blind in the hellish heat.

It would be the next day before the bodies could be removed from the ships. A conservative estimate put the number of dead at 326; the injured at 250. But most who were there agreed that there were far more dead than the official estimates admitted.

UNITED STATES
NEW YORK
BRONX

March 25, 1990

• • • • • • • • • • • • • • • • • •

In the worst mass murder in U.S. history, and the worst fire in New York City since the Triangle Shirtwaist tragedy of 1911, Julio Gonzalez set fire to the Happy Land Social Club in the East Tremont section of the Bronx, New York on March 25, 1990. Eighty-seven people perished in the blaze.

Exactly 79 years to the day after the Triangle Shirtwaist fire, which killed 149 young girls in New York City (see p. 198), the Happy Land Club, an illegal social club crowded with Honduran immigrants, was the scene of an infernal catastrophe that took the lives of 87 people at 3:30 A.M. on Sunday, March 25, 1990.

In March 1990, there were 177 illegal social clubs dotted throughout the five boroughs of New York City. Usually open only on weekends, and catering to groups of people united by ethnicity, nationality, geography or shared interests, they sold liquor illegally, allowed dancing without benefit of cabaret licenses and generally provided congenial, if illegitimate, neighborhood nights out.

The Happy Land Social Club was one of these illegal oases. Located on the west side of Southern Boulevard in the East Tremont section of the Bronx, in the heart of a Honduran community, it sported a stone face, painted red and adorned by a large sign that read:

HAPPY LAND SOCIAL CLUB INC.
LITTLE LEAGUE—PONY
FOR HIRE HALL
ALL SOCIAL EVENTS

A smiling face beamed down from the space between "Happy" and "Land."

The club was 22 feet wide by 58 feet deep and was on two stories. On the left side was the entrance door, which led to a coat-check and admission area, where patrons paid a $5 cover charge. There was a bar at the rear of the downstairs room, and one in the same position upstairs, whose windowless upstairs room most people favored, since it contained a disc jockey and a dance floor. Celebrants paid $3 a drink to talk, sing and dance in the small, low-ceilinged room. A narrow, steep front staircase and a back set of stairs connected the two parts of the club.

"It was like a headquarters for Hondurans," said Steven McGregor, who lived near the club and was interviewed by the *New York Times* after the fire. "They threw parties every weekend."

The club had been pronounced a firetrap by the city fire department, and its landlord had issued an eviction notice 10 months before for nonpayment of rent. On November 21, 1988, the city had ordered the building vacated because it lacked a second exit, a fire alarm and a sprinkler system. In the meantime there had been two arrests made for selling liquor without a license. On November 1, 1989, the police visited the club but found it padlocked. It always was during the week, neighbors said, and it was on a weekday that the police made their visit.

But March 24, 1990 was a Saturday, and the place was packed with noisy, friendly partygoers, except for one disgruntled customer. Early in the morning of Sunday the 25th, 36-year-old Julio Gonzalez came to the club, had two beers and had an argument with his former girlfriend, Lydia Feliciano, who worked there as a coat-check attendant.

Gonzalez was well known at the club and in the neighborhood. In 1980, he had deserted the Cuban Army and had fabricated a record of drug trafficking in Cuba in order to win expulsion to the United States in the 1980 Mariel boatlift. In the intervening 10 years between his arrival in New York City and the fateful night of March 25, 1990, he had worked at and been fired from various jobs. His latest job as a warehouse worker at a lamp company in Long Island City had terminated just six weeks earlier.

Most of the time, he lived as a street person who hustled money washing cars or peddling. He and Ms. Feliciano had lived together for eight years and had recently broken up, and for the past few days he had tried to convince her to come back to him. That night, in his entreaties and demands, he became loud, boisterous and profane. A bouncer, noting the escalating argument, kicked him out.

Gonzalez became furious and shouted a vow that he would shut down the club. He picked up a plastic jug that was sitting near its entrance, walked to a nearby Amoco station and bought $1 worth of gasoline. Returning to the Happy Land, he entered its one street door and encountered a lone man, who was exiting. He pretended to make a phone call on the pay phone in the hallway, until the other man was out of sight, and then poured a trail of gasoline from the street, through the entrance and into the inside hall. He drew out a match, tossed it into the gasoline and watched it ignite. Satisfied that it was burning, he turned and walked home.

Upstairs, the disc jockey, Ruben Valladares, began his favorite Jamaican reggae song, "Young Lover," by Coco Tea.

"The floor got so full that a lot of people couldn't dance," Felipe Figuero, one of the only three people on the second story of the club who would survive, later told a *Times* reporter. "Then you heard it coming up the stairs."

What he heard were shouts, from one of the club's two doormen. (The other was on the dance floor with his girlfriend.) He was yelling "Fire! Fire!" and shoving his way through the mass of humanity.

"Right away, people went crazy," said Figuero. "Some ran this way and that way. Some people didn't make a big deal out of it. I could see a little smoke coming upstairs."

The doorman shoved through the crowd, looking for his girlfriend, and Figuero took up the cry, in Spanish. "Fuego!" he yelled, while his friend, disc jockey Ruben Valladares, turned up the lights and shouted "Fuego!" into a microphone.

"People were already desperate," continued Figuero. "Everybody was running around."

Figuero headed for the stairs. "Everyone saw me go for it," he said. "I yelled 'Down, let's go!' There were a lot of people around those stairs, but nobody followed me. I could hear all the cries, lots of people saying 'Mama!' I heard something explode, like a light."

It was the fire, roaring up and onto the second story. Figuero plunged down the stairs, into the smoke, threw himself against the crash bar of the back entrance to the club and found himself on the sidewalk with Ms. Feliciano and several patrons from the downstairs room.

A minute later, Ruben Valladares exploded through the door, his clothes in bright flames. "He let out some screams that I remember too much," Figuero said. "I didn't even know who he was—he was so burned." Valladares would survive, with burns over 50% of his body.

The fire had been set at 3:30 A.M. The alarm was turned in at 3:41 A.M. According to Albert Scardino, New York City Mayor David Dinkins' press secretary, fire equipment was there within three minutes. But it was already too late for 87 people.

Nineteen died from burns or smoke inhalation on the stairs or in the ground-floor room. But the greater number perished in a mountain of humanity that resembled the mass murders in the gas chambers of Auschwitz. The upstairs room, so low-ceilinged that the 5-foot, 6-inch tall Felipe Figuero could stand flat-footed and touch the mirrored, revolving globe suspended above its dance floor, contained precious little air under ordinary circumstances. When the flames reached it, they abruptly sucked all of the oxygen out of the room, and all of the second-floor victims died in seconds of suffocation and smoke inhalation.

"It was shocking," First Deputy Mayor Norman Steisel told reporters afterward. "None of the bodies I saw showed signs of burns. They looked waxen." "Some looked like they were crying," one of the fire fighters from Ladder Company 58 told reporters. "Some were horrified. Some looked like they were in shock. There were some people holding hands. There were some people who looked like they were trying to commiserate and hug each other. Some people had torn their clothing in their panic to get out."

Later, emergency crews would break a hole through the wall of the upstairs room and into a construction office next door. They would drag the bodies through it and then take them to nearby Public School 67, which was turned into a temporary morgue. All day Sunday, its corridors were choked with grieving relatives and friends, who identified their loved ones through Polaroid pictures supplied by police officials.

Detectives, acting on information supplied by eyewitnesses, arrested Julio Gonzalez at his home that day. He offered no resistance and was brought before Bronx Criminal Court Judge Alexander W. Hunter Jr. at 2 A.M. on March 26. There, Bronx District Attorney Robert T. Johnson charged Gonzalez with 87 counts of arson felony-murder and 87 counts of murder by depraved indifference to human life.

He went to trial in July 1991, pleading not guilty by reason of insanity. Justice Burton B. Roberts of the state supreme court denied a motion by the defense to suppress Gonzalez's admissions to detectives that he had set the fire, as well as physical evidence that included his sneakers containing residue from the gasoline that had been used to fuel the fatal blaze.

On August 19, 1991, the jury found Julio Gonzalez guilty on all charges, and he was sentenced to 25 years to life in prison, the maximum penalty under the law.

Harry S. Murdock, Kate Claxton and two unidentified actors plead vainly with panicking audience members to stay calm during the Brooklyn Theatre fire on December 5, 1876. Frank Leslie's Illustrated Newspaper

UNITED STATES
NEW YORK
BROOKLYN

December 5, 1876

• • • • • • • • • • • • • • • •

A gaslight ignited scenery in the fly space of the Brooklyn Theatre in Brooklyn, New York on December 5, 1876. Two hundred ninety-five died; hundreds were injured.

Actor Harry S. Murdock may never be remembered for the memorable roles he played. But in theater annals, his performance in the face of disaster on the evening of December 5, 1876 at the Brooklyn Theatre will probably never be equaled. In fact, the entire cast of *The Two Orphans,* which was playing to a capacity audience of 900 that night, behaved in the best "show must go on" tradition.

Like practically all theater fires of the 19th and early 20th centuries (see pp. 156, 161 and 187), this one began in the fly space above the stage. It was noticed by stagehands as it began, partway through the performance, and rapidly spread to scenery and drapery not visible to the audience. The stagehands did what they could with their coats and hands, but there was no fire hose backstage, and the waterbuckets that were supposed to be filled every day for just such an emergency were empty.

One of the stagehands whispered to the actors through an upstage curtain, "Fire," and simultaneously, a patron, seeing a wisp of smoke near the top of the proscenium arch, yelled "Fire."

Murdock, who was playing the part of a cripple, immediately gained the use of both legs, walked calmly to the stage apron and said, "Now, now. None of that."

Another actor J. N. Studley, added his assurances. "There is a small flame," he said, "but it will be put out. Please stay calm and keep your seats."

And that is what a few in the first rows of the orchestra did. But behind them, in the gallery and the balcony, where most fatalities occur in theater fires, there was bedlam. "The dress circle and galleries," commented *Frank Leslie's Illustrated Newspaper* after the blaze, "seemed from the stage to be filled with raving lunatics."

In one last desperate attempt to calm the increasingly panicky audience, the play's star, Kate Claxton, entreated, "We are between you and the fire. Sit still, for God's sake, sit still."

But it was too late for that. The patrons on the orchestra floor and the actors did remain calm, and most of them escaped through the ground-floor exits. But not all. By the time the last of the orchestra patrons had reached the entrance foyer, flames and smoke had bellowed out from the stage, igniting the drapery in the auditorium, ringing the balcony with flame and then entering it. The balcony patrons stampeded down a narrow staircase to the foyer floor and poured into the crowd of exiting ground-floor audience members.

A huge pileup ensued, and children, women and men who fell were trampled underfoot. Some women fainted, and their inert bodies were carried over the heads of the crowd by desperate husbands and escorts. Hundreds were trapped and began clawing their way down the staircase to the lower floor.

Meanwhile, keeping his aplomb, Harry Murdock went back to his dressing room, calmly removed his makeup and changed into evening street clothes, complete with cape and top hat. The other actors, sensing the danger, had long since left by emergency stage exits. When Murdock finally emerged from his dressing room and attempted to descend the stairs to the street, he was met with a wall of fire.

Again, calmly, according to witnesses, he shrugged and turned back. The fire department had arrived by now, and firemen were rescuing frantic patrons who had smashed windows and were struggling toward fireladders. Murdock flung open the window of his dressing room and began to squirm through it. Halfway there, the window closed on his midsection, wedging him tight. Wordlessly, he turned and began to free himself, shoving the window upward while firemen hosed down his face and upper torso. He got the window loose, but then, abruptly, he disappeared inside the building. The fire had burned away the floor beneath him, and Murdock, along with scores of other hapless, trapped patrons, plunged to the basement of the theater. There, hours later, his charred corpse would be found, fused into a pile of other victims.

The wooden theater was a total loss. It burned into the night, and the next day was spent transferring the remains of hundreds of dead to coffins and, when they ran out, to bags. Two hundred ninety-five people were buried in a cylindrical ditch in Greenwood Cemetery. Hundreds more were injured, and an unknown number were incinerated beyond discovery.

UNITED STATES
NEW YORK
NEW YORK

March 17, 1899

• • • • • • • • • • • • • • • • • •

New York's Windsor Hotel was totally destroyed by a fire on March 17, 1899 caused by a combination of a carelessly thrown match igniting dining room curtains, a stubborn policeman and St. Patrick's Day crowds. Ninety-two died; there is no record of the number of injuries.

The seven-story Windsor Hotel, located at 46th Street and Fifth Avenue in New York City, was an unprepossessing, boxlike structure that nevertheless housed its 250 guests comfortably and safely—that is, until St. Patrick's Day of 1899. And it very well might have continued to do so for a goodly number of years if it had not been for the carelessness of one of the 300 extra spectators added to the registered roster of guests and the unforgivable stubborness of a New York city policeman.

It was the practice of the management of the Windsor in the late 19th century to open the doors of the hotel to a certain number of unregistered guests to allow them an unimpeded and somewhat more luxurious view of the annual St. Patrick's Day Parade on Fifth Avenue than they might have had were they on the jammed sidewalk. This was the case on March 17, 1899. Unregistered guests outnumbered registered ones by 50, and the combined total of 550 festively crowded the hotel.

Partway through the afternoon, a careless spectator lit a cigar and nonchalantly tossed the still-burning match out of a window facing 46th Street. The wind blew the match into a lower-story window, where it ignited a set of curtains in the dining room. An alert headwaiter saw the fire start and attempted to beat it out. Unable to extinguish it, he summoned a porter to tell the manager that there was a fire in the dining room. Wasting no time, the head-

Firemen try desperately to bring the Windsor Hotel fire on March 17, 1899 under control. The holiday crowds, a stubborn policeman and a carelessly thrown match combined to totally destroy the famous New York City hotel. New York Public Library (Brown Brothers)

waiter dashed through the lobby and out to the sidewalk, which was seven deep in spectators. The alarm box was on the opposite side of Fifth Avenue, and the frantic headwaiter shoved his way through the crowd and reached the curb in seconds. There he met one of New York's finest, on duty to maintain crowd control.

The waiter explained his mission. He had to cross the street, through the marchers, and turn in a fire alarm. The Windsor Hotel was on fire. The policeman looked at him askance. He'd seen this sort of con job before. He shoved the waiter back into the crowd. Frantically, the headwaiter tried to explain again. Once more, the policeman shoved him back. The harried man tried to circumvent the policeman, but the upholder of the law grabbed him by the arm, threatening to arrest him.

At that moment, after precious minutes of time had been wasted, someone in the sidewalk crowd yelled, "Fire! The Windsor Hotel is on fire!" The policeman looked up. Flames and smoke were pouring from the hotel. Now he himself ran across Fifth Avenue, through the paraders, smashed the window on the alarm box and pulled its lever.

It would be another half hour, at least, before the fire department would be able to maneuver itself through the throngs of parade watchers. By that time, the Windsor fire would be totally out of control. Fourteen frantic, trapped people flung themselves from upper-story windows. Another 78 died from asphyxiation or the flames. The hotel would burn completely to the ground, a $1 million loss, which might have been prevented if one obstinate policeman had unbent for a moment.

UNITED STATES
NEW YORK
NEW YORK

June 15, 1904

• • • • • • • • • • • • • • • •

See MARITIME DISASTERS, *General Slocum.*

UNITED STATES
NEW YORK
NEW YORK

March 25, 1911

• • • • • • • • • • • • • • • •

One of the most tragic fires of all time, the Triangle Shirtwaist Factory fire in New York City on March 25, 1911, began unexplainably in a rag bin but was compounded by overcrowding, inadequate, decaying or bolted fire exits and fire escapes and a wholesale ignoring of safety regulations. One hundred forty-five died; scores were injured.

One of the grisliest and saddest fires ever to take place lasted a mere 18 minutes. If it had begun only 30 minutes later, it might have only consumed three floors of the 10-story Asch Building, located on the northwest corner of Greene Street and Washington Place in New York City. Instead, it took the lives of 145 young and trusting immigrant employees of the Triangle Shirtwaist Factory.

The factory, a sweatshop in the worst sense of the word, was located on the top three floors of the Asch Building and was owned and operated by Max Blanck and Isaac Harris. There were almost 800 such factories in New York in 1911. Because of a shortage of appropriate factory space, the top floors of existing buildings were commandeered as loft factories.

Working conditions were unbearable by today's standards—standards that began to be established as a result of the Triangle Shirtwaist Factory fire. On the eighth and ninth floors of the Triangle Shirtwaist loft, young women worked elbow to elbow at sewing machines that were arranged in long lines. The backs of the chairs on one line touched the backs of those on the next, making it difficult to move about. A few men, called cutters, worked at long tables nearby.

Most of the young workers were between 13 and 20 years old, and practically all were Italian, Russian, Hungarian and German immigrants who could speak little or no English. Most had worked up from messenger status, for which they had been paid $4.50 a week. They moved up to sewing on buttons for $6 a week and from there to the position of machine operator at $12. By working overtime—13 hours a day, seven days a week—a few facile girls could and did earn as much as $18 a week.

There were exits from the building, but they were criminally inadequate. There were four elevators, but only one operated efficiently. Access to the elevator was down a long, narrow corridor that was made narrower by piled remnants, so that the girls would have to pass, single file, by inspectors, who examined their purses to make sure they did not steal anything.

There were two stairways leading to ground level, but the Washington Place doors were bolted shut and could not be opened from the inside—again, another device to keep the employees from stealing. The other door opened inward.

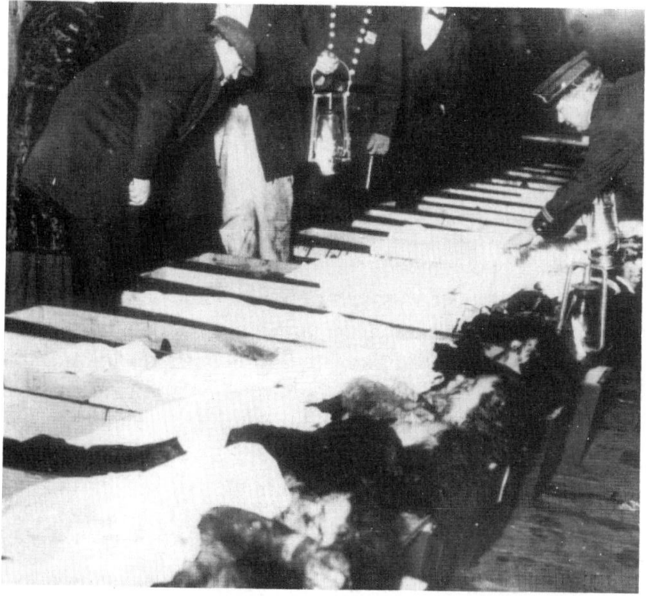

The bodies of young women burned to death in the Triangle Shirtwaist fire of March 25, 1911 in New York City are lined up in the morgue for identification. New York Public Library (Brown Brothers)

The only other exit was a decrepit fire escape, a foot and a half wide and rotting. After the blaze, it was estimated that it would have taken three hours for those working on the top three floors to descend it.

The Triangle Shirtwaist Factory had several fire buckets full of water lined up at its walls; there was a fire hose, but it had rotted to pieces long ago; there was a No Smoking sign, but it was regularly ignored and unenforced.

For years, safety regulators were aware of the dangerous conditions that existed in the brick buildings from Canal Street north to Eighth Street. A fire in one such building had taken the life of Assistant Fire Chief Charles W. Krueger. But the efforts of Fire Chief Edward Croker were frustrated by Wall Street interests, factory owners and the apathy of the city government.

The Triangle Shirtwaist owners were particularly arrogant in their defiance. They, after all, had been responsible for destroying the shirtwaist strike in 1910. It had started there and spread until 40,000 workers were out in the industry. Triangle refused to sign a contract and was credited with finally breaking the strike.

At 4:40 on Saturday afternoon, March 25, 1911, roughly 600 workers were working an overtime shift to make up for a backlog in orders. The narrow aisles were stacked with baskets of cut goods of lace and silk. On the cutting tables, layers of linen and cotton fabric were piled high. Huge bins were filled with scrap and waste material; the floor was littered with remnants. On overhead lines, finished shirtwaists were hung.

The shift was almost over; some employees had already begun to draw on their coats. And then, for a reason that has never been established, the fire started, in a rag bin on the Greene Street side of the eighth floor. It was tiny, and nobody noticed it until it had gotten an impressive, fatal start.

One of the women workers spotted it then and screamed "Fire!" Factory manager Samuel Bernstein and foreman-tailor Max Rother, who were on the Washington Place side of the eighth floor, heard the cry and, grabbing fire buckets, raced to the fire. But it had gained too much headway to be snuffed out by two buckets of water. Other men rolled out the hose, which rotted away in their hands. The valve was rusted shut.

Now the flames leaped upward, igniting the shirtwaists that were hung overhead. Women shoved at one another, knocking over chairs as they tried to squeeze toward the exit from the room. The fire vaulted to a cutting table, setting a blaze there. The narrow hallway to the elevators became jammed with crying, terrorized women. The elevator held only 12 people, and its operator, Giuseppe Zito, could only make four or five round-trips before his car was rendered immovable by burned cables and the weight of the bodies of those who had flung themselves down the elevator shaft.

Those who got down the narrow staircase to the Greene Street exit ran into the inward-opening door. Scores of bodies piled up against it before some men bodily wrested the door open and shepherded a few frantic workers through.

On the Washington Place side of the building, workers piled up against the unyielding, bolted door. Tearing at one another's clothing, most of them died there as flames roared down the stairwell, burning them alive.

The fire had spread to the ninth floor now, where 300 more workers stampeded to escape the flames. On the 10th floor, in the executive offices, Blanck and Harris, along with Blanck's children and governess, who had come to visit him in his office, got to the roof and made their way to an adjacent building via a fire ladder.

Meanwhile, the eighth floor had become a raging inferno. Those who were trapped at the Washington Place exit were already blackened corpses. Some workers frantically tried to leave via the eighth-floor fire escape. Too flimsy to stand either heat or the weight thrown upon it, the iron ladder warped and then gave way. Those on it fell to the ground.

The fire roared on to the ninth floor. The heat was intense enough to curl sheet-iron shutters on a building 20 feet away.

The fire alarm had been turned in, and in moments, Engine Company Number 18, led by Foreman Howard Ruch, Company Number 72 and Hook and Ladder Company Number 20 were all there. But even though they arrived no more than eight minutes after the blaze began, they were too late. The most horrible phase of the drama had begun before they could get there.

Foreman Bernstein later told a UPI reporter that a shopgirl named Clotilda Terdanova was the first to jump from the building to her death. "She tore her hair and ran from window to window," he said, "until finally, before anyone could stop her, she jumped out. She was young and very pretty. She was to leave us next Saturday to be married three weeks later."

More and more women, some of them clinging together, jumped. It was literally raining bodies. The firemen could not unravel their hoses because of the smashed corpses piling on the sidewalks. Some finally did, and Battalion Chief Edward Worth used his first two lines to cool the building over the heads of the hysterical girls clinging to ledges and standing in windows. Then, a gust of wind sucked flames out of windows and onto the clothes of the trapped girls.

A cry of "Raise your ladders! Raise your ladders!" came from the spectators who had begun to accumulate. A girl on a ninth-floor ledge waved a handkerchief, directing one of the ladders, which ascended toward her. But Chief Croker had warned long ago that their ladders would only reach to the seventh floor of any blazing building, and that is where the ladders stopped that afternoon. The girl, her skirt ablaze, leaped for the ladder 30 feet below her and missed. Her flaming body hit the sidewalk.

All of the fire hoses were now crushed by falling bodies, and no water was reaching the blaze. Company Number 18 spread the first life net, a new one 14 feet long. Three girls dove simultaneously from the ninth floor. When they landed, they ripped the net to shreds and pulled a dozen firemen inward on top of their bodies.

Company Number 20 set up a 20-foot Browder net. Bodies rained on it so rapidly that the tube steel frame buckled and gave way.

Two policemen improvised a blanket and caught one girl dead center. The blanket held for a minute and then gave way, and she crashed against the grating of a skylight.

Another net received a girl who landed safely. Battalion Chief Worth pulled her upright. "She blinked and said nothing," Chief Worth later told reporters; "I told her to 'go right across the street.' She walked ten feet—and dropped. She died in one minute.

"Life nets?" continued Worth. "What good were they? The little ones went through life nets, pavement, and all. I thought they would come down one at a time. I didn't know they would come with arms entwined—three and even four together."

Bill Shepherd, the UPI reporter, wrote of the floods of water from the firemen's hoses that ran into the gutter. "[They] were actually red with blood. I looked upon the heap of dead bodies, and I remembered these girls were shirtwaist makers. I remembered their great strike of last year, in which these same girls had demanded more sanitary conditions and more safety precautions in the shops. These dead bodies were the answer."

In 18 minutes, it was over. The doors on the ninth floor were chopped down, and the firemen quickly extinguished the flames. All of the damage had been done in the first 10 minutes. Firemen found 49 burned or suffocated bodies on the ninth floor. Thirty-six more were found at the bottom of the elevator shaft. Fifty-eight lay on the sidewalk. Two more would die of their injuries. All in all, 145 innocent, exploited young immigrants would perish in those terrible 10 minutes.

The reaction to the tragedy was immediate and immense. The Waistmakers Union organized a mass funeral for the victims, and 10,000 mourners attended. New York's East Side, from which most of the dead had come, seethed with anger. On April 5, more than 80,000 people marched up Fifth Avenue, following an empty hearse pulled by six horses draped in black.

The testimony at the trial of Harris and Blanck brought forth horrifying admissions. Safety expert H. F. Porter, who had pleaded with the Triangle owners to institute fire drills, told the *New York Times,* "One man whom I advised to install a fire drill replied to me: 'Let 'em burn. They're a lot of cattle, anyway.' "

In December, a grand jury exonerated the Triangle owners of manslaughter charges, claiming that the bolted door might have been locked by an employee. The *New York Times* erupted in an editorial. "The monstrous conclusion of the law is that the slaughter was no one's fault," it thundered, "that it couldn't be helped, or perhaps even that, in the fine legal phrase which is big enough to cover a multitude of defects of justice, it was 'an act of God!' This conclusion is revolting to the moral sense of the community."

But the country was shocked, and labor gained much. The International Ladies Garment Workers Union was formed as a direct result of the tragedy. The day of the sweatshop was nearing an end. Uniform fire and factory codes, led by New York's Sullivan-Hoey Fire Prevention Law of October 1911, were instituted all over the country. Fire Chief Edward Croker turned in his badge in order to lead a crusade for safety. Nothing would be quite the same in either fire prevention or factory working conditions ever again, and it had taken a tragedy of incredible proportions to bring this about.

UNITED STATES
OHIO
COLLINWOOD

March 4, 1908

• • • • • • • • • • • • • • • •

The fire that began unexplainably in the boiler room of the Lake View School in Collinwood, Ohio on March 4, 1908 turned tragic because of blocked and faulty exits. One hundred seventy-six died; scores were injured.

The Lake View School in the Cleveland suburb of Collinwood was a daytime home for 325 students. On March 4, 1908, 176 of them died by burning or asphyxiation, trapped behind a front door that opened inward and a rear door that was bolted shut.

The fire's origins were never established. It began, apparently, in the boiler room, which was located directly under the steps of the front staircase of the three-story school. Two young girls discovered the smoke first and reported this to a janitor who turned in the fire alarm and than ran for his life, apparently locking the rear door of the school behind him and thus condemning to death by burning scores of children.

The fire spread swiftly; the building was constructed entirely of wood and other inflammable materials. The first-floor, first-grade classroom of teacher Grace Fiske was, because it was located over the boiler room, the first to be invaded by smoke and flames. Fire burst through the closed classroom door, and Ms. Fiske, assessing the situation, directed her hysterical class to the windows and the fire escape beyond them. When some did not respond immediately, she gathered them up and shoved them toward the windows. Others, who ran berserk around the room, she picked up in her arms and carried to the windows. Most of the children in the class escaped, but some recalcitrant ones—and their teacher, who went back into the flames to try to rescue them—were burned to death.

Meanwhile, the fire was spreading rapidly throughout the building, racing through the narrow hallways and igniting drapes in the auditorium. (One small boy would later try to escape by climbing, hand over hand, along the top of the stage curtain. He would fall to his death halfway across.) Fire drills seemed to have meant little to the children. They and some of their teachers ran helter-skelter into the halls and piled up in massive, fatal drifts against both the front and rear exits. A Miss Golmar, finding the staircases blocked, deserted her class; she climbed over struggling children and through a rear window to safety.

Eventually, the back door was battered in by Henry Ellis, a real estate broker, and I. E. Cross, a train superintendent. They encountered a huge pile of charred bodies, with more children climbing on every minute. "Flames reached out from the walls to catch first one and then another child," said Ellis later to UPI. Both men hauled dozens of still-living people from the pile, including Pearl Lynn, a teacher, who, leading her children to the door, stumbled and fell, and was buried beneath the hill of bodies and still survived.

Mrs. John Phillips, whose daughter went to the school, dashed to it when told of the fire. The front door had been pried partially open by the time she arrived, and she saw her daughter struggling near the top of the mass of children jammed against it on the inside. She reached for the child's hands and pulled but could not free her. She stroked her head, "trying," as she said later, "to keep the fire from burning her hair. I stayed there and pulled at her," she went on, "and tried to keep the fire from her till a heavy piece of glass fell on me, cutting my hand nearly off. Then I fell back and my girl died before my face."

The fire department arrived, but there was little they could do, and that little was diminished by their ancient equipment. Neither their ladders nor the water from their hoses would reach above the first floor, and the roaring inferno of the schoolhouse was now a heartrending sight, with bedlam inside and the faces of children at the windows being overcome, one by one, by flames or smoke. Eight thousand spectators—practically the entire population of Collinwood—eventually crowded into the schoolyard, some of them jeering and kicking the firemen as they put forth their futile efforts.

Charles G. McIlrath, the chief of Collinwood's police force, arrived just as his eight-year-old son Hugh appeared on the fire escape, leading a group of younger children to safety. The fire escape ladder ended eight feet from the ground, and Chief McIlrath reached up and lowered those who were afraid to jump to the ground. His son, meanwhile, ran back into the school to rescue more, while his father pleaded with him to jump to safety. The boy's body was later found on a stairway. His arms were around two smaller, dead children.

It would be three hours before the fire burned down enough for rescue teams to enter the building. What they found was appalling. All night, bodies and some few injured children were carried from the wreckage of the school. A makeshift morgue for the 176 killed was fashioned at the Lake Shore Depot.

A coroner's inquest was held, and the coroner asked for prosecution of the builders of the school for erecting it with narrow hallways and escape doors that opened inward. The builders were never brought to trial or account.

UNITED STATES
OHIO
COLUMBUS

April 21, 1930

• • • • • • • • • • • • • • • • • • •

Arson and overcrowding conspired to intensify the fire in the Ohio State Penitentiary on April 21, 1930. Three hundred twenty-one died; 130 were injured in the resultant blaze.

Most of the prisoners had been locked in their cells at the Ohio State Penitentiary on the evening of April 21, 1930. The prison, like most penitentiaries in the first years of the Great Depression, was severely overcrowded. Forty-three hundred inmates were imprisoned in accommodations built for 1,500. The Ohio State Penitentiary, one of the largest prisons in the country, was also one that had been under fire for 12 years by prison authorities for not only its overcrowding but its substandard conditions.

Thus, partially to accommodate its critics, the prison was undergoing a token expansion. A minuscule construction project, designed to increase its capacity, had begun in the west cell block. A cat's cradle of scaffolding stood outside the older building, and it was here that a fire began. A year later two convicts would admit having set the blaze as a protest against being forced to work on the scaffolding. They had poured oil on a pile of garments stored beneath the structure and ignited it with a candle stolen from the chapel.

The flames, fanned by a stiff breeze, quickly spread to the six-tiered cell block that housed approximately 800 prisoners. Running up the scaffolding, the flames leaped to the roof, eating their way through the tar paper and timber and showering sparks on the prisoners in the upper layer of cells. Bedding and mattresses began to ignite, and prisoners, trapped in their cells, screamed in fear, pleading to be let out of their fiery cubicles. The guards, following the orders of head guard of the upper tier Thomas Watkinson, refused to unlock the cells.

Some of the prisoners in the lower rows of cells had not yet been locked in for the night. Hearing the yells of their fellow prisoners, smelling the smoke and seeing the raining cinders, some of these prisoners refused to be locked up. The guards, again mindlessly following orders, tried to force them into their cells.

A riot resulted. Prisoners wrestled guards to the floor, slammed them up against walls and generally managed to drive them back from the first-tier cell block. The smoke grew more dense, obscuring the fighting and choking the combatants, but the prisoners finally forced the guards back to the door leading to the safety of the prison yard. It was a logical, humane solution that some of the lockstepped guards still resisted.

One obstinately tried to bar the only other door to the yard. Two convicts, John Sherman and Charley Simms, grabbed him and ripped his keys from him. Dashing to the second and third tiers, they began to unlock locked cells. They managed to free 68 men and direct them to the yard before, almost overcome by the increasing smoke, they had to abandon the effort and run for the yard themselves.

The sixth tier was a horror. Finally realizing the murderousness of their stubbornness, two guards, Thomas Little and George Baldwin, pleaded with chief guard Watkinson to unlock the cells. The roof had begun to crack, and each cell was now an oven. Some men had already died, turned into human torches when pieces of the roof caved in on them in their confined spaces. Watkinson still refused, citing his orders.

Finally, the two guards wrestled Watkinson to the floor and took his keys from him. But it was too late. The bars on the cells and their doors had become red hot, and the locks had fused together. The keys would not work.

Now, with a sickening roar, the roof collapsed entirely into the cell block, incinerating every single prisoner there.

One hundred sixty-eight men burned alive while Little and Baldwin watched helplessly. Not one man survived. "I saw their faces," recalled one guard for reporters, "wreathed in smoke that poured from their cells. With others I tried to get them out, but we could not move the bars. Soon flames broke into the cellrooms and the convicts dropped before our eyes. They were literally burned alive."

On other tiers, more rational behavior took place, as prisoners and guards used sledges and crowbars to pry open cell doors. There were heroic rescues. Frank Ward, an ex-policeman, now a prisoner, alone released 136 men; "Big Jim" Morton, a bank robber, at liberty in the yard when the fire began, rushed into the cell block time and again to drag out convicts who were half dead from the smoke. Morton himself was eventually overcome and had to be carried to the yard.

Despite the frantic rescue efforts, men continued to die. A fireman described the scene to reporters afterward: "While we were trying to cut through the steel, the trapped prisoners climbed up the bars of the cells pleading with us to save them. We could hardly see through the smoke. We were driven back and these men died before our eyes. They were overcome toward the end and did not scream, so I think they were unconscious by the time the fire reached them."

Firemen faced dual danger when they arrived at the prison. Four thousand convicts, enraged at the fate of their fellow prisoners who had been locked into their iron deathtraps, barred the firemen from fighting the fire. A standoff ensued, while the fire grew to horrendous proportions. Finally, National Guardsmen and federal troops, summoned by prison officials, moved in with bayonets.

Fire fighters began to put out the blaze, but now, prisoners began to pelt the firemen with rocks. The firemen turned their hoses on the prisoners, forcing them back. But the riot now began to take on insane proportions. Some convicts tried to set fire to a fire truck. Others succeeded in igniting the Catholic chapel and a woolen mill. Firemen managed to put out both fires before they caused extensive damage. When an entering ambulance was rushed by 20 convicts, the warden issued a "shoot to kill" order, and the riot quieted.

Firemen finally extinguished the conflagration, and they and prison officials entered the smoldering building. A horrendous sight greeted them. There were the crushed and incinerated corpses of the 168 men of the sixth tier, and in isolated other cells, the agony-twisted and charred remains of hundreds more.

Of the 800 prisoners housed in the cell block, 321 were dead, and 130 were severely injured.

The shocking details of the early minutes of the fire were made public. Watkinson, accused of signing the death warrants of 168 men, denied respo
he was merely carrying out the ord
tain John Hall. Hall denied ever gi
Watkinson was suspended from his j

It was revealed that the fire alarm w
box outside the prison wall, long after t
a firm upper hand. The main cage doo
cells, which was usually unlocked, was foun
locked all during the conflagration. Thus, there
indication that someone had locked it after t
started.

The Reverend Albert O'Brien, the prison's C
chaplain, issued a written condemnation: "The disast
a crime on the part of the state—a greater crime than
of those dead boys ever committed against the state,"
wrote.

The *Columbus Evening Dispatch* noted the horrendous overcrowding and editorialized: "For many years successive legislatures have dawdled over the prison problem while defenseless human lives remained in jeopardy."

The *Cleveland Plain Dealer* echoed this. "The State must abandon a policy of neglect and indifference," it stated. "The cries of men behind steel bars, held in a vise for creeping flames to destroy, are ringing in Ohio ears. The State is more cruel than we believe if the cries are unanswered."

Ironically, with all of its loss of life, the fire caused a mere $11,000 in damage to the west cell block of the Ohio State Penitentiary.

UNITED STATES
WISCONSIN
PESHTIGO

October 8, 1871

• • • • • • • • • • • • • • • • •

The worst forest fire in U.S. history destroyed the entire town of Peshtigo, Wisconsin on October 8, 1871. No specific cause was recorded, but it was probably a combination of smoldering fires, a drought, indiscriminate logging and the burning of debris by railroads. Two thousand six-hundred and eighty-two people died in Peshtigo and the rest of Wisconsin, and hundreds were injured.

On October 8, 1871, the very day that the Great Chicago Fire began in Mrs. O'Leary's barn, the worst forest fire in the history of the United States started, 250 miles to the north of Chicago. It would claim 2,682 lives and level an area of 400 square miles of forest.

Peshtigo, built in the midst of an enormous forest a few miles from Green Bay, was a hugely successful logging town

1. It boasted 350 houses, three hotels, two churches, aloons, a dozen stores, a sawmill and a woodenware y. The Peshtigo River ran through the heart of town, a large wooden bridge allowed those on one side of settlement to get to the other. Most of Peshtigo's pop- tion of 2,000 was in the logging business, and they looked rward to the not too distant day when the Chicago and Northwestern Railroad would link their town with Milwaukee and Chicago.

All of the spring and summer preceding the fire was relentlessly dry. Early in July, a day of rain held out false hope. From then until September, no more rain fell. Springs began to dry up; rivers fell. During the summer, a number of small, fussy fires smoldered in dry peat bogs and in the webwork of roots that dried-up swamps revealed.

In August, citizens of Peshtigo carved a fireline out of the forest ringing the city. Accomplishing this, they felt safer, and when, on September 5, rain finally fell, they felt even more secure. But the rain was shortlived and inadequate, turning the forest into a steaming jungle. It was ripe for a forest fire, and the forest dwellers and logging interests only increased the danger by two foolish activities.

First, figuring that the rivers would soon be filled with water from expected rains, the logging interests continued to harvest trees. Limbs and slashings carpeted the forest floor.

Second, railroads cutting through the forest south of the city ignored the dryness of the brush around them and burned their debris.

Whether the final fire began from the spontaneous combustion of marsh gases, or the small smoldering fires finally burst into full-blown flames, or the railroaders kindled it with their fires, or a careless forest person began it, no one would ever determine. In fact, the fire itself received little notice in the press, except in the pages of Luther B. Noyes's three-month-old *Marinette and Peshtigo Eagle,* which published a Fire Extra on October 14 and has supplied practically all of the information on this fire for historians. The national Fourth Estate was too busy at the time with the Chicago Fire.

But to the people of Peshtigo, on the chilly Sunday of October 8, 1871, the approaching fire was very real. A pall of brownish smoke hung over them as they went to church to hear sermons warning of Judgment Day.

By seven o'clock that night, the wind had picked up, and ashes were beginning to fall on the city in a steady rain, much as if a volcano were erupting nearby. When the townspeople left services an hour later, a steady, full-throated roar could be heard nearby in the forest. Frightened, many of them went home, closed their doors and windows against the smoke and waited.

Meanwhile, farmers in the forest were in dire trouble. The flames of the fire were undeniably visible to them. By seven o'clock, huge tongues of flames licked at a score of farms and then rushed forward, consuming them. The network of paths through the woods became impassable, and forest animals began to mix with farm animals as they tried to escape the advancing fire.

One farmer gathered his wife and five children together into a wagon and tried to outrace the flames. They overtook them, killing everyone but the farmer.

By 9:00 P.M., just as the Chicago fire was starting, church bells began to toll in Peshtigo, warning of the approaching inferno, which was now brutally apparent. The night was rimmed in the crimson glow of the fire advancing from the south. Cinders began to fall more rapidly on the city, setting small fires. The fire department shuttled between them, putting some out, being beaten back by others.

Now women began to gather up their children and, wrapping them in covers, fled to the streets with them. Sparks ignited trees within the city. Some townspeople began to turn toward the Peshtigo River.

Suddenly, a tornado-like gale whipped around the city, scattering a rain of fire. Sheets of flame and huge firebrands began to fly through it. Balls of burning grass uprooted from the swamps and explosions of methane gas from the marshes rocked the night air.

The fleeing townspeople turned into a mob. Men joined the women and children. Those on one side of the river tried to reach the other side, and those on that side tried to cross the bridge at the identical moment. Two frantic, terrified mobs met each other at midspan, milling, fighting, tearing at each other. The bridge groaned and collapsed, flinging the mob into the river, where many drowned.

In the midst of this, the telegraph operator at the railroad station received some news that caused him to dash out into the street and inform nearby fire fighters: "This fire is bigger than we thought. We just got a message on the telegraph from Green Bay. Chicago is burning!"

The fire fighters figured that it was indeed Judgment Day.

The firestorm erupted in another destroying wind. Flames roared through the city. Houses were bowled over. Roofs exploded from the tops of houses and flew through the superheated air. Burning trees became flaming battering rams. And the wall of fire roared on.

The air was so hot now that a person could burst into flames without being touched by fire at all. People simply became human torches, incinerated on the spot. Vacuum pockets developed in the air, and those who ran into them lost their breath, collapsed and died within a few steps.

Bizarre incidents flared up as easily as the fires set by the fire storm. One husky husband running through the streets toward the river with his wife in his arms collided with someone in the semidarkness brought on by the smoke. They all crashed to the ground. Frantically, he picked up his wife and continued toward the river. Reaching it, he plunged in up to his shoulders and set her down on her feet.

But it was not his wife. She was a total stranger. In the confusion after his fall, he had picked up the wrong woman. His wife was now a blackened corpse by the side of a road.

Another man dragged a heavy bed with his wife, who was suffering from a fever, in it to the river, where he submerged it to a depth that covered his wife's body but left her pillowed head above the surface. The family huddled together there all night and survived.

Still another man, realizing he was too far from the river to make it, decided to take refuge in a horse watering trough. He was boiled alive.

Terrified cattle stampeded through the streets, trampling some people. A hysterical man, rather than face death by fire, killed his wife and children and then slit his own throat. Another fastened a noose around his neck and hanged himself in his well. Seventy people huddled together in the middle of a cornfield were burned to death. And on the banks of the Peshtigo River that night, several pregnant woman gave premature birth.

The fire raged till dawn, unchecked. T. J. Teasdale, one of the survivors gave his story to the *Marinette and Peshtigo Eagle:*

> *When the fire struck the town it seemed to swallow up and drown everything . . . a fierce, devouring, pitiless rain of fire and sand, so hot as to ignite everything it touched . . .*
>
> *Within three hours of the time the fire struck, Peshtigo was literally a sand desert, dotted over with smoking ruins. Not a hencoop or dry goods box was left . . . Cattle and horses were burned in their stalls. The Peshtigo Company's barn burned with over fifty horses in the stable. A great many men, women and children were burned in the streets, and in places so far away from anything combustible that it would seem impossible they should burn. But they were burned to a crisp. Whole families, heads of families, children were burned, and remnants of families were running hither and thither, wildly calling and looking for their relatives after the fire.*

Peshtigo was no more. Monday morning dawned silently. No dogs barked, no cows mooed, no birds sang. Even the fish in the river were dead and floating on its surface.

By afternoon, a steamer from nearby Marinette, which had miraculously escaped the fire, arrived with food and clothing and the news that 23 other towns had been destroyed by the same inferno—Casco, DePere, Shite Rock, Ahnepee, Elm Creek, Forestville, Little Sturgeon Bay, Lincoln, Brussels and Rosiere among them.

That night, it began to rain. It was more than the usual rain that follows a fire storm. It would be the beginning of 15 years of the most bountiful rainfall in the history of Wisconsin.

The survivors in Peshtigo set about rebuilding their city and retilling their land. Within three years, the town would be rebuilt as a dairy center, which it is today. But the worst forest fire in the history of the nation would claim 1,182 lives in Peshtigo alone, and 1,500 others in the state of Wisconsin—an unenviable, unbroken record.

MARITIME DISASTERS

• • • • •

THE WORST RECORDED MARITIME DISASTERS

• • • • •

* Detailed in text

Atlantic Ocean
- * *Andrea Doria/Stockholm* (1956)
- *Guiding Star* (1855)
- * *Lusitania* (1915)
- *Monarch of the Sea* (1866)
- * *Morro Castle* (1934)
- * *Titanic* (1912)

Baltic Sea
- * *Wilhelm Gustloff* (1945)

Bay of Gibraltar
- * *Utopia* (1891)

Canada
- Nova Scotia
- Halifax
- * *Atlantic* (1873)
- * *Mont Blanc* (1917) (see EXPLOSIONS)
- Sable Island
- * *La Bourgogne* (1898)
- Wingo Sound
- * *St. George/Defence* (1811)
- Quebec
- St. Lawrence River
- * *Empress of Ireland* (1914)

Cape of Good Hope
- * *St. James* (1586)

Caribbean Sea
- Near Veracruz, Mexico
- * Grand Fleet (1591)

Chile
- Valparaiso
- *L'Orriflame* (1770)

China
- Chusan Islands
- * *Hsin Yu* (1916)
- *Tai Ping* (1949)
- Manchuria
- Chinese Army vessel (1949)
- Swatow Harbor
- * *Hong Koh* (1921)
- Woosung
- * *Kiangya* (1948)
- Yangtze River
- Chinese troop carrier (1926)
- *Hsin Hsu-tung* (1928)

English Channel
- * Spanish Armada (1588)

France
- La Rochelle
- * *Afrique* (1920)

Great Britain
- England
- Spithead
- * *Royal George* (1792)
- Woolwich
- * *Princess Alice* (1878)
- Scotland
- * Rockall
- *Norge* (1904)

Gulf of Finland
- *Leffort* (1857)

Gulf of Mexico
- Flota de Nueva Espana (1590)

Hispaniola
- Spanish fleet (1502)

Holland
- Texel River
- * *Minotaur* (1810)

Hong Kong
- River steamer (1945)

India
- Indian Ocean
- *Blenheim* (1807)
- Madras
- * *Comorta* (1902)
- Manihari Ghat
- * Passenger ferry (1988)

Italy
- Leghorn
- * *Queen Charlotte* (1800)

Japan
- Hakodate
- * *Toyo Maru* (1954)
- Hokkaido
- *Indigirka* (1939)
- Sasebo
- *Mikasa* (1905)
- South coast
- * *Ertogrul* (1890)
- *Kichemaru* (1912)
- Tokyo Bay
- * *Kawachi* (1918)

Java Sea
- * *Tamponas II* (1981)

Labrador
- Egg Island
- * English Armada (1711)

Martinique
- French-Dutch convoy (1776)

Mexico
- Veracruz
- Flota de Neuva Espana (1600)
- *Neustra Senora de la Concepcion* (1732)

New Zealand
- Auckland
- * *Cospatrick* (1874)

North Sea
- *York* (1803)

Philippines
- Tablas Strait
- * *Dona Paz/Victor* (1987)

Turkey
- Constantinople
- *Neiri Shevket* (1850)

United States
- Florida
- Coast
- * *Capitanas* (1715)
- Gulf of Florida
- Narvaez expedition (1528)
- Keys
- Spanish convoys (1622)
- Tampa
- Spanish expedition (1559)
- Illinois
- Chicago
- * *Eastland* (1915)
- New York
- New York
- * *General Slocum* (1904)
- Tennessee
- Memphis
- * *Sultana* (1865) (see EXPLOSIONS)

Venezuela
- Aves Island
- French fleet (1678)

West Indies
- Mona Passage
- *Sisters* (1787)

CHRONOLOGY

* Detailed in text

1502
July
Hispaniola
Spanish fleet

1528
Sept. 22
Gulf of Florida
Narvaez expedition

1559
Tampa, Florida
Spanish expedition

1586
Cape of Good Hope
* *St. James*

1588
August–October
English Channel
* Spanish Armada

1590
July
Gulf of Mexico
Flota de Nueva Espana

1591
Aug. 10
Caribbean Sea near Veracruz
* Grand Fleet

1600
Sept. 12
Veracruz
Flota de Nueva Espana

1622
Sept. 6
Florida Keys
Spanish convoys

1678
May 3
Aves Island, Venezuela
French fleet

1711
Aug. 22
Egg Island, Labrador
* English Armada

1715
July 31
Florida coast
* Capitanas

1732
January
Veracruz
Nuestra Senora de la Concepcion

1770
Valparaiso, Chile
L'Orriflame

1776
Sept. 6
Martinique
French-Dutch convoy

1787
Mona Passage, West Indies
Sisters

1792
Aug. 29
Spithead, Great Britain
* *Royal George*

1800
Mar. 17
Leghorn, Italy
* *Queen Charlotte*

1803
North Sea
York

1807
Feb. 1
Indian Ocean
Blenheim

1810
Dec. 22
Texel River, Holland
* *Minotaur*

1811
Dec. 24
Wingo Sound, Nova Scotia, Canada
* *St. George/Defence*

1850
Oct. 23
Constantinople, Turkey
Neiri Shevket

1855
Jan. 9
Atlantic Ocean
Guiding Star

1857
Sept. 23
Gulf of Finland
Leffort

1865
Mar. 26
Memphis, Tennessee
* *Sultana* (see EXPLOSIONS)

1866
April 3
Atlantic Ocean
Monarch of the Sea

1873
April 1
Halifax, Nova Scotia
* *Atlantic*

1874
Nov. 17
Auckland, New Zealand
* *Cospatrick*

1878
Sept. 3
Woolwich, Great Britain
* *Princess Alice*

1890
Sept. 19
South coast, Japan
* *Ertogrul*

1891
Mar. 17
Bay of Gibraltar
* *Utopia*

1898
July 4
Sable Island, Nova Scotia
* *La Bourgogne*

1902
April
Madras, India
* *Camorta*

1904
June 15
New York, New York
* *General Slocum*
June 28
Rockall, Scotland
* *Norge*

1905
Sept. 10
Sasebo, Japan
Mikasa

1912
April 14
Atlantic Ocean
* *Titanic*
Sept. 28
Mikasa, Japan
Kichemaru

1914
May 29
St. Lawrence River, Quebec,
* *Empress of Ireland*

1915
May 1
Atlantic Ocean
* *Lusitania*
July 24
Chicago, Illinois
* *Eastland*
1916
Aug. 29
Chusan Islands, China
* *Hsin Yu*
1917
Dec. 30
Halifax, Nova Scotia
* *Mont Blanc* (See EXPLOSIONS)
1918
July 12
Tokyo Bay, Japan
* *Kawachi*
1920
Jan. 12
La Rochelle, France
* *Afrique*
1921
Mar. 18
Swatow Harbor, China
* *Hong Koh*
1926
Oct. 16
Yangtze River
Chinese troop carrier
1928
Aug. 15
Chusan Islands, China
Hsin Hsu-Tung
1934
Sept. 8
Atlantic Ocean
* *Morro Castle*
1939
Dec. 12
Hokkaido Island
Indigirka
1945
Jan. 30
Baltic Sea
* *Wilhelm Gustloff*
Nov. 8
Hong Kong, China
Chinese river steamer
1948
Dec. 3
Woosung, China
* *Kiangya*
1949
Jan. 27
Chusan Islands, China
Tai Ping
1954
Sept. 26.
Hakodate, Japan
* *Toyo Maru*
1956
July 25
Atlantic Ocean
* *Andrea Doria/Stockholm*
1981
Jan. 27
Java Sea
* *Tamponas II*
1987
Dec. 20
Tablas Strait, Philippines
* *Dona Paz/Victor*
1988
Aug. 6
Manihari Ghat, India
* Indian passenger ferry

MARITIME DISASTERS

For those who could afford it, there was no more romantic or peaceful way to travel abroad than on a transatlantic ocean liner. Even in the late 1960s, when jet travel was beginning to make ocean travel obsolete, it remained a remnant of a more gracious, less frantic age, when time was not the tyrannical monarch of a person's life and a little bouillon calmed both the stomach and the nerves.

Those leviathans of the North Atlantic and the South Pacific were self-contained cities, and like the great cities of the world, each had its own personality. The Cunard Line, for instance, was definitely British and guarded the doors between first, cabin and tourist class. On the French Line, sybaritic considerations—a shortage of men for the after-dinner revels in first class, for instance—sometimes relaxed those same barriers. The Italian Line was similarly relaxed, as was the round-the-world Moore-McCormick Line.

But what distinguished these liners from the dull world as it was, was a sense of opulence married to a sense of fun. Although the present resurgence of cruise liners is a welcome testament to people's need for the sea, they are really pale imitations of the real thing. Floating summer camps, they cannot begin to approximate the dignified feeling of comfort and relaxation unto relief that life aboard the grand transatlantic liner offered its passengers.

Perhaps it was the long tradition of sailing that reaches back to the Phoenicians that made it so comfortable and even insular. There was a feeling of being cared for that was almost familial, and perhaps that was necessary, for the sea has been, and always will be, the master of all it surveys, borders on, or floats.

Aboard one of these posh, floating metropolises, one never really felt threatened by the sea, only occasionally tormented. Storms at sea were only fun for the very stalwart, and there were those to whom even the gentle sway of the grand saloon was too much for their centers of equilibrium. Seasickness is not fun, as anyone who has experienced it will attest.

But that was the only drawback to this supremely romantic and restful way of travel.

Still, disasters did occur at sea, and this section details the worst of them. Interestingly enough, only one—the *Andrea Doria/Stockholm* collision (see p. 214)—occurred in the last three decades of transatlantic-transpacific travel.

Unlike air crashes, disasters at sea have rarely killed everyone aboard. Except in cases of wholesale stupidity and criminal neglect, as in the events involving the *Titanic* (see p. 219) or the *General Slocum* (see p. 240), adequate lifeboats and life preservers are provided, and mandated safety precautions and drills assure passengers that there is at least some chance of surviving a disaster at sea.

Storms have, naturally, been the scourge of sailors since the Phoenicians. Some of the earlier maritime disasters were caused by hurricanes. The sinking of the entire Spanish Armada in the English Channel in 1588, with its staggering death toll (see p. 230), and the equally dramatic demise of the English Armada off the coast of Labrador in 1711 (see p. 236) were, at least partially, the result of storms.

But even in these cases, the enormous loss of life would have been avoided had it not been for the misjudgment of commanding officers. In fact, as in all disasters involving the transportation of large numbers of people, be it by rail, air or sea, so-called human error has proven to be the most pervasive culprit. Captains have driven their ships into storms and onto reefs, ignored warnings and sped recklessly through fogs. And their ships have sunk, sometimes with them aboard.

In addition, this incompetency, recklessness or downright stupidity has often been compounded by cowardice. The nameless captain who slammed the Portuguese packet *St. James* onto the rocks of South Africa in 1586 (see p. 227) leaped into the first lifeboat, leaving all of his passengers behind; the crew of the French liner *La Bourgogne,* after colliding with another ship because its captain refused to slow down in a heavy fog, saved themselves by deliberately drowning hundreds of passengers (see p. 225). In still other circumstances, such as the fire aboard the *General Slocum* and the *Dona Paz* (see p. 238), the parsimonious shortcuts taken by profit-motivated steamship companies accounted for needless deaths.

But these are the bizarre extremes. Although the tragedy of the *Titanic* proved conclusively that there is no such thing as an unsinkable ship, most passenger liners, lake steamers and even ferries have the good manners to take their time in sinking, thus giving their passengers a reasonable chance of surviving. And with increasingly precise navigation equipment developed by the middle of the century, sea travel has become one of the safest and most gracious ways of travel yet evolved.

A pity, then, that speed proved to be the one barrier reef upon which all the ocean liners of the world except one would founder. The *Queen Elizabeth II,* at a whopping premium and with an assurance that passengers only need to take their time across the North Atlantic in one direction and can wing themselves back by Concorde, still plies the sea-lanes between New York and Southampton. But that is it, at least for now.

Gone are the riotous midnight sailings of the 1920s, the heart-stopping thrill of immigrants and returning expatriates at seeing the Statue of Liberty rise up in a morning mist as the ship on which they sailed eased in on the early tide to New York Harbor; gone are pulse-slowing, leisurely ways to get from here to there.

And gone, too, are yearly compendiums of present-day disasters at sea. And that is just about the only positive effect of the demise of the once-bustling traffic of transatlantic and transpacific ocean liners.

The criterion for inclusion in this section was a purely mathematical one. Since most passenger ships carry upwards of 3,000 passengers, a cutoff figure of 100 deaths was employed (an exception is the 1956 sinking of the *Andria Doria,* which is included in this book despite a lower number of fatalities.) Sadly enough, there were more than enough maritime disasters that fit within that parameter.

As in other categories of man-made catastrophes, wartime sinkings were, with one exception, not recorded. The one exception, the torpedoing of the German transport *Wilhelm Gustloff* by an unidentified Soviet submarine in the waning years of World War II (see p. 222), is so monumental in its all-time record toll of human life that no book that pretends to be comprehensive could ignore it, despite the fact that, to this day, little more than the bare statistics are available.

• • • • • • • • • • • • • • •

ATLANTIC OCEAN

July 25, 1956

• • • • • • • • • • • • • • • •

The Andrea Doria *sank to the bottom of the Atlantic Ocean on July 25, 1956 after the SS* Stockholm *rammed it. Forty-three passengers, all aboard the* Andrea Doria, *died.*

The *Andrea Doria* was the pride of the Italian Line, a 29,083-ton floating marvel. Eleven decks high and 697 feet long, she was outfitted with no less than 31 public rooms, air conditioning and—a first for ocean liners—three outdoor pools. The first luxury ship built by Italy after World War II, she contained not only up-to-date appointments and safety features but also a hand-decorated interior that glowed with good taste and luxury. Apropos of the clientele it hoped to attract, the Italian Line assigned the *Andrea Doria,* with her captain, Piero Calamai, to the fashionable Genoa–New York run, which called at Cannes, Naples and Gibraltar. Her maiden voyage, on January 14, 1953, was a triumph, and from then until July 1956, she made 50 uneventful but memorable transatlantic crossings.

On July 17, 1956, the *Andrea Doria* departed from Genoa on her 51st transatlantic trip. By the time she cruised out of Gibraltar, she was carrying 190 first-class passengers, 267 cabin-class passengers, 677 tourist-class passengers and a crew of 572. Her hold contained 410 tons of freight, nine automobiles, 522 pieces of baggage and 1,754 bags of mail.

The crossing was smooth and festive. July at sea was easy, with none of the stormy weather of midwinter cross-

The stern of the* Andrea Doria *tips to starboard just before the ocean liner sinks beneath the surface of the Atlantic after its collision with the SS* Stockholm *on July 25, 1956. Library of Congress

ings. The only difficulty at this time of year was fog, which wrapped itself around the *Andrea Doria* when it approached the U.S. coast on July 25, its last full day before docking in New York in the early morning of the 26th. By 9 P.M. that evening, the ship was nearing Nantucket Light, and the visibility was virtually zero. The captain ordered the ship's speed lowered from 26 knots to 21. The two radar repeaters on the bridge whirred with green calmness. Anything significant, animate or inanimate, would show up on their screens.

Meanwhile, the small 12,644-ton Swedish-American liner *Stockholm*, which had left New York at 11:30 that morning, was cruising eastward at 18 knots, bound for Europe. It was in the same clinging, soupy fog that enveloped the *Andrea Doria* and bound for the same sea-lane.

At 10:40 P.M., the *Stockholm* appeared as a tiny green blip on the *Andrea Doria*'s radar screen. It drew steadily closer, headed for the *Andrea Doria*'s starboard side. But the other ship should be outfitted with radar, too, the officers on the bridge of the *Andrea Doria* assumed, and would turn to avoid a collision.

As fate would have it, the *Stockholm* had neither radar nor a senior officer on the bridge. Third Officer Ernst Johannsen-Carstens was manning the controls, alone.

Horrified, the captain and officers of the *Andrea Doria* watched their radar screen as the other ship continued to bear down on them. The captain ordered the fog horn to be sounded at 100-second intervals. Still the other ship came on, and at 11:45 P.M., it burst through the wall of fog, its lights blinding the *Andrea Doria*'s wheelhouse crew.

Captain Calamai ordered the *Andrea Doria* to turn hard to port, but the ship responded lazily, and by that time the collision was a certainty. With no pause whatsoever, the *Stockholm* plowed full force into the *Andrea Doria*'s starboard side, ripping an enormous, 30-foot-deep wound in her side. She was ripped open from her upper deck down to her double-bottom tanks. Pivoting as the *Andrea Doria* dragged her along, the *Stockholm* did further damage before her captain, H. Gunnar Nordenson, reached the wheelhouse and ordered a reversal of engines and a closing of the watertight doors.

As the *Stockholm* pulled away, thousands of tons of water rushed into the gash in the *Andrea Doria*'s side, and the ship began to list 18 degrees to starboard, which rendered all of her lifeboats on that side of the ship useless. Only eight lifeboats remained to handle the 1,706 people aboard.

The captain made a quick decision and chose not to issue an abandon-ship order. Panic, he reasoned, would be a bigger enemy than the sea at that moment. Instead, he radioed an immediate SOS to all ships in the area, and within minutes the French Liner *Ile de France*, the destroyer escort *Allen*, the freighter *Cape Ann*, the navy transport *Pvt. William H. Thomas* and the *Stockholm* all rushed to the aid of the stricken ship, which continued to list and take on water.

The *Ile de France*, with a suitable dramatic flourish, appeared with every light ablaze, and the passengers aboard the *Andrea Doria* gave her a healthy cheer of welcome.

The rescue operations went on all night. By 4:30 A.M., the *Andrea Doria* was completely abandoned. One thousand six hundred sixty-three persons had been rescued. Forty-three were killed in the collision, some as they slept in their starboard cabins. At 10:09 A.M., the proudest ship in the Italian Line slid beneath the surface of the Atlantic and settled to the bottom, some 225 feet below.

For several months, the ship lines battled in court, blaming each other for the catastrophe. In January 1957, just before the *Andrea Doria*'s engineering officers were to appear, both shippers agreed to settle out of court. The Italian Line feared that the revelation of the presence of a faulty watertight door would bring up lawsuits by its passengers.

As it turned out, the Italian Line had nothing to fear. Two and a half decades later, filmmaker and adventurer Peter Gimbel dove into the wreck of the *Andrea Doria* and salvaged its safe, which Gimbel opened on television in 1984. In later dives, he and his crew surveyed the point of impact from the *Stockholm*. It had hit at precisely the location of the supposedly faulty watertight door. There was nothing left of it. Functioning or not, the door obviously had not sent the *Andrea Doria* to the bottom. A hole in the bottom of the generator room revealed, according to Gimbel, "80 feet of her hull . . . open to the sea." Nothing could have kept the ship afloat after that.

ATLANTIC OCEAN

May 1, 1915

• • • • • • • • • • • • • • •

A torpedo from a German U-boat sank the Cunard liner Lusitania *on May 1, 1915 in the Atlantic Ocean off the coast of Ireland. One thousand one hundred ninety-eight drowned or were killed by the explosion.*

The transatlantic steamship companies vied with one another throughout the lush years of transatlantic ship travel to win the "Blue Riband" for having the fastest ship afloat. In the early years of the century, the "riband" floated back and forth between Germany, America and Great Britain. In 1903, the German Lloyd Lines possessed it, and it was then that the British Admiralty helped the Cunard Line to build two of the most luxurious and fastest liners afloat. In return, Cunard agreed to include fittings that would allow the ships to be taken over by the Admiralty and used as armed cruisers during wartime.

The first of the two ships was the *Lusitania,* which began its maiden voyage on September 7, 1907 from Liverpool. She was the largest ship afloat at the time and one of the most luxurious. And by the end of her second westbound voyage, on October 5, 1907, she was also the fastest. At an average speed of 23.99 knots, from Queenstown to Ambrose Light, she had clearly won the Blue Riband for England.

In November 1907, the *Lusitania*'s sister ship, the *Mauretania,* was launched, and proved to be the *Lusitania*'s only serious competition. The two passed the ribbon back and forth until 1909, when the *Mauretania* won it and kept it for the next 22 years.

In May 1913, as war drew closer in Europe, the *Lusitania* was secretly refitted. The number one boiler room was converted to a powder magazine, and a second magazine was carved out from part of the mail room. The shelter deck was adapted to accommodate four six-inch guns on either side. When war broke out, in September 1914, the *Lusitania* entered the Admiralty fleet as an armed auxiliary cruiser but continued to make the Liverpool—Queenstown–New York run on a monthly basis.

During the last few days of April, she was loaded, at New York, with 1,248 cases of three-inch shrapnel shells, 4,927 boxes of cartridges, 1,639 ingots of copper, 74 barrels of fuel oil and several tons of food supplies. She was obviously not setting out on an exclusively peaceful ocean crossing, and most of the 2,165 passengers were blissfully

The gigantic hole ripped in the hull of the* Lusitania *by a torpedo from a German U-boat on May 1, 1915. Illustrated London News

unaware of the lethal and dangerous cargo upon which they were sitting, sipping their bouillon.

The ship left New York at noon on May 1, 1915 with Captain William Thomas Turner on the bridge. It was her 101st crossing. All went well and serenely until May 6, when Captain Turner received bulletins from the Admiralty advising him of German submarine activity off the Irish coast. The captain ordered all of the lifeboats hanging on davits to be swung out and lowered to the promenade deck, doubled the watch on the bridge, bow and stern and blacked out all of the passenger portholes.

The cruiser *Juno* was supposed to escort the *Lusitania* from the vicinity of the Irish coast to home port, but for some unexplained reason, she was never ordered out.

On Friday afternoon, May 7, 1915, Kapitan-Leutnant Walter Schwieger gazed through the periscope of his submarine, *U-20,* and spotted the *Lusitania,* steaming straight ahead at a conservative 18 knots. At 2:10 P.M., the *U-20* fired one torpedo, which struck the *Lusitania* on its starboard side, squarely behind the ammunition-loaded number-one boiler room. Within seconds, there was a larger explosion as the ammunition cache ignited.

The *Lusitania* immediately began to list to starboard, rendering her lifeboats on that side useless. Passengers

A contemporary painting depicts survivors of the Lusitania **disaster floating in the North Atlantic. One thousand one hundred ninety-eight passengers aboard the luxury liner were either drowned or killed by the explosion.** Illustrated London News

scrambled to the usable lifeboats, but there were far too few to take the passengers off the fast-sinking ship. It only took 18 minutes for the *Lusitania* to go down off Old Head at Kinsale, Ireland. Out of 1,159 passengers and 702 crew members, only 374 passengers and 289 crew members survived. One thousand one hundred ninety-eight were either drowned or killed in the twin explosions.

Survivors sued Cunard for negligence, but on August 23, 1918 a court in New York exonerated the line, stating: "The cause of the *Lusitania* sinking was the illegal act of the Imperial German government, through its instrument, the submarine commander." By then, the *Lusitania* had become a rallying cry of indignation, particularly useful in convincing those in the United States not inclined to join the war in Europe that it was a necessity.

ATLANTIC OCEAN

September 8, 1934

• • • • • • • • • • • • • • • •

Negligence on the part of the crew and the ship line was responsible for the fire that eventually sank the Morro Castle *in the Atlantic Ocean on September 8, 1934. One hundred thirty-seven died.*

In the pre-Castro 1930s, the run between the casinos of Havana, Cuba and New York was a simple and short one, and the Ward Line provided two luxurious and fast ships to make the trip even more enjoyable: the *Morro Castle* and the *Oriente*. Launched in 1930, they plied the short route often enough for their crews and captains to grow careless.

On the *Morro Castle,* for instance, passengers never remembered a lifeboat drill. Captain Robert Wilmott ordered the removal of several fire hoses from the promenade deck because a woman had slipped on the water from a leaky hydrant and threatened to sue the company.

Ironically, the tragic fire that would consume the *Morro Castle* and kill 137 of its passengers would start on that very deck.

The early September 1934 voyage of the *Morro Castle* was an unusual one. On September 7, Captain Wilmott, a rotund and rollicking man who loved the socializing portion of his duties more than the naval ones, climbed into his bathtub to ready himself for dinner. He never climbed out. While bathing, he suffered a fatal heart attack.

This left the running of the ship to First Officer William Warms, a company man if there ever was one, as the events of that night would prove. Around midnight of the seventh, John Kempf, a fireman from Long Island, smelled smoke in the writing room, and stewardess Harriet Brown noticed that the linen locker, used to store stationery and winter blankets, was "intolerably hot."

But it would be 2:45 A.M. on the eighth before steward Daniel Campbell would finally pull open the linen closet door, see the flames and collect some crew members to battle the blaze. By the time an alert reached the bridge of the ship, the flames had eaten through thin wooden partitions into a ventilator shaft. From here, the fire spread quickly to other ventilating and elevator shafts. Fed by a 20-mile-an-hour wind against which the liner was plowing at a brisk 19.2 knots, the flames began to eat at the insulation of the electrical wiring, creating short circuits that crippled the phone and alarm system. Stewards walked through the corridors banging on pots and pans to waken the passengers.

But on the bridge, confusion had set in. Captain Warms reasoned that they were only half an hour from shore (they were off the coast of Asbury Park, New Jersey), and by the time they reached the Ambrose Channel, all would be in the hands of other fire fighters. But his optimism was ill timed. The fire was raging out of control now, and the passengers were gathering in the stern. The captain sent out no SOS but did attempt to steer the ship out of

The Morro Castle *burns out of control off the coast of New Jersey on September 8, 1934. Sweeping safety reforms for ships at sea resulted from this tragedy caused by careless crew members.* Library of Congress

the wind to prevent the flames from feeding into the staterooms. No sooner had he given the order to change course when everything aboard the *Morro Castle* went dead. The electric pumps stopped. The foghorn and the whistle became inoperable. The gyropilot and the steering gear refused to respond. Thus, the ship was dark and out of control, drifting in a flaming arc.

It was now 3:31 A.M., and 200 of the 316 passengers were huddled in the stern. No one officially connected with the ship had given them information or directions. Some passengers had brought their life preservers; some had not.

The crew was apparently busy saving itself. Seamen began by lowering boat number 10. Seven crew members and three women jumped into the boat, which had space for 48. The number-one boat was lowered. It loaded 29 crew members and two passengers. Number three contained 16 crew members and one passenger; number 11 hit the water with 16 crewmen and no passengers; number five with four crewmen and no passengers. And so it went. Six boats came ashore in New Jersey between 6 and 9 A.M. Their available space totaled 408; they carried 85 persons, most of them crew. Back on the ship, six other boats burned on their davits, as did seven balsa rafts.

Meanwhile, Captain Warms argued with his radiomen. Afraid that his company would have to pay salvage fees, he refused to send out an SOS. Finally, at 3:17, he gave permission to send out a "standby" signal. At 3:24, as the batteries in the emergency transmitter were going dead, the radioman took matters into his own hands and sent out the one and only SOS, 28 minutes after chaos had gotten the upper hand.

Receiving the signal, Coast Guard boats set out immediately from several stations in New Jersey, but the boats were dories, and they would take a long time to reach the stricken ship. Three nearby vessels, from seven to 20 miles away, caught the message and attempted to radio back, but by that time, the *Morro Castle*'s radio was dead.

By 5 A.M., passengers began to leap into the water. Some survived; most drowned. At dawn, the first Coast Guard dory arrived, and its five oarsmen hauled as many survivors aboard as they could. The *Monarch of Bermuda,* which was 20 miles away at the time of the call, arrived at 7:30 and launched four boats that picked up 71 survivors; the *Andrea S. Luckenbach* fished 21 out of the water; the *City of Savannah,* 65. John Bogan, the owner of the fishing smack *Paramount,* hauled 67 into his small boat and later told reporters, "It was the most horrible sight I ever saw. The water was full of dead."

Captain Warms and 14 men were taken aboard the cutter *Tampa.* In his first words to the captain he insisted that he would not be responsible for tow charges.

The maddening irresponsibility continued on shore. A Ward Line attorney met the crew and warned them against making any public statements. Later, in court, the company claimed the disaster was an act of God. When this defense was rejected by the court, they then tried to characterize it as a Communist plot to burn up the ship. No evidence of a plot was discovered, but plenty of evidence of malfeasance aboard the *Morro Castle* was revealed in court: No fire drills, watchmen who were too busy serving passengers to make their rounds and the improper storing of inflammable material were only some of the violations aboard the *Morro Castle.* Backed into a corner, Ward Line attorneys insisted that, despite the fact that 92 of the first 98 evacuees of the ship were crewmen, it was the vessel, and not Ward Line employees, that failed.

Finally, on February 26, 1937, the courts decreed that lawsuits amounting to $13,512,261.11 would be settled for $1,200,000.

Some good did come out of the *Morro Castle* disaster. Legislation forcing the United States to accept the International Convention for Safety of Life at Sea was passed by Congress. In addition, sweeping reforms were made in the entire U.S. merchant marine. Sprinkler systems were made mandatory throughout passenger ships, radio laws were modernized and the Federal Marine Inspection Service was enlarged.

ATLANTIC OCEAN

April 14, 1912

• • • • • • • • • • • • • • • • • • •

Overconfidence in design and a collision with an iceberg caused the sinking of the "unsinkable" Titanic *on April 14, 1912. One thousand five hundred seventeen died.*

A virtually unsinkable ship.

The *Titanic,* announced the British White Star Line, would not only be the most luxurious liner afloat. Its individual watertight compartments would also make it virtually impossible for the new and giant liner to sink at sea. The company of course knew that if more than five of the watertight compartments were breached at once, the *Titanic* would sink. But the odds against that were astronomical, and so the maiden voyage of this truly titanic liner—882.5 feet long, 92.5 feet broad and 104 feet high, capable of a cruising speed of 30 knots, with crystal chandeliers and sweeping staircases, inlaid wood in first class, a special lounge for the servants of the wealthy and the most up-to-date marine machinery available—was perfection at sea. However there were not enough lifeboats.

A contemporary newspaper illustration captures survivors in lifeboats and the* Titanic *poised before its final plunge to the bottom of the North Atlantic on the night of April 14, 1912. Daily Sphere

That was only one of many human failings that caused the terrible tragedy of the sinking of the *Titanic,* which has been recounted over and over in books and on film. Its last hours were packed with enough foolishness, bravery and cowardice to fill at least half a shelf of adventure novels. And the lessons learned from them would make transatlantic travel considerably safer for future voyagers.

The *Titanic* was sister ship to the *Olympic,* built in the same Irish shipyard and launched shortly after its sibling. The *Olympic* had been in service for almost a year when the *Titanic* made ready for its maiden voyage on April 10, 1912. Its itinerary: Southampton to Cherbourg to Queenstown to New York. Its complement after leaving Queenstown: 322 passengers in first class, 277 in second class, 709 in third class and a crew of 898. Total: 2,206. Its lifeboat capacity: 20 lifeboats with a total capacity of *1,178.*

The passenger list was democratic enough: Third class contained immigrants; second class contained the middle class; and the first-class list was packed with the world famous and the wealthy, including John Jacob Astor, Isador Straus and Benjamin Guggenheim.

The beau monde was eager to try new inventions, such as the radio. Thus, on Sunday, April 14, as the *Titanic* was nearing the end of its silken smooth and memorable maiden voyage, the radio room aboard the *Titanic* was flooded with personal messages to be forwarded to Cape Race and on to America. John Phillips, the wireless operator, was inundated with them, so much so that he grew careless about the repeated warnings sent by ships in the area about the presence of icebergs.

It had been a warm winter, and an unusual number of icebergs had broken off the polar cap and were floating southward. Still, the White Star Line had charted a course for the *Titanic* that they felt would carry it safely away from the ice and its dangers. At noon, Phillips received a message from the *Baltic.* "Have had moderate variable winds and clear fine weather since leaving," it read. "Greek steamer *Athenai* reports passing icebergs and large quantities of field ice today in Latitude 41.51 degrees north, Longitude 49.52 degrees west."

In the first in a string of stupidities, the message was passed, not to the bridge, but to White Star president Bruce Ismay, who was aboard for this celebratory voyage. He showed it around to the ladies in the first-class lounge but then stuffed it into his pocket and forgot it until 7:15 that evening, when he finally delivered it to the chart-room.

More messages poured into the radio room from the passengers, and these missives took precedence over two receptions from two other ships, either one of which might have saved the *Titanic.* At 7:30, the freighter *Californian* radioed the *Antillian,* reporting three large icebergs. At 9:30, the *Meshaba* contacted the *Titanic* directly, warning that "much heavy pack ice and a great number of large icebergs" lay ahead. Neither of these messages was delivered to the bridge.

At 11 P.M. the *Titanic* received one last warning. Just before he shut down his radio for the night, the radioman aboard the *Californian* directly contacted the *Titanic* to announce that the *Californian* was totally hemmed in by ice and had stopped engines. It was close enough to the *Titanic* to see its lights. Radioman John Phillips, his patience worn to a nub by the mountain of transmissions he had made that day, snapped back, "Shut up, shut up, I am busy!"—thus sealing the fate of the *Titanic* and the 2,000 aboard.

Meanwhile, Captain Edward Smith, denied the information he should have been receiving, was working on the instinct that had made him an experienced and respected captain. Sensing the sharp drop in temperature, he posted six lookouts to watch for ice and kept the speed at a steady 22.5 knots. First Officer William Murdock also kept sharp eyes out for ice.

At 11:40 P.M., lookout Frederick Fleet yelled out, "Iceberg! Right ahead!"

Murdock snapped out the order to Quartermaster Hitchens, "Turn the wheel hard-a-starboard!" Then he yanked the engine-room telegraph to full speed astern and pushed the button closing all of the watertight doors.

Silent seconds passed. Nothing occurred. And then a telltale shudder ran through the ship, sending it trembling from bow to stern. The ship had missed colliding directly with the iceberg. But an underwater knifelike edge of ice had struck the *Titanic*'s steel plates on her starboard side, and sliced a gash beneath the water line long enough to flood the first six compartments, which included the number-five and number-six boiler rooms.

Passengers in third class felt the collision, knew what had happened and panicked. Those in second class were moderately alarmed. Some were amused. Some who had left their portholes open found chunks of ice on their bunks. In first class, the passengers still up and about merely watched the iceberg glide by and went back to playing cards.

Captain Smith, conferring with Thomas Andrews, the designer of the *Titanic,* immediately knew the worst had happened. The ship could have stayed afloat if up to four of her watertight compartments flooded. But with *six* flooded and filling, there was no hope. She would definitely sink.

At 11:50, Captain Smith ordered radioman Phillips to send out the CQD international call for help. Second operator Bride suggested to Phillips that he also tap out the new SOS signal. Phillips did, and the *Titanic* became the first vessel in distress to use the new code.

The North German Lloyd steamer *Frankfurt* answered first. Shortly after this, the Cunard Liner, *Carpathia,* some 58 miles away, received the distress call and immediately changed course, stoking her boilers to the bursting point and disregarding her own safety by steaming full speed toward the ailing *Titanic.* It would be the *Carpathia* that would rescue most of the survivors.

Meanwhile, the icy Atlantic was pouring into the *Titanic* at frightening speed. In the first 10 minutes, the water rose 14 feet above the keel.

At 12:10, Captain Smith ordered the lifeboats to be uncovered and women and children to be placed in them first. There had been no lifeboat drill; no instruction in donning life jackets had been given. The passengers were bewildered. But only the top officers and Bruce Ismay knew the worse truth: There were 1,028 fewer spaces in the lifeboats than there were people aboard. The outlook was catastrophic. Before the night was out, more than half the persons climbing toward what they fully expected would be rescued would be dead.

Fifth Officer Harold Lowe was in charge of guiding passengers onto lifeboats, and by all accounts, he was unable to maintain the kind of even-handed calmness necessary to bring about an orderly and efficient evacuation. The first lifeboat, number 14, was launched with 55 people aboard. But it would be one of the fuller boats. Number one carried only 12 people—Sir Cosmo and Lady Duff

Gordon, her secretary, two Americans, six stokers and Symons, one of the lookout men. And so it went, with an average of 40 people per lifeboat that should have carried 65.

The first-class passengers, first at the lifeboats, were treated with preference. Only four of the women in first class died, three of them by choice when they refused to leave their husbands. Of the 93 women in second class, 15 survived; out of 179 women in third class, only 81 were saved. In fact, at one point, the doors between the third-class section and the upper-class sections were locked. Eventually, the rioting third-class passengers broke through.

There was an almost eerie calmness about the way some passengers met their deaths. Mr. and Mrs. Isador Straus, two millionaires, sat side by side as the ship went down; John Jacob Astor saw his wife safely into a lifeboat and then settled into a chair in the sumptuous first-class lounge to face his fate; Benjamin Guggenheim and his valet went to their cabins, donned evening dress and sat in splendor as they awaited the inevitable.

Only after the last first-class woman was in a boat were the third-class passengers allowed onto the boat deck. Some leaped from escape ladders into the water. Others milled about without direction.

Meanwhile, down below, last, frantic efforts were being made to pump out two of the watertight compartments. They failed, and shortly after midnight, the captain ordered the crew to abandon ship. The last lifeboat, a collapsible one, carried four crewmen and 45 passengers, including White Star president Ismay, who leaped into the boat at the last minute, despite the fact that there were still women and children who had not been taken into the lifeboats.

One thousand five hundred seven passengers were still aboard the ship, and some of them now leaped into the frigid water. Captain Smith had ordered distress rockets to be launched into the sky, and the *Californian*, a mere 20 miles away, saw them and did nothing. Its captain thought they were celebratory.

Chaos continued on the ship and in the sea. Most of the half-empty lifeboats did nothing to rescue those who were struggling, drowning, and freezing in the water. In lifeboat number five, the women refused to allow the officer to search for survivors, despite the fact that they were in the midst of them. In lifeboat number six, just the opposite occurred; women pleaded with crewmen to try to rescue survivors in the water, but the crewmen rowed stoically away from the *Titanic*. Only Fifth Officer Lowe apparently made a concerted effort to rescue the drowning swimmers. He tied his lifeboat to three others and a collapsible craft and circled around to pick up whomever he could. But he was one of the last to leave the ship, and he only plucked four survivors from the icy Atlantic. Only 13 were pulled out of the water by 18 partially loaded lifeboats.

At 2:20 A.M., the *Titanic* began her final dive. The boilers exploded and, loosed from their anchoring supports, rushed forward. With the sound, according to one survivor, of a long freight train leaving the tracks, the huge, unsinkable ship pointed her bow toward the bottom, rose almost perpendicular to the surface of the black water around her and slid beneath the surface. Her decks were full of passengers; her band, who had tried to maintain calm by playing ragtime tunes during the evacuation, struck up the Episcopal hymn "Autumn"; Captain Smith, who had decided to retire from the sea after this voyage, remained on the bridge and went down with his ship.

A whirling vortex was created, drowning some of the swimming survivors. The rest, who would live, pulled on the oars of their lifeboats, away from the spot where the *Titanic* once sailed.

Within an hour, the *Carpathia*, with all of her lights ablaze, arrived on the scene. Between 4:45 and 8:30, she rescued 705 survivors from the lifeboats. There were no survivors left alive in the sea.

At 5:40 A.M., the radio operator aboard the *Californian* opened his radio channels and learned, to his horror, what had happened less than 20 miles away.

Bruce Ismay, who had locked himself up in the doctor's cabin as soon as he had been brought aboard the *Carpathia*, was later exonerated by the British board of inquiry, although he was severely chastised by the American one. The blame for the *Titanic*'s sinking was placed on the captain and his senior officers for failure to take notice of the four ice warnings that had been received. None of them could answer the charges; all had gone down with the ship.

The captain of the *Californian* was also blamed for not going to the aid of the *Titanic*, even though the radio was, as was the custom in 1912, shut down for the night when the distress calls went out.

The horrific tragedy did produce some positive safety measures for future transatlantic passengers. The required number of lifeboats was revised to accommodate the maximum—rather than the minimum —number of passengers aboard. Boat drill became mandatory. And most important, international regulations requiring radios to remain open and functioning 24 hours a day were instituted, so that cataclysms like that of the *Titanic* could never occur again.

The story of the *Titanic* did not end with the official inquiry. Full of irony, cowardice, bravery and noble self-sacrifice, it became not only the model for seagoing adventure stories for decades to come but also the object of speculation for adventurers. On September 1, 1985, a team of American and French researchers, jointly sponsored by the American Woods Hole Oceanographic Institute and the French Institute for Research and Exploitation of the Sea, finally reached the wreck of the *Titanic,* 73 years after it plunged 13,000 feet to the bottom of the North Atlantic. Murky television and still pictures revealed a ravaged but impressive hulk. Eleven more dives in 1986, in the submersible *Alvin,* revealed that the *Titanic* had split in two on its way to the bottom. Both pieces of the ship were standing upright on the ocean bottom, with the 300-foot bow section embedded in 50 feet of mud some 1,800 feet away from the stern, and both of them in such total darkness that hardly any marine life lived on or near them.

Even now, intrigue and controversy swirl around the *Titanic.* Talk of salvage has arisen on one side of opinion. Relatives of those who perished argue that the wreck is really a gigantic tomb, the final resting place of 1,517 people, and should remain undisturbed.

The oceanographers have refused to reveal the exact location of the wreck, lest fortune hunters try to rob the ship of the staggering wealth that supposedly sank with it. And so, the *Titanic* continues to generate its own unique and legendary aura, a mysterious, glamorous source of stories and speculation.

BALTIC SEA

January 30, 1945

• • • • • • • • • • • • • • • • • •

The most tragic and underreported maritime disaster in history occurred on January 30, 1945 when an unidentified Soviet submarine torpedoed the Wilhelm Gustloff, *loaded with refugees, in the Baltic Sea. Five thousand three hundred forty-eight people died—some records say 7,200.*

Inexplicably, the worst, most tragic maritime disaster of all time, one that may have killed nearly five times the number of those drowned in the *Titanic* tragedy and more than the sinking of the entire English and Spanish armadas in the 16th century, has gone virtually unrecorded. Missing from all but a few histories of World War II, it is given a glancing reference every now and then in stories of other, lesser sinkings. It took place during World War II, but even exhaustive studies of naval warfare of that period fail to mention it. It is almost as if the world has drawn a curtain of shame around this, possibly the most tragic of all disasters that ever occurred at sea.

The *Wilhelm Gustloff* was a passenger liner that belonged to Germany's Labor Front. Named after Wilhelm Gustloff, the Swiss official of the Nazi Party who was murdered on February 2, 1936, it was launched on July 25, 1937. An imposing ship, weighing 25,484 tons, it was 695 feet long and 78 feet wide, had 10 decks and accommodated 1,465 passengers and a crew of 417.

Before it could be put into service as a passenger liner, the *Wilhelm Gustloff* was absorbed by the navy of the Third Reich and did not sail on its maiden voyage until March 23, 1938. Fitted out as a hospital ship and troop carrier, it was berthed in Gotenhafen, in the north of Germany, on the Baltic Sea.

By 1945, as World War II was drawing to a close, the sea war between Germany and the Allies was largely over. The Soviet fleet had not been particularly effective. Its main force, bottled up in the Gulf of Finland by the German Navy, did manage, nevertheless, to delay the Nazi advance through Poland and the eastern USSR. In the Baltic Sea it launched raids on small surface vessels and aircraft, mosquito fleets of motor-torpedo boats and other light craft and some submarines.

By late January 1945, the *Wilhelm Gustloff* had been repeatedly bombed and repaired and pressed back into service.

At 7 P.M. on January 30, 1945, she left the harbor of Gdynia, Poland, a few miles north of Danzig (now Gdansk). Jammed on all 10 of its decks, including the open ones, were German military personnel, technicians, female merchant sailors and an enormous number of civilian refugees trying to escape the advance of the Russian troops toward Danzig.

She must have rested extremely low in the frigid January water. Various reports said that she had up to 10,000 passengers and crew aboard. The official German estimate, reported in *Das Groose Lexicon Des Zweiten Welterkriegs,* was 6,600—which seems more plausible, considering that she was originally designed to carry a total of 1,882, including crew.

It was a bitterly cold night; one can only imagine the monumental discomfort of those crammed on the open deck. Their only comfort was the knowledge that the voyage was to be a short one, to Kiel-Flensburg, on the sheltered peninsula of Germany that juts up and almost joins Denmark.

Two hours from Gdynia, barely into the Baltic, and off Stolpmunde, the *Wilhelm Gustloff* was torpedoed by an unidentified Soviet submarine. At precisely 9:08, she received the full force of the submarine's torpedoes. There was no hope for most of the passengers. One thousand two hundred fifty-two of them did manage to find spaces in lifeboats and rafts (some accounts, broadcast by Finnish radio, said that only 900 did), and these survived.

But the crammed decks and compartments of the hapless ship were jammed with far more people than there were spaces in the lifeboats. The ship sank swiftly. The temperature at the time was −18 degrees centigrade, or slightly less than 0 degrees Fahrenheit.

According to German historians 5,348 (or 7,700 according to other historical sources) passengers were left stranded on its ice-encrusted deck, without a means of escape. They perished instantly and passed into a black abyss of almost totally unrecorded history.

BAY OF GIBRALTAR

March 17, 1891

• • • • • • • • • • • • • • • • •

A storm-caused collision with the British battleship Amson *caused the sinking of the steamer* Utopia *on March 17, 1891 in the Bay of Gibraltar. Five hundred seventy-six passengers and crew died.*

The British steamer *Utopia* of the Anchor Line was a sturdy enough steamer. It had made numerous transatlantic crossings before picking up a full complement of some 800 Italian immigrants bound for America on March 16, 1891.

By the next day, the ship had stopped for supplies at Gibraltar, and was ready to clear the harbor. A raging gale had blown up the night before, and there were various advisories cautioning ships to remain in port. But the *Utopia* ignored them, and chose instead to try for the open sea.

It never made it out of the harbor at Gibraltar. Caught in the violent sea and winds, it was slammed into the iron-plated bow of the British battleship *Amson.* It might as well have had a hole blown in its side. Within minutes, the enormous swells raised by the storm poured thunderously into the *Utopia,* and she began to sink.

Panicked, some of the immigrants leaped overboard into the stormy sea. They drowned immediately. But even those who remained on board the ship, or took to lifeboats, were not assured of safety. Although six ships, including the *Rodney,* the *Amson,* the *Immortalite* and the *Freya* rushed to the rescue, 576 people—half crew and half passengers—died, either from drowning or exposure to the stormy waters.

CANADA
NOVA SCOTIA
HALIFAX

April 1, 1873

• • • • • • • • • • • • • • • • •

A huge storm, shortage of fuel and a foundering on reefs converged to cause the sinking of the liner Atlantic *near Halifax, Nova Scotia on April 1, 1873. Five hundred sixty died.*

"To think that while hundreds of men were saved, every woman should have perished. It's horrible. If I'd been able

The steamer* Utopia *after its collision with the British battleship* Amson *in the Bay of Gibraltar on March 17, 1891. Five hundred seventy-six passengers and crew died in the tragedy. Illustrated London News

to save just one I could bear the disaster, but to lose every woman on board, it's too terrible, it's too terrible."

These were the words of Captain John A. Williams, the severely chastened commander of the luxurious steam-and-sail liner *Atlantic,* as he appeared before a Canadian board of inquiry in April 1873. His ship had gone down off Halifax, Nova Scotia, partially because of the weather, mostly because of his lack of judgment and attention. That not one woman survived, and that only one child—pulled by his hair through a porthole by an alert crewman—could not be blamed upon the captain. That was the fault of one of the largest cases of mass cowardice in recorded history.

The *Atlantic* was a modern ship by 1870s standards. Four hundred thirty-five feet long, with a displaceable tonnage of 3,607, she was powered not only by a full complement of sails but by four 150-horsepower engines. She was a heavy ship, with three eight-foot iron decks, a hold filled with tons of coal, luxurious appointments and a capacity of 1,200 passengers and crew. In late March 1873, a mere two years old, she set sail from Queenstown, England bound for New York with a load of 975 passengers and crew. The passengers were mostly aristocratic; the captain was an experienced sailor who depended more on his instincts than on charts and who, as with many sea captains of the time, had little experience with steam engines.

The first four days out from Queenstown were balmy and tranquil ones. But from then on, the North Atlantic was whipped to a deadly froth by high winds. Turbulent seas forced the captain to reduce speed to a snail's crawl of three knots, and this, plus the power needed to stay on course in heavy seas, burned an enormous amount of coal. When the ship was 1,100 miles from port in New York, the captain was informed that only 419 tons of coal were

A Currier and Ives lithograph captures the* Atlantic *foundering on a reef near Halifax, Nova Scotia on April 1, 1873. New York Public Library

left. He remained unruffled. He was used to relying on sail for power, and if they ran out of coal, he assumed that they could always use that.

But the storm stubbornly persisted, and when the coal supply dwindled to an inadequate 100 tons, they were still 460 miles from New York, and the winds were far too strong and capricious to be employed. Captain Williams decided to divert to Halifax, Nova Scotia to resupply the ship with enough coal to get it to New York. However, Captain Williams had never been to Nova Scotia, and he failed to consult the charts that would have revealed the extreme hazards in getting there.

At 11:50 P.M. on April 1, 1873, he sited a red light. Thinking it was the Sambro Light, poised at the entrance of Halifax Harbor, he turned his ship over to Third Officer Cornelius Brady and went to bed.

Third Mate Brady knew no more about the dangers of Nova Scotia than did Captain Williams. The red light was not Sambro Light at all. It was Peggy's Point Light, meant to warn ships away from the razor-sharp reefs that surrounded it.

So, as the Captain retired, the ship was put on a course directly for the reefs of Peggy's Point—a mistake that would never have been made had either officer consulted the charts that were on the ship's bridge.

At 3:00 A.M., a lookout saw the telltale signs: Waves were breaking on rocks ahead of them—dead ahead. The lookout sang out, the captain rolled out of his bunk and the *Atlantic* crashed headlong into a string of reefs that ripped her open from bow to stern. Three hundred passengers on the lower decks were drowned immediately in their bunks.

Those on the upper levels, awakened by the impact, ran out onto the decks. It was a frigid night, with blasts of cold air from the Arctic freezing even the salt spray on the ship's halyards and decks. The men, in an inexplicably universal display of pusillanimity, abandoned their wives and children and climbed the rigging, hoping to escape the waves that were already washing over the deck, transporting some who were there into the freezing water.

Once awakened, Captain Williams acted quickly. He ordered a line rigged between the foundered ship and the shore, and the crew began to transport passengers by rope to the snow-covered beach.

But then, an inexplicable circumstance began to unfold. It could not have been lost on Captain Williams or his crew that the only people they were transporting were men and that by the time they were through every last woman and child had either drowned or frozen to death. One small boy, John Henly, was grabbed by his hair by Richard Reynolds, a crew member, but that would be the only child to survive. Four hundred fifteen men, including 60 crew members and Captain Williams, made it safely to shore and survived.

The captain was relieved of his command by his employer, the British White Star Line, and would pass into obscurity after his ignominious failure in the face of a disaster he himself had at least partially caused.

CANADA
NOVA SCOTIA
SABLE ISLAND

July 4, 1898

• • • • • • • • • • • • • • • • •

Collision in a heavy fog with the British steel bark Cromartyshire *off Sable Island, Nova Scotia on July 4, 1898 sent the French liner* La Bourgogne *to the bottom of the North Atlantic. Five hundred sixty died.*

In 1896, Guglielmo Marconi invented the wireless. By 1904, it had replaced flags by day, lights by night, and horns in fog as the principal means of communication between ships at sea. Thus, those 560 passengers and crew who needlessly died aboard the French liner *La Bourgogne* on Independence Day, 1898 missed, by six years, a safety device that might have prevented the horrendous collision, in a heavy fog, that sent them and their ship to the bottom of the icy waters off Nova Scotia.

On July 3, 1898, a day out of New York on the way to Le Havre, a dense fog settled over the *Bourgogne.* Captain Jean-Paul Deloncle did not order a reduction in speed at all. It was his job to arrive in Le Havre on time, and he was determined to adhere to the schedule. Oswald Kirkner, a passenger, later told London reporters: "Few of the passengers had crossed the Atlantic more than once, but even as amateurs most of us realized we were moving too fast. By midmorning on July 3, visibility had dropped to forty yards. Still, there were no indications that our captain intended to reduce speed."

Not only was the ship moving too fast for safety under the weather conditions, but she was also far off course—some 150 miles north of her assigned route and dangerously near Sable Island, an exposed sandbar one mile wide and 20 miles long. The cause of more than 200 wrecks, it was called "the graveyard of the Atlantic."

Meanwhile, the British steel bark *Cromartyshire,* operating under sail, was groping its way through the fog at a comfortable four knots, sounding its foghorn every minute. It would be the wife of the *Cromartyshire*'s captain who would first hear the horn on the *Bourgogne.* She warned her husband, who alerted the first mate. But it was already too late. As Mrs. Henderson, the wife of the *Cromarty-*

Lifeboats from the French liner* La Bourgogne *go over the side after its collision, in a heavy fog, with the British steel bark* Cromatyshire *off Sable Island on July 4, 1898. The bark limped home; the liner sank, drowning 560. Illustrated London News

shire's captain, later told a board of inquiry: "Suddenly, the huge hull of an ocean greyhound loomed up in the mist going at least seventeen knots. Our signal system was hopelessly inadequate. Almost as soon as I caught the first glimpse of the big ship there was a fearful crash . . ."

The sailing ship was relatively undamaged. But its bowsprit had ripped open a huge hole in the side of the liner, smashing in the starboard boiler hold and engine room. It was 5:10 in the morning, and the *Bourgogne* was sinking and listing to starboard, which made the launching of her port boats impossible.

Still, had the following deplorable events not occurred, most of the passengers might have been saved. The *Cromartyshire* was nearby and ready to take survivors aboard.

Instead, panic and cowardice on the part of the crew of the *Bourgogne* turned the collision into a catastrophe. No attempt was made to effect an orderly evacuation. Instead, crew members commandeered the functioning lifeboats, beating off hysterical passengers, killing some and drowning others.

Charles Duttwellers, a survivor who had been beaten away from a crew-occupied lifeboat, was finally plucked from the water by a small boat from the *Cromartyshire*. He later told reporters, "I saw women shoved away from boats with oars and boathooks. Members of the crew assaulted many passengers with any implement that came handy. If no instrument was to be had they punched the men and women helpless in the water with their fists."

Dozens of other survivors told similar stories. John Burgi managed to battle his way into a lifeboat and place his aged mother into the boat. "Sailors fighting for their own lives threw my poor old mother into a watery grave," he later told reporters. "They threw me out of the boat five times. Then they beat me with oars and shoved me under the boat. I managed to stay afloat for nine hours and was finally rescued by a party from the vessel that had rammed the liner."

Captain Deloncle and all of his senior officers went down with the ship. But out of 300 women, only one—Mrs. A. D. Lacasse of Plainfield, New Jersey—survived. And out of the 165 survivors of the collision, 100 were crew members. Five hundred and sixty others drowned that awful night.

August Pongi, one of the survivors, summed it up succinctly. "From beginning to end," he told the board of inquiry, "the whole business was a lasting disgrace to the French merchant marine."

CANADA
NOVA SCOTIA
WINGO SOUND

December 24, 1811

• •

Heavy storms off the Baltic station in Wingo Sound caused the sinking of the British warships St. George *and* Defence *on December 24, 1811. Two thousand died.*

The Christmas Eve sinking of the British warships *St. George* and *Defence* was probably inevitable, given the weather conditions. Storms had kept them in port, along with a small flotilla of other British warships, at the Baltic station from early November, their assigned sailing date, until December 17, 1811.

Even then, the break in the weather was only comparative, and from there until they approached Wingo Sound, they encountered a series of steadily escalating storms.

On December 24, the worst of the storms hit. It was of hurricane intensity, with ice-laden winds of nearly 100 miles per hour. The flotilla was devastated and scattered, and its two lead ships, the *St. George* and *Defence,* devoid of masts and sails, were sent to the bottom with all but 14 of their men. These managed to get off in a small boat to shore, but more than 2,000 others, on board and below decks on the two ships, went down in a blizzard that made it difficult to distinguish between sky and sea.

When, weeks later, parts of the hulls of the two ships broke loose from either mud or the rest of the ship and floated to the surface, a grisly sight greeted those who flocked to the location of the wreck. There, laid out as if they had been placed there, were 500 bodies, including that of the commanding officer, Admiral Reynolds.

CANADA
QUEBEC
ST. LAWRENCE RIVER

May 29, 1914

• • • • • • • • • • • • • • • • • •

The collision in a fog with the Norwegian collier Storstad *sank the* Empress of Ireland *in the St. Lawrence River on May 29, 1914. One thousand twenty-seven died.*

The *Empress of Ireland* and her sister ship *Empress of Britain* were the two fastest ships on the Liverpool-Quebec run when they were commissioned in 1906. Not a particularly luxurious liner, the *Empress of Ireland* was an efficient, comfortable ship that accumulated an unspectacular but safe record of crossings between its commissioning and May 28, 1914, the beginning of its last voyage.

Under the command of Captain Edward Kendall, the *Empress of Ireland* left Quebec at 4:30 P.M. on Thursday, May 28, 1914 with 1,057 passengers and 420 crew members. By approximately 1:30 A.M. on May 29, as its passengers slept, it had reached Father Point, on the St. Lawrence River, and dropped off its pilot.

It was a calm night, and the *Empress* left the pilot station headed for the open sea. Approximately eight miles away, the Norwegian collier *Storstad,* loaded with 11,000 tons of Nova Scotia coal, was making its slow way toward the *Empress.* First Mate Alfred Toftenes of the *Storstad* reckoned that the two ships would pass at a safe distance.

Suddenly a thick fog bank drifted from the land onto the river. Within minutes, it had enveloped both ships, making them invisible to each other. Still, there was no cause for alarm. If each kept on her appointed course, nothing would happen.

Captain Kendall decided to take no chances. He ordered his ship to go full speed astern, which stopped it dead in the water. Meanwhile, Captain Thomas Anderson of the *Storstad,* who had been informed by Toftenes that it was "hazy," slowed his ship but did not stop. Instead, he exchanged blasts of the whistle with the *Empress* and pressed on. It was the first of two errors in judgment that would, in a very few minutes, climax in catastrophe.

Both captains strained to see in the darkness and chowder-thick fog. They could see nothing until it was too late. Abruptly, the *Storstad* broke through the fog. Her course was heading her straight for the *Empress,* and within seconds her bow collided with the liner squarely amidships. Coated with ice, the steel bow sliced through the steel plates of the *Empress* as if she were a piece of cake. Captain Kendall ordered his engines full speed ahead in an effort to beach his ship, but the engines failed to respond.

And now, Captain Anderson, on the *Storstad,* made his second error in judgment. Instead of ordering his engines to reverse, he kept on moving ahead, plowing further into the *Empress,* crushing passengers and crewmen in their bunks and forcing the *Empress* to keel over, which drowned passengers and rendered half of her lifeboats unlaunchable.

Later, in the inquiry, Captain Anderson stated that his mysterious actions were intended to keep the hole he had created watertight by "holding [the *Storstad*'s] bow against the side of the *Empress,* and thus preventing the entrance of water into the vessel."

It of course did not. Just the opposite occurred. Tons of water roared into the *Empress,* and she sank in 14 minutes. Miraculously, 217 passengers and 248 crew members managed to clamber to safety. But 1,027 others drowned or were killed by the invading bow of the *Storstad.* It was, at that time, the greatest passenger toll in maritime history during peacetime.

The board of inquiry placed the blame squarely on Captain Anderson's shoulders. But Captain Kendall was not blameless. Canadian Pacific rules stated that in the event of fog or snow on the St. Lawrence, hands were to be stationed at the watertight doors, ready to close them. Captain Kendall ordered no such precautions to be taken when he sighted the fog, and the fact that all of the watertight doors were open during and after the collision accounted, at least in part, for the rapid sinking of the *Empress of Ireland* and the staggering loss of life.

CAPE OF GOOD HOPE

1586

• • • • • • • • • • • • • • • • • •

A combination of reckless sailing and cowardice combined to sink the Portuguese sailing ship St. James *off the Cape of Good Hope in 1586. Four hundred fifty died.*

There are two important pieces missing from the story of the wreck of the Portuguese sailing vessel *St. James.* Lost in the interstices of time, the name of its captain and the details of the final rescue of 60 survivors of the ship seem available nowhere, thus preventing the tale from being well made. Nevertheless, the story is bizarre enough to be recounted.

The captain of the *St. James* was noted as a heavy wine drinker and a reckless man at the wheel of a sailing ship. His philosophy was to use full sail at all times and leave the rest to fate.

Sometime in the spring of 1586, he was sailing his ship the *St. James,* with his usual reckless abandon, through the Cape of Good Hope. Passengers and crew alike both counseled and begged the captain to use some common sense. The ship was running before a heavy wind; darkness had descended, and they were nearing Madagascar, with its seafront pockmarked with reefs.

The captain apparently turned a deaf ear and near midnight ran his ship and its passengers onto a reef. The ship held stubbornly fast and began to break up. It was obvious that she was going nowhere but to the bottom of the sea. Passengers panicked and scrambled for the lifeboats, which were in woeful disrepair.

The captain knew which lifeboat was seaworthy, and he gathered Admiral Fernando Mendoza, who happened to be aboard, and a few crewmen. Elbowing women and children out of the way, they leaped into the one and only launchable lifeboat. As they sailed away from the shrieking passengers, this abominable group yelled back assurances that they would send help from shore, which was fifty miles away. Neither they nor anyone else would return to the stricken ship with its approximately 500 passengers.

A small group of determined survivors finally managed to repair a damaged lifeboat and launch it. But it was fearfully overcrowded and rode low in the water. Frantic passengers dove over the side of the ship and swam after the foundering boat. Those on board used knives, hatchets and sabers to fend off the drowning and desperate others who tried to save themselves.

The lifeboat was still overloaded, however, and those aboard appointed a Portuguese nobleman as executioner. With highborn calm, he silently pointed at those who seemed too weak to pull their share of the oars. The condemned were tossed overboard by the rest.

After 20 days of this, the now comfortably loaded lifeboat came ashore on the east coast of Africa. Reaching a village near the beach, they came upon the cowardly captain and his party of survivors. The natives of the village were hostile, captured all of the outcasts from the *St. James,* tortured some, killed others and turned the rest free.

The captain and the admiral were among those freed, and they reached Mozambique safely. The captain, absolved of any negligence—possibly because of the friendly testimony of Admiral Mendoza—was given another ship to command, which he managed, several years later, to wreck in much the same way. But this time the captain died in the disaster.

Sixty people survived the wreck of the *St. James,* but the details of which people they were, whether they were taken off the wreck of the ship or whether they were solely the lifeboat sailors who were released by the hostile natives, is unclear. What is known is that 450 perished, and certainly most of them on the *St. James,* which had been first wrecked and then abandoned by its captain.

CARIBBEAN SEA
NEAR VERACRUZ, MEXICO

August 10, 1591

• • • • • • • • • • • • • • • •

A major hurricane sank the Spanish grand fleet in the Caribbean Sea near Veracruz on August 10, 1591. Five hundred died.

Cuba, discovered by Columbus in 1492, was conquered by Spain in 1511, and under the leadership of Diego de Velazquez, it became both a major staging area for Spanish exploration of the Americas and an assembly point for the treasure ships carrying looted plunder back to Spain. Loaded with tons of gold and silver, these galleons were the target of choice of pirates and brigands, who laid in wait just over the local curve of the horizon as the Spanish ships left Havana Harbor.

Thus, by the late 1500s, Spain took to combining its treasure ship crossings into one grand, annual transatlantic run. A flotilla of ships, called the Grand Fleet, would manage the yearly trip relatively unscathed by pirates.

There was one hazard that no kind of convoy could avoid, however, and that was the weather. In 1591, four major hurricanes roared through the Caribbean, and one of them coincided precisely with the annual sailing, from Havana, of the Grand Fleet. Caught in the middle of the storm, the fleet was buffeted and battered cruelly by enormous swells and mast-splitting winds. A dozen vessels with 500 Spanish sailors and soldiers and an untold tonnage of treasure were sent to the bottom of the sea in one afternoon, and it was a sorry-looking remainder of the Grand Fleet that limped back to Havana Harbor for repairs.

The late 1500s had not been kind to the Spanish fleet. A mere three years before, the Spanish Armada had sunk in the English Channel (see p. 230) with an enormous loss of life.

CHINA
CHUSAN ISLANDS

August 29, 1916

• • • • • • • • • • • • • • • • • •

Collision in a deep fog off the Chusan Islands between the cruiser Hsin-Yu *and the cruiser* Hai-Yung *sent the* Hsin-Yu *to the bottom on August 29, 1916. One thousand Chinese soldiers aboard died.*

The period from 1900 to 1917, when it entered World War I, was a tumultuous one for China. The Boxer Rebellion, the revolution fomented by Sun Yat-sen and the threat from Japan kept the military in constant motion.

On the fog-shrouded evening of August 29, 1916, a major convoy of troops entered the vicinity of the Chusan Islands in the Strait of Formosa, bound for Fu-chou. It was an orderly grouping, with the exception of the cruiser *Hai-Yung*. The captain of this particular vessel apparently lost his way in the fog and, instead of remaining on course, began to zigzag frantically through the cautiously proceeding flotilla.

After narrowly missing two other ships, the *Hai-Yung* rammed the cruiser *Hsin-Yu* directly amidships, slicing it almost in two. The 1,000 Chinese soldiers aboard did not have a chance of rescue. They were pitched into the water and drowned or were ground up by the screws of the *Hai-Yung*. Only nine sailors, 20 soldiers and a foreign engineer survived the collision and sinking of the *Hsin-Yu*.

CHINA
SWATOW HARBOR

March 18, 1921

• • • • • • • • • • • • • • • • • •

Fighting among passengers aboard the steamer Hong Koh *in Swatow Harbor sank the ship on March 18, 1921. More than 1,000 died from drowning or fighting.*

Violent animosity between the residents of two Chinese cities caused one of the grisliest maritime disasters of all time on March 18, 1921.

The steamer *Hong Koh*, under British command and captained by Captain Harry Holmes, approached the port of Swatow at low tide that day. Its public rooms and decks were packed with Chinese residents of Amoy and Swatow. Fistfights and arguments had already broken out between the residents of the two cities, and a general feeling of ill will pervaded the voyage. Captain Holmes welcomed the harbor pilot aboard with a sense of relief.

But his peace was short-lived. The pilot announced in no uncertain terms that a sandbar would not allow the *Hong Koh*, which drew 22 feet, to reach the harbor of Swatow. And he would not, under any circumstances, attempt to take the ship across the bar.

The captain announced to the disgruntled passengers that the ship would have to proceed to Amoy, unload and then return to Swatow. The Swatow residents rioted, smashing furniture and portholes.

The captain ordered his crew to station themselves in the bow of the ship with guns and a hot-water hose aimed at the rioting passengers. "On the count of three, we will fire!" announced Captain Holmes, his entire concentration and that of his crew on quelling the insurgence aboard his ship. What nobody realized was that the *Hong Koh* was drifting toward a razor-edged reef. Within moments, it piled up on the rocks with a terrible sound of metal scraping against stone. And within seconds, the reef had opened a gash beneath the waterline of the steamer, causing her to list to starboard.

The momentarily chastened passengers, refueled by fear, now began to set upon one another in earnest, each fighting for a place in the lifeboats that were being lowered. Knives, hatchets and axes flashed and fell, as hundreds of people scrambled for the lifeboats. Hundreds were murdered on the spot, and the decks were covered with blood.

The demoralized Captain Holmes ordered his crew to fire over the heads of the rioting crowds. It made no difference whatsoever. People were hacked to pieces as they tried to climb into boats; those in the boats were swamped by overwhelming crowds trying to take their places. Lifeboats tangled in their halyards and spilled their human contents into the water. Others were smashed to kindling against the side of the ship.

Captain Holmes was the only British citizen aboard the *Hong Koh*. He ordered his officers to remain with him as the ship began to slip beneath the waves, but none did. They managed to crowd, unscathed, into the last lifeboat. Captain Holmes accompanied his ship to the bottom of Swatow Harbor. Around the sinking ship floated the bodies of over 1,000 people.

CHINA
WOOSUNG

December 3, 1948

• • • • • • • • • • • • • • • • • •

The overloaded and ancient steamer Kiangya, *bearing refugees, collided with an unexploded Japanese mine near*

Woosung on December 3, 1948. The mine detonated, sinking the ship and killing 2,750 passengers.

The worst officially recorded marine disaster to that date took place as the Communist armies of Mao Tse-tung were sweeping the mainland clean of Chiang Kai-shek's Nationalist forces. It was the end of the Chinese Civil War, when the major cities were falling like November leaves—Nanking, Hankou, Canton, Chungking and now Shanghai.

On the morning of December 3, 1948, refugees, attempting to escape to Ningpo, were rioting on the Shanghai waterfront, bargaining, pleading, demanding, even killing for the opportunity to leave the city, whose outskirts were already occupied by the invading Communist army.

The aged and rusting coastal steamer SS *Kiangya* had arrived early that day from Nanking with a passenger load of 2,250 people. The *Kiangya* was designed to carry 1,186, but all rules and regulations were being broken that day to accommodate the screaming, terrified refugees who poured out of various Chinese cities in search of safety.

Thus, the crew of the *Kiangya* paid little heed to the passengers on board the ship throwing their already purchased tickets to the milling, shouting refugees on the pier at Shanghai. Some tickets reached the docks. Others fell into the scum-coated waters of the port. Fights erupted over those that landed on the piers; desperate men dove after those that hit the water.

By 6:30 P.M., when the *Kiangya* lumbered away from its pier, there were more than 3,450 passengers on its decks and in its state- and public rooms. There was hardly an inch of space on any of its decks.

As darkness deepened, most of the 3,450 aboard attempted to make themselves comfortable for the night. But scarcely had this happened when a huge flash of light, flames and smoke enveloped the ship. A concussion set off a vibration that rattled the entire length of the vessel, and then a sickening settling to port began, as tons of water roared through the gaping hole ripped in the *Kiangya*'s hull by a forgotten, abandoned Japanese mine, left over from World War II. The *Kiangya,* lying low in the water, had collided directly with it, and the mine had blown a hole in its hull.

The ship began to sink immediately and swiftly. Those who could, fought their way upward to the top decks, racing the rising water level that had already drowned hundreds below decks. Again, the shoving and fighting that had taken place on the piers of Shanghai was repeated on the decks of the *Kiangya.* The aged and the weak succumbed first and were unceremoniously flung overboard to make room for the strong.

No radio transmission was possible; the radio room had been decimated by the explosion of the mine. Thus the sinking ship had to hope for river traffic to find it and rescue those who were steadily climbing to the very top decks of the sinking ship. The *Hwafoo* first sighted the ship and sent out the first SOS, which attracted the SS *Mouli.*

Its captain approached with some trepidation. Seeing the 700 hysterical passengers clustered on the *Kiangya,* he feared that they would swamp his own vessel. Sensing this, officers aboard the stricken ship quieted the crowd, and an orderly transfer took place.

The next day, the river was dragged for bodies. More than 1,000 were returned to Shanghai and stacked on the piers of the now Communist-controlled city. Two thousand seven hundred fifty died in this, one of the most unexpected and tragic of all maritime catastrophes.

ENGLISH CHANNEL

August–October, 1588

• • • • • • • • • • • • • • • •

A succession of hurricane-force winds, faulty decisions and the wounds of war sank the Spanish Armada between August and October 1588 in the English Channel. At least 4,000 died.

"God has seen fit to direct the course of events other than we would have wished," wrote Don Alonzo Perez de Guzman, duke of Medina Sidonia, as the once proud Spanish Armada shambled home, half its ships sunk and anywhere from 4,000 to 10,000 of its men dead. That final discrepancy is possibly a testament to the disarray of everything about Philip II's plan to invade England, overthrow the Protestant Elizabeth I and establish himself as ruler of England.

Preparations for the invasion began in 1586, under the direction of the Marques de Santa Cruz, but the course of events to which Medina Sidonia later referred began to take a hand in 1567, with a surprise attack by Sir Francis Drake. This delayed the evolution of the attack plans, and the unexpected death of Santa Cruz delayed them still further.

Still, Philip, goaded by Pope Pius V, was determined. He appointed Medina Sidonia to head up the armada—a peculiar choice, considering that the duke was schooled in neither navigation nor naval warfare, and he confessed to violent seasickness every time he left land. Perhaps it was not God who determined the course of events at all.

In any case, the 130 ships and 30,000 sailors and soldiers set out from Lisbon in May 1588 bound for Flanders,

Between August and October 1588, the Spanish Armada was pummeled by hurricane-force winds in the English Channel. By the end of October, it had been totally destroyed, with a loss of life of at least 4,000. New York Public Library

where they were to meet the army of Alessandro Farnese, duke of Parma and, combining forces, overwhelm England. However, a series of skirmishes with the English, combined with the ordinarily foul weather of the English Channel, scattered the armada, which never did make contact with the duke of Parma and his forces.

Disgruntled, down by four ships, Medina Sidonia put his lack of navigational skills to immediate use and determined to sail home via Scotland and the west coast of Ireland. The first fatality of that decision was the *Gran Grifon,* the *capitanas* of the armada. It foundered on the rocks of Fair Isle, taking 1,000 men to the bottom.

The ragtag remnants of the armada sailed on, its ships patched and its supplies running low. Somewhere out of the Hebrides, Medina Sidonia ordered all animals on board any of the ships flung overboard—an odd order, considering that the animals could have been slaughtered for food for his starving men.

The winds blew steadily and relentlessly, tattering the already torn sails of some of the ships of the armada. The *Santa Maria de la Rosa,* vice-flagship of the fleet and a huge galley, powered by sails and galley slaves—mostly captured British seamen—was in particularly bad shape by September, with half her crew down with disease and most of her hull leaking from the cannon holes in her sides.

Her captain, Martin de Villafranca, determined that she would never make it to Spain and endeavored to find shelter and a harbor off Kerry. The winds rose to hurricane force and drove his hapless ship ashore near Dunmore Head, between Great Basket Island and Beginish. Two other Spanish ships, the *San Juan de Portugal* and the *San Juan,* were already at anchor and slowly sinking into the shallow water of the harbor when the *Santa Maria de la Rosa* skidded into sight, firing its guns for assistance. Her sails were in shreds, her mast splintered. She dropped anchor, but the wind and sea had done their worst. Marcos de Aramburu, the commander of the *San Juan,* wrote in his ship's log, "In an instant we saw she was going to the bottom while trying to hoist the foresail and immediately she went down with the whole crew, not a soul escaping—a most extraordinary and terrible occurrence."

He was not quite right. Three hundred soldiers and sailors did perish as the ship went down, but one Genoese seaman, Giovanni de Monana, rode a plank to shore, where he was captured by the English.

The *San Juan de Portugal* did send raiding parties ashore, captured some provisions and again set sail for Spain. It reached home, but before it did, 200 of its crew died on board of disease and starvation.

Meanwhile, at Killybegs, Admiral Alonso Martinez de Leyva, having lost his own ships, the *Santa Ana* and the *La Rata Santa Maria Encoronada,* in storms off Loughros Bay of Donegal, put his and other men to work patching up the giant galley *Girona.* The harbor was littered with the wrecks of the ships of many nationalities, and the admiral did admirable work. He rebuilt its masts, patched its decks and hull and loaded on cannons, stores and 1,300 men.

On October 26, 1588, the *Girona* sailed out of Killybegs, north to Scotland and back down the channel. And the next day, October 27, an enormous hurricane hit her. Her rudder split in two, she foundered side to the wind and went down off what later became known as Port-na-Spagna. Every one of the 1,300 men aboard, including Admiral de Reyva, drowned.

Sixty-three ships of the Spanish Armada sank during the three months of their ill-fated voyage. Sixty-five, in horrendous shape, made it home. At least 4,000 men died at sea. And Elizabeth remained on the throne in England. It was not one of Spain's finest hours.

FRANCE
LA ROCHELLE

January 12, 1920

• • • • • • • • • • • • • • • • • •

A combination of engine trouble and heavy seas sank the French steamer Afrique *near La Rochelle, France on January 12, 1920. Five hundred fifty-three died.*

The *Afrique,* a small, two-masted, one-funnel steamer owned by the French Compagnie des Chargeurs Renuis and based in Marseilles, sailed the colonial route between France and its West African colonies.

The *Afrique* left Bordeaux on January 11, 1920 with 458 passengers and a crew of 127 bound for Dakar. On the evening of Saturday, January 12, she developed engine trouble in the Bay of Biscay. Her engineers worked feverishly when a heavy sea rose around the ship. The high swells, powered by heavy winds, swept the *Afrique* shoreward, straight for the Roche-Bonnie Reefs, 50 miles from La Rochelle.

The *Afrique*'s radio operator immediately sent out SOS messages, which reached the *Ceylon,* a sister ship of the *Afrique,* the SS *Lapland* and the Belgian liner *Anversville.* But the heavy seas and winds and the shallow water around the reefs kept the three ships from getting close enough to rescue the passengers and crew.

Shortly after midnight of the 13th, two lifeboats were launched from the *Afrique* with great difficulty. They carried a mere 32 people. They were all taken aboard the *Ceylon* to safety, but they would be the only survivors. At 3 A.M., the *Afrique* slipped off the reef, was washed into deep water and sank, taking 553 passengers and crew to their deaths. It was the worst French maritime disaster since the loss of the *La Bourgogne* in 1898 with 560 fatalities (see p. 225).

GREAT BRITAIN
ENGLAND
SPITHEAD

August 29, 1792

• • • • • • • • • • • • • • • • • •

Gross and fatal misjudgment by workmen caused the sinking of the battle frigate Royal George *while it was in port at Spithead, England on August 29, 1792. More than nine hundred died.*

One of the worst marine disasters in history took place, ironically enough, in port.

The *Royal George,* England's most celebrated and valuable battle frigate, had a long list of admirals at its helm and an array of 100 guns stationed on either side of its multiple masts. On August 29, 1792 it was in port at Spithead undergoing routine repairs. A small pipe beneath the waterline on the starboard side had ruptured, and while workmen crawled through the ship, sailors lounged about and merchants sold their wares to the admiralty aboard the *Royal George.* While this was happening, the ship was tipping dangerously to port.

A brisk breeze suddenly picked up, a momentary squall that would ordinarily have no effect on an upright *Royal George.* In port, however, she was at the mercy of swells that poured unchecked into her open portside gun ports. Tons of water cascaded into the vessel within minutes, and she sank like a stone, taking the 1,300 men aboard with her. Four hundred managed to swim to safety, but more than 900 drowned, trapped in the giant hull of the *Royal George,* which sank in a lethal whirlpool in shallow water in the port of Spithead.

GREAT BRITAIN
ENGLAND
WOOLWICH, RIVER THAMES

September 3, 1878

• • • • • • • • • • • • • • • • • •

The excursion steamer Princess Alice, *loaded with celebrants, collided with the steam collier* Bywell Castle *near Woolwich on the River Thames on September 3, 1878. Six hundred forty-five died.*

Steamer excursions were popular pastimes in the late 19th century, and the regally appointed river steamer *Princess Alice* was one of Britain's most popular excursion boats. Berthed at North Woolwich pier, the steamer regularly made day trips from London Bridge to Gravesend and Sheerness. Those aboard were entertained by music on its deck, games in the parlors or tippling in its oversized saloon, reserved, in the 1870s, for men only.

On the morning of September 3, 1878, the *Princess Alice* left London Bridge with 700 holiday-minded merrymakers bound for Gravesend.

At 6:00 P.M., the ship blew several blasts on its whistle and pulled back into the Thames to begin the sail home to North Woolwich pier. Captain William Grinstead decided to hug the south side of the river to avoid a two-knot ebb tide that was working against the ship midstream.

This particular night, the maneuver put the *Princess Alice* on a collision course with the steam collier *Bywell Castle.*

The tragic collision of the excursion steamer* Princess Alice *and the steam collier* Bywell Castle *near Woolwich on the River Thames on September 3, 1878. Six hundred forty-five died in one of the worst steamship wrecks in history. Illustrated London News

There were no regulations in 1878 regarding the proper order of passing (port to port is the regulation today), but it was generally agreed that passenger ships had the right of way.

The *Bywell* moved to port, toward the shore, expecting the *Princess Alice* to pass it in midstream. Instead, the excursion steamer continued to hug the shore, heading directly for the *Bywell Castle.* Too late, both pilots spun their wheels, trying to avert a collision. Both ships unleashed huge blasts on their horns; lanterns waved hysterically; shouts and screams were exchanged.

And then, with a horrific shriek, the *Bywell Castle* plowed into the *Princess Alice* directly amidships, crumpling her, splintering her decks and ripping an enormous hole in her hull from top to bottom. The steamer split in two and started to sink immediately.

The force of the impact catapulted screaming passengers into the water, where they were soon joined by others frantically trying to escape from the sinking vessel and by the bodies of those who had drowned instantly below decks. No one was wearing a life preserver; rescue lines were flung over the side of the *Bywell Castle,* but few survivors from the steamer reached them. Within two minutes, the *Princess Alice* had sunk to the bottom of the Thames, carrying 645 persons to a watery death.

Two boards of inquiry were held. One placed the blame on Captain Grinstead for "improper starboarding." The second placed the responsibility on both captains.

GREAT BRITAIN
SCOTLAND
ROCKALL

June 28, 1904

• • • • • • • • • • • • • • • • • •

Faulty judgment by the captain was responsible for the sinking of the liner Norge *after it ran on the rocks of Rockall, Scotland on June 28, 1904. Five hundred fifty died.*

The Scandinavian-American Line steamship *Norge* was an old but reliable liner, acquired from Thingvalla, another Danish line that cruised the North Atlantic. Launched in 1881 as the *Pieter de Coninck,* it served that line for eight years and then was sold to the Scandinavian-American Line, which renamed it and put it into service between Stettin, Copenhagen, Christina, Christinsand and New York.

She was a small ship, capable of carrying 1,100 passengers (50 in first class, 150 in second class and 900 in steerage) at a very conservative top speed of 11 knots.

On June 22, 1904, the *Norge* left Copenhagen with 700 emigrants and a crew of 80. Six days later, she had only made the coast of Scotland, near Rockall Island. The weather was foggy, and that night she ran onto the rocks that ring the island. The ship was not extensively damaged at first, but the captain, attempting to free the ship by reversing her engines, ripped several huge holes in both sides of her hull.

The *Norge* immediately sent out distress signals, but before help could arrive, she sank, taking 550 persons, most of them emigrants who were trapped below decks, down with her.

HOLLAND
TEXEL RIVER

December 22, 1810

• • • • • • • • • • • • • • • •

Driven inland by a hurricane, the British frigate Minotaur *broke up on the banks of the Texel River in Holland on December 22, 1810. Five hundred seventy died.*

The British frigate *Minotaur* was carrying a full load of cargo, passengers and 74 cannon when it encountered a raging hurricane off the coast of Holland on the night of December 22, 1810. Controlling the ship was impossible; its captain cut sail and tried to ride the storm out.

But near midnight, the enormous sea drove the *Minotaur* up on the sandbanks near the entrance of the Texel River. Battered repeatedly by waves, the ship began to break up, and by 2:00 A.M. on December 23, it was apparent that she was going down, and quickly.

Passengers and crew made for the lifeboats and found, to their horror, that only two were seaworthy. The others were in such disrepair that they would have sunk upon launching. One hundred ten people, the maximum capacity of the two boats, survived. But 570 others, frantically searching the ship for something—anything—that might float and to which they might cling, perished as the ship was beaten to pieces by a relentless and savage sea.

INDIA
MADRAS

April 1902

• • • • • • • • • • • • • • • • • •

A cyclone sank the British steamer Camorta *in the Gulf of Martaban near Madras, India in April 1902. Seven hundred thirty-nine died.*

The British India Steam Navigation Company was formed in 1862 to service passengers and mail between India and England. It proved successful, and this service was later expanded to Australia, East Africa and the Persian Gulf.

In 1880, the iron-hulled steamer *Camorta,* built in Glasgow, joined the fleet. Capable of making 11 knots, she was a reliable, hardworking ship that plied the India-England route from 1880 to 1883, made one trip to Australia in 1883, was transferred in early 1886 to the Netherlands India Steam Navigation Company and then was transferred back again to the British India Company in late 1886, where she remained.

In April 1902 (the precise date is unavailable from all existing records), the *Camorta* departed from Madras with 650 passengers and a crew of 89 bound for England. She did not get far. In the Gulf of Martaban (now called Mannar), between Ceylon (now Sri Lanka) and India, the *Camorta* ran into a giant killer cyclone.

The ship barely had a chance to send out a distress signal before being overwhelmed by the storm-whipped sea. She went down with the entire ship's complement. There were no survivors, and no trace ever found of her.

INDIA
MANIHARI GHAT

August 6, 1988

• • • • • • • • • • • • • • • • • •

An overloaded passenger ferry capsized near Manihari Ghat, India on August 6, 1988. More than four hundred died.

A passenger ferry overcrowded with more than 565 pilgrims set out from Manihari Ghat, a city in the state of Bihar, 200 miles northwest of Calcutta, to reach a religious site of the Hindu god Shiva on Saturday, August 6, 1988. There had been days of monsoons, and the Ganges River was swollen and turbulent.

Still, the officers and crew of the ferryboat allowed it to be dangerously packed with hundreds more than it could safely accommodate.

The ferry was in midstream when the waters seemed to wrest control of the boat away from its crew. Within seconds of reaching the halfway point of its short voyage, it tilted, held a precarious balance for a moment and then capsized, spilling its passengers into the roaring river waters.

It was over in an instant, and all aboard were left to their own will and strength to survive. One hundred fifty people swam to safety or were rescued by frantic witnesses who set out in small boats to try to fish the flailing swimmers out of the monsoon-swollen Ganges.

The following day, the Indian government sent divers from New Delhi to recover the bodies of the more than 400 who drowned. Cranes freed the hulk of the ferry, which was broken into several pieces. Scores of the drowned were trapped within the wreckage of the ferry itself. Others washed up at various places on the banks of the Ganges miles from the accident site. Still others were never found.

ITALY
LEGHORN

March 17, 1800

• • • • • • • • • • • • • • • •

A carelessly thrown match started the fire that caused the sinking of the British frigate Queen Charlotte *near Leghorn, Italy on March 17, 1800. Seven hundred died.*

The British frigate *Queen Charlotte* was massive, a huge and impressive sailing ship bristling with cannon and tall with square sails. But this impressive leviathan fell victim to a carelessly set fire on March 17, 1800 while she was sailing off the coast of Leghorn, Italy. According to a report in the *London Times,* the fire was set "by some hay which was lying under the half deck, having been set on fire by a match in a tub, which was usually kept there for signal guns."

Within minutes the fire had turned the between-decks area into a raging conflagration. A Lieutenant Dundras took several squads of men into the area to work the pumps, but while he and his men were working, the fire spread above decks to the sails. After a few more minutes, it had eaten through the wooden deck. Within moments, the enormous iron cannons crashed through the weakened wooden decking, falling through and crushing Dundras and his men below.

The ship sank quickly, taking 700 men—most of her crew—to the bottom. The handful of survivors were rescued by an unidentified American ship.

JAPAN
HAKODATE

September 26, 1954

• • • • • • • • • • • • • • • •

Bad judgment sent the giant passenger ferry Toyo Maru *out from Hakodate into the teeth of a typhoon in the Sea of Japan on September 26, 1954. The ferry sank, drowning seven hundred ninety-four.*

Giant passenger ferries ply the Taugaru Strait between Hokkaido and Honshu, the main island of Japan. The huge northern city of Hakodate, with its 300,000 plus population, feeds these ferries daily with workers and families traveling across a strait known for its strong currents.

September 26, 1954 was not the kind of day for a ferry to have even been out of dock. A raging typhoon was roaring through the Sea of Japan. Nevertheless, the ferry *Toyo Maru,* with nearly 1,000 people aboard, was in the strait when the typhoon struck.

It capsized immediately, broke apart and smashed against the rocks near Hakodate. Miraculously, 196 passengers survived by clinging to pieces of the ferry. But 794 others were carried to the bottom with most of the ship.

JAPAN
SOUTH COAST

September 19, 1890

• • • • • • • • • • • • • • • •

A plot to assassinate a Turkish political figure sent the ramshackle ship Ertogrul *out in adverse weather off the south coast of Japan on September 19, 1890. It sank, drowning five hundred and eighty-seven.*

In late August 1890, Osman Pasha, a high-ranking Turkish official, departed on a political mission to the mikado of Japan. Why such a powerful man as the pasha should agree to board the *Ertogrul,* a notoriously ramshackle ship navigated by a ragtag crew and incompetent officers, is probably the most mysterious part of this mystery story. It is possible that he was spirited aboard. But if this is so, why then did he complete his mission in Japan, after chugging from the Mediterranean and through the Sea of Japan, on a ship whose engines constantly broke down and that leaked and pitched as if she were about to come apart in an instant?

Partially recorded history draws a veil over the whole matter, except to record the end of the story in some detail. On September 19, 1890, the *Ertogrul* left Japan, heading for home, her unarmored, wooden-framed hulk powered by two 300-horsepower engines that were barely able to get it up to 10 knots.

A squall came up in the Sea of Japan, and the ship finally began to disintegrate, a situation that had been predicted by the sailors and officers of the fleet of seaworthy ships owned by Turkey before she left. It was also a circumstance that was probably assured by several in Constantinople, since, according to the stories told by some of the 66 survivors of the wreck, Osman Pasha was last heard pounding on the inside of the door of his stateroom. The door had been mysteriously locked from the outside, and no key was available. So, the *Ertogrul* became his watery coffin and that of 586 others who also went down with the ship.

JAPAN
TOKYO BAY

July 12, 1918

• • • • • • • • • • • • • • • • • • •

An unexplained explosion sent the battleship Kawachi *to the bottom of Tokyo Bay on July 12, 1918. Five hundred died.*

The *Kawachi* was a formidable battleship. Built in 1912, this 21,420-ton leviathan was 500 feet long and 84 feet in the beam and sported not only a full complement of 12- and six-inch guns but five 18-inch torpedo launchers as well.

The *Kawachi* only sailed for six years. On July 12, 1918, as she was entering Tokuyama Bay, 150 miles northeast of Nagasaki, she suddenly blew up. What was left sank immediately. There was never a definitive answer to the mystery of the explosion, which killed 500 sailors and officers, but an elaborate investigation concluded that a fire in a below-decks magazine could have set off a series of explosions that eventually ignited the big one. None of the 400 survivors, however, could verify this version of a disaster that still remains unexplained.

JAVA SEA

January 27, 1981

• • • • • • • • • • • • • • • • • • •

A fire in its hold led to the sinking of the Tamponas II *in the Java Sea on January 27, 1981. Five hundred eighty died.*

The *Tamponas II* was purchased from Japan in 1980 by the Indonesian government–owned Pelni Shipping Corporation. Government-owned passenger ships, stripped of unnecessary equipment to allow as many people as possible to crowd aboard, ply between the islands, and the 6,139-ton, 10-year-old *Tamponas II* was one of the youngest ships in an otherwise aging fleet.

By all accounts, the Pelni Shipping Corporation was not a company that made a priority of safety. In fact, after the tragedy of the *Tamponas II,* its master complained bitterly to the Indonesian newspaper *Sinar Harapan* that its vessels, and particularly the *Tamponas II,* were not given nearly enough time between voyages for maintenance. The company, stated the captain, had ignored his complaints that four days between trips were not enough to keep the ships in safe running condition.

On Sunday night, January 25, 1981, the *Tamponas II,* with 1,054 passengers and 82 crew members aboard, was plying its way from Jakarta to the Celebes port city of Ujang Pandang, 1,000 miles to the east, when a fire broke out in a hold that contained 166 automobiles.

For 24 hours the crew battled the fire, but by early Tuesday morning, it had gotten out of control, spread to the engine room and caused an explosion. Most of the passengers huddled on the deck, as the sea began to swell with an approaching storm.

An SOS went out from the *Tamponas II,* which was by now halfway between Surabaya in east Java and the southern tip of the island of Borneo. The *Sanghi,* a passenger ship nearby, was the first to arrive on the scene, just as the stern of the *Tamponas* went down. There were no lifeboats or rafts aboard the ship, and passengers had to leap into the turbulent waters.

One hundred forty-nine were fished from the water by the *Sanghi.* Three other rescue vessels, including two Indonesian minesweepers, picked up the rest of the 471 survivors, which included 28 crew members and the captain.

As night fell on the evening of the 27th and the storm intensified, 60 rubber rafts were tossed into the water, in the hope that survivors would cling to them. None did, and by the 29th, the full fury of the monsoon hit and made the search for either survivors or bodies impossible. Six hundred twenty people survived the sinking of the *Tamponas II.* Five hundred eighty died.

LABRADOR
EGG ISLAND

August 22, 1711

• • • • • • • • • • • • • • • • • • •

Storms off Egg Island, Labrador were responsible for the sinking of the English Armada on August 22, 1711. Two thousand British sailors died.

The English Armada passed into history ignominiously, the victim of bad judgment, deliberately dangerous navigation and heavy storms off Egg Island, Labrador.

It all began on April 29, 1711, when the enormous British fleet of 61 warships and transports carrying nearly 10,000 sailors, troops and their families set sail from England under the command of Admiral Sir Hovendon Walker. Sealed orders from Queen Anne revealed that the armada was to attack and capture the most heavily protected stronghold in the Western Hemisphere, the fortress at Quebec. It was to be a sneak attack.

Given the size of the fleet and the presence of General John Hill, it seemed a mission destined for success and glory, which would be a total turnaround from the humbling defeats the British had heretofore suffered in previous attacks against Quebec.

The armada stopped first in Boston for provisions and then headed up the Massachusetts coast. Part way there, the first misstep occurred. The fleet overtook a French sloop, the *Neptune,* commanded by a Captain Paradis. She was on her way to Quebec, and with almost unbelievable naivete, Admiral Walker decided that Paradis would be their ideal guide to Quebec, just the man to guide them through the treacherous waters of St. Lawrence Bay.

Counseled against it, Walker persisted and paid Paradis 500 pistoles for his piloting expertise.

So, at breakneck speed, the armada, led by a loyal Frenchman, headed toward an encounter with Frenchmen. At approximately 10 P.M. on the night of August 22, 1711, a heavy fog descended upon the fleet, scattering its normally tight formation. By the time the fog was blown away by gale-force winds and a biting storm, the eight transports of the armada had been blown onto the razor-sharp reefs that surrounded Egg Island.

Every one of the eight transports was dashed upon the rocks, which split the wooden ships asunder. Within minutes, pounding surf smashed them apart still further, and more than 2,000 women, children, sailors and soldiers were swept into the black and freezing waters. Most of the bodies were later discovered washed up on the shore.

The warships and Admiral Walker were luckier. Faster and more maneuverable than the transports, they had missed the reefs and the island. But Paradis, the Frenchman, had fled, and there were no longer enough troops to safely mount an attack on the French garrison at Quebec, which had probably already been alerted.

In ignominy and defeat, Walker turned his remaining ships around and headed back to England, where he would fall into disgrace and be forced to spend the rest of his days in the colonies.

There were some survivors of the wrecks, apparently. Along with the skeletons on the shore, French inhabitants a year later discovered other skeletons huddled in hollow tree trunks and in shelters constructed of branches of shrubs. None survived long enough to leave Egg Island alive.

NEW ZEALAND
AUCKLAND

November 17, 1874

Faulty navigation worsened a fire aboard the Cospatrick *near Auckland, New Zealand on November 17, 1874. Four hundred sixty-eight died.*

The 1,200-ton *Cospatrick* was a lithe and agile sailing frigate, grandly outfitted with a teak hull and three masts. Used as a luxury passenger liner for its first years, it was then used to lay submarine cable in the Persian Gulf in 1856. By the 1870s, the *Cospatrick* had been purchased from its original owner, the Blackwell Company, by Shaw, Savill & Company, which made a business of transporting immigrants in steerage conditions from Great Britain to Australia and New Zealand.

On September 11, 1874, she left England with 429 immigrants. The crossing was long, uneventful and on schedule. But on November 17, off the coast of Auckland, a small fire broke out in the boatswain's cabin, which was also used to store oil and paints. It was not a huge fire, and the crew was able to bring it under control.

And then, for some unexplained reason, either the captain or the helmsman brought the ship squarely into the wind. Fed by this wind, the fire exploded through the roof of the cabin and ignited the headsails. Minutes later, the entire bow section of the boat was enveloped in flames.

It took little time for the immigrants below to clamber above. They massed on deck as the fire spread from halyard to halyard and rail to rail. The crew began to lower lifeboats, but this was almost as disastrous as the fire itself. The first boat, overloaded with frantic passengers, some of whom leaped into it as it was being lowered, foundered and sank. The second boat caught fire as it was being lowered. Only two boats containing 81 passengers and crew got off the *Cospatrick*. The remainder burned in their checks.

It took 36 hours for the ship to smolder to its gunwales. Before that, the masts burned through and collapsed the deck, crushing and burning scores of immigrants still trapped aboard the ship. The captain, his wife and his small son all drowned.

The two lifeboats, with Second Mate Henry MacDonald in charge, drifted for three days without provisions. On the fourth day, a storm drove them apart, and one apparently sank. Neither it nor its passengers were ever found.

By November 26, only five survivors remained alive—MacDonald, three crewmen and one passenger. On that afternoon, they were sighted by the British *Sceptre*, which drew alongside and took them aboard.

PHILIPPINES
TABLAS STRAIT

December 20, 1987

• • • • • • • • • • • • • • • • •

Allowing an apprentice officer to pilot the monumentally overcrowded passenger ferry Dona Paz *through the crowded Tablas Strait in the Philippines on December 20, 1987 caused one of the worst maritime disasters in history, the collision of the ferry with the tanker* Victor. *Both ships were set afire, and at least 3,000 died.*

It was Sunday, December 20, 1987 when the 2,215-ton ferry *Dona Paz*, owned by the Sulpicio Lines, left Tacloban, on Leyte Island, horrendously overloaded with Filipinos anxious to spend Christmas in Manila with their relatives and friends.

As night fell, the 3,000 passengers that crowded the cabins and three decks of the *Dona Paz* (she was designed to carry 1,424 passengers and 50 crew members) attempted to make themselves comfortable. It was not an easy task. Up to four people shared individual cots; hundreds sprawled on mats they had laid out in the ship's corridors; hundreds more sat, shoulder to shoulder, on the decks of the ship.

It was a dark, moonless night, but an uneventful one for 265 miles of the 375-mile trip from Tacloban to Manila. According to the Coast Guard inquiry, by 10 P.M. only an apprentice officer was on the bridge, piloting the boat through the busy Tablas Strait, 110 miles south of Manila. The other officers were watching television or drinking beer.

At 10 P.M., the ferry was just off Mindoro Island, in the busiest part of the strait. And at precisely that hour, the *Dona Paz* collided head-on with the 629-ton Philippine tanker *Victor*, bound for Masbate Island with 8,300 barrels of oil. Within seconds, the heavier, more powerful ferry had ripped into the hull of the *Victor*, peeling open its compartments and smashing into the oil it was carrying.

Barely a minute later, the *Victor* exploded with a horrendous roar, sending flaming oil onto the *Dona Paz* and igniting the surface of the water surrounding the two foundering ships.

"I went to a window to see what happened, and I saw the sea in flames," one of the survivors, 42-year-old Paquito Osabel, told a reporter later. "I shouted to my companions to get ready, there is fire. The fire spread rapidly and there were flames everywhere. People were screaming and jumping. The smoke was terrible. We couldn't see each other and it was dark. I could see flames, but I jumped."

Both ships sank, almost instantly. Many of those passengers who did not drown were burned. Even those who jumped into the water were soon coated with flaming oil and perished. Pampilio Culalia, who leaped into the water, leaving his 14-year-old daughter, 10-year-old niece and his brother behind, sobbed, "I saw the ship in flames and [as I swam away] I wanted to kill myself. But God shook me and woke me."

Of the more than 3,000 passengers aboard the *Dona Paz*, only 24 survived. Of the 13 crewmen aboard the *Victor*, two were fished from a sea that was littered with the charred corpses of those who had tried to escape. All were suffering from serious burns.

For seven hours, the *Don Eusebio*, a passenger ship, circled the area, searching in vain for survivors. A search mission of five commercial vessels, two naval patrol craft and three U.S. Air Force helicopters covered a wide area, looking for signs of life. They found nothing either.

The next morning, decomposing bodies began washing ashore on Mindoro Island, and for the next week, as Christmas came and went, hundreds of charred, bloated bodies began to float to the surface. But thousands more would never be recovered.

"This is a national tragedy of harrowing proportions," said Philippine president Corazon Aquino. "Our sadness is all the more painful because the tragedy struck with the approach of Christmas," she added.

It was the worst sea disaster in Philippine history and one of the worst marine disasters in the history of the world. There were twice the number of casualties of the *Titanic* (see p. 219), and it was only eclipsed in the 20th century by the torpedoing of the *Wilhelm Gustloff* in 1945 (see p. 222).

UNITED STATES
FLORIDA
COAST

July 31, 1715

• • • • • • • • • • • • • • • • •

A hurricane off the coast of Florida sank the twin capitanas, *the two leaders of a Spanish flotilla, on July 31, 1715. More than 1,000 died on the two ships.*

Spanish ships sailing from the New World to the Old were usually carrying plunder from the ancient civilizations Spain conquered in Central and South America. Low in the water from the weight of gold and silver, they were targeted by pirates, who infested the Caribbean like locusts in a plague year. For this reason, the large convoys were named armadas; they were armed to the gunwales and then some. As many soldiers as sailors strolled the decks of the galleons, ready to stave off any attack.

The armada that was scheduled to leave Havana Harbor on July 24, 1715 was particularly well armed, since it was heavy with appropriated treasure. No less than 4,000 chests of gold, silver, emeralds, silks, pearls and porcelain nested in the holds of the 11 ships. There were 14 million newly minted gold and silver pesos from Veracruz and emeralds and gold bars from Colombia and Peru. It was more than a king's ransom, and it was all destined for the treasury of King Philip of Spain.

But all the cannons in the kingdom, manned by the 2,000 soldiers and sailors aboard the 11 ships, were worthless before a storm. And in the Florida Straits, this armada ran into a gigantic one.

There had been no warning when they left Havana under benign and balmy skies. But by July 29, the weather had turned murky. A swell began to rock the boats, and the humidity rose. Oppressive, heavy air signaled that a hurricane was on the way.

It struck with full force at 2:00 A.M. on July 31, 1715. Hundred-mile-per-hour winds slammed into the ships, driving them shoreward onto the reefs off the Florida coast. Every captain knew that the best defense was to sail for the open sea, to ride out the storm. The *Grifon*, under the captaincy of Antonio Darie, managed to do this and survived.

But it was the only ship that did. Ten ships, loaded with a fortune, were crazily whirled counterclockwise in the vortex of the storm.

Masts collapsed first, crushing those on the decks beneath them. Then, the pounding of the waves and the wind ripped the riggings from the vessels. All 10 ships sank. Three hundred Indians from Florida and Central America were pressed into service as slave divers. Forced to dive until exhaustion, fully half of them drowned in the effort to retrieve six million of the 14 million-peso treasure that had sunk beneath the sea in the Florida Straits.

UNITED STATES
ILLINOIS
CHICAGO

July 24, 1915

• • • • • • • • • • • • • • • •

Faulty design, greed and an unequal distribution of passengers combined to capsize the excursion steamer Eastland *at its dock in Chicago on July 24, 1915. Eight hundred fifty-two picnickers died.*

"I thought the damned ship would take the turns on her side like a skipping stone."

So wrote naval architect W. J. Wood after maneuvering the excursion steamer *Eastland* through its "S curve" configuration, designed to reveal any dangerous listing capabilities. Wood found plenty, as his succinct observation attests. So did John Deveraux York, another naval architect, who on August 2, 1913 wrote to the harbormaster of the Port of Chicago, "You are aware of the conditions of the S.S. *Eastland,* and unless structural defects are remedied to prevent listing, there may be a serious accident."

Neither the authorities nor the St. Joseph–Chicago Steamship Company, the owner of the *Eastland,* apparently paid attention to these warnings from experts. The *Eastland* was too much of a money-maker, ferrying thousands of holiday merrymakers from Chicago on excursions to picnic grounds on the banks of Lake Michigan.

No less than 7,300 people, most of them employees of the Western Electric Company, possessed excursion tickets for the annual picnic of the Hawthorne Club on July 24, 1915. It would take five steamers to transport them from the Port of Chicago to Michigan City, Indiana.

The excursion began early, at 6:00 A.M. Bands played, whistles blew and more than 3,500 picnickers dashed aboard the *Eastland,* which was to lead the flotilla that day. The *Eastland* was only licensed to carry 2,500 passengers, but company officials let it fill over its capacity.

Passengers, eager to be snapped by a professional photographer who was poised on a bridge, crowded to the port rail. The boat began to list—dangerously.

Chief engineer Joseph M. Erickson noted this and opened the ballast tank on the starboard side. But no sooner had he done this than the passengers rushed to the *starboard* railing. He opened the port ballast tanks. But the listing continued and worsened. Sailors were dispatched to the deck to try to redistribute the passengers. It was useless. They were having too much fun, and there were too many of them to heed the instructions of the crew.

Now the list to port increased, alarmingly. The 60 crew members, seeing it and knowing what would happen next, jumped ship, literally, landing safely on the dock. Captain Harry Pedersen, on the bridge, shouted to his absent crew to open the inside doors and get the people off the ship.

It was too late. As the formerly festive group of picnickers screamed and began to slide toward the port rail, the *Eastland* tipped and capsized. Passengers, provisions, furniture, everything crashed toward the port side of the hull as the *Eastland* settled onto the river bottom. A mere eight feet of her starboard side jutted above the water, a metal

The capsized hulk of the* Eastland *lies on its side in the Chicago River while rescuers search for survivors. Eight hundred fifty-two died in this "accident that never should have been allowed to happen." Library of Congress

island that was crowded with panic-stricken excursionists, who clawed and clung to one another.

Hundreds had already drowned, crushed by the tons of water that roared into the *Eastland* through its open portholes. Rescuers on the shore threw anything that was loose and floatable to the thrashing and terrified people.

Workmen using acetylene torches nearby rushed to the scene and immediately went to work cutting a hole in the *Eastland*'s hull, where pounding had been heard.

No sooner had J. H. Rista, a torchman, sliced into the hull when Captain Pedersen arrived on the scene, shouting to the workman to stop cutting holes in his ship. The workmen surrounded the captain, who continued to yell irrationally, and attempt to pull the torchmen away from their rescue work. Finally, police arrested Pedersen and Dell Fisher, his first mate, who had joined the captain in his crazy interference tactics. "After I got rid of Pedersen," Rista later testified before the board of inquiry, "we took out forty people, all alive, out of that hole he had tried to stop me from cutting."

The 40 were fortunate. Eight hundred fifty-two hapless picnickers drowned, and their bodies were hauled off to the Second Regiment Armory for identification.

Hundreds of lawsuits were filed against the company. They would stumble through the Illinois court system for 20 years and finally be thrown out. Astonishingly, the courts eventually ruled that the fault lay with the engineer, who had "neglected to fill the ballast tanks properly."

UNITED STATES
NEW YORK
NEW YORK

June 15, 1904

• • • • • • • • • • • • • • • • •

A wholesale disregard of safety measures, coupled with mindlessness, caused the fatal burning of the steamer General Slocum *in New York Harbor on June 15, 1904. One thousand thirty-one people died, according to the New York City Police Department.*

President Theodore Roosevelt fired the chief inspector of the U.S. Steamboat Inspection Service because of it. The most sweeping reforms ever instituted in U.S. maritime history were the result of it. Operators of excursion steamers from that point forward would think twice before valuing operating costs over human life.

Those were the positive results of the horrific tragedy of the *General Slocum* on June 15, 1904. The dark side was the long litany of criminal stupidity practiced by its captain, crew and owners, all of which came to light in the exhaustive investigation that followed.

The *General Slocum* was one of a number of excursion steamers that gave pleasure to thousands at the turn of the century. Thirteen years old in 1904, she featured huge, Mississippi-style side wheels that powered her at roughly 18 miles per hour. She was a favorite among church and civic groups to take their members on annual picnics and sails.

On June 15, 1904, a bright and beautiful late spring day, St. Mark's German Lutheran Church, located on Sixth Street in Manhattan, assembled 1,360 children, teachers and chaperones for its annual Sunday school voyage and picnic to Locust Point, just beyond Throg's Neck in the Bronx.

At 9:00 A.M. on the 15th, the throng assembled on the pier at Third Street and the East River. Allowing all 1,360 aboard would dangerously overload the boat, but Captain William Van Schaick ignored this, thus committing the first of a string of stupidities.

The worst, however, had happened long before June 15. In violation of all safety regulations, a forward storeroom had been cluttered with cans of oil and barrels filled with leftover excelsior from a previous shipment of crockery.

This volatile, flammable combination was ignited shortly after the ship left its pier either by an oiler passing through with a burning torch on his way to the engine room or by a crew member who lit a lamp and dropped the match. (The crew, almost to a man, was composed of former deckhands and truck drivers; experience was at a premium aboard the *General Slocum.*)

Meanwhile, the white and yellow steamer moved serenely upstream, through Hellgate and toward the Bronx. As she neared 83rd Street, Frank Perditsky, a 14-year-old picnicker, noticed smoke coming from one of the holds in the bow. According to sworn testimony, he shoved his way through the crowd and approached a "man with gold braid on his cap"—which was enough to identify Captain Van Schaick.

Reporting excitedly that he had seen "smoke coming out of the boiler room," he was dismissed airily by the captain, who told him to "shut up and mind your own business."

The captain later ordered First Mate Edward Flanagan, a former ironworker, to take a seaman and investigate.

The* General Slocum *after the fire that killed more than 1,000. New York Historical Society

An artist's rendering of the horrendous burning of the steamer* General Slocum *in New York Harbor on June 15, 1904. One thousand thirty-one people died, according to the New York City Police Department. New York Public Library

They found the smoke, all right, but the door to the room from which it was coming was locked. Flanagan got a key and opened the door, and the air he let in caused the smoldering fire to burst into flames.

There was a fire hose nearby, which Flanagan grabbed. But no water emerged from it when he turned the valve. Precious minutes were lost as crewmen went for the donkey engine used to build up water pressure. Even with this working correctly, no water came from the hose, which had neither been used nor inspected since the launching of the ship 13 years before.

Flanagan now had the presence of mind to unscrew the nozzle of the hose. As he did, a solid rubber washer fell out. It had been installed to prevent water from dripping on the deck—another mistake which would be repeated 30 years later aboard the *Morro Castle* (see p. 217). Flanagan now rescrewed the nozzle onto the hose. The water pressure forced water into it, and its aged and unused linen casing burst apart, soaking the crewmen who held it.

At this point the fire was absolutely out of control. The sensible thing to do would have been to head sharply for shore, where the smoke from the fire had already been noticed and an alarm turned in to the 138th Street Station of the New York City Fire Department. Firemen had already laid hose out to the end of the longest pier.

But Captain Van Schaick continued on, ordering the pilot to steer for North Brother Island. His rationale, expressed in later testimony, was "a moral responsibility not to risk setting buildings on fire." There was a sand beach on North Brother Island, and it was possible to beach the boat there in shallow water and presumably disembark the now-uneasy passengers who were crowding the decks of the ship.

But Pilot Van Wart fumbled the landing, missed the stretch of sand and steamed the *General Slocum* instead into a rocky cove. He now ran her up on the rocks. Thus, her blazing bow was in the shallows, while her stern, which offered the only safe exit, was in water 30 feet deep.

The fireboat *Zophar Mills* had been alerted and was on its way, but it was a full mile astern of the flaming excursion steamer. The tugboats *John Wade* and *Walter Tracy* were also on their way, but they were three-quarters of a mile away in another direction.

Terror and further malfeasance were now sealing the fate of the horrified passengers. The 10 lifeboats were lashed so thoroughly that the adults among the passengers could not budge them, and no crewmen offered to help. Children fought with one another for life preservers, which were supposed to be of regulation solid cork. Instead, to save money, the Knickerbocker Company, which owned the ship, had substituted granulated cork fitted with seven-inch bars of cast iron to make them come up to the weight standard. They were worse than useless; children leaping into the water with the life preservers on were pulled to the bottom by the iron weights.

But by now, children were dying in other ways. Some were trampled underfoot in the panic on deck. Others leaped into the water and were chewed up by the still-turning paddle wheels. And then, the flames ate through the decks. They collapsed, sending hundreds more into the burning bowels of the ship.

By 11:30 A.M. it was over. More than 600 bodies were recovered, some of them burned beyond recognition. From then until midnight, delivery wagons and coal carts were pressed into service to supplement the ambulances and hearses that carried bodies and the injured to hospitals and morgues in the Bronx.

The next day, cannon were brought from the Brooklyn Navy Yard to be fired over the water. The vibrations from the explosions loosened more bodies that were sunk in the mud of the river bottom.

Many of the dead were buried in a mass grave in the Lutheran Cemetery in Queens. To this day, every June 15, a memorial service is held for the dead. The exact figure was never precisely determined. According to the U.S. Steamboat Inspection Service (whose head President Roosevelt would fire), it was "only 938." The New York City Police asserted firmly that the figure was 1,031.

A coroner's jury finally charged Captain Van Schaick, Mate Flanagan and the inspector responsible for checking the ship's fire-fighting equipment with first degree manslaughter. The officers of the Knickerbocker Company were charged as accessories.

Only Captain Van Schaick received a sentence, for criminal negligence, of 10 years at hard labor in the federal penitentiary at Sing Sing. In 1908, President Roosevelt pardoned him because of his advanced age.

NUCLEAR AND INDUSTRIAL ACCIDENTS

• •

THE WORST RECORDED NUCLEAR AND INDUSTRIAL ACCIDENTS

* Detailed in text

Germany
- * Oppau
  - Badische Anilinfabrick Company (1921)

Great Britain
- England
- * Liverpool
  - Windscale Plutonium Plant (1957)

India
- * Bhopal
  - Union Carbide Pesticide Plant (1984)

Japan
- * Tsuruga
  - Nuclear power plant (1981)

Switzerland
- Lucends Vad
  - Underground reactor (1969)

United States
- Alabama
- Brown's Ferry
  - Nuclear power plant (1975)
- Idaho
- * Idaho Falls
  - Idaho Nuclear Engineering Laboratory (1961)
- Michigan
- Detroit
  - Sodium cooling plant (1966)
- Minnesota
- Monticello
  - Nuclear power plant (1971)
- New York
- Rochester
  - Ginna Steam Plant (1982)
- Oklahoma
- * Gore
  - Sequoyah Fuels Corporation Plant (1986)
- Pennsylvania
- * Middletown
  - Three Mile Island Nuclear Power Plant (1979)
- Tennessee
- Erwin
  - Nuclear fuel plant (1979)

USSR
- * Kasli
  - Nuclear waste Dump (1957)
- * Pripyat
  - Chernobyl nuclear power plant (1986)

CHRONOLOGY

* Detailed in text

1921
- *Sept. 20*
  - * Oppau, Germany; Badische Anilinfabrick Co.

1957
- * Kasli, USSR; Nuclear waste dump
- *Oct. 10*
  - * Liverpool, England; Windscale Plutonium Plant

1961
- *Jan. 3*
  - * Idaho Falls, Idaho; Idaho Nuclear Engineering Laboratory

1966
- *Oct. 5*
  - Detroit, Michigan; Sodium cooling plant

1969
- *Jan. 21*
  - Lucends Vad (Switzerland; Underground reactor

1971
- *Nov. 19*
  - Monticello, Minnesota; Nuclear reactor

1975
- *Mar. 22*
  - Brown's Ferry, Alabama; Nuclear reactor

1979
- *Mar. 28*
  - * Middletown, Pennsylvania; Three Mile Island Nuclear Power Plant
- *Aug. 7*
  - Erwin, Tennessee; Nuclear fuel plant

1981
- *Mar. 8*
  - * Tsuruga, Japan; Nuclear power plant

1982
- *Jan. 25*
  - Rochester, New York; Ginna Steam Plant

1984
- *Dec. 3*
  - * Bhopal, India; Union Carbide Pesticide Plant

1986
- *Jan. 4*
  - * Gore, Oklahoma; Sequoyah Fuels Corporation Plant
- *April 16*
  - * Pripyat, USSR; Chernobyl nuclear power plant

• • • • •

NUCLEAR AND INDUSTRIAL ACCIDENTS

• • • • •

There is no more timely disaster than a nuclear accident. Fortunately, only one actual meltdown has occurred so far, at Chernobyl (see p. 263), but the nuclear age is young. And because so little is known about both its short- and long-term consequences, no disaster is more frightening.

Ever since Enrico Fermi put one of Albert Einstein's theories to work, the world has experienced a steadily increasing and intensifying series of nuclear accidents. The worst so far is the latest; the very worst is, alas, yet to come.

In a positive sense, nuclear disasters have made us more cautious. Three Mile Island, for instance, put the brakes on the proliferation of nuclear power plants; the Chernobyl disaster brought it to a virtual standstill. Without arguing the relative virtue of atomic power, the very fact that huge public outcries have followed each of these disasters forces government and industry to concentrate more on safety practices than ever before and to be more public about these practices or the lack of them.

For if there is a single thread that runs through all the industrial and nuclear accidents of this section, it is a failure to pay proper attention to safety precautions. From Oppau, Germany in 1921, to Bhopal, India in 1984, to Chernobyl in 1986, safety precautions were either ignored, circumvented or, as in the case of Chernobyl, dismantled.

Monumental carelessness on the part of both management and labor also runs through these accidents. Not one of the industrial plants examined—*not one of them*—had a workable evacuation plan in place for the innocent populace that lived around the plant. In each case, evacuations had to be made up as they went along, and in each case, these evacuations were delayed enough to increase the number and severity of casualties, often enormously.

In each case, human error was the trigger that brought about the cataclysms that ensued. And if the similarity in cause and effect of man-made catastrophes has proved anything, it is that human error is at the root of virtually every man-made disaster. With industrial and nuclear disasters, this human error is compounded, all too frequently, by human greed, by political and governmental expediency, by economic considerations and by deliberate misinformation or withholding of information.

And this is the final dimension that characterizes nuclear disasters and makes them unique: In every case, from the absolutely tight lid that was kept on every detail of the Kasli disaster in Russia's Ural Mountains in 1957 through Windscale, Three Mile Island and Chernobyl, official silence or deliberate downplaying of casualty statistics and, what is far worse, the danger posed by radiation is consistent enough to be policy.

Admittedly, some of this has come from ignorance. But an equal amount has also come from governmental design, explained away as a desire not to create panic in the populace. This policy has resulted in hundreds of lawsuits against governments by the families of victims who have died agonizing and puzzling deaths long after the incident that had been passed off as posing little or no danger to the public at large. And until this pervasive policy is changed, casualty figures from nuclear accidents will continue to multiply as governments continue to use nuclear power, which is cheap and abundant, without spending the proper amount of time on researching methods of preventing disasters and their consequent effects.

The criteria for inclusion in this section were based on the effect the disaster had on the innocent. Certainly, industrial accidents are a frequent occurrence, and that is regrettable and recordable. Certainly, the life of a worker in a factory is not worth more nor less than a person living down the road from the factory. But there are certain compensations involved in injuries or deaths suffered by those employed by an industry.

In the case of each of the included industrial and nuclear accidents in this section, huge numbers of innocent people who had either nothing or very little to do with the industry were victims of the disaster. And that was the reason for that happening's inclusion.

GLOSSARY OF NUCLEAR TERMS

• • • • •

chain reaction The process that occurs when uranium atoms split, emitting neutrons that split other uranium atoms in a continuum, or chain.

china syndrome A meltdown through the reactor floor, accompanied by a large explosion. The worst possible kind of reactor accident.

cladding The metal that encases the nuclear fuel material.

condenser The heat exchanger in which steam is transformed into water by the removal of heat and the transference of the steam to a cooling pond.

control rods Carbon rods that are dropped between fuel rods, neutralizing the fission, thus slowing or stopping the chain reaction.

coolant Usually water, which removes nuclear-generated heat from the core.

core The place in a reactor in which the nuclear fuel is contained and nuclear reaction occurs.

curie A measure of radioactivity based on disintegration over time.

emergency core cooling system Any sort of system that is present to cool the core in the event that the regular cooling system malfunctions or fails to function.

fission The splitting of a heavy atomic nucleus. This forms two lighter "fission fragments" and smaller particles, such as neutrons. In a nuclear reactor, the energy released from the fission provides heat, and part of this heat is converted into electricity.

fuel pellet The basic form of uranium used in reactors.

fuel rod A stainless steel tube holding uranium fuel pellets.

fusion The opposite of fission, and the energy source of stars. In this process, atomic nuclei, such as those of hydrogen, are fused, releasing nuclear energy.

meltdown Second to an explosion, this is the most catastrophic occurrence in a nuclear accident. When the cooling systems—primary or emergency—fail to keep the temperature in a reactor within controllable limits, either the metal rods containing the pellets or the pellets themselves melt. Then the core melts into a glowing radioactive mass, capable of smashing through the wall or the floor of the reactor's containment walls and releasing a massive surge of radiation.

millirad One thousandth of a rad.

millirem A term used to describe the measuring of the absorption of radiation by human beings. The average person undergoes, as a result of exposure to everything from dental X rays to cosmic rays, 100 to 200 millirems of radiation per year. One chest X ray causes an exposure of from 20 to 30 millirems.

rad The standard unit of an absorbed dose of radiation.

radioactivity The spontaneous disintegration of the nucleus of an atom, which in turn emits radiation. The radiant energy is in the form of particles, or rays, as alpha (positively charged particles), beta (negatively charged electrons) and gamma rays (elements of electromagnetic radiation, resembling X rays, and considerably more penetrating than other forms of radiation).

reactor The core and its protective shell, or container.

rem An abbreviation of "roentgen equivalent, man." A measure of the quantity of any ionizing radiation that contains the same biological effectiveness as one rad of X rays.

uranium A metal with radioactive properties, used as a fuel because it has the ability to undergo continuous fission.

• • • • • • • • • • • • • • •

GERMANY
OPPAU

September 20, 1921

• • • • • • • • • • • • • • •

An error in mixing chemicals, producing explosive gas, caused the giant explosion in the Badische Anilinfabrick Company plant in Oppau, Germany on September 20, 1921. Five hundred died; 1,500 were injured, many seriously.

The cataclysmic explosion of the Badische Anilinfabrick works at 7:30 A.M. on September 20, 1921 in Oppau, Germany released more than an odd, green, evil-smelling

A soup kitchen is set up and utilized by survivors and families of victims of the gigantic explosion at the Badische Anilinfabrick Company plant in Oppau Germany on September 20, 1921. Five hundred died; 1,500 were injured, many seriously. Library of Congress

gas into the atmosphere. Mystery surrounded the explosion; wartime activities at the plant were unveiled during the post-explosion investigation; speculation that nuclear experiments were being conducted in the plant still persists. The complex mystery of it all has never been solved.

The Badische plant was built in 1913, shortly before the start of World War I. Almost from the very beginning, it was engaged in aiding the German war effort. First, it saved Germany from a military collapse, when, in the spring of 1915, it supplied artificial nitrates when the British blockade cut off the Chile saltpeter supply. Then, expanded, it manufactured most of the chlorine and phosgene used by the German army when it engaged in poison gas attacks in World War I.

After the war, it was converted into a sprawling, imposing complex that covered acres and employed between 10,000 and 15,000 people. It bustled with profitable activity, utilizing chemicals to produce nitrates for dyes and artificial fertilizer. It employed the so-called Haber process, in which nitrogen was extracted from the air and then, in the presence of a catalyst, mixed under high compression with hydrogen. This converted the nitrogen into ammonia, nitric acid, nitrates, fertilizers and ammonium sulfates.

According to Major Theodore W. Sill, a member of the Interallied Mission appointed to study the German chemical industry after the war, the Oppau plant had a long history of accidental explosions. Despite the fact that German engineers developed a new type of steel capable of holding hydrogen under pressure, a compound that could remain solid against 2,000 pounds of pressure per square inch when the hydrogen and nitrogen gases were compressed, under a temperature running from 500 to 600 degrees, the tanks *did* erupt. In September 1917, one of the compression tanks blew, killing approximately 100 workers; the concussion from the explosion was powerful enough to kill workmen crossing a bridge half a mile away.

But that was small compared with the cataclysmic eruption that took place in the early morning of September 20, 1921.

The shifts changed every morning at 7:30 A.M. at this monster plant surrounded by a small town of 6,500, most of whom either worked in the plant or were family members of workers in the plant.

It was a cold and crisp day, and the departing shift was just concluding its duties. Three trains pulled onto the siding alongside the plant, preparatory to discharging hundreds of workers for the incoming shift.

And then, with a thunderous roar, the main building of the huge plant exploded. According to eyewitnesses, the entire structure lifted from its foundations and then descended in 1,000 pieces on those who managed to survive the first blast.

The three trains that had just pulled into the siding were catapulted into the air. They sank back onto the siding and were immediately buried under the descending girders, bricks and tiles of the fragmented factory building.

Immediately after the first explosion, a second, slightly lesser one occurred, leveling more factory buildings and sending voluminous, sickening clouds of chemical smoke into the air.

Outside the factory sites, the village of Oppau was leveled, as if it had been bombed from the air. The shock waves spread over a 50-mile radius throughout the Mannheim-Ludwigshafen district. At Eisenheim, a train just leaving the station was blown off its tracks and plowed through the wooden sheds, where French soldiers of the Army of Occupation were quartered. Twelve soldiers were killed and several were injured by the freak accident caused by the explosion's concussive force.

The nearby villages of Frankenthal and Edigheim were also leveled, and a steady stream of bandaged refugees began to pour from them, headed toward the hospitals in Mannheim.

Fires spread immediately from the explosion site and moved on into the surrounding villages. Firemen wearing gas masks made their way to the huge, funnel-shaped crater that was once a factory. Their task was multiple: putting out fires, rescuing those who had been injured, putting mutilated animals out of their misery, hauling the bodies and pieces of bodies out of the debris. As they worked, ground water rapidly filled the crater, making the retrieval of bodies or the survival of the injured within it impossible.

Seventy thousand people attended the mass funeral that took place in Ludwigshafen Cemetery in Mannheim, and expressions of bewildered gratitude came from Germans over the international outpouring of grief, concern and comfort.

But then the questions arose: Did the explosion, like those that occurred during the war, come about because of a tank giving way under the giant pressure of uniting nitrogen and hydrogen? Scientists in Berlin speculated that the cause of the catastrophe was "extreme heat, generated by some hitherto unknown gas explosive, [which] must have led to the decomposition and subsequent explosion of a large quantity of ammonia and sulphate of saltpeter which forms the basis of artificial fertilizer."

True enough, some scientists said, but what was that other "unknown gas explosive"? What sort of experimentation was taking place at Oppau? Why did the second explosion take place? And what accounted for the enormous devastation, the likes of which no one had yet seen?

The events of the following years may have explained it. The beginnings of bombs that would stagger the imagination might very well have been given their first public airing at Oppau in September 1921. All during World War II, the nuclear triggering device that would control this awesome power was the subject of a race between the Germans and the Allied powers. The Allies won, and won the war. And humankind, for better or worse, entered the atomic age.

GREAT BRITAIN
ENGLAND
LIVERPOOL

October 10, 1957

• • • • • • • • • • • • • • • •

The overheating of uranium cartridges releasing radioactive iodine caused widespread radioactive contamination surrounding the Windscale Plutonium Plant near Liverpool, England on October 10, 1957. Thirty-three cancer deaths have occurred; more are expected. There was a temporary suspension of the milk and beef industries of northwestern England.

The Windscale plutonium factory in the Cumberland country of northwest England manufactured plutonium for use in nuclear reactors and atomic bombs and produced certain by-products that were used in medicine. Powered by the nearby Calder Hall atomic power plant, it was thought to be, in 1957, a model of clean and efficient productivity.

But the accident that took place on October 10, 1957, which was England's first nuclear accident—and one of the first in the peacetime world—was the forerunner of hundreds of nuclear accidents that would release radioactivity into the atmosphere. In 1957 the world was naive to the hazards, and little space was given to the accident.

But as its aftermath extended and deepened, so did the awareness of its significance.

At 4:15 P.M. on Thursday, October 10, 1957, the number-one pile of uranium at Windscale overheated, and as its temperature rose, it released radioactive iodine-131 vapor and some oxidized uranium particles into the air. It would be 15 minutes before the red-hot uranium pile would be discovered; that part of the plant had been shut down for maintenance.

Shortly after it was discovered, workers wearing gas masks and other protective equipment were assigned to use carbon dioxide to extinguish the fire. It was ineffectual.

A sense that this was no ordinary fire began to grow. All of the plant's off-duty safety workers were called back, and all of the roads to the plant were blocked off. By 5:15, safety experts issued conciliatory statements to the press, claiming that all danger had departed.

By 9:00 A.M. on the 11th, it was decided to use water to damp down the fire. Two plant officials and a local fire chief hauled a hose to the top of the containment dome and aimed it at the fire. No one knew quite what would happen, and plant workers all over the complex crouched behind steel and concrete barriers.

Fortunately, the water worked, but it also released huge clouds of radioactive steam through the stacks and into the atmosphere. The worst was over, everyone thought; there had been neither an explosion nor a meltdown.

By midday of October 11, nearly all of the 3,000 workers at the plant and the nearby Calder Hall atomic energy plant were sent home. They had been exposed to radiation, and it was obvious that a reevaluation of the situation was needed.

Significant quantities of radioactive iodine-131 had been released into the atmosphere over a 200-mile radius, and at 2 A.M. on Sunday, October 13, police began to knock on the doors of the farmhouses in Cumberland. The milk from their cows, the police warned them, might be radioactive.

By Tuesday the 15th, the milk ban was extended from a 14-square-mile area to 200 square miles, including 600 dairy farms. Approximately 30,000 gallons of milk, worth $11,000, were dumped into the Irish Sea each day until the end of October, and all distribution of milk from the contaminated area was immediately halted.

Beyond that, hundreds of cows, goats and sheep were confiscated, shot and buried. Farmers who slaughtered their animals for meat were told to send the thyroid glands to the Atomic Energy Commission for testing.

Farmers in the area now began to make public the tales they had exchanged among themselves: Even before the accident, sterilization had occurred in their cattle. W. E. Hewitson, a dairy farmer in Yottenfews, stated that he had changed bulls four times in four years, but only a third of his cows either calved or gave milk.

Then it became apparent that the radioactive iodine-131 that safety experts first said had drifted out to sea had not done so at all. There was a marked increase in the radioactivity of the atmosphere after the accident at the Windscale plant.

Several months later, British officials conceded to a United Nations conference at Geneva that nearly 700 curies of cesium and strontium had also been released into the air over England and northern Europe, in addition to 20,000 curies of iodine-131. The iodine dose represented more than 1,400 times the quantity American officials later claimed had been released during the 1979 accident at Three Mile Island (see p. 260).

As was so often the case, there were no official follow-up studies regarding the health of residents of the 200-mile area near the plant. When a local health officer, Frank Madge, used a Geiger counter to confirm abnormal radiation levels in mosses and lichens, representatives of the British Atomic Energy Authority discouraged publication of his findings.

Private studies of health data in downwind European countries later indicated a clear impact of the accident on infant-mortality rates. Dr. Ernest Sternglass, interviewed by Harvey Wasserman and Norman Solomon for their study, *Killing Our Own*, remarked, "[It was] as if a small bomb had been detonated in northern Great Britain."

As late as 1981, while the Windscale plant continued to operate without modification, British scientist E. D. Williams stated in the January 1981 issue of *Health Physics Journal* that there were "high cesium levels in people eating fish caught in the path of the Windscale effluent."

By 1990, 33 cancer deaths in the vicinity of the Windscale plant had been directly attributed to the 1957 accident.

INDIA
BHOPAL

December 3, 1984

• • • • • • • • • • • • • • • • •

The worst industrial accident in history, the explosion at the Union Carbide Pesticide Plant in Bhopal, India on December 3, 1984, was caused by a combination of faulty maintenance, laxity in management, outdated equipment, faulty judgment and social factors. At least 2,000 died; 200,000 were injured.

For years, India has been a place where a patina of the present is layered over an ancient civilization, used to conducting itself in ancient ways. The teachings of Kashmir Shaivism go back 3,000 years, and the lyrics of Brahmin chants are in Sanskrit. Oxen carts still haul produce; electricity is still a distant stranger to parts of the country.

When the government of a new, free India was formed, its character was, at least in part, shaped by the country's spiritual leader, Mohandas Gandhi. Although television now permeates India as it does all over the world, the most popular program—the one that brought the entire country to a virtual standstill—was a dramatization of the great and ancient Hindu spiritual epic, the *Mahabharata.*

Thus, there is always a sense of difference, a feeling of, if not compromise, at least accommodation when Western ideas or industries introduce themselves into India. And, sometimes, those accommodations carry with them a certain carelessness.

Although Western industries find that locating their plants in Third World countries is profitable because labor is cheap, there are also trade-offs. The labor is usually both cheap and unskilled. And because of the distance from the source, some equipment that exists in these plants goes too long without updating, replacement or even maintenance. Finally, there is the danger that a kind of casualness, a slowing down of the metabolism that is more in tune with the pace of ancient life than of modern life, works against the constant, concentrated vigilance that can prevent industrial disaster by preparing for it.

This was at least a factor in the complex series of events that led up to the worst industrial accident in the history of the world early in the morning of December 3, 1984. The disaster took place in the Union Carbide Pesticide Plant in Bhopal, a small city in the north central region of Madhya Pradesh, in India, midway between New Delhi and Bombay.

The plant, a boon to this economically depressed city, was located in its slum section, a community called Jai Prakash Nagar.

At 2:45 P.M. on Sunday, December 2, while children played in the dirt outside the huts crammed together near the plant's entrance, about 100 workers reported for duty for the eight-hour late shift.

The plant, which manufactured the pesticide Sevin, had been closed down for some time and had been reactivated only a week before. It was still working at a partial pace, carrying through the process of making the pesticide, which consisted of a mix of carbon tetrachloride, methyl isocyanate and alpha-napthol.

The methyl isocyanate, MIC, was stored in three partially buried tanks, each with a 15,000-gallon capacity.

One of the tanks, number 610, was giving the workers trouble. For some reason they could not determine, the chemical could not be forced out of the tank. Nitrogen was pumped into the tank to force the MIC into the Sevin plant, but each time this was done, the nitrogen leaked out.

There was a greater problem with tank number 610, however, and this, plus a leak that had not been repaired in seven days, would set the stage for a major catastrophe.

First of all, MIC must, to maintain stability and be nonreactive, be kept at a low temperature. A refrigeration unit designed to keep it at that temperature had, for a still-unexplained reason, been turned off. The chemical was thus warmer than the four degrees Fahrenheit recommended in the plant's operating manual, but just how much warmer was impossible to tell, since the instruments monitoring it were old and unreliable.

In addition, the money-losing plant had undergone further cost-cutting procedures in the past months, and this included the curtailment of maintenance on the noncomputerized, behind-the-times equipment. And finally, new supervisors and operators were in key positions.

As a result of this laxity, tank number 610, besides having a faulty valve and not being maintained at the proper temperature, was also overfilled.

Other pieces of the scenario began to come together. At about 9:30 P.M. that night, a supervisor ordered a worker to clean a 23-foot section of pipe that filtered crude MIC before it went into the storage tanks. The worker did this by connecting a hose to the pipe, opening a drain and turning on the water. It flowed into the pipe, out the pipe drains and onto the floor, where it entered a floor drain. It flowed continuously for three hours.

All of the workers and presumably the new supervisor knew that water reacts violently with MIC. They also knew that there was a leaky valve not only in tank number 610 but also in the pipe that was being washed. Rahaman Khan, the worker who washed out the pipe, later told the *New York Times,* "I knew that valves leaked. I didn't check to see if that one was leaking. It was not my job."

It is generally conceded that it was the water flowing from the hose that triggered the horror that was to follow.

At 10:30, a pressure reading was taken on tank 610. It was two pounds per square inch, which was normal.

At 10:45, the next shift arrived. The water was still running.

At 11:00 P.M., the pressure had climbed to 10 pounds per square inch, five times what it had been a half hour before. Something was obviously wrong. But no one did anything about it, because it was still within acceptable limits. In fact, some workers later testified that that was the usual temperature and pressure of the MIC at the plant.

Then, too, there was the problem of the instruments. Shakil Qureshi, the MIC supervisor on duty, later noted that he thought that one of the readings was probably wrong. "Instruments often didn't work," he said. "They got corroded. Crystals would form on them."

But by 11:30 P.M., the eyes and noses of the workers informed them that something was indeed wrong. Their eyes began to tear. They knew MIC was leaking, but this happened on the average of once a month. They often relied on these symptoms to inform them that a leak had occurred. Suman Dey, a worker, later told reporters, "We were human leak detectors."

V. N. Singh, another worker, discovered the leak at approximately 11:45 P.M. He noticed a drip of liquid about 50 feet off the ground, which was accompanied by some yellowish white gas. Mr. Singh informed his supervisor, Mr. Qureshi, who said that he would look into it after his tea break.

The tea break began for everyone at 12:15. And while this ancient custom went on for 20 minutes, the disaster continued to unfold unchecked.

From 12:40 A.M. on December 3, events began to take place with lightning rapidity. The smell of gas rose alarmingly. Workers choked on it. The temperature gauge on tank number 610 rose above 77 degrees Fahrenheit, the top of the scale. The pressure gauge was visibly inching upward toward 40 pounds per square inch, a point at which the emergency relief valve on the MIC tank was scheduled to burst open.

At 12:45 P.M., the pressure gauge read 55 pounds per square inch, 15 points from the top of the scale. Supervisor Qureshi ordered all the water in the plant turned off, and it was only then that the water in the hose that had been running for three hours was finally found and turned off.

But it was far too late. The water reacted with the MIC, and the leak burst forth. Panicked workers dashed to and fro, blinded and coughing.

An alarm sounded, and within minutes the fire brigade arrived to place a water curtain around the escaping gas. But the curtain reached only 100 feet in the air. The top of the stack through which the gas was now spewing into the atmosphere was 120 feet high, and the gas fountained another 10 feet above that.

A vent gas scrubber, a device designed to neutralize the escaping gas, was turned on. But its gauges showed that no caustic soda was flowing into it. Or, perhaps, the gauge was broken. Who knew at this point? In either case, the gas, instead of being neutralized, was shooting out of the scrubber stack and was being carried on the high winds southward from the plant into the surrounding slums.

There were four buses parked by the road leading out of the plant. Drivers were supposed to man them in an emergency and load and evacuate workers and people who lived near the plant. But no drivers appeared. They, along with the terrified workers, were running from the plant.

At 1 A.M., Mr. Qureshi had run out of ideas. He called S. P. Choudhary, the assistant factory manager, who instructed him to turn on the flare tower, which was designed to burn off escaping gas.

But, explained Mr. Qureshi, with all that gas in the air, turning on the flare would cause a huge explosion. At any rate, a four-foot, elbow-shaped piece of pipe was missing from the flare. It had corroded and was due to be replaced as soon as the part arrived from the United States.

An alternative would have been to dump the MIC into a spare storage tank. There were two spares that were supposed to be empty. But they were not. Both contained MIC.

The workers who remained and tried to control the leak now donned oxygen masks. It was the only way they could breathe. Visibility was down to one foot. The supervisor, unable to find a mask, he said, opted to run away from the plant. He found a clear area, scaled a six-foot fence topped by barbed wire, vaulted over it and fell to the other side, breaking his leg. He was later transported to a hospital, with many, many others.

The gas poured unchecked out of the leak until 2:30 A.M. Jagannathan Mukund, the factory manager, arrived at 3 A.M., and only then, because, he later stated, the telephones were out of order, did he send a man to inform the police about the accident. The company had a policy, he said, of not involving the local authorities in gas leaks.

And to be fair, the sleeping populace *did* hear the emergency sirens going off, but they sounded so often in false alarms, that the people in the surrounding slums ignored them and went back to sleep—some of them for the last time.

Outside the factory, people were dying by the hundreds, some in their sleep. Others, panicked, choking, blinded, ran into the cloud of gas, inhaling more and more of it until they dropped dead. Thousands of terrified animals perished where they stood.

The outside temperature was only 57 degrees Fahrenheit which kept the lethal cloud of gas close to the ground, rather than allowing it to rise and dissipate into the atmosphere, as it would have under warmer conditions.

The gas crept into open shacks, killing the weak and the frail immediately. Others woke, vomited and groped blindly to get outdoors, where they filled their lungs with the searing chemical vapor.

"I awoke when I found it difficult to breathe," said Rahis Bano to a reporter afterward. "All around me my neighbors were shouting, and then a wave of gas hit me."

She fell down, vomiting, and her two sons, whom she was carrying, rolled on the floor. She revived herself and grabbed one son. He and she would survive; the son she left behind would die.

Rivers of humanity, tens of thousands of people, stumbled about. Some were trampled. Others simply gave up and sat down. As the cloud spread southeastward, it enveloped the Bhopal railroad station. Ticket takers, trainmen and passengers died where they stood.

A hill was located in the center of the city, and thousands rushed toward it, thinking they could climb above the gas. "There were cars, bicycles, auto rickshaws, anything that would move on the road trying to get up the hill," said one survivor. "I saw people just collapsing by the side of the road."

New hazards presented themselves; many of the fleeing refugees were run over by cars and buses and emergency vehicles. The police, instead of helping, heightened the panic by roaring through the crowds, their police van loudspeakers shouting, "Run! Run! Poison gas is spreading!"

Hospitals were immediately filled. Doctors and nurses tried to save as many as they could, but Hamida Hospital recorded a death a minute until it finally gave up trying to keep count. Dr. N. H. Trivedi, deputy superintendent of the hospital, told the *Times,* "People picked up helpless strangers, their best friends, their relatives, and brought them in here. They did far more than the police and official organizations."

Most hospitals placed two stricken people in one bed, until there was finally no more room, and emergency clinics were set up in stores and on streets.

When dawn finally broke over Bhopal, it lit a scene of cataclysmic destruction. Thousands of bodies—human and animal—littered the streets. No birds sang. The only movement was from trucks sent out to pick up the dead and to search houses for more dead and dying.

Between 2,000 and 2,500 had died, and more than 200,000 would be afflicted for years, possibly for the rest of their lives, with the aftereffects of the Bhopal tragedy. Some were permanently blinded. Others could not sleep, had difficulty breathing or digesting food and had trouble functioning.

For a week, the suffering continued in Bhopal's hospitals and clinics. Children between one and six years old seemed to suffer most. The tragedy was made worse by the inability of either medical specialists or parents to do anything. Relatives watched mutely from doorways as doctors placed intravenous feeding tubes in the children's arms and oxygen tubes in their noses and mouths.

For weeks, sirens wailed, cremations took place one after another and bodies were buried in mass graves. The worst panic took place 10 days after the accident, on December 13, when Union Carbide announced that it would start the plant up again on Sunday, December 16 to neutralize what remained of the MIC.

Bhopal, normally a city of 900,000, was already depleted. Besides the 2,000 dead and the 200,000 injured, 100,000 others had fled after the disaster. Now 100,000 more took to trains, buses, cars, planes, auto rickshaws, two-wheeled tongas and their own feet to put a distance between themselves and what they perceived to be the site of another possible catastrophe.

Two thousand paramilitary troops and special armed police officers were brought in by the Indian government to supplement the local police force in an effort to prevent the looting of vacated homes and to maintain order in the clinics and refugee camps.

Most of the dead came from Jai Prakash Nagar and Kali Parade, the two slum neighborhoods adjacent to the plant, but the brisk night breeze carried the fatal fumes much farther than that.

A year after the accident, residents of Bhopal who had been affected by MIC were still suffering. According to authorities in India, an estimated 10 to 20% of the 200,000 people injured were still seriously affected. Many were having trouble breathing, sleeping, digesting food and undertaking simple tasks, just as they had right after the leak occurred.

They suffered memory loss, nausea, nerve damage, including tremors, and damage to kidneys, liver, stomach and spleen. A year later, 40% of those afflicted were in the same condition, 40% had improved and 20% had worsened. Medical studies predicted that these would be long-term, perhaps lifelong, afflictions.

The relief effort had become bureaucratic and sometimes contradictory. Cortisone injections were given by one medical team; cough medicine and aspirin by another. One health expert, Rashmi Mayur of the Urban Institute in Bombay, averred that he had come across one victim who had been able to get 250 pills in one day from seven different doctors.

What ultimately became apparent in the tragic unfolding of this disaster was that ignorance was also a culprit. Even as people were dying, Union Carbide factory doctors were telling local physicians that MIC, which is used in 20 to 25% of all the world's pesticides, only caused lung and eye irritation. And none of these company doctors had informed the local medical workers ahead of time that a simple antidote for the effects of the chemical was to merely cover the face with a wet cloth. "Had we known this," police superintendent Swaraj Puri later told reporters, "many lives might have been saved."

Six months before the accident, the National Academy of Sciences had said that little or nothing was known about the health effects of most of the 54,000 chemicals used in commercial products, thus making treatment and prevention difficult at the very best.

Afterward, concerted efforts were made to find causes and blame, and there was more than enough to go around. Officials of Union Carbide were arrested when they arrived in India and then freed. They were later charged with criminal negligence, as was the plant supervisor. The government of India filed suit against Union Carbide in the federal district court in Manhattan, seeking compensation for the victims of the disaster. The suits are still pending.

It was generally acknowledged that the seeds of the tragedy were planted in 1972 when, under government pressure to reduce imports and loss of foreign exchange, the company proposed to manufacture and store MIC at the plant in Bhopal. Both the local government and the company agreed, at that time, that the risks would not be high.

Dr. S. R. Kamat, a prominent Bombay expert on industrial health and the hazards of development, probably summed it up most succinctly and accurately: "Western technology came to this country but not the infrastructure for that technology," he told the *New York Times* on February 2, 1985. "A lot of risks have been taken here, " he went on. "Machinery is outdated. Spare parts are not included. Maintenance is inadequate. Bhopal is the tip of an iceberg, an example of lapses not only in India but by the United States and many other countries."

JAPAN
TSURUGA

March 8, 1981

• • • • • • • • • • • • • • • •

A leak from a disposal building at the nuclear power plant at Tsuruga, Japan on March 8, 1981 caused widespread radiation contamination. Fifty-nine workers were exposed to radiation, and Japan's fishing industry was temporarily suspended.

The nuclear power plant at Tsuruga, Japan, a seacoast city of 60,000 located on the far west coast of Japan, opposite Tokyo, was in chronic trouble in the early spring of 1981. And Japan's Atomic Power Commission, like the atomic power commissions of the United States (see Three Mile Island, p. 260) and Great Britain (see Windscale, p. 252), spent as much time misinforming the public as it did in investigating the mishap.

On March 8, a huge leakage of radioactive waste occurred in a disposal building adjacent to the main plant. The first newspaper report did not appear until April 18, more than a month from the time that 16 *tons* of the waste had spilled into the adjoining Wakasa Bay, which flows into the Sea of Japan.

The April 18 bulletin merely stated that a crack in a pipe or the storage tanks themselves "might have allowed waste water to seep into general drainage pipes into the Wakasa Bay."

Shortly thereafter, the Ministry of International Trade and Industry also announced that it had found radioactivity levels 10 times normal in seaweed near drainage outlets, and the Kyodo News Service accompanied the news release with the discomforting information that the amount of cobalt-60 discovered in the seaweed and the soil surrounding the plant was "5,000 times the previous highest reading . . . the effects on the human body could be serious if the radioactive waste has spread throughout the bay."

It would not be until April 21, six and a half weeks after the mishap, that the Japan Atomic Power Company would make its first statement, in which it acknowledged that some waste-contaminated water had leaked onto the floor of the plant and that 56 men who had been put to work mopping up the water with buckets and rags "had been exposed to radiation at levels considerably below government limits," an assessment the Ministry of Trade and Industry immediately disputed. The announcement went on to speculate that the plant's executives might be indicted on criminal charges.

Finally, two days later, the Tsuruga company released more detailed information, which had been withheld, a company spokesman avowed, because of "Japanese emotionalism toward anything nuclear."

The accident, according to the account released by the company, occurred when an operator apparently forgot to shut off a valve, which in turn let water run through a radioactive sludge tank, which overflowed and splashed on the floor of the power plant and then seeped into the general sewage system.

Akira Machida, the plant's general manager, attempted to downplay the accident by comparing it with Three Mile Island. "[It was] nowhere near as serious as America's Three Mile Island," he told reporters, but then he acknowledged that the biggest blunder was in failing to report it to the authorities.

Further revelations came swiftly. Forty-five other workers had been exposed to radiation in January, when another pipe had broken in the plant. Thirty-one other accidents had occurred since the plant had opened in 1970.

But the worst was yet to come. Fish and fish products from the immediate area of Tsuruga had been recalled following the March 8 mishap, but no one knew how widespread the contamination of the waters of the Sea of Japan had been. (Several years later, mutant forms of fish continued to be caught in the area, indicating that there was far more contamination than first reports indicated.) Japanese officials could not have forgotten the 1954 furor when 23 fishermen and the tuna catch aboard the Japanese fishing boat *Lucky Dragon* were victims of acute radiation exposure after the U.S. test explosion of a hydrogen bomb near Rongelap Atoll in the Marshall Islands. But their silence in 1981 seemed to indicate that they had.

Finally, in May, the chairman of the board and the president of the Japan Atomic Power Company resigned, accepting the responsibility for the leakages. A government investigation blamed human error, faulty equipment and structural weaknesses.

It would be Japan's first and last nuclear accident so far. That human carelessness and cover-up should figure at all in the nuclear industry of the first country in the world to suffer a nuclear holocaust made it enormously significant, and a discouraging comment on the pervasiveness of human carelessness.

UNITED STATES
IDAHO
IDAHO FALLS

January 3, 1961

• • • • • • • • • • • • • • •

Sabotage was suspected but never proved in the chemical explosion that blew apart the reactor core at the Idaho Nuclear Engineering Laboratory in Idaho Falls on January 3, 1961. Three died.

The explosion that shattered the core of an atomic reactor at the National Reactor Testing Station, part of the Idaho Nuclear Engineering Laboratory at Idaho Falls, Idaho, is significant in two ways: First, it was the first nuclear accident to occur in the United States. And second, it was symptomatic of conditions that would cause future disasters at other nuclear plants around the world.

The Idaho Nuclear Engineering Laboratory is a huge complex in which research and development projects are conducted for the military, spent nuclear submarine fuel is recycled and military radioactive wastes are stored.

Because of the military and therefore largely secret character of the operations of the facility, details remain sketchy.

At 9:02 P.M., Mountain Standard Time, on January 3, 1961, three military technicians were at work, operating a new-style reactor known as Stationary Low Power Reactor Number 1. The reactor was a two-year-old prototype of a small mobile unit that was being developed as a heat and power facility for the armed forces in remote areas.

Suddenly, the core of the reactor blew. A fuel rod shot out of the reactor, piercing the body of one of the technicians and pinning him to the reactor containment, high above the core. The other two men were blown apart and had to be buried in pieces in lead-lined coffins. The radiation level within the container building was so high that it would be weeks before officials dared enter it, even in protective garb.

The cause of the accident was later determined to be "human error," causing an accidental overloading of one chemical against others. In 1981, Stephen Hanauer of the Nuclear Regulatory Commission, in an interview with Harvey Wasserman and Norman Solomon, authors of *Killing Our Own,* a study of atomic radiation in the United States, indicated that "the 'accident' may have been caused deliberately by one of the technicians in a bizarre suicide-murder plot stemming from a love triangle at the plant." More atrocious happenings than this have occurred, but there has, so far as this author knows, been no further substantiation of this steamy analysis of the events of January 3, 1961.

What is known, however, is that the Idaho plant had, as have most nuclear and industrial facilities experiencing accidents, a history of sloppiness. In the late 1960s, it was charged with accidentally dumping concentrated uranium on a nearby road. From 1952 to 1970, its management deliberately tossed 16 billion gallons of liquid waste into wells that fed directly into the water table below, causing radioactive contamination seven and one half miles away.

During the 1978 World Series, the plant supervisor was consumed by watching the games on a portable TV, which had been sneaked into the plant against regulations, and neglected to notice a dangerous buildup of radioactivity in a small nearby uranium-processing column. Or, perhaps even if the game had not gobbled up his attention, he would not have noticed the imbalance in the column, since one recording chart of the plant's monitoring devices had run out of paper two weeks before, and the paper had not been replaced.

At 8:45 P.M., high-radiation alarms were tripped by a bursting force of radiation from the afflicted column. The supervisor and others escaped to uncontaminated areas, and the column was brought under control, but not before 8,000 curies of radioactive iodine, krypton and xenon had been released into the atmosphere—an amount that could easily threaten the health of anyone downwind of the plant.

The plant supervisor was later fired, and an investigation of worker alienation and low morale at the plant indicated that these were major factors leading to both the 1961 and 1978 accidents.

UNITED STATES
OKLAHOMA
GORE

January 4, 1986

• • • • • • • • • • • • • • • •

Faulty judgment was the culprit in the chemical leak at the Sequoyah Fuels Corporation Plant at Gore, Oklahoma on January 4, 1986. One died.

The bald statistics of the chemical leak released by a storage tank rupture at the Sequoyah nuclear fuel processing plant in Gore, Oklahoma on January 4, 1986 are unimpressive. But its magnitude goes far beyond its statistics, in a remarkable and disquieting resemblance to the far more cataclysmic disaster at the Union Carbide plant in Bhopal, India two years before (see p. 253). The very vastness of that catastrophe was supposed to be a lesson in safety, maintenance and preparedness. But the accident in Gore confirmed the axiom that lessons unlearned become errors recommitted.

The facts are these: At about 9:30 A.M. on Saturday, January 4, 1986, workers at the Sequoyah nuclear fuel plant, which is owned by the oil and natural-gas manufacturing company Kerr-McGee, discovered that they had overfilled a shipping container with liquid uranium hexafluoride. The substance is used as a raw material for nuclear fuel, and it was to be shipped in solid form for further processing.

The error was caused by a faulty instrument, which caused a container that was rated to hold 27,500 pounds of the substance to be loaded to a weight of 29,700 pounds.

A decision was made to heat the container enough to convert some of the substance to gas, so that the excess could be removed. For some reason never explained, the heating process was delayed until *two hours* after the discovery of the overfill.

Finally, at 1:30 P.M., the workers moved the container into an outdoor steam chest and began to heat it. Several workers remained nearby, in the production building. One of them, James Harrison, had just mounted a flight of stairs to the top of the building. Suddenly, the tank exploded. The uranium hexafluoride, now partially a gas, shot skyward, merged with the moisture in the air and fractured into two components: uranyl fluoride, a heavy white powder, and hydrofluoric acid, a highly corrosive gas. Both were initially radioactive, but as soon as the uranyl fluoride powder fell to the ground, only it remained radioactive.

The gaseous hydrofluoric acid, a lethally corrosive substance, was drawn immediately by the ventilation equipment into the production building where the workers were stationed. Thirty-one workers were immediately exposed to the corrosive cloud. They ran, stumbling and gasping, from the building, while the cloud outside, powered by 25- to 30-mile-per-hour winds, began to drift outward over the open countryside, where it would affect 77 unsuspecting people and send them to Sequoyah Memorial Hospital.

James Harrison, the worker who had climbed the staircase inside the production building, was trapped above the slowly rising cloud of gas. His only escape was a route directly through it, and he chose to plunge forward, through the cloud and down the stairs. Before he reached the bottom, he had been blinded and scalded and was choking from the fumes.

He was immediately rushed in an ambulance to the hospital, while the gas, which is widely used in industry to etch glass and make plastics, including Teflon, was working within his body. The gas coagulates proteins on contact and can almost instantly create second- and third-degree burns when it touches the skin. Even in a diluted form, it can burn or irritate the mucous lining of the lungs.

By the time he reached the hospital, Harrison's exposed skin was laced with horrible burns. The corneas of his eyes had been seared by the acid, blinding him. Four hours after arriving at the hospital, Harrison's lungs swelled and hemorrhaged from the effects of the acid gas, and he died.

Others, including motorists and the local sheriff, who had been affected when he responded to the emergency situation at the plant, were treated with oxygen, asthma medication and breathing therapy. They survived, as did nearby residents, a fifth of them children, who were exposed to the gas cloud as it grew more diluted and drifted downwind from the plant.

The 30 plant workers who had been exposed to the uranyl fluoride were given alkaline treatments—two Alka Seltzers every four hours—to treat its presence in their kidneys.

Safety-clothed cleanup men were sent out to scrub down highways and dig up topsoil that had been contaminated by radiation, and the investigation began.

Within weeks, the pattern that characterized the Bhopal disaster began to reassert itself. The plant, it turned out, had been cited for a number of safety violations—15 since 1978. The cylinder rupture was not without precedent. In 1960, 17,800 pounds of liquid uranium hexafluoride from a ruptured cylinder that was being heated at a government uranium plant in Peducah, Kentucky had injured 21 men. In 1966, one worker had been hospitalized when 3,844 pounds of uranium hexafluoride escaped from a cylinder after a valve had been improperly turned at a government uranium processing plant in Fernald, Ohio. In 1978, 21,125 pounds escaped from a ruptured cylinder that was being improperly moved at a government plant in Portsmouth, Ohio. And a mere two years earlier, in 1984, the horrendous leak at the Union Carbide installation in Bhopal, India had devastated a countryside, killing over 2,000 people and injuring 200,000.

One would think that the history of accidents preceding the event at Gore, Oklahoma would have precluded it. But apparently not. Kerr-McGee, like Union Carbide, was not making much money on the plant and had resorted to cost-cutting shortcuts. As in Bhopal, uncared for and aging instruments did not work properly and thus contributed to the catastrophe.

But that was just the beginning. The similarities multiplied. Both happened with a weekend crew in charge. In both cases, the process used was a clear violation of company regulations, and yet a supervisor took part in it. In both cases, despite repeated instructions from regulators, the plants had failed to develop evacuation plans. In both cases, innocent people beyond the perimeters of the plant were unexpectedly afflicted with the effects of carelessness, cost cutting and human error.

Thus the parallels were massive and discouraging and presaged an uncomfortable future for populaces living near chemical processing plants.

UNITED STATES
PENNSYLVANIA
MIDDLETOWN

March 28, 1979

• • • • • • • • • • • • • • • •

The worst nuclear disaster in the history of the United States was blamed on human error, which was in turn caused by design flaws. No deaths or injuries occurred at the plant; there is still contention over infant and fetus mortality after the radiation spread. The chief casualty was the growth of the National Atomic Power Program.

The worst nuclear disaster in U.S. history occurred in one of America's youngest nuclear power plants. The Three Mile Island Unit Two Nuclear Power Generator, owned by the Metropolitan Edison Company and located on an island in the Susquehanna River, approximately 11 miles south of Harrisburg, Pennsylvania, began operation on December 28, 1978. According to a letter sent by consumer advocate Ralph Nader to President Jimmy Carter, the plant was rushed into service in order to obtain a tax break of $40 million, despite the fact that, during its initial break-in period, the reactor was experiencing mechanical failures and other problems.

Nader was, and still is, opposed to public nuclear power, and that undoubtedly skewed his evaluation of the birth of the plant. Still, there must have been a basic core of truth in his accusations, for just slightly more than three months after it began operating, the Three Mile Island generator showed its flaws in a dramatic and terrible way, by leaking radiation over an enormous area and by narrowly missing that most dreaded of nuclear accidents, a reactor meltdown.

At 3:58 A.M. on Wednesday, March 28, 1979, the first of a chain of mishaps occurred at the plant. A pump that provided steam to the electric turbines broke down. This in turn shut down another pump that circulated water through the reactor, which in turn raised the temperature of the reactor, which opened a relief valve designed to bleed off the increased pressure brought about by the rise in temperature. Within the reactor, some of the cladding, or sheaths around the fuel rods, melted. The uranium pellets in them apparently did not.

By this time, alarms were sounding in the control room, and operators, unschooled in this sort of unprecedented emergency, began to make wrong decisions, while the system itself malfunctioned. The relief valve failed to close, and consequently pressure in the reactor dropped low enough to allow the water to vaporize.

Then, a major error was committed. An operator opened a valve allowing water from this system to enter a waste tank where it created enough pressure to rupture the plumbing. Sixty thousand gallons of radioactive water flooded the reactor to a depth of eight feet.

A second human error followed rapidly. The emergency core cooling system kicked in, but an operator shut it off.

Now, a pump flooded an auxiliary building with contaminated water, causing a release of steam. Within moments, radioactive steam poured up the vent stack and into the atmosphere.

Inexplicably, it would take operators almost three hours to act on these events. It would be 7 A.M. before state authorities would be informed and another hour before the authorities would declare a "general emergency."

Even this general emergency was, as in the Windscale disaster (see p. 252) minimized, presumably to prevent panic. Margaret Reilly, of Pennsylvania's Department of Radiation Protection, in one of the most monumental understatements of all time, likened the escape of radiation to "a gnat's eyelash."

However, authorities were aware that a minimum of a million millirems per hour of radiation was present inside the reactor building at Three Mile Island, a lethal dose for anyone directly exposed to it. Monitors 1,000 feet from the vent stacks, where the radioactive steam was spewing into the air, showed levels of 365 millirems of beta and gamma rays per hour.

Three months later, Albert Gibson, a Radiation Support section chief who would coauthor the Nuclear Regulatory Commission's final report on Three Mile Island emissions, testified, "All radiation monitors in the vent stack, where as much as 80 percent of the radiation escaped, went off the scale the morning of the accident. The trouble with those monitors is they were never contemplated for use in monitoring accidents like Three Mile Island."

Besides the beta and gamma emissions, there were bursts of strontium and iodine-131, which characteristically settles on grass, is eaten by cows and thus enters the milk supply.

On Thursday, holding tanks filled to overflowing with radioactive water were opened, pouring 400,000 gallons of water containing xenon-133 and xenon-135 into the Susquehanna River, while federal nuclear officials assured the public that the gases posed "little hazard to persons living downstream of the . . . plant."

By the end of Thursday, March 29, detectable levels of increased radiation were measured over a four-county area, and officials at the plant admitted that, contrary to their early assessment, 180 to 300 of the 36,000 fuel rods in the reactor had melted.

At 9 A.M. on Friday, March 30, the Pennsylvania Emergency Management Agency reported that there had been a new, "uncontrolled release" of radiation—a puff of contaminated steam.

Because of intense radioactivity within the reactor, the temperature had risen high enough in places to break up the water molecules into hydrogen and oxygen, forming a large bubble of hydrogen, which, if large enough, could prevent further reduction, therefore inhibiting the ability of the circulating water to cool down the fuel rods.

Thus, a meltdown was possible, and becoming more probable.

Now, Governor Richard Thornburgh issued a directive that advised pregnant women and small children to evacuate and stay at least five miles away from the Three Mile Island facility.

In 23 schools, children were pulled from classes, crammed into cafeterias and ordered not to open windows. From these gathering points, they were transported in sealed school buses to other schools 10 to 15 miles away. ("It was sure hot in that bus with all those windows up," said nine-year-old Kim Hardy, from Etters, a community within the five-mile radius.) Parents were then informed of their children's whereabouts.

Fright, but no panic, abounded. An air-raid siren shrieked in Harrisburg shortly before noon, setting off a midday traffic jam of jittery state employees. The alarm was explained away by the governor's office as either a malfunction or the overzealous response of a civil defense official to Governor Thornburgh's directive.

Meanwhile, towns near the plant, such as Goldboro, had been emptying out ever since the beginning of the accident. A small leak of people from the villages had turned into a torrent by Friday, the 30th. Gasoline stations were jammed; telephone switchboards were so overloaded that callers received nothing but busy signals.

Fifteen mass-care centers were established in counties surrounding the Middletown area.

Back at the plant, officials were tensely monitoring the bubble of hydrogen, trying to decide whether to allow it to sink to the bottom of the containment vessel by drawing off water—and thus risking a further increase of temperature and the consequent possibility of a meltdown—or starting up the reactor again and trying to saturate the bubble with steam, which would break it up.

A third, venting method was tried, and on Saturday, the 31st, the bubble was reduced enough so that a combination of safety rods and water could hasten the "cold shutdown" of the reactor. The danger of a meltdown passed.

By Monday, April 9, the Nuclear Regulatory Commission (NRC) declared the Three Mile Island crisis at an end and said it was safe for pregnant women and young children to return to their homes, despite the fact that the reactor was still leaking small quantities of radiation into the air and that readings of radiation emissions were still above average.

Schools were reopened, government offices returned to business as usual and the civil defense forces were taken off full alert. It would be months before the reactor would be entirely shut down, and further instrument failure would lengthen that process, too.

But the book on Three Mile Island was not closed, by any means. First, there was the business of assigning responsibility for the accident. On May 11, 1979, the NRC issued a report blaming the operators for "inadvertently turn[ing] a minor accident into a major one because they could not tell what was really happening inside the reactor." This juxtaposition of human, instrument and design error ran through the NRC report like a fugue.

The accident began when someone forgot to reopen a set of valves, and operators failed to notice the mistake. Operators apparently paid attention mainly to the pressurizer water indicator, which was misleading them, and failed to watch other instruments that should have informed them that something was wrong. Operators apparently failed to follow the procedure for dealing with a stuck-open pressure relief valve, and so forth.

But in its conclusions, the NRC removed some of the onus from the operators. "Human factors engineering has not been sufficiently emphasized in the design and layout of the control rooms," it admitted in its summary.

In February 1984, Metropolitan Edison Company pleaded guilty to charges that it knowingly used "inaccurate and meaningless" test methods at the Unit Two reactor prior to the accident. The company then disciplined 17 employees—among them a former vice president, shift supervisors, control room operators, shift foremen and managers—for manipulating records of the tests. The penalties ranged from letters of reprimand to the loss of two weeks' pay.

Another aspect of the continuing story of Three Mile Island was the effect on the surrounding population.

As in practically every nuclear accident, there was no evacuation plan in place when the disaster occurred. To compound this, reports released during and after the accident were, either deliberately or inadvertently, misinformation. Despite the admirable motivation of preventing needless panic, the "gnat's eyelash" analogy seems irresponsible in light of the later findings of other scientists and investigators.

Although the NRC continued to maintain that there had been and was still no significant intensification of radiation as a result of the Three Mile Island accident, Dr. Ernest Sternglass, a University of Pittsburgh Medical School professor of radiology, in a paper presented at the Fifth World Congress of Engineers and Architects at Tel Aviv, Israel in 1980, stated that figures from Harrisburg and Holy Spirit hospitals showed that infant deaths in the vicinity of Three Mile Island had *doubled,* from six during February through April 1979 to 12 in May through July.

Furthermore, Dr. Sternglass observed, data from the U.S. Bureau of Vital Statistics showed that there were "242 [infant] deaths above the normally expected number in Pennsylvania and a total of 430 in the entire northeastern area of the United States." He based his linkage on the large amounts of iodine-131 released into the atmosphere and the peaking of infant mortality within a matter of months after the release of the I-131.

Dr. Sternglass went on to charge that, as NRC investigator Joseph Hendrie had confirmed on March 30, 1979, individual areas where the steam plume touched the ground were "husky" and in the range of 120 millirems per hour or more, which was easily enough to cause severe damage to fetuses in the womb.

In addition, Dr. Sternglass noted that doses of I-131 had impacted people in the path of the plume in Syracuse, Rochester and Albany, New York, and each city had suffered rising infant deaths.

"My daughter got real sick," Becky Mease of Middletown told an NRC panel. "She had diarrhea for three days straight and headaches and she became anemic. I didn't know what to do. My little girl is still getting colds and sinus problems. Now if that's not because of that power plant, you tell me what it is."

Deaths in the Middletown area from thyroid cancer (the thyroid gland is particularly affected by iodine-131) are still monitored by families and organizations. No absolute link has been established, but those who were affected feel that the cause was the accident and the radiation it released into the Pennsylvania countryside. Some cancer victims have sued the Metropolitan Edison Company.

And finally, the third reason for the continued interest in Three Mile Island is the ongoing impact it has had on the nuclear energy industry in America. Prior to Three Mile Island, antinuclear activists were relatively quiescent. On May 6, 1979, after the accident, a crowd of 65,000 demonstrators arrived at the Capitol in Washington, D.C. to demand the cessation of building and the closing of nuclear power plants in the United States.

The Three Mile Island disaster opened the door to an escalation of protest activity that became rocket powered after the Chernobyl disaster (see p. 263). It was responsible for the abandonment of the Shoreham Nuclear Energy plant on Long Island, and the virtual halt in construction of nuclear power plants nationwide in the 1980s.

USSR
KASLI
1957

• • • • • • • • • • • • • • • • • •

Military and Soviet secrecy has muffled the details of an explosion in a nuclear waste dump near Kasli, in the Ural Mountains of the USSR, sometime in 1957, but a chemical or steam explosion has been theorized as its cause. Hundreds were said to have died; tens of thousands were afflicted.

What was perhaps the most cataclysmic nuclear disaster in the world remains, to this day, unofficially recorded and officially nonexistent, according to the Soviet government. Even the U.S. Central Intelligence Agency, which apparently knew of the disaster shortly after it occurred, suppressed any mention of it and in fact denied its existence for 20 years, until the Freedom of Information Act forced it to open its files on the subject.

So it is only possible to piece together the fragments of this cataclysm, largely through the diligent research of Dr. Zhores Medvedev, a Soviet emigre scientist who, in 1976, first brought the news of the explosion to the West.

In an article titled "Two Decades of Dissidence" in the British journal *New Scientist,* Dr. Medvedev told of "an enormous explosion, like a violent volcano," in a radioactive-waste dump in the Ural Mountains near the town of Kasli, or Kyshtym, as Dr. Medvedev called it. "The nuclear reactions had led to an over-heating in the underground burial grounds," he continued. "The explosion poured radioactive dust and materials high up into the sky . . . Tens of thousands of people were affected, hundreds dying, though the real figures have never been made public. The large [50-kilometer-square] area, where the accident happened, is still considered dangerous and is closed to the public."

The official response to the article was swift and negative. *Tass* denied it. Sir. John Hill, the chairman of the United Kingdom Atomic Energy Authority, wrote a letter to the *Times* of London calling the story "rubbish."

But one month later, Lev Tumerman, another Russian emigre, wrote a letter to the *Jerusalem Post* relating a ride through the same countryside in the Urals in 1960. "On both sides of the road as far as one could see the land was 'dead,' " wrote Tumerman, "no villages, no towns, only the chimneys of destroyed houses, no cultivated fields or pastures, no herds, no people . . . nothing."

Signs warned him to proceed without stopping for the next 30 kilometers and to drive through at maximum speed. "An enormous area, some hundreds of square kilometers, had been laid waste," he concluded.

Finally, in 1979, Dr. Medvedev published *Nuclear Disaster in the Urals.* In it, he quoted Soviet scientists who made post-catastrophe studies of plant and animal life and subsequent weather patterns in the area. All confirmed the explosion and its consequent radiation contamination.

Within weeks, a special report was released by the Oak Ridge National Laboratory that confirmed the Soviet scientists' reports and stated that a system of 14 lakes had been contaminated by the Kasli blast and that 30 small towns that had been on Soviet maps of the southern Ural region before 1957 were no longer there.

Investigation by reporters of newly released CIA files revealed anecdotal confirmation from survivors who were in the area. One described a huge explosion that shook the ground and spewed a huge cloud of red dust into the air, which settled on the leaves of trees. "Very quickly," the eyewitness said, "all the leaves curled up and fell off the trees," as did vegetables that were covered with the red radioactive dust.

"All stores in Kamensk-Uralskiy which sold milk, meat and other foodstuffs were closed as a precaution against radiation exposure," said another, "and new supplies were brought in two days later by train and truck. The food was sold directly from the vehicles and the resulting queues were reminiscent of those during the worst shortages during World War II."

That was only the beginning. As the effects of the widespread radiation contamination began to be felt, another witness reported, "The people in Kamensk-Uralskiy grew hysterical with fear, and with incidence of unknown 'mysterious' diseases breaking out."

Homes were burned to the ground to prevent their owners from reentering them, and these displaced people "were allowed to take with them only the clothes in which they were dressed."

"One of the current topics of conversation at the time," said another survivor, "was whether eating fish or eating crabs from the radioactive rivers of the area was more dangerous . . . Hundreds of people perished and the area became and will remain radioactive for years."

American officials tended to soft-pedal the implications for worldwide storage of nuclear waste. Despite more realistic warnings against risks of nuclear dumping, Richard Corrigan, a spokesperson for the Ford administration in Washington, wrote in the *National Journal* of August 1979, "They [the Russians] don't know what they're doing and we do."

It was cheerful news, but disarmingly simplistic when compared with the facts of Windscale (see p. 252) and two catastrophes that were yet to come: Three Mile Island (see p. 260) and Chernobyl (see following entry).

USSR
PRIPYAT

April 26, 1986

• • • • • • • • • • • • • • • • • •

The worst recorded nuclear accident in history, that of the Chernobyl nuclear power plant in Pripyat, USSR on April 26, 1986, was the result of human error in conducting a test of the system. Thirty-one died in the explosion and fire; more than 100,000 were evacuated from the vicinity of the plant, and casualties are yet to be finally calculated.

"An accident has occurred at the Chernobyl nuclear power plant as one of the reactors was damaged. Measures are being taken to eliminate the consequences of the accident. Aid is being given to those affected. A government commission has been set up."

Two days after the stupendous disaster at the Chernobyl nuclear power plant, located 70 miles north of Kiev, the capital of the Ukraine, the Soviet government released this terse, businesslike and uninformative announcement.

Some of the facts and some of the effects of this, the worst nuclear disaster in history, had already drifted out of the Soviet Union, on winds bringing radioactive waste to Scandinavia, then eastern Europe, then western Europe and finally to the rest of the world, including the United States.

The situation at Chernobyl was frightening. With four 1,000-megawatt reactors in operation, it was one of the largest and oldest of the Soviet Union's 15 or so civilian nuclear stations. There, a cascade of awesome human errors had set in motion, as surely as uranium brought about a chain reaction, a series of events the likes of which the world had yet to experience.

At 1 A.M. on Friday, April 25, operators of the number-four reactor, which had gone on line in 1983, began to reduce its power in preparation for an operations test. The test was designed to measure the amount of residual energy produced by the turbine and generator after the nuclear reactor had been shut down. The conclusion of the test would tell these engineers how long the turbine and generator would be able to run if, in some sort of emergency, the reactor were shut down.

It was a routine test. The valves on the main steam line between the reactor and the turbine were to be closed, thus stopping power to the turbine, and the residual energy would then be measured until the turbine stopped.

While this was happening, steam would still be produced by the reactor, which would be slowly reduced to a fraction of its potential power. That steam could either be released into the atmosphere through bypass valves or condensed back to water in a cooling unit. If the operators decided to rerun the test, they could open the valves to the turbine and close the bypass valves.

The difficulty with the process was that, if the reactor continued to operate, certain "perturbations,"as nuclear experts euphemistically call them, could take place in the reactor, which could in turn increase the pressure and cause the unit to be automatically shut down. Or, they could reduce the pressure, causing the automatic flooding of the reactor with emergency cooling water.

In other words, no one could tell just what would happen in the reactor under these circumstances, but the operators at Chernobyl, determined to carry through their test without a shutdown of the reactor, *shut off all of the emergency safety systems.*

As astounding as that seems, this is exactly what happened at 2 P.M. on Friday, the 25th, as the reactor was reduced to 7% capacity. The reactor's emergency cooling system was shut off. Then the power regulating system and the automatic shutdown system were disconnected. It was a little like a fire department responding to a burning fire and then dismantling the fire alarms and fire escapes and going home.

What the operators did was in violation of regulations, but they did it anyway—as countless other operators in other industrial and nuclear accidents had and would—and continued with their routine testing through the afternoon and evening. And all the while, the "perturbations" went on in the reactor.

Some time during this process, a reactor operator received a computer printout that indicated the reactor was in extremely serious danger of overheating unless it was shut down immediately. He ignored it.

Control rods were withdrawn, lowering the power in the reactor below the minimum required by the unit's operating manual. Xenon gases began to build up as the temperature rose in the reactor.

At 1:22 A.M. on Saturday, April 26, these same operators noticed that the power level had risen to the point at which, had the emergency system been engaged, it would have shut down. The operators noted it and kept on testing. If they had stopped at that moment, if they had heeded the warnings the instruments were clearly giving them and reengaged the safety system, the disaster would not have occurred. But they blundered on, ignoring the obvious.

Exactly one minute and 40 seconds later, the reactor blew. There was a loud bang as the control rods began to fall into place. At that instant, the operators knew exactly what was about to happen. They desperately tried to drop the rest of the control rods to stop the runaway chain reactions that were taking place in the reactor, the splitting by radiation of superhot water and the reactions caused by the superheating of its graphite shell.

But it was too late. The control rods drop by gravity, and that takes time, and the operators of the reactor had used up all the time there was. Twenty seconds later, the fuel atomized. Three explosions tore through the reactor, blowing off its top, sending its 1,000-ton steel cover plate rocketing into the air and ripping off the tops of all 1,661 channels, which were attached to the cover plate and contained the nuclear fuel. The channels became like "1,000 howitzers pointed at the sky," according to Dr. Herbert J. C. Kouts, the chairman of the Department of Nuclear Energy at Brookhaven National Laboratory on Long Island. Powered by these nuclear howitzers, a huge fireball shot up into the sky. The graphite caught fire and burned, fiercely and wildly. The reactor was completely out of control and beginning to melt down.

Flames continued to shoot over 1,000 feet into the air. This would continue for two days and nights. The operators within the building were doomed. Emergency alarms went off all through the complex, in which 4,500 workers were employed.

Miles away, a startled populace witnessed a gigantic fireworks display of hot radioactive material being flung into the night sky and onto the winds that would eventually carry this material far enough to contaminate a huge nearby area and, eventually, to a much lesser and varying degree, much of the rest of the world.

The reactor continued to burn, while emergency teams hauled off the dead and the radiated. Others, their boots sinking in molten bitumen, uselessly attempted to battle the blaze. But, as in other nuclear accidents around the world, evacuation of the populace was delayed, while scientists debated the seriousness of the situation.

Finally, at 1:50 P.M., on Sunday, April 27, fully 36 hours after the accident, the local radio station at Pripyat announced that a full-scale evacuation was to begin immediately. The city of 40,000 was to be totally abandoned, and 1,100 buses, some of them commandeered from Kiev, undertook the task. To prevent panic, rallying points were not used. The city was emptied within two hours and 20 minutes.

The countryside around Pripyat, a region of wooded steppes, small villages and moderately productive farms, was less thickly populated. Between Pripyat and Chernobyl lay the Kiev reservoir, fed by the Pripyat River. And at this point, radioactive matter was falling like lethal rain onto the thinly settled countryside and into this reservoir that supplied water to the 2,500,000 people of Kiev, Russia's third largest city.

Meanwhile, at the plant, workers were shutting down the other three reactors. The fire continued to burn unchecked. Twenty-five percent of the radiation leaked in the accident was released in the first 24 hours of the fire. The fire would continue for eight days.

On Monday morning, April 28, Swedish monitoring stations detected unusually high levels of xenon and krypton and concluded that, considering the prevailing winds, an atomic accident had occurred in the Soviet Union. Sweden demanded that the Soviets comply with international agreements to notify other nations immediately after a nuclear accident that might threaten those countries with radiation.

It was not until 9 P.M. that night that the Soviets released the terse statement quoted at the beginning of this entry, a masterpiece of noninformation.

But the truth began to seep out. On Tuesday, Soviet diplomats in Europe and Scandinavia approached private nuclear agencies, asking advice on fighting graphite fires. United Press International, frustrated by the silence from official sources, quoted a Kiev woman who communicated with them by telephone. "Eighty people died immediately and some 2,000 people died on the way to hospitals," she told UPI. "The whole October Hospital in Kiev is packed with people who suffer from radiation sickness."

A Dutch radio operator reported a message received from a Soviet ham broadcaster. "We got to know that not one, but two reactors are melted down, destroyed and burning. Many, many hundreds are dead and wounded by radiation, but maybe many, many more," he said, ending with a plea. "Please tell the world to help us," he concluded.

This was clearly at odds with the official version of events, which placed the dead at two and the injured at 197.

Now, the heavier products of radiation, the ones that the atmosphere could not dissipate easily and were lethal to human beings, were beginning to fall on Europe. Among a score of elements detected in the fallout were cesium-134 and iodine-131, both easily assimilated by the body and both thought to cause cancer.

By Wednesday, April 30, European countries began to take steps to preserve their own people. In Austria, mothers in the province of Carinthia were being advised to keep infants and small children indoors. The Polish government banned the sale of milk from grass-fed cows and issued iodine tablets to infants, children and pregnant mothers in order to protect the thyroid gland against poisoning from iodine-131. In Sweden, officials warned people not to drink water from casks that collected rain water for summer cottages and banned the import of fresh meat, fish and vegetables from the Soviet bloc countries. Evacuation plans were activated for citizens who were traveling or working in the area within 200 miles of Chernobyl. A group of American students studying in Kiev boarded planes for Moscow, then London, then the United States.

By Thursday, May 1, the Soviet bulletins noted that 18 people were in critical condition and that the fire was cooling down. In an effort to control it still further, civil defense forces began to drop bags of wet sand from helicopters hovering over the gaping hole in the top of the reactor. The radioactivity levels within the building were still too high to allow human beings, even in protective gear, to enter.

International help came swiftly. Dr. Robert Gale, the head of the International Bone Marrow Transplant Registery, left Los Angeles for Kiev on May 1. Two days later, his associate, Dr. Richard Champlin, and Dr. Paul Terasaki, a tissue-typing expert, joined him. They would have much work to do with the hundreds hospitalized from the accident.

Wind patterns were affecting the radiation levels reported in various European countries. In Sweden, it fluctuated between normal and five times the normal amount. Traces of iodine-131 were detected in rainwater samples in the Pacific Northwest region of the United States, but they were not deemed dangerous.

By Monday, May 5, the Soviet government announced that dikes were being built along the Pripyat River to prevent potential contamination and that the leakage of radiation from the plant had virtually stopped.

This was not the case, as later studies would indicate. In a report released the following September, a study prepared by the Lawrence Livermore National Laboratory in California asserted: "The nuclear disaster at Chernobyl emitted as much long-term radiation into the world's air, topsoil and water as all the nuclear tests and bombs ever exploded." Cesium, a product associated with health effects such as cancer and genetic disease, does not break down into a harmless form for more than 100 years, and it was sent into the atmosphere in quantities, the study estimated, that were as much as 50% more than the total of hundreds of atmospheric tests and the two nuclear bombs dropped on Japan at the end of World War II.

On May 9, the Soviets began the monumental task of encasing the still smoldering wreck of a reactor in concrete. It involved tunneling under the reactor, in order to prevent a "China syndrome" style of meltdown, which would immediately contaminate the groundwater near the reactor. The massive job was begun by dropping thousands of tons of sand, boron, clay, dolomite and lead from helicopters into the graphite core. Then the huge sarcophagus of concrete was poured and erected.

As May gave way to June, Soviet authorities attempted to protect citizens from the continuing effects of exposure to radiation. On May 15, 25,000 students in the Kiev area received an early vacation when all of the elementary schools and kindergartens were closed early for the summer.

Officials told residents of Kiev to keep their windows closed, mop floors frequently and wash their hands and hair often to reduce the chance of radiation contamination. And for the first time, these authorities acknowledged the dissemination of radiation over the rest of Europe.

The Russian children would be transported by the state to "Pioneer" camps scattered from the Moscow suburbs to the Crimea. More than 60,000 children, in fact, joined the first evacuees from Pripyat, who, like 12-year-old Olya Ryazanova, remembered a fire-blackened nuclear power plant, "a sort of mist, a misty cloud around it," and booted workers washing down the road in front of her home.

On May 15, the day the schools closed, the radioactive cloud had, after first blowing north to Scandinavia and Byelorussia, reversed itself and was hovering over Kiev. Crowds had formed at railroad stations and airports, most of them women and children, and the government had added extra trains and flights out of the city.

As more accurate information began to filter out of the Soviet Union, the scope of the disaster continued to grow. Hans Blix, the head of the International Atomic Energy Agency, confirmed that at least "204 persons, including nuclear power station personnel and firefighters, were affected by radiation from the first degree to the fourth degree." The government newspaper *Izvestia* revealed that more than 94,000 people had been evacuated. Eventually, the official number of dead would be set at 31.

It was learned that a full month before the disaster, a Ukrainian journal had reported management failures and labor dissatisfaction at Chernobyl. Because coal was becoming scarce in the Soviet Union, construction at the plant was speeded up in 1984, and it was suggested that this haste—a fifth nuclear reactor was already under construction at the time of the accident—was partially responsible for the tragedy.

But ultimately, the blame was focused on human error, and in June, *Pravda* announced that the director and chief engineer of the plant had been dismissed for mishandling the disaster and that other top officials were accused of misconduct ranging from negligence to desertion.

As with any nuclear catastrophe, the story of Chernobyl had no quick ending. In 1991, as of this writing, five and a half years after the accident, Pripyat is a ghost town, a place from which everyone has departed forever, and the sarcophagus that encases the 171 tons of coagulated and resolidified uranium fuel is becoming outdated. Its contents will remain radioactive and dangerous for at least 150 years, and the 20-story-high cube of concrete and steel that was hastily executed to bury that radiation has a life span of only 25 years.

The exploded generator's tortured and twisted mass of nuclear fuel can be viewed through special periscopes. According to a reporter for the *New York Times*, it resembles a "nightmarish cave, of great uranium magma oozings solidified into what workers already are nicknaming 'elephant's feet' of deadly radioactive permanence."

In addition to the rebuilding of the gigantic sarcophagus, scientists, workers and officials are faced with the problem of the 800 burial pits of other contaminated material, including trees, topsoil and even entire houses. Some of them are close to Pripyat's water supply, and if the city is ever to live again, these pits will also have to be encapsulated with clay, concrete and steel, or perhaps decontaminated. But scientists are still uneasy about disturbing the now quiescent nuclear debris.

In recent years, the independent Soviet republics have demanded that three nuclear power generators still operating at the Chernobyl plant be closed by 1995.

Today, the long-term effects of the radiation are just beginning to manifest themselves. Data show that 150,000 people, many of whom used the obviously contaminated Kiev water system, are suffering from some sort of thyroid illness. Sixty thousand of these are children, and of these, 13,000 have what is termed "very serious" problems requiring ongoing treatments.

Power plant workers now live in a new town, Slavutich, located 35 miles east of the plant, where even the tree bark has been scrubbed clean of radiation. Still, hot spots have been discovered here and there in the new village, and workers must change their clothes three times en route, twice a day, as they traverse the 18-mile "hot-zone" around the plant.

Near Chernobyl, 500 tons of dangerously irradiated beef have been stored in 40 refrigerated boxcars ever since the disaster. No one knows what to do with it.

Alarming medical data are being gathered. Sickness rates are reported up 45% over 1988, and the death rate is even higher. No conclusive evidence of linkage has been released, however.

Officials from Pripyat have been quoted in Radio Liberty's "Report on the U.S.S.R." as saying that the death toll in the cleanup was probably more than 300. But the official total still stands at 31. Even so, all experts agree, this figure will continue to rise for years, perhaps generations, to come.

RAILWAY DISASTERS

. . . .

THE WORST RECORDED RAILWAY DISASTERS

* Detailed in text

Algeria
- Algiers (1982)

Argentina
- * Buenos Aires (1970)

Bangladesh
- * Jessore (1972)
- * Maizdi Khan (1989)

Brazil
- * Aracaju (1946)
- * Mangueira (1958)
- Nova Iguacu (1951)
- * Pavuna River (1952)
- * Tangua (1950)

Burma
- Toungoo (1965)

Canada
- Ontario
  - * Hamilton (1857)
- Quebec
  - * St. Hilaire (1864)

Chile
- Mapocho River (1899)

China
- Canton (1947)
- Loyang (1935)
- Yencheng (1938)

Costa Rica
- Virilia River (1926)

Czechoslovakia
- * Pardubice (1960)

France
- * Lagny (1933)
- Les Couronnes (1903)
- * Modane (1917)
- St. Nazaire (1871)
- * Versailles (1842)
- * Vierzy (1972)

Germany
- * Laangenweddingen (1967)
- * Magdeburg (1939)

Great Britain
- England
  - * Harrow-Wealdstone (1952)
- Scotland
  - * Dundee (1879)
  - * Gretna Green (1915)

India
- Bhosawal (1867)
- * Hyderabad (1954)
- Jasidih (1950)
- Lahore (1891)
- Madras (1902)
- * Mahbubnagar (1956)
- * Mansi (1981)
- Marudaiyar (1956)
- Moradabad (1908)
- * Patna (1937)

Indonesia
- Java
  - * East Priangan (1959)

Ireland
- * Armagh (1889)

Italy
- * Salerno (1944)
- Voghera (1962)

Jamaica
- * Kendal (1957)

Japan
- Osaka (1940)
- Sakuragicho (1951)
- * Tokyo (1962)
- * Yokohama (1963)

Mexico
- Behesa (1916)
- * Cazadero (1945)
- * Cuartla (1881)
- Encavnacion (1907)
- Guadalajara
  - * (1915)
  - * (1955)
- Mexico City
  - (1895)
  - (1919)
- * Saltillo (1972)
- Tepic (1982)

Netherlands
- Woerden (1962)

New Zealand
- * Waiouri (1953)

Pakistan
- * Gambar (1957)
- Sind Desert (1954)

Poland
- * Nowy Dwor (1949)
- Pzepin (1952)

Portugal
- * Custoias (1964)

Romania
- Bucharest (1918)
- Costesi (1913)

Russia
- Odessa (1876)
- Petrograd (1920)
- Tcherny (1882)

South Africa
- Orlando (1949)

Spain
- Aguadilla (1944)
- * Lebrija (1972)
- San Arsenslo (1903)

Switzerland
- * Bale (1891)

Turkey
- Philippopolis (1879)

United States
- Colorado
- * Eden (1904)
- Connecticut
- * South Norwalk (1853)
- Illinois
- * Chatsworth (1887)
- Massachusetts
- * Revere (1871)
- New Jersey
- * Atlantic City (1896)
- * Hackettstown (1925)
- * Hightstown (1833)
- * Woodbridge (1951)
- New York
- * Angola (1867)
- * Brooklyn (1918)
- * Queens (1950)
- Ohio
- * Ashtabula (1876)
- Pennsylvania

CHRONOLOGY

* Detailed in text

1833
Nov. 11
Hightstown, New Jersey
1842
May 8
* Versailles, France
1853
May 6
* South Norwalk, Connecticut
1856
July 17
* Camp Hill, Pennsylvania
1857
Mar. 17
Hamilton, Ontario
1864
June 29
* St. Hilaire, Quebec
July 15
* Shohola, Pennsylvania
1867
June 26
Bhosawal, India
Dec. 18
* Angola, New York
1871
Feb. 25
St. Nazaire, France
Aug. 26
* Revere, Massachusetts
1876
Jan. 8
Odessa, Russia
Dec. 29
* Ashtabula, Ohio
1879
Jan. 11
Philippopolis, Turkey
Dec. 28
* Dundee, Scotland
1881
June 24
* Cuartla, Mexico
1882
July 13
Tcherny, Russia
1887
Aug. 10
* Chatsworth, Illinois
1888
Oct. 10
* Mud Run, Pennsylvania
1889
June 12
* Armagh, Ireland
1891
June 14
* Bale, Switzerland
Dec. 8
Lahore, India
1895
Feb. 28
Mexico City, Mexico
1896
July 30
* Atlantic City, New Jersey
1899
Aug. 24
Mapocho River, Chile
1902
Sept. 11
Madras, India
1903
June 27
San Arsenslo, Spain
Aug. 10
Les Couronnes, France
Dec. 23
* Laurel Run, Pennsylvania
1904
Aug. 7
* Eden, Colorado
Sept. 24
* Hodges, Tennessee
1907
Sept. 19
Encavnacion, Mexico
1908
May 8
Moradabad, India
1910
Mar. 1
Wellington, Washington
1913
Dec. 6
Costesi, Romania
1915
Jan. 18
* Guadalajara, Mexico
May 22
* Gretna Green, Scotland
1916
Nov. 19
Behesa, Mexico
1917
Dec. 12
* Modane, France
1918
July 9
* Nashville, Tennessee
Oct. 15
Bucharest, Romania
Nov. 2
* Brooklyn, New York
1919
Oct. 5
Mexico City, Mexico
1920
Dec. 22
Petrograd, Russia
1925
June 16
* Hackettstown, New Jersey
1926
Mar. 15
Virilia River, Costa Rica
1933
Dec. 23
* Lagny, France
1935

Sept. 24
Loyang, China
1937
July 16
* Patna, India
1938
April 5
Yencheng, China
1939
Dec. 22
* Magdeburg, Germany
1940
Jan. 28
Osaka, Japan
1944
Mar. 2
* Salerno, Italy
Nov. 7
Aguadilla, Spain
Dec. 31
* Ogden, Utah
1945
Feb. 1
* Cazadero, Mexico
1946
Mar. 20
* Aracaju, Brazil
1947
July 10
Canton, China
1949
April 28
Orlando, South Africa
Oct. 22
* Nowy Dwor, Poland
1950
April 6
* Tangua, Brazil
May 7
Jasidih, India
Nov. 22
* Queens, New York
1951
Feb. 6
* Woodbridge, New Jersey
April 4
Sakuragicho, Japan
June 8
Nova Iguacu, Brazil
1952
Mar. 4
* Pavuna River, Brazil
July 9
Pzepin, Poland
Oct. 8
* Harrow-Wealdstone, England
1953
Dec. 24
* Waiouri, New Zealand
1954
Jan. 21
Sind Desert, Pakistan
Sept. 24
* Hyderabad, India
1955
April 3
* Guadalajara, Mexico
1956
Sept. 2
* Mahbubnagar, India
Nov. 23
Marudaiyar, India
1957
Sept. 1
* Kendal, Jamaica
Sept. 29
* Gambar, Pakistan
1958
May 8
* Mangueira, Brazil
1959
May 28
* East Priangan, Java
1960
Nov. 14
* Pardubice, Czechoslovakia
1962
May 3
* Tokyo, Japan
May 31
Voghera, Italy
1963
Nov. 9
* Yokohama, Japan
1964
July 26
* Custoias, Portugal
1965
Dec. 9
Toungoo, Burma
1967
June 6
* Laangenweddingen, East Germany
1970
Feb. 1
* Buenos Aires, Argentina
1972
June 4
* Jessore, Bangladesh
June 16
* Vierzy, France
July 21
* Lebrija, Spain
Oct. 9
* Saltillo, Mexico
1974
Aug. 30
* Zagreb, Yugoslavia
1981
June 6
* Mansi, India
1982
Jan. 27
Algiers, Algeria
July 11
* Tepic, Mexico
1989
Jan. 15
* Maizdi Khan, Bangladesh

RAILWAY DISASTERS

As the first means of mechanical transportation, the railroad enjoyed a long period of unchallenged supremacy and comparative safety. Slow speeds, a conservative amount of track mileage, and a small number of passengers combined to keep the accidents and the casualty numbers low.

The very first days of rail travel were, in fact, restricted entirely to traffic in and out of mines. The first recorded railway's existence is an illustration of a narrow-gauge mine railway at Leberthal in Alsace, included in *Cosmographae Universalis,* by Sebastian Munster, published in 1550. The first railway of any consequence seems to have been a line made of balks of timber from coal pits at Wollaton and Strelley near Nottingham, England in the late 16th century. True to tradition, it was designed to take the coal from the pits to the River Trent, outside Nottingham.

It would be another three centuries before railways were used to transport people. The first railway in the world to carry fare-paying passengers was the Ostermouth Railway (also known as the Swansea & Mumbles Railway), which opened for business in April 1806 in Ostermouth, England. Horses and sails were used to move the cars, at speeds slow enough for the railway to eventually, once the novelty wore thin, lose customers to horse buses skimming along a turnpike road next to the railway. It was the last and only time that a railroad lost out to buses.

The first railroad to be built in America came about in 1795, when a short length of wooden track was laid on Beacon Hill in Boston to carry building material for the State House. By 1825, John Stevens tested the first steam locomotive in America on a circular track at his home at Hoboken, New Jersey. Stevens would, four years later, begin service on America's first steam-powered railway, the Pennsylvania Railroad. Within a couple of years, the B & O would best Stevens, with a verticle boiler that developed 1.43 horsepower. Small wonder that the early days of railroading were relatively accident free.

Still, by 1833, the wrecks began. On November 9 of that year, a carriage overturned on the Camden & Amboy main line between Spotswood and Hightstown, New Jersey, and 12 of 24 passengers, including Commodore Vanderbilt, the later head of the New York Central, were seriously injured see p. 302).

Other European, South American and Asian countries developed rail lines at the same time, with the same primitive signal systems, laminated iron rails, brittle cast iron wheels and link and pin couplings between cars. Still, until midcentury, most accidents were caused by derailments caused by separating rails, slow-motion collisions and cows wandering onto the tracks.

But by 1853, railways, particularly in America, were catastrophes waiting to happen. With its land grant policy, in which railroads were given land and loans only as track mileage was completed, the U.S. government actually encouraged flimsy and hasty railroad construction. As a result, practically every government-subsidized road was poorly and dangerously built. Whereas the English were constructing their railroads carefully and safely in the middle of the 19th century, with an eye for permanence, laying double rows of tracks and erecting substantial bridges, viaducts and tunnels and eliminating curves and grades, the American way was to put it all up quickly and expediently.

Thus, the foundation for the major categories of train wrecks was laid simultaneously with the hasty laying of track: Head-on and rear-end collisions were the result of single tracks and primitive signal systems; derailments came about through sloppy track laying and brittle wheels and axles; bridge disasters came about from poorly designed and hastily built bridges; telescopes resulted from a lethal link and pin coupling method between cars; crossing accidents resulted from lack of communication on the lines; fires resulted from a combination of superheated steam boilers in the engines and wooden cars heated by coal stoves and illuminated by oil lamps.

Many of these failings that would cause grisly accidents and terrible loss of life before the turn of the century would be corrected. Cheap steel would bring sound rails, bridges, wheels and axles. Automatic electric signals, double track and the Westinghouse brake would reduce the danger of collisions. The Miller platform and buffer method of coupling cars through tension and compression would reduce telescoping of passenger cars. The adoption of electric lighting and steam heating at the end of the century would reduce the fire hazard greatly, and the adoption of all-steel passenger cars in 1907 would virtually eliminate it in all but the Third World.

Even so, the most up-to-date technology cannot cancel out human failure. As more sophisticated signal devices were developed, signal men, conductors and engineers sometimes ignored them, resulting in catastrophe. As the possibility of higher speeds was introduced through more advanced equipment, engineers misjudged track conditions and drove their high-speed trains off the rails, into abutments or off bridges.

More recently, societal conditions have been responsible for train wrecks. The overcrowding of trains in Bangladesh and India, where poverty dictates that train and bus travel are the only means by which enormous segments of the populace can travel, has resulted in calamitous tragedies, with enormous loss of life. Inebriated train operators have also become a hazard. And drug use has necessitated mandatory random drug testing for American railroads.

Despite the hazards, railroading remains a relatively safe mode of transportation. As the technology of railroading has developed mightily in Europe and Japan, safety has increased along with the rate of speed. The demands of the superfast trains of France and Japan have dictated that new and safer roadbeds and configurations be built. Although the United States lags behind France and Japan in high-speed rail technology the very restricted nature of the use of railroads in this country, its safety record has improved since the 19th century. Again, social change will dictate not only the development of rail travel in this country but also its safety.

Like the other disaster categories in the book, events in this section were chosen in terms of human, not material, loss. An arbitrary cutoff figure of 50 deaths was used, and the only deviations from this figure occurred when historic firsts were deemed important enough to be included.

• • • • • • • • • • • • • • •

ARGENTINA
BUENOS AIRES

February 1, 1970

• • • • • • • • • • • • • • • •

Human error caused the collision of an express train and a commuter train near Buenos Aires, Argentina on February 1, 1970. One hundred forty-two died; hundreds were injured.

On Sunday night, February 1, 1970, a cross-country express train of Argentina's Bartolome Mitre railroad, composed of two diesel locomotives and 21 passenger coaches containing 500 people, was nearing the end of its 1,000-mile journey from the northern city of San Miguel de Tucuman to Buenos Aires. It was traveling at 65 miles per hour and was 50 minutes behind schedule.

Ahead of it, a commuter train, packed with 700 weekenders returning to Buenós Aires from the fashionable northern suburb of Zarate, had experienced mechanical difficulty and was stalled five miles outside the Pacheco station, which was 18 miles from Buenos Aires.

A signalman, Maximo Bianco, on duty near the crash site should have warned the approaching express of the stalled commuter train. But for some reason he did not, and the express plowed into the back of the stalled local train at 65 miles an hour.

"We were going very, very fast," said survivor Maria Isabel Algoden, "when all of a sudden everything exploded and people went everywhere."

The last five cars of the commuter train were crushed beyond recognition. Other cars telescoped into one another, mangling their occupants and upending some of the coaches. Wreckage was strewn over a wide area on either side of the tracks outside Pacheco.

Rescue crews were dispatched immediately. Firemen installed mobile power stations to illuminate the wreckage, and air force helicopters flew blood plasma, medical kits and surgical instruments to the macabre, floodlit scene.

Ambulances, trucks, commercial buses and private cars were pressed into service to transport the injured to an emergency hospital that was set up in the Pacheco railroad station. There, doctors from Buenos Aires labored to save whomever they could. The less seriously injured were taken into Buenos Aires and its hospitals.

The dead were first lined up along the tracks and then taken to the Pacheco and Benavidez stations, where they were displayed for identification purposes. One hundred forty-two persons died, most of them in the rear cars of the commuter train. Hundreds more were injured.

At first, authorities blamed terrorists. Only 90 minutes before the crash occurred, terrorists had attacked a railroad station three miles from the site of the collision and had made off with $400. Some link between the two incidents was thought to exist.

But further investigation led to the arrest of signalman Maximo Bianco and two of his fellow workers for failing to engage the warning signals that would have informed the engineer of the express that the commuter train was stalled in front of him. Once more, human error had caused a tragic rail accident.

BANGLADESH
JESSORE

June 4, 1972

• • • • • • • • • • • • • • • • •

Human error caused the collision of an express train with a standing train in the station at Jessore, Bangladesh on June 4, 1972. Seventy-six were killed on the train and the station platform; 500 were hospitalized.

Trains in Bangladesh and India are frequently loaded beyond capacity. It is not unusual to see passengers on the roofs of cars, between cars or hanging outside the cars' compartments. And this was the condition of an express train that left Khulna, a port town in the southern part of Bangladesh, headed north to the city of Jessore on June 4, 1972.

Despite its overload, the express made good time and entered the city limits of Jessore at nearly full speed. But the Jessore stationmaster threw a wrong switch, and the express was channeled onto the same track as that of a waiting train in the station. The moving train plowed into the standing one at maximum speed. The impact of the collision flung the locomotive off the track, and 10 coaches behind it telescoped into one another, hurtling ahead into the splintered remnants of the stationary train.

Passengers on the moving train were flung to the tracks and the station platform. Those in the waiting train were trapped or crushed. Seventy-six died immediately. More than 500 others received injuries serious enough to hospitalize them.

BANGLADESH
MAIZDI KHAN

January 15, 1989

• • • • • • • • • • • • • • • • •

Bangladesh's worst train disaster, the collision of an overloaded express train with a mail train near Maizdi Khan on January 15, 1989 was caused by human error—the switching of both trains onto the same track. One hundred thirty-six died; more than 1,000 were injured.

On January 15 in Tongi, a city in central Bangladesh, hundreds of thousands of pilgrims gathered for a Muslim religious festival. The devout came from all over Bangladesh to take part in the ceremonies, and a train, filled to overflowing with more than 2,000 pilgrims, made its way north from Dhaka to Tongi and then southeast to Chittagong. Passengers were everywhere—in seats, in the aisles, on the platforms, on the roofs of the cars. It was not an unusual occurrence, but in this case it was a terribly dangerous one.

Several days before, a new signal system had been initiated on this line, and later official explanations blamed what was about to occur on railroad personnel being confused by the new system.

The express bearing the more than 2,000 pilgrims had almost reached Tongi. It was speeding at 50 miles per hour, near the village of Maizdi Khan, when suddenly a mail train appeared, headed in the opposite direction on the same track. There was no time for either train to brake, although the mail train had almost stopped. They crashed head-on.

The impact flung the diesel locomotives of both trains off the tracks, and the first two coaches of each train were carried with the locomotives. Other cars telescoped into one another, picking off the passengers on the roofs as if they were billiard balls. "I saw coaches flying up to 15 feet as the collision occurred," said a soldier who, with some 250 other military men, was involved in winter exercises near the tracks. "It was a terrible scene with hundreds of passengers—men, women and children—shouting for help."

The carnage was appalling. Bodies, some of them without limbs or heads, were strewn over the countryside. Screams and moans filled the air. The soldiers were the first on the scene, and they pulled more than 100 dead passengers from the mangled cars and laid them side by side along the tracks.

Medical teams and ambulances arrived, but the job was overwhelming. More than 1,000 were injured, 100 of them critically enough to require hospitalization. Hundreds were taken to hospitals in Tongi, five miles north of Maizdi Khan; hundreds more were taken to Chaka, the capital, 22 miles to the south.

Police were brought in to control the crowd of thousands, who thronged the fields around the wreckage trying to find loved ones among the rows of bodies. Twenty-six would die in the hospitals. A total of 136 would perish, and more than 1,000 would be injured in this, Bangladesh's worst railway accident.

BRAZIL
ARACAJU

March 20, 1946

• • • • • • • • • • • • • • • •

The worst train wreck in Brazil's history occurred near Aracaju on March 20, 1946 when an overcrowded commuter train derailed. One hundred eighty-five died; several hundred were injured.

Brazil's worst train wreck also caused a bizarre aftermath. An overcrowded suburban commuter train carrying 1,000 passengers was apparently too heavy to negotiate a steep incline near Aracaju, the capital of the Brazilian coastal state of Sergipe. It derailed; its cars uncoupled, telescoped and piled up at the bottom of the incline.

Hundreds were trapped in the crushed cars; 185 died and several hundred were injured.

Grief-stricken relatives descended on the scene and discovered the surviving passengers. Enraged at the accident, they turned on the engineer. The thoroughly terrified man fled on foot and finally surrendered himself to authorities in the nearby town of Laranjetras. Several of the survivors, blaming him for the crash, tried to lynch him, the engineer told the local police, who took him into protective custody.

BRAZIL
MANGUEIRA

May 8, 1958

• • • • • • • • • • • • • • • •

Human error—a wrong switch thrown—caused the head-on collision of two commuter trains near Mangueira, Brazil on May 8, 1958. One hundred twenty-eight died; more than 300 were injured.

It was pouring on May 8, 1958 in the suburbs north of Rio de Janeiro. A driving, torrential downpour limited the visibility of anyone caught in it. Thus, the terrible head-on collision of two commuter trains late that afternoon could have been partially blamed on the weather. But a post-accident inquiry laid the vast majority of the blame on officials of the state-operated Central do Brasil line, and Brazilian president Juscelino Kubitschek immediately dismissed three top officials of the line.

The accident occurred as a crowded commuter train pulled out of the station at Mangueira. Picking up speed, it raced onward, its packed cars warm and light in comparison with the driving rain that was mercilessly pelting the train. It was an ordinary run, made countless times by both the passengers and the engineer. But shortly after he pushed his train to full speed, the engineer was suddenly blinded by an oncoming headlight. Somewhere along the chain of command, a wrong switch had been thrown, and the outgoing commuter train had been routed onto the same track. The two trains crashed head-on at high speed.

Both leaped skyward. Cars were telescoped or flung on their sides by the enormous impact. Rescue workers, nurses and physicians from Rio de Janeiro, 10 miles to the south, toiled in the driving rain to pry open cars, following the moans and screams of survivors beneath the mass of tangled, smoking steel.

It would be daylight of the next day before some sort of accurate casualty figures could be reached. One hundred twenty-eight people died, and more than 300 were injured, some of them critically.

In a bizarre postscript, hundreds of hysterically indignant residents of the northern suburbs of Rio de Janeiro rioted on the night following the crash, venting their frustration and fury on railroad stations along the route of the two trains. They completely wrecked the station at Engenho de Dentro, the most populous town, and attempted to tear down three other stations but were finally repelled by police in riot gear.

BRAZIL
PAVUNA RIVER

March 4, 1952

• • • • • • • • • • • • • • • •

Overloading, outdated equipment and unrepaired track caused the collision of two suburban trains on the Pavuna River bridge in Brazil on March 4, 1952. One hundred nineteen died; hundreds were injured.

The rebuilt Pavuna River bridge, the scene of an appalling wreck in 1950, was the site of a second train crash on the morning of March 4, 1952.

The suburban trains of the Central Railroad of Brazil were habitually overloaded in the 1950s, and a general overhaul of conditions on the line was being discussed in 1952 by the joint Brazil–United States Commission for Economic Development. But the Brazilians on the commission gave priority to improving the long-distance distribution of food and raw materials over the state of suburban rail traffic.

It was nevertheless a frustrating problem for Brazilian workers and industry chiefs who saw thousands of man-hours lost while workers waited for trains on which they often could not find room.

Thus, a dangerously overloaded train composed mostly of old and decrepit wooden coaches left Rio de Janeiro at 8:30 A.M. on March 4, 1952 bound for Juiz de Fora in the state of Minas Geras, 100 miles north of Rio. Not only was every seat taken and the aisles full, but clusters of passengers were clinging to the outsides of the wooden cars and riding the bumpers between them. Fatal accidents occurred daily on the line because of this practice, but a shortage of equipment, authorities complained, prevented any improvement.

The rolling stock was not the only part of the Central Railroad in need of repair and replacement. Some of its rails were in dire need of repair. The day before the coach train left for Juiz de Fora, a freight train had derailed in the middle of the Pavuna River bridge, but there had been no casualties and no inspection of the tracks at the site of the derailment.

At 8:40 A.M., just 10 minutes after the coach train left the station at Rio, several of its wooden cars crossed that same piece of defective track. Like the cars of the freight train, they derailed, swinging across the parallel track of the bridge reserved for trains traveling in the opposite direction.

At that precise moment, a modern electric suburban train loaded with commuters thundered onto the bridge, headed into Rio. It smashed directly into the wooden coaches with their hapless passengers packed inside and clinging to the outside. The cars splintered into thousands of fragments. Bodies were sent spinning through the air, onto the tracks, over the side of the bridge and into the river.

One hundred nineteen would die in the three cars, and hundreds more would be cruelly injured. A squadron of ambulances was sent out from Rio de Janeiro, together with rescue squads from four fire stations. Local buses and even trucks were pressed into service. A special train was sent to bring the bodies back to the capital, and special police squads, mindful of the riots associated with major crashes (see p. 278), were stationed in a perimeter around Rio's Dom Pedro Segundo Station, where the ill-fated train had originated.

Investigations were initially hampered. The engineer, it seemed, uncoupled the locomotive and fled in it, abandoning it some miles down the track. A peculiarity in Brazilian law stated that an engineer, if arrested at the scene of an accident, could be held indefinitely without bail, but if he succeeded in escaping arrest for 48 hours, he could remain free unless his responsibility was formally established by the court. He was set free, but later charged and imprisoned.

BRAZIL
TANGUA

April 6, 1950

• • • • • • • • • • • • • • • •

A lack of warning signals and torrential rains were responsible for a passenger train plunging through a weakened bridge over the Indios River near Tangua, Brazil on April 6, 1950. One hundred ten died; 40 were injured.

Torrential rains soaked the ground and filled the rivers to overflowing near Rio de Janeiro in early April 1950. A 22-car midnight train left Rio on April 5, jammed with Holy Week vacationers bound for Victoria in Espirito Santo State. The train on the Leopoldina Railway was a modern one, with the comforts of some sleepers. By 1:30 A.M., it had reached the vicinity of Tangua, some 55 miles from Rio, and most of the passengers were asleep.

It was at this point that the tracks crossed the Indios River, which days of downpours had swollen until it overflowed its banks on either side. If a warning system had existed, the engineer would not have been permitted to take his train across the railway bridge at Tangua. But no such system existed, and the train eased its way across the bridge.

The bridge's foundations, however, had been hopelessly undermined by the raging floodwaters of the Indios. The train only reached the halfway point when the bridge gave way. The locomotive, two baggage cars and three coaches uncoupled themselves and plunged into the river, wrapped in the girders of the bridge. Miraculously the other passenger cars remained on the tracks.

There were more than 200 passengers in the first three cars, and all of them sank immediately beneath the white water of the Indios. Some were able to escape by swimming through broken windows and open doors. These survivors together with trainmen and passengers from the remainder of the train worked feverishly in the dark, rainy night to free some of the injured. Forty were saved. But 110 died, trapped in the sunken cars or swept away in the turbulent water.

The bodies were taken by rail to Rio de Janeiro and Nietheroy for identification. Highway access to the scene of the wreck was blocked by landslides. The following day, a railway crane was dispatched to grapple the three sunken passenger cars, baggage cars and engine from the still-raging river. It would take three days to recover the train.

CANADA
ONTARIO
HAMILTON

March 17, 1857

• • • • • • • • • • • • • • • • •

Failure to maintain a railroad bridge caused a train to break through the bridge and fall into the Des Jardines Canal near Hamilton, Ontario on March 17, 1857. Sixty died; 20 were injured.

One of the major rail disasters of the 19th century occurred on the night of March 17, 1857 when the engine, tender and two coaches of a train burst through the rotted timbers of the Des Jardines Canal bridge, plummeted 18 feet through the frigid winter air and smashed through the ice of the canal.

The bridge was a rickety affair, and engineers of the Great Western of Canada line that traversed it were grimly aware that there was no guardrail to prevent derailed trains from plunging off its sides. Had there been one on the bridge, the 1857 disaster might have been prevented, for the train was a local and traveling at a slow speed.

However, the engine appeared to have struck something at the entrance to the bridge and derailed itself onto the timbers. These gave way immediately, and with a huge sigh of steam and an enormous clatter of splitting wood, the entire train stove through the bottom of the bridge, hurtling toward the frozen canal.

The engine was the first to break through the ice. It was lost in the water immediately. The baggage car somehow uncoupled itself and slid harmlessly across the ice to the far shore, injuring its three occupants only slightly.

The two coaches followed the engine; one flipped over on its roof, which splintered when it smashed into the steel of the locomotive's boiler. The other drove like a battering ram into the other car, killing every one of its occupants. The only survivors, aside from the fortunate three in the baggage car, were rescued from the second car. They were dug from the wreckage that night by scores of rescuers from Hamilton who worked by the light of locomotive lamps and torchlights. They improvised stretchers made from ladders to raise the injured from the icy canal to the remains of the bridge. Some survivors were found floating on pieces of ice; others wandered dazed on the intact surface; still others were hauled, half drowned and in shock, from the interior of the second coach. Altogether, 60 persons died and 20 were injured in the wreck.

CANADA
QUEBEC
ST. HILAIRE

June 29, 1864

• • • • • • • • • • • • • • • • •

The worst bridge disaster in North America occurred at St. Hilaire, Canada on June 29, 1864 as a result of human negligence; the engineer of a passenger train failed to stop before crossing the open St. Hilaire drawbridge. Ninety were killed; more than a hundred were injured.

The number of railway disasters that have occurred because of disregard of rules is legion and chilling, and the worst bridge disaster on the North American continent occurred for just that reason. An 11-car train of Canada's Grand Trunk Railway left Quebec on June 29, 1864 loaded with 354 passengers, most of them recent German and Norwegian immigrants.

The St. Hilaire drawbridge, over which the train was to pass, hovered 45 feet above a heavily traveled canal. Because of the constant use of the drawbridge, the company had a strict regulation stating that all trains were to come to a full stop before crossing.

The engineer of this particular train apparently ignored both his own eyes and company regulations. Approaching the drawbridge—which had been opened to accommodate a string of six barges—at full speed, the engineer had no chance of preventing the entire train from plunging 45 feet into the canal below.

The engine smashed a hole through one barge, sinking it and dragging it partway to the bottom of the canal. The following cars splayed crazily, some diving straight into the water, others landing on the barges. Ninety people, trapped in the cars of the train, were killed in the crash, but the engineer responsible for the tragedy was miraculously thrown clear of the wreck and survived.

A train of the Great Western line of Canada plunged through a rickety bridge and into the Des Jardines Canal, near Hamilton, Ontario, on March 17, 1857. Sixty died. Illustrated London News

CZECHOSLOVAKIA
PARDUBICE

November 14, 1960

• • • • • • • • • • • • • • • • •

Both engineers of two passenger trains ignored speed and right-of-way regulations and collided near Pardubice, Czechoslovakia on November 14, 1960. One hundred ten died; 106 were injured.

The village of Pardubice, located 68 miles east of Prague, Czechoslovakia, was the scene of a horrendous head-on collision of two speeding passenger trains on the night of November 14, 1960. Tight restrictions on news gathering in this Communist bloc country prevented details from reaching the rest of the world.

What *was* revealed was that both engineers ignored speed and right-of-way regulations, and the two trains collided at top speed shortly after 6 P.M. just outside Pardubice. Both trains derailed, and 110 people were killed. One hundred six others, seriously injured, were taken to hospitals.

FRANCE
LAGNY

December 23, 1933

• • • • • • • • • • • • • • • • •

Heavy fog and excessive speed combined to cause the collision of a Strasbourg-bound express with the stationary Nancy express and a commuter train near Lagny, France on December 23, 1933. One hundred ninety-one died; 280 were injured.

It was the night before Christmas Eve of 1933. A heavy fog fed by the frost-covered ground made it slow going for motorists on the roads surrounding Paris. Even within the city, the haloed streetlights were barely effective.

A commuter train making its tortuous way through the fog stalled near the village of Lagny, 15 miles east of Paris, and the Nancy express, brimming over with students on holiday and other merrymakers leaving Paris early for Christmas, pulled up behind it. The revelers aboard the train—among them two members of the Chamber of Deputies, Henri Rollin and Gaston Poitevin—were unfazed. It was warm in the wooden cars; it was safe. And to assure this safety, trainmen set up red flares along the track, supplementing them with torpedoes.

But the fog was heavier than anyone could have imagined. The Strasbourg express, traveling on the same main line as both the commuter train and the Nancy express and already an hour late, was making 65 miles an hour—an excessive speed on this part of the line under good conditions and an insane speed in the heavy fog of the night of December 23.

The engineer of the Strasbourg-bound train saw no flares and heard no torpedoes. At 65 miles an hour, his train slammed into the rear of the stationary Nancy express, crushing the wooden cars to splinters and flinging bodies, luggage and chunks of cars onto the frosted ground on either side of the tracks. By the time the Strasbourg train stopped, it had plowed through every car on the Nancy train, telescoping whatever it left of each coach.

The devastation was indescribable. The dead and dying strewed the tracks. Hardly anyone was left alive in the Nancy train, and not a single person was injured on the Strasbourg express.

The inhabitants of Lagny rushed to the site of the accident. Local doctors did what they could. Rescuers built fires along the track to illuminate the grisly scene and began to haul the dead from the pile of charred and blood-soaked wood that had once been a passenger train.

Partway through their efforts, they froze in their activity as the sound of another train approaching at a high rate of speed pierced the fog. Dozens of flares had been set up to warn off other trains on the main line. The engineer of the Meaux express claimed later that, in the fog, the lights looked green, but a strange presentiment caused him to look again. The fog cleared for a moment, and he saw the red flares. He slammed on the brakes so suddenly that passengers on the train were thrown from their seats. With a huge shrieking of brakes, it stopped a mere 350 yards short of the wreckage of the Strasbourg and Nancy trains.

Had it not been for the reflexes of the engineer of the fourth train, the carnage would have been worse. As it was, 191 died, 200 were taken to Paris hospitals and 80 others were transported to hospitals and private homes in Lagny, Pomponna and Torigny by rescue trains, fleets of ambulances and private cars. It was, and would remain, one of the gravest accidents in the history of French railroads.

FRANCE
MODANE

December 12, 1917

• • • • • • • • • • • • • • • • •

A military order to move a severely overloaded troop train near Modane, France on December 12, 1917 resulted in the derailment and plunge of the train into a gorge. More than 1,000 soldiers were killed; hundreds were injured.

It would be 15 years before there would be a full accounting of one of the worst railway disasters in history. The reason: It occurred in wartime, the train was loaded with servicemen and the responsibility for the wreck lay squarely on the shoulders of the military officers in charge.

In early December 1917, a troop train was packed far beyond its safe capacity with more than 1,200 war-weary French soldiers on their way home for Christmas. The war had been going badly for the French, and this respite was seen as a necessary one for morale.

Alarmed at the weight and balance problems resulting from the overloading, the engineer refused to leave the station until the load was decreased. A French staff officer confronted the engineer, warning him that he would be court-martialed for refusing to follow orders if he did not pull his train out immediately. The engineer remained adamant, citing safety regulations. The officer produced a pistol and warned that the engineer's offense was a capital one and that he would therefore have him executed for refusing to obey wartime orders. Faced with this ultimatum, the engineer agreed to begin what would be a fatal journey.

The overweight train, loaded with celebrating soldiers, navigated the flat portion of its journey uneventfully. But part of its return trip would take it through the Alps in the southeastern corner of France. It entered the steeply graded Mount Cenis Tunnel near the village of Mondane. Partway through the tunnel, the overloaded train wrested itself away from the engineer's control and accelerated far beyond safe limits.

At the bottom of the grade at the end of the tunnel was a wooden bridge and a sharp curve. Below it was an immense and deep gorge. The train blasted the bridge to tinder, shot off the rails and fell sickeningly into the gorge below. When it struck bottom, it burst into flames, which consumed the entire train in a matter of minutes. More than 1,000 soldiers died in the crash and the flames. Hundreds were injured. Only a handful of survivors emerged from this monumental and avoidable disaster. Ironically, one of these survivors was the engineer.

A lithograph captures the first recorded major railway disaster in the world: the rear-end collision of two excursion trains leaving the celebration of King Louis Philippe's birthday on May 8, 1842; 54 were killed. New York Public Library

FRANCE
VERSAILLES

May 8, 1842

• • • • • • • • • • • • • • • • • •

A rear-end collision of two excursion trains in Versailles, France on May 8, 1842 killed 54 passengers. The cause was a combination of overloading and a broken axle on the lead train.

The first recorded major railway disaster in the world occurred in the late afternoon of May 8, 1842 following the celebration of King Louis Philippe's birthday. Thousands of Parisians had traveled by rail and spent the day on the grounds of Versailles, wining and dining and witnessing a regal ceremony held in the midst of the royal palace's fountains.

When the ceremonies ended, there was a rush to board the spartan wooden coaches of the return train to Paris. Extra engines had been added to accommodate the anticipated crowds, and the first train to leave needed at least two locomotives to pull the enormous load of passengers that had been jammed into its cars and then, in the practice of the day, locked in.

Shortly after leaving Versailles, the lead engine on the first train broke an axle. The engine nosedived to the tracks, stopping instantly. The second engine then plowed into the first, bursting its boiler and setting both engines afire. Traveling at full speed, the wooden coaches careened into the two engines and split asunder. Moments later, the fire from the boilers had spread to them, sending them up in huge pyres of oily flame.

Locked in or crushed beneath the splintered cars, scores of helpless passengers were incinerated by the furious fire that roared through the entire train. The official death toll was listed at 54, but according to unofficial sources the number exceeded 100.

FRANCE
VIERZY

June 16, 1972

• • • • • • • • • • • • • • • • • •

Two trains crashed into the collapsed Vierzy tunnel in France on June 16, 1972. One hundred seven died; 90 were injured.

The Vierzy tunnel, located sixty miles northeast of Paris, has stood for nearly two centuries, not an unusual age for structures in Europe. But this one was apparently not constructed with the usual care of its contemporaries, and on June 16, 1972 it collapsed with a roar.

Moments later, two trains traveling in opposite directions entered the heavily used tunnel. Both were moving at top speed; both crashed into an immense pile of fallen rock and shattered ceiling timbers almost simultaneously. The locomotives of both trains climbed the rock pile and shot skyward through the jagged hole in the ceiling of the tunnel. The following cars remained on the tracks but telescoped into one another.

Help arrived almost immediately, but fear of igniting the diesel fumes that permeated the tunnel forced rescuers to move slowly and carefully. The slightest spark could have set off an explosion that would have dwarfed the train wreck in catastrophic consequences. Thus, it would be three days before 107 bodies and 90 injured passengers would be pried from the tangled wrecks that jutted half in and half out of the remains of the Vierzy railway tunnel.

GERMANY
LAANGENWEDDINGEN

June 6, 1967

• • • • • • • • • • • • • • • • • •

The failure to report a defective grade crossing in Laangenweddingen, East Germany caused the collision of a commuter train and a gasoline truck at the crossing on June 6, 1967. Eighty-two were killed; 51 were injured.

The grade crossing alongside the railroad station in the little town of Laangenweddingen, located near Magdeburg, 80 miles southwest of Berlin and 20 miles from the West German border, was defective in July 1967. The barrier, which should have lowered and prevented vehicles from crossing the tracks, snagged repeatedly on an overhead telephone line and failed to close. There was a crossing guard, and it was his duty to report this sort of danger to his supervisor, who would order the proper repairs to be made. But from the time of the first discovery of the defective crossing gate, no such warning had been issued. At 8 P.M. on the evening of July 6, 1967, the lack of a report resulted in tragedy.

That night, a gasoline truck, owned by the East German state-operated oil corporation and loaded with 4,000 gallons of gasoline, approached the grade crossing. Seeing no barrier, the driver assumed that it was safe to cross the tracks and so drove ahead.

At that instant, a double-decker commuter train roared into sight. There was no time for the train to stop or the truck to dislodge itself. The train slammed full speed into the truck; it exploded in an incendiary spectacle that shot flames to enormous heights. The cars of the train were set afire; the explosion blew apart the engine and the first four coaches, which were heavily loaded with children.

Flaming gasoline poured into the cars, onto the tracks and onto the roof of the railroad station, which caught fire and burned to the ground. Inside the trains, children were burned to cinders instantly. Seventy-nine people died on the spot; three more died of their injuries later in the local hospitals at Magdeburg and Bahrendorf. Fifty-one were injured, and Red Cross volunteers, doctors, firemen and policemen labored for hours cutting away wreckage and pulling the injured and the dead from the twisted mass of fused and still-hot metal.

An investigation was immediately initiated, and five days later, the crossing operator and his supervisor were arrested and charged with manslaughter. The results of their trial were never released by the East German authorities.

GERMANY
MAGDEBURG

December 22, 1939

• • • • • • • • • • • • • • • •

The ignoring of a signal by the engineer of the Berlin express caused him to crash at full speed into the rear of the Cologne express near Magdeburg, Germany on December 22, 1939. One hundred thirty-two died; 109 were injured.

The collision of two express trains on the morning of December 22, 1939 near Magdeburg, Germany revealed as much about the price the German people were paying for war, even in its early stages, as it did about human error's responsibility for railway accidents.

From 1920 until 1936, German railways were models of efficiency to the world. But with the ascension of Hitler and his Third Reich, this would take a dramatic turn. Although military efficiency was consistently high in the early days of World War II, it would be at an elevated and, in this case, tragic cost to German civilians.

By 1939, three years into the Nazi regime, there was tremendous congestion on German railways, which had never before been subject to quite so much strain with quite so many untrained personnel. Not only was the rail system overloaded with troop transports, military supply and personnel trains and freight traffic, it was also deprived, because of military conscription, of its best trained men. Their places were taken by reemployed pensioners, promotions among the present personnel and hastily trained workers pressed into service from other industries.

During the Christmas season of 1939, this situation was exacerbated by extra holiday, troop transport and troop leave trains, which had to be switched into the normal schedule. In addition, the normally crowded passenger trains were filled to capacity on December 22.

On that morning, because of holiday demands, the Cologne express made an unscheduled stop at the Genthin station, just outside Magdeburg. There was a thick early morning mist that considerably reduced visibility.

At Genthin, an automatic stop signal lit, announcing the presence and the location of the Berlin-Cologne train in the station. But the engineer of the Berlin-Neunkirchen express either ignored or did not see the signal and ran through it at high speed. The express rammed the rear of the stopped Cologne train, slamming three of its third-class coaches to the roadbed and demolishing its baggage car. The locomotive of the Berlin-Neunkirchen train, deflected by the impact, left the rails and overturned, carrying five telescoping cars with it. The engineer was killed instantly, and a fireman was gravely injured.

The Third Reich immediately clamped a lid of silence on the details of the wreck; because America was not yet at war with Germany, however, some American journalists managed to file stories at least giving the outlines of it. The brief communique from official sources admitted to 132 dead and 109 injured, but witnesses at the scene estimated a far larger casualty figure.

GREAT BRITAIN
ENGLAND
HARROW-WEALDSTONE

October 8, 1952

• • • • • • • • • • • • • • • •

Ignoring signals by the engineer of one train caused the multiple collision in the Harrow-Wealdstone station, near London, on October 8, 1952. The worst crash in the history of British Rail, to that date, it killed 112 and injured 165.

The worst crash in British Rail history took place at the worst possible time—at the height of the morning commuter rush hour. An estimated 1,000 persons jammed the platform of the Harrow-Wealdstone station, some 11 miles west of London, on the morning of October 8, 1952. Most were waiting the arrival of the local from Tring and West Hertfordshire to London, but a few had arrived early to board the many commuter shuttles that used this customarily crowded station.

The local loaded up at 8:19 and was just pulling out of the station when the Night Scot, an express from Perth to London, late and trying to make up time, roared into the station on the same track as the local. It had ignored the clear signals set by signalman A. G Armitage at Harrow number one box and, oblivious, hurtled into the rear of the local train, flinging coaches everywhere and ripping an enormous hole in a footbridge that ran beneath the tracks.

According to observers, bodies seemed to fly through the air, and some dropped through the hole in the footbridge. It was a catastrophic scene, but not the end of the carnage. Seconds later, the Manchester express, also late and trying to make up time, sped into the station on an adjacent track that was now blocked with some of the cars of the demolished commuter train. The express, powered by two enormous engines, careened into the cars. Both engines left the tracks, soared vertically into the air and came down directly on the platform, which was crowded with waiting commuters.

Scalding gouts of steam erupted everywhere. Severed electric lines rained sparks and swung lethally over the scene. Within minutes, thousands of rescuers rushed to the station, freeing those who were reachable, bandaging horribly mangled bodies, administering morphine to those who were trapped or maimed or dying.

It would be two days and nights before the two rear coaches of the local would be reached, by cutting with acetylene torches, and there the rescue operation reached its most hopeless nadir. There were few survivors and scores of dead in these two cars alone.

One hundred twelve died; 165 were seriously injured in that morning of horror at the normally placid commuter stop of Harrow-Wealdstone.

GREAT BRITAIN
SCOTLAND
DUNDEE

December 28, 1879

• • • • • • • • • • • • • • • • • • •

Storms caused the buckling of the Tay River Bridge near Dundee, Scotland on December 28, 1879. Seventy-five people were killed when a train plunged through it; there were no survivors.

The Tay River Bridge at Dundee, Scotland was completed in 1877, and it was hailed worldwide as a triumph of engineering skill. The longest bridge in the world, it was also the most modern, the strongest, the most graceful.

A view from the storm-damaged Tay River Bridge near Dundee, Scotland following the plunge into the river of the Edinburgh express on December 28, 1879. London Illustrated News

But a mere two years after its completion, it would be the scene of one of the saddest disasters in the history of rail travel, one in which there was not a single survivor.

The train that left Edinburgh at 4:15 P.M. on December 28, 1879 was traveling in hard conditions. A raging storm with hurricane-force winds had lashed the countryside all day, battering at houses and seawalls and swelling streams and rivers. One of the rivers that was at least three times its normal depth was the Tay, and its boiling waters had been ramming the pilings of the Tay River railbridge since the storm began.

The train started to cross the multiple-span bridge at 6:15 and traversed almost half of its length before disaster struck. Midway through the central span, the train lurched as girders began to buckle beneath it. Thirteen girders gave way, pulling the structure out from beneath the wheels of the train and flinging it 88 feet into the river below.

It was only a matter of minutes before the waters closed over the train, leaving nothing in evidence but stray pieces of it, floating bits and pieces of luggage and boards from the cars that shattered on the rocks or were crushed by the steel girders that hurtled downward once the train had shaken them loose.

Seventy-five people—all the passengers and crew—died in this wreck.

GREAT BRITAIN
SCOTLAND
GRETNA GREEN

May 22, 1915

• • • • • • • • • • • • • • • • •

Human error on the part of a signalman caused the crash of a troop train and 2 passenger trains near Gretna Green, Scotland on May 22, 1915. Two hundred twenty-seven were killed; 223 were injured.

The year 1915 was one of grim records. In January, a troop train plunged into a ravine in Guadalajara, Mexico, resulting in Mexico's worst train wreck (see p. 294). On May 22, Great Britain's worst railway disaster took place at Gretna Green, in Scotland.

Whereas the Mexican tragedy was caused by forces of nature, the wreck in Scotland was reportedly the fault of one man, a signalman who threw the wrong switch.

Gretna Green is a small town in which several tracks of the Caledonian Railway intersect. At 6:00 A.M. on May 22, 1915, a troop train loaded with 500 soldiers bound for the Western front roared into view. The signalman waved it on, and into a direct collision course with a local train traveling in the opposite direction. Within minutes, both trains hit head-on, turning the engines into mangled, hissing interweavings of steel and telescoping a series of passenger cars into one another.

The signalman had no sooner left his post to try to assist in rescue efforts when the London-Glasgow express appeared. With no signal to slow it, the express rammed both trains, igniting heavy ammunition and gas cylinders that were being carried in a baggage car of the troop train.

Within an instant, the wreckage was turned into an exploding inferno in which human beings were incinerated by the score.

A horrendous consequence of the soldiers' battle dress made rescue a dangerous proposition. Each of the soldiers was wearing an ammunition belt, and the heat of the fire began to set off the belts, causing them to explode, thus killing not only the wearer of the belt but rescuers in the vicinity.

The burned-out hulk of one of the cars of a troop train that collided with a passenger train near Gretna Green, Scotland on May 22, 1915. Two hundred twenty-seven were killed and 223 injured in the wreck, caused by a signalman's faulty judgment. London Illustrated News

Fire brigades, swarms of rescuers, nurses and doctors toiled all day and night to try to save whomever they could. Arms and legs were set, transfusions were given, battlefield operating rooms were set up and amputations were performed on the spot. Long before they got to the war, most of this company was decimated. Out of 500 soldiers and hundreds of civilians, 227 died and 223 were wounded. It was a catastrophe of immense proportions, one of the worst of the war, and it occurred, ironically, hundreds of miles and a channel from the battlefields.

INDIA
HYDERABAD

September 24, 1954

• • • • • • • • • • • • • • • •

Monsoon rains weakened a bridge over the Vasanti River near Hyderabad, India, causing it to give way beneath a train on September 24, 1954. One hundred thirty-seven were killed; 100 were injured.

The eight-car Hyderabad to Kazipet express had not traveled far from Hyderabad in the minutes just after midnight on September 24, 1954. There were 319 persons aboard, many of them dozing in the fetid heat. It was the end of the monsoon season; rains had produced floods everywhere, and one of the rivers that was at flood stage was the Vasanti, outside Hyderabad.

The tracks crossed the Vasanti via a bridge 50 miles east of Hyderabad. The bridge had been weakened by the floodwaters, but other trains had crossed it safely that day. The express was not so lucky. It had almost reached the other side of the bridge when the span swayed, groaned and gave way beneath the weight of the train.

The engine and seven of its eight cars plunged into the river with the bridge. The far end of the span gave way first, thus forcing the cars to telescope into one another

The overcrowding of trains in India contributes greatly to the abnormally high death tolls in that country's train wrecks. United Nations

on their way down. Some people were crushed before they reached the river; others were trapped and drowned.

Salvage crews worked all night and through the following day. More than 100 injured people managed to swim to safety or were dragged from the swollen river by rescuers. One hundred thirty-seven died, either in the train or in the waters of the river. Bodies washed up miles from the scene of this, the worst railway wreck to date in Indian history.

INDIA
MAHBUBNAGAR

September 2, 1956

• • • • • • • • • • • • • • • • • • •

Monsoon rains weakened a bridge over a gorge near Mahbubnagar, India, and a train was flung into the gorge as the bridge collapsed on September 2, 1956. One hundred twelve were killed; hundreds were injured.

Monsoon season in India turns placid ponds into seas and barely visible streams into raging rivers. This was the case in the province of Hyderabad in September 1956, at the beginning of the yearly monsoons.

The Central Rail line of India traverses several of these normally inconsequential streams via bridges. In the southwest portion of India, near the large city of Hyderabad, these bridges are often extended nearly 100 feet in the air, traversing sickeningly deep gorges.

Such was the case between the cities of Secunderbad and Dhone. The Central Line passed 85 feet in the air over a normally placid stream. But on September 2, 1956 this stream had become a torrent, and its incessant battering had weakened the support struts of the towering trestle bridge that spanned the gorge near Mahbubnagar. A guard on duty that night would have stopped the passenger train that reached the bridge at midnight had he been there. But unfortunately, when the train arrived, he was a mile away, checking on another bridge weakened by the monsoons.

The engine traversed the span without incident. But the resulting vibrations traveled down the struts of the bridge, and within seconds after the locomotive reached the other side, the entire steel structure gave way. The tender and first two cars plummeted like stones to the bottom of the gorge, followed by girders from the bridge, which landed on the train, burying and crushing it. One hundred twelve persons were believed to have perished, either from the fall or from drowning. Hundreds more were injured.

INDIA
MANSI

June 6, 1981

• • • • • • • • • • • • • • • • • • •

The worst train wreck in India's history was caused by an engineer's decision to brake for a cow on the tracks on the rainy night of June 6, 1981 near Mansi. Two hundred sixty-eight bodies were recovered; more than 300 were missing.

Cows are sacred in India. To harm one is forbidden. And the engineer of a nine-car passenger train passing near Mansi, in the northeastern state of Bihar, 250 miles northwest of Calcutta, on the monsoon-whipped Saturday of June 6, 1981 was certainly aware of this. A devout Hindu, he would not, under any circumstances, add further bad karma to the cycle of his lives by harming a cow. And yet, on that rainswept night, as his train, loaded with more than 1,000 passengers, approached a bridge over the Baghmati River, there it was: a cow standing on the track.

The engineer applied the brakes, too suddenly, too fast and at just the wrong place. The momentum of the train carried it forward; the following cars, sliding on rain-slick rails, on a roadbed that had been made, by the heavy rains, soft and insecure, derailed and whipped forward. Seven of the nine coaches and the locomotive plunged over the embankment, off the bridge and into the whirling waters below. It was over in an instant; the cars catapulted downward one after the other, careening and crashing into one another before they sank swiftly into the monsoon-swollen river.

Survivors in the last two cars which remained on the tracks moaned as they faced the fate of the others. There was nothing to be done but to run for help to take out the bodies. There was no sign of life in the river below.

Within hours, help arrived. Fifty-nine divers, 110 soldiers and scores of villagers from Mansi and other nearby settlements searched the wreckage and the riverbanks for miles and for days. Two hundred sixty-eight bodies were found, but more than 300 passengers from the tragically fated seven cars were missing and assumed dead. It was the worst railway wreck in the history of India.

INDIA
PATNA

July 16, 1937

• • • • • • • • • • • • • • • • • • •

A monsoon-softened track bed accounted for the derailment of a passenger train near Patna, India on July 16, 1937. One hundred seven were killed; 65 were injured.

One of India's worst train wrecks occurred in daylight in clear weather on July 16, 1937. The Delhi-Calcutta express had reached the vicinity of Patna, some 275 miles northwest of Calcutta in the Vindhya Mountain range, without incident. The monsoon season had begun, and there were reports of flooding, but none of the rivers in the vicinity had reached the extreme flood stage.

Still, the monsoons had apparently softened part of the roadbed on a stretch of track that ran adjacent to a steep and precipitous embankment. The engine lost traction and leaped from the tracks, carrying seven of the train's nine cars down the embankment. Rolling and pitching down the steep slope, the first two cars became uncoupled from the last three and landed at the bottom of the ravine. The force of the impact telescoped one car completely into the other. Seconds later, the remaining five cars landed on top of the engine and the first two coaches, crushing them completely.

"Bodies were strewn around as if it were a battlefield," was the description one observer gave reporters. The passengers in the seven cars involved in the accident were all Indians; the last two cars were occupied by Europeans, and for some unexplained or fortuitous reason, these two became uncoupled and remained safely on the tracks. The occupants of these cars immediately set about rescuing as many as they could from the cataclysmic pileup at the bottom of the ravine. One hundred seven passengers were dead, and 65 were injured.

INDONESIA
JAVA
EAST PRIANGAN

May 28, 1959

• • • • • • • • • • • • • • • • • •

The uncoupling of several cars of a passenger train in an act of sabotage sent the cars careening into a ravine in East Priangan on the island of Java on May 28, 1959. One hundred forty were killed; 125 were injured.

Sabotage was responsible for the worst train wreck in the history of Indonesia, in which a trainload of innocent passengers plunged into a ravine in the East Priangan regency of West Java province on the island of Java.

Indonesia in 1959 was a country in ferment. Under pressure from the United Nations, the Dutch had given way to Nationalist pressure in 1949, and an independent republic of Indonesia was formed. Sukarno was elected president of a parliamentary form of government, but his administration was marked by inefficiency, injustice, corruption and chaos. Inflation soared in the 1950s, and economic depravation spawned a popular revolt. It began in Sumatra in 1958, and widespread disorders caused Sukarno to become more and more authoritarian. In May 1959, there were numerous incidents that killed both the innocent and the involved. Sukarno would dissolve parliament in 1960.

One of these incidents was the train wreck of May 28 in West Java. The Bandjar-Bandung express was loaded with 500 passengers and, early that morning, was traveling through mountainous terrain, slashed by ravines hundreds of feet deep. The train was not moving fast; there were numerous curves and steep inclines, and it was on just such an incline that someone uncoupled the engine from the entire complement of passenger cars.

Set free, the cars rolled backward, gaining speed alarmingly. There were apparently no independent braking devices on them, and in moments the cars left the tracks, careened crazily on the edge of a precipice and then plunged hundreds of feet into a ravine.

Miraculously, some passengers escaped uninjured, but 140 were killed and 125 seriously injured in the wreck.

At first, the conductor was charged with negligence, but further investigation determined that an unidentified person (he or she would never be captured and brought to trial) had uncoupled the cars from the engine. Speculation grew that Sukarno might have invented the charges to cover up still another example of inefficiency or corruption in his government, but the dissolution of parliament in 1960 forestalled any possibility of a public inquiry.

IRELAND
ARMAGH

June 12, 1889

• • • • • • • • • • • • • • • • • •

A faulty decision by a conductor led to the collision of two excursion trains near Armagh, Ireland on June 12, 1889. Three hundred were killed; hundreds were injured.

Two excursion trains left Armagh in Northern Ireland on the morning of June 12, 1889 loaded with more than 1,200 holiday-spirited youngsters from the local Methodist Church Sunday school. They were headed for the resort village of Warrenpoint on Carlingford Bay. The distribution of the seven- to 16-year-old picnickers between the two trains was decidedly uneven: The first train was jammed with 970 children and teachers, crammed into 13 cars and two vans. The remaining 300 or so climbed into the relative comfort of the wooden cars of the second train.

It all began peacefully enough. The first train spun its wheels, spouted steam, strained and departed on schedule.

Shortly after this, the half-empty second section eased out of the Armagh station.

But soon afterward, the first train encountered Kilooney Ridge, a normally navigable but steep slope. The overloaded train made it halfway up the ridge, but the sheer weight of its cargo finally ground it to a halt. The engineer, Thomas Magrath, increased the steam. The train groaned forward a foot and then stopped again.

The second train eased along behind the first, and its engineer, seeing that the lead train was stalled, slowed and waited at the Annaclare bridge.

Meanwhile, the conductor of the first train was in the midst of making a strange decision. Reasoning that the only way to move his train forward was to lighten the load, he ordered the last seven coaches uncoupled. Both the engineer and the assistant conductor argued vehemently against it. It was obvious that those cars would continue to roll back into the waiting second train.

But for some reason, the conductor's aberrant reasoning won, and the assistant conductor uncoupled the coaches. They began to slip back, first slowly, then swiftly, as the conductor, now apparently having second thoughts, commanded men to run alongside, shoving rocks in the wheels to slow the cars.

It was a futile effort. The cars began to careen downhill at breakneck speed, heading straight for the engine of the second train. Within minutes, the last car smashed into the engine, splitting asunder with a horrendous tearing of wood against metal. The other cars telescoped into it, flinging pieces of carriages and passengers down a 70-foot embankment.

With the exception of two men and two girls, every person in the last two cars was killed. Hundreds lay on the slope, some terribly injured. It would be hours before rescuers from the village would be able to clear the bodies from the wreckage and transport the injured to hospitals.

The conductor who caused all of this was brought before a Board of Trade inquiry and given a reprimand.

ITALY
SALERNO

March 2, 1944

• • • • • • • • • • • • • • • • • •

The stalling of a train in a tunnel near Salerno, Italy on March 2, 1944 caused the death by asphyxiation of more than 400 passengers and crew.

Ordinarily, railroad wrecks are the result of head-on and rear-end collisions, derailments, collapsed bridges or switching errors. These are the most common hazards, and there are safety regulations and precautions to prevent them. But no one could predict the circumstances that would lead to one of the most tragic train wrecks in the history of European rail travel.

On March 2, 1944, at the height of World War II, a train loaded to capacity with military and civilian passengers approached Salerno, Italy. A long tunnel marks the last few meters into the city, and for a reason never explained, this train stalled midway through the tunnel. The fumes from the engine accumulated and spread through the cars, killing over 400 passengers. Trapped and asphyxiated in their seats, they had no chance of escaping the lethal contamination.

JAMAICA
KENDAL

September 1, 1957

• • • • • • • • • • • • • • • • • •

Mechanical failure caused the derailing of a train near Kendal, Jamaica on September 1, 1957. One hundred seventy-five died; more than 750 were injured.

An S-curve in a track outside Kendal, Jamaica is an anathema to train engineers. It appears suddenly and unexpectedly and has been the scene of numerous accidents caused by errors in judgment on the part of trainmen. In 1938, a train failed to negotiate it, leaped from the tracks and crashed, claiming 85 lives.

The tragic train wreck of September 1, 1957 would occur in precisely the same spot. This accident involved a 12-car train loaded with 1,500 passengers returning from a holiday excursion to Montego Bay. The vacationers were all from Kingston and were part of a trip organized by Catholic agencies in that city.

The train approached the curve at 11:15 P.M. on a balmy, absolutely clear evening. It was traveling at a high but not excessive rate of speed and should have been able to negotiate the curve. But two factors apparently conspired to cause the tragedy. First, the train's brakes failed to hold—or so the engineer, Garnish Lurch, told investigators later.

Second, the coupling between the third and fourth cars was faulty. It had been loosening at intervals on the way to Montego Bay, and yard workers there had tightened it, but apparently not enough. At the middle of the S-curve, the coupling let go, and the momentum whipped both the engine and all of the cars from the tracks.

The locomotive and first three cars landed on level ground, and their occupants received only injuries. But the last nine cars dove headlong into a ravine. The force smashed cars into other cars, ripping tops and sides from the carriages and flinging occupants through smashed windows or holes in the cars' sides. One car's momentum actually sent it climbing up the far side of the ravine, where it hung precariously while rescuers climbed gingerly through it searching for survivors or hauling off bodies.

More than 750 were injured and 175 died in the worst train wreck in Jamaica's history.

JAPAN
TOKYO

May 3, 1962

• • • • • • • • • • • • • • •

Human error—the running of a signal—caused the collision of a freight train and a commuter train near Tokyo on May 3, 1962. One hundred sixty died; more than 300 were injured.

Three miles north of Tokyo and just outside the Mikawashima station, at 9:30 P.M. on Constitution Day, May 3, 1962, a freight train ran through a blocking signal, designed to keep it from entering an occupied track, jumped the tracks and sideswiped a six-car electric commuter train. The commuter train, packed with celebrants, was outbound from Tokyo.

"Blue electric sparks filled the air and then everything went dark," Shoji Iwasaki, a factory worker and survivor, told the *New York Times.* "People stumbled about, wailing and screaming. I broke a window glass and jumped out and started to climb down the embankment."

The embankment was a 30-foot incline next to the tracks. It was the only means of escape, and most of the stunned passengers who, like the young man, had managed to crawl through the automatically opened emergency doors, or through broken windows, either stumbled onto the freight tracks or began to crawl down the embankment.

And then, tragedy struck.

A second, nine-car commuter train rammed into the wreckage of the first commuter train and the freight engine. Cars were hurled in several directions. The freight cars were destroyed and the boiler of the steam locomotive exploded with a dreadful roar, spewing scalding steam in all directions. It spread through the leading cars of the commuter train, scalding the survivors of the first wreck.

"The other train came crashing into our wreckage," continued Iwasaki. "The leading car toppled down and pulled four others after it. It rolled down the embankment, pinning and crushing many people who were fleeing for safety. It was horrible."

Cars continued to tumble down the embankment, grinding fleeing passengers beneath them and piling up, finally, at the bottom of the incline. "It rained bodies," one observer recalled.

Rescuers arrived under a thick, superheated fog of spent steam. The grisly business of removing the dead and the injured went on through the night and into the next day. One hundred sixty people died in the catastrophic wreck, and more than 300 were injured.

Three weeks later, following an investigation, nine railwaymen were indicted on charges of criminal negligence.

JAPAN
YOKOHAMA

November 9, 1963

• • • • • • • • • • • • • • • • • •

A cracked rail was responsible for a three-train collision near Yokohama, Japan on November 9, 1963. One hundred sixty-two died; 72 were injured.

Two horrendous tragedies occurred on the same crisp autumn day in Japan in 1963. Early on Saturday, November 9, an explosion rocked through a coal mine in Omuta, killing 446 men. Six hours later, three trains were involved in a colossal collision outside Yokohama. One hundred and sixty-two people perished in this wreck.

At 10 P.M. that night, a fast-moving freight train traveling on Japan's main north-south Tokaido trunk line derailed when the train passed over a section of track that contained a cracked section of rails. Three of the freight train's cars flung themselves across two adjacent passenger train tracks.

At almost the same instant, two passenger trains, traveling in opposite directions, roared into the site. One was a commuter train headed south, from Yokohama to its southern suburbs. It plowed into the three derailed cars, smashing them to timber, and shot off the southbound track directly into the path of a northbound train, headed for Tokyo. With a horrible screeching of steel, this train was sent sideways off its rails.

Cars telescoped on both commuter trains, and overhead electric lines, ripped from their fastenings by the crash, sent firework displays of sparks fanning into the night sky. Small fires started and were quickly extinguished by a rain that had just begun to fall.

Rescue workers with searchlights rushed to the scene within minutes. Firemen and medical workers cut away twisted and fused pieces of the passenger train, trying to separate the cars and open up escape routes for survivors.

A steady stream of ambulances sped the injured to the 13 Yokohama hospitals in the area, while Japanese television broadcast lists of the dead and injured throughout the night. One hundred sixty-two died and 72 were injured, 48 of them critically. A 28-year-old American, William Scott of Colorado Springs, Colorado, was among the dead.

November was an election month in Japan, and the two disasters became political fodder, particularly for the foes of Premier Hayato Ikeda's conservative government. Until the November 21 election, investigations, charges and countercharges of negligence and irresponsibility flew back and forth, while the grieving relatives buried their dead.

MEXICO
CAZADERO

February 1, 1945

• • • • • • • • • • • • • • • •

Human error—a faulty switch setting—caused the collision of an excursion train and a freight train in Cazadero, Mexico on February 1, 1945. One hundred died; 70 were injured.

At 11:00 P.M. on January 31, 1945, a trainload of religious pilgrims left Mexico City bound for San Juan de Los Lagos, south of Aguascalientes and about 300 miles northwest of Mexico City. A religious festival for the Virgin Mary was to be held there the next day, and the pilgrims were confident that they would arrive by sunrise, in order to participate in the festivities and the devotional services.

The special excursion train provided by the National Railways was not a comfortable one. It was old and contained wooden coaches that had seen years of service. The seats were hard and spartan and not necessarily designed for a good night's sleep. But the pilgrims were content. It was, for some of them, the high point of their lives.

By 12:47 on the morning of February 1, the excursion train had reached the tiny hamlet of Cazadero, 100 miles north of Mexico City. It was plainly marked. Lanterns hung from its rear cars. But a fast-moving freight train, misdirected onto the same track by a faulty switch setting, overtook the excursion train just outside Cazadero and smashed into it. The nine coaches were swept off the track like debris as the steam locomotive of the freight careened forward and then left the rails itself.

Three cars burst into flames instantly, burning alive most of their occupants. Other passengers were flung to the tracks or the roadbed. Still others were trapped in the other cars.

Rescuers from Cazadero and neighboring towns rushed to the scene, extinguishing the fires and attempting to drag survivors and bodies from the charred and tangled wreckage. News of the wreck was telegraphed to Mexico City, and a relief train loaded with doctors and supplies set out immediately. By the time it arrived, most of the injured had been taken to San Juan del Rio, 20 miles from Cazadero, where a small regional hospital was overwhelmed by the rush of casualties. One hundred pilgrims were killed; 70 were seriously injured in still another railway wreck caused by human error.

MEXICO
CUARTLA

June 24, 1881

• • • • • • • • • • • • • • • •

Faulty judgment on the part of an engineer caused the plunge of a train through a weakened bridge near Cuartla, Mexico on June 24, 1881. A fire compounded the tragedy. Two hundred sixteen died; 40 were injured.

The most tragic train wreck in Mexican history was also one of the grisliest of all railroad accidents.

On June 24, 1881, a troop train, loaded with more than 300 soldiers and 60 civilians, approached a wooden bridge that spanned the rain-swollen San Antonio River near Cuartla. According to reports in the *New York Times,* there was some consternation among some of the passengers as they noted that the swirling floodwaters had almost reached the tracks along the embankment.

The bridge was not inundated, but the river was only a few feet beneath the trestle's tracks and moving swiftly. Nevertheless, the engineer chose to proceed.

Within minutes, the bridge began to sway, made top-heavy by the train's weight and weakened considerably by the force of the floodwaters. Moments later, it gave way, toppling the train and its contents toward the river. But the engine and cars did not plunge directly into the roiling waters. They careened into the embankment, thus saving the train's occupants from drowning.

But their safety was only momentary. A freight car full of brandy requisitioned for military personnel aboard the train split open and poured its contents onto the engine and the passenger cars below. Sparks from the engine ignited the brandy, which turned the first few wooden cars into horrific infernos. Burning liquid poured into the open cars, setting fire to the military men trapped inside.

Most of the 60 civilians, all of whom were in the last cars of the train, escaped either unscathed or with varying degrees of injuries. But the soldiers in the first cars died horribly, "wrapped," according to the *Times* reporter, "in a sheet of flame." The engineer and conductor were both scalded to death by the steam from the engine's boiler.

Forty of the civilians were seriously injured; 216 passengers, most of them soldiers, died in this, one of the grimmest of all transportation disasters.

MEXICO
GUADALAJARA

January 18, 1915

• • • • • • • • • • • • • • • • • •

Loss of control by the engineer on a steep grade accounted for the derailment of a train near Guadalajara, Mexico on January 18, 1915. Over 600 died; scores were injured.

Even in the best of times, the military tends to obfuscate the precise details of incidents that result in great loss of life to that military's personnel. In 1915, Mexico was awash with civil unrest and violence. President Victoriano Huerta had resigned, partly because of U.S. military intervention under President Woodrow Wilson, and one of the revolutionaries, Venustiano Carranza, was the ostensible head of the country. But bands of brigands, led by Francisco "Pancho" Villa and Emiliano Zapata, continued to terrorize the countryside.

Still, Carranza hoped to present a face of relative order in a country that had been split asunder by civil war, and so, when a railroad wreck of awesome proportions and horrendous fatalities occurred near Guadalajara on January 18, 1915, he and his military aides made certain that the world received no official news of it.

The only report of this tragedy came from a letter written in February 1915 by American missionary Mrs. John Howland to the American Board of Commissions for Foreign Missions.

Guadalajara province was secured by Carranza's troops on the 18th of January, and as a reward to his troops, Carranza ordered that their families be sent by train from Colima to join them. The train carried 20 cars, but this was inadequate to accommodate the number of people. "The roofs [were] covered with men and women and many slung under the cars in a most perilous position even for ordinary travel," wrote Mrs. Howland.

"At the top of the steepest grade, coming down," she continued, "the engineer lost control, the cars rushed down the long incline, throwing off human freight on both sides and finally plunging into an abyss.

"Nine hundred people were on the train and only six were unhurt. More than six hundred were killed outright," the letter concludes, thus making this one of the most lethal train wrecks of the world.

MEXICO
GUADALAJARA

April 3, 1955

• • • • • • • • • • • • • • • • • •

No reason was given for the derailment of a passenger train over a gorge near Guadalajara, Mexico on April 3, 1955. Three hundred were killed; hundreds were injured.

An astounding death toll of 300 persons made the April 3, 1955 calamity near Guadalajara one of Mexico's worst train wrecks. Certainly the horror of it ranks it as one of the world's worst railway catastrophes.

The popular night express from Guadalajara to the popular Pacific coast resort of Manzanillo, due west of Mexico City, was packed on the first weekend in April 1955. It was Holy Week, and thousands of vacationers were vacating the cities. A large number of Mexicans headed for the Pacific beaches, including Manzanillo. All weekend long, trains ran with passengers standing in the aisles and vestibules.

The night express was no exception. On April 3 it was packed, and there was a holiday mood aboard as it rounded a curve headed for a bridge that spanned a 600-foot-deep canyon near the little town of Alsaba.

Suddenly, celebration turned to tragedy as nine cars derailed and plunged into the canyon, tumbling over one another, telescoping at the bottom, crushing 300 passengers and injuring hundreds more.

It would be a day before rescuers could climb down the steep sides of the ravine and extricate survivors from the tangled mass of twisted steel at the foot of the canyon.

MEXICO
SALTILLO

October 9, 1972

• • • • • • • • • • • • • • • • • •

Drunkenness in the cab and excessive speed were the causes of the derailment of a passenger train near Saltillo, Mexico on October 9, 1972. Two hundred eight were killed; hundreds were injured.

More than 1,600 Mexicans made the 60-mile pilgrimage by train from Saltillo and Monterey to the shrine of

St. Francis at Catorce, in the central part of Mexico, on Wednesday, October 9, 1972. It was the saint's day, and the pilgrims, composed of entire families from grandparents to grandchildren, made requests and promises at the shrine and then joined the festival celebrating the Day of St. Francis.

When the festivities and the ceremonies were over, they boarded the train for the short night journey back to Saltillo and Monterey.

In the locomotive of the train, far more secular activities were happening. The engineer and four crewmen had procured tequila and some women in a small whistlestop. A party continued through most of the journey.

By the time the train neared Saltillo, the engineer and his companions were thoroughly drunk and, unfortunately, wreckless. At 10 P.M., the train rumbled down a moderately steep grade that led to a bridge two and a half miles south of Saltillo. The track curved at a six-degree angle before it reached the bridge, and because of this, the posted speed limit was 35 miles per hour.

The train was doing 75 miles per hour as it entered the curve. The locomotive fairly flew off the track, derailing 13 of the 22 passenger cars behind it. Most of them overturned, and four of them burst immediately into flames. "There were cars cut in half," said a policeman who arrived on the scene shortly after the catastrophe occurred, "bodies everywhere, and women and children crying and screaming, 'Get me out of here!'"

Dazed survivors and injured staggered about in the darkness, stunned and in pain. The screams of the dying and injured were like a grim chorus. Some survivors found the engineer and his companions, who were still drunk. Enraged, they grabbed the engineer and, ripping loose a cord from within the crushed and flaming coaches, attempted to lynch him and the train's conductor. A special inspector, Arnulfo Ochoa, intervened and promised to have the authorities deal with the dazed and shaken engineer and conductor, whom he then shepherded off to an arriving ambulance. Blood tests at the hospital to which they were taken confirmed their extreme drunkenness.

The long and ghastly job of cutting through the twisted and tangled wreckage began immediately and would continue for two days. Policemen, firemen, Red Cross workers, soldiers and civilian volunteers from a wide area worked through the night, the next day and the following night to extricate some who were trapped and would live. Cars were piled upon cars, and rubble was everywhere.

Two hundred eight persons died and hundreds were injured in this, one of the worst rail crashes in Mexican history.

MEXICO
TEPIC

July 11, 1982

An eroded roadbed accounted for the derailment of a train near Tepic, Mexico on July 11, 1982. One hundred twenty died; hundreds were injured.

The weather was bad on the night of July 11, 1982 in the mountainous regions of western Mexico. A train carrying 1,560 passengers from Nogales, on the Arizona border, to Guadalajara had safely negotiated much of the treacherous track that hugged the sides of mountains and sometimes ascended as much as 1,000 feet above the gorges below.

Jose Louis Velasco, the engineer, was a careful man, and there was probably nothing he could have done to avert what happened that night. A section of roadbed at the top of an 800-foot ravine had eroded. Fatefully, the weight of this particular train caused it to give way. Ten cars tipped, balanced for a moment and then plunged into the ravine. Coaches piled upon coaches, crushing those and their occupants under them. Others telescoped. Amazingly, some passengers were flung from the wreckage and so survived.

Rescue crews arrived on the scene, but the steepness of the mountain, the imminent danger of mudslides and the blinding rain hampered their efforts. Rescue helicopters were finally called in and airlifted the most gravely injured to hospitals in Guadalajara. Once this had been accomplished, the griın job of cutting the corpses out of the mangled wreckage began.

One hundred twenty people, including one American, died in the crash. Hundreds more were injured.

NEW ZEALAND
WAIOURI

December 24, 1953

A swollen river caused by a volcanic eruption caused the bridge accident of a train near Waiouri, New Zealand on December 24, 1953. One hundred fifty five died; there is no record of survivors.

The eruption of the 9,000-foot-high volcano Mount Ruapehu, near Waiouri, New Zealand, in December 1953 was described by seismologists as "minor." And in the scale of volcanic activities it undoubtedly was.

The eruption was, however, intense enough to send millions of gallons of water barreling down the River

Wangaehu, which in turn weakened the Tangiwai Railroad Bridge. On Christmas Eve it was about to be crossed by the Wellington-Auckland express, a nine-car passenger train loaded with hundreds of well-wishers on their way to welcome Queen Elizabeth II, who was making a rare visit to New Zealand.

Partway across the span, the train broke through the sagging and swaying trestle and plunged into the roaring river. Some cars floated, momentarily, but most sank like boulders, drowning 155 hapless passengers.

PAKISTAN
GAMBAR

September 29, 1957

• • • • • • • • • • • • • • • • • •

Inadequate signals caused the collision of a passenger train and an oil train in Gambar, Pakistan on September 29, 1957. Three hundred died; 150 were injured.

Nearly 300 people were burned to death or died from the collision, shortly before midnight of September 29, 1957, of a Karachi-bound passenger train and a stationary oil train at Gambar, near Montgomery, West Pakistan. More than 150 were injured as the overcrowded, speeding passenger train crashed into the oil train, which was stopped in the yards of the Gambar railroad station.

Apparently, there were inadequate signals, and the passenger train had been routed onto the wrong track. By the time the engineer of the passenger train realized his situation, he had driven his locomotive full force into the oil train, which exploded with a thunderous roar, collapsing the railroad station and literally blowing apart the passenger train's engine and forward coaches.

The search for bodies and survivors went on through the entire night of September 29, and by daylight it was apparent that it would go on for hours more. The charred, smoking wreckage contained the bodies of hundreds; others had been blown into the countryside. It would be one of the worst rail wrecks in Pakistan's history.

POLAND
NOWY DWOR

October 22, 1949

• • • • • • • • • • • • • • • • • •

Excessive speed was blamed for the derailment of a passenger train near Nowy Dwor, Poland on October 22, 1949. Two hundred were killed; 400 were injured.

Not much news seeped through the government censorship agencies of the Eastern bloc during the Cold War. Soviet authorities were particularly loathe to admit tragedies that occurred. So for years and years, as far as the rest of the world knew, no train wrecks, air crashes, ship sinkings or other disasters that are the unfortunate consequence of modern-day living occurred in the countries of the Eastern bloc.

Occasionally, however, news did leak out, from "unofficial sources." In late October 1949, news came from Poland of its worst rail wreck in 30 years, and one of the worst of the century. Two hundred people were killed and nearly 400 were injured when the Danzig-Warsaw express, traveling at excessive speed, left the rails on a curve near the town of Nowy Dwor, northwest of Warsaw.

No further details were ever provided to the world outside Poland.

PORTUGAL
CUSTOIAS

July 26, 1964

• • • • • • • • • • • • • • • • • •

The overloading of a passenger car caused its derailment in Custoias, Portugal on July 26, 1964. Ninety-four died; 92 were injured.

The worst train accident in the history of Portugal occurred because of the overloading of one passenger car. Designed to carry a maximum of 70 passengers, one of the cars of the Automara express was packed with 161 holiday revelers on their way from the seaside resort of Povoa de Varzim to Oporto, Portugal on July 26, 1964.

A short six miles from the end of their journey, near the village of Custoias, the overloaded car came uncoupled, jumped the track and raced down an embankment. It would take seven hours to excavate the smashed debris of the car and unearth survivors and the dead. Sixty-nine people died instantly in the accident; 92 were seriously injured, and of those, another 25 died in the hospital, bringing the total of dead to 94.

SPAIN
LEBRIJA

July 21, 1972

• • • • • • • • • • • • • • • • • •

Human error—the ignoring of a signal—caused the collision of two trains near Lebrija, Spain on July 21, 1972. Seventy-six died; scores were injured.

Servicemen seem to have suffered the most casualties in the world's worst train disasters. The reasons are logical.

Until very recently, troops have been transported primarily by train. Off-duty servicemen on leave generally return home from camp in large numbers, frequently on overcrowded trains.

The latter was the case on July 21, 1972, when the Madrid-Cadiz express, carrying more than 500 passengers in its 14 cars, slammed into a similarly packed local train making its way out of the station at Lebrija.

The post-crash investigation revealed that the engineer of the local, which was loaded with Spanish sailors on leave, had ignored a signal and moved directly into a collision course with the express, which had the right of way. The local sustained most of the damage and all of the fatalities, but there were 103 people injured on both trains, some of them seriously. The 76 dead—all sailors on the local—were pulled from the wreckage by other servicemen either on the trains or from the American Polaris submarine base, which was located very near the site of the wreck.

SWITZERLAND
BASEL

June 14, 1891

• • • • • • • • • • • • • • • •

A collapsed bridge caused the accident of June 14, 1891 in Basel, Switzerland. One hundred twenty were killed; scores were injured.

The train, consisting of two engines and 12 wooden carriages, departed from Basel en route to Delsburg and began to move across the newly constructed Monchenstein bridge at a normal and respectable rate of speed. The Birs River, which the bridge crossed, was placid; there was no indication that a strong current or a storm-swollen cataract had weakened the bridge.

Yet it collapsed, immediately after the two engines had cleared the span. The three carriages directly behind the engines uncoupled themselves from the remaining cars and plunged to the river, twisting as they went and flipping the engines over on their sides. The engineers and stokers were crushed to death.

Behind them, 120 passengers were killed instantly, trapped and drowned in the wreckage in the river. The occupants of the third car were seriously injured but at least survived.

The rescue work proceeded very slowly. Some bodies were disentangled from the wreckage and laid out for identification. But many, many more were left in the wreckage, and for weeks they would drift one by one to the surface and come ashore in the small riverfront villages downstream from the crash site.

UNITED STATES
COLORADO
EDEN

August 7, 1904

• • • • • • • • • • • • • • • •

Swollen rivers caused the wreckage of one bridge to collide with another, collapsing it just as a train passed over it near Eden, Colorado on August 7, 1904. Ninety-six died; scores were injured.

Collisions of trains are not uncommon. But collisions of bridges are quite another phenomenon, destined for the record books. And such an occurrence resulted in one of the United States' more terrible train disasters.

Much of the land of the American West is scarred with arroyos—gullies that once contained a river or small stream. Pacific train number eight, which because of the St. Louis World's Fair had earned itself the nickname World's Fair Flyer, crossed a number of these arroyos on its trip from Denver to St. Louis and back again. Arroyos were usually just part of the scenery, and the bridges that forded them were maintained in a desultory manner, as were the wagon bridges, some of which were never maintained but left to age in the relentlessly extreme weather.

The beginning of August 1904 brought heavy rains to Colorado, and the normally dry arroyos were no longer unobtrusive. They overflowed with boiling mountain streams, tumbling toward valleys miles away. On the night of August 7, the World's Fair Express paused momentarily at the small mountain town of Eden and then pushed on toward St. Louis.

If its only task had been to cross Steele's Hollow Bridge, its trip would have been as serene as it usually was. But on this particular night, coincidence conspired with nature and brought about a catastrophe. Just as the seven-coach express began its traverse of the railroad trestle, an ancient wagon bridge a short distance upstream collapsed with a roar.

Propelled by the floodwaters in the arroyo, the timbers of the wagon bridge acted like battering rams and slammed into Steele's Hollow Bridge just as the train was in midspan. Trestle and train collapsed simultaneously and were flung into the water. Nothing was left of the three main spans of the bridge. The train's locomotive, baggage car and chair and smoking cars dove into the stream together. A quick-thinking porter, seeing the disaster occurring ahead of him, grabbed the air brakes on the two sleepers and

One of the oddest of all railway wrecks took place as a result of the collision of two bridges—one wrecked by floodwaters, one an innocent bystander over an arroyo near Eden, Colorado. Trestle and train were both flung into the floodwaters on August 7, 1904. Frank Leslie's Illustrated Newspaper

dining car, saving himself and his fellow passengers from the horrible fate of those in the rest of the train.

Frank Mayfield, the fireman of the train, was thrown clear. He landed on the embankment and was knocked unconscious. Later, his eyewitness account describing the wreck and early rescue attempts formed the basis of most news accounts of the disaster.

What he saw were pullman cars sitting serenely on the tracks, no sign of the engine, and passenger cars with their roof burst open by the impact. Passengers and wrecked cars alike were driven miles downstream by the raging floodwaters, and the army of more than 500 rescuers would spend days and nights digging debris and bodies out of the muddy river banks. Ninety-six died and scores were injured in this freak accident.

UNITED STATES
CONNECTICUT
SOUTH NORWALK

May 6, 1853

• • • • • • • • • • • • • • • • • •

Disregard of both a signal and a speed limit caused the bridge accident over the Norwalk River near South Norwalk, Connecticut on May 6, 1853. Forty-six were killed; 25 were injured.

The year 1853 was a bad year for drawbridge accidents in the United States. Two occurred that year; one was minor, with neither an injury nor the loss of life. But the other was horrendous and is generally considered to be the worst U.S. railroad accident until that time.

The second wreck took place on a drawbridge spanning the Norwalk River near South Norwalk, Connecticut at approximately 10:30 on the morning of May 6, 1853. The bridge was a well-marked one, with a warning tower consisting of a 40-foot pole from which a red ball the size of a basketball was suspended. If the ball was lowered and visible, it was safe for the trains of the New York and New Haven railroad to proceed. If raised out of sight, it signaled that the drawbrige was open.

At 10:15 that morning, the steamboat *Pacific* whistled to pass the closed bridge. The bridge tender, a man named Harford, raised the warning ball for trains and opened the bridge, allowing the *Pacific* to steam through.

Meanwhile, an express passenger train bound for Boston from New York shot through the Norwalk station, trying to make up lost time. Its engineer was one Edward Tucker, and his safety record was anything but spotless. It was he, in fact, who had been the engineer in the New York and New Haven's first wreck, in 1849, its first year of existence. He had been severely injured in the head-on collision in Greenwich, Connecticut, although an investigative team had concluded that he had put his train on the wrong track on the advice of his conductor.

Still, that accident was caused by inattention to signals, and perhaps that had something to do with the tragedy Tucker was about to cause as he sped his express toward the Norwalk River Bridge.

It was a clear morning. Visibility was unlimited and unimpeded. Once a curve had been negotiated, there were 3,000 feet of straight track to the bridge, during which the warning tower was visible at all times. But for some reason, no one—engineer, conductor or fireman—saw it or, apparently, looked for it. "It's not my duty to look for it," fireman George Elmer testified later.

The train roared on at full throttle, despite the posted 10-mile-per-hour speed limit.

Approximately 370 feet from the edge of the 60-foot gap between the tracks' end and the stone tower of the wooden drawbridge, Tucker saw the river—and no bridge. He blew two blasts of his whistle, the signal to the brakemen in the passenger cars to apply the hand brakes. But the brakemen had seen the coming catastrophe at the same time as Tucker had, and instead of applying the brakes, they jumped for their lives.

Showing a similar disregard of responsibility, the conductor, fireman and engineer all leaped from the train without a word of warning to the passengers.

The railroad employees rolled free just as the locomotive shot into space, leaped across the 60-foot gap and smashed into the bridge's concrete pier. The tender, two baggage cars and two passenger cars followed. The remaining passenger cars would have also made the leap had it not been for passengers in the last two coaches who grabbed the idle hand brakes and brought their cars to a squealing stop. The third passenger car, caught at the edge of the precipice, cracked open like a rectangular egg, spewing seats, luggage, floor and ceiling timbers and terrified passengers into the Norwalk River. One eyewitness told the *New York Times,* "Many of the seats and the dislodged window sashes, with a crowd of timber fragments, were propelled, some of them, fully across the gulf, and two of the passengers, who were seated just at the spot where the car snapped asunder, were thrown a full twenty feet forward and pitched with frightful force upon the ruins of the second and first cars."

The steamboat *Pacific* stopped immediately and set about trying to rescue survivors, who were frantically swimming to the surface. Sailors and passengers alike on the *Pacific* dove into the waters to assist survivors as the wrecked passenger cars shifted and began to sink.

Meanwhile, on shore, a group of South Norwalk citizens had witnessed not only the accident but the bailing out of the train's crew. The group surrounded engineer Edward Tucker, who had broken his leg in his leap for life. One mob member had already produced a lynch rope, but he was challenged by other men who felt that hanging was too good and that shooting would be the proper fate for Tucker. The argument lasted just long enough to allow the police to arrive and extricate Tucker from the mob.

The same afternoon, a jury was convened, and although Tucker vowed that the warning ball was not in place, other witnesses stated that it was, and both he and the directors of the railroad were found guilty of extreme negligence.

No criminal charges were pressed, but public indignation forced New York and New Haven officials to require all trains henceforth to come to a full stop before every drawbridge. In addition, Connecticut set up the state's first Board of Railroad Commissioners to investigate all railroad accidents and impose stricter safety rules for railroads.

Forty-six people died in this tragedy, and 25 were injured. There would be more bridge accidents in the future, but this dramatic one would initiate a growing movement toward stricter railroad regulation and safety practices.

UNITED STATES
ILLINOIS
CHATSWORTH

August 10, 1887

• • • • • • • • • • • • • • • • •

Human negligence led to the weakening of a railroad bridge, which caused an excursion train to fall through it at Chatsworth, Illinois on August 10, 1887. Eighty-two died. There is no record of injuries.

In the same way that the terrible South Norwalk bridge disaster of 1853 (See previous entry) brought about regional safety precautions, the even more disastrous bridge accident of August 10, 1887 at Chatsworth, Illinois raised the responsibility for these regulations to the federal level, with the Interstate Commerce Commission and later the U.S. Department of Transportation.

In this event, as in the earlier disaster, human negligence was the prime culprit. This time, however, it was not the engineer of the train but the head of a railroad track-work gang who was responsible for the needless loss of 82 lives.

Timothy Coughlin was the man in charge of a railroad gang cleaning dry brush from the tracks near a small 15-foot wooden trestle that spanned a shallow, usually dry culvert near Chatsworth, Illinois on August 10, 1887. Their method was to collect the weeds in piles and burn them.

At quitting time, Coughlin cautioned his men to make sure the fire was out; but once he gave the order, he failed to follow it up by checking each of the smoldering piles. That night, an excursion train of the Toledo, Peoria & Western Railroad left Peoria bound for Niagara Falls. It was packed with residents of the farmlands of central Illinois, on their way to a holiday at the falls. As the train sped through Illinois shortly after midnight, its engineer spotted what seemed to be a brushfire on the tracks ahead of him. Too late, he realized that it was a wooden bridge burning. The smoldering remnants of the burned weeds that Coughlin's crew had left that afternoon had set the trestle on fire.

The engineer reversed the engine and whistled for brakes. But he was going too fast and it was too late to prevent the engine from plunging straight into the flames. The lead locomotive made it across the gulf safely, but the weight of the second engine snapped the fire-weakened timber supporting the tracks, and the entire wooden bridge folded in upon itself and the train, toppling both into the creek. Nine passenger cars crashed, one on top of the other, splintering apart and crushing some of their occupants. The 10th car, a sleeper, managed to brake to a stop at the edge of the trestle, but the speed of the train drove the second sleeper into it, telescoping both cars and killing most of the occupants.

It was an inferno of a wreck, needless in its cause, horrendous in its consequences and so impressive to the people of the Midwest at that time that it became part of its regional folklore. "The Bridge Was Burned at Chatsworth," attributed to T. P. Westendorf, contained the following vivid description of that flaming night:

The mighty crash of timbers
A sound of hissing steam
The groans and cries of anguish
A woman's stifled scream.
The dead and dying mingled,
With broken beams and bars
An awful human carnage
A dreadful wreck of cars.

UNITED STATES
MASSACHUSETTS
REVERE

August 26, 1871

• • • • • • • • • • • • • • • • • • • •

Outdated equipment was responsible for the collision of two excursion trains in Revere, Massachusetts on August 26, 1871. Thirty-two died; more than 100 were injured.

One of the best known of all American railroad accidents was noted not for its immense casualty figures (32 were killed) but for the impact it had on the public. It occupied the newspapers and minds of mid-Victorian America for months afterward.

August 26, 1871 was an unusually busy Saturday for the Eastern Railroad out of Boston, mainly because of three weekend events: two major religious revival meetings and, in an interesting juxtaposition, a military muster. Because of the crush of people, 192 trains left the Eastern's Boston depot each day of the weekend.

The main line ran from Boston north to Salem via Lynn, with several branches along the north shore. At 8:30 on Saturday evening, August 26, a slow-moving local switched onto this main line from a branch near Revere, Massachusetts. It was a particularly dark night, and according to later reports in the *New York Times,* the engineer of an express, moving at 30 miles per hour, did not see the rear of the slow-moving local until his train was almost upon it. He immediately hit the outdated hand brakes. Although other railroads had already switched to the new Neihouse air brake, the Eastern had not, and the old hand brakes were useless on rails that were slick from rain.

American newspapers fed the insatiable appetite of the public for months following the collision of two excursion trains in Revere, Massachusetts on August 26, 1871. Frank Leslie's Illustrated Newspaper

With a roar, the express slammed into the rear of the local, forcing the engine two-thirds of the way through the rear car. Steam pipes on the engine's boiler erupted, blasting live steam into the car and searing its occupants. Simultaneously, hot coals from the firebox mixed with the smashed kerosene lamps in the two last cars, setting the wood of these carriages on fire. Flames engulfed both coaches. Thirty-two passengers were either crushed to death or incinerated by the consuming fire, and more than 100 were injured, some of them critically.

Boston erupted with cries of "deliberate murder" directed against the railroad's management. Resultant lawsuits nearly bankrupted the company, forcing it finally to modernize and monitor its equipment.

UNITED STATES
NEW JERSEY
ATLANTIC CITY

July 30, 1896

• • • • • • • • • • • • • • • • •

Human error was blamed for the broadside collision of the Philadelphia express with a West Jersey excursion train at "Death Trap," a track intersection in Atlantic City, New Jersey, on July 30, 1896. Sixty were killed; hundreds were injured.

> *When I was at the crossing, I saw the train coming with unslackened speed, and I shouted to [my fireman] Newell, "My God, Morris, he's not going to stop!" Then I followed the first impulse, and leaped from my seat to the floor, and then to the step. I hesitated about jumping after I was on the step, and then, through some unaccountable impulse, I sprang back into the cab. Had I leaped I would have been buried beneath the wreck . . . When the crash came, my engine broke loose and ran down the track. When I ran back, the sights and sounds I witnessed unnerved me, and I have been in a tremble ever since. I shall never forget the sight of that Reading engine as she rushed toward us.*

Thus engineer John Greiner described to reporters the moment of impact of a broadside collision that took place early in the evening of July 30, 1896 at "Death Trap," an insidious and potentially lethal intersection of tracks located at Atlantic City, New Jersey.

For years, trains of the West Jersey and Pennsylvania lines had had close calls at the crossing, saved only by the alertness of signalmen who gave the white light for safety and the red light for danger to trains approaching Death Trap.

Around 7:00 P.M. on July 30, 1896, the West Jersey excursion train, a slow mover out of Atlantic City, approached Death Trap and was given the white light to proceed. Engineer Greiner of the West Jersey train was aware that the Philadelphia express of the Reading line was approaching the same intersection from another direction and at high speed, but he followed his signals and proceeded to enter the intersection.

He had done everything right. Upon leaving the drawbridge just before the crossing, he had whistled for signal instructions and had received them, and then had eased himself into the notorious crossing.

What was going through the mind of Edward Farr, the engineer of the Philadelphia express, will never be known. But it must have had nothing to do with heeding signals. Despite the clear red light that should have prevented him from entering the crossing, he barrelled in at 50 miles per hour, seemingly unaware that there was another train—the Jersey excursion train—directly in front of him. He smashed full force into the side of the second car of the Jersey train, lifting it from the tracks and hurtling it down an embankment and then into a marsh. The second, third and fourth cars telescoped into one another and spun off the tracks and down the embankment.

The express train's engine ricocheted off the cars it had devastated and, carrying the first car of the express with it, hurtled into a ditch, where it immediately set fire to the wooden cars into which it smashed. Its boiler exploded, sending scalding steam into the wreckage and killing some of those who had survived the initial impact.

It was a grisly sight. All of the wooden cars caught fire. The speed of the express flung bodies like discarded dolls, through windows and from one end of smashed cars to the other. Engineer Farr was dismembered, and parts of his body were found the length of the car behind the engine. Individual acts of heroism abounded, as passengers and rescuers alike risked the fire that consumed the scene.

By dawn, the boardwalk was littered with bodies and bandaged survivors. Sixty people were killed; hundreds were injured, and many were mutilated for life.

UNITED STATES
NEW JERSEY
HACKETTSTOWN

June 16, 1925

• • • • • • • • • • • • • • • • • •

A collision with a mudslide caused the wreck of an excursion train in Hackettstown, New Jersey on June 16, 1925. Thirty-eight died; 38 were injured.

The wreck that occurred when an excursion train from Chicago to Hoboken, New Jersey ran into a mudslide at 3:30 A.M. on June 16, 1925 would have been a minor accident had the engine been a diesel. But 1925 was the age of steam, and the violent explosion of the train's boiler turned a mishap into a disaster.

The train, consisting of two coaches, four pullmans and a diner, was crammed with 182 German-Americans on their way to the port of Hoboken. From there, the celebrators would board the SS *Republic* for a summer holiday in Germany.

By 3:30 on June 16, all of the passengers, thoroughly relaxed by an afternoon and evening of celebration, were serenely asleep. The engineer had encountered a huge cloudburst around 3:00 A.M., but by 3:30 it had passed, and he had opened the throttle in order to utilize the downslope of Rockport Sag to pick up momentum. It was necessary. The upgrade in Hackettstown lost both speed and time for trains on rigid schedules.

Under normal conditions, this was an easy, expected routine. But this night, the cloudburst had caused an immense mudslide partway along Rockport Sag. Mud covered both the embankment and the tracks, and the engine's headlight failed to pick this up until it was already on top of the mud. For 160 feet, the engine careened crazily, barely remaining on the track. A siding switch was hidden beneath the mud.

The engine struck the switch and derailed. It instantly churned down a 12-foot embankment, carrying the first four cars with it. Reaching the bottom, the engine toppled over on its side, killing the engineer, the two firemen and the head trainman instantly. The first and second cars slammed crossways, one on the engine, the other across the tracks, and the first two pullmans derailed on either side of the mud pile.

Aside from the railroad employees, one other known passenger, a decapitated woman, was the only fatality at that moment. But then the engine's boiler exploded, shooting steam through the cars and horribly scalding the awakening passengers within.

Their screams brought rescuers from the surrounding farms to the scene, which had now turned nightmarish. Scores of charred bodies and survivors so badly burned they pleaded for either morphine or death were dragged from the destroyed cars. One man, his face completely burned away, was reported by a local paper to have withdrawn a roll of bills from his pocket and roamed the accident site offering money to anyone who would put a bullet through his head.

Thirty-eight passengers died; 38 more were taken to hospitals with serious injuries. The remaining 100 or so passengers were put aboard another train to continue their trip toward their now-ruined holiday.

UNITED STATES
NEW JERSEY
HIGHTSTOWN

November 11, 1833

• • • • • • • • • • • • • • • •

A broken axle caused the first derailment in U.S. history in Hightstown, New Jersey on November 11, 1833. One person was killed; several were injured.

The first passenger-car wreck in U.S. history took place on November 11, 1833 in Hightstown, New Jersey on the Camden & Amboy line. Only one passenger was killed, but the effects of this accident were curious and far reaching.

The accident occurred when the train, roaring along at 25 miles an hour—a high speed for its time—snapped an axle on one of the passenger cars. Instantly, all of the cars on the train derailed, and the wooden coaches, careening off the track, broke apart. The passengers were tossed around, bruised and cut, and some were flung from the cars. James C. Stedman, a jeweler from Raleigh, North Carolina, became the first passenger fatality in U.S. railroad history when he died, several hours later, from injuries received in the accident.

Two prominent men happened to be aboard the ill-fated train that day. One, ex-president John Quincy Adams, escaped uninjured. The other, Commodore Cornelius Vanderbilt, was flung from his carriage and rolled down a 30-foot embankment. One of his lungs was punctured and several of his ribs were broken. He was transported back to his home in New York, where he was reported to hover between life and death for a month.

When the commodore recovered, he vowed never to invest a penny of his enormous fortune in railroads. He was convinced that they were a bad and dangerous investment.

He later changed his mind greatly. In 1862, at the age of 68, when his fortune from steamboats had climbed to $11 million, Commodore Vanderbilt decided to forget his accident and invest in railroads. By the time he died, 15 years later, he controlled the entire New York Central system.

UNITED STATES
NEW JERSEY
WOODBRIDGE

February 6, 1951

• • • • • • • • • • • • • • • •

Speed was the culprit in the derailing of an express train at Woodbridge, New Jersey on February 6, 1951. Eighty-four died; more than 100 were injured.

Rescue workers struggle to pull survivors from the Pennsylvania Railroad wreck in Woodbridge, New Jersey in February 1951. Wheels and shattered cars are strewn over the embankment from which the train hurtled when a temporary wooden trestle buckled. American Red Cross

While a new railway bridge was being built over the New Jersey Turnpike, traffic on the Pennsylvania Railroad's Jersey Shore line was diverted to a winding bypass. In the shape of an S, the diversion carried the caveat: "Trains and engines must not exceed a speed of 25 miles per hour."

So much for warnings, especially when they are offset by a company schedule that requires commuter trains to make the 35-mile run from Newark to Red Bank in 44 minutes, including stops at various points on the Jersey Shore.

On February 6, 1951, The Broker, one of the Pennsylvania's most posh and popular commuter trains, set out on its usual trip between Newark and Red Bank. It was one of the last trains on the Pennsylvania to be pulled by a steam locomotive, and its engineer was Joseph Fitzsimmons, a 47-year-old veteran with a superior record of safety.

What caused Fitzsimmons to favor his timetable over a clearly stated speed limit will forever remain a mystery. Not even the inquiry after the accident could reveal that information from the befuddled engineer.

At 5:43 P.M. on February 6, pulling seven cars packed with commuters, he plunged into the beginning of the S-curved diversion at 50 miles per hour. The violent lurching caused by the navigation of the first part of the curve galvanized conductor "Honest John" Bishop into immediate action. He tried to shove his way through the crowd of commuters to the emergency stop lever. But by then the locomotive had plunged on into the tight conclusion of the S-curve, and within seconds it had shot off the track, become momentarily airborne as it cleared an embankment and then crashed on its side, hauling all seven cars with it.

Fitzsimmons was thrown clear. His fireman and the passengers in the twisted steel cars fared considerably worse. Pandemonium reigned in the cars, where some commuters had already died and others were dying. Passengers kicked, pummeled and clawed their way through broken windows and mangled doors. Eighty-four died in the crash, most of them in the first four cars. More than 100 were injured.

UNITED STATES
NEW YORK
ANGOLA

December 18, 1867

• • • • • • • • • • • • • • • • • •

Defective equipment caused the derailing of the Lake Shore express near Angola, New York on December 18, 1867. Forty-three were killed; hundreds were injured.

For months after it occurred, the "Angola Horror," as the newspapers in Buffalo and elsewhere called the derailment wreck of December 18, 1867, was given a great deal of ghoulish treatment in the national tabloid press and magazines. The city of Buffalo did nothing to dissuade the tabloids and in fact added to the grisly carnival. It held a mass funeral for the accident victims in the Exchange Street depot a mere three days before Christmas of that year.

It was truly a horror, an avoidable tragedy caused by a defective axle on the rear car of the eastbound Lake Shore express on the afternoon of December 18, 1867.

Speeding to make up time, the train approached the bridge spanning Three Sisters Creek near Angola, New York without incident. But just before it reached the bridge, a wheel on the bent axle hit the "frog," or upthrusting part of a switch. The jolt was enough to derail the car, which in turn derailed the car ahead of it.

Swinging crazily on and off the track, the last car finally slammed into a bridge abutment. The impact burst the car's coal stove apart, scattering red-hot coals around the car and on some of the passengers. Within minutes the wooden coach was ablaze, and all of its 42 passengers were burned alive.

Meanwhile, the detached second car was dragged half on and half off the track for 300 feet before it broke loose from the rest of the train and plummeted down an embankment. Amazingly, though the car was smashed apart, only one passenger was killed.

UNITED STATES
NEW YORK
BROOKLYN

November 2, 1918

• • • • • • • • • • • • • • • • • •

Excessive speed, outdated equipment, defective brakes and an overworked motorman combined to cause the derailment of a Brooklyn Rapid Transit train outside Malbone Tunnel in Brooklyn, New York on November 2, 1918. Ninety-seven died; 95 were injured.

Three conditions conspired to both cause and worsen the crash of a Brooklyn Rapid Transit train that derailed just outside the Malbone Street Tunnel in Brooklyn during rush hour on November 2, 1918.

First, most of the cars on the train were ancient wooden ones that had not been replaced by the steel coaches the Public Service Commission had ordered for the line. After the accident, in which all of the fatalities and injuries occurred in the wooden cars and none in the steel ones of the train, Public Service commissioner Travis H. Whitney accused New York mayor John F. Hylan of dragging his feet and not signing an agreement that would have mandated the steel cars.

Second, the motorman, 25-year-old Edward Anthony Lewis, was exhausted. He had just recovered from influenza. His baby had just died. That day he had already put in a full shift as a train dispatcher and was working overtime as a motorman during rush hour to earn extra money.

And finally, and most crucial of all, the train's brakes were defective and failed to hold when Lewis applied them.

The train, loaded with office workers—most of them women—on their way home, approached the Malbone Street Tunnel at about 30 miles per hour. The posted speed limit was 6 miles per hour, but Lewis, in his testimony at the inquiry, said that the brakes failed, and instead of slowing, the train picked up speed.

On a curve, just before the tunnel's entrance, the train left the track. The lights simultaneously went out in the cars. The decrepit wooden coaches shattered as they capsized and piled into one another, crushing and impaling their passengers on jagged pieces of walls, flooring and ceilings. In all, 97 people, most of them women, were killed, and 95 more were injured, many of them critically.

UNITED STATES
NEW YORK
QUEENS

November 22, 1950

• • • • • • • • • • • • • • • • • •

Defective equipment was responsible for the rear-end collision of two Long Island Railroad trains in Queens, New York on November 22, 1950. Seventy-nine were killed; 363 were seriously hurt.'

The Long Island Railroad, a subsidiary commuter line of the Pennsylvania Railroad, has never been known for its reliability or modernity. It is therefore both gratifying and amazing to note that there have been few major accidents on the LIRR.

The worst wreck to occur on the line occurred during rush hour on November 22, 1950 on a stretch of track just outside the Richmond Hill section of Queens. A local 12-car train bound for Hempstead was ordered, by overhead signals, to slow before entering the station. The motorman, William Murphy, heeded the signals and slowed to 15 miles per hour. According to Murphy, the brakes began to grab at this speed, eventually stopping the train dead.

Just before the stretch of track on which the Hempstead train was stalled was a blind curve, and so Bertram Biggam, the rear car flagman, debarked from the back of the train with a red lamp to warn off any approaching trains.

Eventually, the Hempstead train was given the go-ahead signal, and Murphy revved its electric motors. Biggam abandoned his task and climbed back aboard the train. But the brakes appeared to be locked. The train stayed in place.

Just then, the Babylon express, traveling at 40 miles per hour, rounded the curve. Its motorman, Benjamin Pokorney, had received the same go-ahead signal that Murphy had received and had no reason to believe that the track was not clear. The express smashed into the rear of the Hempstead train, burrowing under and into the last car, flinging it into the air and killing almost everyone in that car and then plowing ahead through subsequent passenger coaches.

Mayhem resulted. Pokorney was killed, but it would be hours before his body could be dug from beneath the mountain of twisted debris. All in all, 79 people died, most of them in the last car of the Hempstead train, and an astonishing 363 were seriously injured.

The Long Island Railroad would be branded a "disgraceful common carrier" by New York mayor Vincent Impellitari and forced to pay out $11 million in damage suits. It then began a decades-long improvement program that has yet to be completed.

UNITED STATES
OHIO
ASHTABULA

December 29, 1876

• • • • • • • • • • • • • • • •

A collapsed bridge caused a train to plunge into a gorge near Ashtabula, Ohio on December 29, 1876. Eighty were killed; 68 were injured.

No charges of wrongdoing were ever filed against the Lake Shore and Michigan Southern Railway following the collapse of a 152-foot iron trestle bridge outside Chicago on the night of December 28, 1876. And yet, two days after the inquiry, Charles Collins, its chief engineer and one of the two men responsible for the safety of the bridge, committed suicide. Five years later, Amasa Stone, the designer of the bridge and president of the line, also committed suicide.

The natural conclusion was that both facts and blame were missing from the inquiry, the first and the model for subsequent boards of inquiry into any railroad accidents involving the deaths of passengers.

The famous Ashtabula Bridge Disaster, as it was destined to be called, was the most deadly railroad accident up to that time, and it took place on the same line (Commodore Vanderbilt's Lake Shore Road) and in the same season as the Angola Horror (see p. 304).

There was a blinding snowstorm on the night of December 29, 1876, which slowed the Pacific Express from New York to Chicago to a 10-mile-per-hour crawl. It was an 11-car train, composed of two engines, three sleepers, a smoker, a parlor car, two coaches and four baggage cars. The first engine, nicknamed Socrates, was piloted by 17-year veteran Daniel McGuire, and he was having great difficulty seeing several feet ahead of him. Drifting snow and sheets of wind-whipped snow had all but eliminated his visibility.

At 7:30 P.M., he reached the iron truss bridge that reached from one embankment of the Ashtabula Creek to the other. He inched across the span and reached the other side with the front wheels of his engine when he felt a sickening, sinking sensation. The struts and underpinnings of the bridge had gone soft and were collapsing under the weight of the train.

McGuire raced his engine and managed to drive Socrates on to safe terrain. But the sudden momentum uncoupled the engine behind him, and it and the rest of the train began the long plummet to the bottom of the creek. The engine plunged into the deep ravine first, followed by car after car, telescoping and splintering apart as they smashed into one another. Almost instantly, the burning coal stoves that heated each of the cars ignited the sperm oil from their illuminating lamps, sending up huge exclamations of flames and incinerating the passengers in their seats and berths.

McGuire slid down through the snowdrifts of the embankment and encountered the injured engineer of the second engine, "Dad" Folsom. "It's another Angola Horror," said Folsom, and it was, only worse. Out of almost 200 passengers, 80 died, 19 of them so badly burned that they would never be identified. Only 52 escaped uninjured. The magnitude of this Christmas season tragedy prompted the Ohio state legislature, and eventually the

Human error, inadequate signals and missed schedules conspired to cause this monstrous head-on collision of an excursion and a passenger train near Camp Hill Station, Pennsylvania on July 17, 1856. Sixty-six children on the excursion train were killed. Frank Leslie's Illustrated Newspaper

federal legislature, to establish permanent boards to investigate fatal accidents.

UNITED STATES
PENNSYLVANIA
CAMP HILL

July 17, 1856

• • • • • • • • • • • • • • • • • •

Missed schedules, inadequate signals and human error were responsible for the head-on collision of two trains near Camp Hill, Pennsylvania on July 17, 1856. Sixty-six children on an excursion train died; 60 were injured.

In the 1850s and 1860s, it was not uncommon for passengers to take seats in the middle of a train because they believed that this midway location was the least vulnerable to either a head-on or rear-end collision. They had reasons to be cautious, and not the least of these had to do with the most serious and violent train wreck in the United States in terms of human casualties: a head-on collision that took place near dawn on July 17, 1856 in Camp Hill, Pennsylvania.

Before sunrise on that particular day, some 1,500 children of Philadelphia's St. Michael's Church gathered at the Master Street Station, preparatory to boarding two trains for a massive picnic-outing at Fort Washington. One train would leave at 5:00 A.M., the other at 8:00 A.M.

Naturally, there was a huge rush to board the first train; none of the 1,500 children of Irish-American immigrants wanted to wait more than three hours in a train station before beginning the trip to the picnic grounds. The priests succeeded in regaining order and loading 600 young people on the 5:00 A.M. train, pulled by the locomotive *Shackamaxon,* with 21-year-old engineer Henry Harris at the throttle.

It took longer than anticipated to load the train; once the doors had been closed, they had to be opened again to accommodate more passengers who adamantly refused to wait, and it would be 5:30 before the train would ultimately leave the Master Street Station. The delay would be a fatal one.

During the chaos in the Master Street Station, the regular local train from Gwynedd to Philadelphia was making its slow way along the single track of the North Pennsylvania (now the Reading) Railroad. It was the practice then to pull trains that did not have the right of way onto sidings. This right of way was determined by schedules. If a train was on schedule, it had the right of way. If it was more than 15 minutes behind, it was required to pull to the siding and let the train going in the opposite direction through—a dangerous practice that depended on accurate watches and the discretion of conductors.

The conductor aboard the local was William Vanstavoren, a young man who had trained under conductor Alfred Hoppel, who, ironically, was the conductor on the excursion train headed in the opposite direction.

Both conductors had reason to be nervous. The local, scheduled to depart from Fort Washington at 6:00 A.M., left at 6:14. The excursion train was a half hour late. Told that the special had not passed through, Vanstavoren, according to the subsequent inquiry, ordered his engineer, William Lee, to proceed anyway. Lee reportedly challenged this order, and Vanstavoren assured him, "It's all right. Just sound your whistle like hell and go slow."

Lee did just this, inching his three-car train (one engine, a baggage car and a passenger car carrying 12 passengers) at 10 miles per hour toward Philadelphia. The passengers, nervous at the sound of the whistle and the slow speed, wisely moved to the back of the car.

At Camp Hill, at the entrance to an S-curve sandwiched between two 20-foot embankments, Lee spotted the excursion train coming directly toward them. It was clipping along at 35 miles per hour, confident that it had the right of way. Lee slammed on his brakes and applied reverse throttle and then jumped, as did his fireman.

Henry Harris, at the controls of the excursion train, saw the almost stationary local at the same time, but it was far too late to avoid a collision. He and his fireman also jumped, but Harris neglected to even try to apply either brakes or reverse throttle. He miscalculated his jump, landed between the tender and the engine and the first car and was crushed to death in the impact that occurred seconds later.

With a roar, the engine of the excursion train slammed into the engine of the local, bursting both boilers and catapulting both engines first into the air and then backward onto the wooden coaches of their trains. The passengers aboard the local had long since abandoned the train and escaped uninjured. But the children aboard the excursion train were trapped in the wooden cars, which instantly splintered and caught fire. Children were flung through broken windows and to either end of the collapsing, fiery infernos.

Hoppel, the conductor of the excursion train, was thrown clear, and he oversaw the fire-fighting efforts of volunteer fire departments from Camp Hill and Chestnut Hill, who were able to save five of the cars of the special. The others burned to the wheels. Sixty-six children were killed, and 60 more were critically injured.

Conductor Hoppel would be arrested and tried for murder but would be acquitted. Conductor Vanstavoren, distraught beyond sanity, repeated over and over, "All of it, all of it is my fault." Along with some trainman companions, he ran to Edge Hill, commandeered a handcar and then borrowed a buggy that he drove into Philadelphia. Once there, he found a pharmacy, bought arsenic and morphine, went to the offices of the railroad and swallowed the poison. An hour later, he died.

"Railroad Butchery," was the description of the wreck in the *New York Times.* The reason for it all was an inadequate warning system that broke down as a result of the faulty judgment of two good men.

UNITED STATES
PENNSYLVANIA
LAUREL RUN

December 23, 1903

• • • • • • • • • • • • • • • •

Debris on the tracks was the initial cause of the huge train wreck of December 23, 1903 near Laurel Run, Pennsylvania. Sixty-four died; nine were injured.

One of the more bizarre railroad wrecks of the 20th century took place in a driving snowstorm on December 23, 1903 just outside the tiny hamlet of Laurel Run, Pennsylvania. The Duquesne Limited from Pittsburgh to Connellsville, which enjoyed the reputation of being the fastest train on the B & O line, had gained its stature by averaging speeds of 60 miles per hour. It was traveling at just this speed on the night of December 23, despite a steady snow that had reduced visibility to nearly zero.

But snow or not, the Duquesne Limited would not have been able to avoid the catastrophe it was hurtling toward that night. A slow-moving freight of the Nickel Plate line, moving in the opposite direction on a parallel track, had lost practically an entire gondola load of heavy railroad ties. The engineer of the train was unaware of this as he passed the Limited going in the other direction.

Minutes later, the speeding passenger train rounded a curve and plowed, full speed, into the mountain of wooden ties. The engine became airborne, climbing the ties and twisting off the tracks, carrying the baggage car with it. A smoker, running just behind the baggage car, leaped over the baggage car and rammed the engine, slicing off its steam dome and sending scalding steam into the smoker.

The sleeper behind the smoker roared on, ripping up track as it went, and came to rest, precariously poised, on the edge of an embankment. The dining car followed this, toppling over and strewing its occupants around like jack-straws. Dining steward Benjamin Nicholas, dazed by the crash, pulled himself together instantly and became one of the two heroes on the scene.

After seeing to the inhabitants of the dining car, Nicholas crawled through the smoker and its 40 dead and dying occupants and reached the engine, which was still erupting steam. Tearing his coat to shreds, he stuffed it into the ruptured pipe and then climbed down and turned off the engine's boiler valve.

Thomas J. Baum, the train's baggage master, was trapped in the baggage car, which, after colliding with the engine, had ricocheted into the Youghiogheny River. Severely injured, he freed himself and climbed the embankment just in time to hear conductor Louis Hilgot, whose face had been burned into an unidentifiable mass, shout to anyone who could hear that Number 49 was due behind them and would have to be flagged down.

Despite his injuries, Baum dragged himself to the tracks behind the wreck. There he could plainly hear the approaching engine of Number 49, charging through the snowstorm. Baum ripped off his coat and, with a package of pocket matches, set it afire and waved it at the approaching train. Number 49 saw the signal and ground to a stop just three feet from where Baum, faint from loss of blood and exhaustion had collapsed on the tracks.

Rescuers from Number 49, including two detectives who arrested several men who were looting the dead, rushed to the scene. Sixty-four persons, all of them men, and most of them passengers in the smoker, were killed. Nine were injured. And 500 yards of track on both roadbeds were reduced to twisted, jagged steel.

UNITED STATES
PENNSYLVANIA
MUD RUN

October 10, 1888

• • • • • • • • • • • • • • • • •

Outdated equipment accounted for the rear-end collision of two trains at Mud Run, Pennsylvania on October 10, 1888. Sixty-four died; 100 were injured.

"Telescoping," or the passing of cars into and sometimes through one another like the joints of a telescope, was one of the most feared and calamitous consequences of head-on or rear-end collisions in 19th-century America. The culprit was the American system of link and pin coupling, which allowed car platforms to bounce at varying levels. In England, powerful compression coupled the cars, and telescoping was virtually unknown. But it would be 1869 before the Miller platform and buffer—a locking together of the car sills by a strong tension-compression coupling—would be invented, and decades before it would be universally employed in America.

The eight excursion trains that hauled 5,000 members of the Total Abstinence Union of Wilkes-Barre, Pennsylvania from Wilkes-Barre over the Lehigh Valley line to the mountains near Hazelton on October 10, 1888 were not top-of-the-line equipment. All of the passenger cars were wooden and rickety; each of them was outfitted with outmoded link and pin couplings. Even the first engine on the seventh excursion train contained only steam brakes, and the engineer had to signal, by a whistle to the engineer of the second engine, to apply them. Each of these factors would add up to a catastrophe.

The eight special excursion trains took the 5,000 merrymakers to the Laurentian campgrounds in the morning and back in the evening at 10-minute intervals, a separation that was twice the usual space between trains in 1888 and thus thought to be safe. As further precautionary measures, two brakemen were stationed as lookouts in each engine cabin, and extra brakemen were assigned to the rear of each train.

Train number six of the eight-train contingent contained, in its last car, a group of particularly joyous celebrants, who had apparently been less than abstemious during the day. Shortly beyond the station at Mud Run, this train was halted. Hannigan, its brakeman, debarked and walked the 400 feet from the rear of the last car of loud celebrants to the edge of the station platform and hung out a red warning light.

Train number seven, meanwhile, was approaching Mud Run, tooling along at a conservative 20 miles per hour. The track curved into the station at Mud Run, and the signals read all clear ahead. But train number six was still halted, and as the seventh train rounded the curve, brakeman Hannigan's pathetically small warning light suddenly appeared.

Henry Cook, the engineer of the seventh train's first engine, spotted the warning when he was almost abreast of it. Too late, he blasted his brake signal, simultaneously applying his steam brakes. But the train scarcely slowed. With a horrendous screeching of splintering wood, it rammed into the rear of the sixth train, telescoping the

The shattered, twisted, burned-out remains of the last car of the number six train of the Lehigh Valley line excursion of the celebrating Total Abstinence League in Mud Run, Pennsylvania on October 10, 1888. Most of the 64 victims of the crash were crushed in this last car when train number seven rear-ended it. Library of Congress

last car halfway through the next one. Two hundred passengers were trapped in these cars, and 64, most of whom were in the last coach, were killed instantly, crushed by the impact and folding together of the two cars. One hundred other passengers were badly injured, some of them dismembered.

"Oh! What a tongue can tell or pen picture this most dreadful calamity," wrote Matt J. Meredith, in a commemorative book titled *First Anniversary of the Mud Run Disaster.* "The roasting, scalding engine under which were crushed those poor young children," he went on, in antique style, and with less than punctilious accuracy (most of the dead were adults), "and the car ahead being telescoped and the lives crushed out of those who but a few moments since were full of life. Oh, God, why visit upon your unhappy children such a death."

UNITED STATES
PENNSYLVANIA
SHOHOLA

July 15, 1864

• • • • • • • • • • • • • • • • • •

A 13 ½-hour departure delay caused the head-on collision of a troop train and a passenger train at Shohola, Pennsylvania on July 15, 1864. Seventy-four were killed; there is no record of the injured.

A Union Army troop train carrying hundreds of Confederate prisoners of war was scheduled to leave Jersey City, New Jersey at 4:30 A.M. on July 15, 1864 bound for a Union prisoner of war camp in Elmira, New York. But when the departure time arrived, it was discovered that three Confederate prisoners were missing. A full-scale search was launched through the trains, through the station yards of Jersey City and through the ship that had transported the prisoners up the coast to Jersey City.

The search would take all day, and it would be after 5 P.M. before the three would be found, hiding out in the hold of the ship that had brought them there. The 18-car military train would then depart from Jersey City 13½ hours late, well off schedule.

The Erie track near Shohola, Pennsylvania is a single one, and on that single track, heading in the opposite direction that night, was an enormous 50-car coal train. It had been telegraphed a go-ahead from the control operator at the Lackawaxen station and was proceeding at full throttle.

The two trains met head-on at a curve in the tracks near Shohola. Both engines were catapulted off the tracks, ending up in a steamy tangle on an embankment. The cars of both trains telescoped into one another, smashing asunder. The coal cars, traveling at a greater speed and containing greater mass and weight than the passenger cars, crushed both cars and occupants instantly upon impact. Seventy-four passengers (51 prisoners, 19 guards and four engine crew members) were killed, thus making this one of the most mortally catastrophic head-on collisions in the history of railroading in the United States.

UNITED STATES
TENNESSEE
HODGES

September 24, 1904

• • • • • • • • • • • • • • • • • •

Human error was blamed for the collision of two trains at Hodges, Tennessee on September 24, 1904. Sixty-three died; there is no record of the injured.

Train number 12 from Bristol to Chattanooga and train number 15 from Chattanooga to Bristol traveled the same single track on the Southern line. The schedule always allowed smooth passage. At New Market, a station away from Hodges, Tennessee, depending on the signals and the time, one of the two trains would take to a siding, allowing the other to pass.

On the afternoon of September 24, 1904, the signals and the schedule clearly indicated that number 12 had the right of way. But for some reason that died with them, the engineer and stoker of number 15 ignored both signals and their orders and steamed straight ahead, at full throttle, through New Market.

A few minutes later, at Hodges, number 15 slammed head-on into number 12, flinging engines and cars off the tracks on either side. Sixty-three passengers and crew members would die in the conflagration that resulted, and the blame would be fixed on the dead engineer of number 15.

UNITED STATES
TENNESSEE
NASHVILLE

July 9, 1918

• • • • • • • • • • • • • • • •

Human error was responsible for the worst rail crash in number of fatalities in U.S. history, a head-on collision of an express and a workers' train near Nashville, Tennessee on July 9, 1918. One hundred one were killed and 100 were injured.

There is an ironic circumstance of history surrounding the worst railroad crash in number of fatalities in the United States. Practically all of the victims of the crash were black. It took place in Tennessee. And it took place in July 1918, exactly 12 months before the Chicago race riots that would kill 31 and injure more than 500, in a tense atmosphere of racial tension in the nation.

Thus, the terrible wreck of July 9, 1918 in Nashville went virtually unnoticed, while the subway disaster in Brooklyn in November of that same year (see p. 304), which claimed four fewer lives, received enough attention for history books to incorrectly indicate that it was the nation's worst train wreck in terms of fatalities.

The disaster occurred shortly after 7 A.M. on the morning of July 9, between the Shops and Harding stations on the fringes of Nashville. Train number one of the Nashville, Chattanooga & St. Louis line, loaded with black workers in Tennessee's munitions plants, was a low-priority train that had orders to remain on the double tracks at Shops and allow Train number four to rocket by on the single express track. Following this, it was to pull onto the track for its short trip to Harding, where the munitions plant was located.

Engineer Kennedy waited while a freight sped by, and speculation afterward was that he mistook it for the express—a shaky assumption, considering the experience of Kennedy.

For whatever reason, Kennedy, after the freight disappeared, pulled out onto the single track and pushed his engine on, pulling several ancient wooden passenger cars, at 50 miles per hour toward Harding.

He traveled a very short distance before slamming full force into express number four, traveling at 50 miles per hour in the opposite direction. The roaring head-on collision reduced the two engines to steaming scrap metal in an instant. The first two cars of number one telescoped and shot into the engines, shattering into jagged splinters, killing every occupant of each car.

One hundred one people were killed and 100 more were injured, and the papers of the nation would hardly mention it.

UNITED STATES
UTAH
OGDEN

December 31, 1944

• • • • • • • • • • • • • • • •

An engineer's heart attack was the cause of a rear-end collision near Ogden, Utah on December 31, 1944. Fifty died and more than 80 were injured.

Human error of the most uncontrollable sort was apparently responsible for an appalling rear-end crash that took place in the early morning hours of December 31, 1944 on the salt marshes near Great Salt Lake in Ogden, Utah. The engineer of the second section of the Pacific Limited of the Southern Pacific line suffered a heart attack just before plowing into the rear of the first section.

The two trains were loaded with soldiers on holiday furlough and civilians intent on celebrating New Year's Eve in San Francisco. The first section was a comfortable distance ahead of the second. This was 1944; signals and safety precautions were sophisticated.

Then, shortly after dawn, an express ahead of the first section signaled that it was having difficulty. It slowed and then stopped; its brakeman debarked from the last car and set a series of warning flares along the tracks behind the halted train.

Morning mists were drifting off Great Salt Lake, across the tracks and into the marshes. The flares were shrouded in them, removing their sharp definition, and thus their shock capability. Still, they were visible to an alert engineer.

However, as surviving crewmen described later, James McDonald, the engineer of the second section, seemed to be moving and reacting sluggishly as he drove his train at 65 miles per hour straight for the rear of the stationary first section of the Limited. When it came into view and the men around him began to shout, he applied the brakes. But by then, it was too late.

The engine slammed into the last car of the parked train, demolishing it and shoving it off the track. The next car, a Pullman, miraculously escaped destruction, but the following two cars were catapulted into the marshes.

Fifty people were killed, 29 of them in the last car of the first section. More than 80 were injured. More might have died from their injuries if it hadn't been for two army hospital cars attached to the first section, which were far enough forward in the 18-car train to remain undamaged and serviceable. McDonald, examined by company doctors, was found to have had a heart attack.

YUGOSLAVIA
ZAGREB

August 30, 1974

• • • • • • • • • • • • • • •

Drinking in the cab of a train caused the crash of a train at high speed into the station at Zagreb, Yugoslavia on August 30, 1974. One hundred seventy-five were killed; there was no official report of injuries.

The worst rail accident in the history of Yugoslavia took place in the station at Zagreb on the night of August 30, 1974.

A solitary passenger train, the Belgrade to Dortmund express, traveling at nearly 55 miles per hour, roared into the station at Zagreb that night, its engine at full throttle. A subsequent board of inquiry would accuse the train's two engineers of drunkenness, and to the horrified witnesses of this cataclysm, it was the only plausible explanation for the bizarre scene that unfolded before them.

Out of control, the train crashed into the station platform and derailed, splaying its cars onto the platform and adjacent tracks. Electric power cables, used for commuter lines, exploded into sparks and fell on the metal cars, electrocuting some of the occupants as they tried to escape.

It would be hours before 50 passengers, trapped by the power lines and the overturned cars, could be rescued. They were the lucky ones. A staggering 150 passengers were killed by the crash and 25 others were electrocuted. The two engineers were acquitted of drunkenness but received reprimands for speeding.

SPACE DISASTERS

THE WORST RECORDED SPACE DISASTERS

* Detailed in text

United States
Florida
* Cape Canaveral (1967)
* Atlantic Ocean (1986)

USSR
* (1967)
* (1971)

CHRONOLOGY

* Detailed in text

1967
Jan. 27
* Cape Canaveral, Florida; Fire in space capsule
April 23
* USSR; *Soyuz I* crash

1971
June 30
* USSR; *Soyuz II* tragedy

1986
Jan. 28
* Atlantic Ocean; Explosion of *Challenger*

SPACE DISASTERS

Thankfully, this section is a brief one. In the more than two decades of its existence, modern space exploration has claimed only 15 lives—21 if you count the six American astronauts who died in airplane accidents and other ancillary activities. And perhaps there are other casualties never reported by the Soviet space program.

None of these lost lives are those of innocent victims. Even schoolteacher Christa McAuliffe volunteered and knew full well the hazards she faced when she entered the Challenger. That, of course, is little comfort to the surviving families of those who died, but when examined against the entire landscape of human disaster, it does, at least, circumscribe catastrophes in space.

Space exploration has been largely dominated by the two world superpowers—the United States and the USSR. From that monumental moment in 1957, when *Sputnik I* was launched, the exploration of space moved from the pages of science fiction stories to the front pages of newspapers and from there to the imaginations of the world. To those who had trouble flying in an airliner and who now watched astronauts on the moon, the leap in achievement seemed almost beyond comprehension. But the public loved it. Reservations for the first passenger flight to the moon sold at a brisk clip in New York City in the early 1960s.

That the race between the two superpowers to put a man in space, then men on the moon, then people on space stations, then people on Mars and other planets would eventually extract its toll in human tragedy was scarcely believable in the early days of the space race. Even the high economic cost failed to dampen the exciting, adventurous enthusiasm of scientists and nonscientists alike. Up went the satellites, space stations and space shuttles, until outer space began to resemble an ill-tended backyard, full of floating garbage left by those who played in it.

It would take a tragedy the size of the 1986 *Challenger* explosion to sober up the world, it seemed. The adolescent love affair with outer space ended for many that January day. Experiment, the world learned, carries with it danger and responsibility.

In our eagerness to explore outer space, we had perhaps neglected some of the inner space of thoughtful preparation, both in technology and our own emotional and mental development. We had, in short, not paid enough attention to the natural priorities that regard the preservation of human life as the highest goal.

It was a sad, sobering and perhaps overdue moment. Looking back at the terrible deaths of those who had been killed before in the space race, it was easier to see what was ahead. More exploration, certainly. More monumental achievements. But caution on the way to them.

Ironically enough, one of the lessons that has been learned from the four space tragedies that have occurred so far is that, as in civilian airline travel, the most dangerous moments in any flight occur during takeoff and landing. With the exception of the fire on the launchpad at Cape Canaveral that killed astronauts Grissom, White and Chaffee, all took place in the first few seconds of blastoff or the last few seconds of landing.

Thus, as this is written, more and more launchings are being aborted on the launchpad, as we learn from our disasters. It is only the beginning for the space program. And it is only the beginning of the chronicle of its disasters and achievements.

UNITED STATES
FLORIDA
CAPE CANAVERAL

January 27, 1967

• • • • • • • • • • • • • • • • •

Three Apollo I *astronauts perished in a simulation exercise at Cape Canaveral, Florida on January 27, 1967 when a fire caused by a spark from a faulty wire ignited the pure oxygen in their space capsule.*

The *Apollo I* astronauts, America's first men on the moon, were selected carefully: Virgil Grissom was 40 years old, an Air Force lieutenant colonel, and one of the seven original Mercury astronauts. Edward I. White II was 36, a lieutenant colonel in the Air Force and the first American to "walk" in space. Roger B. Chaffee was 31 and a Navy lieutenant commander. This was to be his first spaceflight.

The Apollo space program, first introduced by President John F. Kennedy in May 1961 and designed to place a man on the moon by 1970, had operated since its inception on the razor-thin edge of uncertainty. An expensive, extensive program, it was constantly being scrutinized by Congress and the administration when budget-tightening time came.

The Apollo program itself had undergone a series of technical glitches that had also delayed the program and increased its budget demands. In fact, the moon shot for which Grissom, White and Chaffee were preparing in January 1967 had been postponed twice, in February 1966 and November 1966.

In January, it seemed as if they were headed toward a "go," and a series of simulations that precede any space launching began. The space capsule had been positioned atop its booster rocket for several days of trial blastoffs.

Early in the morning of January 27, 1967, flight controllers arrived at the Mission Control Center in Houston and took their seats at the communication consoles. Simultaneously, at Cape Canaveral's Kennedy Space Center, workers in the blockhouse and launchpad prepared the capsule and rocket for a takeoff simulation.

At 1 P.M., the three astronauts, in full space regalia, climbed into the 12 × 13 foot spacecraft poised 218 feet in the air atop its *Saturn I* rocket. The orange gantry surrounded the linked space vessels and the connections that linked them. All that was missing was the fuel in the spacecraft and the rocket.

For two hours, until approximately 3 P.M., the astronauts checked the instruments in the cockpit and then signaled that they were ready for the hatch to be closed and locked over their heads.

Apollo astronauts* (left to right) *Gus Grissom, Ed White and Roger Chaffee shortly before the tests on the launchpad that ended in their deaths by fire on January 27, 1967. NASA

For the next few hours they would be undergoing what was known as a "plugs out" simulation of the countdown, blastoff and first three hours of spaceflight. "Plugs out" meant that, as in a real blastoff, all the electrical and life-support connections between the spacecraft and the gantry would be severed, and the spacecraft would then depend completely on its own inner power.

Two days before, the astronauts had undergone a similar "plugs out" exercise, except that in that one, the pure oxygen with which the space capsule would ultimately be filled was not pumped in. Instead, the hatch was left open, and the mixture of gases—predominantly nitrogen and oxygen—that characterizes earth's atmosphere was allowed to drift in.

However, this one would be closer to the real thing. NASA (the National Aeronautics and Space Administration) had decided to use pure oxygen in the space capsule rather than a mixture of gases, because the equipment would be simpler to install and would weigh less. Some scientists in the organization and out were disquieted by this choice. Pure oxygen is highly combustible, particularly at the pressure volume of 18 pounds per square inch that was contemplated for the Apollo. Although the Gemini craft flew with pressure at five pounds per square inch, the Apollo scientists decided to increase this to approximate the 15-pound-per-square-inch pressure volume of the earth's atmosphere.

At approximately 6:00 P.M., with the hatch closed and the oxygen level at 16, there was a loss of communication between Houston and the astronauts. It was worked on and corrected, and the simulated blastoff was scheduled for 6:41 P.M. The astronauts were in their seats—Colonel

Grissom was in the command pilot's seat on the left, Colonel White was in the middle and Commander Chaffee occupied the right seat.

At 6:31, a casual voice, never identified, came over the communication system to the blockhouse at Cape Canaveral and the control center in Houston. "Fire—I smell fire." the voice said.

Two seconds passed.

"Fire in the cockpit!" shouted the unmistakable voice of Colonel White.

Three more seconds of silence elapsed.

A hysterical cry came over the intercom: "There's a bad fire in the spacecraft!"

There was the sickening sound of scuffling, frantic movement and unintelligible shouting. The craft was filling up with black smoke, and it was starting to glow from the heat within—all within 11 seconds.

Finally, one last communication blasted from the intercom. It was the strangled voice of Commander Chaffee. "We're on fire!" he pleaded. "Get us out of here!"

And those were the last words from the astronauts, who were burning to death, while a camera dispassionately recorded, in minute detail, their death throes.

They didn't have a chance. A faulty wire near Grissom's couch had ignited a spark, which had ignited the pure oxygen, setting a fire that burned at 2,500 degrees Fahrenheit. They were roasted alive and asphyxiated at the same time, in 21 seconds. The only way they could have opened the hatch would have been to unscrew it with a ratchet tool, an operation that would have taken at least 90 seconds.

Rescue workers with gas masks tried to get to the white-hot capsule and open the hatch, but they were beaten back by the heat and incredibly dense smoke.

Five minutes later, rescuers clad in asbestos were finally able to enter the capsule, where they encountered a grisly sight. The astronauts had struggled out of their restraining harnesses. What was left of Colonel Grissom and Colonel White—little more than their bones—was found lying at the hatch. Commander Chaffee lay below. Pieces of skin containing intact fingerprints were grafted to the hatch. Grissom and White had been tearing at it with their bare hands. There was nothing left of the astronauts' space suits. They had been burned completely through.

"[There may have been a small fire] at first largely absorbed by the spacecraft structure," said Dr. Robert C. Seamans Jr., deputy administrator of NASA, before a congressional panel investigating the tragedy. "It may have continued for as long as 10 seconds," he continued. This would encompass the first cries of alarm from the astronauts. "A more intense fire may have then developed," he went on, "causing the rapid increase in cabin pressure. This fire was probably extinguished by the depletion of oxygen."

The astronauts died, then, in a space of time somewhere between 12 and 20 seconds, not without suffering terribly.

Lieutenant Colonel White, Lieutenant Colonel Grissom and Lieutenant Commander Chaffee were all given heroes' burials in Arlington National Cemetery, a fitting honor for the first American casualties of the space age.

UNITED STATES
FLORIDA
ATLANTIC OCEAN

January 28, 1986

• • • • • • • • • • • • • • • •

While millions watched, the Challenger *space shuttle exploded on blastoff over the Atlantic Ocean near Cape Canaveral on January 28, 1986, killing all seven astronauts aboard. A combination of low temperatures, O-rings that malfunctioned, and NASA's determination to launch the shuttle caused the disaster.*

In the age of modern telecommunication, we have become accustomed to seeing history as it happens. Millions watched while Jack Ruby killed Lee Harvey Oswald on television, live. The evening news carried the Vietnam War into our living rooms, and, as violence escalated in American society, the theory was postulated that, since that time when war appeared on our TV screens as information, we had become a nation inured to violence, numbed by actuality-as-television-drama.

But nobody who was sitting before a television set on the morning of January 28, 1986 was immune to the escalating horror they witnessed as the space shuttle *Challenger* and its seven occupants exploded in a million fragments, 74 short seconds after they had taken off from Cape Canaveral, Florida. The personal shock and loss ran like an electric current through practically everyone in the nation, for this was the famous first flight that would take an ordinary citizen into space. Schoolteacher Christa McAuliffe was the Everywoman of the 20th century, and she was also the victim of one of its worst tragedies. Not since the assassination of John F. Kennedy 23 years before had such a shared sense of loss and sadness and bewilderment united ordinary people on the street.

The *Challenger* flight was a storybook mission. The space shuttle was a known quantity. It had succeeded before; it would succeed again. America felt good about its space program. The fact that there was a predominantly civilian crew aboard *Challenger* was, of itself, a positive sign. We

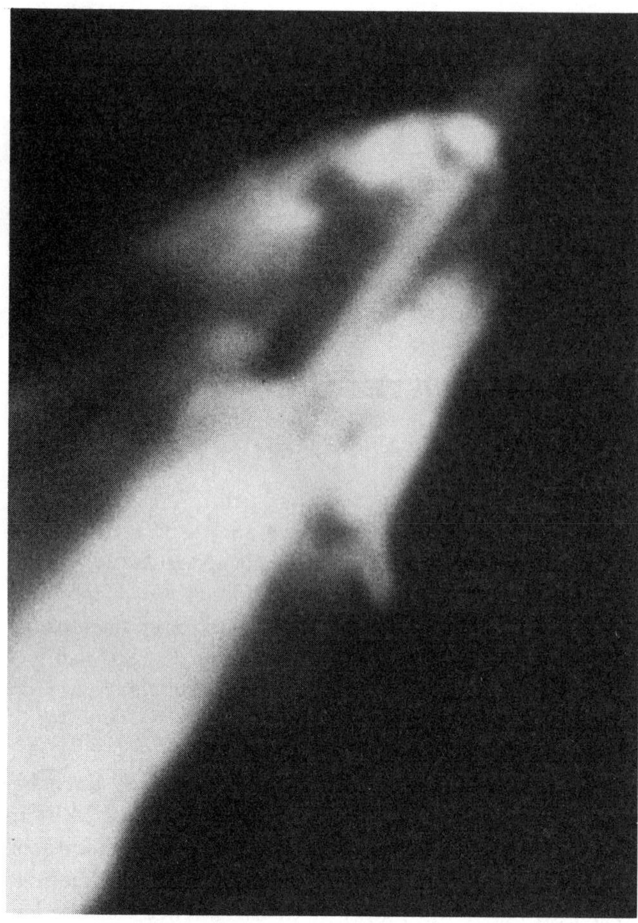

The tragic explosion of Challenger, *73 seconds after takeoff on January 28, 1986. The death of all seven crew members halted the U.S. space program for two and a half years.* NASA

had turned the corner toward space travel for the common person.

Scheduled to fly the *Challenger* that January day were mission commander Francis R. (Dick) Scobee; the pilot, Commander Michael J. Smith of the Navy; Lieutenant Colonel Ellison S. Onizuka of the Air Force; Dr. Ronald E. McNair, a physicist; Dr. Judith Resnik, an electrical engineer; Gregory B. Jarvis, another electrical engineer; and science teacher Christa McAuliffe.

Behind the scenes, the scenario was a little less sanguine. Bad weather at the Kennedy Space Center in Florida had already caused two postponements in three days of the *Challenger* launching.

It had originally been scheduled to leave on Sunday morning, January 26. But the weather reports on Saturday had been ominous, predicting heavy rain, and so the Sunday launch was scrubbed. As it turned out, the weather forecasters were wrong, and it was a balmy, blissful day, ideal for a space launch. But the cancellation, once put in motion, had to stand.

On Monday, January 27, the skies clouded up, but meteorologists predicted a clearing trend, so the *Challenger* astronauts suited up and boarded the ship. But a handle on the shuttle latch malfunctioned. Mindful of the Apollo disaster (see p. 318), those in command dispatched workers to free or replace the recalcitrant handle.

It would take the workers two hours to complete the job, and by then, stiff winds had blown up and the launch was again postponed, this time to 9:38 Tuesday morning, January 28, 1986.

But even that launch date and time were the subject of long and worried conferences. The winds that had postponed the January 27 launch preceded a cold front that was about to visit Florida. The forecast, issued in mid-afternoon of the 27th, called for freezing temperatures throughout the night.

"When we saw those predicted temperatures, I just knew we had to talk about it," recalled Allan J. McDonald, an engineer who represented Morton Thiakol Inc., shuttle contractors and the manufacturer of the booster rockets. Mr. McDonald argued vehemently that evening against proceeding with the countdown. He and other Morton Thiakol engineers were concerned about the effect of the cold weather on the solid-fuel booster rockets. Their concern was focused on the O-rings, the rubber seals that contained the booster's hot gases.

These seals were obviously critical, and they had had a history of problems. A double set of synthetic rubber Os shaped like giant washers, they fit around the circumference of the rocket casing and were intended to fill the tiny gap that remained after two steel rocket segments were bolted together. In the past, the enormous pressures during blastoff had sometimes dislodged these seals. Besides, they had never been tested at temperatures lower than 53 degrees Fahrenheit.

So when McDonald got on the phone to Utah to confer with other engineers at Morton Thiakol, he returned with a unanimous recommendation for delay. The engineers suspected that cold weather could only heighten the chances of a failure of the O-ring seals. The rubber, they argued, would harden and shrink at these low temperatures, increasing the likelihood that the seals would open up. The consequences, they concluded, could be catastrophic.

NASA took this under advisement, but NASA was under pressure to proceed with this launch. They were scheduled to conduct 15 shuttle flights in 1986, which was six more than in any previous year. This was to be the symbolic 25th flight, which would demonstrate that it was safe and that space vehicles could be reused. And it was to be the first flight with an ordinary citizen aboard.

According to later testimony, NASA brought extreme pressure on Morton Thiakol to agree to a go-ahead. Finally, Morton Thiakol reluctantly agreed.

As the weather forecast predicted, the temperature fell below freezing. At 6 A.M., it was 27 degrees on the launchpad, and the shuttle's external tank was coated with frost and ice. A special ice team checked the shuttle and boosters three times—at 1:30 A.M., 7 A.M. and 11 A.M. They noted readings of seven and nine degrees in the right-hand booster rocket, much lower than in the left booster—an indication that liquid hydrogen might have been leaking from that rocket. In fact, there were indications that temperatures on the strut connecting the rocket to the external fuel tank were as low as eight degrees below zero. All of this could have signaled danger, but the ice team's mandate was merely to check for excess ice, and so their infrared temperature readings were not reported to high-level officials who made the decision about lifting off.

At 9:07 A.M., the seven astronauts boarded the shuttle. The photograph that will remain as one of the public's permanently stored images of that day shows them smiling, cheery and waving. It was a historic occasion, and the excitement was written on each of their faces.

They climbed into the shuttle, arranged themselves at their stations and drew on extra gloves. It was cold in the spaceship.

Shortly after they settled in place, the astronauts were told that the liftoff had again been put on hold to wait for the sun to warm up and melt some of the ice on the capsule and rockets. The delay would last for two hours.

The crew waited patiently—Francis R. (Dick) Scobee, the commander, and Commander Michael J. Smith at the controls, Dr. Judith Resnik in the center of the shuttle at the flight engineer position, Lieutenant Colonel Ellison Onizuka to her right, and in the mid-deck, Christa McAuliffe, Dr. Donald McNair and Gregory Jarvis.

At T minus nine minutes, the countdown was resumed. It was 38 degrees on the launchpad, 15 degrees colder than it had been for any previous launching at the cape, or anywhere else. At 6.6 seconds before liftoff, the *Challenger*'s three main engines roared to life. At zero, the two 149-foot booster rockets ignited.

"Liftoff," announced the commentator in Houston. "Liftoff of the 25th space shuttle mission, and it has cleared the tower."

Several thousand spectators, including family members of some of the crew, shivered and cheered as the boosters and the shuttle began their slow ascent into the heavens. It all looked so easy and smooth and impressive.

But less than a second into the flight, there was trouble. A puff of black smoke shot out of the lower part of the right booster, at a location covered by a seal. And this was probably the cause of the coming tragedy. The puff of smoke went undetected at the time, and was only found when photos were examined the next day.

Twelve to 13 seconds after liftoff, the smoke, which had spread and blackened, disappeared. The computers monitoring the mission registered no warnings or problems.

At 40 seconds into the flight, when the main engines had been throttled down to 65% thrust, the shuttle encountered heavy, shifting winds. It responded by automatically pivoting the booster and main engine nozzles to maintain the correct trajectory.

At 52 seconds, the three engines began their steady throttling up to full power. "Challenger, go with throttle up," Mission Control radioed.

"Roger, go with throttle up," responded Scobee, calmly.

At 59 seconds, the *Challenger* reached its maximum dynamic pressure, when the vibrations of thrusting rockets, the momentum of the ascent and the force of wind resistance combined to exert incredible stresses on the shuttle structure. At this moment, the O-rings would be tested to the extreme.

A new plume of smoke now appeared on the lower side of the right booster. The pressures, which should have been equal between the two boosters, started to diverge. The right booster's pressure dropped alarmingly, indicating a leak. The fire in the O-ring was being fed by escaping fuel. Both the primary and backup seals had ruptured, and at 73.175 seconds into the mission, there were flashes of light and a series of explosions. At 73.621 seconds, there was a sudden surge of pressure in the main engines. Intense heat shut down one of them.

Now the superheated propulsive gases set off a chain of events that led to the explosion of propellants in the huge primary fuel tank. Flames from the leak severed the struts that held the rocket's base to the fuel tank. As the booster pivoted outward, its nose swung in and ruptured the tank, releasing its hydrogen, and a fierce explosion occurred. The shuttle and its rockets were consumed in an immense fireball.

At this moment, the *Challenger* was about nine miles above the earth and seven miles out over the Atlantic Ocean from the Florida coast. Spectators looked on in horror as the shuttle, soaring so serenely against the crystalline blue of the morning sky, suddenly blew apart in a huge orange flash and then, trailing a white plume, arched over and fell back to earth. On thousands of TV screens, including the ones in Christa McAuliffe's school, the identical, horrible scene was unfolding.

From Houston, at Mission Control, there was a long, terrible pause. "Obviously a major malfunction," stated Stephen Nesbitt, the public relations officer describing the

The ill-fated* Challenger *crew* (left to right, front row) *Michael J. Smith, Francis (Dick) Scobee and Ronald McNair;* (rear) *Ellison Onizuka, Christa McAuliffe, Gregory Jarvis and Judith Resnik. NASA

liftoff. "We have no downlink," he added, meaning that all communication with the *Challenger* had ceased. There was a long pause, and then Nesbitt came back on the line. "We have a report," he said, "from the flight dynamics officer that the vehicle has exploded."

Debris would rain down on the Atlantic for hours, making immediate salvage operations impossible. It would be March 10 before Navy divers would find the crew compartment, with its crew inside, in 100 feet of water, 15 miles northeast of Cape Canaveral. The cabin, it was learned, had remained intact until it hit the ocean, where it broke apart on impact. It is believed that the seven were alive and perhaps conscious during that long, nine-mile plunge to the surface of the ocean. It was theorized that the seven had met their deaths either through the shock of the initial blast, the sudden depressurization of the cabin or by the force of the tumbling, nine-mile descent.

In whatever way, they were gone, the U.S. space program would be thrown into confusion and reassessment. It would be a long, long time, experts predicted, and many, many safety precautions, before another *Challenger* would be launched from the pad at Cape Canaveral into another blue sky of another clear Florida morning.

USSR

April 23, 1967

• • • • • • • • • • • • • • • • • •

A defective parachute caused the crash of Soyuz I *on April 23, 1967 in the USSR. Vladimir Komarov, its sole astronaut, was killed in the crash.*

Vladimir M. Komarov was a Muscovite who had served in the Soviet Air Force from the age of 15 but was almost dropped from the Soviet space program because of a heart murmur. The tall, dark-haired astronaut was a jet fighter pilot with a scholarly nature that had, in 1954, won him admission to the Zhukovsky Air Force Engineering Academy in Moscow.

His training as an aeronautical engineer made him an ideal candidate for space, and in the fall of 1964, he and two companions, scientist Konstantin P. Feoktistov and doctor Boris B. Yegrow, tested the first of the eight-ton Vosknod spaceships. The three made 16 orbits of the earth that fall, and Komarov proved that his physical disability had been either exaggerated or cured.

In 1967, Komarov was selected to test the *Soyuz I,* the first Soviet-launched spaceship in two years. It would make him the first Soviet astronaut to make two trips in space.

There had been tragedies and near tragedies in the space programs of both the United States and the USSR before this trip. Early in 1967, three U.S. astronauts had been killed in a fire during ground tests of the Apollo capsule (see p. 318). In March 1965, Colonel Pavel I. Belyayev, guiding the *Vosknod 2* to earth, was suddenly faced with the failure of the spaceship's equipment for automatically controlled reentry into the earth's atmosphere. Fortunately, manual controls were available, and he was able to land it safely in a dense forest several hundred miles from the intended landing site.

As was the practice in the Soviet Union, Komarov's wife Valentina was not informed of her husband's mission to fly the *Soyuz I* until after it had been launched. "When Velodya goes away on an assignment, he doesn't say where he is going or why," she later related. "And this time as well, he just flew off. I felt, of course, that something was about to happen."

The launchpad from which the colonel and his *Soyuz I* craft were launched was only a few yards from an obelisk marking the site of the launching of *Sputnik I,* on October 4, 1957 at Baikonur, the Soviet Union's space center in Kazakhstan, 1,200 miles southeast of Moscow.

It was the practice of Soviet astronauts not to wear space suits in flight, and Colonel Komarov arrived on the morning of April 23 two hours before blastoff wearing a bright blue nylon pullover, sports trousers and light shoes.

The launching was a textbook one, and the colonel entered orbit easily. After the first circle of the earth, he reportedly radioed to ground control a message that sounds anything but spontaneous: "This ship is a major creative achievement of our designers, scientists, engineers and workers," he said. "I am proud that I was given the right to be the first to test it in flight."

U.S. tracking stations were monitoring the experiment closely, and partway into the flight, they were aware that all was not well aboard the *Soyuz I*. It was not responding as easily as the colonel's sanguine statement indicated, and it was clear, according to U.S. space officials, that the flight would not extend beyond 24 hours.

The experiment had actually included the launching of a second space vehicle, to dock with the colonel's ship, but that was apparently scrubbed early in the colonel's flight.

Real problems began to develop when Colonel Komarov began reentry procedures. According to U.S. observers, he tried to bring his ship in on the 16th orbit, after 24 hours of flight, but he was unable to do so because he could not maneuver it properly to fire the braking rockets.

The colonel and his craft circled the world twice more, while he fought to control the tumbling spaceship. Finally, on the 18th orbit, the retrorockets fired, and he appeared to be coming in successfully. "Well done!" was the cry from ground control.

"Everything is working fine," replied Komarov, who was over Africa at this moment.

When the spaceship reached 23,000 feet, its landing parachute was to be deployed. But the frantic tumbling in outer space had taken its toll. The parachute lines had become hopelessly tangled, and the parachute did not open. And the *Soyuz I* streaked toward the earth at a frightening rate of speed.

Colonel Komarov struggled to regain control of the ship, but there was no backup for an unopened parachute. He died on impact.

Moscow mourned; thousands passed his bier, which was placed on public display. Two days later, in a ceremony attended by every top dignitary in the Soviet government, his ashes were placed in an urn, and he was buried in the Kremlin wall. The Russian space program would be set back another year by this.

USSR

June 30, 1971

• • • • • • • • • • • • • • • • •

A faulty valve or hatch seal caused a sudden decompression during the landing of the Soyuz II *spacecraft in the USSR on June 30, 1971. All three astronauts aboard were killed.*

On June 5, 1971, the *Soyuz II* spacecraft with Lieutenant Colonel Georgi T. Dobrovolsky, Vladislav N. Volkov and Viktor I. Patsayev aboard was launched into earth orbit. Its mission, though heavily censored by the Soviets, was thought to be to attempt a linkup with the unmanned Salyut space station and to conduct some secret, in-space experiments—which included a study of the earth from space and an examination of the long-term effects of weightlessness on human beings.

The blastoff was uneventful, and the astronauts docked at the Salyut station smoothly. First, the docking mechanism was locked, and pressure was equalized between the two vehicles. Then, floating through the hatch of the docking tunnel, Viktor I. Patsayev, the 37-year-old civilian test engineer who had been trained specifically for work on orbital stations, entered the Salyut laboratory.

While Mr. Patsayev began to connect electrical and hydraulic lines between the craft, the other engineer, Vladislav Volkov, followed him through the crew transfer tunnel. The Soyuz commander, Lieutenant Colonel Dobrovolsky, at first stayed in the ferry craft to handle communications with ground control while the systems on the Salyut were connected. Finally, he, too, swam through the air of the crew tunnel.

Once aboard, all of the men reported that they were in good spirits and then began their task of setting up an outer space experimental laboratory, the first of its kind, in or out of this world.

There was great optimism on the part of Soviet leaders. Premier Aleksei Kosygin said, to them and the world, "We express confidence that you will cope well with this responsible and complex assignment, whose fulfillment will be a major contribution to implementation of plans for developing space for the good of the Soviet people and the whole of mankind."

The laboratory was soon in place, in a 55,000-pound space station orbiting around the earth every 88.2 minutes. The astronauts' habitat was not exactly grand; there was a pressurized module of the station, including its crew quarters of 3,500 cubic feet, or the size of a 40-foot house trailer. In addition, there was a service module with a propulsion system for orbital corrections, linked by hydraulic lines.

Once establishing themselves, the three space explorers settled down to a daily routine. Although, as usual, very few details were conveyed to the rest of the world, it seemed that this was going to be a sustained mission. This was confirmed when the crew was ordered to place the station into a higher orbit, which would reduce the pull of the rarefied atmosphere and prolong the lifetime of the station.

The station was amply stocked with food, treated for preservation over a long period of time.

On June 9, four days into the mission, Lieutenant Colonel Dobrovolsky conducted an in-space fashion show, floating upside down and pedaling the air and demonstrating, for TV, a new tension suit designed to keep muscles in condition on long spaceflights.

Once more, the orbit was raised, and it was obvious that the Soviets were attempting to set an in-space endurance record. For the next few days, the astronauts followed a strict regimen: Following breakfast, and their usual morning exercises, they took samples of their own blood, ran a set of cardiovascular tests and checked the calcium content in their bones—an important experiment, since weightlessness causes a washing out of calcium from the bones.

The afternoons were devoted to experiments with a gamma telescope to study cosmic rays and to make spectographic studies of the earth's natural formations.

The experiment lengthened enough to be relegated to the back pages of the world's newspapers and to disappear entirely from TV news broadcasts. By June 27, the three had lived in space for 23 days, five days beyond the previously known capacity of a person to endure weightlessness in spaceflight and record normal pulse, blood pressure and respiration rate.

Soviet doctors continued to monitor the men. "Each day is now a step into the unknown," said one doctor.

And then it was time to come home. Tass, the Soviet news agency, reported that on June 29, the order was given to return, and the three astronauts "transferred the materials of scientific research and the logs" to the *Soyuz II* for return to earth.

"After completing the transition operation, the astronauts took their seats in the *Soyuz II* ship, checked the onboard systems and prepared the ship for unlinking from the Salyut station," the communique continued.

At 9:28 P.M., Soviet time, the two vehicles separated.

"The crew of the *Soyuz II,*" said Tass, "reported to earth the unlinking operation passed without a hitch and all the systems were functioning normally."

At 1:35 A.M., June 30, the *Soyuz II* reentered the earth's atmosphere. "Its braking engine was fired and functioned throughout the estimate time," Tass went on. "Communication with the crew ceased according to the set program."

The spacecraft braked, the parachute system was put into motion and the soft-landing engines were fired. "The flight of the descending apparatus ended in a smooth landing in the pre-set areas," Tass said.

And now, the tragic ending began to unfold. "Landing simultaneously with the ship, a helicopter-borne recovery group, upon opening the hatch," said Tass dispassionately, "found the crew of the Soyuz II spaceship . . . in their seats, without any signs of life."

They had died, apparently on reentry, without a word to ground control about its happening or its causes.

A board of inquiry looked into the disaster, and the mystery was soon solved. At the moment they landed, a faulty valve or a hatch seal fault in the crew module had caused sudden decompression, and all three had died instantly from the abrupt change in pressure.

The tragedy would stall the Soviet space program for a full two years. Coming as it did after the death of Colonel Vladimir Komarov (see p. 322), it was a stunning, staggering blow to world public confidence in the possibility of probing outer space safely.

BIBLIOGRAPHY

Brown, Walter R. and Norman D. Anderson. *Fires.* Reading, Mass.: Addison-Wesley, 1976.

Brown, Walter R., Billye W. Cutchen and Norman D. Anderson. *Catastrophes.* Reading, Mass.: Addison-Wesley, 1979.

Butler, Hal. *Inferno!* Chicago: Henry Regnery Co., 1975.

Butler, Joyce. *Wildfire Loose.* Kennebunkport, Me.: Durrell Publications, 1987.

"Captain X." *Safety Last: The Dangers of Commercial Aviation.* New York: Dial Press, 1972.

Carlson, Kurt. *One American Must Die.* New York: Congdon and Weed, 1986.

Clarke, James W. *American Assassins.* Princeton, N.J.: Princeton University Press, 1982.

Davie, Michael. *Titanic.* New York: Alfred Knopf, 1987.

Demaris, Ovid. *Brothers in Blood: The International Terrorist Network.* New York: Charles Scribner's Sons, 1977.

Dobkin, Marjorie Housepian. *Smyrna 1922.* Kent, Ohio: Kent State University Press, 1988.

Dobson, Christopher and Ronald Payne. *The Never Ending War: Terrorism in the '80s.* New York: Facts On File, 1987.

———. *The Terrorists.* New York: Facts On File, 1982.

Dunbar, Seymour. *A History of Travel in America.* Indianapolis: Bobbs-Merrill, 1946.

Eddy, Paul, Elaine Potter and Bruce Page. *Destination Disaster: From the Tri-Motor to the DC-10: The Risk of Flying.* New York: Quadrangle, 1976.

Edwardes, Michael. *British India.* New York: Taplinger Publishing Co., 1967.

Emerson, Steven and Brian Duffy. *The Fall of Pan Am 103.* New York: G. P. Putnam's Sons, 1990.

Farrington, S. Kip Jr. *Railroading around the World.* New York: Castle Books, 1955.

Gadney, Reg. *Cry Hungary! Uprising 1956.* New York: Atheneum, 1986.

Garrison, Webb. *Disasters That Made History.* New York: Abingdon Press, 1973.

Godson, John. *Unsafe at Any Height.* New York: Simon and Schuster, 1970.

Grayland, Eugene C. *There Was Danger on the Line.* Auckland, New Zealand: Belvedere, 1954.

Hamilton, James A. B. *British Railway Accidents of the Twentieth Century.* London: Unwin, 1967.

Hamlyn, Paul. *Railways.* London: Hamlyn Publishing Group Ltd., 1970.

Hartunian, Abraham H. *Neither to Laugh nor to Weep: A Memoir of the Armenian Genocide.* Boston: Beacon Press, 1968.

Hooper, Finley. *Roman Realities.* Detroit: Wayne State University Press, 1979.

Howland, S. A. *Steamboat Disasters and Railroad Accidents in the United States.* Worcester, Mass.: Dorr, 1846.

Hyams, Edward. *Terrorists and Terrorism.* New York: St. Martin's Press, 1974.

Hyde, George E. *A Life of George Brent.* Norman, Okla.: University of Oklahoma Press, 1968.

Jerrome, Edward G. *Tales of Railroads.* Belmont, Calif.: Fearon Pittman Publishers, 1959.

Johnson, Thomas P. *When Nature Runs Wild.* Mankato, Minn.: Creative Education Press, 1968.

Kelner, Joseph, with James Munves. *The Kent State Coverup.* New York: Harper and Row, 1970.

Kennett, Frances. *The Great Disasters of the 20th Century.* London: Marshall Cavendish Books Ltd., 1981.

Larimer, J. McCormick. *The Railroad Wrecker.* Muskogee, Okla.: Muskogee Press, 1909.

Lattimer, John H. *Kennedy and Lincoln.* New York: Harcourt Brace Jovanovich, 1980.

Lenz, Harry M. III. *Assassinations and Executions, An Encyclopedia of Violence, 1865–1986.* New York: McFarland, 1988.

Longstreet, Stephen. *City on Two Rivers; Profiles of New York—Yesterday and Today.* New York: Hawthorn Publishers, 1975.

Marshall, John. *Rail Facts and Feats.* New York: Two Continents Publishing Group, 1974.

Marx, Joseph Laurence. *Crisis in the Skies.* New York: David McKay, 1970.

Matthews, Rupert. *The Fire of London.* New York: The Bookwright Press, 1989.

McClement, Fred. *Anvil of the Gods.* New York: J. B. Lippincott, 1964.

———. *It Doesn't Matter Where You Sit.* New York: Holt, Rinehart & Winston, 1969.

McKee, Alexander. *Dresden, 1945: The Devil's Tinderbox.* New York: E. P. Dutton, 1984.

Medvedev, Zhores. *Nuclear Disaster in the Urals.* New York: Vintage, 1980.

Meltzer, Milton. *The Terrorists.* New York: Harper and Row, 1983.

Michener, James. *Kent State; What Happened and Why.* New York: Random House, 1971.

Morris, John V. *Fires and Firefighters.* New York: Bramhall House, 1955.

Nash, Jay Robert. *Darkest Hours.* New York: Nelson-Hall, 1976.

Nock, Oswald, S. *Historic Railway Disasters.* London: Allan, 1966.

Obenzinger, Hilton. *New York on Fire.* Seattle: Real Comet Press, 1989.

Pryce-Jones, David. *The Hungarian Revolution.* New York: Horizon Press, 1970.

Reed, Robert C. *Train Wrecks.* New York: Bonanza Books, 1968.

Rolt, Lionel T. *Red for Danger.* London: Bodley Head, 1955.

Sayre, Nora. *Sixties Going on Seventies.* New York: Arbor House, 1973.

Sobel, Lester A., ed. *Political Terrorism.* New York: Facts On File, 1975.

Soboul, Albert. *The French Revolution, 1787–1799.* New York: Vintage, 1975.

Sterling, Claire. *The Terrorism Network.* New York: Holt, Rinehart and Winston, 1981.

Stover, John F. *American Railroads.* Chicago: Chicago University Press, 1961.

Wasserman, Harvey et al. *Killing Our Own.* New York: Delacorte Press, 1982.

With, Emile. *Railroad Accidents.* Boston: Little Brown, 1856.

INDEX

J

K

N

T

U